MICROECONOMICS

CANADA IN THE GLOBAL ENVIRONMENT

FOURTH EDITION

MICROECONOMICS

CANADA IN THE GLOBAL ENVIRONMENT

FOURTH EDITION

MICHAEL PARKIN
ROBIN BADE

Addison
Wesley
Longman

Toronto

Canadian Cataloguing in Publication Data

Parkin, Michael, 1939-
    Microeconomics: Canada in the global environment

4th ed.
Includes index.
ISBN 0-201-61385-9

1. Microeconomics. 2. Canada—Economic conditions—1991- . I. Bade, Robin.
II. Title.

HM172.P37 2000   338.5   C99-931983-3

ISBN: 0-201-61385-9

Vice President and Editorial Director: Patrick Ferrier
Senior Acquisitions Editor: Dave Ward
Developmental Editor: Suzanne Schaan
Production Editor: Nicole Mellow
Copy Editor: Gail Marsden
Production Coordinator: Deborah Starks
Permissions: Susan Wallace-Cox
Photo Research: Cheryl Freedman
Art Director: Mary Opper
Cover and Interior Design: Anthony Leung
Cover Image (globe): Tony May TSI Imaging/Tony Stone Images
Cover Image (inset): Frederick Charles/Tony Stone Images
Page Layout: Bill Renaud
Illustrator: Richard Parkin

    2 3 4 5   04 03 02 01

Printed and bound in the United States of America.

Statistics Canada information is used with the permission of the Minister of Industry, as Minister responsible for Statistics
Canada. Information on the availability of the wide range of data from Statistics Canada's regional offices, its World Wide
Web site at **http://www.statcan.ca**, and its toll-free access number **1-800-263-1136**.

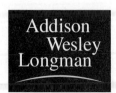

Michael Parkin received his training as an economist at the Universities of Leicester and Essex in England. Currently in the Department of Economics at the University of Western Ontario, Canada, Professor Parkin has held faculty appointments at Brown University, the University of Manchester, the University of Essex, and Bond University. He is a past president of the Canadian Economics Association and has served on the editorial boards of the *American Economic Review* and the *Journal of Monetary Economics* and as managing editor of the *Canadian Journal of Economics*. Professor Parkin's research on macroeconomics, monetary economics, and international economics has resulted in over 160 publications in journals and edited volumes, including the *American Economic Review*, the *Journal of Political Economy*, the *Review of Economic Studies*, the *Journal of Monetary Economics*, and the *Journal of Money, Credit and Banking*. He became most visible to the public with his work on inflation that discredited the use of wage and price controls. Michael Parkin also spearheaded the movement toward European monetary union.

About the Authors

Robin Bade earned degrees in mathematics and economics at the University of Queensland and her Ph.D. at the Australian National University. She has held faculty appointments in the business school at the University of Edinburgh and Bond University and in the economics departments at the University of Manitoba, the University of Toronto, and the University of Western Ontario. Her research on international capital flows appears in the *International Economic Review* and the *Economic Record*.

Professor Parkin and Dr. Bade are joint authors of *Modern Macroeconomics* (Prentice-Hall), an intermediate text, and have collaborated on many research and textbook writing projects. They are both experienced and dedicated teachers of introductory economics.

To our students

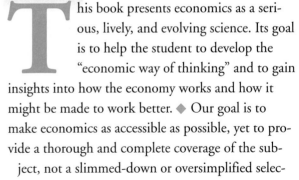

Preface

This book presents economics as a serious, lively, and evolving science. Its goal is to help the student to develop the "economic way of thinking" and to gain insights into how the economy works and how it might be made to work better. ◆ Our goal is to make economics as accessible as possible, yet to provide a thorough and complete coverage of the subject, not a slimmed-down or oversimplified selection. ◆ We are conscious that many students find economics hard, so we place the student at centre stage and write for the student. We use a style and language that doesn't intimidate and that allows the student to concentrate on the substance. ◆ We open each chapter with a clear statement of learning objectives, a real-world student-friendly vignette to grab attention, and a brief preview. We illustrate principles with examples that are selected to hold the student's interest and to make the subject lively. And we put principles to work by using them to illuminate current real-world problems and issues. ◆ We present some new ideas, such as dynamic comparative advantage, game theory, the modern theory of the firm, public choice theory, rational expectations, new growth theory, and real business cycle theory. But we explain these topics with familiar core ideas and tools. ◆ Today's course springs from today's issues—the information revolution, the Asian recession, and the expansion of global trade and investment. But the principles that we use to understand these issues remain the core principles of our science. ◆ Governments and international agencies place renewed emphasis on long-term fundamentals as they seek to sustain economic growth. This book reflects this emphasis. ◆ To enable students to access the latest information on the national and global economy, we have developed a companion Web site. And to provide active learning opportunities, we have developed the tutorials and quizzes on the accompanying *Economics in Action* CD.

The Fourth Edition Revision

Economics: Canada in the Global Environment, Fourth Edition, retains all the improvements achieved in its predecessor with its emphasis on core principles, coverage of recent economic developments, brief yet accessible explanations, and strong pedagogy. New to this edition are:

- Revised and updated micro content
- Revised and updated macro content
- In-text review quiz
- Parallel end-of-chapter problems
- Part wrap-up

Revised and Updated Micro Content

The major revisions in the micro chapters are:

1. What Is Economics? (Chapter 1): A new photo-intensive introduction to the issues and methods of economics.

2. The Economic Problem (Chapter 3): Improved explanation of increasing opportunity cost and simplified explanation of the gains from trade.

3. Elasticity (Chapter 5): A new predictions-oriented treatment of the elasticity of demand and supply.

4. Efficiency and Equity (Chapter 6): New chapter studies the efficiency and the fairness of market outcomes using the tools of demand and supply.

5. Markets in Action (Chapter 7): Now includes explicit discussion of efficiency and equity issues.

6. Organizing Production (Chapter 10): A briefer and more complete statement of the nature of the firm, the essence of its problem, its objectives and constraints, its costs and economic profit.

7. Monopoly (Chapter 13): New explanations of single-price and price discriminating cases including efficiency and distributional aspects of each type and monopoly policy issues.

8. Monopolistic Competition (Chapter 14): A more extensive discussion of the role and effects of selling costs and advertising.

9. Demand and Supply in Resource Markets (Chapter 15): New compact yet complete coverage of all factor markets and now includes simple explanation of net present value and investment decision.

10. Market Failure and Public Choice (Chapter 18): Includes a simpler treatment of public goods and more extensive coverage on taxes.

Revised and Updated Macro Content

The major revisions in the macro chapters are:

1. Measuring Employment and Unemployment (Chapter 23): A new chapter (based on Chapter 31 of the Third Edition) that covers the measurement issues in the labour market.

2. Aggregate Supply and Aggregate Demand (Chapter 24): Reorganized and simplified to better explain the supply-side fundamentals.

3. Money, Banking, and Interest Rates (Chapter 27): New section on interest rates and expenditure plans.

4. Monetary Policy (Chapter 28): A new explanation of the distinction between interest rate targeting and money supply targeting.

5. Fiscal and Monetary Interactions (Chapter 29): First part extensively revised and now organized around the *AS–AD* and money market models to provide greater continuity.

6. The Economy at Full Employment (Chapter 31): A new chapter that begins to build the story of the aggregate supply side of the economy and that explains how changes in population, capital, and technology change potential GDP, employment, and the real wage rate. This chapter provides the foundation for the theory of aggregate supply and is the jumping-off point for Chapter 32 on economic growth.

7. The Business Cycle (Chapter 33): Simplified explanation of aggregate demand theories and a new section, the Japanese recession of the 1990s.

8. Thorough and extensive updating to reflect the Canadian economy and the global economy at the end of the 1990s including events such as the evolution of the federal budget from deficit to surplus, the ongoing expansion of the North American economy, recession in Asia, and turmoil in global financial markets.

In-Text Review Quiz

We have replaced the in-text Review of the previous editions with a Review Quiz. These brief quizzes invite students to revisit the material they have just studied with a set of questions in mind. We hope that these quizzes will encourage a more critical and thoughtful rereading of any material that proves difficult for the student.

Parallel End-of-Chapter Problems

We have reworked the end-of-chapter problems and created pairs of parallel problems. We have provided the solutions to the odd-numbered problems on the Student Resource CD and on the Parkin-Bade Web site. Also, these solutions together with those to the even-numbered problems are available to instructors on the Instructor Resource CD. This arrangement provides help to students and flexibility to instructors who want to assign problems for credit.

Part Wrap-Up

A new feature at the *end* of each part:

- Explains how the chapters relate to each other and fit into the larger picture.
- Provides a biographical sketch of the economist who developed the central idea and places the original contribution in its historical context.
- Presents an interview with a leading contemporary economist.

Features to Enhance Teaching and Learning

HERE, WE DESCRIBE THE CHAPTER FEATURES that are designed to enhance teaching and learning. Each chapter contains:

Chapter Objectives

A list of learning objectives enables students to see exactly where the chapter is going and to set their goals before they begin the chapter. We link these goals directly to the chapter's major headings.

After studying this chapter, you will be able to:

- **Explain the fundamental economic problem**
- **Define the production possibility frontier**
- **Define and calculate opportunity cost**
- **Explain the conditions in which resources are used efficiently**
- **Explain how economic growth expands production possibilities**
- **Explain how specialization and trade expand production possibilities**

Chapter Opener

A one-page student-friendly, attention-grabbing vignette raises questions that both motivate and focus the chapter.

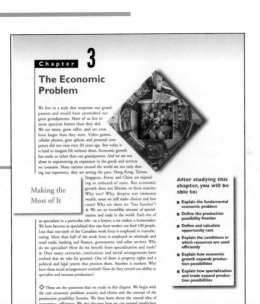

In-Text Review Quiz

A review quiz at end of most major sections enables students to determine whether a topic needs further study before moving on.

REVIEW QUIZ

- What is marginal cost and how is it measured?
- What is marginal benefit and how is it measured?
- How does the marginal benefit from a good change as the quantity of that good increases? Why?
- What is the relationship between marginal cost and the production possibility frontier?
- What conditions must be satisfied if resources are used efficiently? Why?

Key Terms

Highlighted terms within the text simplify the student's task of learning the vocabulary of economics. Each highlighted term appears in an end-of-chapter list with page numbers, an end-of-book glossary, bold-faced in the index, in the *Economics in Action* software on the Student Resource CD, and on the Parkin-Bade Web site.

Key Figures and Tables

An icon ◆ identifies the most important figures and tables, and the end-of-chapter summary lists them. Instructor's overhead transparencies also contain enlarged images of most of these key figures.

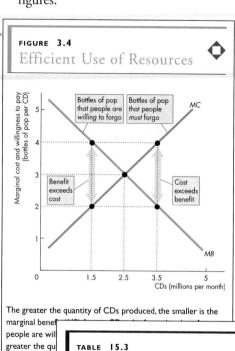

FIGURE 3.4
Efficient Use of Resources ◆

The greater the quantity of CDs produced, the smaller is the marginal benef... ... ... people are will... greater the qu... ginal cost (MC... must give up t... equals margina...

TABLE 15.3
A Firm's Demand for Labour ◆

The Law of Demand

(Movements along the demand curve for labour)

The quantity of labour demanded by a firm

Decreases if:	Increases if:
■ The wage rate increases	■ The wage rate decreases

Changes in Demand

(Shifts in the demand curve for labour)

A firm's demand for labour

Decreases if:	Increases if:
■ The firm's output price decreases	■ The firm's output price increases
■ A new technology decreases the marginal product of labour	■ A new technology increases the marginal product of labour

(Changes in the prices of other resources have an ambiguous effect on the demand for labour.)

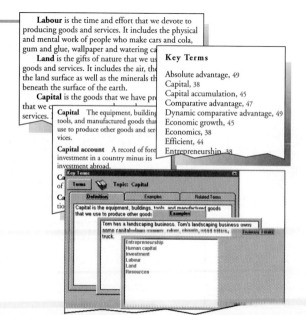

Diagrams That Show the Action

This book has set new standards of clarity in its diagrams. Our goal has always been to show "where the economic action is." The diagrams in this book continue to generate an enormously positive response, which confirms our view that graphical analysis is the most important tool available for teaching and learning economics. But many students find graphs hard to work with. For this reason, we have developed the entire art program with the study and review needs of the student in mind. The diagrams feature:

- Shifted curves, equilibrium points, and other important features highlighted in red
- Colour-blended arrows to suggest movement
- Graphs paired with data tables
- Diagrams labelled with boxed notes
- Extended captions that make each diagram and its caption a self-contained object for study and review

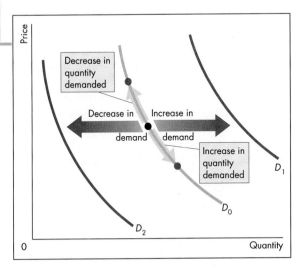

Reading Between the Lines

Each chapter contains an economic analysis of a significant news article together with a set of critical thinking questions that relate to the issues raised in the article.

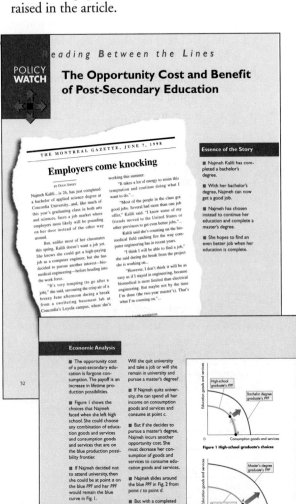

End-of-Chapter Study Material

Each chapter has a concise summary organized by major topics, lists of key terms, figures, and tables (all with page references), problems, and critical thinking questions. Items identified by an icon 💻 link to the *Economics in Action* software CD included with the text. Items identified by an icon 〰 link to the Parkin-Bade Web site at **http://www.econ100.com**. Our hope is to encourage students to keep up-to-date and to become comfortable and efficient in their use of the Internet to access information.

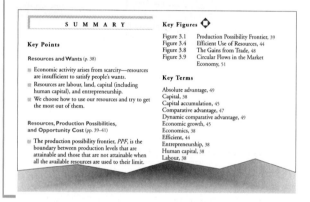

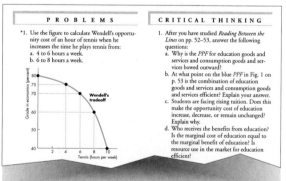

For the Instructor

THIS BOOK ENABLES YOU TO ACHIEVE THREE objectives in your principles course:

- ■ Focus on the core ideas.
- ■ Explain the issues and problems of our time.
- ■ Choose your own course structure.

Focus on the Core Ideas

You know how hard it is to encourage a student to think like an economist. But that is your goal. Consistent with this goal, the text focuses on and repeatedly uses the central ideas: choice, tradeoff, opportunity cost, the margin, incentives, the gains from voluntary exchange, the forces of demand, supply, and equilibrium, the pursuit of economic rent, and the effects of government actions on the economy.

Explain the Issues and Problems of Our Time

Students must use the core ideas and tools if they are to begin to understand them. And there is no better way to motivate students than by using the tools of economics to explain the issues that confront students in today's world. These issues include the environment, immigration, widening income gaps, the productivity growth slowdown, budget surpluses and deficits, restraining inflation, watching for the next recession, avoiding protectionism, and the long-term growth of output and incomes.

Choose Your Own Course Structure

You want to teach your own course. We have organized this book to enable you to do so. We demonstrate the book's flexibility in the "Flexibility Chart" and "Alternative Sequences" tables that appear on pp. xvii–xviii. You can use this book to teach a traditional course that blends theory and policy or a current policy issues course. Your micro course can emphasize theory or policy. The choices are yours.

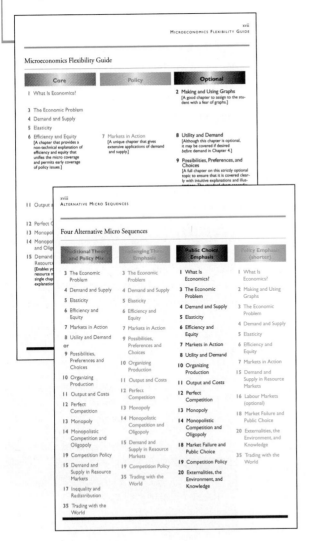

Instructor's Resource CD

Our *Instructor's Resource CD* contains an Instructor's Manual, Computerized Test Bank, and PowerPoint Lecture Presentations.

Instructor's Manual

An Instructor's Manual includes teaching notes and solutions to end-of-chapter problems.

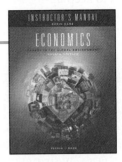

Computerized Test Bank

The Test Bank by Harvey King has been revised and updated by Kam Hon Chu of Memorial University and Glen Stirling of the University of Western Ontario. The Test Bank is accessed using Diploma, a highly acclaimed test generating and grade management software. The questions in the computerized Test Bank are also available in a printed Test Bank.

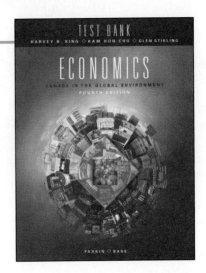

PowerPoint Lecture Presentations

A full-colour Microsoft PowerPoint Lecture Presentation by Vicky Barham of the University of Ottawa breaks the chapters into lecture-size bites and includes key figures from the text, animated graphs, and speaking notes. The presentation can be used electronically in the classroom or can be printed to create hard-copy Transparency Masters. The lecture presentation is available for Windows to qualified adopters of the text (contact your Pearson Education sales representative).

Other Instructor Resources

Economics in Action Software

Instructors can use *Economics in Action* interactive software in the classroom. Its full-screen display option turns its many analytical graphs into "electronic transparencies" for live graph manipulation in lectures. Its real-world data sets and graphing utility bring animated time-series graphs and scatter diagrams to the classroom.

Overhead Transparencies

Full-colour overhead transparencies of enlarged key figures from the text will improve the clarity of your lectures. They are available to qualified adopters of the text (contact your Pearson Education sales representative).

For the Student

Study Guide

The fourth edition *Study Guide* by Avi Cohen (York University) and Harvey King (University of Regina) is carefully coordinated with the main text and the Test Bank. Each chapter of the Study Guide contains:

- Key concepts
- Helpful hints
- Self-Test with True/false/uncertain and Multiple-choice questions, and Short-answer problems, many of which are Critical Thinking problems.
- Detailed solutions.

Each part allows students to test their cumulative understanding with questions that go across chapters and work a sample mid-term examination.

Economics in Action Interactive Software

With *Economics in Action* Release 4.0 that accompanies the Fourth Edition, students will have fun working the tutorials, answering questions that give instant explanations, and testing themselves ahead of their midterm tests. One of our students told us that using *EIA* is like having a private professor in your dorm room!

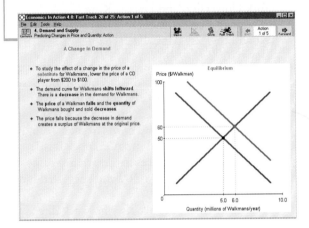

The Parkin-Bade Web Site

The Parkin-Bade Web site provides online quizzes, study tips, office hours, links, electronic *Reading Between the Lines*, a *Point-Counterpoint* feature that encourages students to participate in contemporary policy debates, and much more. You can reach the site at **http://www.econ100.com**.

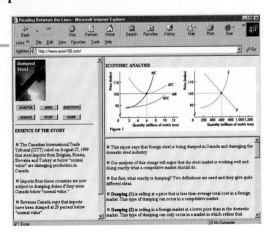

Reviewers

Syed Ahmed, Red Deer Community College; **Benjamin Amoah,** University of Guelph; **Terri Anderson,** Fanshawe College; **Torben Andersen,** Red Deer College; **Syed Ashan,** Concordia University; **Keith Baxter,** Bishop's University; **Andy Baziliauskas,** University of Winnipeg; **Karl Bennett,** University of Waterloo; **Ronald Bodkin,** University of Ottawa; **Caroline Boivin,** Concordia University; **Paul Booth,** University of Alberta; **John Boyd,** University of British Columbia; **John Brander,** University of New Brunswick; **Larry Brown,** Selkirk College; **Lutz-Alexander Busch,** University of Waterloo; **Beverly Cameron,** University of Manitoba; **Norman Cameron,** University of Manitoba; **Emanuel Carvalho,** University of Waterloo; **Francois Casas,** University of Toronto; **Robert Cherneff,** University of Victoria; **Saud Choudhry,** Trent University; **Louis Christofides,** University of Guelph; **Kam Hon Chu,** Memorial University of Newfoundland; **George Churchman,** University of Manitoba; **Avi Cohen,** York University; **Rosilyn Coulson,** Douglas College; **Brian Coulter,** University College of the Fraser Valley; **Stanya Cunningham,** Concordia University College of Alberta; **Douglas Curtis,** Trent University; **Garth Davies,** Olds College; **Vaughan Dickson,** University of New Brunswick (Fredericton); **Mohammed Dore,** Brock University; **Byron Eastman,** Laurentian University; **Fahira Eston,** Humber College; **Brian Ferguson,** University of Guelph; **Len Fitzpatrick,** Carleton University; **Peter Fortura,** Algonquin College; **Donald Garrie,** Georgian College; **David Gray,** University of Ottawa; **Michael Hare,** University of Toronto; **Rod Hill,** University of New Brunswick; **Susan Kamp,** University of Alberta; **Peter Kennedy,** Simon Fraser University; **Harvey King,** University of Regina; **Patricia Koss,** Concordia University; **Robert Kunimoto,** Mt. Royal College; **David Johnson,** Wilfrid Laurier University; **Eva Lau,** University of Waterloo; **Gordon Lee,** University of Alberta; **Scott Lynch,** Memorial University; **Dan MacKay,** SIAST; **Keith MacKinnon,** York University; **S. Manchouri,** University of Alberta; **Raimo Martalla,** Malaspina University College; **Dennis McGuire,** Okanagan University College; **Rob Moir,** University of New Brunswick (St. John); **Joseph Muldoon,** Trent University; **David Murrell,** University of New Brunswick (Fredericton); **Robin Neill,** Carleton University; **A. Gyasi Nimarko,** Vanier College; **Sonia Novkovic,** Saint Mary's University; **John O'Brien,** Concordia University; **Kit Pasula,** Okanagan University College; **Arne Paus-Jenssen,** University of Saskatchewan; **Stephen Rakoczy,** Humber College; **Don Reddick,** Kwantlen University College; **E. Riser,** Memorial University; **Roberta Robb,** Brock University; **Nick Rowe,** Carleton University; **Michael Rushton,** University of Regina; **Balbir Sahni,** Concordia University; **Brian Scarfe,** University of Regina; **Marlyce Searcy,** SIAST Palliser; **Judith Skuce,** Georgian College; **Peter Sinclair,** Wilfred Laurier University; **Stan Shedd,** University of Calgary; **Ian Skaith,** Fanshawe College; **George Slasor,** University of Toronto; **Bert Somers,** John Abbott College; **Lewis Soroka,** Brock University; **Glen Stirling,** University of Western Ontario; **Tony Ward,** Brock University; **Bruce Wilkinson,** University of Alberta; **Russell Uhler,** University of British Columbia; **A. Wong,** Grant McEwan Community College; **Ayoub Yousefi,** University of Waterloo; **Weiqiu Yu,** University of New Brunswick (Fredericton)

Acknowledgments

WE THANK OUR CURRENT AND FORMER COLLEAGUES and friends at the University of Western Ontario who have taught us a great deal. They are: Audra Bowlus, Jim Davies, Jeremy Greenwood, Ig Horstmann, Peter Howitt, Greg Huffman, David Laidler, Phil Reny, Chris Robinson, John Whalley, and Ron Wonnacott. We also thank Doug McTaggart and Christopher Findlay, co-authors of the Australian edition, and Melanie Powell and Kent Matthews, co-authors of the European edition. Suggestions arising from their adaptations of earlier editions have been helpful in preparing this edition.

We thank the several thousand students whom we have been privileged to teach. The instant response that comes from the look of puzzlement or enlightenment has taught us, more than anything else, how to teach economics.

This new edition has been developed during the merger of two outstanding Canadian publishers, Addison-Wesley Canada and Prentice-Hall Canada into the new Pearson Education Canada. We have been privileged to work with both publishers for many years and have come to know well their contrasting styles and strengths. Chief Executive Officer Tony Vander Woude and Chief Operating Officer Alan Reynolds have managed this merger with vision and sensitivity both to the individuals involved and the economic realities that the publishing industry faces today. Tony and Alan have been champions of our project from its inception in the mid-1980s and we want to place on record once more our deep gratitude to them for their support and for ensuring that despite upheavals, we are provided with the best editors in the industry.

We first want to say thank you to those of our former Addison-Wesley team who did not join the new company. They are John More, Ron Doleman, and Linda Scott. John and Ron worked with us from day one and became (and remain) dear friends. We can see their stamp on this edition and believe that it will survive and be visible in many subsequent editions. Linda died during the development of this edition, but she, too left many indelible marks. She was a truly outstanding editor and friend who we greatly miss.

Second, we thank our new editors and helpers at Pearson Education. Patrick Ferrier, Vice President and Editorial Director, has provided overall direction. Dave Ward, Senior Acquisitions Editor and our sponsoring editor, has ably coordinated the arrangements for this edition and worked tirelessly to champion our cause. Suzanne Schaan, Developmental Editor, and Joan MacMillan have brought creative and professional direction to the development effort on this edition. Nicole Mellow, our Production Editor, has managed a tight production schedule and been extremely responsive to our need to keep revising up to the last possible minute.

We thank our outstanding colleagues and friends who have written the supplements and in other ways helped to make this text and package as accurate and useful as possible. Avi Cohen and Harvey King have written a superb Study Guide. And once again, they have played a crucial role in the creation of other supplements and in the overall revision process. Kit Pasula and Glen Stirling have provided valuable suggestions and caught slips and errors in their accuracy review of near-final pages. Lutz-Alexander Busch pointed out an error in the entry deterrence game that is described on pp. 308-309 and suggested how it might be fixed.

Finally, we thank the people who work directly with us. Our assistant, Jeannie Gillmore, has performed too many tasks to list. A few include finding news articles and writing the first drafts of most of the *Reading Between the Lines* features, checking the end-of-chapter problems and solutions, preparing and checking the glossary, and ensuring the accuracy of *Economics in Action* and the quizzes on our Web site.

Jane McAndrew provided excellent library help. Richard Parkin created the electronic art files for the text, CD, and Web site and offered many ideas that improved the illustrations. Laurel Davies created, edited, and checked the accuracy of the *Economics in Action* database. Jessica Dooley read and suggested improvements to the interview with Martin Dooley that appears on pp. 198–200.

Classroom experience will test the value of this book. We would appreciate hearing from teachers and students about how we can continue to improve it in future editions.

Robin Bade
Michael Parkin
London, Ontario, Canada
michael.parkin@uwo.ca
robin@econ100.com

Microeconomics Flexibility Guide

Core	Policy	Optional
1 What Is Economics?		2 Making and Using Graphs [A good chapter to assign to the student with a fear of graphs.]
3 The Economic Problem		
4 Demand and Supply		
5 Elasticity		
6 Efficiency and Equity [A chapter that provides a non-technical explanation of efficiency and equity that unifies the micro coverage and permits early coverage of policy issues.]	7 Markets in Action [A unique chapter that gives extensive applications of demand and supply.]	8 Utility and Demand [Although this chapter is optional, it may be covered if desired *before* demand in Chapter 4.]
		9 Possibilities, Preferences, and Choices [A full chapter on this strictly optional topic to ensure that it is covered clearly with intuitive explanations and illustrations. The standard short appendix treatment of this topic makes it indigestible.]
11 Output and Costs		10 Organizing Production [This chapter may be skipped or assigned as a reading.]
12 Perfect Competition		
13 Monopoly		
14 Monopolistic Competition and Oligopoly		
15 Demand and Supply in Resource Markets [Enables you to cover all the resource market issues in a single chapter. Includes an explanation of present value.]	17 Inequality and Redistribution	16 Labour Markets
	18 Market Failure and Public Choice [Introduces the role of government in the economy and explains the positive theory of government.]	
	19 Competition Policy	
	20 Externalities, the Environment, and Knowledge	35 Trading with the World

Four Alternative Micro Sequences

Brief Contents

Contents

Summary (Key Points, Key Figures and Tables, and Key Terms), Problems, and Critical Thinking appear at the end of each chapter.

Don't Throw This Out!

This is your Online Resource Access Code for
EconomicsCentral

Welcome to **EconomicsCentral**, *Pearson Education Canada's online resource for economics students! You'll want to bookmark this site, because you'll find **actual past exams**, **tutorials** for difficult topics, an **online tutor** to help you with those tough questions, dynamic **Weblinks**, and much more, all right here.*

What do you

do with this

access code?

1. **Locate the Site:**
   Launch your web browser and type **www.pearsoned.ca/economics** into the location area.

2. **Use your Pearson Education Canada access code:**
   The first time you access the site, you will be required to register using this access code. Type in the access code on this page (one word per box) and follow the steps indicated. During registration, you will choose a personal User ID and password for logging into the site. Your access code can be used only once to establish your subscription, which is non-transferable. Once your registration has been confirmed, you need to enter only your personal User ID and password each time you enter the site. **This code is valid for 4 months of access to *EconomicsCentral*.**

   Warning: Once you enter your access code, registration processing may take up to 3 minutes to complete. If you do not wait for confirmation before proceeding, the access code will become invalid.

3. **Log onto the site:**
   Once your registration is confirmed, follow the **EconomicsCentral** link to log on with your newly-established User ID and Password.

CSBY-STOSS-THOLE-PICON-RELAX-CEASE

This pincode is only valid with the purchase of a new book.
For help using this access code, please e-mail us at

online.support@pearsoned.com

What Is Economics?

A Day in Your Life

From the moment you wake up each morning to the moment you fall asleep again each night, your life is filled with *choices*. Your first choice is when to get up. Will you start running the moment the alarm goes off, or will you linger for a few minutes and listen to the radio? What will you wear today? You check the weather forecast and make that decision. Then, what will you have for breakfast? Will you drive to school or take the bus? Which classes will you attend? Which assignments will you complete? What will you do for lunch? Will you play tennis, swim, run, or skate today? How will you spend your evening? Will you study, relax at home with a video, or go to the movies? ◆ You face decisions like these every day. But on some days, you face choices that can change the entire direction of your life. What will you study? Will you major in economics, business, law, or film? ◆ While you are making your own decisions, other people are making theirs. And some of the decisions that other people make will have an impact on your own subsequent decisions. Your school decides its course offerings for next year. Steven Spielberg decides what his next movie will be. General Motors decides what new models to introduce and how many of this year's models to produce. A team of eye doctors decides on a new experiment that will lead them to a cure for nearsightedness. Parliament decides to cut defence spending and to lower taxes. The Bank of Canada decides to lower interest rates. ◆ All these choices and decisions by you and everyone else are examples of economics in your life.

◇ This chapter takes a first look at the subject you are about to study. It defines economics. Then it expands on that definition with five big questions that economists try to answer and eight big ideas that define the economic way of thinking. These questions and ideas are the foundation on which your course is built. The chapter concludes with a description of how economists go about their work, the scientific method they use, and the pitfalls they try to avoid. When you have completed your study of this chapter, you will have a good sense of what economics is about and you'll be ready to start learning economics and using it to gain a new view of the world.

After studying this chapter, you will be able to:

■ Define economics

■ Explain the five big questions that economists seek to answer

■ Explain eight ideas that define the economic way of thinking

■ Describe how economists go about their work

A Definition of Economics

⌐ ALL ECONOMIC QUESTIONS AND PROBLEMS ARISE
from **scarcity**—they arise because our wants exceed
the resources available to satisfy them.

We want good health and long life, material
comfort, security, physical and mental recreation, and
knowledge. None of these wants is completely satisfied for everyone, and everyone has some unsatisfied
wants. While many people have all the material comfort they want, many others do not. And no one feels
entirely satisfied with her or his state of health and
expected length of life. No one feels entirely secure,
even in the post–Cold War era, and no one has
enough time for sport, travel, vacations, movies,
theatre, reading, and other leisure pursuits.

The poor and the rich alike face scarcity. A child
wants a 75¢ can of soft drink and a 50¢ pack of gum
but has only $1.00 in her pocket. She experiences
scarcity. A student wants to go to a party on Saturday
night but also wants to spend that same night catching up on late assignments. He experiences scarcity. A
millionaire wants to spend the weekend playing golf
and attending a business strategy meeting and cannot
do both. She experiences scarcity. Even parrots face
scarcity—there just aren't enough crackers to go
around!

Faced with scarcity, we must *choose* among the
available alternatives. Economics is sometimes called
the *science of choice*. More formally, **economics** is the
science that studies the choices that people make
when wants exceed the available resources—when
resources are scarce.

Not only do I want a cracker—we all want a cracker!

Big Economic Questions

⌐ ALL ECONOMIC CHOICES CAN BE SUMMARIZED IN
five big questions about the goods and services we
produce. These questions are: What? How? Who?
Where? When?

1. What?

What goods and services are produced and in what
quantities? **Goods and services** are all the things that
we value and are willing to pay for. We produce a
dazzling array of goods and services that range from
necessities such as houses to leisure items such as
camping vehicles and equipment. We build more
than a million new homes every year. And these
homes are more spacious and better equipped than
they were 20 years ago. We make several million new
leisure vehicles, tents, portable microwaves, refrigerators, telephones, television sets, and VCRs, all of
which make outdoor living and vacations more
attractive and more comfortable.

What determines whether we build more homes
or make more camping gear and develop more camp-
sites? How do these choices change over time? And
how are they affected by the ongoing changes in technology that make an ever-wider array of goods and
services available to us?

others, they use a laser scanner. One farmer keeps track of his livestock feeding schedules and inventories by using paper and pencil records, while another uses a personal computer. GM hires workers to weld auto bodies in some of its plants and uses robots to do the job in others.

Why do we use machines in some cases and people in others? Do mechanization and technological change destroy more jobs than they create? Do they make us better off or worse off?

2. How?

How are goods and services produced? In a vineyard in France, basket-carrying workers pick the annual grape crop by hand. In a vineyard in Ontario, a machine and a few workers do the same job that a hundred French grape harvesters do. Look around you and you will see many examples of this phenomenon—the same job being done in different ways. In some supermarkets, checkout clerks key in prices. In

3. Who?

Who consumes the goods and services that are produced? Who consumes the goods and services produced depends on the incomes that people earn. Doctors earn much higher incomes than nurses and medical assistants. So, doctors get more of the goods and services produced than nurses and medical assistants.

You probably know about many other persistent differences in incomes. Men, on the average, earn more than women. College graduates, on the average, earn more than high school graduates do. Canadians, on the average, earn more than Europeans, who in turn earn more on the average than Asians and Africans. But there are some significant exceptions. The people of Japan and Hong Kong now earn an amount similar to that of Canadians. And there is a lot of income inequality throughout the world.

What determines the incomes we earn? Why do doctors earn larger incomes than nurses? Why do women and minorities earn less than white males?

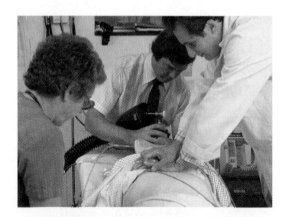

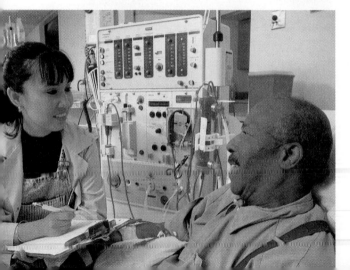

4. Where?

Where are goods and services produced? The Kellogg Company, of Battle Creek, Michigan, makes breakfast cereals in 20 countries and sells them in 160 countries. Kellogg's business in Japan is so huge that it has a Japanese language Web site to promote its products! Honda, the Japanese auto producer, makes cars and motorcycles on most continents. "Globalization through localization" is its slogan. But it produces some cars in one country and ships them for sale in another. Canadians even import some cars from Japan.

In today's global economy, people who are separated by thousands of miles cooperate to produce many goods and services. Software engineers in the Ottawa Valley work via the Internet with programmers in India. American Express card charge slips are processed in Barbados. But there is a lot of local concentration of production as well. Most North American carpets are made in Dalton, Georgia. And most Canadian movies are made in Toronto.

What determines where goods and services are produced? And how are changing patterns of production location changing the jobs we do and the wages we earn?

5. When?

When are goods and services produced? On a building site, there is a surge of production activity and people must work overtime to keep production flowing fast enough. An auto factory closes for the summer, temporarily lays off its workers, and its production dries up.

Sometimes, economy-wide production slackens off and even shrinks in what is called a *recession*. At other times, economy-wide production expands rapidly. We call these ebbs and flows of production the *business cycle*. When production falls, jobs are lost and unemployment climbs. Once, during the Great Depression of the 1930s, production fell so much that 20 percent of the work force was jobless.

During the past few years, production has decreased in Russia and its Central and Eastern European neighbours as these countries try to change the way they organize their economies.

In contrast, in Canada and the United States, production has expanded rapidly during the 1990s and unemployment has fallen. Is this burst of rapid expansion a sign of a "new economy" as some people claim, or is it just another example of a period of temporary expansion that will eventually end?

What makes production rise and fall? When will production fall again in Canada? Can the government prevent production from falling?

R E V I E W   Q U I Z

- How would you define economics?
- What is scarcity? Give some examples of rich people and poor people facing scarcity.
- Give some examples, different from those in the chapter, of each of the five big economic questions.
- Why do you care about *what* goods and services are produced? Give some examples of goods that you value highly and goods on which you place a low value.
- Why do you care about *how* goods and services are produced? [Hint: Think about cost.]
- Why do you care about *who* gets the goods and services that are produced?
- Why do you care about *where* or *when* goods and services are produced?

These five big economic questions give you a sense of what economics is *about*. They tell you about the *scope of economics*. But they don't tell you what economics *is*. They don't tell you how economists *think* about these questions and seek answers to them. Let's find out how economists approach economic questions by looking at some big ideas that define the *economic way of thinking*.

Big Ideas of Economics

WE CAN SUMMARIZE THE ECONOMIC WAY OF thinking in eight big ideas. Let's study them.

1. Choice, Tradeoff, and Opportunity Cost

A choice is a tradeoff—we give up something to get something else—and the highest-valued alternative we give up is the opportunity cost of the activity we choose.

Whatever we choose to do, we could have done something else instead. We trade off one thing for another. **Tradeoff** means giving up something to get something else. The highest-valued alternative we give up to get something is the **opportunity cost** of the activity chosen. "There's no such thing as a free lunch" is not just a clever throwaway line. It expresses the central idea of economics—that every choice involves a cost.

We use the term *opportunity cost* to emphasize that when we make a choice in the face of scarcity, we give up an opportunity to do something else. The opportunity cost of any action is the highest-valued alternative forgone. The action that you choose not to do—the highest-valued alternative forgone—is the cost of the action that you choose to do.

You can quit school right now or you can remain in school. If you quit and take a job at McDonald's, you might earn enough to buy some CDs, go to the movies, and spend lots of free time with your friends. If you remain in school, you can't afford these things. You will be able to buy these things later, and that is one of the payoffs from being in school. But for now, when you've bought your books, you have nothing left for CDs and movies. And doing assignments means that you've got less time for hanging around with your friends. The opportunity cost of being in school is the alternative things that you would have done if you had quit school.

Opportunity cost is the highest-valued alternative forgone. It is not *all* the possible alternatives forgone. For example, your economics lecture is at 8:30 on a Monday morning. You contemplate two alternatives to the lecture: staying in bed for an hour or jogging for an hour. You can't stay in bed and jog for that same hour. The opportunity cost of attending the lecture is the forgone hour in bed *or* the forgone hour of jogging. If these are the only alternatives you consider, then you have to decide which one you would do if you did not go to the lecture. The opportunity cost of attending a lecture for a jogger is a forgone hour of exercise; the opportunity cost of attending a lecture for a late sleeper is a forgone hour in bed.

2. Margins and Incentives

We make choices in small steps, or at the margin, and choices are influenced by incentives. Everything that we do involves a decision to do a little bit more or a little bit less of an activity. You can allocate the next hour between studying and e-mailing your friends. But the choice is not "all-or-nothing." You must decide how many minutes to allocate to each activity. To make this decision, you compare the benefit of a little bit more study time with its cost—you make your choice at the **margin**.

The mother of a young child must decide how to allocate her time between being with her child and working for an income. Like your decision about study time, this decision too involves comparing the benefit of a little bit more income with the cost of a little bit less time with her child.

The benefit that arises from an increase in an activity is called **marginal benefit**. For example, suppose that a mother is working 2 days a week and is thinking about increasing her work to 3 days. Her marginal benefit is the benefit she will get from the additional day of work. It is *not* the benefit she gets from all 3 days. The reason is that she already has the benefit from 2 days work, so she doesn't count this benefit as resulting from the decision she is now making.

The cost of an increase in an activity is called **marginal cost**. For the mother of the young child, the marginal cost of increasing her work to 3 days a week is the cost of the additional day not spent with her child. It does not include the cost of the 2 days she is already working.

To make her decision, the mother compares the marginal benefit from an extra day of work with its marginal cost. If the marginal benefit exceeds the marginal cost, she works the extra day. If the marginal cost exceeds the marginal benefit, she does not work the extra day.

By evaluating marginal benefits and marginal costs and choosing only those actions that bring greater benefit than cost, we use our scarce resources in the way that makes us as well off as possible.

Our choices respond to incentives. An **incentive** is an inducement to take a particular action. The inducement can be a benefit—a carrot—or a cost—a stick. A change in opportunity cost—in marginal cost—and a change in marginal benefit changes the incentives that we face and leads to changes in our actions.

For example, suppose the daily wage rate rises and nothing else changes. With a higher daily wage rate, the marginal benefit of working increases. For the young mother, the opportunity cost of spending a day with her child has increased. She now has a bigger incentive to work an extra day a week. Whether or not she does so depends on how she evaluates the marginal benefit of the additional income and the marginal cost of spending less time with her child.

Similarly, suppose the cost of day care rises and nothing else changes. The higher cost of day care increases the marginal cost of working. For the young mother, the opportunity cost of spending a day with her child has decreased. She now has a smaller incentive to work an extra day a week. Again, whether or not she changes her actions in response to a change in incentives depends on how she evaluates the marginal benefit and marginal cost.

The central idea of economics is that by looking for changes in marginal cost and marginal benefit, we can predict the way choices will change in response to changes in incentives.

3. Voluntary Exchange and Efficient Markets

Voluntary exchange makes both buyers and sellers better off, and markets are generally an efficient way to organize exchange.

When you shop for food, you give up some money in exchange for a basket of vegetables. But the food is worth the price you have to pay. You are better off having exchanged some of your money for the vegetables. The food store receives a payment that makes its operator happy too. Both you and the food store operator gain from your purchase.

Similarly, when you work at a summer job, you receive a wage that you've decided is sufficient to compensate you for the leisure time you must give up. But the value of your work to the firm that hires you is at least as great as the wage it pays you. So again, both you and your employer gain from a **voluntary exchange**.

You are better off when you buy your food. And you are better off when you sell your labour during the summer vacation. Whether you are a buyer or a seller, you gain from voluntary exchange with others. What is true for you is true for everyone. Everyone gains from voluntary exchange.

In our economy, exchanges take place in **markets** and for money. We sell our labour in exchange for an income in the labour market. And we buy the goods and services we've chosen to consume in a wide variety of markets—markets for vegetables, coffee, movies, videos, muffins, haircuts, and so on. At the other side of these transactions, firms buy our labour and sell us the hundreds of different consumer goods and services we buy.

Markets are **efficient** in the sense that they send resources to the place where they are valued most highly. For example, a frost kills Florida's orange crop and sends the price of orange juice through the roof. This increase in price, with all other prices remaining unchanged, increases the opportunity cost of drinking orange juice. The people who place the highest value on orange juice are the ones who keep drinking it. People who place a lower value on orange juice now have an incentive to substitute other fruit juices.

Markets are not the only way to organize the economy. An alternative is called a command system. In a **command system**, some people give orders (commands) and other people obey those orders. A command system is used in the military and in many firms. And it was used in the former Soviet Union to organize the entire economy. But the market is a superior method of organizing an entire economy.

4. Market Failure

The market does not always work efficiently and government action is sometimes necessary to make the use of resources efficient.

Market failure is a state in which the market does not use resources efficiently. If you pay attention to the news media, you might get the impression that the market almost never does a good job. It makes credit card interest rates too high. It makes the wages of fast-food workers too low. It causes the price of coffee to go through the ceiling every time Brazil has a serious frost. It increases the world price of oil when political instability threatens the Middle East. These examples are not cases of market failure. They are examples of the market doing its job of helping us to allocate our scarce resources and ensure that they are used in the activities in which they are most highly valued.

Buyers never like it when prices rise. But sellers love it. And sellers never like it when prices fall. But buyers are happy. Rising and falling prices make news because they bring changes in fortunes. Some people win and some lose. Everyone gains from voluntary exchange, as you've just seen, but other things remaining the same, the higher the price, the more the seller gains and the less the buyer gains.

Because a high price brings a bigger gain to the seller, there is an incentive for sellers to try to control a market. When a single producer controls an entire market, the producer can restrict the quantity available and raise the price. This action brings market failure. The quantity of the good available is too small. Some people believe that Intel restricts the quantity of computer chips when it introduces a new design in order to get a high price for it. Eventually, the price falls, but at first, Intel sells its new design for a high price and makes a bigger profit.

Market failure can also arise when producers don't take into account the costs they impose on other people. For example, when foreign boats take huge quantities of cod from the North Atlantic, they deplete the stock of fish and destroy jobs and fishing communities in Newfoundland. If these costs were taken into account, the cod catch would be smaller.

Market failure can also arise because some goods, such as national defence, must be consumed equally by everyone. None of us has an incentive voluntarily to pay our share of the cost of such a good. Instead, we try to free ride on everyone else. But if everyone tries to free ride, no one gets a ride!

To overcome market failure, governments intervene in markets. They discourage the production and consumption of some goods and services (such as tobacco and alcohol) by taxing them. They encourage the production and consumption of some goods and services (such as health care and education) by subsidizing them. And they directly provide some goods and services (such as national defence).

5. Expenditure, Income, and the Value of Production

For the economy as a whole, expenditure *equals* income and *equals* the value of production.

When you buy a coffee milk shake, you spend $2. But what happens to that money? The server gets some of it in wages, the owner of the building gets some of it as rent, and the owner of the milk bar gets some of it as profit. The suppliers of the milk, ice cream, and coffee also get some of your $2. But these suppliers spend part of what they receive on wages and rent. And they keep part of it as profit. Your $2 of **expenditure** creates exactly $2 of **income** for all the people who have contributed to making the milk shake, going all the way back to the farmer in Brazil who grew the coffee beans.

Your expenditure generates income of an equal amount. The same is true for everyone else's expenditure. So, for the economy as a whole, total

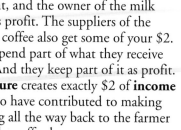

expenditure on goods and services equals total income. One way to value the things you buy is to use the prices you pay for them. So the value of all of the goods and services bought equals total expenditure. Another way to value the items you buy is to use the cost of production. This cost is the total amount paid to the people who produced the items—the total

income generated by your expenditure. But we've just seen that total expenditure and total income are equal, so they also equal the **value of production**.

6. Living Standards and Productivity Growth

Living standards improve when production per person increases.

By automating a car production line, one worker can produce a greater output. But if one worker can produce more cars, then more people can enjoy owning a car. The same is true for all goods and services. With increased output per person, we enjoy a higher standard of living and buy more goods and services.

The dollar value of production can increase for any of three reasons: because prices rise, because production per person—**productivity**—increases, or because the population increases.

But only an increase in productivity brings an improvement in living standards. A rise in prices brings higher incomes, but only in dollars. The extra income is just enough to pay the higher prices, not enough to buy more goods and services. An increase in population brings an increase in *total* production, but not an increase in production per person.

7. Inflation: A Monetary Problem

Prices rise in a process called **inflation** when the quantity of money increases faster than production. This process leads to a situation in which "too much money is chasing too few goods." As people bring more money to market, sellers see that they can raise their prices. But when these sellers go to buy their supplies, they find that the prices they face increase. With too much money around, money starts to lose value.

In some countries, inflation has been rapid. One such country is Poland. Since 1990, prices in Poland have risen more than seven-fold. In Canada, we have moderate inflation of about 1 percent a year.

Some people say that by increasing the quantity of money, we can create jobs. The idea is that if more money is put into the economy, when it is spent, businesses sell more and so hire more labour to produce more goods and services.

Initially, an increase in money might increase production and create jobs. But eventually, it only increases prices and leaves production and jobs unchanged.

8. Unemployment: Productive and Wasteful

Unemployment can result from market failure and be wasteful. But some unemployment is productive.

Unemployment is ever present. Sometimes its rate is low and sometimes it is high. Also, unemployment fluctuates over the business cycle.

Some unemployment is normal and efficient. We choose to take our time finding a suitable job rather than rushing to accept the first one that comes along. Similarly, businesses take their time in filling vacancies. The unemployment that results from these careful searches for jobs and workers improves productivity because it helps to assign people to their most productive jobs.

Some unemployment results from fluctuations in expenditure and can be wasteful.

R E V I E W   Q U I Z

- Give some examples of *tradeoffs* that you have made and the *opportunity costs* you've incurred today.
- Give some examples of *marginal cost* and *marginal benefit*.
- How do markets enable both buyers and sellers to gain from exchange and why do markets sometimes fail?
- For the economy as a whole, why does expenditure equal income and the value of production?
- What makes living standards rise?
- What makes prices rise?
- Is unemployment always a problem?

What Economists Do

ECONOMISTS USE THE EIGHT BIG IDEAS THAT YOU have just studied to search for answers to the five big questions that you reviewed at the start of this chapter. But how do they go about their work? What special problems and pitfalls do they encounter? And do they always agree on the answers?

Microeconomics and Macroeconomics

Economists approach their work from either a micro or a macro perspective. These two perspectives define the two major branches of the subject:

■ Microeconomics
■ Macroeconomics

Microeconomics is the study of the decisions of individual people and businesses and the interaction of those decisions in markets.

Macroeconomics is the study of the national economy and the global economy. It seeks to explain *average* prices and *total* employment, income, and production.

You can take either a micro or a macro view of the spectacular display of national flags in a Korean sports stadium. The micro view is of a single participant and the actions he or she is taking. The macro view is the patterns formed by the joint actions of all the individuals participating in the entire display.

Microeconomics seeks to explain the prices and quantities of individual goods and services. It also studies the effects of government regulation and taxes on the prices and quantities of individual goods and services. For example, microeconomics studies the forces that determine the prices of cars and the quantities of cars produced and sold. It also studies the effects of regulations and taxes on the prices and quantities of cars.

Macroeconomics studies the effects of taxes, government spending, and the government budget surplus or deficit on total jobs and incomes. It also studies the effects of money and interest rates.

Economic Science

Economics is a social science (along with political science, psychology, and sociology). A major task of economists is to discover how the economic world works. In pursuit of this goal, economists (like all scientists) distinguish between two types of statements:

■ What *is*
■ What *ought* to be

Statements about what *is* are called *positive* statements. They say what is currently believed about the way the world operates. A positive statement might be right or wrong. And we can test a positive statement by checking it against the facts. When a

chemist does an experiment in her laboratory, she is attempting to check a positive statement against the facts.

Statements about what *ought* to be are called *normative* statements. These statements depend on values and cannot be tested. When Parliament debates a motion, it is ultimately trying to decide what ought to be. It is making a normative statement.

To see the distinction between positive and normative statements, consider the controversy over global warming. Some scientists believe that centuries of the burning of coal and oil are increasing the carbon dioxide content of the earth's atmosphere and leading to higher temperatures that eventually will have devastating consequences for life on this planet. "Our planet is warming because of an increased carbon dioxide buildup in the atmosphere" is a positive statement. It can (in principle and with sufficient data) be tested. "We ought to cut back on our use of carbon-based fuels such as coal and oil" is a normative statement. You may agree with or disagree with this statement, but you can't test it. It is based on values. Health-care reform provides an economic example of the distinction. "Universal health care will cut the amount of work time lost to illness" is a positive statement. "Every Canadian should have equal access to health care" is a normative statement.

The task of economic science is to discover and catalogue positive statements that are consistent with what we observe in the world and that enable us to understand how the economic world works. This task is a large one that can be broken into three steps:

■ Observation and measurement
■ Model building
■ Testing models

Observation and Measurement   First, economists keep track of the amounts and locations of natural and human resources, of wages and work hours, of the prices and quantities of the different goods and services produced, of taxes and government spending, and of the quantities of goods and services bought from and sold to other countries. This list gives a flavour of the array of things that economists can observe and measure.

Model Building   The second step toward understanding how the economic world works is to build a model. An **economic model** is a description of some aspect of the economic world that includes only those features of the world that are needed for the purpose at hand. A model is simpler than the reality it describes. What a model includes and what it leaves out result from *assumptions* about what is essential and what are inessential details.

You can see how ignoring details is useful—even essential—to our understanding by thinking about a model that you see every day, the TV weather map. The weather map is a model that helps to predict the temperature, wind speed and direction, and precipitation over a future period. The weather map shows lines called isobars—lines of equal barometric pressure. It doesn't show the highways. The reason is that our theory of the weather tells us that the pattern of air pressure, not the location of the highways, determines the weather.

An economic model is similar to a weather map. It tells us how a number of variables are determined by a number of other variables. For example, an economic model of the 1994 Los Angeles earthquake might tell us the effects of the earthquake and the government's relief efforts on the number of houses and apartments, rents and prices, jobs, and commuting times.

Testing   The third step is testing the model. A model's predictions may correspond to or be in conflict with the facts. By comparing the model's predictions with the facts, we are able to test a model and develop an economic theory. An **economic theory** is a generalization that summarizes what we think we understand about the economic choices that people make and the performance of industries and entire economies. It is a bridge between an economic model and the real economy.

A theory is created by a process of building and testing models. For example, meteorologists have a theory that if the isobars form a particular pattern at a particular time of the year (a model), then it will snow (reality). They have developed this theory by repeated observation and by carefully recording the weather that follows specific pressure patterns.

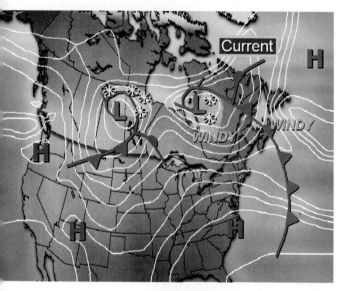

Economics is a young science. It was born in 1776 with the publication of Adam Smith's *The Wealth of Nations* (see pp. 58–59). Over the past 225 years, economics has discovered many useful theories. But in many areas, economists are still looking for answers. The gradual accumulation of economic knowledge gives most economists some faith that their methods will, eventually, provide usable answers to the big economic questions.

But progress in economics comes slowly. Let's look at some of the obstacles to progress in economics.

Obstacles and Pitfalls in Economics

We cannot easily do economic experiments. And most economic behaviour has many simultaneous causes. For these two reasons, it is difficult in economics to unscramble cause and effect.

Unscrambling Cause and Effect By changing one factor at a time and holding all the other relevant factors constant, we isolate the factor of interest and are able to investigate its effects in the clearest possible way. This logical device, which all scientists use to identify cause and effect, is called *ceteris paribus*. *Ceteris paribus* is a Latin term that means "other things being equal" or "if all other relevant things remain the same." Ensuring that other things are equal is crucial in many activities, including athletic events, and all successful attempts to make scientific progress use this device.

Economic models (like the models in all other sciences) enable the influence of one factor at a time to be isolated in the imaginary world of the model. When we use a model, we are able to imagine what would happen if only one factor changed. But *ceteris paribus* can be a problem in economics when we try to test a model.

Laboratory scientists, such as chemists and physicists, perform experiments by actually holding all the relevant factors constant except for the one under investigation. In the non-experimental sciences such as economics (and astronomy), we usually observe the outcomes of the *simultaneous* operation of many factors. Consequently, it is hard to sort out the effects of each individual factor and to compare the effects with what a model predicts. To cope with this problem, economists take three complementary approaches.

First, they look for pairs of events in which other things were equal (or similar). An example might be to study the effects of employment insurance on the unemployment rate by comparing Canada with the United States on the presumption that the people in the two economies are sufficiently similar. Second, economists use statistical tools—called *econometrics*. And third, when they can, they perform experiments. This relatively new approach puts real subjects (usually students) in a decision-making situation and varies their incentives in some way to discover how they respond to one factor at a time.

Economists try to avoid *fallacies*—errors of reasoning that lead to a wrong conclusion. But two fallacies are common, and you need to be on your guard to avoid them. They are the

- Fallacy of composition
- *Post hoc* fallacy

Fallacy of Composition The fallacy of composition is the (false) statement that what is true of the parts is true of the whole or that what is true of the whole is true of the parts. Think of the true statement, "Speed kills," and its implication, going more slowly saves lives. If an entire freeway moves at a lower speed, everyone on the highway has a safer ride.

But suppose that one driver only slows down and all the other drivers try to maintain their original speed. In this situation, there will probably be more accidents because more cars will change lanes to overtake the slower vehicle. So, in this example, what is true for the whole is not true for a part.

The fallacy of composition arises mainly in macroeconomics, and it stems from the fact that the parts interact with each other to produce an outcome for the whole that might differ from the intent of the parts. For example, a firm lays off some workers to cut costs and improve its profits. If all firms take similar actions, incomes fall and so does spending. The firm sells less, and its profits don't improve.

Post Hoc Fallacy Another Latin phrase—*post hoc ergo propter hoc*—means "after this, therefore because of this." The *post hoc* fallacy is the error of reasoning that a first event *causes* a second event because the first occurred before the second. Suppose you are a visitor from a far-off world. You observe lots of people shopping in early December and then you see them opening gifts and partying on Christmas day. Does the shopping cause Christmas, you wonder. After a deeper study, you discover that Christmas causes the shopping. A later event causes an earlier event.

Unravelling cause and effect is difficult in economics. And just looking at the timing of events often doesn't help. For example, the stock market booms, and some months later the economy expands—jobs and incomes grow. Did the stock market boom cause the economy to expand? Possibly, but perhaps businesses started to plan the expansion of production because a new technology that lowered costs had become available. As knowledge of the plans spread, the stock market reacted to *anticipate* the economic expansion. To disentangle cause and effect, economists use economic models and data and, to the extent that they can, perform experiments.

Economics is a challenging science. Does the difficulty of getting answers in economics mean that anything goes and that economists disagree on most questions? Perhaps you've heard the joke: "If you laid all the economists in the world end to end, they still wouldn't reach agreement." Does the joke make a valid point?

Agreement and Disagreement

Economists agree on a remarkably wide range of questions. And surprisingly, the agreed view of economists often disagrees with the popular and sometimes politically correct view. When Bank of Canada Governor Gordon Thiessen testifies before Parliament, his words are rarely controversial among economists, even when they generate endless debate in the media.

Here are 12 propositions[1] with which at least 7 out of every 10 economists broadly agree:

■ Tariffs and import restrictions make most people worse off.

■ A large federal budget deficit has an adverse effect on the economy.

■ Cash payments to welfare recipients make them better off than do transfers-in-kind of equal cash value.

■ A minimum wage increases unemployment among young workers and low skilled workers.

■ A tax cut can help to lower unemployment when the unemployment rate is high.

■ The distribution of income should be more equal.

■ Inflation is primarily caused by a rapid rate of money creation.

■ The government should restructure welfare along the lines of a "negative income tax."

■ Rent ceilings cut the availability of housing.

■ Pollution taxes are more effective than pollution limits.

■ The redistribution of income is a legitimate role for the federal government.

■ The federal budget should be balanced on the average over the business cycle, but not every year.

Which are positive and which are normative? Notice that economists are willing to offer their opinions on normative issues as well as their professional views on positive questions. Be on the lookout for normative propositions dressed up as positive propositions.

R E V I E W   Q U I Z

▨ What is the distinction between microeconomics and macroeconomics? Provide an example (not in the chapter) of a micro issue and a macro issue.

▨ What is the distinction between a positive statement and a normative statement? Provide an example (different from those in the chapter) of each type of statement.

▨ What is a model? Can you think of a model that you might use (probably without thinking of it as a model) in your everyday life?

▨ What is a theory? Why is the statement, "It might work in theory but it doesn't work in practice" a silly statement? [Hint: Think about what a theory is and how it is used.]

▨ What is the *ceteris paribus* assumption and how is it used?

▨ Try to think of some everyday examples of fallacies.

◇ You are now ready to start *doing* economics. As you get into the subject, you will see that we rely heavily on graphs. You must be comfortable with this method of reasoning. If you need some help with it, take your time in working carefully through Chapter 2. If you are already comfortable with graphs, then you are ready to jump right into Chapter 3 and begin to study the fundamental economic problem, scarcity.

---

[1]These are propositions generally supported or supported with provisions by more than 7 out of 10 economists according to a survey by Richard M. Alston, J.R. Kearl, and Michael B. Vaughan, "Is There a Consensus Among Economists," *American Economic Review*, 82, (May 1992), pp. 203–209. We have simplified the language in some cases and you should check the original for the exact propositions and percentages agreeing.

S U M M A R Y

Key Points

A Definition of Economics (p. 2)

▪ Economics is the *science of choice*—the science that explains the choices that we make to cope with scarcity.

Big Economic Questions (pp. 2–5)

▪ Economists try to answer five big questions about goods and services:
1. What?
2. How?
3. Who?
4. Where?
5. When?
What are the goods and services produced, *how*, are they produced, *who* consumes them, and *where* and *when* are they produced?

▪ These questions interact to determine the standards of living and the distribution of well-being in Canada and around the world.

Big Ideas of Economics (pp. 6–11)

▪ A choice is a tradeoff and the highest-valued alternative forgone is the opportunity cost of what is chosen.

▪ Choices are made at the margin and are influenced by incentives.

▪ Markets enable both buyers and sellers to gain from voluntary exchange.

▪ Sometimes government actions are needed to overcome market failure.

▪ For the economy as a whole, expenditure equals income and equals the value of production.

▪ Living standards rise when production per person increases.

▪ Prices rise when the quantity of money increases faster than production.

▪ Unemployment can result from market failure but can also be productive.

What Economists Do (pp. 12–16)

▪ Microeconomics is the study of individual decisions, and macroeconomics is the study of the economy as a whole.

▪ Positive statements are about what *is* and normative statements are about what *ought* to be.

▪ To explain the economic world, economists build and test economic models.

▪ Economists use the *ceteris paribus* assumption to try to disentangle cause and effect, and they are careful to avoid the fallacy of composition and the *post hoc* fallacy.

▪ Economists agree on a wide range of questions about how the economy works.

Key Terms

Ceteris paribus, 14
Command system, 8
Economic model, 13
Economic theory, 13
Economics, 2
Efficient, 8
Expenditure, 10
Goods and services, 2
Incentive, 7
Income, 10
Inflation, 11
Macroeconomics, 12
Margin, 7
Marginal benefit, 7
Marginal cost, 7
Markets, 8
Market failure, 9
Microeconomics, 12
Opportunity cost, 6
Productivity, 10
Scarcity, 2
Tradeoff, 6
Unemployment, 11
Value of production, 10
Voluntary exchange, 8

PROBLEMS

*1. You plan to go to school this summer. If you do, you won't be able to take your usual job that pays $6,000 for the summer and you won't be able to live at home for free. The cost of your tuition will be $2,000, textbooks $200, and living expenses $1,400. What is the opportunity cost of going to summer school?

2. You plan a major adventure trip for the summer. You won't be able to take your usual summer job that pays $6,000 and you won't be able to live at home for free. The cost of your travel on the trip will be $3,000, film and video tape will cost you $200, and your food will cost $1,400. What is the opportunity cost of taking this trip?

*3. The local mall has free parking, but the mall is always very busy and it usually takes 30 minutes to find a parking space. Today when you found a vacant spot, Harry also wanted it. Is parking really free at this mall? If not, what did it cost you to park today? When you parked your car today, did you impose any costs on Harry? Explain your answers.

4. A city has built a new parking garage. There is always a free parking spot but it costs $1 a day. Before the new garage was built, it usually took 15 minutes of cruising to find a parking space. Compare the opportunity cost of parking in the new garage with that in the old parking lot. Which is less costly and by how much?

CRITICAL THINKING

1. Use the link on the Parkin-Bade Web site to visit *Resources for Economists on the Internet*. This site is a good place from which to search for economic information on the Internet. Visit the "general interest" sites and become familiar with the types of information that they contain.

2. Use the link on the Parkin-Bade Web site to visit *Statistics Canada*. Use this site to keep informed about the Canadian economy and about the economy of your own province and city.

a. What is the number of people employed in your area?

b. Has employment increased or decreased?

c. What is income per person in your area?

3. This man is homeless and you can see all his possessions in the photograph.

Use the five big questions and the eight big ideas of economics to organize a short essay about the economic life of the man in the photograph. Does he face scarcity? Does he make choices? Can you interpret his choices as being in his own best interest? Can either his own choices or the choices of others make this man better off? If so, how?

4. Use the link on the Parkin-Bade Web site to visit the *National Post*.

a. What is the top economic news story today?

b. With which of the five big questions does it deal? [Hint: It must deal with at least one of them and might deal with more than one.]

c. Which of the eight big ideas seem to be relevant to understanding this news item?

d. Write a summary of the news item using as much as possible of the economic vocabulary that you have learned in this chapter and that is in the key terms list on p. 17.

Chapter 2

Making and Using Graphs

British Prime Minister Benjamin Disraeli is reputed to have said that "There are three kinds of lies: lies, damned lies, and statistics." One of the most powerful ways of conveying statistical information is in the form of a graph. And like statistics, graphs can lie. But the right graph does not lie. It reveals a relationship that would otherwise be obscure. ◆ Graphs are a modern invention. They first appeared in the late eighteenth century, long after the discovery of logarithms and calculus. But today, in the age of the personal computer and video display, graphs have become as important as

Three Kinds of Lies

words and numbers. How do economists use graphs? What types of graphs do they use? What do graphs reveal and what can they hide? ◆ The big questions that economics tries to answer—questions that you studied in Chapter 1—are difficult ones. They involve relationships among a large number of variables. Almost nothing in economics has a single cause. Instead, a large number of variables interact with each other. It is often said that in economics, everything depends on everything else. Changes in the quantity of ice cream consumed are caused by changes in the price of ice cream, the temperature, and many other factors. How can we make and interpret graphs of relationships among several variables?

◆ In this chapter, you are going to look at the kinds of graphs that economists use. You are going to learn how to make them and read them. You are also going to learn how to determine the magnitude of the influence of one variable on another by calculating the slope of a line and of a curve. ◆ There are no graphs or techniques used in this book that are more complicated than those explained and described in this chapter. If you are already familiar with graphs, you may want to skip (or skim) this chapter. Whether you study this chapter thoroughly or give it a quick pass, you can use it as a handy reference and return to it whenever you feel that you need extra help understanding the graphs that you encounter in your study of economics.

After studying this chapter, you will be able to:

■ Make and interpret a time-series graph, a scatter diagram, and a cross-section graph

■ Distinguish between linear and nonlinear relationships and between relationships that have a maximum and a minimum

■ Define and calculate the slope of a line

■ Graph relationships among more than two variables

Graphing Data

GRAPHS REPRESENT A QUANTITY AS A DISTANCE on a line. Figure 2.1 gives two examples. A distance on the horizontal line represents temperature, measured in degrees Celsius. A movement from left to right shows an increase in temperature. A movement from right to left shows a decrease in temperature. The point marked 0 represents zero degrees Celsius. To the right of 0, the temperatures are positive. To the left of 0, the temperatures are negative (as indicated by the minus sign in front of the numbers).

A distance on the vertical line represents altitude or height, measured in thousands of metres above sea level. The point marked 0 represents sea level. Points above 0 represent metres above sea level. Points below 0 (indicated by a minus sign) represent metres below sea level.

There are no rigid rules about the scale for a graph. The range of the variables being graphed determines the scale.

The main point of a graph is to enable us to visualize the relationship between two variables. And to accomplish this, we set two scales perpendicular to each other, like those in Fig. 2.1.

The two scale lines are called *axes*. The horizontal line is called the *x*-axis or horizontal axis, and the vertical line is called the *y*-axis or vertical axis. The letters *x* and *y* appear on the axes of Fig. 2.1. Each axis has a zero point, which is shared by the two axes. This zero point, common to both axes, is called the *origin*.

To show something in a two-variable graph, we need two pieces of information. We need the value of the variable *x* and the value of the variable *y*. For example, off the coast of British Columbia on a winter's day, the temperature is 10 degrees. Call this value *x*. A fishing boat is located at 0 metres above sea level. We'll call this value *y*. These two bits of information appear as point *a* in Fig. 2.1. A climber at the top of Mount McKinley on a very cold day is 6,194 metres above sea level in a zero degree gale. These two pieces of information appear as point *b*. The position of the climber on a warmer day might be at the point marked *c*. This point represents the peak of Mt. McKinley when the temperature is 10 degrees.

Two lines, called coordinates, can be drawn from point *c* in the graph. One of these lines runs from *c* to the horizontal axis. This line is called the *y*-coordinate. Its length is the same as the value marked off on the *y*-axis. The other of these lines

FIGURE 2.1

Making a Graph

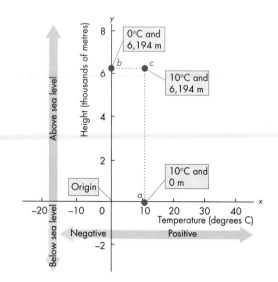

All graphs have axes that measure quantities as distances. Here, the horizontal axis (*x*-axis) measures temperature. A rightward movement shows an increase in temperature. The vertical axis (*y*-axis) measures height. An upward movement shows an increase in height. Point *a* represents a fishing boat at sea level (0 on the *y*-axis) on a day when the temperature is 10° (10° on the *x*-axis). Point *b* represents a climber at the top of Mt. McKinley (6,194 metres above sea level on the *y*-axis) on a day when the temperature on Mt. McKinley is 0° (0° on the *x*-axis). Point *c* represents a climber at the top of Mt. McKinley, 6,194 metres above sea level (on the *y*-axis) on a day when the temperature on Mt. McKinley is 10° (on the *x*-axis).

runs from *c* to the vertical axis. This line is called the *x*-coordinate. Its length is the same as the value marked off on the *x*-axis. To describe a point in a graph, we simply use the values of its *x*- and *y*-coordinates.

Graphs like that in Fig. 2.1 can be used to show any type of quantitative data about two variables. Economists use graphs similar to the one in Fig. 2.1 to reveal and describe the relationships among economic variables. To do so, they use three main types of graph, which we'll now study. They are:

■ Scatter diagrams
■ Time-series graphs
■ Cross-section graphs

Scatter Diagrams

A **scatter diagram** plots the value of one economic variable against the value of another variable. Such a graph is used to reveal whether a relationship exists between two economic variables. It is also used to describe a relationship.

Consumption and Income   Figure 2.2(a) shows a scatter diagram of the relationship between consumption and income. The *x*-axis measures average income, and the *y*-axis measures average consumption. Each point shows consumption per person and income per person (on the average) in Canada in a given year from 1985 to 1998. The points for the fourteen years are "scattered" within the graph. Each point is labelled with a two-digit number that shows us its year. For example, the point marked 88 shows us that in 1988, income per person was $25,750 and consumption per person was $14,700.

The dots in this graph form a pattern, which reveals a positive relationship between these two variables. That is, when income increases, consumption also increases.

Phone Calls and Price   Figure 2.2(b) shows a scatter diagram of the relationship between the number of international phone calls made from Canada and the average price per minute.

The dots in this graph reveal that as the price per minute falls, the number of calls increases.

Unemployment and Inflation   Figure 2.2(c) shows a scatter diagram of inflation and unemployment in Canada. The dots in this graph form a pattern that shows us there is no clear relationship between these two variables. By its lack of a distinct pattern, the graph shows us there is no simple relationship between inflation and unemployment in Canada.

Correlation and Causation   A scatter diagram that shows a clear relationship between two variables, such as Fig. 2.2(a) or Fig. 2.2(b), tells us that the two variables have a high correlation. When a high correlation is present, we can predict the value of one variable from the value of the other variable. But correlation does not imply causation. Sometimes a high correlation is just a coincidence, but sometimes

---

FIGURE   2.2

Scatter Diagrams

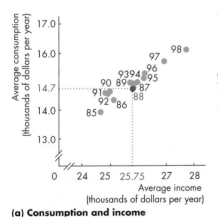

(a) Consumption and income

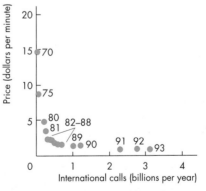

(b) International phone calls and prices

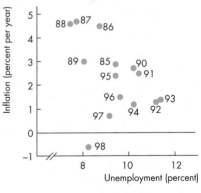

(c) Unemployment and inflation

A scatter diagram reveals the relationship between two variables. Part (a) shows the relationship between consumption and income between 1985 to 1998. Each point shows the values of the two variables in a specific year. For example, in 1988, average income was $25,750 and average consumption was $14,700. The pattern formed by the points shows that as income increases, so does consumption. Part (b) shows the

relationship between the price of an international phone call and the number of phone calls made per year between 1970 and 1993. This graph shows that as the price of a phone call has fallen, the number of calls made has increased. Part (c) shows the inflation rate and unemployment rate in Canada between 1985 and 1998. This graph shows that inflation and unemployment are not closely related.

it does arise from a causal relationship. It is likely, for example, that increasing income causes increasing consumption (Fig. 2.2a) and that falling phone call prices cause more calls to be made (Fig. 2.2b).

Breaks in the Axes Two of the graphs you've just looked at, Fig. 2.2(a) and Fig. 2.2(c), have breaks in their axes, as shown by the small gaps. The breaks indicate that there are jumps from the origin, 0, to the first values recorded.

In Fig. 2.2(a), the breaks are used because the lowest value of consumption exceeds $10,000 and the lowest value of income exceeds $15,000. With no breaks in the axes, there would be a lot of empty space, all the points would be crowded into the top right corner, and we would not be able to see whether a relationship exists between these two variables. By breaking the axes, we are able to see the relationship.

Putting a break in the axes is like using a zoom lens to bring the relationship into the centre of the graph and magnify it so that it fills the graph.

Misleading Graphs Breaks can be used to highlight a relationship. But they can also be used to mislead and create a wrong impression—to make a graph that lies. The most common way of making a graph lie is to use axis breaks and to either stretch or compress a scale. The most effective way to see the power of this kind of lie is to make some graphs that use this technique. For example, redraw Fig. 2.2(a) but make the *y*-axis that measures consumption run from zero to $45,000 and keep the *x*-axis the same as the one shown. The graph will now create the impression that despite huge income growth, consumption has barely changed.

To avoid being misled, it is a good idea to get into the habit of always looking closely at the values and the labels on the axes of a graph before you start to interpret it.

Time-Series Graphs

A **time-series graph** measures time (for example, months or years) on the *x*-axis and the variable or variables in which we are interested on the *y*-axis. Figure 2.3 shows an example of a time-series graph. In this graph, time (on the *x*-axis) is measured in years, which run from 1968 to 1998. The variable that we are interested in is the price of coffee and it is measured on the *y*-axis.

A time-series graph conveys an enormous amount of information quickly and easily, as this example illustrates. It shows:

- The *level* of the price of coffee—when it is *high* and *low*. When the line is a long way from the *x*-axis, the price is high. When the line is close to the *x*-axis, the price is low.

- How the price *changes*—whether it *rises* or *falls*. When the line slopes upward, as in 1976, the price is rising. When the line slopes downward, as in 1978, the price is falling.

- The *speed* with which the price is changing—whether it is rising or falling *quickly* or *slowly*. If the line is very steep, then the price is rising or falling quickly. If the line is not steep, the price rises or falls slowly. For example, the price rose very quickly in 1976 and 1977. The price went up again in 1993 but slowly. Similarly, when the price was falling in 1978, it fell quickly, but during the early 1980s, it fell more slowly.

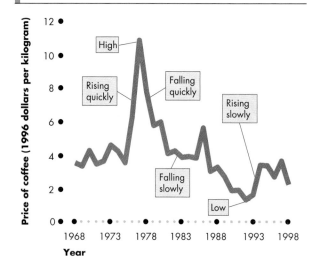

FIGURE 2.3

A Time-Series Graph

A time-series graph plots the level of a variable on the *y*-axis against time (day, week, month, or year) on the *x*-axis. This graph shows the price of coffee (in 1996 dollars per kilogram) each year from 1968 to 1998. It shows us when the price of coffee was *high* and when it was *low*, when the price *rose* and when it *fell*, and when it changed *quickly* and when it changed *slowly*.

A time-series graph also reveals whether there is a trend. A **trend** is a general tendency for a variable to rise or fall. You can see that the price of coffee had a general tendency to fall from the mid-1970s to the early 1990s. That is, although there were ups and downs in the price, there was a general tendency for it to fall.

A time-series graph also lets us compare different periods quickly. Figure 2.3 shows that the 1980s were different from the 1970s. The price of coffee fluctuated more violently in the 1970s than it did in the 1980s. This graph conveys a wealth of information, and it does so in much less space than we have used to describe only some of its features.

Comparing Two Time Series Sometimes we want to use a time-series graph to compare two different variables. For example, suppose you want to know whether the balance of the government's budget fluctuates with the unemployment rate. You can examine the government's budget balance and the unemployment rate by drawing a graph of each of them on the same time scale. But we can measure the government's budget balance either as a surplus or as a deficit. Figure 2.4(a) plots the budget surplus. The scale of the unemployment rate is on the left side of the figure, and the scale of the government's budget surplus is on the right. The orange line shows unemployment, and the blue line shows the government's budget surplus. This figure shows that the unemployment rate and the government's budget surplus move in opposite directions. For example, when the unemployment rate decreases, the budget surplus increases.

Figure 2.4(b) uses a scale for the government's budget balance measured as a deficit. That is, we flip the right-side scale over. This figure shows that the unemployment rate and the budget deficit move in the same direction. The budget deficit and the unemployment rate increase together and decrease together.

Scatter Diagram for Comparing Two Time Series We can compare two time series in a graph like Fig. 2.4 or in a scatter diagram like Fig. 2.2. Which is better? There is no right answer to this question. If the purpose of the graph is to show *both* the way two variables have changed over time and how they are related to each other, then the time-series graph does the better job. But if the purpose of the graph is to check the strength of the relationship between two variables, then a scatter diagram does a better job. A relationship that looks strong in a time-series graph often looks weak in a scatter diagram.

FIGURE 2.4
Time-Series Relationships

(a) Unemployment and budget surplus

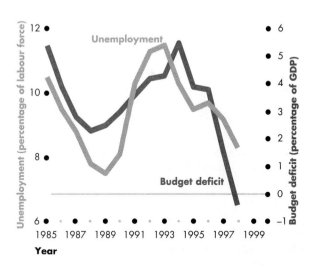

(b) Unemployment and budget deficit

These two graphs show the unemployment rate and the balance of the government's budget. The unemployment line is identical in the two parts. Part (a) shows the budget surplus—taxes *minus* spending—on the right scale. It is hard to see a relationship between the budget surplus and unemployment. Part (b) shows the budget as a deficit—spending *minus* taxes. It inverts the scale of part (a). With the scale for the budget balance inverted, the graph reveals a tendency for unemployment and the budget deficit to move together.

Cross-Section Graphs

A **cross-section graph** shows the values of an economic variable for different groups in a population at a point in time. Figure 2.5 is an example of a cross-section graph. It shows the unemployment rate across ten cities in Canada in 1998. This graph uses bars rather than dots and lines, and the length of each bar indicates the percentage of the labour force in the city unemployed. Figure 2.5 enables you to compare the unemployment rates in these ten cities. And you can do so much more quickly and clearly than by looking at a list of numbers.

The cross-section graph in Fig. 2.5 is also an example of a *bar chart*. We often use bars rather than lines in cross-section graphs, but there are no fixed rules about whether to use lines, dots, or bars. It is a matter of taste.

You've now seen how we can use graphs in economics to show economic data and to reveal relationships between variables. Next, we're going to learn how to use graphs in a more abstract way. We'll learn how economists use graphs to construct and display economic models.

FIGURE 2.5
A Cross-Section Graph

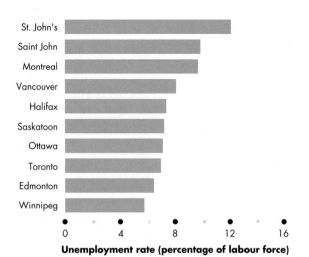

Unemployment rate (percentage of labour force)

A cross-section graph shows the level of a variable across the members of a population. This graph shows the unemployment rate in ten Canadian cities in May 1998.

Graphs Used in Economic Models

THE GRAPHS USED IN ECONOMICS ARE NOT always designed to show real-world data. Often they are used to show general relationships among the variables in an economic model.

An **economic model** is a stripped down, simplified description of an economy or of a component of an economy such as a business or a household. It consists of statements about economic behaviour that can be expressed as equations or as curves in a graph. Economists use models to explore the effects of different policies or other influences on the economy in ways that are similar to the use of model airplanes in wind tunnels and models of the climate.

You will encounter many different kinds of graphs in economic models, but there are some repeating patterns and once you've learned to recognize these patterns, you will instantly understand the meaning of a graph. Here, we'll look at the different types of curves that are used in economic models, and we'll see some everyday examples of each type of curve. The patterns to look for in graphs are:

- Variables move in the same direction
- Variables move in opposite directions
- Variables have a maximum or a minimum
- Variables are unrelated

Let's look at these four cases.

Variables That Move in the Same Direction

Figure 2.6 shows graphs of the relationships between two variables that move up and down together. A relationship between two variables that move in the same direction is called a **positive relationship** or a **direct relationship**. Such a relationship is shown by a line that slopes upward.

Figure 2.6 shows three types of relationships, one that has a straight line and two that have curved lines. But all the lines in these three graphs are called *curves*. Any line on a graph—no matter whether it is straight or curved—is called a *curve*.

A relationship shown by a straight line is called a **linear relationship**. Figure 2.6(a) shows a linear relationship between the distance travelled in 5 hours

---

FIGURE 2.6

Positive (Direct) Relationships

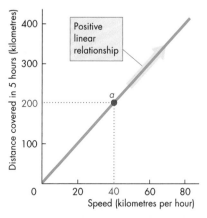

(a) Positive linear relationship

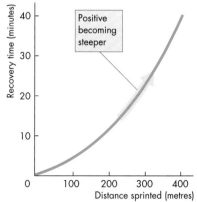

(b) Positive becoming steeper

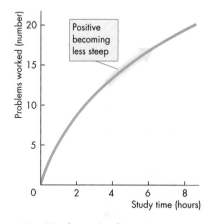

(c) Positive becoming less steep

Each part of this figure shows a positive (direct) relationship between two variables. That is, as the value of the variable measured on the *x*-axis increases, so does the value of the variable measured on the *y*-axis. Part (a) shows a linear relationship—as the two variables increase together, we move along a straight line. Part (b) shows a positive relationship such that as the two variables increase together, we move along a curve that becomes steeper. Part (c) shows a positive relationship such that as the two variables increase together, we move along a curve that becomes flatter.

---

and speed. For example, point *a* shows us that we will travel 200 kilometres in 5 hours if our speed is 40 kilometres an hour. If we double our speed to 80 kilometres an hour, we will travel 400 kilometres in 5 hours.

Part (b) shows the relationship between distance sprinted and recovery time (the time it takes the heart rate to return to its normal resting rate). This relationship is shown by a curved upward-sloping line that starts out quite flat but becomes steeper as we move along the curve away from the origin. The reason this curve slopes upward and becomes steeper is because the additional recovery time needed from sprinting an additional 100 metres increases. It takes less than five minutes to recover from 100 metres but more than 10 minutes to recover from the third 100 metres.

Part (c) shows the relationship between the number of problems worked by a student and the amount of study time. This relationship is shown by an upward-sloping curved line that starts out quite steep and becomes flatter as we move away from the origin. Study time becomes less productive as you increase the hours worked and become more tired.

Variables That Move in Opposite Directions

Figure 2.7 shows relationships between things that move in opposite directions. A relationship between variables that move in opposite directions is called a **negative relationship** or an **inverse relationship**.

Part (a) shows the relationship between the number of hours available for playing squash and the number of hours for playing tennis. One extra hour spent playing tennis means one hour less playing squash and vice versa. This relationship is negative and linear.

Part (b) shows the relationship between the cost per kilometre travelled and the length of a journey. The longer the journey, the lower is the cost per kilometre. But as the journey length increases, the cost per kilometre decreases, and the fall in the cost is smaller, the longer the journey. This feature of the relationship is shown by the fact that the curve slopes downward, starting out steep at a short journey length and then becoming flatter as the journey

FIGURE 2.7

Negative (Inverse) Relationships

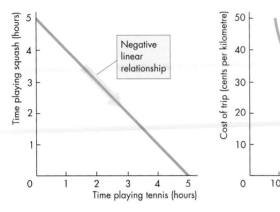

(a) Negative linear relationship

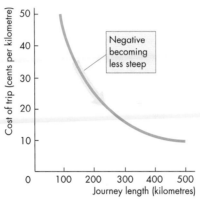

(b) Negative becoming less steep

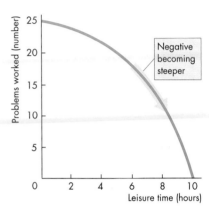

(c) Negative becoming steeper

Each part of this figure shows a negative (inverse) relationship between two variables. Part (a) shows a linear relationship—as one variable increases and the other variable decreases, we move along a straight line. Part (b) shows a negative relationship such that as the journey length increases the curve becomes less steep. Part (c) shows a negative relationship such that as leisure time increases, the curve becomes steeper.

length increases. This relationship arises because some of the costs are fixed, such as auto insurance, and the fixed costs are spread over a longer journey.

Part (c) shows the relationship between the amount of leisure time and the number of problems worked by a student. Increasing leisure time produces an increasingly large reduction in the number of problems worked. This relationship is a negative one that starts out with a gentle slope at a small number of leisure hours and becomes steeper as the number of leisure hours increases. This relationship is a different view of the idea shown in Fig. 2.6(c).

Variables That Have a Maximum or a Minimum

Many relationships in economic models have a maximum or a minimum. For example, firms try to make the maximum possible profit and to produce at the lowest possible cost. Figure 2.8 shows relationships that have a maximum or a minimum.

Part (a) shows the relationship between rainfall and wheat yield. When there is no rainfall, wheat will

not grow, so the yield is zero. As the rainfall increases up to 10 days a month, the wheat yield also increases. With 10 rainy days a month, the wheat yield reaches its maximum at 2 tonnes per hectare (point *a*). Rain in excess of 10 days a month starts to lower the yield of wheat. If every day is rainy, the wheat suffers from a lack of sunshine and the yield falls back to zero. This relationship is one that starts out sloping upward, reaches a maximum, and then slopes downward.

Part (b) shows the reverse case—a relationship that begins sloping downward, falls to a minimum, and then slopes upward. An example of such a relationship is the gasoline cost per kilometre as the speed of travel varies. At low speeds, the car is creeping along in a traffic snarl-up. The number of kilometres per litre is low, so the gasoline cost per kilometre is high. At very high speeds, the car is travelling faster than its most efficient speed, and again the number of kilometres per litre is low and the gasoline cost per kilometre is high. At a speed of 100 kilometres an hour, the gasoline cost per kilometre travelled is at its minimum (point *b*). This relationship starts out sloping downward, reaches a minimum, and then slopes upward.

FIGURE 2.8

Maximum and Minimum Points

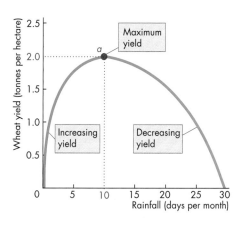

(a) Relationship with a maximum

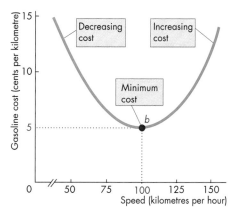

(b) Relationship with a minimum

Part (a) shows a relationship that has a maximum point, *a*. The curve slopes upward as it rises to its maximum point, is flat at its maximum, and then slopes downward. Part (b) shows a relationship with a minimum point, *b*. The curve slopes downward as it falls to its minimum, is flat at its minimum, and then slopes upward.

Variables That Are Unrelated

There are many situations in which no matter what happens to the value of one variable, the other variable remains constant. Sometimes we want to show the independence between two variables in a graph and Fig. 2.9 shows two ways of achieving this.

In describing the graphs in Fig. 2.6 through 2.9, we have talked about the slopes of curves. Let's look more closely at the concept of slope.

FIGURE 2.9

Variables That Are Unrelated

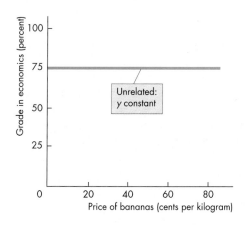

(a) Unrelated: *y* constant

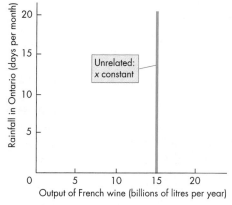

(b) Unrelated: *x* constant

This figure shows how we can graph two variables that are unrelated to each other. In part (a), a student's grade in economics is plotted at 75 percent regardless of the price of bananas on the *x*-axis. The curve is horizontal. In part (b), the output of the vineyards of France in a year does not vary with the rainfall in Ontario. The curve is vertical.

The Slope of a Relationship

WE CAN MEASURE THE INFLUENCE OF ONE variable on another by the slope of the relationship. The **slope** of a relationship is the change in the value of the variable measured on the *y*-axis divided by the change in the value of the variable measured on the *x*-axis—or, slope equals rise over run. We use the Greek letter Δ (*delta*) to represent "change in." Thus Δ*y* means the change in the value of the variable measured on the *y*-axis, and Δ*x* means the change in the value of the variable measured on the *x*-axis. Therefore the slope of the relationship is

$$\Delta y\,/\,\Delta x.$$

If a large change in the variable measured on the *y*-axis (Δ*y*) is associated with a small change in the variable measured on the *x*-axis (Δ*x*), the slope is large and the curve is steep. If a small change in the variable measured on the *y*-axis (Δ*y*) is associated with a large change in the variable measured on the *x*-axis (Δ*x*), the slope is small and the curve is flat.

We can make the idea of slope sharper by doing some calculations.

The Slope of a Straight Line

The slope of a straight line is the same regardless of where on the line you calculate it. Thus the slope of a straight line is constant. Let's calculate the slopes of the lines in Fig. 2.10. In part (a), when *x* increases from 2 to 6, *y* increases from 3 to 6. The change in *x* is +4—that is, Δ*x* is 4. The change in *y* is +3—that is,

---

FIGURE 2.10
The Slope of a Straight Line

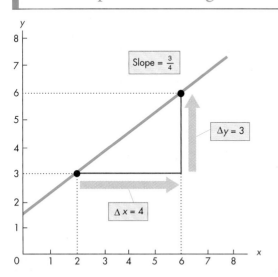

(a) Positive slope

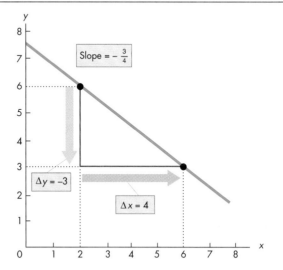

(b) Negative slope

To calculate the slope of a straight line, we divide the change in the value of the variable measured on the *y*-axis (Δ*y*) by the change in the value of the variable measured on the *x*-axis (Δ*x*), as we move along the curve. Part (a) shows the calculation of a positive slope. When *x* increases from 2 to 6, Δ*x* equals 4. That change in *x* brings about an increase in *y* from 3

to 6, so Δ*y* equals 3. The slope (Δ*y*/Δ*x*) equals 3/4. Part (b) shows the calculation of a negative slope. When *x* increases from 2 to 6, Δ*x* equals 4. That increase in *x* brings about a decrease in *y* from 6 to 3, so Δ*y* equals –3. The slope (Δ*y*/Δ*x*) equals –3/4.

Δy is 3. The slope of that line is

$$\frac{\Delta y}{\Delta x} = \frac{3}{4}.$$

In part (b), when x increases from 2 to 6, y decreases from 6 to 3. The change in y is *minus* 3—that is, Δy is –3. The change in x is *plus* 4—that is, Δx is 4. The slope of the curve is

$$\frac{\Delta y}{\Delta x} = \frac{-3}{4}.$$

Notice that the two slopes have the same magnitude (3/4), but the slope of the line in part (a) is positive (+3/+4 = 3/4), while the slope in part (b) is negative (–3/+4 = – 3/4). The slope of a positive relationship is positive; the slope of a negative relationship is negative.

The Slope of a Curved Line

The slope of a curved line is trickier. The slope of a curved line is not constant. Its slope depends on where on the line we calculate it. There are two ways to calculate the slope of a curved line: You can calculate the slope at a point or you can calculate the slope across an arc of the line. Let's look at the two alternatives.

Slope at a Point   To calculate the slope at a point on a curve, you need to construct a straight line that has the same slope as the curve at the point in question. Figure 2.11 shows how this is done. Suppose you want to calculate the slope of the curve at point a. Place a ruler on the graph so that it touches point a and no other point on the curve, then draw a straight line along the edge of the ruler. The straight red line is this line, and it is the tangent to the curve at point a. If the ruler touches the curve only at point a, then the slope of the curve at point a must be the same as the slope of the edge of the ruler. If the curve and the ruler do not have the same slope, the line along the edge of the ruler will cut the curve instead of just touching it.

Now that you have found a straight line with the same slope as the curve at point a, you can calculate the slope of the curve at point a by calculating the slope of the straight line. Along the straight line, as x increases from 0 to 4 ($\Delta x = 4$), y increases from 2 to 5

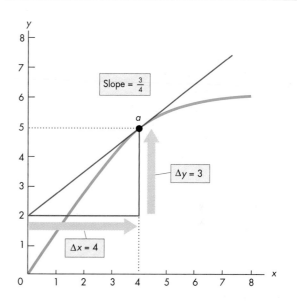

FIGURE 2.11

Slope at a Point

Slope = $\frac{3}{4}$

a

$\Delta y = 3$

$\Delta x = 4$

To calculate the slope of the curve at point a, draw the red line that just touches the curve at a—the tangent. The slope of this straight line is calculated by dividing the change in y by the change in x along the line. When x increases from 0 to 4, Δx equals 4. That change in x is associated with an increase in y from 2 to 5, so Δy equals 3. The slope of the red line is 3/4. So the slope of the curve at point a is 3/4.

($\Delta y = 3$). Therefore the slope of the line is

$$\frac{\Delta y}{\Delta x} = \frac{3}{4}.$$

Thus the slope of the curve at point a is 3/4.

Slope Across an Arc   An arc of a curve is a piece of a curve. In Fig. 2.12, you are looking at the same curve as in Fig. 2.11. But instead of calculating the slope at point a, we are going to calculate the slope across the arc from b to c. You can see that the slope at b is greater than the slope at c. When we calculate the slope across an arc, we are calculating the average slope between two points. As we move along the arc from b to c, x increases from 3 to 5 and y increases from 4 to 5.5. The change in x is 2 ($\Delta x = 2$), and the

FIGURE 2.12

Slope Across an Arc

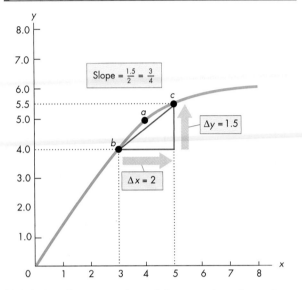

To calculate the average slope of the curve along the arc *bc*, draw a straight line from *b* to *c*. The slope of the line *bc* is calculated by dividing the change in *y* by the change in *x*. In moving from *b* to *c*, Δx equals 2 and Δy equals 1.5. The slope of the line *bc* is 1.5 divided by 2, or 3/4. So the slope of the curve across the arc *bc* is 3/4.

change in *y* is 1.5 ($\Delta y = 1.5$). Therefore the slope of the line is

$$\frac{\Delta y}{\Delta x} = \frac{1.5}{2} = \frac{3}{4}.$$

Thus the slope of the curve across the arc *bc* is 3/4.

This calculation gives us the slope of the curve between points *b* and *c*. The actual slope calculated is the slope of the straight line from *b* to *c*. This slope approximates the average slope of the curve along the arc *bc*. In this particular example, the slope across the arc *bc* is identical to the slope of the curve at point *a*. But the calculation of the slope of a curve does not always work out so neatly. You might have some fun constructing counterexamples.

You now know how to make and interpret a graph. But so far, we've limited our attention to graphs of two variables. We're now going to learn how to graph more than two variables.

Graphing Relationships Among More Than Two Variables

WE HAVE SEEN THAT WE CAN GRAPH THE relationship between two variables as a point formed by the *x*- and *y*-coordinates in a two-dimensional graph. You may be thinking that although a two-dimensional graph is informative, most of the things in which you are likely to be interested involve relationships among many variables, not just two. For example, the amount of ice cream consumed depends on the price of ice cream and the temperature. If ice cream is expensive and the temperature is low, people eat much less ice cream than when ice cream is inexpensive and the temperature is high. For any given price of ice cream, the quantity consumed varies with the temperature, and for any given temperature, the quantity of ice cream consumed varies with its price.

Figure 2.13 shows a relationship among three variables. The table shows the number of litres of ice cream consumed each day at various temperatures and ice cream prices. How can we graph these numbers?

To graph a relationship that involves more than two variables, we use the *ceteris paribus* assumption.

Ceteris Paribus The Latin phrase **ceteris paribus** means "other things remaining the same." Every laboratory experiment is an attempt to create *ceteris paribus* and isolate the relationship of interest. We use the same method to make a graph.

Figure 2.13(a) shows what happens to the quantity of ice cream consumed when the price of ice cream varies while the temperature is held constant. The line labelled 21°C shows the relationship between ice cream consumption and the price of ice cream if the temperature is 21°C. The numbers used to plot that line are those in the third column of the table in Fig. 2.13. For example, if the temperature is 21°C, 10 litres are consumed when the price is 60¢ a scoop, and 18 litres are consumed when the price is 30¢ a scoop. The curve labelled 32°C shows consumption as the price varies if the temperature is 32°C.

We can also show the relationship between ice cream consumption and temperature while the price of ice cream remains constant, as shown in Fig. 2.13(b). The curve labelled 60¢ shows how the con-

FIGURE 2.13
Graphing a Relationship Among Three Variables

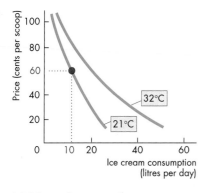

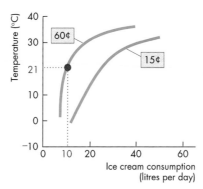

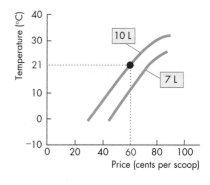

(a) Price and consumption at a given temperature

(b) Temperature and consumption at a given price

(c) Temperature and price at a given consumption

Price (cents per scoop)	Ice cream consumption (litres per day)			
	–10°C	**10°C**	**21°C**	**32°C**
15	12	18	25	50
30	10	12	18	37
45	7	10	13	27
60	5	7	**10**	20
75	3	5	7	14
90	2	3	5	10
105	1	2	3	6

The quantity of ice cream consumed depends on its price and the temperature. The table gives some hypothetical numbers that tell us how many litres of ice cream are consumed each day at different prices and different temperatures. For example, if the price is 60¢ a scoop and the temperature is 21°C, 10 litres of ice cream are consumed. This set of values is highlighted in the table and each part of the figure. To graph a relationship among three variables, the value of one variable is held constant.

Part (a) shows the relationship between price and consumption when temperature is held constant. One curve holds temperature at 32°C and the other at 21°C. Part (b) shows the relationship between temperature and consumption when price is held constant. One curve holds the price at 60¢ a scoop and the other at 15¢ a scoop. Part (c) shows the relationship between temperature and price when consumption is held constant. One curve holds consumption at 10 litres and the other at 7 litres.

sumption of ice cream varies with the temperature when the price of ice cream is 60¢ a scoop, and a second curve shows the relationship when ice cream costs 15¢ a scoop. For example, at 60¢ a scoop, 10 litres are consumed when the temperature is 21°C and 20 litres when the temperature is 32°C.

Figure 2.13(c) shows the combinations of temperature and price that result in a constant consumption of ice cream. One curve shows the combination that results in 10 litres a day being consumed, and the other shows the combination that results in 7

litres a day being consumed. A high price and a high temperature lead to the same consumption as a lower price and a lower temperature. For example, 10 litres of ice cream are consumed at 32°C and 90¢ a scoop, at 21°C and 60¢ a scoop and at 10°C and 45¢ a scoop.

◆ With what you have learned about graphs, you can move forward with your study of economics. There are no graphs in this book that are more complicated than those that have been explained here.

MATHEMATICAL NOTE: EQUATIONS TO STRAIGHT LINES

IF A STRAIGHT LINE IN A GRAPH DESCRIBES THE relationship between two variables, we call it a **linear relationship**. Figure 1 shows the linear relationship between a person's expenditure and income. This person spends $100 a week (by borrowing or spending previous savings) when income is zero. And out of each dollar earned, this person spends 50 cents (and saves 50 cents).

All linear relationships are described by the same general equation. We call the quantity that is measured on the horizontal (or x-axis) x and we call the quantity that is measured on the vertical (or y-axis) y. In the case of Fig. 1, x is income and y is expenditure.

A Linear Equation

The equation that describes a straight-line relationship between x and y is:

$$y = a + bx.$$

In this equation, a and b are fixed numbers and they are called *constants*. The values of x and y vary so these numbers are called *variables*. Because the equation describes a straight line, it is called a **linear equation**.

The equation tells us that when the value of x is zero, the value of y is a. We call the constant a the y-axis intercept. The reason is that on the graph the straight line hits the y axis at a value equal to a. Figure 1 illustrates the y-axis intercept.

For positive values of x, the value of y exceeds a. The constant b tells us by how much y increases above a as x increases. The constant b is the slope of the line.

Slope of Line

As we explain in the chapter, the **slope** of a relationship is the change in the value of y divided by the change in the value of x. We use the Greek letter Δ (*delta*) to represent "change in." Thus Δy means the change in the value of the variable measured on the y-axis, and Δx means the change in the value of the variable measured on the x-axis. Therefore the slope of the relationship is

$$\Delta y \,/\, \Delta x.$$

To see why the slope is b, suppose that initially the value of x is x_1, or $200 in Fig. 2. The corresponding value of y is y_1, also $200 in Fig. 2. The equation to the line tells us that

$$y_1 = a + bx_1. \qquad (1)$$

Now the value of x increases by Δx to $x_1 + \Delta x$ (or $400 in Fig. 2). And the value of y increases by Δy to $y + \Delta y$ (or $300 in Fig. 2).

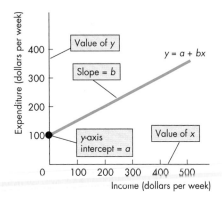

Figure 1 Linear relationship

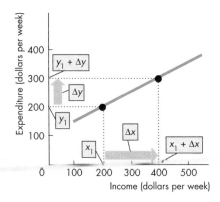

Figure 2 Calculating slope

The equation to the line now tells us that

$$y_1 + \Delta y = a + b(x_1 + \Delta x) \qquad (2)$$

To calculate the slope of the line, subtract equation (1) from equation (2) to obtain:

$$\Delta y = b \Delta x \qquad (3)$$

and now divide equation (3) by Δx to obtain:

$$\frac{\Delta y}{\Delta x} = b.$$

So, the slope of the line is b.

Position of Line

The y-axis intercept determines the position of the line on the graph. Figure 3 illustrates the relationship between the y-axis intercept and the position of the line on the graph. The y-axis measures saving and the x-axis measures income. When the y-axis intercept, a, is positive, the line hits the y-axis at a positive value of y—as the blue line does. When the y-axis intercept, a, is zero, the line hits the y-axis at the origin—as the purple line does. When the y-axis intercept, a, is negative, the line hits the y-axis at a negative value of y—as the red line does. As the equations to the three lines show, the value of the y-axis intercept does not influence the slope of the line.

Positive Relationships

Figure 1 shows a positive relationship—the two variables x and y move in the same direction. All positive relationships have a slope that is positive. In the equation to the line, the constant b is positive. In this example, the y-axis intercept, a, is 100. The slope b equals $\Delta y/\Delta x$, which is 100/200 or 0.5. The equation to the line is:

$$y = 100 + 0.5x.$$

Negative Relationships

Figure 4 shows a negative relationship—the two variables x and y move in the opposite direction. All negative relationships have a slope that is negative. In the equation to the line, the constant b is negative. In the example in Fig. 4, the y-axis intercept, a, is 30. The slope, b, equals $\Delta y/\Delta x$, which is $-20/2$ or -10. The equation to the line is:

$$y = 30 + (-10)x$$

or,

$$y = 30 - 10x.$$

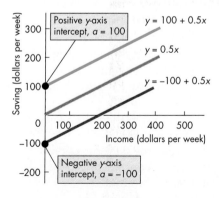

Figure 3 The *y*-axis intercept

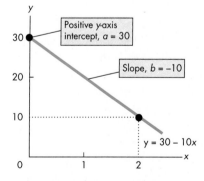

Figure 4 Negative relationship

SUMMARY

Key Points

Graphing Data (pp. 20–24)

- Time-series graphs show trends, cycles, and other fluctuations in economic data.
- Scatter diagrams show the relationship between two variables. They show whether two variables are positively related, negatively related, or unrelated.
- Cross-section graphs show how variables change across the members of a population.

Graphs Used in Economic Models (pp. 24–27)

- Graphs are used to show relationships among variables in economic models.
- Relationships can be positive (an upward-sloping curve), negative (a downward-sloping curve), positive and then negative (have a maximum point), negative and then positive (have a minimum point), or unrelated (a horizontal or vertical curve).

The Slope of a Relationship (pp. 28–30)

- The slope of a relationship is calculated as the change in the value of the variable measured on the y-axis divided by the change in the value of the variable measured on the x-axis—that is, $\Delta y/\Delta x$.
- A straight line has a constant slope.
- A curved line has a varying slope. To calculate the slope of a curved line, we calculate the slope at a point or across an arc.

Graphing Relationships Among More Than Two Variables (pp. 30–31)

- To graph a relationship among more than two variables, we hold constant the values of all the variables except two.
- We then plot the value of one of the variables against the value of another.

Key Figures ◆

Key Terms

REVIEW QUIZ

- What are the three types of graphs used to show economic data?
- Give an example of a time-series graph.
- List three things that a time-series graph shows quickly and easily.
- Give three examples, different from those in the chapter, of scatter diagrams that show a positive relationship, a negative relationship, and no relationship.
- Draw some graphs to show the relationships between two variables:
  a. That move in the same direction.
  b. That move in opposite directions.
  c. That have a maximum.
  d. That have a minimum.
- Which of the relationships in the previous question is a positive relationship and which is a negative relationship?
- What are the two ways of calculating the slope of a curved line?
- How do we graph a relationship among more than two variables?

PROBLEMS

Use the following data on the Canadian economy in problems 1, 2, 3, and 4. Column A is the year, column B is the inflation rate, column C is the interest rate, column D is the growth rate of output, column E is the unemployment rate.

	A	B	C	D	E
1	1980	9.6	12.7	1.4	7.5
2	1981	10.8	17.8	3.8	7.6
3	1982	8.7	13.8	-3.4	11.0
4	1983	5.0	9.3	3.3	11.9
5	1984	3.1	11.1	6.4	11.3
6	1985	2.6	9.5	5.4	10.5
7	1986	2.4	9.0	2.6	9.5
8	1987	4.7	8.2	4.1	8.8
9	1988	4.6	9.4	4.9	7.8
10	1989	4.8	12.0	2.5	7.5
11	1990	3.1	12.8	0.0	8.1
12	1991	2.7	8.9	–1.9	10.3
13	1992	1.4	6.5	1.0	11.3
14	1993	1.8	4.9	2.3	11.5
15	1994	0.2	5.4	4.7	10.3
16	1995	2.2	7.0	2.6	9.5
17	1996	1.6	4.2	1.2	9.7
18	1997	1.6	3.3	3.8	9.2
19	1998	1.0	4.7	4.2	8.3

*1. a. Draw a time-series graph of the inflation rate.
   b. In which year(s) (i) was inflation highest? (ii) was inflation lowest? (iii) did it increase? (iv) did it decrease? (v) did it increase most? and (vi) did it decrease most?
   c. What was the main trend in inflation?

2. a. Draw a time-series graph of the interest rate.
   b. In which year(s) (i) was the interest rate highest? (ii) was it lowest? (iii) did it increase? (iv) did it decrease? (v) did it increase most? and (vi) did it decrease most?
   c. What was the main trend in the interest rate?

3. Draw a scatter diagram to show the relationship between the inflation rate and the interest rate. Describe the relationship.

4. Draw a scatter diagram to show the relationship between the growth rate of output and the unemployment rate. Describe the relationship.

*5. Draw a graph to show the relationship between the two variables x and y:

x	0	1	2	3	4	5	6	7	8
y	0	1	4	9	16	25	36	49	64

   a. Is the relationship positive or negative?
   b. Does the slope of the relationship increase or decrease as the value of x increases?
   c. Think of some economic relationships that might be similar to this one.

6. Draw a graph that shows the relationship between two variables x and y:

x	0	1	2	3	4	5
y	50	48	44	32	16	0

   a. Is the relationship positive or negative?
   b. Does the slope of the relationship increase or decrease as the value of x increases?
   c. Think of some economic relationships that might be similar to this one.

*7. In problem 5, calculate the slope of the relationship between x and y when x equals 4.

8. In problem 6, calculate the slope of the relationship between x and y when x equals 3.

*9. In problem 5, calculate the slope of the relationship across the arc when x increases from 3 to 4.

10. In problem 6, calculate the slope of the relationship across the arc when x increases from 4 to 5.

*11. Calculate the slope of the relationship shown at point a in the following figure.

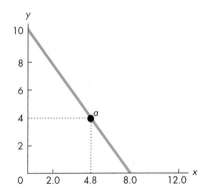

12. Calculate the slope of the relationship shown at point *a* in the following figure.

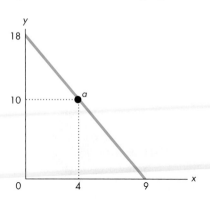

*13. Use the following figure to calculate the slope of the relationship:

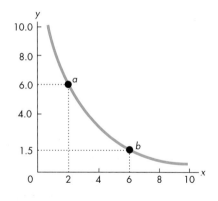

  a. At points *a* and *b*.
  b. Across the arc *ab*.

14. Use the following figure to calculate the slope of the relationship:

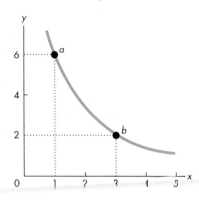

  a. At points *a* and *b*.
  b. Across the arc *ab*.

*15. The table gives the price of a balloon ride, the temperature, and the number of rides a day.

Price	Balloon rides (number per day)		
(dollars per ride)	10°C	20°C	30°C
5.00	32	40	50
10.00	27	32	40
15.00	18	27	32
20.00	10	18	27

Draw graphs to show the relationship between
  a. The price and the number of rides, holding the temperature constant.
  b. The number of rides and temperature, holding the price constant.
  c. The temperature and price, holding the number of rides constant.

16. The table gives the price of umbrellas, rainfall, and the umbrellas purchased.

Price	Umbrellas (number per day)		
(dollars per umbrella)	0 mm	2 mm	10 mm
10	7	8	12
20	4	7	8
30	2	4	7
40	1	2	4

Draw graphs to show the relationship between
  a. The price and the number of umbrellas purchased, holding rainfall constant.
  b. The number of umbrellas purchased and rainfall, holding the price constant.
  c. Rainfall and the price, holding the number of umbrellas purchased constant.

17. Visit the Parkin-Bade Web site and find the Consumer Price Index (CPI) for the latest 12 months. Make a graph to show whether the CPI is rising or falling and whether the rate of rise or fall is increasing or decreasing.

18. Visit the Parkin-Bade Web site and find the unemployment rate for the latest 12 months. Make a graph to show whether the unemployment rate is rising or falling and whether the rate of rise or fall is increasing or decreasing.

3

The Economic Problem

We live in a style that surprises our grandparents and would have astonished our great grandparents. Most of us live in more spacious homes than they did. We eat more, grow taller, and are even born larger than they were. Video games, cellular phones, gene splices, and personal computers did not exist even 20 years ago. But today it is hard to imagine life without them. Economic growth has made us richer than our grandparents. And we are not alone in experiencing an expansion in the goods and services we consume. Many nations around the world are not only sharing our experience, they are setting the pace. Hong Kong, Taiwan, Singapore, Korea, and China are expanding at unheard-of rates. But economic growth does not liberate us from scarcity. Why not? Why, despite our immense wealth, must we still make choices and face costs? Why are there no "free lunches"?
◆ We see an incredible amount of specialization and trade in the world. Each one of us specializes in a particular job—as a lawyer, a car maker, a homemaker. We have become so specialized that one farm worker can feed 100 people. Less than one-sixth of the Canadian work force is employed in manufacturing. More than half of the work force is employed in wholesale and retail trade, banking and finance, government, and other services. Why do we specialize? How do we benefit from specialization and trade?
◆ Over many centuries, institutions and social arrangements have evolved that we take for granted. One of them is property rights and a political and legal system that protects them. Another is markets. Why have these social arrangements evolved? How do they extend our ability to specialize and increase production?

◇ These are the questions that we study in this chapter. We begin with the core economic problem: scarcity and choice and the concept of the production possibility frontier. We then learn about the central idea of economics—efficiency. We also discover how we can expand production by accumulating capital and by specializing and trading with each other.
◆ What you will learn in this chapter is the foundation on which all economics is built. You will receive big dividends from a careful study of this material.

Making the Most of It

After studying this chapter, you will be able to:

- ■ Explain the fundamental economic problem

- ■ Define the production possibility frontier

- ■ Define and calculate opportunity cost

- ■ Explain the conditions in which resources are used efficiently

- ■ Explain how economic growth expands production possibilities

- ■ Explain how specialization and trade expand production possibilities

Resources and Wants

TWO FACTS DOMINATE OUR LIVES:

- We have limited resources.
- We have unlimited wants.

These two facts define **scarcity**, a condition in which the resources available are insufficient to satisfy people's wants.

Scarcity is a universal fact. It confronts each one of us individually, and it confronts our families, local communities, and nations.

The fundamental economic problem is to use our limited resources to produce the items that we value most highly. **Economics** is the study of the *choices* people make to cope with *scarcity*. It is the study of how we each individually try to get the most out of our own limited resources and of how in that endeavour we interact with each other. Let's look a bit more closely at our limited resources and unlimited wants.

Limited Resources

The resources that can be used to produce goods and services are grouped into four categories:

1. Labour
2. Land
3. Capital
4. Entrepreneurship

Labour is the time and effort that we devote to producing goods and services. It includes the physical and mental work of people who make cars and cola, gum and glue, wallpaper and watering cans.

Land is the gifts of nature that we use to produce goods and services. It includes the air, the water, and the land surface as well as the minerals that lie beneath the surface of the earth.

Capital is the goods that we have produced and that we can now use to produce other goods and services. It includes highways, buildings, dams and power projects, airports and jumbo jets, car production lines, shirt factories, and cookie shops.

Capital also includes **human capital**, which is the knowledge and skill that people obtain from education and on-the-job training. You are building human capital right now as you work on your economics course and other subjects. And your human capital will continue to grow when you get a full-

time job and become better at it. Human capital improves the *quality* of labour.

Entrepreneurship is the resource that organizes labour, land, and capital. Entrepreneurs make business decisions, bear the risks that arise from these decisions, and come up with new ideas about what, how, where, and when to produce.

Our limited resources are converted into goods and services by using the technologies available. These technologies are limited by our knowledge—our human capital—and by our other resources.

Unlimited Wants

Our wants are limited only by our imaginations and are effectively unlimited. We want food and drink, clothing, housing, education, and health care. We want some of these things so badly that we call them *necessities*. But we also want many other things. We want cars and airplanes, movie theatres and videos, popcorn and pop, Walkmans and CDs, books and magazines, restaurant meals, vacations at the beach and in the mountains, music and poetry, and instant telecommunication across the globe.

Some of these wants are less pressing than others, but they are all wants. We even want things that are technologically impossible today but about which we fantasize. We want to live longer and healthier lives. Some of us want to hitch-hike the galaxy and be beamed around the universe.

Because our wants exceed our resources, we must make choices. We must rank our wants and decide which wants to satisfy and which to leave unsatisfied. We try to get the most out of our resources.

R E V I E W   Q U I Z

- What is scarcity?
- What is the fundamental economic problem?
- Can you provide a definition of economics?
- What are the resources that can be used to produce goods and services?
- How do we cope with the fact that our wants cannot be satisfied with the resources available?

We'll begin our study of the choices people make by looking at the limits to production and at a fundamental implication of choice—opportunity cost.

Resources, Production Possibilities, and Opportunity Cost

EVERY WORKING DAY, IN MINES, FACTORIES, shops, and offices and on farms and construction sites across Canada, 15 million people produce a vast variety of goods and services valued at around $27 billion. The quantities of goods and services that can be produced are limited by our available resources and by technology. That limit is described by the production possibility frontier.

The **production possibility frontier** (*PPF*) is the boundary between those combinations of goods and services that can be produced and those that cannot.

To illustrate the production possibility frontier in a graph, we focus our attention on two goods at a time. In focusing on two goods, we hold the quantities produced of all the other goods and services constant—a device called the *ceteris paribus* assumption. That is, we look at a *model* of the economy in which everything remains the same except for the production of the two goods we are currently considering.

Let's look at the production possibility frontier for two goods that most students buy—bottles of pop and CDs.

Production Possibility Frontier

The *production possibility frontier* for pop and CDs shows the limits to the production of these two goods, given the total resources available to produce them. Figure 3.1 shows this production possibility frontier. The table lists some combinations of the quantities of CDs and pop that can be produced given the resources available, and the figure graphs these combinations. The quantity of CDs produced is shown on the *x*-axis and the quantity of pop produced is shown on the *y*-axis. (The numbers are hypothetical.)

Because the *PPF* shows the *limits* to production, we cannot attain the points outside the frontier. They are points that describe wants that cannot be satisfied. We can produce at all the points *inside* the *PPF* and *on* the *PPF*. They are attainable points.

Suppose that in a typical month, 4 million CDs and 5 million bottles of pop are produced. Figure 3.1 shows this combination as point *e* and as possibility *e* in the table. Figure 3.1 also shows other production possibilities. For example, we might stop producing

FIGURE 3.1

Production Possibility Frontier

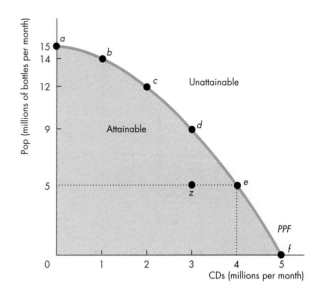

Possibility	CDs (millions per month)		Pop (millions of bottles per month)
a	0	and	15
b	1	and	14
c	2	and	12
d	3	and	9
e	4	and	5
f	5	and	0

The table lists six points on the production possibility frontier for CDs and pop. Row *a* tells us that if we produce no CDs, the maximum quantity of pop we can produce is 15 million bottles a month. The rows of the table are graphed as points *a, b, c, d, e,* and *f* in the figure. The line passing through these points is the production possibility frontier (*PPF*). It separates the attainable from the unattainable. We can produce at any point inside the orange area or on the frontier. Points outside the frontier are unattainable. Points inside the frontier such as point *z* are inefficient because it is possible to use the available resources to produce more of either or both goods.

CDs and move all the people who produce them into bottling pop. This case is shown as point *a* in the figure and possibility *a* in the table. The quantity of pop produced increases to 15 million bottles a month, and CD production dries up. Alternatively, we might close down the bottling plants and switch all the resources into producing CDs. In this situation, we produce 5 million CDs a month. This case is shown as point *f* in the figure and possibility *f* in the table.

Production Efficiency

We achieve **production efficiency** if we cannot produce more of one good without producing less of some other good. When production is efficient, we are at a point *on* the *PPF*. If we are at a point *inside* the *PPF*, such as point *z*, production is *inefficient* because we have some *unused* resources or we have some *misallocated* resources or both.

Resources are unused when they are idle but could be working. For example, we might leave some of the bottling plants idle or some workers might be unemployed.

Resources are *misallocated* when they are assigned to tasks for which they are not the best match. For example, we might assign skilled bottling machine operators to work in a CD factory and skilled CD makers to work in a bottling plant. We could get more CDs *and* more bottles of pop from these same workers if we reassigned them to the tasks that more closely match their skills.

If we produce at a point inside the *PPF* such as *z*, we can use our resources more efficiently to produce more CDs, more pop, or more of *both* CDs and pop. But if we produce at a point *on* the *PPF*, we are using our resources efficiently and we can produce more of one good only if we produce less of the other. We face a *tradeoff*.

Tradeoff

On the production possibility frontier, every choice involves a **tradeoff**—we must give up something to get something else. On the *PPF* in Fig. 3.1, we must give up some pop to get more CDs (or give up some CDs to get more pop).

Tradeoffs arise from scarcity and occur in every imaginable real-world situation. At any given point in time, we have a fixed amount of labour, land, capital, and entrepreneurship. By using our available technologies, we can employ these resources to produce goods and services. But we are limited in what we can produce. This limit defines a boundary between what we can attain and what we cannot attain. This

boundary is the real-world's production possibility frontier, and it defines the tradeoffs that we must make. On our real-world *PPF*, we can produce more of any one good or service only if we produce less of some other goods or services.

When doctors say we must spend more on AIDS and cancer research, they are suggesting a tradeoff—more medical research for less of some other things. When Jean Chrétien says he wants to spend more on education and health care, he is suggesting a tradeoff: more education and health care for less national defence or less private spending (because of higher taxes). When your parents say that you should study more, they are suggesting a tradeoff: more study time for less leisure or less sleep. When an environmental group argues for less logging, it is suggesting a tradeoff: greater conservation of endangered wildlife for less paper.

All tradeoffs involve a cost—an opportunity cost.

Opportunity Cost

The **opportunity cost** of an action is the highest-valued alternative forgone. We can make the concept of opportunity cost more precise by using the production possibility frontier. Along the frontier, there are only two goods, so there is only one alternative forgone—some quantity of the other good. Given our current resources and technology, we can produce more CDs only if we produce fewer bottles of pop. The opportunity cost of producing an additional CD is the number of bottles of pop we must forgo. Similarly, the opportunity cost of producing an additional bottle of pop is the quantity of CDs we must forgo.

For example, at point *c* in Fig. 3.1, we produce fewer CDs and more bottles of pop than at point *d*. If we choose point *d* over point *c*, the additional 1 million CDs *cost* 3 million bottles of pop. One CD costs 3 bottles of pop.

We can also work out the opportunity cost of choosing point *c* over point *d* in Fig. 3.1. If we move from point *d* to point *c*, the quantity of pop produced increases by 3 million bottles and the quantity of CDs produced decreases by 1 million. So if we choose point *c* over point *d*, the additional 3 million bottles of pop *cost* 1 million CDs. One bottle of pop costs 1/3 of a CD.

Opportunity Cost Is a Ratio Opportunity cost is a ratio. It is the decrease in the quantity produced of one good divided by the increase in the quantity produced of another good as we move along the production possibility frontier.

Because opportunity cost is a ratio, the opportunity cost of producing pop is equal to the *inverse* of the opportunity cost of producing CDs. Check this proposition by returning to the calculations we've just worked through. When we move along the *PPF* from *c* to *d,* the opportunity cost of a CD is 3 bottles of pop. The inverse of 3 is 1/3, so if we decrease the production of CDs and increase the production of pop by moving from *d* to *c,* the opportunity cost of a bottle of pop must be 1/3 of a CD. You can check that this number is correct. If we move from *d* to *c,* we produce 3 million more bottles of pop and 1 million fewer CDs. Because 3 million bottles cost 1 million CDs, the opportunity cost of 1 bottle of pop is 1/3 of a CD.

Increasing Opportunity Cost   The opportunity cost of a CD increases as the quantity of CDs produced increases. Also, the opportunity cost of pop increases as the quantity of pop produced increases. This phenomenon of increasing opportunity cost is reflected in the *shape* of the *PPF*—it is bowed outward.

When a large quantity of pop and a small quantity of CDs are produced—between points *a* and *b* in Fig. 3.1—the frontier has a gentle slope. A given increase in the quantity of CDs *costs* a small decrease in the quantity of pop, so the opportunity cost of a CD is a small amount of pop.

When a large quantity of CDs and a small quantity of pop are produced—between points *e* and *f* in Fig. 3.1—the frontier is steep. A given increase in the quantity of CDs *costs* a large decrease in the quantity of pop, so the opportunity cost of a CD is a large amount of pop.

The production possibility frontier is bowed outward because resources are not all equally productive in all activities. Production workers with many years of experience working for PepsiCo are very good at producing pop but not very good at making CDs. So if we move these people from PepsiCo to Maxell, we get a small increase in the quantity of CDs but a large decrease in the quantity of pop.

Similarly, plastics engineers and production workers who have spent many years working for Maxell are good at producing CDs but not so good at bottling pop. So if we move these people from Maxell to PepsiCo, we get a small increase in the quantity of pop but a large decrease in the quantity of CDs. The more we try to produce of either good, the less productive are the additional resources we use to produce that good and the larger is the opportunity cost of a unit of that good.

Increasing Opportunity Costs Are Everywhere
Just about every activity that you can think of is one with an *increasing* opportunity cost. Two examples are the production of food and the production of health-care services. We allocate the most skilful farmers and the most fertile land to the production of food. And we allocate the best doctors and least fertile land to the production of health-care services. If we shift fertile land and tractors away from farming to hospitals and ambulances and ask farmers to become hospital porters, the production of food drops drastically and the increase in the production of health-care services is small. The opportunity cost of a unit of health-care services rises. Similarly, if we shift our resources away from health-care towards farming, we must use more doctors and nurses as farmers and more hospitals as hydroponic tomato factories. The decrease in the production of health-care services is large, but the increase in food production is small. The opportunity cost of a unit of food rises.

This example is extreme and unlikely, but these same considerations apply to any pair of goods that you can imagine: housing and diamonds, wheelchairs and golf carts, pet food and breakfast cereals.

REVIEW QUIZ

- How does the production possibility frontier illustrate scarcity?
- How does the production possibility frontier illustrate production efficiency?
- How does the production possibility frontier show that every choice involves a tradeoff?
- How does the production possibility frontier illustrate opportunity cost?
- Why is opportunity cost a ratio?
- Why does the *PPF* for most goods bow outward so that opportunity cost increases as the quantity produced of a good increases?

We've seen that production possibilities are limited by the production possibility frontier. And we've seen that production on the *PPF* is efficient. But there are many possible quantities we can produce on the *PPF*. How do we choose among them? How do we know which point on the frontier is the best one?

Using Resources Efficiently

How do we decide whether to spend more on AIDS and cancer research? Whether to vote for an education and health-care package or a tax cut? Whether to join an environmental group and press for a greater conservation of endangered wildlife?

These are big questions that have enormous consequences. But you can see the essence of the answer by thinking about the simpler question: How do we decide how many CDs and how many bottles of pop to produce?

We decide by calculating and comparing two numbers:

- Marginal cost
- Marginal benefit

Marginal Cost

Marginal cost is the opportunity cost of producing *one more unit* of a good or service. You've seen how we can calculate opportunity cost as we move along the production possibility frontier. The marginal cost of a CD is the opportunity cost of *one* CD—the quantity of pop that must be given up to get one more CD—as we move along the *PPF*.

Figure 3.2 illustrates the marginal cost of a CD. If all the available resources are used to produce pop, 15 million bottles of pop and no CDs are produced. If we now decide to produce 1 million CDs, how much pop do we have to give up? You can see the answer in Fig. 3.2(a). To produce 1 million more CDs, we move from *a* to *b* and the quantity of pop decreases by 1 million bottles to 14 million a month. So the opportunity cost of the first 1 million CDs is 1 million bottles of pop.

If we decide to increase the production of CDs to 2 million, how much pop must we give up? This time, we move from *b* to *c* and the quantity of pop decreases by 2 million bottles. So the second million CDs costs 2 million bottles of pop.

You can repeat this calculation for an increase in the quantity of CDs produced from 2 million to 3 million, then to 4 million, and finally to 5 million. Figure 3.2(a) shows these opportunity costs as a series of steps. Each additional million CDs costs more bottles of pop then the preceding million did.

We've just calculated the opportunity cost of CDs in blocks of 1 million at a time and generated the steps

FIGURE 3.2

Opportunity Cost and Marginal Cost

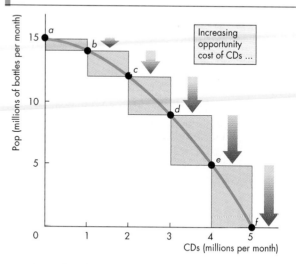

(a) PPF and opportunity cost

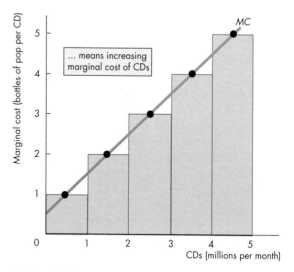

(b) Marginal cost

Opportunity cost is measured along the *PPF* in part (a). If the production of CDs increases from zero to 1 million, the opportunity cost of the first 1 million CDs is 1 million bottles of pop. If the production of CDs increases from 1 million to 2 million, the opportunity cost of the second 1 million CDs is 2 million bottles of pop. The opportunity cost of CDs increases as the production of CDs increases. Marginal cost is the opportunity cost of producing one more unit. Part (b) shows the marginal cost of a CD as the *MC* curve.

in Fig. 3.2(a). If we now calculate the opportunity cost of CDs one at a time, we obtain the *marginal cost* of a CD. In Fig. 3.2(b), the line labelled *MC* shows the marginal cost of a CD. The marginal cost of each additional CD in terms of forgone bottles of pop increases, so the marginal cost curve slopes upward.

Marginal Benefit

To use our resources efficiently, we must compare the marginal cost of a CD with its marginal benefit. **Marginal benefit** is the benefit that a person receives from consuming one more unit of a good or service. The marginal benefit from a good or service is measured as the maximum amount that a person is willing to pay for one more unit of it. It is a general principle that the more we have of any good or service, the smaller is our marginal benefit from it —the principle of *decreasing marginal benefit*.

To understand the principle of decreasing marginal benefit, think about your own marginal benefit from CDs. If CDs were very hard to come by and you can buy only one or two a year, you might be willing to pay a high price to get one more CD. But if CDs are readily available and you have as many as you can use, you are willing to pay almost nothing for yet one more CD.

In everyday life, we think of prices as money—as dollars per CD. But you have just been thinking about cost as opportunity cost, which is not a dollar cost but a cost in terms of a forgone alternative. You can also think about prices in the same terms. The price you pay for something is not the number of dollars you give up, but the goods and services that you would have bought with those dollars.

To see this idea more clearly, let's continue with the example we used to study the *PPF* and opportunity cost—CDs and pop. The marginal benefit from a CD can be expressed as the number of bottles of pop that a person is willing to forgo to get a CD. Figure 3.3 illustrates the marginal benefit from CDs. Marginal benefit is the way people feel about different quantities of goods and we can't derive it from the *PPF*. The numbers in Fig. 3.3 are *assumed*.

In row *a*, 0.5 million CDs a month are available and at that quantity, people are willing to pay 5 bottles of pop for a CD. As the quantity of CDs available increases, the amount that people are willing to pay for a CD falls. When 4.5 million CDs a month are available, people are willing to pay only 1 bottle of pop for a CD.

FIGURE 3.3
Marginal Benefit

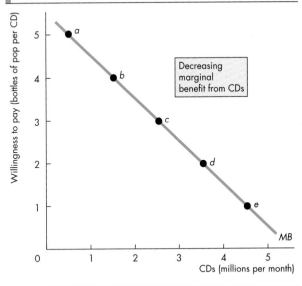

Possibility	CDs (millions per month)	Willingness to pay (bottles per CD)
a	0.5	5
b	1.5	4
c	2.5	3
d	3.5	2
e	4.5	1

The fewer the number of CDs available, the more pop people are willing to give up to get an additional CD. If only 0.5 million CDs a month are available, people are willing to pay 5 bottles of pop for a CD. But if 4.5 million CDs a month are available, people will pay only 1 bottle of pop for a CD. Decreasing marginal benefit is a universal feature of people's preferences.

The marginal benefit from a CD and the opportunity cost of a CD are both measured in bottles of pop. But they are not the same concept. The *opportunity cost* of a CD is the amount of pop that people *must forgo* to get another CD. The *marginal benefit* from a CD is the amount of pop that people are *willing to forgo* to get another CD.

You now know how to calculate marginal cost and marginal benefit. Let's use these concepts to discover the efficient quantity of CDs to produce.

Efficient Use of Resources

Resource use is **efficient** when we produce the goods and services that we value most highly. That is, when we are using our resources efficiently, we cannot produce more of any good without giving up something that we value even more highly.

We always choose *at the margin*. We compare marginal cost and marginal benefit. If the marginal benefit from a good exceeds the marginal cost of the good, we increase production of that good. If marginal cost exceeds marginal benefit, we decrease production of the good. And if marginal benefit equals marginal cost, we stick with the current production.

This principle is just like the decisions you make when you go shopping. You have $10 to spend and are thinking about buying a CD or a box of floppy disks. You figure that you will get more value from the CD than from the floppy disks, so you spend your $10 on the CD. You have allocated scarce resources to their highest-value use. The marginal benefit from a CD is greater than (or equal to) its marginal cost, the box of floppy disks. The marginal benefit from a box of floppy disks is less than its marginal cost. No matter what the goods or services, if you can afford it and you think it is worth the price, you buy it. If you think it not worth its price, you pass it up.

We can illustrate an efficient use of resources by continuing to use the example of pop and CDs. Figure 3.4 shows the marginal cost and marginal benefit of CDs. Suppose we produce 1.5 million CDs a month. The marginal cost of a CD is 2 bottles of pop. But the marginal benefit from a CD is 4 bottles of pop. Because someone values an additional CD more highly than it costs to produce, we can get more value from our resources by moving some of them out of pop production and into CD production.

Now suppose we produce 3.5 million CDs a month. The marginal cost of a CD is now 4 bottles of pop. But the marginal benefit from a CD is only 2 bottles of pop. Because an additional CD costs more to produce than anyone thinks it is worth, we can get more value from our resources by moving some of them away from CD production and into pop production.

But suppose we produce 2.5 million CDs a month. Marginal cost and marginal benefit are now equal at 3 bottles of pop. This allocation of resources between CDs and pop is efficient. If more CDs are produced, the forgone pop is worth more than the additional CDs. If fewer CDs are produced, the forgone CDs are worth more than the additional pop.

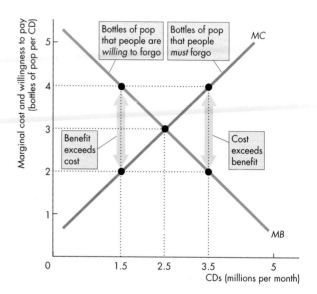

FIGURE 3.4
Efficient Use of Resources

The greater the quantity of CDs produced, the smaller is the marginal benefit (*MB*) from a CD—the fewer bottles of pop people are willing to give up to get an additional CD. But the greater the quantity of CDs produced, the greater is the marginal cost (*MC*) of a CD—the more bottles of pop people must give up to get an additional CD. When marginal benefit equals marginal cost, resources are being used efficiently.

REVIEW QUIZ

- What is marginal cost and how is it measured?
- What is marginal benefit and how is it measured?
- How does the marginal benefit from a good change as the quantity of that good increases? Why?
- What is the relationship between marginal cost and the production possibility frontier?
- What conditions must be satisfied if resources are used efficiently? Why?

You now understand the limits to production and the conditions under which resources are used efficiently. Your next task is to study the expansion of production possibilities.

Economic Growth

DURING THE PAST 30 YEARS, PRODUCTION PER person in Canada has doubled. Such an expansion of production is called **economic growth**. Can economic growth enable us to overcome scarcity and avoid opportunity cost? You are going to see that economic growth does not overcome scarcity and avoid opportunity cost. You are also going to see that the faster we make production grow, the greater is the opportunity cost of economic growth.

The Cost of Economic Growth

Two key factors influence economic growth: technological change and capital accumulation. **Technological change** is the development of new goods and of better ways of producing goods and services. **Capital accumulation** is the growth of capital resources.

As a consequence of technological change and capital accumulation, we have an enormous quantity of cars that enable us to produce more transportation than when we had only horses and carriages. We have satellites that make global communications possible on a scale that is much larger than that produced by the earlier cable technology. But new technologies and new capital have an opportunity cost. To use resources in research and development and to produce new capital, we must decrease our production of consumption goods and services. Let's look at this opportunity cost.

Instead of studying the *PPF* of CDs and pop, we'll hold the quantity of pop produced constant and examine the *PPF* for CDs and CD-making machines. Figure 3.5 shows this *PPF* as the blue curve *abc*. If we devote no resources to producing CD-making machines, we produce at point *a*. If we produce 3 million CDs a month, we can produce 6 CD-making machines at point *b*. If we produce no CDs, we can produce 10 CD-making machines a month at point *c*.

The amount by which our production possibilities expand depends on the resources we devote to technological change and capital accumulation. If we devote no resources to this activity (point *a*), the frontier remains at *abc*—the blue curve in Fig. 3.5. If we cut the current production of CDs and produce 6 machines a month (point *b*), then in the future, we'll have more capital and our *PPF* rotates outward to the

FIGURE 3.5

Economic Growth

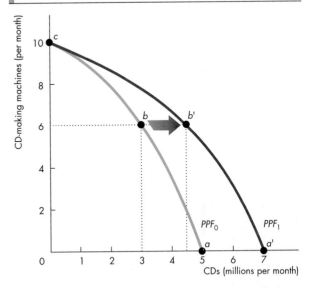

PPF_0 shows the limits to the production of CDs and CD-making equipment, with the production of all other goods and services remaining the same. If we devote no resources to producing CD-making machines and produce 5 million CDs a month, we remain stuck at point *a*. But if we decrease CD production to 3 million a month and produce 6 CD-making machines a month, at point *b*, our production possibilities will expand. After a year, the production possibility frontier shifts outward to PPF_1 and we can produce at point *b'*, a point outside the original *PPF*. We can shift the *PPF* outward but we cannot avoid opportunity cost. The opportunity cost of producing more CDs in the future is fewer CDs today.

position shown by the red curve. The fewer resources we devote to producing CDs and the more resources we devote to producing machines, the greater is the expansion of our production possibilities.

Economic growth is not free. To make it happen, we devote resources to producing new machines and fewer resources to producing CDs. In Fig. 3.5, we move from *a* to *b*. There is no free lunch. The opportunity cost of more CDs in the future is fewer CDs today. Also, economic growth is no magic formula for abolishing scarcity. On the new *PPF*, we continue to face opportunity costs.

The ideas about economic growth that we have explored in the setting of the CD industry also apply to nations. Let's look at two examples.

Economic Growth in Canada and Hong Kong

If as a nation we devote all our resources to producing consumer goods and none to research and capital accumulation, our production possibilities in the future will be the same as they are today. To expand our production possibilities in the future, we must devote fewer resources to producing consumption goods and some resources to accumulating capital and developing technologies so we can produce more consumption goods in the future. The decrease in today's consumption is the opportunity cost of an increase in future consumption.

The experiences of Canada and Hong Kong make a striking example of the effects of our choices on the rate of economic growth. In 1968, the production possibilities per person in Canada were two and a half times those in Hong Kong (see Fig. 3.6). Canada devoted one-fifth of its resources to accumulating capital and the other four-fifths to consumption. In 1968, Canada was at point *a* on its *PPF*. Hong Kong devoted two-fifths of its resources to accumulating capital and three-fifths to consumption. In 1968, Hong Kong was at point *a* on its *PPF*.

Since 1968, both countries have experienced economic growth, but growth in Hong Kong has been more rapid than in Canada. Because Hong Kong devoted a bigger fraction of its resources to accumulating capital, its production possibilities have expanded more quickly than Canada's production possibilities expanded.

In 1998, the *PPF* per person in Canada and Hong Kong are similar. If Hong Kong continues to devote a similar proportion of its resources to accumulating capital (at point *b* on the 1998 *PPF*), it will continue to grow more rapidly than Canada and its frontier will move out beyond our own. But if Hong Kong increases its consumption and decreases its capital accumulation (moving to point *c* on its 1998 production possibility frontier), then its rate of economic growth will slow.

Canada is typical of the rich industrial countries, which include the United States, Western Europe, and Japan. Hong Kong is typical of the fast-growing Asian economies, which include Taiwan, Thailand, South Korea, and China. Growth in these countries has slowed during the past two years, but before the slowdown, these countries expanded production by between 5 percent and almost 10 percent a year. If these high growth rates are restored, these other

countries will eventually close the gap on Canada as Hong Kong has done.

FIGURE 3.6
Economic Growth in Canada and Hong Kong

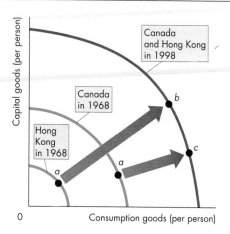

In 1968, the production possibilities per person in Canada were much larger than those in Hong Kong. But Hong Kong devoted more of its resources to accumulating capital than did Canada, so its production possibility frontier has shifted out more quickly than has that of Canada. In 1998, the two production possibilities per person were similar.

R E V I E W   Q U I Z

- What are the two key factors that generate economic growth?
- How does economic growth influence the production possibility frontier?
- What is the opportunity cost of economic growth?
- Why has Hong Kong experienced faster economic growth than Canada has?

Next, we're going to study another way we expand our production possibilities—the amazing fact that buyers and sellers gain from specialization and trade.

Gains from Trade

PEOPLE CAN PRODUCE FOR THEMSELVES ALL THE goods that they consume, or they can concentrate on producing one good (or perhaps a few goods) and then trade with others—exchange some of their own goods for those of others. Concentrating on the production of only one good or a few goods is called *specialization*. We are going to discover how people gain by specializing in the production of the good in which they have a *comparative advantage* and trading with each other.

Comparative Advantage

A person has a **comparative advantage** in an activity if that person can perform the activity at a lower opportunity cost than anyone else. Differences in opportunity costs arise from differences in individual abilities and from differences in the characteristics of other resources.

The range of individual ability is enormous. But no one excels at *everything*. One person is an outstanding pitcher but a poor catcher; another person is a brilliant lawyer but a poor teacher. In almost all human endeavours, what one person does easily, someone else finds difficult. The same applies to land and capital. One plot of land is fertile but has no mineral deposits; another plot of land has outstanding views but is infertile. One machine has great precision but is difficult to operate; another machine is fast but often breaks down.

Although no one excels at everything, some people excel and can outperform others in many activities. But such a person does not have a *comparative* advantage in every activity. For example, Robertson Davies was a better actor than most people. But he was an even better writer. So his *comparative* advantage was writing.

Because people's abilities and the quality of their resources differ, they have different opportunity costs of producing various goods. Such differences give rise to comparative advantage. Let's explore the idea of comparative advantage by looking at two CD factories, one operated by Tom and the other operated by Trish.

Tom's Factory To simplify the story, suppose that CDs have just two components: a disc and a plastic case. Suppose that Tom has two production lines: one

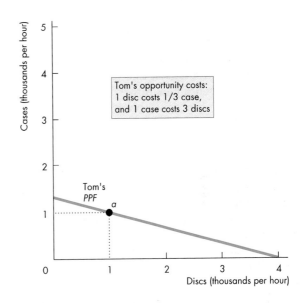

FIGURE 3.7

Production Possibilities in Tom's Factory

Tom's opportunity costs:
1 disc costs 1/3 case,
and 1 case costs 3 discs

Tom can produce discs and cases along the production possibility frontier *PPF*. For Tom, the opportunity cost of 1 disc is 1/3 of a case and the opportunity cost of 1 case is 3 discs. If Tom produces at point *a*, he can produce 1,000 cases and 1,000 discs an hour.

for discs and one for cases. Figure 3.7 shows Tom's production possibility frontier for discs and cases.

Tom's *PPF* in Fig. 3.7 is a straight line rather than a bowed out curve. This situation arises when resources are equally useful in each activity. We use this situation here because it lets us focus on comparative advantage without worrying about varying opportunity cost along the *PPF*.

Tom's *PPF* in Fig. 3.7 tells us that if Tom uses all his resources to make discs, he can produce 4,000 discs an hour. It also tells us that if Tom uses all his resources to make cases, he can produce 1,333 cases an hour. But to produce cases, Tom must decrease his production of discs. For each 1 case produced, he must decrease his production of discs by 3.

Tom's opportunity cost of producing 1 case is 3 discs.

Similarly, if Tom wants to increase his production of discs, he must decrease his production of cases. And for each 1,000 discs produced, he must decrease his production of cases by 333. So

Tom's opportunity cost of producing 1 disc is 0.333 cases.

Trish's Factory The other factory, operated by Trish, can also produce cases and discs. But Trish's factory has machines that are custom-made for case production, so they are more suitable for producing cases than discs. Also, Trish's work force is more skilled in making cases.

This difference between the two factories means that Trish's production possibility frontier—shown along with Tom's *PPF* in Fig. 3.8—is different from Tom's. If Trish uses all her resources to make discs, she can produce 1,333 discs an hour. If she uses all her resources to make cases, she can produce 4,000 cases an hour. To produce discs, Trish must decrease her production of cases. For each 1,000 additional discs produced, she must decrease her production of cases by 3,000.

Trish's opportunity cost of producing 1 disc is 3 cases.

Similarly, if Trish wants to increase her production of cases, she must decrease her production of discs. For each 1,000 additional cases produced, she must decrease her production of discs by 333. So

Trish's opportunity cost of producing 1 case is 0.333 discs.

Suppose that Tom and Trish produce both discs and cases and that each produces 1,000 discs and 1,000 cases—1,000 CDs—an hour. That is, each produces at point *a* on their production possibility frontiers. Total production is 2,000 CDs an hour.

In which of the two goods does Trish have a comparative advantage? Recall that comparative advantage is a situation in which one person's opportunity cost of producing a good is lower than another person's opportunity cost of producing that same good. Trish has a comparative advantage in producing cases. Trish's opportunity cost of a case is 0.333 discs, whereas Tom's is 3 discs.

You can see her comparative advantage by looking at the production possibility frontiers for Trish

FIGURE 3.8
The Gains from Trade

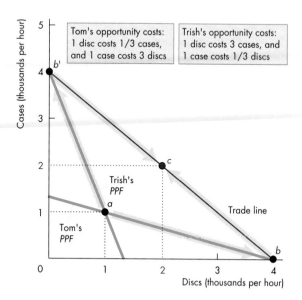

Tom and Trish each produce at point *a* on their respective *PPF*s. Trish has a comparative advantage in cases, and Tom has a comparative advantage in discs. If Trish specializes in cases, she produces at point *b'* on her *PPF*. If Tom specializes in discs, he produces at point *b* on his *PPF*. They exchange cases for discs along the red "Trade line." Trish buys discs from Tom for less than her opportunity cost of producing them, and Tom buys cases from Trish for less than his opportunity cost of producing them. Each goes to point *c*—a point outside his or her *PPF*—where each has 2,000 CDs an hour. Tom and Trish increase production with no change in resources.

and Tom in Fig. 3.8. Trish's production possibility frontier is steeper than Tom's. To produce one more case, Trish gives up fewer discs than Tom. Hence Trish's opportunity cost of a case is less than Tom's. This means that Trish has a comparative advantage in producing cases.

Tom's comparative advantage is in producing discs. His production possibility frontier is less steep than Trish's. This means that Tom gives up fewer cases to produce one more disc than Trish does. Tom's opportunity cost of producing a disc is 0.33 cases, which is less than Trish's 3 cases. So Tom has a comparative advantage in producing discs.

Achieving the Gains from Trade

Because Trish has a comparative advantage in cases and Tom in discs, they can both gain from specialization and exchange. If Tom, who has a comparative advantage in disc production, puts all his resources into that activity, he can produce 4,000 discs an hour—point *b* on his *PPF*. If Trish, who has a comparative advantage in producing cases, puts all her resources into that activity, she can produce 4,000 cases an hour—point *b'* on her *PPF*. By specializing, Tom and Trish together can produce 4,000 cases and 4,000 discs an hour, double their total production without specialization. By specialization and exchange, Tom and Trish can get *outside* their production possibility frontiers.

To achieve the gains from specialization, Tom and Trish must trade with each other. Suppose they agree to the following deal: Each hour, Trish produces 4,000 cases, Tom produces 4,000 discs, and Trish supplies Tom with 2,000 cases in exchange for 2,000 discs. With this deal in place, Tom and Trish move along the red "Trade line" to point *c*. At this point, each produces 2,000 CDs an hour—double their previous production rate. These are the gains from specialization and trade.

Both parties share the gains. Trish, who can produce discs at an opportunity cost of 3 cases per disc can buy discs from Tom for a price of 1 case per disc. Tom, who can produce cases at an opportunity cost of 3 discs per case, can buy cases from Trish at a price of 1 disc per case. Trish gets her discs more cheaply, and Tom gets his cases more cheaply.

Absolute Advantage

Suppose that Trish invents and patents a production process that makes her *four* times as productive as she was before in the production of both cases and discs. With her new technology, Trish can produce 16,000 cases an hour (4 times the original 4,000) if she puts all her resources into that activity. Alternatively, she can produce 5,332 discs (4 times the original 1,333) if she puts all her resources into that activity. Trish now has an **absolute advantage** in producing *both* goods—she can produce more of both goods than Tom can produce.

But Trish does not have a *comparative* advantage in both goods. She can produce four times as much of *both* goods as before, but her *opportunity cost* of 1

disc is still 3 cases. And this opportunity cost is higher than Tom's. So Trish can still get discs at a lower cost by exchanging cases for discs with Tom.

A key point to recognize is that it is *not* possible for *anyone* to have a comparative advantage in *everything*. So gains for specialization and trade are always available when opportunity costs diverge.

Dynamic Comparative Advantage

At any given point in time, the resources and technologies available determine the comparative advantages that individuals and nations have. But just by repeatedly producing a particular good or service, people become more productive in that activity, a phenomenon called **learning-by-doing**. Learning-by-doing is the basis of *dynamic* comparative advantage. **Dynamic comparative advantage** is a comparative advantage that a person (or country) possesses as a result of having specialized in a particular activity and, as a result of learning-by-doing, having become the producer with the lowest opportunity cost.

Hong Kong and Singapore are two countries that have pursued dynamic comparative advantage vigorously. They have developed industries in which initially they did not have a comparative advantage but, through learning-by-doing, became low opportunity cost producers in those industries. A specific example is Singapore's decision to develop a genetic engineering industry. Singapore probably did not have a comparative advantage in genetic engineering initially. But it might develop one as its scientists and production workers become more skilled in this activity.

R E V I E W   Q U I Z

- What gives a person a comparative advantage in producing a good?
- Why is it not possible for anyone to have a comparative advantage at everything?
- What are the gains from specialization and trade?
- Explain the source of the gains from specialization and trade.
- Distinguish between comparative advantage and absolute advantage.
- What is dynamic comparative advantage and how does it arise?

The Market Economy

INDIVIDUALS AND COUNTRIES GAIN BY SPECIALIZ-
ing in the production of those goods and services in
which they have a comparative advantage and then
trading with each other. This source of economic
wealth was identified by Adam Smith in his *Wealth of
Nations*, published in 1776—see pp. 58–59.

To enable billions of people who specialized in
producing millions of different goods and services
to reap these gains, trade must be organized. But
trade need not be *planned* or *managed* by a central
authority. In fact, when such an arrangement has
been tried, as it was for 60 years in Russia, the result
has been less than dazzling.

Trade is organized by using social institutions.
Two key ones are:

- Property rights
- Markets

Property Rights

Property rights are social arrangements that govern
the ownership, use, and disposal of resources, goods,
and services. *Real property* includes land and buildings—the things we call property in ordinary
speech—and durable goods such as plant and equipment. *Financial property* includes stocks and bonds
and money in the bank. *Intellectual property* is the
intangible product of creative effort. This type of
property includes books, music, computer programs,
and inventions of all kinds and is protected by copyrights and patents.

If property rights are not enforced, the incentive
to specialize and produce the goods in which each
person has a comparative advantage is weakened, and
some of the potential gains from specialization and
trade are lost. If people can easily steal the production
of others, then time, energy, and resources are devoted
not to production, but to protecting possessions.

Establishing property rights is one of the greatest
challenges facing Russia and other Eastern European
nations as they seek to develop market economies.
Even in countries where property rights are well
established, such as Canada, protecting intellectual
property is proving to be a challenge in the face of
modern technologies that make it relatively easy to
copy audio and video material, computer programs,
and books.

Markets

In ordinary speech, the word *market* means a place
where people buy and sell goods such as fish, meat,
fruits, and vegetables. In economics, a *market* has a
more general meaning. A **market** is any arrangement
that enables buyers and sellers to get information and
to do business with each other. An example is the
market in which oil is bought and sold—the world
oil market. The world oil market is not a place. It is
the network of oil producers, oil users, wholesalers,
and brokers who buy and sell oil. In the world oil
market, decision makers do not meet physically. They
make deals throughout the world by telephone, fax,
and direct computer link.

In the example we've just studied, Trish and Tom
get together and do a deal. They agree to exchange
cases for discs. But in a market economy, Trish sells
cases to a dealer in plastic products and she buys discs
from a dealer in electronic recording media. Similarly,
Tom buys cases and sells discs in these same two
markets. Tom can use Trish's cases and Trish can
use Tom's discs and yet be unaware of the
other's existence.

Circular Flows in the Market Economy

Figure 3.9 identifies two types of markets: goods
markets and resource markets. *Goods markets* are
those in which goods and services are bought and
sold. *Resource markets* are those in which productive
resources are bought and sold.

Households decide how much of their labour,
land, capital, and entrepreneurship to sell or rent in
resource markets. They receive incomes in the form
of wages, rent, interest, and profit. Households also
decide how to spend their incomes on goods and services produced by firms. Firms decide the quantities
of resource to hire, how to use them to produce
goods and services, what goods and services to produce, and in what quantities.

Figure 3.9 shows the flows that result from these
decisions by households and firms. The red flows are
the resources that go from households through
resource markets to firms and the goods and services
that go from firms through goods markets to households. The green flows in the opposite direction are
the payments made in exchange for these items.

How do markets coordinate all these decisions?

FIGURE 3.9

Circular Flows in the Market Economy

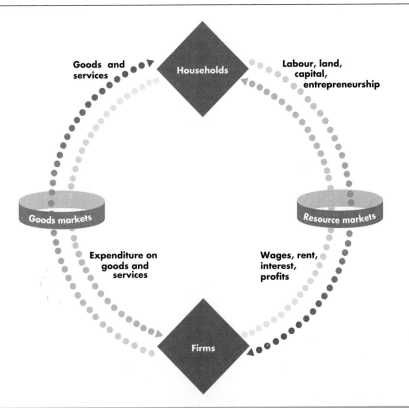

Households and firms make economic choices. Households choose the quantities of labour, land, capital, and entrepreneurship to sell or rent to firms in exchange for wages, rent, interest, and profits. Households also choose how to spend their incomes on the various types of goods and services available. Firms choose the quantities of resources to hire and the quantities of the various goods and services to produce. Goods markets and resource markets coordinate these choices of households and firms. Resources and goods flow clockwise (red) and money payments flow counterclockwise (green).

Coordinating Decisions

Markets coordinate individual decisions through price adjustments. To see how, think about your local market for hamburgers. Suppose that some people who want to buy hamburgers are not able to do so. To make the choices of buyers and sellers compatible, buyers must scale down their appetites or more hamburgers must be offered for sale (or both must happen). A rise in the price of hamburgers produces this outcome. A higher price encourages producers to offer more hamburgers for sale. It also encourages some people to change their lunch plans. Fewer people buy hamburgers, and more buy hot dogs. More hamburgers (and more hot dogs) are offered for sale.

Alternatively, suppose that more hamburgers are available than people want to buy. In this case, to make the choices of buyers and sellers compatible, more hamburgers must be bought or fewer hamburgers must be offered for sale (or both). A fall in the price of a hamburger achieves this outcome. A lower price encourages

firms to produce a smaller quantity of hamburgers. It also encourages people to buy more hamburgers.

R E V I E W   Q U I Z

■ Why are social arrangements such as markets and property rights necessary?
■ What are the main functions of markets?

◇ You have now begun to see how economists approach economic questions. Scarcity, choice, and divergent opportunity cost explain why we specialize and trade and why property rights and markets have developed. You can see the lessons you've learned in this chapter all around you. *Reading Between the Lines* on pp. 52–53 gives an example. It explores the *PPF* of a student like you and the choices that students must make that influence their own economic growth—the growth of their incomes.

The Opportunity Cost and Benefit of Post-Secondary Education

THE MONTREAL GAZETTE, JUNE 7, 1998

Employers come knocking

BY DOUG SWEET

Najmeh Kalili...is 26, has just completed a bachelor of applied science degree at Concordia University...and, like much of this year's graduating class in both arts and sciences, faces a job market where employers most likely will be pounding on her door instead of the other way around.

But, unlike most of her classmates this spring, Kalili doesn't want a job yet. She knows she could get a high-paying job as a computer engineer, but she has decided to pursue another interest—biomedical engineering—before heading into the work force.

"It's very tempting (to go after a job)," she said, savouring the crisp air of a breezy June afternoon during a break from a sweltering basement lab at Concordia's Loyola campus, where she's working this summer.

"It takes a lot of energy to resist this temptation and continue doing what I want to do."...

"Most of the people in the class got good jobs. Several had more than one job offer," Kalili said. "I know some of my friends moved to the United States or other provinces to get even better jobs."...

Kalili said she's counting on the biomedical field catching fire the way computer engineering has in recent years.

"I think I will be able to find a job," she said during the break from the project she is working on...

"However, I don't think it will be as easy as if I stayed in engineering, because biomedical is more limited than electrical engineering. But maybe not by the time I'm done (the two-year master's). That's what I'm counting on."...

Essence of the Story

■ Najmeh Kalili has completed a bachelor's degree.

■ With her bachelor's degree, Najmeh can now get a good job.

■ Najmeh has chosen instead to continue her education and complete a master's degree.

■ She hopes to find an even better job when her education is complete.

■ The opportunity cost of a post-secondary education is forgone consumption. The payoff is an increase in lifetime production possibilities.

■ Figure 1 shows the choices that Najmeh faced when she left high school. She could choose any combination of education goods and services and consumption goods and services that are on the blue production possibility frontier.

■ If Najmeh decided not to attend university, then she could be at point *a* on the blue *PPF* and her *PPF* would remain the blue curve in Fig. 1.

■ When Najmeh attends university she consumes at point *b* on the blue *PPF*.

■ By attending university, Najmeh incurs an opportunity cost. She decreases her consumption of goods and services to increase her consumption of education goods and services.

■ With a completed bachelor's degree, Najmeh's consumption possibilities expand to the red *PPF* in Fig. 1.

■ The blue curve in Fig. 2 is the same *PPF* as the red *PPF* in Fig. 1. It is Najmeh's *PPF* following the completion of her bachelor's degree.

■ Now Najmeh must make another decision.

Will she quit university and take a job or will she remain in university and pursue a master's degree?

■ If Najmeh quits university, she can spend all her income on consumption goods and services and consume at point *c*.

■ But if she decides to pursue a master's degree, Najmeh incurs another opportunity cost. She must decrease her consumption of goods and services to consume education goods and services.

■ Najmeh slides around the blue *PPF* in Fig. 2 from point *c* to point *d*.

■ But with a completed master's degree, Najmeh will expand her production possibilities further.

■ The red *PPF* in Fig. 2 shows the expanded possibilities that Najmeh faces with a graduate degree. Following graduation, she can consume at any point on the red *PPF*.

■ The greater the resources that Najmeh devotes to education, the greater are her future consumption possibilities.

■ Najmeh is expanding her personal *PPF* by incurring a cost. Her economic growth has a cost, but it results in her reaping large returns.

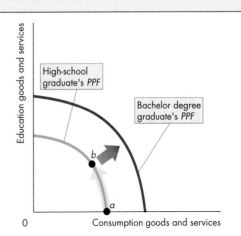

Figure 1 High-school graduate's choices

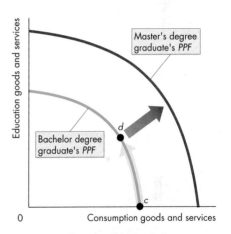

Figure 2 College graduate's choices

■ In September 1997, Prime Minister Chrétien announced the establishment of a Canada Millennium Scholarship Endowment Fund, which will provide thousands of scholarships each year for low- and moderate-income Canadians to attend post-secondary institutions.

■ Why do you think the Prime Minister is concerned about post-secondary education?

■ With such huge returns from education, why don't more people remain in university for longer?

■ What is the opportunity cost of the Prime Minister's plan?

■ Would you vote for or against a tax increase to fund the Millennium Scholarship Endowment Fund?

SUMMARY

Key Points

Resources and Wants (p. 38)

- Economic activity arises from scarcity—resources are insufficient to satisfy people's wants.
- Resources are labour, land, capital (including human capital), and entrepreneurship.
- We choose how to use our resources and try to get the most out of them.

Resources, Production Possibilities, and Opportunity Cost (pp. 39–41)

- The production possibility frontier, *PPF*, is the boundary between production levels that are attainable and those that are not attainable when all the available resources are used to their limit.
- Production efficiency occurs at points on the *PPF*.
- Along the *PPF*, the opportunity cost of producing more of one good is the amount of the other good that must be given up.
- The opportunity cost of all goods increases as the production of the good increases.

Using Resources Efficiently (pp. 42–44)

- The marginal cost of a good is the opportunity cost of producing one more unit.
- The marginal benefit from a good is the maximum amount of another good that a person is willing to forgo to obtain more of the first good.
- The marginal benefit of a good decreases as the amount available increases.
- Resources are used efficiently when the marginal cost of each good is equal to its marginal benefit.

Economic Growth (pp. 45–46)

- Economic growth, which is the expansion of production possibilities, results from capital accumulation and technological change.
- The opportunity cost of economic growth is forgone current consumption.

Gains from Trade (pp. 47–49)

- A person has a comparative advantage in producing a good if that person can produce the good at a lower opportunity cost than everyone else can.
- It is *not* possible for *anyone* to have a comparative advantage at *everything*.
- People gain by specializing in the activity in which they have a comparative advantage and trading with others.

The Market Economy (pp. 50–51)

- Property rights and markets enable people to gain from specialization and trade.
- Markets coordinate decisions and help to allocate resources to *higher* valued uses.

Key Figures

Key Terms

PROBLEMS

*1. Use the figure to calculate Wendell's opportunity cost of an hour of tennis when he increases the time he plays tennis from:
a. 4 to 6 hours a week.
b. 6 to 8 hours a week.

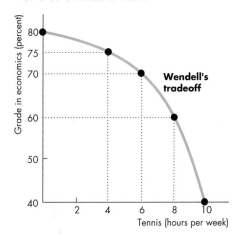

2. Use the figure to calculate Mary's opportunity cost of an hour of skating when she increases her time spent skating from:
a. 2 to 4 hours a week.
b. 4 to 6 hours a week.

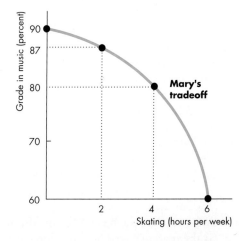

*3. In problem 1, describe the relationship between the time Wendell spends playing tennis and the opportunity cost of an hour of tennis.

4. In problem 2, describe the relationship between the time Mary spends skating and the opportunity cost of an hour of skating.

*5. Wendell, in problem 1, has the following marginal benefit curve:

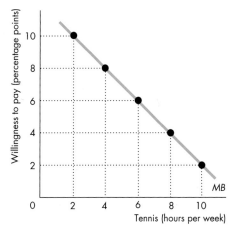

a. If Wendell uses his time efficiently, what grade will he get?
b. Why would Wendell be worse off getting a higher grade?

6. Mary, in problem 2, has the following marginal benefit curve:

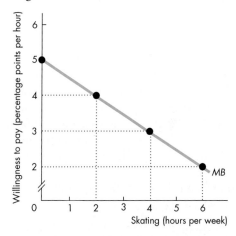

a. If Mary uses her time efficiently, how much skating will she do?
b. Why would Mary be worse off spending fewer hours skating?

*7. Leisureland's production possibilities are

Food (kilograms per month)		Sunscreen (litres per month)
300	and	0
200	and	50
100	and	100
0	and	150

a. Draw a graph of Leisureland's production possibility frontier.

b. What are Leisureland's opportunity costs of producing food and sunscreen at each output in the table?

8. Jane's Island's production possibilities are:

Corn (kilograms per month)		Cloth (metres per month)
3	and	0
2	and	2
1	and	4
0	and	6

a. Draw a graph of the *PPF* on Jane's Island.
b. What are Jane's opportunity costs of producing corn and cloth at each output in the table?

*9. In problem 7, to get a litre of sunscreen people are willing to give up 5 kilograms of food if they have 25 litres of sunscreen; 2 kilograms of food if they have 75 litres of sunscreen; and 1 kilogram of food if they have 125 litres of sunscreen.
a. Draw a graph of Leisureland's marginal benefit from sunscreen.
b. What is the efficient use of sunscreen?

10. In problem 8, to get a metre of cloth Jane is willing to give up 0.75 kilograms of corn if she has 2 metres of cloth; 0.50 kilograms of corn if she has 4 metres of cloth; and 0.25 kilograms of corn if she has 6 metres of cloth.
a. Draw a graph of Jane's marginal benefit from cloth.
b. What is Jane's efficient quantity of cloth?

*11. Busyland's production possibilities are:

Food (kilograms per month)		Sunscreen (litres per month)
150	and	0
100	and	100
50	and	200
0	and	300

Calculate Busyland's opportunity costs of food and sunscreen at each output in the table?

12. Joe's Island's production possibilities are:

Corn (kilograms per month)		Cloth (metres per month)
6	and	0
4	and	1
2	and	2
0	and	3

What are Joe's opportunity costs of producing corn and cloth at each output in the table?

*13. In problems 7 and 11, Leisureland and Busyland each produce and consume 100 kilograms of food and 100 litres of sunscreen per month; and they do not trade. Now the countries begin to trade with each other.
a. What good does Leisureland sell to Busyland and what good does it buy from Busyland?
b. If Leisureland and Busyland divide the total output of food and sunscreen equally, what are the gains from trade?

14. In problems 8 and 12, Jane's Island produces and consumes 1 kilogram of corn and 4 metres of cloth. Joe's Island produces and consumes 4 kilograms of corn and 1 metre of cloth. Now the islands begin to trade.
a. What good does Jane sell to Joe and what good does Jane buy from Joe?
b. If Jane and Joe divide the total output of corn and cloth equally, what are the gains from trade?

CRITICAL THINKING

1. After you have studied *Reading Between the Lines* on pp. 52–53, answer the following questions:
a. Why is the *PPF* for education goods and services and consumption goods and services bowed outward?
b. At what point on the blue *PPF* in Fig. 1 on p. 53 is the combination of education goods and services and consumption goods and services efficient? Explain your answer.
c. Students are facing rising tuition. Does this make the opportunity cost of education increase, decrease, or remain unchanged? Explain why.
d. Who receives the benefits from education? Is the marginal cost of education equal to the marginal benefit of education? Is resource use in the market for education efficient?

2. Use the links on the Parkin-Bade Web site and obtain data on the tuition and other costs of enrolling in a graduate program and on job opportunities for graduates. Why doesn't everyone go to graduate school?

Understanding the Scope of Economics

You are living at a time that future historians will call the *Information Revolution*. We reserve the word "Revolution" for big events that influence all future generations. ◆ During the *Agricultural Revolution*, which occurred 10,000 years ago, people learned to domesticate animals and plant crops. They stopped roaming in search of food and settled in villages and eventually towns and cities, where they developed markets in which to exchange their products. ◆ During the *Industrial Revolution*,

Your Economic Revolution

which began 240 years ago, people used science to create new technologies. This revolution brought extraordinary wealth for some but created conditions in which others were left behind. It brought social and political tensions that we still face today. ◆ During today's *Information Revolution*, people who have the ability and opportunity to embrace the new technologies are prospering on an unimagined scale. But the incomes and living standards of the less educated are falling behind and social and political tensions are increasing. Today's revolution has a global dimension. Some of the winners live in previously poor countries in Asia, and some of the losers live here in Canada. ◆ So you are studying economics at an interesting

time. Whatever *your* motivation is for studying economics, *our* objective is to help you to do well in your course, to enjoy it, and to develop a deeper understanding of the economic world around you. ◆ There are three reasons why we hope that we both succeed. ◆ First, a decent understanding of economics will help you become a full participant in the Information Revolution. Second, an understanding of economics will help you play a more effective role as a citizen and voter and enable you to add your voice to those who are looking for solutions to our social and political problems. And third, you will enjoy the sheer fun of *understanding* the forces at play and how they are shaping our world. ◆ If you do find economics interesting, think seriously about majoring in the subject. A degree in economics gives the best training available in problem solving, offers lots of opportunities to develop conceptual skills, and opens doors to a wide range of graduate courses, including the MBA, and to a wide range of jobs. You can read more about the benefits of an economics degree in Robert Whaples' essay in your *Study Guide*.

◈ Economics as a discipline was born during the Industrial Revolution. We'll look at its birth and meet its founder, Adam Smith. Then we'll talk with one of today's leading economists, Professor John Whalley of the University of Western Ontario.

Probing the Ideas

The Sources of Economic Wealth

The Economist

Adam Smith *was a giant of a scholar who contributed to ethics and jurisprudence as well as economics. Born in 1723 in Kirkcaldy, a small fishing town near Edinburgh, Scotland, Smith was the only child of the town's customs officer (who died before Adam was born).*

His first academic appointment, at age 28, was as Professor of Logic at the University of Glasgow. He subsequently became tutor to a wealthy Scottish duke, whom he accompanied on a two-year grand European tour, following which he received a pension of £300 a year—ten times the average income at that time.

With the financial security of his pension, Smith devoted ten years to writ-ing An Inquiry into the Nature and Causes of **The Wealth of Nations**, *which was published in 1776. Many people had written on economic issues before Adam Smith, but he made eco-nomics a science. Smith's account was so broad and authoritative that no subse-quent writer on economics could advance ideas without tracing their connections to those of Adam Smith.*

"It is not from the benevolence of the butcher, the brewer, or the baker that we expect our dinner, but from their regard to their own interest."

<small>ADAM SMITH,
The Wealth of Nations</small>

The Issues

Why are some nations wealthy while others are poor? This question lies at the heart of economics. And it leads directly to a second question: What can poor nations do to become wealthy?

Adam Smith, who is regarded by many scholars as the founder of eco-nomics, attempted to answer these questions in his book *The Wealth of Nations*. Smith was pondering these questions at the height of the Industrial Revolution. During those years, new technologies were invented and applied to the manufacture of cot-ton and wool cloth, iron, transporta-tion, and agriculture.

Smith wanted to understand the sources of economic wealth, and he brought his acute powers of observa-tion and abstraction to bear on the question. His answer:

- The division of labour
- Free markets

The division of labour—breaking tasks down to simple tasks and becom-ing skilled in those tasks—is the source of "the greatest improvement in the productive powers of labour," said Smith. The division of labour became even more productive when it was applied to creating new technologies. Scientists and engineers, trained in extremely narrow fields, became spe-cialists at inventing. Their powerful skills accelerated the advance of tech-nology, so by the 1820s, machines could make consumer goods faster and more accurately than any craftsman could. And by the 1850s, machines could make other machines that labour alone could never have made.

But, said Smith, the fruits of the division of labour are limited by the extent of the market. To make the market as large as possible, there must be no impediments to free trade both within a country and among countries. Smith argued that when each person makes the best possible economic choice, that choice leads as if by "an invisible hand" to the best outcome for society as a whole. The butcher, the brewer, and the baker each pursue their own interests but, in doing so, also serve the interests of everyone else.

Then ...

Adam Smith speculated that one person, working hard, using the hand tools available in the 1770s, might possibly make 20 pins a day. Yet, he observed, by using those same hand tools but breaking the process into a number of individually small operations in which people specialize—by the **division of labour**—ten people could make a staggering 48,000 pins a day. One draws out the wire, another straightens it, a third cuts it, a fourth points it, a fifth grinds it. Three specialists make the head, and a fourth attaches it. Finally, the pin is polished and packaged. But a large market is needed to support the division of labour: one factory employing ten workers would need to sell more than 15 million pins a year to stay in business.

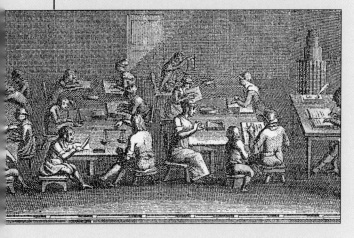

... and Now

If Adam Smith were here today, the computer chip would fascinate him. He would see it as an extra-ordinary example of the productivity of the division of labour and of the use of machines to make machines that make other machines. From a design of a chip's intricate circuits, cameras transfer an image to glass plates that work like stencils. Workers prepare silicon wafers on which the circuits are printed. Some slice the wafers, others polish them, others bake them, and yet others coat them with a light-sensitive chemical. Machines transfer a copy of the circuit onto the wafer. Chemicals then etch the design onto the wafer. Further processes deposit atom-sized transistors and aluminum connectors. Finally, a laser separates the hundreds of chips on the wafer. Every stage in the process of creating a computer chip uses other computer chips. And like the pin of the 1770s, the computer chip of the 1990s benefits from a large market—a global market—to buy chips in the huge quantities in which they are produced efficiently.

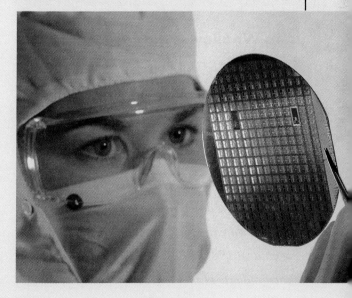

Many economists have worked to refine the big themes that Smith began. One of these economists is John Whalley, whom you can meet on the following pages.

Talking with
John Whalley

John Whalley *is Professor of Economics and Director of the Centre for the Study of International Economic Relations at the University of Western Ontario and Professor of International and Development Economics and Director of the Development and International Economics Research Centre at the University of Warwick, England. He is also a Research Associate at the National Bureau of Economic Research. Born in England in 1947, Professor Whalley was an undergraduate at the University of Essex and a graduate student at Yale University. He received his Ph.D. in 1973 and began his academic career at the London School of Economics. He came to Canada in 1976. Professor Whalley is a prolific scholar. He has published 30 books and more than 200 articles on globalization, economic development, taxes, global environmental issues, and income and wealth distribution and has developed*

new tools for computing the quantitative effects of policy actions.

Professor Whalley is an all-round economist. He works on theoretical problems, he measures the quantitative effects of policies, and he advises governments and international agencies on the consequences of alternative policy choices.

Robin Bade and Michael Parkin talked with Professor Whalley about his work, how it connects with the insights of Adam Smith, and the contribution that he and other economists are making to try to improve living standards and economic relations among nations in today's world.

Professor Whalley, what first attracted you to economics?

I was attracted to economics by the opportunity to make some small contribution to improving the economic well-being of individuals and communities around the world. It seems at first sight simply unbelievable that so many people live in such appalling conditions, and that the world is such an unequal place. And yet understanding the how and why of where we are, and what to do about it, involves many subtleties of argument that only economics as a discipline offers.

What have economists learned during the past 200 years about the "nature and causes of the wealth of nations" that would surprise Adam Smith?

There are many surprises: One is that since Smith's day the period which has seen the most rapid elevation of living standards has been that with the highest (not lowest) degree of government intervention in the economy; and that the richest countries (in the OECD) have substantially more regulation, control, and taxation than the very poorest. Another is the level and sophistication of formal argument in economic logic relative to Smith's time.

What are the challenges and benefits of globalization in today's world?

The great challenge of globalization is to exploit and harness the gains of economic integration for the greater good. This includes increased trade, investment flows, and global production for a single market. For now, removal of transborder restrictions on labour flows is the missing element in globalization. This has to be done in such a way that regulatory functions within existing nation states are taken up by new global institutions (globally redistributive taxation, global regulation of banks, global antitrust arrangements). The greatest challenge posed by globalization is marginalization; the lack of progress in and even regress in the very poorest countries (many in Africa). Other challenges involve the global environment, which is deteriorating both within countries, and globally; and the volatility we have seen on global financial markets of late (Asia 1997).

You have made many visits to Russia and studied at close hand that country's economic problems. How bad is Russia's economic performance? Why can't the Russian economy deliver for its people a standard of living that is similar to that in Canada?

By most statistical measures, Russia has suffered a fall in per capita income since the end of communism of nearly 50 percent (the World Bank puts it closer to 35 percent). This has been mirrored in other former Soviet Union countries, such as Ukraine, Belorusse, and Moldova; but in more remote former republics (Georgia, Armenia, Azerbaijan, Tadjikstan) the fall has been even larger (up to 70 percent). How and why this has occurred is a major challenge for the next generation of economists to understand. At one level, Russia followed almost exactly what Western neo-classical economists prescribed (privatization, establish legal structures, open up to trade, remove price controls). The result has been little short of catastrophic.

Why is Russian doing so much worse than China?

In China, few of the prescriptions of Western neo-classical economists have been followed and the

economy has grown rapidly (up to 10 percent in some years). The contrast between Russia and China could hardly be more dramatic. It is true that Russia has had trouble collecting taxes, and it experienced hyperinflation in 1993–1995. Also, the equipment and machinery that Russia inherited from communism was not able to produce products that could compete on world markets, and it has had to be scrapped to a large degree. China has had large foreign investment, Russia almost none. In my view, modern neo-classical economics has no clear explanations for why these phenomena have occurred, just as it does not for the onset of Asian growth first in Korea and Taiwan in the late 1950s, and then in Singapore and Hong Kong later. Any discipline needs unsolved mysteries to give it focus and dynamism, and explaining the economic performance in Russia in the late 1990s is certainly one.

The greatest challenge posed by globalization is marginalization; the lack of progress in and even regress in the very poorest countries

What is your assessment of NAFTA? Has it raised living standards in Canada, the United States, and Mexico?

Like Russia, NAFTA is also a great paradox. When Canada signed the Free Trade Agreement with the United States in 1987, the average tariff that Canadian products faced in U.S. markets was less than 1 percent. We had good access to U.S. markets, and we were trying to make that access more secure.

But many of the same trade irritants and conflicts that troubled us before NAFTA (such as those in softwood lumber and steel) have remained. But equally since the days of NAFTA, Canada's trade with the United States has grown from 75 percent to 85 percent of our total trade. And our international trade has increased from 30 percent to almost 45 percent of our total production.

Something has clearly happened, but at the same time other OECD countries have experienced increases in the percentage of their production traded. Studies seem to indicate that rationalization has happened in Canada since 1987 (a smaller number of larger plants producing for an integrated North American market, rather than for a smaller Canadian market). But it is hard to see how this has been driven principally by reductions in trade barriers. Some people talk about the psychological effect of NAFTA raising awareness of larger markets, but this is an unsatisfactory explanation for economists. More challenges!

Like Russia, NAFTA is also a great paradox.

China would like to join the World Trade Organization. What exactly is the WTO, and why is China so anxious to join it?
The World Trade Organization is a body in Geneva that oversees the main agreements between governments not to restrict international trade and organizes periodic negotiating rounds to lower trade barriers. It also arbitrates trade disputes between countries.

China wants to join the WTO principally to receive the WTO benefit of most favoured nation status (a guarantee that a nation will not be discriminated against in trade by other WTO countries). There are many other factors, but an equally interesting question is why so many countries are reluctant to let China into the WTO.

With your graduate school friend and colleague John Shoven (Charles R. Schwab Professor of Economics at Stanford University), you developed quantitative general equilibrium analysis, a branch of economics that now keeps hundreds of economists around the world busy. Can you describe the purpose of this work and perhaps provide a glimpse at how it is done?
You are right that I have worked a lot on numerical general equilibrium analysis, much of it with my friend John Shoven at Stanford. This work seeks to apply theoretical structures to real-world policy and other issues using computer-based models of economics, and computational techniques. These techniques include calibration procedures that we developed during the 1970s, and counterfactual equilibrium solution methods pioneered by Herbert Scarf of Yale. John and I were both students of Scarf, and he influenced us greatly.

What are some of the main lessons that we have learned from quantitative general equilibrium analysis? Have these lessons been used in any concrete ways to make the world economy more efficient?
The applications of these methods are all over the discipline: tax policy, trade policy, environmental policy, economic history, and developmental policy. Macroeconomics began to use similar techniques during the 1980s, though macroeconomists calibrate and use their models in different ways.

There are many policy implications that have been drawn from this work. They were influential in the Canada–U.S. Free Trade debate during the 1980s, for example, and in higher-level economics courses you may encounter them.

What is your advice to a student who is just setting out to study economics? How should he or she approach the subject? What are the other subjects that should be studied alongside economics?
My advice is to strike a balance between analysis (application of deductive logic) and accumulation of information/facts. Don't let analytics become the sole driver of your work. Keep focussed and relevant. On the other hand, don't adopt an approach that is descriptive; look for analytical content and lines of logical development. Most policy debates, in my view, are settled by some convincing analytical argument but it must be supported by factual material and be placed in the right context.

Other subjects to study should also, in my view, reflect balance. These days math and computer science are very important, but so too are history and sociology. Build a portfolio of mutually reinforcing subjects once you know what sub-discipline in economics you want to study: geography for economic development, law for industrial organization, statistics for macroeconomics.

Chapter 4

Demand and Supply

Slide, rocket, and roller coaster—rides at Canada's Wonderland? No. Commonly used descriptions of price changes. ◆ CD players have taken a price slide from around $1,100 (in today's money) in 1983 to less than $200 today. And during these years, the quantity of CD players bought has increased steadily. What caused this price slide? Why didn't brisk buying keep the price high? ◆ Occasionally, a price will rocket upward. But a price rocket, like a satellite-launching rocket, has a limited life. It eventually runs out of fuel. One spectacular price rocket occurred in 1993 and 1994 when the price of coffee shot skyward from $1.30 a kilogram in 1993 to $4.60 a kilogram in 1994. Why did the price of coffee rise so spectacularly? ◆ Over longer periods, the price of coffee along with the prices of bananas and other agricultural commodities rise and fall like a roller coaster ride. ◆ The prices of some things are steady. For example, the price of an audiocassette tape has not changed much. But despite its steady price, people buy more and more tapes each year. Why do we buy more tapes even though their price is no lower than it was a decade ago? And why do firms sell more tapes even though they can't get higher prices for them? ◆ Economics is about the choices people make to cope with scarcity. These choices are guided by costs and benefits and are coordinated through markets. ◆ The tool that explains how markets work is demand and supply. It is the main tool of economics and it is used to study issues as diverse as wages and jobs, rents and housing, pollution, crime, consumer protection, education, welfare, the value of money, and interest rates.

Slide, Rocket, and Roller Coaster

◇ Your careful study of this topic will bring big rewards in both your further study of economics and your everyday life. Once you understand demand and supply, you will view the world through new eyes. When you have completed your study of demand and supply, you will be able to explain how prices are determined and make predictions about price slides, rockets, and roller coasters. But first, we're going to take a closer look at the idea of price. Just what is a price?

After studying this chapter, you will be able to:

- Distinguish between a money price and a relative price
- Explain the main influences on demand
- Explain the main influences on supply
- Explain how prices and quantities bought and sold are determined by demand and supply
- Explain why some prices fall, some rise, and some fluctuate
- Use demand and supply to make predictions about price changes

Price and Opportunity Cost

ECONOMIC ACTIONS ARISE FROM SCARCITY— wants exceed the resources available to satisfy them. Faced with *scarcity*, we must make choices. And to make choices, we compare *costs* and *benefits*. Choices are influenced by opportunity costs. Producers only offer items for sale if the price is high enough to cover their opportunity cost. And consumers respond to changing opportunity cost by seeking cheaper alternatives to expensive items.

We are going to study the way people respond to *prices* and the forces that determine prices. But to pursue these tasks, we need to understand the relationship between a price and an opportunity cost.

In everyday life, the *price* of an object is the number of dollars that must be given up in exchange for it. Economists refer to this price as the *money price*.

The *opportunity cost* of an action is the highest-valued alternative forgone. If, when you buy a cup of coffee, the highest-valued thing you forgo is some gum, then the opportunity cost of buying a coffee is the *quantity* of gum forgone. We can calculate this quantity from the money prices of coffee and gum.

If the money price of coffee is $1 a cup and the money price of gum is 50¢ a pack, then the opportunity cost of one cup of coffee is two packs of gum. To calculate this opportunity cost, we divide the price of a cup of coffee by the price of a pack of gum and find the *ratio* of one price to the other. The ratio of one price to another is called a **relative price**, and a *relative price is an opportunity cost*.

We can express the relative price of coffee in terms of gum or any other good. The normal way of expressing a relative price is in terms of a "basket" of all goods and services. To calculate this relative price, we divide the money price of a good by the money price of a "basket" of all goods (called a *price index*). The resulting relative price is expressed in the buying power of money in a particular year. It tells us the opportunity cost of an item in terms of how much of the "basket" we must give up to buy it.

Figure 4.1 shows the money price and the relative price of wheat. The money price (green) has fluctuated but has tended to rise. The relative price (red) peaked in 1974 and has tended to fall since that year.

The theory of demand and supply that we are about to study determines *relative prices*, and the word "price" means *relative price*. When we predict

FIGURE 4.1

The Price of Wheat

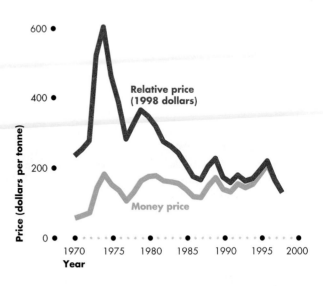

The money price of wheat—the number of dollars that must be given up for a tonne of wheat—has fluctuated between $55 and $207. But the *relative* price or *opportunity cost* of wheat, expressed in 1998 dollars, has fluctuated between $126 and $596 and has tended to fall. The behaviour of the money price obscures the fall in the relative price of wheat.

Sources: International Monetary Fund, *International Financial Statistics*, Washington, DC, 1999

that a price will fall, we do not mean that its *money* price will fall—although it might. We mean that its *relative* price will fall. That is, its price will fall *relative* to the average price of other goods and services.

R E V I E W   Q U I Z

▓ Explain the distinction between a money price and a relative price.

▓ Why is a relative price an opportunity cost?

▓ Can you think of an example of a good whose money price and relative price have risen?

▓ Can you think of an example of a good whose money price and relative price have fallen?

Let's now begin our study of demand and supply, starting with demand.

Demand

IF YOU DEMAND SOMETHING, THEN YOU

- Want it,
- Can afford it, and
- Have made a definite plan to buy it.

Wants are the unlimited desires or wishes that people have for goods and services. How many times have you thought that you would like something "if only you could afford it" or "if it weren't so expensive"? Scarcity guarantees that many—perhaps most—of our wants will never be satisfied. Demand reflects a decision about which wants to satisfy.

The **quantity demanded** of a good or service is the amount that consumers plan to buy during a given time period at a particular price. The quantity demanded is not necessarily the same amount as the quantity actually bought. Sometimes the quantity demanded is greater than the amount of goods available, so the quantity bought is less than the quantity demanded.

The quantity demanded is measured as an amount per unit of time. For example, suppose that you consume one cup of coffee a day. The quantity of coffee that you demand can be expressed as 1 cup per day or 7 cups per week or 365 cups per year. Without a time dimension, we cannot tell whether a particular quantity demanded is large or small.

What Determines Buying Plans?

The amount of any particular good or service that consumers plan to buy depends on many factors. The main ones are:

- The price of the good
- The prices of related goods
- Expected future prices
- Income
- Population
- Preferences

We first look at the relationship between the quantity demanded and the price of a good. To study this relationship, we keep all other influences on consumers' planned purchases the same and ask: How does the quantity demanded of the good vary as its price varies, other things remaining the same?

The Law of Demand

The law of demand states:

Other things remaining the same, the higher the price of a good, the smaller is the quantity demanded.

Why does a higher price reduce the quantity demanded? For two reasons:

- Substitution effect
- Income effect

Substitution Effect   When the price of a good rises, other things remaining the same, its *relative* price—its opportunity cost—rises. Although each good is unique, it has *substitutes*—other goods that can be used in its place. As the opportunity cost of a good rises, people buy less of that good and more of its substitutes.

Income Effect   When a price changes and all other influences on buying plans remain unchanged, the price rises *relative* to people's incomes. So faced with a higher price and an unchanged income, people cannot afford to buy all the things they previously bought. They must decrease the quantities demanded of at least some goods and services. Normally, the good whose price has increased is one of those that people buy in a smaller quantity.

To see the substitution effect and the income effect at work, think about the effects of a change in the price of tapes. Many different goods provide a service similar to that provided by a tape. For example, a compact disc, a pre-recorded tape, a radio or television broadcast, and a live concert all provide similar services to a tape. Suppose that a tape initially sells for $3 each and then the price doubles to $6. People now substitute compact discs and pre-recorded tapes for blank tapes—the substitution effect. And faced with a tighter budget, they buy fewer tapes as well as less of other goods and services—the income effect. The quantity of tapes demanded decreases for these two reasons.

Now suppose the price of a tape falls to $1. People now substitute blank tapes for compact discs and pre-recorded tapes—the substitution effect. And with a budget that now has some slack from the lower price of a tape, they buy more tapes as well as more of other goods and services—the income effect. The quantity of tapes demanded increases for these two reasons.

Demand Curve and Demand Schedule

You are now about to study one of the two most used curves in economics, the demand curve. And you are going to encounter one of the most critical distinctions: the distinction between *demand* and *quantity demanded*.

The term **demand** refers to the entire relationship between the quantity demanded and the price of a good, and it is illustrated by the demand curve and the demand schedule. The term *quantity demanded* refers to a point on a demand curve—the quantity demanded at a particular price.

Figure 4.2 shows the demand curve for tapes. A **demand curve** shows the relationship between the quantity demanded of a good and its price, when all other influences on consumers' planned purchases remain the same.

The table in Fig. 4.2 is the demand schedule for tapes. A *demand schedule* lists the quantities demanded at each different price when all the other influences on consumers' planned purchases—such as other prices, income, population, and preferences—remain the same. For example, if the price of a tape is $1, the quantity demanded is 9 million tapes a week. If the price of a tape is $5, the quantity demanded is 2 million tapes a week. The other rows of the table show the quantities demanded at prices of $2, $3, and $4.

We graph the demand schedule as a demand curve with the quantity demanded on the horizontal axis and the price on the vertical axis. The points on the demand curve labelled *a* through *e* represent the rows of the demand schedule. For example, point *a* on the graph represents a quantity demanded of 9 million tapes a week at a price of $1 a tape.

Willingness and Ability to Pay Another way of looking at the demand curve is as a willingness-and-ability-to-pay curve. And the willingness-and-ability-to-pay is a measure of *marginal benefit*.

If a small quantity is available, the highest price that someone is willing and able to pay for one more unit is high. But as the quantity available increases, the marginal benefit of each additional unit falls and the highest price that someone is willing and able to pay also falls along the demand curve.

In Fig. 4.2, if 2 million tapes are available each week, the highest price that someone is willing to pay for the 2 millionth tape is $5. But if 9 million tapes are available each week, someone is willing to pay $1 for the last tape bought.

FIGURE 4.2

The Demand Curve

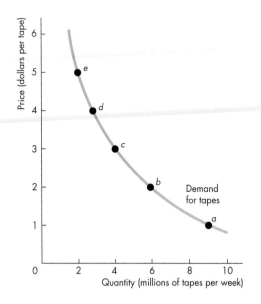

	Price (dollars per tape)	Quantity (millions of tapes per week)
a	1	9
b	2	6
c	3	4
d	4	3
e	5	2

The table shows a demand schedule listing the quantity of tapes demanded at each price if all other influences on buyers' plans remain the same. At a price of $1 a tape, 9 million tapes a week are demanded; at a price of $3 a tape, 4 million tapes a week are demanded. The demand curve shows the relationship between quantity demanded and price, everything else remaining the same.

The demand curve slopes downward: As price decreases, the quantity demanded increases. The demand curve can be read in two ways. For a given price, it tells us the quantity that people plan to buy. For example, at a price of $3 a tape, people plan to buy 4 million tapes a week. For a given quantity, the demand curve tells us the maximum price that consumers are willing and able to pay for the last tape available. For example, the maximum price that consumers will pay for the 6 millionth tape is $2.

A Change in Demand

When any factor that influences buying plans changes, other than the price of the good, there is a **change in demand**. Figure 4.3 illustrates an increase in demand. When demand increases, the demand curve shifts rightward and the quantity demanded is greater at each price. For example, at a price of $5, on the original (blue) demand curve, the quantity demanded is 2 million tapes a week. On the new (red) demand curve, the quantity demanded is 6 million tapes a week. Look closely at the numbers in the table in Fig. 4.3 and check that the quantity demanded is greater at each price.

Let's look at the factors that bring a change in demand. There are five key factors to consider.

1. Prices of Related Goods The quantity of tapes that consumers plan to buy depends in part on the prices of substitutes for tapes. A **substitute** is a good that can be used in place of another good. For example, a bus ride is a substitute for a train ride; a hamburger is a substitute for a hot dog; and a CD is a substitute for a tape. If the price of a substitute for a tape increases, people buy less of the substitute and more tapes. For example, if the price of a CD rises, people buy fewer CDs and more tapes. The demand for tapes increases.

The quantity of tapes that people plan to buy also depends on the prices of complements with tapes. A **complement** is a good that is used in conjunction with another good. Hamburgers and fries are complements. So are spaghetti and meat sauce, and so are tapes and Walkmans. If the price of a Walkman falls, people buy more Walkmans *and more tapes*. It is a fall in the price of a Walkman that increases the demand for tapes in Figure 4.3.

2. Expected Future Prices If the price of a good is expected to rise in the future and if the good can be stored, the opportunity cost of obtaining the good for future use is lower now than it will be when the price has increased. So people retime their purchase—they substitute over time. They buy more of the good before its price is expected to rise (and less after), so the current demand for the good increases.

For example, suppose that Florida is hit by a severe frost that damages the season's orange crop. You expect the price of orange juice to rise. So, anticipating a higher price, you fill your freezer with enough frozen juice to get you through the next six months. Your current demand for frozen orange juice has increased (and your future demand has decreased).

FIGURE 4.3

An Increase in Demand

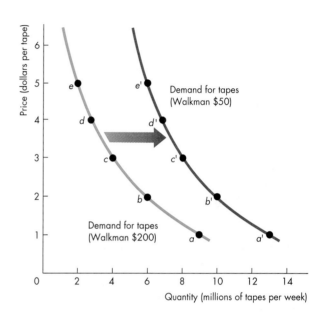

| Original demand schedule | | | New demand schedule | | |
Walkman $200			Walkman $50		
	Price (dollars per tape)	**Quantity** (millions of tapes per week)		**Price** (dollars per tape)	**Quantity** (millions of tapes per week)
a	1	9	a'	1	13
b	2	6	b'	2	10
c	3	4	c'	3	8
d	4	3	d'	4	7
e	5	2	e'	5	6

A change in any influence on buyers' plans other than the price of the good itself results in a new demand schedule and a shift of the demand curve. A change in the price of a Walkman changes the demand for tapes. At a price of $3 a tape (row *c* of the table), 4 million tapes a week are demanded when the Walkman costs $200 and 8 million tapes a week are demanded when the Walkman costs only $50. A *fall* in the price of a Walkman *increases* the demand for tapes because the Walkman is a complement of tapes. When demand *increases*, the demand curve shifts *rightward*, as shown by the shift arrow and the resulting red curve.

Similarly, if the price of a good is expected to fall in the future, the opportunity cost of buying the good now is high relative to what it is expected to be in the future. So again, people retime their purchases. They buy less of the good now before its price falls (and more after), so the current demand for the good decreases.

Computer prices are constantly falling, and this fact poses a dilemma. Will you buy a new computer now, in time for the start of the school year, or will you wait until the price has fallen some more? Because people expect computer prices to keep falling, the current demand for computers is less (and the future demand is greater) than it otherwise would be.

3. Income Another influence on demand is consumer income. When income increases, consumers buy more of most goods, and when income decreases, they buy less of most goods. Although an increase in income leads to an increase in the demand for *most* goods, it does not lead to an increase in the demand for *all* goods. A **normal good** is one for which demand increases as income increases. An **inferior good** is one for which demand decreases as income increases. Long-distance transportation has examples of both normal goods and inferior goods. As incomes increase, the demand for air travel (a normal good) increases and the demand for long-distance bus trips (an inferior good) decreases.

4. Population Demand also depends on the size and the age structure of the population. The larger the population, the greater is the demand for all goods and services. And the smaller the population, the smaller is the demand for all goods and services.

For example, the demand for car parking spaces or movies or tapes or just about anything that you can imagine is much greater in Toronto than it is in Thunder Bay.

Also the larger the proportion of the population in a given age group, the greater is the demand for the types of goods and services used by that age group.

For example, in 1995, there were 1.9 million 20–24 year olds in Canada compared with 2.3 million in 1985. As a result, the demand for college places decreased between 1985 and 1995. During these same years, the number of Canadians aged 85 years and over increased. As a result, the demand for nursing home services increased.

5. Preferences Demand depends on preferences. *Preferences* are an individual's attitudes towards goods

---

TABLE 4.1
The Demand for Tapes

The Law of Demand

The quantity of tapes demanded

Decreases if:	*Increases if:*
■ The price of a tape rises	■ The price of a tape falls

Changes in Demand

The demand for tapes

Decreases if:	*Increases if:*
■ The price of a substitute falls	■ The price of a substitute rises
■ The price of a complement rises	■ The price of a complement falls
■ The price of a tape is expected to fall in the future	■ The price of a tape is expected to rise in the future
■ Income falls*	■ Income rises*
■ The population decreases	■ The population increases

*A tape is a normal good.

---

and services. For example, a rock music fanatic has a much greater preference for tapes than does a tone-deaf workaholic. As a consequence, even if they have the same incomes, their demands for tapes will be very different.

Table 4.1 summarizes the influences on demand and the direction of those influences.

A Change in the Quantity Demanded Versus a Change in Demand

Changes in the factors that influence buyers' plans cause either a change in the quantity demanded or a change in demand. Equivalently, they cause either a movement along the demand curve or a shift of the demand curve.

The distinction between a change in the quantity demanded and a change in demand is the same as that between a movement along the demand curve and a shift of the demand curve.

A point on the demand curve shows the quantity demanded at a given price. So a movement along the demand curve shows a **change in the quantity demanded**. The entire demand curve shows demand. So a shift of the demand curve shows a **change in demand**. Figure 4.4 illustrates and summarizes these distinctions.

Movement Along the Demand Curve   If the price of a good changes but everything else remains the same, there is a movement along the demand curve. Because the demand curve slopes downward, a fall in the price of a good or service increases the quantity demanded and a rise in the price of the good or service decreases the quantity demanded—the law of demand.

In Fig. 4.4, if the price of a good falls when everything else remains the same, the quantity demanded of that good increases and there is a movement down the demand curve D_0. If the price rises when everything else remains the same, the quantity demanded decreases and there is a movement up the demand curve D_0.

A Shift of the Demand Curve   If the price of a good remains constant but some other influence on buyers' plans changes, there is a change in demand for that good. We illustrate a change in demand as a shift of the demand curve. For example, a fall in the price of the Walkman—a complement of tapes—increases the demand for tapes. We illustrate this increase in demand for tapes with a new demand schedule and a new demand curve. If the price of the Walkman falls, consumers buy more tapes regardless of whether the price of a tape is high or low. That is what a rightward shift of the demand curve shows—that more tapes are bought at each and every price.

In Fig. 4.4, when any influence on buyers' planned purchases changes, other than the price of the good, there is a *change in demand* and the demand curve shifts.

Demand *increases* and the demand curve *shifts rightward* (to the red demand curve D_1) if the price of a substitute rises, the expected future price of the good rises, the price of a complement falls, income increases (for a normal good), or the population increases.

Demand *decreases* and the demand curve *shifts leftward* (to the red demand curve D_2) if the price of a substitute falls, the expected future price of the good falls, the price of a complement rises, income decreases (for a normal good), or the population decreases.

For an inferior good, the effects of changes in income are in the direction opposite to those described above.

FIGURE   4.4

A Change in the Quantity Demanded Versus a Change in Demand

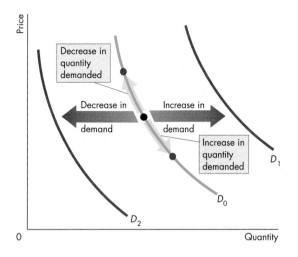

When the price of the good changes, there is a movement along the demand curve and *a change in the quantity demanded*, shown by the blue arrows on demand curve D_0. When some other influence on buying plans changes, there is a *change in demand* and the demand curve shifts. An increase in demand shifts the demand curve rightward (from D_0 to D_1) and a decrease in demand shifts the demand curve leftward (from D_0 to D_2).

REVIEW   QUIZ

- Can you define the *quantity demanded* of a good or service?
- What is the *law of demand* and how do we illustrate it?
- If a fixed amount of a good is available, what does the demand curve tell us about the price that consumers are willing to pay for that fixed quantity?
- Can you list all the influences on buying plans that *change demand* and for each influence say whether it increases demand or decreases demand?
- What happens to the quantity of CDs demanded and the demand for CDs if the price of a CD falls and all other influences on buying plans remain the same?

Supply

IF A FIRM SUPPLIES A GOOD OR SERVICE, THE FIRM

- Has the resources and technology to produce it,
- Can profit from producing it, and
- Has made a definite plan to produce it and sell it.

A supply is more than just having the *resources* and the *technology* to produce something. *Resources and technology* are the constraints that limit what is possible.

Many useful things can be produced, but they are not produced unless it is profitable to do so. Supply reflects a decision about which technologically feasible items to produce.

The **quantity supplied** of a good or service is the amount that producers plan to sell during a given time period at a particular price. The quantity supplied is not necessarily the same amount as the quantity actually sold. Sometimes the quantity supplied is greater than the quantity demanded, so the quantity bought is less than the quantity supplied.

Like the quantity demanded, the quantity supplied is measured as an amount per unit of time. For example, suppose that GM produces 1,000 cars a day. The quantity of cars supplied by GM can be expressed as 1,000 a day, or 7,000 a week, or 365,000 a year. Without the time dimension, we cannot tell whether a particular number is large or small.

What Determines Selling Plans?

The amount of any particular good or service that producers plan to sell depends on many factors. The main ones are:

- The price of the good
- The prices of resources used to produce the good
- The prices of related goods produced
- Expected future prices
- The number of suppliers
- Technology

Let's first look at the relationship between the price of a good and the quantity supplied. To study this relationship, we keep all the other influences on the quantity supplied the same. We ask: How does the quantity supplied of a good vary as its price varies?

The Law of Supply

The law of supply states:

> Other things remaining the same, the higher the price of a good, the greater is the quantity supplied.

Why does a higher price increase the quantity supplied? It is because of *increasing marginal cost*. As the quantity produced of any good increases, the marginal cost of producing the good increases. (You can refresh your memory of increasing marginal cost in Chapter 3, p. 42.)

It is never worth producing a good if the price received for it does not at least cover marginal cost. So when the price of a good rises, other things remaining the same, producers are willing to incur the higher marginal cost and increase production. The higher price brings forth an increase in the quantity supplied.

Let's now illustrate the law of supply with a supply curve and a supply schedule.

Supply Curve and Supply Schedule

You are now going to study the second of the two most used curves in economics, the supply curve. And you're going to learn about the critical distinction between *supply* and *quantity supplied*.

The term **supply** refers to the entire relationship between the quantity supplied and the price of a good, and it is illustrated by the supply curve and the supply schedule. The term *quantity supplied* refers to a point on a supply curve—the quantity supplied at a particular price.

Figure 4.5 shows the supply curve of tapes. A **supply curve** shows the relationship between the quantity supplied of a good and its price, when all other influences on producers' planned sales remain the same. It is a graph of a supply schedule.

The table in Fig. 4.5 sets out the supply schedule for tapes. A *supply schedule* lists the quantities supplied at each different price when all the other influences on producers' planned sales remain the same. For example, if the price of a tape is $1, the quantity supplied is zero—on row *a* of the table. If the price of a tape is $2, the quantity supplied is 3 million tapes a week—on row *b*. The other rows of the table show the quantities supplied at prices of $3, $4, and $5.

FIGURE 4.5

The Supply Curve

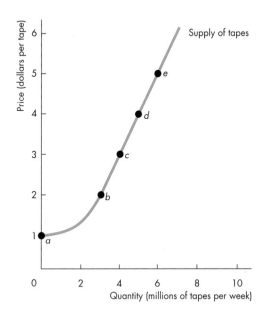

	Price (dollars per tape)	Quantity (millions of tapes per week)
a	1	0
b	2	3
c	3	4
d	4	5
e	5	6

The table shows the supply schedule of tapes. For example, at $2 a tape, 3 million tapes a week are supplied; at $5 a tape, 6 million tapes a week are supplied. The supply curve shows the relationship between the quantity supplied and price, everything else remaining the same. The supply curve usually slopes upward: As the price of a good increases, so does the quantity supplied.

A supply curve can be read in two ways. For a given price, it tells us the quantity that producers plan to sell. For example, at a price of $3 a tape, producers plan to sell 4 million tapes a week. And for a given quantity, it tells us the minimum price that producers are willing to accept for that quantity. For example, the minimum price that producers are willing to accept for the 6 millionth tape is $5.

To make a supply curve, we graph the quantity supplied on the horizontal axis and the price on the vertical axis, just as in the case of the demand curve. The points on the supply curve labelled *a* through *e* represent the rows of the supply schedule. For example, point *a* on the graph represents a quantity supplied of zero at a price of $1 a tape.

Minimum Supply Price Just as the demand curve has two interpretations, so too does the supply curve. The demand curve can be interpreted as a willingness-and-ability-to-pay curve. The supply curve can be interpreted as a minimum-supply-price curve. It tells us the lowest price at which someone can profitably sell another unit.

If a small quantity is produced, the lowest price at which someone can profitably produce one more unit is low. But if a large quantity is produced, the lowest price at which someone can profitably sell one more unit is high.

In Fig. 4.5, if 6 million tapes a week are produced, the lowest price that a producer is willing to accept for the 6 millionth tape is $5. But if only 4 million tapes are produced each week, the lowest price that a producer is willing to accept for the 4 millionth tape is $3.

A Change in Supply

When any factor that influences selling plans changes, other than the price of the good, there is a **change in supply**. Let's look at the five key factors that change supply.

1. Prices of Productive Resources The prices of productive resources influence supply. The easiest way to see this influence is to think about the supply curve as a minimum-supply-price curve. If the price of a productive resource rises, the lowest price a producer is willing to accept rises so supply decreases. For example, during 1996, the price of jet fuel increased and the supply of air transportation decreased. Similarly, a rise in the minimum wage decreases the supply of hamburgers. If the wages of tape producers rise, the supply of tapes decreases.

2. Prices of Related Goods Produced The prices of related goods and services that firms produce influence supply. For example, if the price of pre-recorded tapes rises, the supply of blank tapes decreases. Blank tapes and pre-recorded tapes are *substitutes in produc-*

tion—goods that can be produced by using the same resources. If the price of beef rises, the supply of cowhide increases. Beef and cowhide are *complements in production*—goods that must be produced together.

3. Expected Future Prices If the price of a good is expected to rise, the return from selling the good in the future is higher than it is in the present. So the current supply decreases.

4. The Number of Suppliers Supply also depends on the number of suppliers. The larger the number of firms that produce a good, the greater is the supply of the good. As firms enter an industry, the supply in that industry increases. As firms leave an industry, the supply in that industry decreases. For example, over the past two years there has been a huge increase in the number of firms that produce and manage Web sites. As a result, the supply of Internet and World Wide Web services has increased enormously.

5. Technology New technologies create new products and lower the costs of producing existing products. As a result, new technologies change supply. For example, the development of a new technology for tape production by Sony and Minnesota Mining and Manufacturing (3M) has lowered the cost of producing tapes and increased the supply of tapes.

Figure 4.6 illustrates an increase in supply. When supply increases, the supply curve shifts rightward and the quantity supplied is larger at each and every price. For example, at a price of $2, on the original (blue) supply curve, the quantity supplied is 3 million tapes a week. On the new (red) supply curve, the quantity supplied is 6 million tapes a week. Look closely at the numbers in the table in Fig. 4.6 and check that the quantity supplied is larger at each price.

Table 4.2 summarizes the influences on supply and the directions of those influences.

A Change in Quantity Supplied Versus a Change in Supply

Changes in the factors that influence producers' planned sales cause either a change in the quantity supplied or a change in supply. Equivalently, they cause either a movement along the supply curve or a shift of the supply curve.

FIGURE 4.6

An Increase in Supply

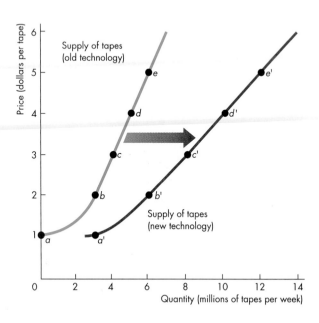

| Original supply schedule | | | New supply schedule | | |
| Old technology | | | New technology | | |
	Price (dollars per tape)	Quantity (millions of tapes per week)		Price (dollars per tape)	Quantity (millions of tapes per week)
a	1	0	a'	1	3
b	2	3	b'	2	6
c	3	4	c'	3	8
d	4	5	d'	4	10
e	5	6	e'	5	12

A change in any influence on sellers' plans other than the price of the good itself results in a new supply schedule and a shift of the supply curve. For example, if Sony and 3M invent a new, cost-saving technology for producing tapes, the supply of tapes changes.

At a price of $3 a tape, 4 million tapes a week are supplied when producers use the old technology (row c of the table) and 8 million tapes a week are supplied when producers use the new technology. An advance in technology *increases* the supply of tapes and the supply curve shifts *rightward*, as shown by the shift arrow and the resulting red curve.

A point on the supply curve shows the quantity supplied at a given price. A movement along the supply curve shows a **change in the quantity supplied**. The entire supply curve shows supply. A shift of the supply curve shows a **change in supply**.

Figure 4.7 illustrates and summarizes these distinctions. If the price of a good falls and everything else remains the same, the quantity supplied of that good decreases and there is a movement down the supply curve S_0. If the price of a good rises and everything else remains the same, the quantity supplied increases and there is a movement up the supply curve S_0. When any other influence on selling plans changes, the supply curve shifts and there is a change in supply. If the supply curve is S_0 and if production costs fall, supply increases and the supply curve shifts to the red supply curve S_1. If the supply curve is S_0 and if production costs rise, supply decreases and the supply curve shifts to the red supply curve S_2.

TABLE 4.2

The Supply for Tapes

The Law of Supply

The quantity of tapes supplied

Decreases if:	*Increases if:*
■ The price of a tape falls	■ The price of a tape rises

Changes in Supply

The supply of tapes

Decreases if:	*Increases if:*
■ The price of a resource used to produce tapes rises	■ The price of a resource used to produce tapes falls
■ The price of a substitute in production rises	■ The price of a substitute in production falls
■ The price of a complement in production falls	■ The price of a complement in production rises
■ The price of a tape is expected to rise in the future	■ The price of a tape is expected to fall in the future
■ The number of tape producers decreases	■ The number of tape producers increases
	■ More efficient technologies for producing tapes are discovered

---

FIGURE 4.7

A Change in the Quantity Supplied Versus a Change in Supply

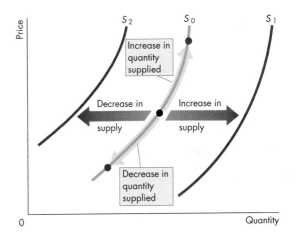

When the price of the good changes, there is a movement along the supply curve and *a change in the quantity supplied*, shown by the blue arrows on supply curve S_0. When any other influence on selling plans changes, there is a shift of the supply curve and a *change in supply*. An increase in supply shifts the supply curve rightward (from S_0 to S_1) and a decrease in supply shifts the supply curve leftward (from S_0 to S_2).

R E V I E W   Q U I Z

■ Can you define the *quantity supplied* of a good or service?

■ What is the *law of supply* and how do we illustrate it?

■ If consumers are willing to buy only a given quantity, what does the supply curve tell us about the price at which firms will supply that quantity?

■ Can you list all the influences on selling plans that *change supply* and for each influence say whether it increases supply or decreases supply?

Your next task is to use what you've learned about demand and supply and learn how prices and quantities are determined.

Market Equilibrium

WE HAVE SEEN THAT WHEN THE PRICE OF A good *rises*, the quantity demanded *decreases* and the quantity supplied *increases*. We are now going to see how prices coordinate the plans of buyers and sellers and achieve an equilibrium.

An *equilibrium* is a situation in which opposing forces balance each other. Equilibrium in a market occurs when the price balances the plans of buyers and sellers. The **equilibrium price** is the price at which the quantity demanded equals the quantity supplied. The **equilibrium quantity** is the quantity bought and sold at the equilibrium price. A market moves towards its equilibrium because:

- Price regulates buying and selling plans
- Price adjusts when plans don't match

Price As a Regulator

The price of a good regulates the quantities demanded and supplied. If the price is too high, the quantity supplied exceeds the quantity demanded. If the price is too low, the quantity demanded exceeds the quantity supplied. There is one price at which the quantity demanded equals the quantity supplied. Let's work out what that price is.

Figure 4.8 shows the market for tapes. The table shows the demand schedule (from Fig. 4.2) and the supply schedule (from Fig. 4.5). If the price of a tape is $1, the quantity demanded is 9 million tapes a week, but no tapes are supplied. The quantity demanded exceeds the quantity supplied by 9 million tapes a week. In other words, at a price of $1 a tape, there is a shortage of 9 million tapes a week. This shortage is shown in the final column of the table. At a price of $2 a tape, there is still a shortage, but only of 3 million tapes a week. If the price of a tape is $5, the quantity supplied exceeds the quantity demanded. The quantity supplied is 6 million tapes a week, but the quantity demanded is only 2 million. There is a surplus of 4 million tapes a week. The one price at which there is neither a shortage nor a surplus is $3 a tape. At that price, the quantity demanded is equal to the quantity supplied: 4 million tapes a week. The equilibrium price is $3 a tape, and the equilibrium quantity is 4 million tapes a week.

Figure 4.8 shows that the demand curve and supply curve intersect at the equilibrium price of

FIGURE 4.8

Equilibrium

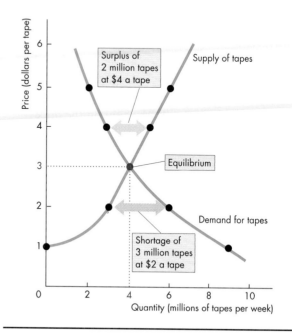

The table lists the quantities demanded and quantities supplied as well as the shortage or surplus of tapes at each price. If the price is $2 a tape, 6 million tapes a week are demanded and 3 million are supplied. There is a shortage of 3 million tapes a week, and the price rises. If the price is $4 a tape, 3 million tapes a week are demanded and 5 million are supplied. There is a surplus of 2 million tapes a week, and the price falls. If the price is $3 a tape, 4 million tapes a week are demanded and 4 million are supplied. There is neither a shortage nor a surplus. Neither buyers nor sellers have any incentive to change the price. The price at which the quantity demanded equals the quantity supplied is the equilibrium price.

Price (dollars per tape)	Quantity demanded	Quantity supplied	Shortage (–) or surplus (+)
	(millions of tapes per week)		
1	9	0	–9
2	6	3	–3
3	4	4	0
4	3	5	+2
5	2	6	+4

$3 a tape. At each price *above* $3 a tape, there is a surplus of tapes. For example, at $4 a tape the surplus is 2 million tapes a week, as shown by the blue arrow. At each price *below* $3 a tape, there is a shortage of tapes. For example, at $2 a tape, the shortage is 3 million tapes a week, as shown by the red arrow.

Price Adjustments

You've seen that if the price is below equilibrium there is shortage and if the price is above equilibrium there is a surplus. But can we count on the price to change and eliminate shortages or surpluses? We can, because such price changes are mutually beneficial to both buyers and sellers. Let's see why the price changes when there is a shortage or a surplus.

A Shortage Forces the Price Up Suppose the price of a tape is $2. Consumers plan to buy 6 million tapes a week, and producers plan to sell 3 million tapes a week. Consumers can't force producers to sell more than they plan, so the quantity actually offered for sale is 3 million tapes a week. In this situation, powerful forces operate to increase the price and move it towards the equilibrium price. Some producers, noticing lines of unsatisfied consumers, move their prices up. Some producers increase their output. As producers push their prices up, the price rises towards its equilibrium. The rising price reduces the shortage because it decreases the quantity demanded and increases the quantity supplied. When the price has increased to the point at which there is no longer a shortage, the forces moving the price stop operating and the price comes to rest at its equilibrium.

A Surplus Forces the Price Down Suppose the price of a tape is $4. Producers plan to sell 5 million tapes a week, and consumers plan to buy 3 million tapes a week. Producers cannot force consumers to buy more than they plan, so the quantity that is actually bought is 3 million tapes a week. In this situation, powerful forces operate to lower the price and move it towards the equilibrium price. Some producers, unable to sell the quantities of tapes that they planned to sell, cut their prices. In addition, some producers scale back production. As producers cut prices, the price falls towards its equilibrium. The falling price decreases the surplus because it increases the quantity demanded and decreases the quantity supplied. When the price has fallen to the point at

which there is no longer a surplus, the forces moving the price stop operating, and the price comes to rest at its equilibrium.

The Best Deal Available for Buyers and Sellers
When the price is below equilibrium, it is forced upward towards the equilibrium. Why don't buyers resist the increase and refuse to buy at the higher price? Because they value the good more highly than the current price and they cannot satisfy all their demands at the current price. In some markets—an example is the market for rental accommodation in Sydney, Australia, as we approach the 2000 Olympic Games—the buyers might even be the ones who force the price upward by offering higher prices to divert the limited quantities away from other buyers.

When the price is above equilibrium, it is bid downward towards the equilibrium. Why don't sellers resist this decrease and refuse to sell at the lower price? Because their minimum supply price is below the current price and they cannot sell all they would like to at the current price. Normally, it is the sellers who force the price downward by offering lower prices to gain market share from their competitors.

At the price at which the quantity demanded and the quantity supplied are equal, neither buyers nor sellers can do business at a better price. Buyers pay the highest price they are willing to pay for the last unit bought, and sellers receive the lowest price at which they are willing to supply the last unit sold.

When people freely make offers to buy and sell, and when demanders try to buy at the lowest possible price and suppliers try to sell at the highest possible price, the price at which trade takes place is the equilibrium price—the price at which the quantity demanded equals the quantity supplied. The price coordinates the plans of buyers and sellers.

REVIEW QUIZ

- What is the *equilibrium price* of a good or service?
- Over what range of prices does a shortage arise?
- Over what range of prices does a surplus arise?
- What happens to the price when there is a shortage?
- What happens to the price when there is a surplus?
- Why is the price at which the quantity demanded equals the quantity supplied the equilibrium price?
- Why is the equilibrium price the best deal available for both buyers and sellers?

Predicting Changes in Price and Quantity

THE DEMAND AND SUPPLY THEORY WE HAVE JUST studied provides us with a powerful way of analysing influences on prices and the quantities bought and sold. According to the theory, a change in price stems from either a change in demand or a change in supply or a change in both. Let's look first at the effects of a change in demand.

A Change in Demand

What happens to the price and quantity of tapes if the demand for tapes increases? We can answer this question with a specific example. Suppose the price of a Walkman falls from $200 to $50. Because the Walkman and tapes are complements, the demand for tapes increases, as is shown in the table in Fig. 4.9. The original demand schedule and the new one are set out in the first three columns of the table. The table also shows the supply schedule for tapes.

The original equilibrium price is $3 a tape. At that price, 4 million tapes a week are demanded and supplied. When demand increases, the price that makes the quantity demanded equal the quantity supplied is $5 a tape. At this price, 6 million tapes are bought and sold each week. When demand increases, both the price and the quantity increase.

Figure 4.9 shows these changes. The figure shows the original demand for and supply of tapes. The original equilibrium price is $3 a tape, and the quantity is 4 million tapes a week. When demand increases, the demand curve shifts rightward. The equilibrium price rises to $5 a tape, and the quantity supplied increases to 6 million tapes a week, as highlighted in the figure. There is an *increase in the quantity supplied* but *no change in supply*—a movement along, but no shift of, the supply curve.

We can reverse the exercise that we've just conducted. If we start at a price of $5 a tape with 6 million tapes a week being bought and sold, we can work out what happens if demand decreases to its original level. Such a decrease in demand might arise from a fall in the price of a CD or a CD player (both substitutes for tapes). The decrease in demand shifts the demand curve leftward. The equilibrium price falls to $3 a tape, and the equilibrium quantity decreases to 4 million tapes a week.

FIGURE 4.9

The Effects of a Change in Demand

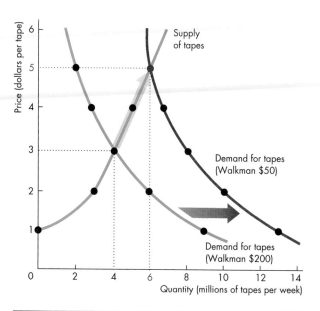

Price (dollars per tape)	Quantity demanded (millions of tapes per week)		Quantity supplied (millions of tapes per week)
	Walkman $200	Walkman $50	
1	9	13	0
2	6	10	3
3	4	8	4
4	3	7	5
5	2	6	6

With the price of a Walkman at $200, the demand for tapes is the blue curve. The equilibrium price is $3 a tape and the equilibrium quantity is 4 million tapes a week. When the price of a Walkman falls from $200 to $50, the demand for tapes increases and the demand curve shifts rightward to become the red curve.

At $3 a tape, there is now a shortage of 4 million tapes a week. The price of a tape rises to a new equilibrium of $5 a tape. As the price rises to $5, the quantity supplied increases, as shown by the blue arrow along the supply curve, to the new equilibrium quantity of 6 million tapes a week. Following an increase in demand, the quantity supplied increases but supply does not change—the supply curve does not shift.

We can now make our first two predictions:

1. When demand increases, both the price and the quantity increase.
2. When demand decreases, both the price and the quantity decrease.

A Change in Supply

Suppose that Sony and 3M introduce a new cost-saving technology in their tape production plants. The new technology increases the supply of tapes. The new supply schedule (the same one that was shown in Fig. 4.6) is presented in the table in Fig. 4.10. What are the new equilibrium price and quantity? The answer is highlighted in the table: The price falls to $2 a tape, and the quantity increases to 6 million a week. You can see why by looking at the quantities demanded and supplied at the original price of $3 a tape. The quantity supplied at that price is 8 million tapes a week, and there is a surplus of tapes. The price falls. Only when the price is $2 a tape does the quantity supplied equal the quantity demanded.

Figure 4.10 illustrates the effect of an increase in supply. It shows the demand curve for tapes and the original and new supply curves. The initial equilibrium price is $3 a tape, and the quantity is 4 million tapes a week. When the supply increases, the supply curve shifts rightward. The equilibrium price falls to $2 a tape, and the quantity demanded increases to 6 million tapes a week, highlighted in the figure. There is an *increase in the quantity demanded* but *no change in demand*—a movement along, but no shift of, the demand curve.

The exercise that we've just conducted can be reversed. If we start out at a price of $2 a tape with 6 million tapes a week being bought and sold, we can work out what happens if supply decreases to its original level. Such a decrease in supply might arise from an increase in the cost of labour or raw materials. The decrease in supply shifts the supply curve leftward. The equilibrium price rises to $3 a tape, and the equilibrium quantity decreases to 4 million tapes a week.

We can now make two more predictions:

1. When supply increases, the quantity increases and the price falls.
2. When supply decreases, the quantity decreases and the price rises.

FIGURE **4.10**

The Effects of a Change in Supply

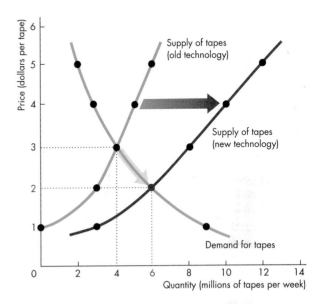

Price	Quantity demanded	Quantity supplied (millions of tapes per week)	
(dollars per tape)	(millions of tapes per week)	old technology	new technology
1	9	0	3
2	6	3	6
3	4	4	8
4	3	5	10
5	2	6	12

With the old technology, the supply of tapes is shown by the blue supply curve. The equilibrium price is $3 a tape, and the equilibrium quantity is 4 million tapes a week. When the new technology is adopted, the supply of tapes increases and the supply curve shifts rightward to become the red curve.

At $3 a tape, there is now a surplus of 4 million tapes a week. The price of a tape falls to a new equilibrium of $2 a tape. As the price falls to $2, the quantity demanded increases, as shown by the blue arrow on the demand curve, to the new equilibrium quantity of 6 million tapes a week. Following an increase in supply, the quantity demanded increases but demand does not change—the demand curve does not shift.

A Change in Both Demand and Supply

You can now predict the effects of a change in either demand or supply on the price and the quantity. But what happens if *both* demand and supply change together? To answer this question, we look first at the case in which demand and supply move in the same direction—either both increase or both decrease. Then we look at the case in which they move in opposite directions—demand decreases and supply increases or demand increases and supply decreases.

Demand and Supply Change in the Same Direction We've seen that an increase in the demand for tapes increases the price of tapes and increases the quantity bought and sold. And we've seen that an increase in the supply of tapes lowers the price of tapes and increases the quantity bought and sold. Let's now examine what happens when both of these changes happen to occur together.

The table in Fig. 4.11 brings together the numbers that describe the original quantities demanded and supplied and the new quantities demanded and supplied after the fall in the price of the Walkman and the improved tape production technology. These same numbers are illustrated in the graph. The original (blue) demand and supply curves intersect at a price of $3 a tape and a quantity of 4 million tapes a week. The new (red) supply and demand curves also intersect at a price of $3 a tape but at a quantity of 8 million tapes a week.

An increase in either demand or supply increases the quantity. So when both demand and supply increase, so does quantity.

An increase in demand raises the price, and an increase in supply lowers the price, so we can't say whether the price will rise or fall when demand and supply increase together. In this example, the price does not change. But notice that if demand increases by slightly more than the amount shown in the figure, the price will rise. And if supply increases by slightly more than the amount shown in the figure, the price will fall.

We can now make two more predictions:

1. When *both* demand and supply increase, the quantity increases and the price might increase, decrease, or remain the same.

2. When *both* demand and supply decrease, the quantity decreases and the price might increase, decrease, or remain the same.

FIGURE 4.11

The Effects of an Increase in Both Demand and Supply

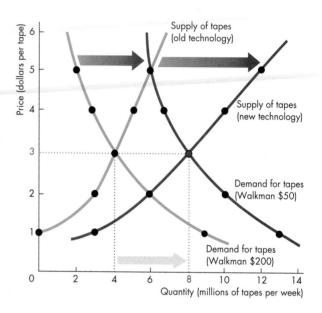

	Original quantities (millions of tapes per week)		**New quantities** (millions of tapes per week)	
Price (dollars per tape)	**Quantity demanded** Walkman $200	**Quantity supplied** old technology	**Quantity demanded** Walkman $50	**Quantity supplied** new technology
1	9	0	13	3
2	6	3	10	6
3	4	4	8	8
4	3	5	7	10
5	2	6	6	12

When a Walkman costs $200 and firms use the old technology to produce tapes, the price of a tape is $3 and the quantity is 4 million tapes a week. A fall in the price of a Walkman increases the demand for tapes, and improved technology increases the supply of tapes. The new supply curve intersects the new demand curve at $3 a tape, the same price as before, but the quantity increases to 8 million tapes a week. These increases in demand and supply increase the quantity but leave the price unchanged.

Demand and Supply Change in Opposite Directions Let's now see what happens when demand and supply change together but move in *opposite* directions. An improved production technology increases the supply of tapes as before. But now the price of a CD player falls. A CD player is a substitute for tapes. With cheaper CD players, more people buy them and switch from buying tapes to buying CDs, and the demand for tapes decreases.

The table in Fig. 4.12 describes the original and new demand and supply schedules. These schedules are shown as the original (blue) and new (red) demand and supply curves in the graph. The original demand and supply curves intersect at a price of $5 a tape and a quantity of 6 million tapes a week. The new supply and demand curves intersect at a price of $2 a tape and at the original quantity of 6 million tapes a week.

A decrease in demand or an increase in supply lowers the price. So when a decrease in demand and an increase in supply occur together, the price falls.

A decrease in demand decreases the quantity and an increase in supply increases the quantity, so we can't say for sure which way the quantity will change when demand decreases and supply increases at the same time. In this example, the decrease in demand and the increase in supply are such that the increase in quantity brought about by an increase in supply is offset by the decrease in quantity brought about by a decrease in demand—so the quantity does not change. But notice that if demand had decreased by slightly more, the quantity would have decreased. And if supply had increased by slightly more, the quantity would have increased.

We can now make two more predictions:

1. When demand decreases and supply increases, the price falls and the quantity might increase, decrease, or remain the same.
2. When demand increases and supply decreases, the price rises and the quantity might increase, decrease, or remain the same.

R E V I E W   Q U I Z

What is the effect on the price of a tape and the quantity of tapes if: (a) the price of a CD rises or (b) the price of a Walkman rises or (c) more firms start to produce tapes or (d) tape producers' wages rise or (e) if any pair of these events occur at the same time? (Draw the diagrams!)

FIGURE 4.12

The Effects of a Decrease in Demand and an Increase in Supply

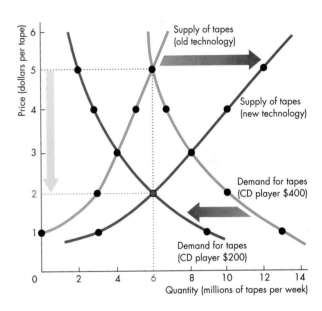

	Original quantities (millions of tapes per week)		New quantities (millions of tapes per week)	
Price (dollars per tape)	**Quantity demanded** CD player $400	**Quantity supplied** old technology	**Quantity demanded** CD player $200	**Quantity supplied** new technology
1	13	0	9	3
2	10	3	6	6
3	8	4	4	8
4	7	5	3	10
5	6	6	2	12

When the price of a CD player is $400 and firms use the old technology to produce tapes, the price of a tape is $5 and the quantity is 6 million tapes a week. A fall in the price of a CD player decreases the demand for tapes, and improved technology increases the supply of tapes. The new supply curve intersects the new demand curve at $2 a tape, a lower price, but in this case the quantity remains constant at 6 million tapes a week. This decrease in demand and increase in supply lower the price but leave the quantity unchanged.

CD Players, Coffee, and Bananas

Earlier in this chapter, we looked at some facts about prices and quantities of CD players, coffee, and bananas. Let's use the theory of demand and supply that we have just studied to explain the movements in the prices and quantities of those goods.

A Price Slide: CD Players   Figure 4.13(a) shows the market for CD players. In 1983, when CD players were first manufactured, very few producers made them and the supply was small. The supply curve was S_0. In 1983, there weren't many titles on CDs and the demand for CD players was small. The demand curve was D_0. The quantities supplied and demanded in 1983 were equal at Q_0, and the price was $1,100 (1994 dollars).

As the technology for making CD players improved and as more and more factories began to produce CD players, the supply increased by a large amount and the supply curve shifted rightward from S_0 to S_1. At the same time, increases in incomes, a decrease in the price of a CD, and an increase in the number of titles on CDs increased the demand for CD players. But the increase in demand was much smaller than the increase in supply. The demand curve shifted rightward from D_0 to D_1. With the new demand curve D_1 and the new supply curve S_1, the equilibrium price fell to $170 in 1994, and the quantity increased to Q_1.

The large increase in supply combined with a smaller increase in demand resulted in an increase in the quantity of CD players and a dramatic fall in the price. Figure 4.13(a) shows the CD player price slide.

A Price Rocket: Coffee   Figure 4.13(b) shows the market for coffee. In the second quarter of 1993, the supply curve for coffee was S_0 and the demand for coffee was D_0. The price of coffee was $1.30 a kilogram and the quantity was Q_0.

Serious back-to-back frosts in Brazil damaged coffee plants and severely cut the harvest. As a result, the supply of coffee decreased. This decrease in supply shifted the supply curve leftward from S_0 to S_1. At the same time that the supply of coffee decreased, the demand for coffee increased. The increase in demand was not large, but higher incomes and a larger population brought some increase in demand. The demand curve shifted rightward from D_0 to D_1. The combined effect of a large decrease in supply and a small increase in demand was a rapid rise in price from $1.30 a kilogram in the second quarter of 1993

to $4.60 a kilogram in the third quarter of 1994. The quantity decreased from Q_0 to Q_1. Figure 4.13(b) shows the coffee price rocket.

A Price Roller Coaster: Bananas   Figure 4.13(c) shows the market for bananas. The demand for bananas—curve D—does not change much over the years. But the supply of bananas, which depends mainly on the weather, fluctuates between S_0 and S_1. With good growing conditions, the supply curve is S_1. With bad growing conditions, supply decreases and the supply curve is S_0. As a consequence of fluctuations in supply, the quantity fluctuates between Q_0 and Q_1. The price of bananas fluctuates between 44 cents per kilogram (1995 cents), the minimum price, and 73 cents per kilogram, the maximum price. Figure 4.13(c) shows the banana price roller coaster.

⬦ You now know the basic theory of demand and supply. By using this theory, you can explain past fluctuations in prices and quantities and also make predictions about future fluctuations. *Reading Between the Lines* on pp. 82–83 shows you the theory in action in the world market for luxury cruises during the New Year vacation season at the turn of the millennium.

You will see lots of news articles that you can better understand by using your knowledge of demand and supply. Watch for stories on frosts in Brazil and the price of coffee, on frosts in Florida and the price of orange juice, or on hurricanes and earthquakes and their effects on the prices of many necessities.

Adam Smith said that each buyer and seller in a market "is led by an invisible hand to promote an end which was no part of his intention." What did he mean? He meant that when each one of us makes decisions to buy or sell in order to achieve the best outcome for ourselves and when our decisions are co-ordinated in free markets, we end up achieving the best outcome for everyone.

Although markets are amazing instruments, it turns out that they do not always work quite so perfectly as Adam Smith imagined. If you go on to study *micro*economics, you will discover the conditions under which markets are efficient and why they sometimes fail to achieve the best possible outcome for everyone. If you go on to study *macro*economics, you will discover the reasons why the market economy produces fluctuations in output and employment and sometimes creates persistent unemployment.

FIGURE 4.13

Price Slide, Rocket, and Roller Coaster

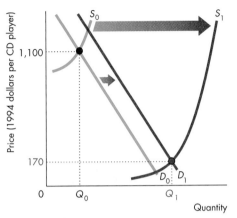

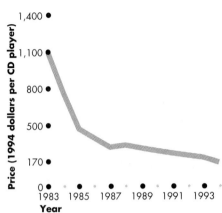

A large increase in the supply of CD players, from S_0 to S_1 combined with a small increase in demand, from D_0 to D_1, resulted in an increase in the quantity of CD players bought and sold from Q_0 to Q_1. The average price of a CD player fell from $1,100 in 1983 to $170 in 1994—a price slide.

(a) Price slide: CD players

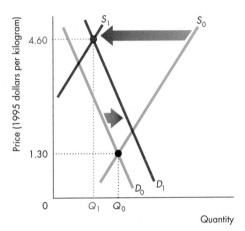

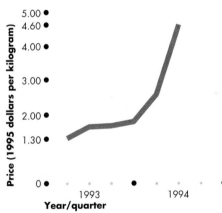

A large decrease in the supply of coffee, from S_0 to S_1, combined with a small increase in the demand, from D_0 to D_1, resulted in a decrease in the quantity, from Q_0 to Q_1, and a rise in the price of coffee from $1.30 a kilogram in the second quarter of 1993 to $4.60 a kilogram in the third quarter of 1994—a price rocket.

(b) Price rocket: coffee

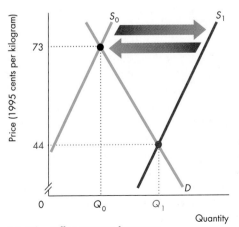

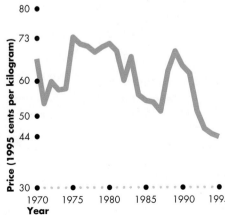

The demand for bananas remains at D. But supply fluctuates between S_0 and S_1. As a result, the price of bananas has fluctuated between 44 cents per kilogram and 73 cents per kilogram—a price roller coaster.

(c) Price roller coaster: bananas

Supply and Demand:
The Millennium Party

VANCOUVER SUN, JULY 18, 1998

Prepare to pay big for millennium party cruise tickets

When Richard Ramlall, of Herndon, Va., started shopping around for a millennium New Year's Eve cruise for himself and 31 friends a couple of months ago, he figured a guy who was willing to shell out $96,000 (based on $3,000 US per person) would be a pretty important client to some dutiful, commission-hungry travel agent. Wrong. After approaching eight different local agencies, Ramlall didn't even merit a return call. He's decided to spend the cash in landlocked Times Square instead.

The problem: While travel industry price-gouging during the "first" millennium celebration (Jan. 1, 2000; the real one, purists insist, follows a year later) isn't limited to cruise lines, Ramlall and numerous other cruisers are finding themselves caught in the kind of once-in-a-thousand-years seller's market in which cruise lines, anticipating a tidal wave of demand, are playing "punish the passengers."...

Expect high prices. Millennium cruisers will pay 25 per-cent more on top of the ... premium already charged for holiday periods. The cheapest cabin on a seven-day Caribbean cruise on Holland America on a slow week costs $1,128; this year's holiday rate is $1,600. For New Year's Eve 1999? The cheapest inside berth on a ship like the Volendam costs $2,740 —but the ship's booked. ...

Early booking discounts are minuscule or absent. Windstar and Princess offer a whopping 10 per cent discount if you book "soon."...

Grand Princess is reportedly sold out for its millennium cruise. Carnival's five-day Caribbean cruise on Jubilee, one of the shortest millennium itineraries available, is almost fully booked. ...

Essence of the Story

■ Demand for millennium cruise tickets is high.

■ During holiday periods, cruise ticket prices are 25 to 35 percent higher than during other periods.

■ Millennium cruisers will pay an additional 25 percent.

■ A 7-day Caribbean cruise in the cheapest cabin costs $1,128 during a slow week, $1,600 during the 1998 holiday period, and $2,740 on the millennium cruise.

Economic Analysis

■ Figure 1 shows the market for cabins on weekly Caribbean cruises. The supply curve is S and initially the demand curve is D_0. The equilibrium is at point a. The price of a cabin is $1,128 and the quantity of cabins occupied is 30,000 a week.

■ During the winter holiday season, the demand for cruises increases. The demand curve shifts rightward from D_0 to D_1.

■ The supply of cabins does not increase, but the quantity of cabins supplied increases. There is a movement up along the supply curve. The equilibrium is at point b. The price of a cabin rises to $1,600 and the quantity of cabins occupied increases to 40,000 a week.

■ The price increase between a normal week and the 1998 holiday season is more than 40 percent.

■ During the millennium holiday period, many people want to experience the "once-in-a-thousand-years" party cruise. The demand for cabins for New Year's celebrations in 1999 is greater than the demand for cabins for New Year's celebrations in 1998.

■ The demand curve shifts rightward from D_1 to D_2.

■ The supply of cabins does not increase, but the quantity of cabins supplied increases. There is a movement up along the supply curve. The equilibrium is at point c. The price of a cabin rises to $2,740 and the quantity of cabins occupied increases to 50,000 a week.

■ Suppose that the price of a cabin on a millennium cruise is $1,600, the same price as the cabin in the 1998 holiday season.

■ Figure 2 shows that when the price is $1,600 60,000 cabins are demanded, but only 40,000 cabins are supplied. There is a shortage of 20,000 cabins.

■ Figure 2 also shows that when only 40,000 cabins are supplied, the highest price that someone is willing to pay for the 40,000th cabin is $3,880.

■ Some people, unable to find a cabin at $1,600, offer to pay more and some cruise ships, noticing lists of prospective passengers, raise their prices.

■ The price rise reduces the shortage because the quantity demanded decreases and the quantity supplied increases.

■ The price will rise until there is no shortage. The equilibrium price is $2,740.

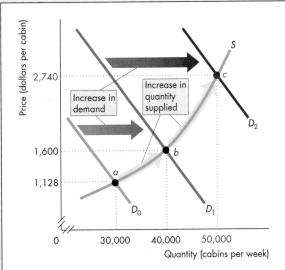

Figure 1 The market for cruises

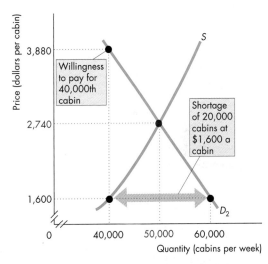

Figure 2 The market for millennium cruises

MATHEMATICAL NOTE: DEMAND, SUPPLY, AND EQUILIBRIUM

Demand Curve

The law of demand states that as the price of a good or service falls, the quantity demanded of it increases. A demand schedule, a demand curve, or a demand equation illustrates the law of demand. When the demand curve is a straight line, a linear equation describes it. A demand equation is

$$P = a - bQ_D,$$

where P is the price and Q_D is the quantity demanded. The a and b are positive constants.

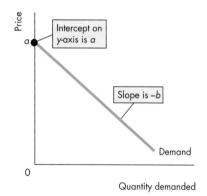

Figure 1 Demand curve

The demand equation tells us three things:

1. The price at which no one is willing to buy the good (Q_D is zero). If the price is a, then the quantity demanded is zero. You can see the price a on the graph. It is the price at which the demand curve hits the y-axis—what we call the demand curve's "intercept on the y-axis."

2. As the price falls, the quantity demanded increases. If Q_D is a positive number, then the price P must be less than a. And as Q_D gets larger, the price P becomes smaller. That is, as the quantity increases, the maximum price that buyers are willing to pay of the good falls.

3. The constant b tells us how fast the maximum price that someone is willing to pay for the good falls as the quantity increases. That is, the constant b tells us about the steepness of the demand curve. The equation tells us that the slope of the demand curve is $-b$.

Supply Curve

The law of supply states that as the price of a good or service rises, the quantity supplied of it increases. A supply schedule, a supply curve, or a supply equation illustrates the law of supply. When the supply curve is a straight line, a linear equation describes it. A supply equation is

$$P = c + dQ_S,$$

where P is the price and Q_S the quantity supplied. The c and d are positive constants.

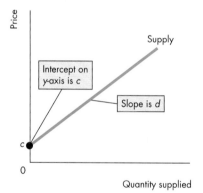

Figure 2 Supply curve

The supply equation tells us three things:

1. The price at which no one is willing to sell the good (Q_S is zero). If the price is c, then the quantity supplied is zero. You can see the price c on the graph. It is the price at which the supply curve hits the y-axis—what we call the supply curve's "intercept on the y-axis."

2. As the price rises, the quantity supplied increases. If Q_S is a positive number, then the price P must be greater than c. And as Q_S increases, the price P gets larger. That is, as the quantity increases, the minimum price that sellers are willing to accept rises.

3. The constant d tells us how fast the minimum price at which someone is willing to sell the good rises as the quantity increases. That is, the constant d tells us about the steepness of the supply curve. The equation tells us that the slope of the supply curve is d.

Market Equilibrium

Demand and supply determined the equilibrium price (P^*) and equilibrium quantity (Q^*) at the intersection of the demand curve and the supply curve.

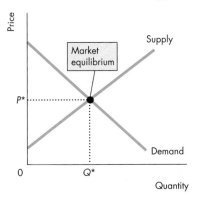

Figure 3 Market equilibrium

We can use the equations to find the equilibrium price and equilibrium quantity. The price of a good will adjust until the quantity demanded equals the quantity supplied. That is,

$$Q_D = Q_S.$$

So at the equilibrium price (P^*) and equilibrium quantity (Q^*),

$$Q_D = Q_S = Q^*.$$

To find the equilibrium price and equilibrium quantity: First substitute Q^* for Q_D in the demand equation and Q^* for Q_S in the supply equation. Then the price is the equilibrium price (P^*), which gives

$$P^* = a - bQ^*$$

$$P^* = c + dQ^*.$$

Notice that

$$a - bQ^* = c + dQ^*.$$

Now solve for Q^*

$$a - c = bQ^* + dQ^*$$

$$a - c = (b + d)Q^*$$

$$Q^* = \frac{a - c}{b + d}.$$

To find the equilibrium price (P^*), substitute for Q^* in either the demand equation or the supply equation.

Using the demand equation,

$$P^* = a - b\left(\frac{a - c}{b + d}\right)$$

$$P^* = \frac{a(b + d) - b(a - c)}{b + d}$$

$$P^* = \frac{ad + bc}{b + d}.$$

Alternatively, using the supply equation,

$$P^* = c + d\left(\frac{a - c}{b + d}\right)$$

$$P^* = \frac{c(b + d) + d(a - c)}{b + d}$$

$$P^* = \frac{ad + bc}{b + d}.$$

An Example

The demand for ice cream cones is

$$P = 800 - 2Q_D.$$

The supply of ice cream cones is

$$P = 200 + 1Q_S.$$

The price of a cone is expressed in cents and the quantities are expressed in cones per day.
To find the equilibrium price (P^*) and equilibrium quantity (Q^*), substitute Q^* for Q_D and Q_S and P^* for P.
That is,

$$P^* = 800 - 2Q^*$$

$$P^* = 200 + 1Q^*.$$

Now solve for Q^*:

$$800 - 2Q^* = 200 + 1Q^*$$

$$600 = 3Q^*$$

$$Q^* = 200.$$

And

$$P^* = 800 - 2Q^*$$

$$P^* = 400.$$

The equilibrium price is $4 a cone, and the equilibrium quantity is 200 cones a day.

SUMMARY

Key Points

Price and Opportunity Cost (p. 64)

■ Opportunity cost is a relative price. We measure a relative price by dividing the price of one good by the price (index) of a basket of all goods.

■ Demand and supply determines relative prices.

Demand (pp. 65–69)

■ Demand is the relationship between the quantity demanded of a good and its price when all other influences on buying plans remain the same.

■ The higher the price of a good, other things remaining the same, the smaller is the quantity demanded—the law of demand.

■ Demand depends on the prices of substitutes and complements, expected future prices, income, population, and preferences.

Supply (pp. 70–73)

■ Supply is the relationship between the quantity supplied of a good and its price when all other influences on selling plans remain the same.

■ The higher the price of a good, other things remaining the same, the greater is the quantity supplied—the law of supply.

■ Supply depends on the prices of resources used to produce a good, the prices of related goods produced, expected future prices, the number of producers, and technology.

Market Equilibrium (pp. 74–75)

■ At the equilibrium price, the quantity demanded equals the quantity supplied.

■ At prices above equilibrium, there is a surplus and the price falls.

■ At prices below equilibrium, there is a shortage and the price rises.

Predicting Changes in Price and Quantity (pp. 76–81)

■ An increase in demand brings a rise in price and an increase in the quantity supplied. (A decrease in demand brings a fall in price and a decrease in the quantity supplied.)

■ An increase in supply brings a fall in price and an increase in the quantity demanded. (A decrease in supply brings a rise in price and a decrease in the quantity demanded.)

■ An increase in demand and an increase in supply bring an increase in the quantity but the price might rise, fall, or remain the same. An increase in demand and a decrease in supply bring a higher price but the quantity might increase, decrease, or remain the same.

Key Figures ◆

Key Terms

P R O B L E M S

*1. What is the effect on the price of a tape and the quantity of tapes sold if:
   a. The price of a CD rises?
   b. The price of a Walkman rises?
   c. The supply of CD players increases?
   d. Consumers' incomes increase?
   e. Workers who make tapes get a pay raise?
   f. The price of a Walkman rises at the same time as workers who make tapes get a raise?

2. What is the effect on the price of hot dogs and the quantity of hot dogs sold if:
   a. The price of a hamburger rises?
   b. The price of a hot dog bun rises?
   c. The supply of hot dog sausages increases?
   d. Consumers' incomes decrease?
   e. The wage of the hot dog seller increases?
   f. The wage of the hot dog seller rises and at the same time prices of ketchup, mustard, and relish fall?

*3. Suppose that one of the following events occurs:
   i. The price of crude oil rises.
   ii. The price of a car rises.
   iii. All speed limits on highways are abolished.
   iv. Robot production cuts car production costs.
   Which of the above events increases or decreases (state which):
   a. The demand for gasoline?
   b. The supply of gasoline?
   c. The quantity of gasoline demanded?
   d. The quantity of gasoline supplied?

4. Suppose that one of the following events occurs:
   i. The price of wool rises.
   ii. The price of a sweater falls.
   iii. A close substitute for wool is invented.
   iv. A new high-speed loom is invented.
   Which of the above events increases or decreases (state which):
   a. The demand for wool?
   b. The supply of wool?
   c. The quantity of wool demanded?
   d. The quantity of wool supplied?

*5. The figure illustrates the market for pizza.
   a. Label the curves in the figure.
   b. What are the equilibrium price of a pizza and the equilibrium quantity of pizza?

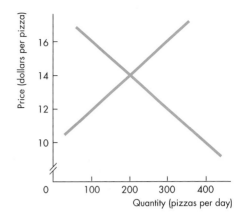

6. The figure illustrates the market for bread.

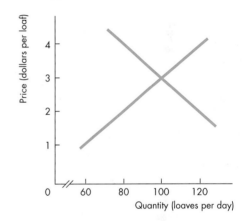

   a. Label the curves in the figure.
   b. What are the equilibrium price of bread and the equilibrium quantity of bread?

*7. The demand and supply schedules for gum are:

Price (cents per pack)	Quantity demanded	Quantity supplied
	(millions of packs a week)	
20	180	60
30	160	80
40	140	100
50	120	120
60	100	140
70	80	160
80	60	180

   a. What are the equilibrium price and quantity of gum?
   b. If gum was 70 cents a pack, describe the situation in the gum market and explain what would happen to the price of gum.

8. The demand and supply schedules for potato chips are:

Price (cents per bag)	Quantity demanded	Quantity supplied
	(millions of bags per week)	
40	170	90
50	160	100
60	150	110
70	140	120
80	130	130
90	120	140
100	110	150
110	100	160

a. What are the equilibrium price and equilibrium quantity of potato chips?
b. If the price of chips was 60 cents a bag, describe the situation in the market for potato chips and explain what would happen to the price of a bag of chips.

*9. In problem 7, suppose that a fire destroys some gum-producing factories and the supply of gum decreases by 40 million packs a week.
a. Has there been a shift in or a movement along the supply curve of gum?
b. Has there been a shift in or a movement along the demand curve for gum?
c. What are the new equilibrium price and quantity of gum?

10. In problem 8, suppose that a new snack food comes onto the market and as a result the demand for potato chips decreases by 40 million bags a week.
a. Has there been a shift in or a movement along the supply curve of chips?
b. Has there been a shift in or a movement along the demand curve for chips?
c. What are the new equilibrium price and quantity of chips?

*11. In problem 9, suppose an increase in the teenage population increases the demand for gum by 40 million packs per week at the same time as the fire occurs. What are the new equilibrium price and quantity of gum?

12. In problem 10, suppose that a flood destroys several potato farms and as a result supply decreases by 20 million bags a week at the same time as the new snack food comes onto the market. What are the new equilibrium price and quantity of chips?

CRITICAL THINKING

1. Study *Reading Between the Lines*, pp. 82–83, and then:
a. Describe how the millennium changes the price of a Caribbean cruise.
b. Draw a figure of demand and supply to explain what happens when there is an increase in demand and no change in supply.
c. Explain why the millennium results in an increase in the quantity of cabins supplied but no change in the supply of cabins.
d. What do you think is happening to bring about an increase in the quantity of cabins supplied? Describe what the cruise line companies are doing to increase the quantity supplied.
e. What do you predict would happen to the price of a cruise if air fares to Australia and the South Pacific were to decrease?
f. What do you predict would happen to the price of a cruise if there were an increase in the price of oil?

2. Use the links on the Parkin-Bade Web site and obtain data on the prices and quantities of wheat.
a. Draw a demand and supply diagram to illustrate the market for wheat in 1998.
b. Show the changes since 1998 in demand and supply and the changes in the quantity demanded and the quantity supplied that are consistent with the price and quantity data.

3. Use the link on the Parkin-Bade Web site to obtain information about the market for California navel oranges in 1999.
a. Explain why the supply of oranges decreased but the demand for oranges did not change. How can the demand not change when the quantity available decreases?
b. Explain the forces that determine the wholesale price and the retail price of oranges.
c. What, if anything, can be done to keep the price of oranges down when a frost occurs?
d. Use the links on the Parkin-Bade Web site and obtain the latest data on the quantity and price of oranges produced and use the demand and supply model to explain the changes in price during the past year.

5

Elasticity

Your pizza business is earning you a good profit but you are worried. You've just learned that a major pizza franchise is planning a big expansion in your neighbourhood. You know that the resulting increase in supply will lower the price of pizza and bring tough competition for you. But how big a price fall will you have to cope with? Will there be little change in pizza consumption and a large fall in price? Or will there be a huge increase in pizza consumption and little change in the price? To answer these questions, you need a measure of the responsiveness of the quantity of pizza demanded to the price of pizza. ◆ Faced with tough competition from your

Predicting Prices

pizzeria, the burger shop next door has cut its prices. How will the lower price of burgers affect the demand for your pizza? Will it wipe you out of business or make only a small dent in your sales? To answer this question, you need a measure of the responsiveness of the demand for your pizza to the price of burgers, a substitute for pizza. ◆ The economy is booming and people's incomes are rising. You know that with more income to spend, people will buy more pizza. But how much more pizza will people buy? Will the higher incomes bring a large increase in your sales or will they make only a small difference? To answer this question, you need a measure of the responsiveness of the demand for pizza to consumers' incomes. ◆ As incomes increase, you expect the demand for pizza to increase. But will the increase in demand bring a rise in price with little change in the quantity bought? Or will it bring a huge increase in pizza consumption with little change in the price? To answer this question, you need a measure of the responsiveness of the quantity of pizza supplied to a change in the price of pizza.

◆ In this chapter, you will learn how to answer questions like the ones just posed. You will learn about elasticity, a measure of the responsiveness of quantities bought and sold to changes in prices and other influences on buyers' and sellers' plans.

After studying this chapter, you will be able to:

■ **Define and calculate the price elasticity of demand**

■ **Use a total revenue test and an expenditure test to estimate the price elasticity of demand**

■ **Explain the factors that influence the price elasticity of demand**

■ **Define and calculate the cross elasticity of demand**

■ **Define and calculate the income elasticity of demand**

■ **Define and calculate the elasticity of supply**

The Price Elasticity of Demand

YOU KNOW THAT WHEN SUPPLY INCREASES, THE equilibrium price falls and the equilibrium quantity increases. But does the price fall by a large amount and the quantity increase by a little? Or does the price barely fall and the quantity increase by a large amount?

The answer depends on the responsiveness of the quantity demanded to a change in the price. You can see why by studying Fig. 5.1, which shows two possible scenarios in a local pizza market. Figure 5.1(a) shows one scenario and Fig. 5.1(b) shows the other.

In both cases, supply is initially S_0. In part (a), the demand for pizza is shown by the demand curve D_a. In part (b), the demand for pizza is shown by the demand curve D_b. Initially, in both cases, the price is $20 a pizza and the quantity of pizza produced and consumed is 10 pizzas an hour.

Now a large pizza franchise opens up and the supply of pizza increases. The supply curve shifts rightward to S_1. In case (a), the price of a pizza falls by an enormous $15 to $5 and the quantity increases by only 3 to 13 pizzas an hour. In contrast, in case (b), the price falls by only $5 to $15 a pizza and the quantity increases by 7 to 17 pizzas an hour.

The different outcomes arise from differing degrees of responsiveness of the quantity demanded to a change in the price. But what do we mean by responsiveness? One possible answer is slope. The slope of demand curve D_a is steeper than the slope of demand curve D_b.

In this example, we can compare the slopes of the two demand curves. But we can't always do so. The reason is that the slope of a demand curve depends on the units in which we measure the price and quantity. And we often must compare the demand curves for different goods and services that are measured in unrelated units. For example, a pizza producer might want to compare the demand for pizza with the demand for pop. Which quantity demanded is more responsive to a price change? This question can't be answered by comparing the slopes of two demand curves. The units of measurement of pizza and pop are unrelated. The question can be answered with a measure of responsiveness that is independent of units of measurement. Elasticity is such a measure.

The **price elasticity of demand** is a units-free measure of the responsiveness of the quantity demanded of a good to a change in its price when all other influences on buyers' plans remain the same.

FIGURE 5.1

How a Change in Supply Changes Price and Quantity

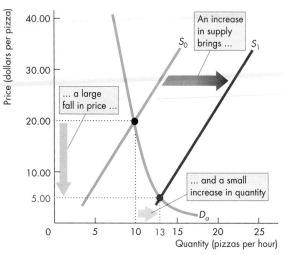

(a) Large price change and small quantity change

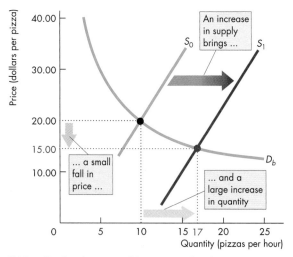

(b) Small price change and large quantity change

Initially, the price is $20 a pizza and the quantity sold is 10 pizzas an hour. Then supply increases from S_0 to S_1. In part (a), the price falls by $15 to $5 a pizza and the quantity increases by only 3 to 13 pizzas an hour. In part (b), the price falls by only $5 to $15 a pizza and the quantity increases by 7 to 17 pizzas an hour. This price change is smaller and quantity change is larger than in case (a). The quantity demanded is more responsive to price in case (b) than in case (a).

Calculating Elasticity

We calculate the *price elasticity of demand* by using the formula:

$$\text{Price elasticity of demand} = \frac{\text{Percentage change in quantity demanded}}{\text{Percentage change in price}}.$$

To use this formula, we need to know the quantities demanded at different prices when all other influences on buyers' plans remain the same. Suppose we have the data on prices and quantities demanded of pizza and calculate the price elasticity of demand for pizza.

Figure 5.2 zooms in on the demand curve for pizza and shows how the quantity demanded responds to a small change in the price. Initially, the price is $20.50 a pizza and 9 pizzas an hour are sold—the original point in the figure. The price then falls to $19.50 a pizza and the quantity demanded increases to 11 pizzas an hour—the new point in the figure. When the price falls by $1 a pizza, the quantity demanded increases by 2 pizzas an hour.

To calculate the price elasticity of demand, we express the changes in price and quantity demanded as percentages of the *average price* and the *average quantity*. By using the average price and average quantity, we calculate the elasticity at a point on the demand curve midway between the original point and the new point. The original price is $20.50 and the new price is $19.50, so the average price is $20. The $1 price decrease is 5 percent of the average price. That is,

$$\Delta P / P_{ave} = (\$1/\$20) \times 100 = 5\%.$$

The original quantity demanded is 9 pizzas and the new quantity demanded is 11 pizzas, so the average quantity demanded is 10 pizzas. The 2 pizza increase in the quantity demanded is 20 percent of the average quantity. That is,

$$\Delta Q / Q_{ave} = (2/10) \times 100 = 20\%.$$

So the price elasticity of demand, which is the percentage change in the quantity demanded (20 percent) divided by the percentage change in the price (5 percent), is 4. That is,

$$\text{Price elasticity of demand} = \frac{\%\Delta Q}{\%\Delta P}$$

$$= \frac{20\%}{5\%} = 4.$$

FIGURE 5.2

Calculating the Elasticity of Demand

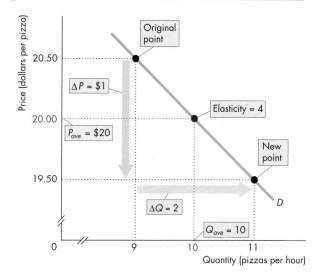

The elasticity of demand is calculated by using the formula*

$$\text{Price elasticity of demand} = \frac{\text{Percentage change in quantity demanded}}{\text{Percentage change in price}}$$

$$= \frac{\%\Delta Q}{\%\Delta P}$$

$$= \frac{\Delta Q / Q_{ave}}{\Delta P / P_{ave}}$$

$$= \frac{2/10}{1/20}$$

$$= 4.$$

This calculation measures the elasticity at an average price of $20 a pizza and an average quantity of 10 pizzas an hour.

*In the formula, the Greek letter delta (Δ) stands for "change in" and %Δ stands for "percentage change in."

Average Price and Quantity We use the *average* price and *average* quantity to avoid having two values for the elasticity of demand at a single point on the demand curve, depending on whether the price falls or rises. If the price falls from $20.50 to $19.50, the $1 price change is 4.9 percent of $20.50. The 2 pizza change in quantity is 22.2 percent of 9, the original quantity. If we use these numbers, the elasticity is 22.2 divided by 4.9, which equals 4.5. If the price rises from $19.50 to $20.50, the $1 price change is

5.1 percent of $19.50. The 2 pizza change in quantity is 18.2 percent of 11, the original quantity. If we use these numbers, the elasticity is 18.2 divided by 5.1, which equals 3.6. By using the *average* price and *average* quantity, we get the same value for the elasticity regardless of whether the price falls or rises.

Percentages and Proportions Elasticity is the ratio of the *percentage* change in the quantity demanded to the percentage change in the price. It is also, equivalently, the proportionate change in the quantity demanded, $\Delta Q/Q_{ave}$, divided by the proportionate change in the price, $\Delta P/P_{ave}$. The percentage changes are the proportionate changes multiplied by 100. So when we divide one percentage change by another, the 100s cancel and the result is the same as we get by using the proportionate changes.

A Units-Free Measure Now that you've calculated a price elasticity of demand, you can see why it is a *units-free measure*. Elasticity is a units-free measure because the percentage change in each variable is independent of the units in which the variable is measured. And the ratio of the two percentages is a number without units.

Minus Sign and Elasticity When the price of a good *rises*, the quantity demanded *decreases* along the demand curve. Because a *positive* change in the price brings a *negative* change in the quantity demanded, the price elasticity of demand is a negative number. But it is the magnitude, or *absolute value*, of the price elasticity of demand that tells us how responsive—how elastic—demand is. To compare elasticities, we use the magnitude of the price elasticity of demand and ignore the minus sign.

Inelastic and Elastic Demand

Figure 5.3 shows three demand curves that cover the entire range of possible elasticities of demand. In Fig. 5.3(a), the quantity demanded is constant regardless of the price. In this case, the price elasticity of demand is zero and the good is said to have **perfectly inelastic demand**. One good that has a very low price elasticity of demand (perhaps zero over some price range) is insulin. Insulin is of such importance to some diabetics that if the price rises or falls, they do not change the quantity they buy.

If the percentage change in the quantity demanded equals the percentage change in the price, then the price elasticity equals 1 and the good is said to have **unit elastic demand**. The demand in Fig. 5.3(b) is an example of unit elastic demand.

Between the cases shown in parts (a) and (b) of Fig. 5.3 is the general case in which the percentage

---

FIGURE 5.3

Inelastic and Elastic Demand

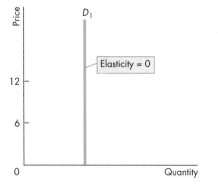
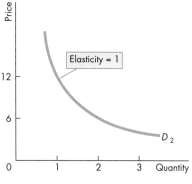
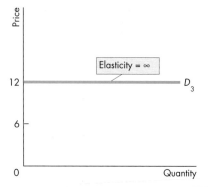

(a) Perfectly inelastic demand   **(b) Unit elastic demand**   **(c) Perfectly elastic demand**

Each demand illustrated here has a constant elasticity. The demand curve in part (a) illustrates the demand for a good that has a zero elasticity of demand. The demand curve in part (b) illustrates the demand for a good with a unit elasticity of demand. And the demand curve in part (c) illustrates the demand for a good with an infinite elasticity of demand.

change in the quantity demanded is less than the percentage change in the price. In this case, the price elasticity of demand is between zero and 1, and the good is said to have **inelastic demand**. Food and housing are examples of goods with inelastic demand.

If the quantity demanded changes by an infinitely large percentage in response to a tiny price change, then the price elasticity of demand is infinity, and the good is said to have **perfectly elastic demand**. Fig. 5.3(c) shows perfectly elastic demand. An example of a good that has a very high elasticity of demand (almost infinite) is marker pens from the campus bookstore and from the convenience store next door to the bookstore. If the two stores offer pens for the same price, some people buy from one and some from the other. But if the bookstore's price is higher than the convenience store's price, even by a small amount, the bookstore will not sell many pens. Pens from the two stores are perfect substitutes.

Between the cases in parts (b) and (c) of Fig. 5.3 is the general case in which the percentage change in the quantity demanded exceeds the percentage change in the price. In this case, the price elasticity is greater than 1 and the good is said to have **elastic demand**. Automobiles and furniture are examples of goods that have elastic demand.

Elasticity Along a Straight-Line Demand Curve

Elasticity and slope are not the same but are related. To understand how they are related, let's look at elasticity along a straight-line demand curve—a demand curve that has a constant slope.

Figure 5.4 illustrates the calculation of elasticity along a straight-line demand curve. First, let's calculate the elasticity when the price falls by $10 from $20 to $10. The average price in this case is $15 and

$$\Delta P/P_{ave} = \$10/\$15.$$

When the price falls from $20 to $10, the quantity demanded increases by 20 pizzas an hour from zero to 20, so the average quantity demanded is 10 and

$$\Delta Q/Q_{ave} = 20/10.$$

Now divide the proportionate change in the quantity demanded by the proportionate change in the price to obtain the elasticity as

$$\frac{\Delta Q/Q_{ave}}{\Delta P/P_{ave}} = \frac{20/10}{10/15} = 3.$$

We can repeat the calculation that we've just done at any price and quantity along the demand curve. Because the demand curve is a straight line, a $10 price fall always increases the quantity demanded by 20 pizzas an hour. So in the elasticity formula, ΔP is $10 and ΔQ is 20 for every average price and average quantity. But the lower the average price, the greater is the average quantity. So the lower the average price, the less elastic is demand.

Check this proposition by calculating the elasticity when the price falls by $10 from $10 to zero. Now the average price is $5 and

$$\Delta P/P_{ave} = \$10/\$5.$$

When the price falls from $10 to zero, the quantity demanded increases by 20 pizzas an hour from 20 to 40, so the average quantity demanded is 30 and

$$\Delta Q/Q_{ave} = 20/30.$$

FIGURE 5.4

Elasticity Along a Straight-Line Demand Curve

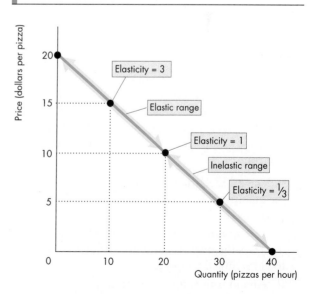

On a straight-line demand curve, elasticity decreases as the price falls and the quantity demanded increases. Demand is unit elastic at the midpoint of the demand curve (elasticity is 1). Above the midpoint, demand is elastic; and below the midpoint, demand is inelastic.

To obtain the elasticity of demand, divide the proportionate change in the quantity demanded by the proportionate change in the price

$$\frac{\Delta Q/Q_{ave}}{\Delta P/P_{ave}} = \frac{20/30}{10/5} = 1/3.$$

Finally, let's calculate the elasticity when the price falls by \$10 from \$15 to \$5. Now the average price is \$10 and

$$\Delta P/P_{ave} = \$10/\$10.$$

When the price falls from \$15 to \$5, the quantity demanded increases by 20 pizzas an hour from 10 to 30, so the average quantity demanded is 20 and

$$\Delta Q/Q_{ave} = 20/20.$$

To obtain the elasticity of demand, divide the proportionate change in the quantity demanded by the proportionate change in the price

$$\frac{\Delta Q/Q_{ave}}{\Delta P/P_{ave}} = \frac{20/20}{10/10} = 1.$$

You've now seen how elasticity changes along a straight-line demand curve. At the midpoint of the curve, the elasticity is 1. Above the midpoint, demand is elastic; and below the midpoint, demand is inelastic.

Total Revenue and Elasticity

Total revenue from the sale of a good equals the price of the good multiplied by the quantity sold. When a price changes, total revenue changes. But a rise in price does not always increase total revenue. The change in total revenue depends on the elasticity of demand.

- If demand is elastic, a 1 percent price cut increases the quantity sold by more than 1 percent and total revenue increases.
- If demand is unit elastic, a 1 percent price cut increases the quantity sold by 1 percent and so total revenue does not change.
- If demand is inelastic, a 1 percent price cut increases the quantity sold by less than 1 percent and total revenue decreases.

Figure 5.5 shows how we can use this relationship between elasticity and total revenue to estimate elasticity using the total revenue test. The **total revenue test** is a method of estimating the price elasti-

FIGURE 5.5

Elasticity and Total Revenue

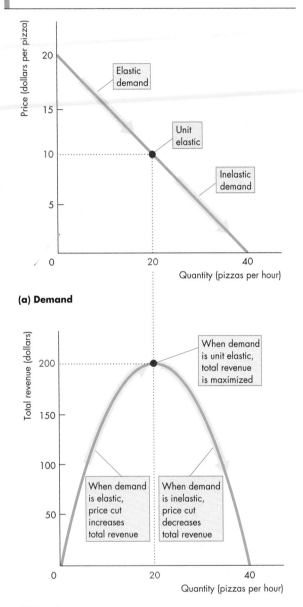

(a) Demand

(b) Total revenue

When demand is elastic, in the price range from \$20 to \$10, a decrease in the price (part a) brings an increase in total revenue (part b). When demand is inelastic, in the price range from \$10 to zero, a decrease in the price (part a) brings a decrease in total revenue (part b). When demand is unit elastic, at a price of \$10 (part a), total revenue is at a maximum (part b).

city of demand by observing the change in total revenue that results from a price change (with all other influences on the quantity sold remaining unchanged).

■ If a price cut increases total revenue, demand is elastic.

■ If a price cut decreases total revenue, demand is inelastic.

■ If a price cut leaves total revenue unchanged, demand is unit elastic.

In Fig. 5.5(a), over the price range from $20 to $10, demand is elastic. Over the price range from $10 to zero, demand is inelastic. At a price of $10, demand is unit elastic. In Fig. 5.5(b), you can see how total revenue changes. At a price of $20, the quantity sold is zero, so total revenue is also zero. At a price of zero, the quantity demanded is 40 pizzas an hour but total revenue is again zero. A price cut in the elastic range brings an increase in total revenue—the percentage increase in the quantity demanded is greater than the percentage decrease in the price. A price cut in the inelastic range brings a decrease in total revenue—the percentage increase in the quantity demanded is less than the percentage decrease in the price. At a unit elasticity, total revenue is at a maximum.

So if when the price of an item falls, you spend more on it, your demand for that item is elastic; if you spend the same amount, your demand is unit elastic; and if you spend less, your demand is inelastic.

The Factors That Influence the Elasticity of Demand

Table 5.1 lists some estimates of actual elasticities in the real world. You can see that these real-world elasticities of demand range from 1.52 for metals, the good with the most elastic demand in the table, to 0.12 for food, the good with the most inelastic demand in the table. What makes the demand for some goods elastic and the demand for others inelastic?

Elasticity depends on three main factors:

■ The closeness of substitutes
■ The proportion of income spent on the good
■ The time elapsed since a price change

Closeness of Substitutes The closer the substitutes for a good or service, the more elastic is the demand for it. For example, oil has substitutes but none that are very close (imagine a steam-driven,

TABLE 5.1 Some Real-World Price Elasticities of Demand	
Good or Service	**Elasticity**
Elastic Demand	
Metals	1.52
Electrical engineering products	1.39
Mechanical engineering products	1.30
Furniture	1.26
Motor vehicles	1.14
Instrument engineering products	1.10
Professional services	1.09
Transportation services	1.03
Inelastic Demand	
Gas, electricity, and water	0.92
Oil	0.91
Chemicals	0.89
Beverages (all types)	0.78
Clothing	0.64
Tobacco	0.61
Banking and insurance services	0.56
Housing services	0.55
Agricultural and fish products	0.42
Books, magazines, and newspapers	0.34
Food	0.12

Sources: Ahsan Mansur and John Whalley, "Numerical Specification of Applied General Equilibrium Models: Estimation, Calibration, and Data," in *Applied General Equilibrium Analysis*, eds. Herbert E. Scarf and John B. Shoven (New York: Cambridge University Press, 1984), 109, and Henri Theil, Ching-Fan Chung, and James L. Seale, Jr., *Advances in Econometrics, Supplement 1, 1989, International Evidence on Consumption Patterns* (Greenwich, Conn.: JAI Press Inc., 1989). Reprinted with permission.

coal-fuelled car or a nuclear-powered jetliner). So the demand for oil is inelastic. Metals have substitutes such as plastics, so the demand for metals is elastic.

The degree of substitutability between two goods also depends on how narrowly (or broadly) we define them. For example, the elasticity of demand for meat is low, but the elasticity of demand for beef, lamb, or chicken is high. The elasticity of demand for personal computers is low, but the elasticity of demand for a Compaq, Dell, or IBM is high.

In everyday language we talk about *necessities* and *luxuries*. A necessity is a good that has poor substitutes and that is crucial for our well-being. So generally, a necessity has an inelastic demand. A luxury is a good that usually has many substitutes, one of which is not buying it. So a luxury generally has an elastic demand.

Proportion of Income Spent on the Good

Other things remaining the same, the greater the proportion of income spent on a good, the more elastic is the demand for it.

Think about your own elasticity of demand for chewing gum and housing. If the price of chewing gum doubles, you consume almost as much gum as before. Your demand for gum is inelastic. If apartment rents double, you shriek and look for more students to share accommodation with you. Your demand for housing is more elastic than your demand for gum. Why the difference? Housing takes a large proportion of your budget and gum takes only a tiny proportion. You don't like either price increase, but you hardly notice the higher price of gum, while the higher rent puts your budget under severe strain.

Figure 5.6 shows the proportion of income spent on food and the price elasticity of demand for food in 10 countries. This figure confirms the general tendency we have just described. The larger the proportion of income spent on food, the larger is the price elasticity of demand for food. For example, in Tanzania, where 62 percent of income is spent on food, the price elasticity of demand for food is 0.77. In contrast, in Canada, where 14 percent of income is spent on food, the elasticity of demand for food is 0.13.

Time Elapsed Since Price Change
The longer the time that has elapsed since a price change, the more elastic is demand. When a price rises, consumers often continue to buy similar quantities of a good for a while. But given enough time, they find acceptable and less costly substitutes. As this process of substitution occurs, the quantity purchased of a good or service that has become more expensive gradually decreases. When a price falls, consumers buy more of the good. But as time passes, they find ever more creative ways of using inexpensive items and demand becomes more elastic. For example, some Japanese farmers have discovered that they can use an inexpensive pager to tell their cows when it is milking time!

FIGURE 5.6

Price Elasticities in 10 Countries

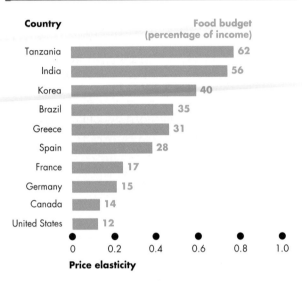

As income increases and the proportion of income spent on food decreases, the demand for food becomes less elastic.

Source: Henri Theil, Ching-Fan Chung, and James L. Seale, Jr., *Advances in Econometrics, Supplement 1, 1989, International Evidence on Consumption Patterns* (Greenwich, Conn.: JAI Press Inc., 1989).

REVIEW QUIZ

- Why do we need a units-free measure of the responsiveness of the quantity demanded of a good or service to a change in its price?
- Define and calculate the price elasticity of demand.
- Why, when we calculate the price elasticity of demand, do we express the change in the price as a percentage of the *average* price and the change in quantity as a percentage of the *average* quantity?
- What is the total revenue test and why does it work?
- What are the main influences on the elasticity of demand that make the demand for some goods elastic and the demand for other goods inelastic?

You've now completed your study of the *price* elasticity of demand. Two other elasticity concepts tell us about the effects of other influences on demand. Let's look at these other elasticities of demand.

More Elasticities of Demand

BACK AT THE PIZZERIA, YOU ARE TRYING TO WORK out how a price cut by the burger shop next door will affect the demand for your pizza. You know that pizzas and burgers are substitutes. And you know that when the price of a substitute for pizza falls, the demand for pizza decreases. But by how much?

You also know that pizza and pop are complements. And you know that if the price of a complement of pizza falls, the demand for pizza increases. So you wonder whether you might keep your customers by cutting the price you charge for pop. But you want to know by how much you must cut the price of pop to hold on to your customers in the face of the cheaper burgers next door.

To answer these questions, you need to calculate the cross elasticity of demand. Let's examine this elasticity measure.

Cross Elasticity of Demand

We measure the influence of a change in the price of substitutes or complements by using the concept of the cross elasticity of demand. The **cross elasticity of demand** is a measure of the responsiveness of the demand for a good to a change in the price of a substitute or complement, other things remaining the same. It is calculated by using the formula

$$\text{Cross elasticity of demand} = \frac{\text{Percentage change in quantity demanded}}{\text{Percentage change in price of a substitute or complement}}.$$

The cross elasticity of demand can be positive or negative. It is positive for a substitute and negative for a complement.

Figure 5.7 illustrates the cross elasticity of demand. Pizza and burgers are substitutes. Because they are substitutes, when the price of a burger falls, the demand for pizza decreases. The demand curve for pizza shifts leftward from D_0 to D_1. Because a *fall* in the price of a burger brings a *decrease* in the demand for pizza, the cross elasticity of demand for pizza with respect to the price of a burger is *positive*. Both the price and the quantity change in the same direction.

FIGURE 5.7

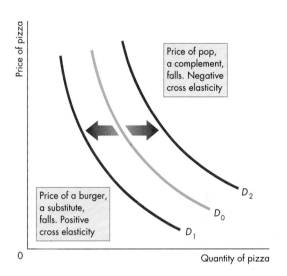

Cross Elasticity of Demand

A burger is a *substitute* for pizza. When the price of a burger falls, the demand for pizza decreases and the demand curve for pizza shifts leftward from D_0 to D_1. The cross elasticity of the demand for pizza with respect to the price of a burger is *positive*. Pop is a *complement* of pizza. When the price of pop falls, the demand for pizza increases and the demand curve for pizza shifts rightward from D_0 to D_2. The cross elasticity of the demand for pizza with respect to the price of pop is *negative*.

Pizza and pop are complements. Because they are complements, when the price of pop falls, the demand for pizza increases. The demand curve for pizza shifts rightward from D_0 to D_2. Because a *fall* in the price of pop brings an *increase* in the demand for pizza, the cross elasticity of demand for pizza with respect to the price of pop is *negative*. The price and quantity change in *opposite* directions.

The magnitude of the cross elasticity of demand determines how far the demand curve shifts. The larger the cross elasticity (absolute value), the greater is the change in demand and the larger is the shift in the demand curve.

If two items are very close substitutes, such as two brands of spring water, the cross elasticity is large. If two items are close complements, such as movies and popcorn, the cross elasticity is large. If two items are somewhat unrelated, such as newspapers and orange juice, the cross elasticity is small, and perhaps zero.

Income Elasticity of Demand

The economy is expanding and people are enjoying rising incomes. This prosperity is bringing an increase in the demand for all types of goods and services. But by how much will the demand for pizza increase?

The answer depends on the income elasticity of demand for the good. The **income elasticity of demand** is a measure of the responsiveness of the demand for a good or service to a change in income, other things remaining the same. It is calculated by using the formula

$$\text{Income elasticity of demand} = \frac{\text{Percentage change in quantity demanded}}{\text{Percentage change in income}}.$$

Income elasticities of demand can be positive or negative and fall into three interesting ranges:

1. Greater than 1 (*normal* good, income elastic)
2. Between zero and 1 (*normal* good, income inelastic)
3. Less than zero (*inferior* good)

Figure 5.8(a) shows an income elasticity of demand that is greater than 1. As income increases, the quantity demanded increases, but the quantity demanded increases faster than income. Examples of goods in this category are ocean cruises, international travel, jewellery, and works of art.

Figure 5.8(b) shows an income elasticity of demand that is between zero and 1. In this case, the quantity demanded increases as income increases, but income increases faster than the quantity demanded. Examples of goods in this category are food, clothing, newspapers, and magazines.

Figure 5.8(c) shows an income elasticity of demand that eventually becomes negative. In this case, the quantity demanded increases as income increases until it reaches a maximum at income *m*. As income continues to increase above *m*, the quantity demanded decreases. The elasticity of demand is positive but less than 1 up to income *m*. Beyond income *m*, the income elasticity of demand is negative. Examples of goods in this category are small motorcycles, potatoes, and rice. Low-income consumers buy most of these goods. At low income levels, the demand for such goods increases as income increases. But as income increases above *m*, consumers replace these goods with superior alternatives. For example, a small car replaces the motorcycle; fruit, vegetables, and meat begin to appear in a diet that was heavy in rice or potatoes.

FIGURE 5.8

Income Elasticity of Demand

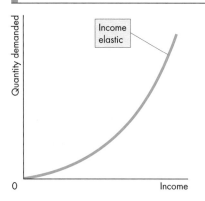

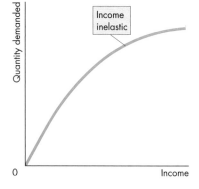

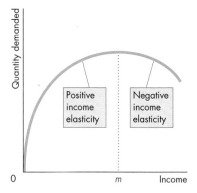

(a) **Elasticity greater than 1**

(b) **Elasticity between zero and 1**

(c) **Elasticity less than 1 and becomes negative**

Income elasticity of demand has three ranges of values. In part (a), income elasticity of demand is greater than 1. As income increases along the x-axis, the quantity demanded increases but by a bigger percentage than the increase in income. In part (b), income elasticity of demand is between zero and 1. As income increases, the quantity demanded increases but by a smaller percentage than the increase in income. In part (c), the income elasticity of demand is positive at low incomes but becomes negative as income increases above level *m*. Maximum consumption of this good occurs at the income *m*.

Real-World Income Elasticities of Demand

Table 5.2 shows estimates of some real-world income elasticities of demand. Necessities such as food and clothing are income inelastic, while luxuries such as airline and foreign travel are income elastic.

But what is a necessity and what is a luxury depends on the level of income. For people with a low income, food and clothing can be luxuries. So the *level* of income has a big effect on income elasticities of demand. Figure 5.9 shows this effect on the income elasticity of demand for food in 10 countries. In countries with low incomes, such as Tanzania and India, the income elasticity of demand for food is high. In countries with high incomes, such as Canada and the United States, it is low.

TABLE 5.2

Some Real-World Income Elasticities of Demand

Elastic Demand

Airline travel	5.82
Movies	3.41
Foreign travel	3.08
Electricity	1.94
Restaurant meals	1.61
Local buses and trains	1.38
Haircuts	1.36
Cars	1.07

Inelastic Demand

Tobacco	0.86
Alcoholic beverages	0.62
Furniture	0.53
Clothing	0.51
Newspapers and magazines	0.38
Telephone	0.32
Food	0.14

Sources: H.S. Houthakker and Lester D. Taylor, *Consumer Demand in the United States* (Cambridge, Mass.: Harvard University Press, 1970), and Henri Theil, Ching-Fan Chung, and James L. Seale, Jr., *Advances in Econometrics, Supplement 1, 1989, International Evidence on Consumption Patterns* (Greenwich, Conn.: JAI Press Inc., 1989). Reprinted with permission.

FIGURE 5.9

Income Elasticities in 10 Countries

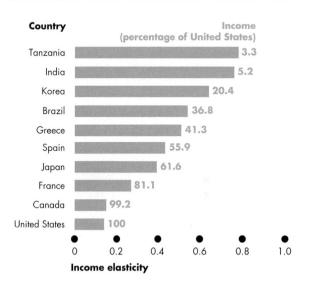

As income increases, the income elasticity of demand for food decreases. For low-income consumers, a larger percentage of any increase in income is spent on food than for high-income consumers.

Source: Henri Theil, Ching-Fan Chung, and James L. Seale, Jr., *Advances in Econometrics, Supplement 1, 1989, International Evidence on Consumption Patterns* (Greenwich, Conn.: JAI Press Inc., 1989).

REVIEW QUIZ

- What does the cross elasticity of demand measure?
- What does the sign (positive versus negative) of the cross elasticity of demand tell us about the relationship between two goods?
- What does the income elasticity of demand measure?
- What does the sign (positive versus negative) of the income elasticity of demand tell us about a good?
- Why does the level of income influence the magnitude of the income elasticity of demand?

You've now completed your study of the *cross elasticity* of demand and the *income elasticity* of demand. Let's look at the other side of a market and examine the elasticity of supply.

Elasticity of Supply

YOU KNOW THAT WHEN DEMAND INCREASES, THE equilibrium price rises and the equilibrium quantity increases. But does the price rise by a large amount and the quantity increase by a little? Or does the price barely rise and the quantity increase by a large amount?

The answer depends on the responsiveness of the quantity supplied to a change in the price. You can see why by studying Fig. 5.10, which shows two possible scenarios in a local pizza market. Figure 5.10(a) shows one scenario and Fig. 5.10(b) shows the other.

In both cases, demand is initially D_0. In part (a), the supply of pizza is shown by the supply curve S_a. In part (b), the supply of pizza is shown by the supply curve S_b. Initially, in both cases, the price is $20 a pizza and the quantity produced and consumed is 10 pizzas an hour.

Now an increase in income and population increase the demand for pizza. The demand curve shifts rightward to D_1. In case (a), the price rises by $20 to $30 a pizza and the quantity increases by only 3 to 13 an hour. In contrast, in case (b), the price rises by only $1 to $21 a pizza and the quantity increases by 10 to 20 pizzas an hour.

The different outcomes arise from differing degrees of responsiveness of the quantity supplied to a change in the price. We measure the degree of responsiveness by using the concept of the elasticity of supply.

Calculating the Elasticity of Supply

The **elasticity of supply** measures the responsiveness of the quantity supplied to a change in the price of a good when all other influences on selling plans remain the same. It is calculated by using the formula

$$\text{Elasticity of supply} = \frac{\text{Percentage change in quantity supplied}}{\text{Percentage change in price}}.$$

We use the same method that you learned when you studied the elasticity of demand. Let's calculate the elasticity of supply for the supply curves in Fig. 5.10.

In Fig. 5.10(a), when the price rises from $20 to $30, the price rise is $10 and the average price is $25, so the price rises by 40 percent of the average price. The quantity increases from 10 to 13, so the increase

FIGURE 5.10

How a Change in Demand Changes Price and Quantity

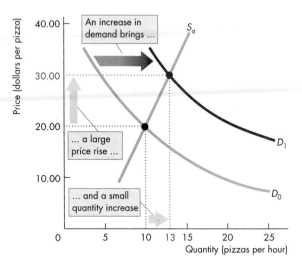

(a) Large price change and small quantity change

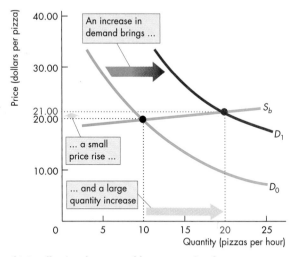

(b) Small price change and large quantity change

Initially, the price is $20 a pizza and the quantity sold is 10 pizzas an hour. Then incomes and population increase and demand increases from D_0 to D_1. In part (a), the price rises by $10 to $30 a pizza and the quantity increases by only 3 to 13 pizzas an hour. In part (b), the price rises by only $1 to $21 a pizza and the quantity increases by 10 to 20 pizzas an hour. This price change is smaller and quantity change is larger than in case (a). The quantity supplied is more responsive to price in case (b) than in case (a).

is 3, the average quantity is 11.5, and the quantity increases by 26 percent. The elasticity of supply is equal to 26 percent divided by 40 percent, which equals 0.65.

In Fig. 5.10(b), when the price rises from $20 to $21, the price rise is $1 and the average price is $20.50, so the price rises by 4.9 percent of the average price. The quantity increases from 10 to 20, so the increase is 10, the average quantity is 15, and the quantity increases by 67 percent. The elasticity of supply is equal to 67 percent divided by 4.9 percent, which equals 13.67.

Figure 5.11 shows the range of supply elasticities. If the quantity supplied is fixed regardless of the price, the supply curve is vertical and the elasticity of supply is zero. Supply is perfectly inelastic. This case is shown in Fig. 5.11(a). A special intermediate case is when the percentage change in the price equals the percentage change in quantity. Supply is then unit elastic. This case is shown in Fig. 5.11(b). No matter how steep the supply curve is, if it is linear and passes through the origin, supply is unit elastic. If there is a price at which sellers are willing to offer any quantity for sale, the supply curve is horizontal and the elasticity of supply is infinite. Supply is perfectly elastic. This case is shown in Fig. 5.11(c).

The Factors That Influence the Elasticity of Supply

The magnitude of the elasticity of supply depends on:

- Resource substitution possibilities
- Time frame for supply decisions

Resource Substitution Possibilities Some goods and services can be produced only by using unique or rare productive resources. These items have a low, and perhaps a zero, elasticity of supply. Other goods and services can be produced by using commonly available resources that could be allocated to a wide variety of alternative tasks. Such items have a high elasticity of supply.

A Van Gogh painting is an example of a good with a vertical supply curve and an elasticity of supply of zero. At the other extreme, wheat can be grown on land that is almost equally good for growing corn. So it is just as easy to grow wheat as corn, and the opportunity cost of wheat in terms of forgone corn is almost constant. As a result, the supply curve of wheat is almost horizontal and its elasticity of supply is very large. Similarly, when a good is produced in many different countries (for example, sugar and beef), the supply of the good is highly elastic.

FIGURE 5.11

Inelastic and Elastic Supply

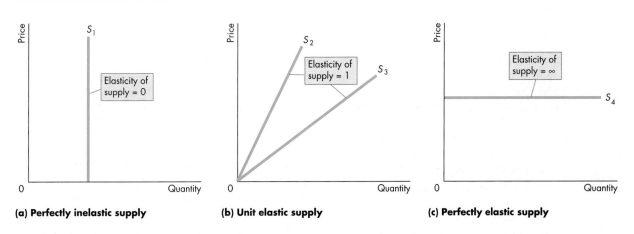

(a) Perfectly inelastic supply

(b) Unit elastic supply

(c) Perfectly elastic supply

Each supply illustrated here has a constant elasticity. The supply curve in part (a) illustrates the supply of a good that has a zero elasticity of supply. The supply curves in part (b) illustrate the supply of goods that have a unit elasticity of supply.

All linear supply curves that pass through the origin have a unit elasticity. The supply curve in part (c) illustrates the supply of a good that has an infinite elasticity of supply.

The supply of most goods and services lies between the two extremes. The quantity produced can be increased but only by incurring higher cost. If a higher price is offered, the quantity supplied increases. Such goods and services have an elasticity of supply between zero and infinity.

Time Frame for Supply Decisions To study the influence of the length of time elapsed since a price change, we distinguish three time frames of supply:

- Momentary supply
- Long-run supply
- Short-run supply

When the price of a good rises or falls, the *momentary supply curve* shows the response of the quantity supplied immediately following a price change.

Some goods, such as fruits and vegetables, have a perfectly inelastic momentary supply—a vertical supply curve. The quantities supplied depend on crop-planting decisions made earlier. In the case of oranges, for example, planting decisions have to be made many years in advance of the crop being available. The momentary supply curve is vertical because, on a given day, no matter what the price of oranges, producers cannot change their output. They have picked, packed, and shipped their crop to market, and the quantity available for that day is fixed.

In contrast, some goods have a perfectly elastic momentary supply. Long-distance phone calls are an example. When many people simultaneously make a call, there is a big surge in the demand for telephone cables, computer switching, and satellite time, and the quantity bought increases (up to the physical limits of the telephone system). But the price remains constant. Long-distance carriers monitor fluctuations in demand and re-route calls to ensure that the quantity supplied equals the quantity demanded without changing the price.

The *long-run supply curve* shows the response of the quantity supplied to a change in the price after all the technologically possible ways of adjusting supply have been exploited. In the case of oranges, the long run is the time it takes new plantings to grow to full maturity—about 15 years. In some cases, the long-run adjustment occurs only after a completely new production plant has been built and workers have been trained to operate it—typically a process that might take several years.

The *short-run supply curve* shows how the quantity supplied responds to a price change when only *some* of the technologically possible adjustments to production have been made. The first adjustment that is usually made is in the amount of labour employed. To increase output in the short run, firms work their labour force overtime and perhaps hire additional workers. To decrease their output in the short run, firms lay off workers or reduce their hours of work. With the passage of time, firms can make additional adjustments, perhaps training additional workers or buying additional tools and other equipment. The short-run response to a price change, unlike the momentary and long-run responses, is not a unique response but a sequence of adjustments.

The short-run supply curve slopes upward because producers can take actions quite quickly to change the quantity supplied in response to a price change. For example, if the price of oranges falls, growers can stop picking and leave oranges to rot on the tree. Or if the price rises they can use more fertilizer and improved irrigation to increase the yields of their existing trees. In the long run, they can plant more trees and increase the quantity supplied even more in response to a given price rise.

REVIEW QUIZ

- Why do we need to measure the responsiveness of the quantity supplied of a good or service to a change in its price?
- Can you define and calculate the elasticity of supply?
- What are the main influences on the elasticity of supply that make the supply of some goods elastic and the supply of other goods inelastic?
- Can you provide examples of goods or services whose elasticity of supply are: (a) zero, (b) greater than zero but less than infinity, and (c) infinity?
- How does the time frame over which a supply decision is made influence the elasticity of supply?

◆ You have now studied the theory of demand and supply, and you have learned how to measure the elasticities of demand and supply. All the elasticities that you've met in this chapter are summarized in Table 5.3. In the next chapter, we are going to study the efficiency of competitive markets. But before doing that, take a look at *Reading Between the Lines*, on pp. 104–105, to see elasticity in action.

TABLE 5.3

A Compact Glossary of Elasticities

Price Elasticities of Demand

A relationship is described as	When its magnitude is	Which means that
Perfectly elastic or infinitely elastic	Infinity	The smallest possible increase in the price causes an infinitely large decrease in the quantity demanded*
Elastic	Less than infinity but greater than 1	The percentage decrease in the quantity demanded exceeds the percentage increase in the price
Unit elastic	1	The percentage decrease in the quantity demanded equals the percentage increase in the price
Inelastic	Greater than zero but less than 1	The percentage decrease in the quantity demanded is less than the percentage increase in the price
Perfectly inelastic or completely inelastic	Zero	The quantity demanded is the same at all prices

Cross Elasticities of Demand

A relationship is described as	When its value is	Which means that
Perfect substitutes	Infinity	The smallest possible increase in the price of one good causes an infinitely large increase in the quantity demanded of the other good
Substitutes	Positive, less than infinity	If the price of one good increases, the quantity demanded of the other good also increases
Independent	Zero	The quantity demanded of one good remains constant, regardless of the price of the other good
Complements	Less than zero	The quantity demanded of one good decreases when the price of the other good increases

Income Elasticities of Demand

A relationship is described as	When its value is	Which means that
Income elastic (normal good)	Greater than 1	The percentage increase in the quantity demanded is greater than the percentage increase in income
Income inelastic (normal good)	Less than 1 but greater than zero	The percentage increase in the quantity demanded is less than the percentage increase in income
Negative income elastic (inferior good)	Less than zero	When income increases, quantity demanded decreases

Elasticities of Supply

A relationship is described as	When its value is	Which means that
Perfectly elastic	Infinity	The smallest possible increase in the price causes an infinitely large increase in the quantity supplied
Elastic	Less than infinity but greater than 1	The percentage increase in the quantity supplied exceeds the percentage increase in the price
Inelastic	Greater than zero but less than 1	The percentage increase in the quantity supplied is less than the percentage increase in the price
Perfectly inelastic	Zero	The quantity supplied is the same at all prices

*In each description, the directions of change may be reversed. For example, in this case: The smallest possible *decrease* in the price causes an infinitely large *increase* in the quantity demanded.

The Price Elasticity of Demand for Computers

THE GLOBE AND MAIL, JUNE 22, 1998

Students show their shopping smarts

University students have been doing their homework when it comes to computer shopping, according to retailers who say more and more students are coming into stores with a clear idea of what they need.

Luckily for students, who tend to shop on a fairly tight budget, computer manufacturers also have been hitting the books to come up with an interesting array of powerful entry-level models at prices that have dropped considerably over the past year.

"Students always want the biggest bang for their buck," says computer salesman Tom Lam at the University of British Columbia Computer Shop.

"They want the most processing power they can get for the least number of dollars."

Manufacturers are battling for market share in the home computer market and that is good news right now for students looking to make their first computer purchase before classes begin in the fall. Prices have dropped and if that's not enough for bargain hunters, incentives aimed at students include package deals

to provide hardware and software upgrades, plus easy terms and low-cost financing.

The average price of a consumer desktop fell about 21 per cent to about $1,800 in the first quarter of this year compared with a year earlier, according to market research firm AC Nielsen Canada. That helped to boost home computer sales in that period by about 17 per cent overall, says AC Nielsen spokesman Kelvin Wayne. Within the postsecondary-school education market, sales were up 22 per cent. ...

UBC's Mr. Lam says students coming into his store on the UBC campus want well-equipped computers with enough power and speed to easily handle the applications they need...

"Pricing is usually the prime concern but students won't pay a low price and take lower quality," Mr. Lam says. "They want the most current specs." That includes fast microprocessing, CD-ROM drives and modems, plus plenty of memory. ...

Essence of the Story

■ The price of a desktop computer fell 21 percent between the first quarter of 1997 and the first quarter of 1998.

■ Home computer sales in the same period increased by 17 percent overall.

■ Computer sales in the same period in the post-secondary student market increased by 22 percent.

■ Students tend to shop on a tight budget but still buy the most processing power they can get for the smallest price.

■ The price elasticity of demand equals the percentage change in the quantity demanded divided by the percentage change in price, using the *average* quantity and *average* price.

■ The percentage changes in price and quantity demanded reported in the news article are most likely percentages of the 1997 price and quantities.

■ The table uses the information in the news article to work out the numbers we need. (The news article does not give quantity data, but our assumptions are consistent with the information in the article.)

■ The first row of the table shows the price and assumed quantities for 1998. The second row shows the percentage changes from 1997. The third row calculates the implied quantities in 1977.

■ The fourth row shows the changes in price and quantities. The fifth row shows the average price and average quantities. The final row shows the implied elasticities of demand.

■ Figure 1 illustrates this calculation for the overall market for computers.

■ When the price falls from $2,280 to $1,800, the quantity demanded

increases from 641,000 to 750,000.

■ The price falls by 23.5 percent of the average price. And the quantity demanded increases by 15.7 percent of the average quantity. So the elasticity of demand is 15.7 percent divided by 23.5 percent, which is 0.67.

■ Figure 2 illustrates the calculation for the postsecondary student market.

■ When the price falls from $2,280 to $1,800, the quantity demanded increases from 82,000 to 100,000.

■ The price falls by 23.5 percent of the average price. And the quantity demanded increases by 19.8 percent of the average quantity. So the elasticity of demand is 19.8 percent divided by 23.5 percent, which is 0.84.

■ The student demand for computers is inelastic. But it is less inelastic than the overall demand. Why?

■ Students tend to have smaller budgets than do other buyers and so spend a greater proportion of their budgets on computers. The greater the proportion of income spent on a good, the more elastic is the demand for it. This is the reason why the students' demand for computers is more elastic than the overall demand.

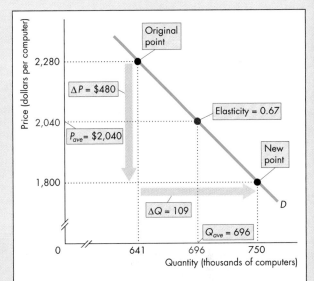

Figure 1 Canadian demand

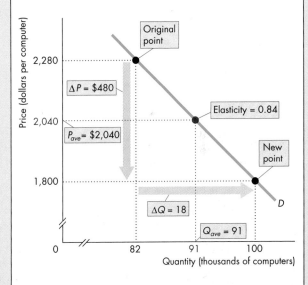

Figure 2 Post-secondary students' demand

	Price	Overall quantity	Students' quantity
1998	$1,800	750,000	100,000
% Δ from 1997	21	17	22
1997	$2,280	641,000	82,000
Change	$480	109,000	18,000
Average	$2,040	696,000	91,000
% of average	23.5	15.7	19.8
Elasticity		0.67	0.84

Table 1 Canadian Computer Markets

SUMMARY

Key Points

The Price Elasticity of Demand (pp. 90–96)

- Elasticity is a measure of the responsiveness of the quantity demanded of a good to a change in its price.
- Price elasticity of demand equals the percentage change in the quantity demanded divided by the percentage change in the price.
- The larger the magnitude of the elasticity of demand, the greater is the responsiveness of the quantity demanded to a given change in the price.
- Price elasticity of demand depends on how easily one good serves as a substitute for another, the proportion of income spent on the good, and the length of time elapsed since the price change.
- If demand is elastic, a decrease in price leads to an increase in total revenue. If demand is unit elastic, a decrease in price leaves total revenue unchanged. And if demand is inelastic, a decrease in price leads to a decrease in total revenue.

More Elasticities of Demand (pp. 97–99)

- Cross elasticity of demand measures the responsiveness of demand for one good to a change in the price of a substitute or a complement.
- The cross elasticity of demand with respect to the price of a substitute is positive. The cross elasticity of demand with respect to the price of a complement is negative.
- Income elasticity of demand measures the responsiveness of demand to a change in income. For a normal good, the income elasticity of demand is positive. For an inferior good, the income elasticity of demand is negative.
- When the income elasticity is greater than 1, as income increases, the percentage of income spent on the good increases.
- When the income elasticity is less than 1 but greater than zero, as income increases, the percentage of income spent on the good decreases.

Elasticity of Supply (pp. 100–102)

- Elasticity of supply measures the responsiveness of the quantity supplied of a good to a change in its price.
- Elasticities of supply are usually positive and range between zero (vertical supply curve) and infinity (horizontal supply curve).
- Supply decisions have three time frames: momentary, long run, and short run.
- Momentary supply refers to the response of sellers to a price change at the instant that the price changes.
- Long-run supply refers to the response of sellers to a price change when all the technologically feasible adjustments in production have been made.
- Short-run supply refers to the response of sellers to a price change after some adjustments in production have been made.

Key Figures and Table

Key Terms

PROBLEMS

*1. Rain spoils the strawberry crop. As a result, the price rises from $4 to $6 a box and the quantity demanded decreases from 1,000 to 600 boxes a week. Over this price range,
   a. What is the price elasticity of demand?
   b. Describe the demand for strawberries.

2. Good weather brings a bumper tomato crop. The price falls from $6 to $4 a basket and the quantity demanded increases from 200 to 400 baskets a day. Over this price range,
   a. What is the price elasticity of demand?
   b. Describe the demand for tomatoes.

*3. The figure shows the demand for videotape rentals.

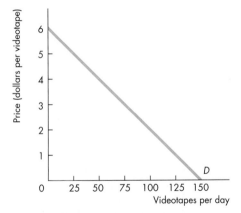

   a. Calculate the elasticity of demand for a rise in rental price from $3 to $5.
   b. At what price is the elasticity of demand equal to 1?

4. The figure shows the demand for pens.

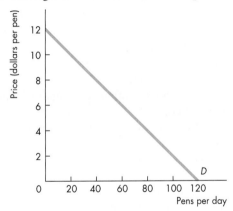

   a. Calculate the elasticity of demand for a rise in price from $2 to $4.

b. At what prices is the elasticity of demand equal to 1, greater than 1, and less than 1?

*5. If the quantity of dental services demanded increases by 10 percent when the price of dental services falls by 10 percent, is the demand for dental services inelastic, elastic, or unit elastic?

6. If the quantity of fish demanded decreases by 5 percent when the price of fish rises by 10 percent, is the demand for fish elastic, inelastic, or unit elastic?

*7. The demand schedule for computer chips is:

Price (dollars per chip)	Quantity demanded (millions of chips per year)
200	50
250	45
300	40
350	35
400	30

   a. What will happen to total revenue if the price of a chip falls from $400 to $350?
   b. What will happen to total revenue if the price of a chip falls from $350 to $300?
   c. At what price is total revenue maximized?
   d. What quantity of chips will be sold at the price that answers problem 7(c)?
   e. At an average price of $350, is the demand for chips elastic or inelastic? Use the total revenue test to answer this question.

8. The demand schedule for coffee is:

Price (dollars per kilogram)	Quantity demanded (millions of kilograms per year)
10	30
15	25
20	20
25	15

   a. What will happen to total revenue if the price rises from $10 to $20 per kilogram?
   b. What will happen to total revenue if the price rises from $15 to $25 per kilogram?
   c. At what price is total revenue maximized?
   d. What quantity of coffee will be sold at the price that answers problem 8(c)?
   e. At an average price of $15 a kilogram, is the demand for coffee elastic or inelastic? Use the total revenue test to answer this question.

*9. In problem 7, at $250 a chip, is the demand for chips elastic or inelastic? Use the total revenue test to answer this question.

10. In problem 8, at $15 a kilogram, is the demand for coffee elastic or inelastic? Use the total revenue test to answer this question.

*11. If a 12 percent rise in the price of orange juice decreases the quantity of orange juice demanded by 22 percent and increases the quantity of apple juice demanded by 14 percent, calculate the cross elasticity of demand between orange juice and apple juice.

12. If a 10 percent fall in the price of beef increases the quantity of beef demanded by 15 percent and decreases the quantity of chicken demanded by 20 percent, calculate the cross elasticity of demand between beef and chicken.

*13. Last year Alex's income increased from $3,000 to $5,000. Alex increased his consumption of bagels from 4 to 8 a month and decreased his consumption of donuts from 12 to 6 a month. Calculate Alex's income elasticity of demand for (i) bagels and (ii) donuts.

14. Last year Judy's income increased from $10,000 to $12,000. Judy increased her demand for concert tickets by 10 percent and decreased her demand for bus rides by 5 percent. Calculate Judy's income elasticity of demand for (i) concert tickets and (ii) bus rides.

□*15. The table gives the supply schedule for long-distance phone calls:

Price (cents per minute)	Quantity supplied (millions of minutes per day)
10	200
20	400
30	600
40	800

Calculate the elasticity of supply when
a. The price falls from 40 cents to 30 cents a minute.
b. The price is 20 cents a minute.

16. The table gives the supply schedule for shoes.

Price (dollars per pair)	Quantity supplied (millions of pairs per year)
120	1,200
125	1,400
130	1,600
135	1,800

Calculate the elasticity of supply when
a. The price rises from $125 to $135 a pair.
b. The price is $125 a pair.

CRITICAL THINKING

1. Study *Reading Between the Lines* on pp. 104–105 on the markets for computers in Canada and then answer the following questions:
   a. What happened to the total revenue from computer sales to post-secondary students during 1997 and 1998?
   b. What happened to the total revenue from computer sales to home computer buyers during 1997 and 1998?
   c. Do you think that the overall computer market has an inelastic demand? Explain why.
   d. If you were a retailer, how would you try to take advantage of the difference in the elasticities of demand between students and other computer buyers?

2. Thinking about the computer market in Canada, what do you predict will happen to the price and quantity during the coming year? Set out your assumptions about changes in supply, changes in demand, the price elasticity of demand, the relevant cross elasticities of demand, the income elasticity of demand, and the elasticity of supply.

3. Use the link on the Parkin-Bade Web site and:
   a. Find the price of gasoline during 1999. Did the price rise or fall?
   b. Use the tools of demand and supply and the concept of elasticity to explain the recent changes in the price of gasoline.
   c. Find the latest price of crude oil.
   d. Use the tools of demand and supply and the concept of elasticity to explain the recent changes in the price of crude oil.

4. Use the link on the Parkin-Bade Web site and:
   a. Find the number of litres in a barrel.
   b. What is the cost of the crude oil in one litre of gasoline?
   c. What are the other costs that make up the total cost of a litre of gasoline?
   d. If the price of crude oil falls by 10 percent, by what percentage would you expect the price of gasoline to change, other things remaining the same?
   e. In light of your answer to part (d), do you think the elasticity of demand for crude oil is greater than, less than, or equal to the elasticity of demand for gasoline?

6

Efficiency and Equity

People constantly strive to get more for less. As consumers, we love to get a bargain. We enjoy telling our friends about the great deal we got on CDs or some other item we bought at a surprisingly low price. Every time we buy something, or decide *not* to buy something, we express our view about how scarce resources should be used. We try to spend our incomes in ways that get the most out of our scarce resources. For example, we balance the pleasure we get from our expenditure on movies against that we get from our textbooks.

More for Less

◆ Is the allocation of our resources between leisure and education, pizza and submarine sandwiches, inline skates and squash balls, and all the other things we buy the right one? Could we get more out of our resources if we spent more on some goods and services and less on others? ◆ Scientists and engineers devote enormous efforts to finding new and more productive ways of using our scarce land, labour, and capital resources to produce goods and services. Workers in factories and on assembly lines make suggestions that increase productivity. Is our economy efficient at producing goods and services? Do we get the most out of our scarce resources in our factories, offices, and shops? ◆ Some firms make huge profits year after year. Microsoft, for example, has generated enough profit over the past ten years to rocket Bill Gates, one of its founders, into the position of being one of the richest people in the world. Is that kind of business success a sign of efficiency? ◆ And is it fair that Bill Gates is so incredibly rich, while others live in miserable poverty?

◆ These are the kinds of questions you'll explore in this chapter. You will first learn some concepts that enable you to think about efficiency more broadly than the everyday use of that word. You will discover that competitive markets can be efficient. But you will also discover some sources of inefficiency that can be addressed with government action. You will also discover that firms that make huge profits, while efficient in one sense, might be inefficient in a broader sense.

After studying this chapter, you will be able to:

■ Define efficiency

■ Distinguish between value and price and define consumer surplus

■ Distinguish between cost and price and define producer surplus

■ Explain the conditions in which competitive markets move resources to their highest-valued uses

■ Explain the obstacles to inefficiency in our economy

■ Explain the main ideas about fairness and evaluate claims that competitive markets result in unfair outcomes

Efficiency: A Refresher

IT IS HARD TO TALK ABOUT EFFICIENCY IN ordinary conversation without generating both disagreement and misunderstanding. Many people see efficiency as a clearly desirable goal. To an engineer, an entrepreneur, a politician, a working mother, or an economist, getting more for less seems like a sensible thing to aim for. But some people think that the pursuit of efficiency conflicts with other goals. They believe the other goals are more worthy of pursuit. Environmentalists worry about contamination from "efficient" nuclear power plants. Car producers worry about competition from "efficient" foreign producers.

Economists use the idea of efficiency in a special way that avoids these disagreements. An **efficient allocation** of resources occurs when we produce the goods and services that people value most highly (see Chapter 3, pp. 42–44). Equivalently, resource use is efficient when we cannot produce more of a good or service without giving up some other good or service that we value more highly.

If people value a nuclear-free environment more highly than they value cheap electric power, it is efficient to use higher-cost, non-nuclear technologies to produce electricity. Efficiency is not a cold, mechanical concept. It is a concept based on value, and value is based on people's feelings.

Think about the efficient quantity of pizza. To produce more pizza, we must give up some other goods and services. For example, we might give up some submarine sandwiches. To get more pizzas, we forgo submarines. If we have fewer pizzas, we can have more submarines. What is the efficient quantity of pizza to produce? The answer depends on marginal benefit and marginal cost.

Marginal Benefit

If we consume one more pizza, we receive a marginal benefit. **Marginal benefit** is the benefit that a person receives from consuming one more unit of a good or service. The marginal benefit from a good or service is measured as the maximum amount that a person is willing to pay for one more unit of it. So the marginal benefit from a pizza is the maximum amount of other goods and services that people are willing to give up in order to get one more pizza. The marginal benefit from pizza decreases as the quantity of pizza consumed increases—the principle of *decreasing marginal benefit.*

We can express the marginal benefit from a pizza as the number of submarine sandwiches that people are willing to forgo to get one more pizza. But we can also express marginal benefit as the dollar value of other goods and services that people are willing to forgo. Figure 6.1 shows the marginal benefit from pizza expressed in this way. As the quantity of pizza increases, the value of other items that people are willing to forgo to get yet one more pizza decreases.

Marginal Cost

If we produce one more pizza, we incur a marginal cost. **Marginal cost** is the opportunity cost of producing *one more unit* of a good or service. The marginal cost of a good or service is measured as

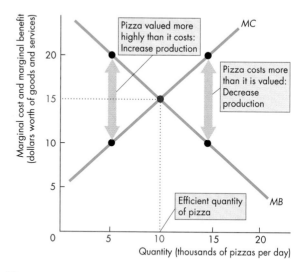

FIGURE 6.1

The Efficient Quantity of Pizza

The marginal benefit curve (MB) shows what people *are willing* to forgo to get one more pizza. The marginal cost curve (MC) shows what people *must* forgo to get one more pizza. If fewer than 10,000 pizzas a day are produced, marginal benefit exceeds marginal cost. Greater value can be obtained by producing more pizzas. If more than 10,000 pizzas a day are produced, marginal cost exceeds marginal benefit. Greater value can be obtained by producing fewer pizzas. If 10,000 pizzas a day are produced, marginal benefit equals marginal cost and the efficient quantity of pizza is available.

the value of the best alternative forgone. So the marginal cost of a pizza is the value of the best alternative forgone to get one more pizza. The marginal cost of a pizza increases as the quantity of pizza produced increases—the principle of *increasing marginal cost*.

We can express marginal cost as the number of submarine sandwiches we must forgo to get one more pizza. But we can also express marginal cost as the dollar value of other goods and services we must forgo. Figure 6.1 shows the marginal cost of pizza expressed in this way. As the quantity of pizza produced increases, the value of other items we must forgo to get yet one more pizza increases.

Efficiency and Inefficiency

To determine the efficient quantity of pizza, we compare the marginal cost of a pizza with the marginal benefit from a pizza. There are three possible cases:

- Marginal benefit exceeds marginal cost.
- Marginal cost exceeds marginal benefit.
- Marginal benefit equals marginal cost.

Marginal Benefit Exceeds Marginal Cost

Suppose the quantity of pizza produced is 5,000 a day. Figure 6.1 shows that at this quantity, the marginal benefit of a pizza is $20. That is, when the quantity of pizza available is 5,000 a day, people are willing to pay $20 for the 5,000th pizza.

Figure 6.1 also shows that the marginal cost of the 5,000th pizza is $10. That is, to produce one more pizza, the value of other goods and services that we must forgo is $10. If pizza production increases from 4,999 to 5,000, the value of the additional pizza is $20 and its marginal cost is $10. By producing this pizza, the value of the pizza produced exceeds the value of the goods and services forgone by $10. Resources are used more efficiently—they create more value—if we produce an extra pizza and fewer other goods and services. This same reasoning applies all the way up to the 9,999th pizza. Only when we get to the 10,000th pizza does marginal benefit not exceed marginal cost.

Marginal Cost Exceeds Marginal Benefit

Suppose the quantity of pizza produced is 15,000 a day. Figure 6.1 shows that at this quantity, the marginal benefit of a pizza is $10. That is, when the quantity of pizza available is 15,000 a day, people are willing to pay $10 for the 15,000th pizza.

Figure 6.1 also shows that the marginal cost of the 15,000th pizza is $20. That is, to produce one more pizza, the value of the other goods and services that we must forgo is $20.

If pizza production decreases from 15,000 to 14,999, the value of the one pizza forgone is $10 and its marginal cost is $20. So by not producing this pizza, the value of the other goods and services produced exceeds the value of the pizza forgone by $10. Resources are used more efficiently—they create more value—if we produce one fewer pizza and more other goods and services. This same reasoning applies all the way down to the 10,001st pizza. Only when we get to the 10,000th pizza does marginal cost not exceed marginal benefit.

Marginal Benefit Equals Marginal Cost

Suppose the quantity of pizza produced is 10,000 a day. Figure 6.1 shows that at this quantity, the marginal benefit of a pizza is $15. That is, when the quantity of pizza available is 10,000 a day, people are willing to pay $15 for the 10,000th pizza.

Figure 6.1 also shows that the marginal cost of the 10,000th pizza is $15. That is, to produce one more pizza, the value of other goods and services that we must forgo is $15.

In this situation, we cannot increase the value of the goods and services produced by either increasing or decreasing the quantity of pizza. If we increase the quantity of pizza, the 10,001st pizza costs more to produce than it is worth. If we decrease the quantity of pizza produced, the 9,999th pizza is worth more than it costs to produce. So when marginal benefit equals marginal cost, resource use is efficient.

R E V I E W   Q U I Z

- If the marginal benefit of pizza exceeds the marginal cost of pizza, are we producing too much pizza and too little of other goods, or too little pizza and too much of other goods? Explain.
- If the marginal cost of pizza exceeds the marginal benefit of pizza, are we producing too much pizza and too little of other goods, or too little pizza and too much of other goods? Explain.
- Explain the relationship between the marginal benefit of pizza and the marginal cost of pizza when we are producing the efficient quantity of pizza.

Does a competitive market in pizza produce the efficient quantity of pizza? Let's answer this question.

Value, Price, and Consumer Surplus

TO INVESTIGATE WHETHER A COMPETITIVE market is efficient, we need to learn about the connection between demand and marginal benefit and between supply and marginal cost.

Value, Willingness to Pay, and Demand

In everyday life we talk about "getting value for money." When we use this expression we are distinguishing between *value* and *price*. Value is what we get, and the price is what we pay.

The **value** of one more unit of a good or service is its *marginal benefit*. Marginal benefit can be expressed as the maximum price that people are willing to pay for another unit of the good or service. The willingness to pay for a good or service determines the demand for it.

In Fig. 6.2(a), the demand curve shows the quantity demanded at each price. For example, when the price of a pizza is $15, the quantity demanded is 10,000 pizzas a day. In Fig. 6.2(b), the demand curve shows the maximum price that people are willing to pay when there is a given quantity. For example, when 10,000 pizzas a day are available, the most that people are willing to pay for a pizza is $15. This second interpretation of the demand curve means that the marginal benefit from the 10,000th pizza is $15.

When we draw a demand curve, we use a *relative* price, not a *money* price. A relative price is expressed in dollar units, but it measures the number of dollars-worth of other goods and services forgone to obtain one more unit of the good in question (see Chapter 4, p. 64). So a demand curve tells us the quantity of other goods and services that people are willing to forgo to get an additional unit of a good. But this is what a marginal benefit curve tells us too. So:

A demand curve is a marginal benefit curve.

We don't always have to pay the maximum price that we are willing to pay. When we buy something, we often get a bargain. Let's see how.

FIGURE 6.2

Demand, Willingness to Pay, and Marginal Benefit

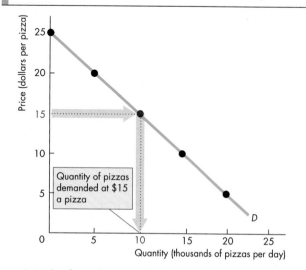

(a) Price determines quantity demanded

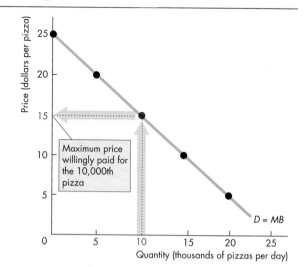

(b) Quantity determines willingness to pay

The demand curve for pizza, D, shows the quantity of pizza demanded at each price, other things remaining the same. It also shows the maximum price that consumers are willing to pay if a given quantity of pizza is available. At a price of $15 a pizza, the quantity demanded is 10,000 pizzas a day (part a). If 10,000 pizzas a day are available, the maximum price that consumers are willing to pay for the 10,000th pizza is $15 (part b).

Consumer Surplus

When people buy something for less than it is worth to them, they receive a consumer surplus. A **consumer surplus** is the value of a good minus the price paid for it.

To understand consumer surplus, look at Lisa's demand for pizza, which is shown in Fig. 6.3. Lisa likes pizza, but the marginal benefit she gets from it decreases quickly as her consumption increases.

Suppose Lisa can buy pizza by the slice and that there are 10 slices in a pizza. If a pizza costs $2.50 a slice (or $25 a pizza), Lisa buys no pizza. She spends her fast-food budget on items that she values more highly than pizza. At $2 a slice, she buys 10 slices (one pizza) a week. At $1.50 a slice, she buys 20 slices a week; at $1 a slice, she buys 30 slices a week; and at 50 cents a slice she buys 40 slices a week.

Lisa's demand curve for pizza in Fig. 6.3 is also her *willingness-to-pay* or marginal benefit curve. It tells us that if Lisa can have only 10 slices a week, she is willing to pay $2 a slice. Her marginal benefit from the 10th slice is $2. If she can have 20 slices (2 pizzas) a week, she is willing to pay $1.50 for the 20th slice. Her marginal benefit from the 20th slice is $1.50.

Figure 6.3 also shows Lisa's consumer surplus from pizza when its price is $1.50 a slice. At this price, she buys 20 slices a week. A price of $1.50 a slice is the most she is willing to pay for the 20th slice, so its marginal benefit is exactly the price she pays for it. But Lisa is willing to pay almost $2.50 for the first slice. Her marginal benefit from this slice is close to $1 more than she pays for it, so her *consumer surplus* from the first slice is almost $1. Lisa's marginal benefit from the 10th slice is $2, so on the 10th slice her consumer surplus is 50 cents.

To calculate Lisa's consumer surplus, we find the consumer surplus on each slice and add these surpluses together. This sum is the area of the green triangle in Fig. 6.3. The base of the triangle is 20 slices a week and the height is $1 a slice, so consumer surplus is

$$\frac{20 \text{ slices per week} \times \$1 \text{ per slice}}{2} = \$10 \text{ per week}.$$

The blue rectangle in Fig. 6.3 is the amount that Lisa pays for pizza, which is $30 a week—20 slices at $1.50 a slice.

All goods and services are like the pizza example you've just studied. Because of decreasing marginal

FIGURE 6.3

A Consumer's Demand and Consumer Surplus

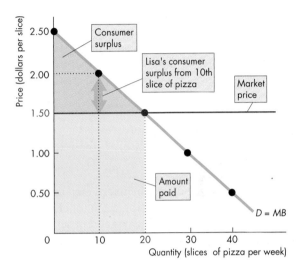

Lisa's demand curve for pizza tells us that at $2.50 a slice, she does not buy pizza. At $2 a slice, she buys 10 slices a week; at $1.50 a slice, she buys 20 slices a week. Lisa's demand curve also tells us that she is willing to pay $2 for the 10th slice and $1.50 for the 20th. She actually pays $1.50 a slice—the market price—and buys 20 slices a week. Her consumer surplus from pizza is $10—the area of the green triangle.

benefit, people receive more benefit from their consumption than the amount they pay.

R E V I E W   Q U I Z

- Explain how we measure the value or marginal benefit of a good or service.
- Explain the relationship between marginal benefit and the demand curve.
- What is consumer surplus and how do we measure it?

You've seen how we distinguish between value—marginal benefit—and price. And you've seen that buyers receive a consumer surplus when marginal benefit exceeds price. Next, we're going to study the connection between supply and marginal cost and learn about producer surplus.

Cost, Price, and Producer Surplus

WHAT YOU ARE NOW GOING TO LEARN ABOUT cost, price, and producer surplus parallels the related ideas about value, price, and consumer surplus that you've just studied.

Firms are in business to make a profit. To do so, they must sell their output for a price that exceeds the cost of production. Let's investigate the relationship between cost and price.

Cost, Minimum Supply Price, and Supply

Firms undertake elaborate schemes to earn profits. Earning a profit means receiving more (or at least receiving no less) for the sale of a good or service than the cost of producing it. Just as consumers distinguish between *value* and *price*, so producers distinguish between *cost* and *price*. Cost is what a producer gives up, and price is what a producer receives.

The cost of producing one more unit of a good or service is its *marginal cost*. Marginal cost is the minimum price that producers must receive to induce them to produce another unit of the good or service. This minimum acceptable price determines supply.

In Fig. 6.4(a), the supply curve shows the quantity supplied at each price. For example, when the price of a pizza is $15, the quantity supplied is 10,000 pizzas a day. In Fig. 6.4(b), the supply curve shows the minimum price that producers must be offered to produce a given quantity of pizza. For example, the minimum price that producers must be offered to get them to produce 10,000 pizzas a day is $15 a pizza. This second view of the supply curve means that the marginal cost of the 10,000th pizza is $15.

Because the price is a relative price, a supply curve tells us the quantity of other goods and services that *sellers must forgo* to produce one more unit of the good. But a marginal cost curve also tells us the quantity of other goods and services that we must

FIGURE 6.4

Supply, Minimum Supply Price, and Marginal Cost

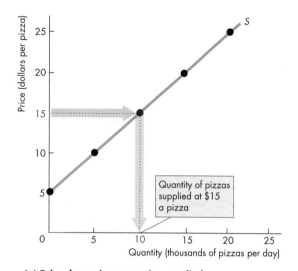

(a) Price determines quantity supplied

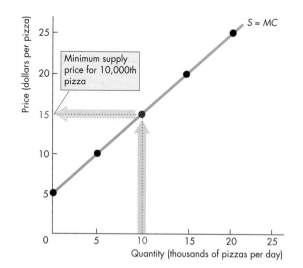

(b) Quantity determines minimum supply price

The supply curve of pizza, S, shows the quantity of pizza supplied at each price, other things remaining the same. The supply curve also shows the minimum price that producers must be offered to get them to produce a given quantity of

pizza. At a price of $15 a pizza, the quantity supplied is 10,000 pizzas a day (part a). To get firms to produce 10,000 pizzas a day, the minimum price they must be offered for the 10,000th pizza is $15 (part b).

forgo to get one more unit of the good. So:

> A supply curve is a marginal cost curve.

Producers don't always receive their minimum supply price. If the price they receive exceeds the cost they incur, producers earn a surplus. This producer surplus is analogous to consumer surplus. Let's look at producer surplus.

Producer Surplus

When a firm sells something for more than it costs to produce, the firm obtains a producer surplus. A **producer surplus** is the price of a good minus the opportunity cost of producing it. To understand producer surplus, look at Max's supply of pizza in Fig. 6.5.

Max can produce pizza or bake bread. The more pizza he bakes, the less bread he can bake. His opportunity cost of pizza is the value of the bread he must forgo. This opportunity cost increases as Max increases his production of pizza. If a pizza sells for only $5, Max produces no pizza. He uses his kitchen to bake bread. Pizza just isn't worth producing. But at $10 a pizza, Max produces 50 pizzas a day, and at $15 a pizza, he produces 100 a day.

Max's supply curve of pizza is also his *minimum supply price* curve. It tells us that if Max can sell only 1 pizza a day, the minimum that he must be paid for it is $5. If he can sell 50 pizzas a day, the minimum that he must be paid for the 50th pizza is $10, and so on.

Figure 6.5 also shows Max's producer surplus. If the price of a pizza is $15, Max plans to sell 100 pizzas a day. The minimum that he must be paid for the 100th pizza is $15. So its opportunity cost is exactly the price he receives for it. But his opportunity cost of the first pizza is only $5. So this first pizza costs $10 less to produce than he receives for it. Max receives a *producer surplus* from his first pizza of $10. He receives a slightly smaller producer surplus on the second pizza, less on the third, and so on until he receives no producer surplus on the 100th pizza.

Figure 6.5 shows Max's producer surplus as the blue triangle formed by the area above the supply curve and beneath the price line. The base of the triangle is 100 pizzas a week and the height is $10 a pizza, so producer surplus is

$$\frac{100 \text{ pizzas per week} \times \$10 \text{ per pizza}}{2} = \$500 \text{ per week.}$$

FIGURE 6.5
A Producer's Supply and Producer Surplus

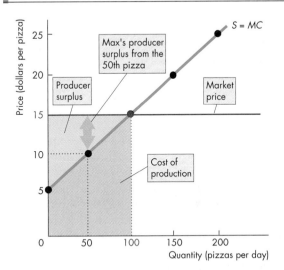

Max's supply curve of pizza tells us that at a price of $5, Max plans to sell no pizza. At a price of $10, he plans to sell 50 pizzas a day; and at a price of $15, he plans to sell 100 pizzas a day. Max's supply curve also tells us the minimum that he must be offered is $10 for the 50th pizza a day and $15 for the 100th pizza a day. If the market price is $15 a pizza, he sells 100 pizzas a day and receives $1,500. The red area shows Max's cost of producing pizza, which is $1,000 a day, and the blue area shows his producer surplus, which is $500 a day.

Figure 6.5 also shows Max's opportunity costs of production as the red area beneath the supply curve.

REVIEW QUIZ

- Explain the relationship between the marginal cost or opportunity cost of producing a good or service and the minimum supply price.
- Explain the relationship between marginal cost and the supply curve.
- What is producer surplus and how do we measure it?

Consumer surplus and producer surplus can be used to measure the efficiency of a market. Let's see how we can use these concepts to study the efficiency of a competitive market.

Is the Competitive Market Efficient?

FIGURE 6.6 SHOWS THE MARKET FOR PIZZA. THE demand curve, *D*, shows the demand for pizza. The supply curve, *S*, shows the supply of pizza. The equilibrium price is $15 a pizza, and the equilibrium quantity is 10,000 pizzas a day.

The market forces that you studied in Chapter 4 (pp. 74–75) will pull the pizza market to this equilibrium. If the price is greater than $15 a pizza, a surplus will force the price down. If the price is less than $15 a pizza, a shortage will force the price up. Only if the price is $15 a pizza is there neither a surplus nor a shortage and no forces operating to change the price.

So the market price and quantity are pulled towards their equilibrium values. But is this competitive equilibrium efficient? Does it produce the efficient quantity of pizza?

Efficiency of Competitive Equilibrium

The equilibrium in Fig. 6.6 is efficient. Resources are being used to produce the quantity of pizza that people value most highly. It is not possible to produce more pizza without giving up some other good or service that is valued more highly. And if a smaller quantity of pizza is produced, resources are used to produce some other good that is not valued as highly as the pizza forgone.

To see why the equilibrium in Fig. 6.6 is efficient, think about the interpretation of the demand curve as a marginal benefit curve and the supply curve as a marginal cost curve. The demand curve tells us the marginal benefit from pizza. The supply curve tells us the marginal cost of pizza. So where the demand curve and the supply curve intersect, marginal benefit equals marginal cost.

But this condition—marginal benefit equals marginal cost—is the condition that delivers an efficient use of resources. It puts resources to work in the activities that create the greatest possible value. So a competitive equilibrium is efficient.

If production is less than 10,000 pizzas a day, the marginal pizza is valued more highly than its opportunity cost. If production exceeds 10,000 pizzas a day, the marginal pizza costs more to produce than the value that consumers place on it. Only when 10,000

FIGURE 6.6

An Efficient Market for Pizza

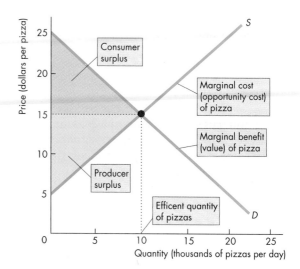

Resources are used efficiently when the sum of consumer surplus and producer surplus is maximized. Consumer surplus is the area below the demand curve and above the market price line—the green triangle. Producer surplus is the area below the price line and above the supply curve—the blue triangle. Here consumer surplus is $50,000 and producer surplus is also $50,000. Total surplus is $100,000. Total surplus is maximized when the willingness to pay equals the opportunity cost. The efficient quantity of pizza is 10,000 per day.

pizzas a day are produced is the marginal pizza worth exactly what it costs. The competitive market pushes the quantity of pizza produced to its efficient level of 10,000 a day. If production is less than 10,000 a day, a shortage raises the price, which stimulates an increase in production. If production exceeds 10,000 a day, a surplus lowers the price, which decreases production.

When the market is using resources efficiently at the competitive equilibrium, the sum of consumer surplus and producer surplus is maximized. At this equilibrium, resources are used in the activities in which they are valued most highly.

Buyers and sellers each attempt to do the best they can for themselves and no one plans for an efficient outcome for society as a whole. Buyers seek the lowest possible price and sellers seek the highest possible price. And the market comes to an equilibrium in which the gains from trade are as large as possible.

The Invisible Hand

Writing in his *Wealth of Nations* in 1776, Adam Smith was the first to suggest that competitive markets send resources to the uses in which they have the highest value—see pp. 58–59. Smith believed that each participant in a competitive market is "led by an invisible hand to promote an end [the efficient use of resources] which was no part of his intention."

You can see the invisible hand at work in the cartoon. The cold drinks vendor has both cold drinks and shade. He has an opportunity cost of each and a minimum supply price of each. The park-bench reader has a marginal benefit from a cold drink and from shade. You can see that the marginal benefit from shade exceeds the marginal cost, but the marginal cost of a cold drink exceeds its marginal benefit. The transaction that occurs creates producer surplus and consumer surplus. The vendor obtains a producer surplus from selling the shade for more than its opportunity cost and the reader obtains a consumer surplus from buying the shade for less than its marginal benefit. In the third frame of the cartoon, both the consumer and the producer are better off than they were in the first frame. The umbrella has moved to its highest-value use.

The Invisible Hand at Work Today

The market economy relentlessly performs the activity illustrated in the cartoon and in Fig. 6.6 to achieve an efficient allocation of resources. And rarely has the market been working as hard as it is today. Think about a few of the changes taking place in our economy that the market is guiding towards an efficient use of resources.

New technologies have cut the cost of producing computers. As these advances have occurred, supply has increased and the price has fallen. Lower prices have encouraged an increase in the quantity demanded of this now less costly tool. The marginal benefit from computers is brought to equality with their marginal cost.

A Florida frost cuts the supply of oranges. With fewer oranges available, the marginal benefit from an orange increases. A shortage of oranges raises their price and so the market allocates the smaller quantity available to the people who value them most highly.

Market forces persistently bring marginal cost and marginal benefit to equality and maximize the sum of consumer surplus and producer surplus.

Obstacles to Efficiency

ALTHOUGH MARKETS GENERALLY DO A GOOD JOB at sending resources to where they are most highly valued, they do not always get the correct answer. Sometimes markets overproduce a good or service, and sometimes they underproduce. The most significant obstacles to achieving an efficient allocation of resources in the market economy are

- Price ceilings and price floors
- Taxes, subsidies, and quotas
- Monopoly
- Public goods
- External costs and external benefits

Price Ceilings and Price Floors A **price ceiling** is a regulation that makes it illegal to charge a price higher than a specified level. An example is a price ceiling on apartment rents, which some cities impose. A **price floor** is a regulation that makes it illegal to pay a lower price than a specified level. An example is the minimum wage. (We study both of these restrictions on buyers and sellers in Chapter 7.)

The presence of a price ceiling or a price floor blocks the forces of demand and supply and results in a quantity produced that might exceed or fall short of the quantity determined in an unregulated market.

Taxes, Subsidies, and Quotas Taxes increase the prices paid by buyers and lower the prices received by sellers. Taxes decrease the quantity produced (for reasons that are explained in Chapter 7, on p. 137). All kinds of goods and services are taxed, but the highest taxes are on gasoline, alcohol, and tobacco.

Subsidies, which are payments by the government to producers, decrease the prices paid by buyers and increase the prices received by sellers. Subsidies increase the quantity produced.

Quotas, which are limits to the quantity that a firm is permitted to produce, restrict output below the quantity that a competitive market produces. Farms are sometimes subject to quotas.

Monopoly A **monopoly** is a firm that has sole control of a market. For example, Microsoft has a near monopoly on operating systems for personal computers. Although monopolies earn large profits, they prevent markets from achieving an efficient use of resources. The goal of a monopoly is to maximize profit. To achieve this goal, it restricts production and raises price. (We study monopoly in Chapter 13.)

Public Goods A **public good** is a good or service that is consumed simultaneously by everyone, even if they don't pay for it. Examples are national defence and the enforcement of law and order. Competitive markets would produce too small a quantity of public goods because of a *free-rider problem*. It is not in each person's interest to buy her or his share of a public good. So a competitive market produces less than the efficient quantity. (We study public goods in Chapter 18.)

External Costs and External Benefits An **external cost** is a cost not borne by the producer but borne by other people. The cost of pollution is an example of an external cost. When an electric power

utility burns coal to generate electricity, it puts sulfur dioxide into the atmosphere. This pollutant falls as acid rain and damages vegetation and crops. The utility does not consider the cost of pollution when it decides the quantity of electric power to supply. Its supply curve is based on its own costs, not on the costs that they inflict on others. As a result, the utility produces more power than the efficient quantity.

An **external benefit** is a benefit that accrues to people other than the buyer of a good. An example is when someone in a neighbourhood paints her home or landscapes her yard. The homeowner does not consider her neighbour's marginal benefit when she decides whether to do this type of work. So the demand curve for house painting and yard improvement does not include all the benefits that accrue. In this case, the quantity falls short of the efficient quantity. (We study externalities in Chapter 20.)

The impediments to efficiency that we've just reviewed and that you will study in greater detail in later chapters result in two possible outcomes:

- Underproduction
- Overproduction

Underproduction

Suppose that one firm owned all the pizza outlets in a city and that it restricted the quantity of pizza produced to 5,000 a day. Figure 6.7(a) shows that at this quantity, consumers are willing to pay $20 for the marginal pizza—marginal benefit is $20. The marginal cost of a pizza is only $10. So there is a gap between what people are willing to pay and what producers must be offered—between marginal benefit and marginal cost.

The sum of consumer surplus and producer surplus is decreased by the amount of the grey triangle in Fig. 6.7(a). This triangle is called deadweight loss. **Deadweight loss** is the decrease in consumer surplus and producer surplus that results from an inefficient level of production.

The 5,000th pizza brings a benefit of $20 and costs only $10 to produce. If we don't produce this pizza, we are wasting almost $10. Similar reasoning applies all the way up to the 9,999th pizza. By producing more pizza and less of other goods and services, we get more value from our resources.

The deadweight loss is borne by the entire society. It is not a loss for the consumers and a gain for the producer. It is a *social* loss.

FIGURE 6.7

Underproduction and Overproduction

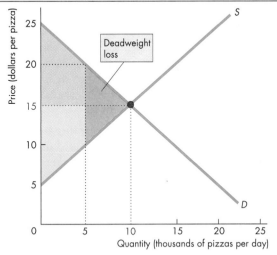

(a) Underproduction

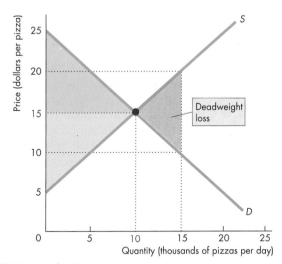

(b) Overproduction

If pizza production is restricted to 5,000 a day, a deadweight loss (the grey triangle) arises. Consumer surplus and producer surplus are reduced to the green and blue areas. At 5,000 pizzas, the benefit of one more pizza exceeds its cost. The same is true for all levels of production up to 10,000 pizzas a day. If production increases to 15,000, a deadweight loss arises. At 15,000 pizzas a day, the cost of the 15,000th pizza exceeds its benefit. The cost of each pizza above 10,000 exceeds its benefit. Consumer surplus plus producer surplus equals the green and blue areas minus the deadweight loss.

Overproduction

Suppose the pizza lobby gets the government to pay the pizza producers a fat subsidy and that production increases to 15,000 a day. Figure 6.7(b) shows that at this quantity, consumers are willing to pay only $10 for that marginal pizza but the opportunity cost of that pizza is $20. It now costs more to produce the marginal pizza than consumers are willing to pay for it. The gap gets smaller as production approaches 10,000 pizzas a day, but it is present at all quantities greater than 10,000 a day.

Again, the grey triangle shows the deadweight loss. The sum of consumer surplus and producer surplus is smaller than its maximum by the amount of deadweight loss. The 15,000th pizza brings a benefit of $10 but costs $20 to produce. If we produce this pizza, we are wasting almost $10. Similar reasoning applies all the way down to the 10,001st pizza. By producing less pizza and more of other goods and services, we get more value from our resources.

REVIEW QUIZ

- Do competitive markets use resources efficiently? Explain why or why not.
- Do markets with a price ceiling or price floor, taxes, subsidies, or quotas, monopoly power, public goods, or externalities result in the quantity produced being the efficient quantity? Explain.
- What is deadweight loss and in what conditions does it occur?
- Does a deadweight loss occur in a competitive market when the quantity produced equals the competitive equilibrium quantity and the resource allocation is efficient? Explain why or why not.

You now know the conditions under which the resource allocation is efficient. You've seen how a competitive market can be efficient, and you've seen some impediments to efficiency. But is an efficient allocation of resources fair? Does the competitive market provide people with fair incomes for their work? And do people always pay a fair price for the things they buy? Don't we need the government to step into some competitive markets to prevent the price from rising too high or falling too low? Let's now study these questions.

Is the Competitive Market Fair?

WHEN A NATURAL DISASTER STRIKES, SUCH AS A severe winter storm or a hurricane, the prices of many essential items jump. The reason the prices jump is that some people have a greater demand and greater willingness to pay while the items are in limited supply. So the higher prices achieve an efficient allocation of scarce resources. News reports of these price hikes almost never talk about efficiency. Instead, they talk about fairness, or more particularly, unfairness. The claim is that it is unfair for profit-seeking dealers to cheat the victims of natural disaster.

Similarly, when low-skilled people work for a wage that is below what most would regard as a "living wage," the media and politicians talk of employers taking unfair advantage of their workers.

How do we decide if something is fair or unfair? You know when *you* think something is unfair. But how do you know? What are the *principles* of fairness?

Philosophers have tried for centuries to answer this question. Economists have offered their answers too. But before we look at the proposed answers, you should know that there is no universally agreed answer.

Economists agree about efficiency. That is, they agree that it makes sense to make the economic pie as large as possible and to bake it at the lowest possible cost. But they do not agree about fairness. That is, they do not agree about what are fair shares of the economic pie for all the people who make it. The reason is that ideas about fairness are not exclusively economic ideas. They touch on politics, ethics, and religion. Nevertheless, economists have thought about these issues and have a contribution to make. So let's examine the views of economists on this topic.

To think about fairness, think of economic life as a game—a serious game. All ideas about fairness can be divided into two broad groups. They are:

■ It's not fair if the *result* isn't fair
■ It's not fair if the *rules* aren't fair

It's Not Fair If the *Result* Isn't Fair

The earliest efforts to establish a principle of fairness were based on the view that the result is what matters. And the idea was that it is unfair if people's incomes are too unequal. It is unfair that bank chairpersons

earn millions of dollars a year while bank tellers earn only thousands of dollars a year. It is unfair that a storeowner enjoys a larger profit and her customers pay higher prices in the aftermath of a winter storm.

There was a lot of excitement during the nineteenth century when economists thought they had made the incredible discovery that equality of incomes was not only fair, but also efficient. If the economic pie is shared equally, it will be the largest it can possibly be. This idea turns out to be wrong, but there is a lesson in the reason that it is wrong. So this nineteenth century idea is worth a closer look.

Utilitarianism The nineteenth century idea that equality is both fair and efficient is called utilitarianism. **Utilitarianism** is a principle that states that we should strive to achieve "the greatest happiness for the greatest number." The people who developed this idea were known as utilitarians. They included the most eminent minds such as David Hume, Adam Smith, Jeremy Bentham, and John Stuart Mill.

Utilitarians argued that to achieve "the greatest happiness for the greatest number," income must be transferred from the rich to the poor up to the point of complete equality—to the point that there are no rich and no poor.

They reasoned in the following way: First, everyone has the same basic wants and a similar capacity to enjoy life. Second, the greater a person's income, the smaller is the marginal benefit of a dollar. The millionth dollar spent by a rich person brings a smaller marginal benefit to that person than the marginal benefit of the thousandth dollar spent by a poorer person. So by transferring a dollar from the millionaire to the poorer person, more is gained than is lost and the two people added together are better off.

Figure 6.8 illustrates this utilitarian idea. Tom and Jerry each have the same marginal benefit curve, *MB*. (Marginal benefit is measured on the same scale of 1 to 3 for both Tom and Jerry.) Tom is at point *a*. He earns $5,000 a year and his marginal benefit of a dollar of income is 3. Jerry is at point *b*. He earns $45,000 a year and his marginal benefit of a dollar of income is 1. If a dollar is transferred from Jerry to Tom, Jerry loses 1 unit of marginal benefit and Tom gains 3 units. So if we take Tom and Jerry together, they are better off. They are sharing the economic pie more efficiently. If a second dollar is transferred, the same thing happens: Tom gains more than Jerry loses. And the same is true for every dollar transferred until they each reach point *c*. At point *c*, Tom and Jerry

FIGURE 6.8
Utilitarian Fairness

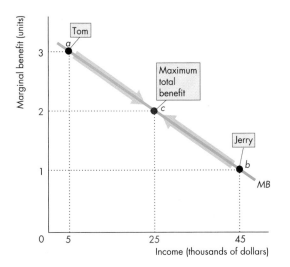

Tom earns $5,000 and has 3 units of marginal benefit at point a. Jerry earns $45,000 and has 1 unit of marginal benefit at point b. If income is transferred from Jerry to Tom, Jerry's loss is less than Tom's gain. Only when each of them has $25,000 and 2 units of marginal benefit (at point c) can the sum of their total benefit increase no further.

each have $25,000 and each have a marginal benefit of 2 units. Now they are sharing the economic pie in the most efficient way. It is bringing the greatest attainable happiness to Tom and Jerry together.

The Big Tradeoff A big problem with the utilitarian ideal of complete equality is that it ignores the costs of making income transfers. Recognizing the cost of making income transfers leads to what is called "the **big tradeoff**," which is a tradeoff between efficiency and fairness.

The big tradeoff is based on the following facts. Income can be transferred from people with high incomes to people with low incomes only by taxing incomes. Taxing people's income from employment makes them work less. It results in the quantity of labour being less than the efficient quantity. Taxing people's income from capital makes them save less. It results in the quantity of capital being less than the efficient quantity. With smaller quantities of both labour and capital, the quantity of goods and services produced is less than the efficient quantity. The economic pie shrinks.

The tradeoff is between the size of the economic pie and the degree of equality with which it is shared. The greater the amount of income redistribution through income taxes, the greater is the inefficiency—the smaller is the economic pie.

There is a second source of inefficiency. A dollar taken from a rich person does not end up as a dollar in the hands of a poorer person. Some of it is spent on administration of the tax and transfer system. The cost of tax-collecting agencies, such as Revenue Canada, and welfare-administering agencies, such as Health Canada and the provincial government welfare departments, must be paid with some of the taxes collected. Also, taxpayers hire accountants, auditors, and lawyers to help them ensure that they pay the correct amount of tax. These activities use skilled labour and capital resources that could otherwise be used to produce goods and services that people value.

You can see that when all these costs are taken into account, transferring a dollar from a rich person does not give a dollar to a poor person. It is even possible that with high taxes, those with low incomes end up being worse off. Suppose, for example, that highly taxed entrepreneurs decide to work less hard and shut down some of their businesses. Low-income workers get fired and must seek other, perhaps even lower-paid, work.

Because of the big tradeoff, those who say that fairness is equality propose a modified version of utilitarianism.

Make the Poorest As Well Off As Possible A Harvard philosopher, John Rawls, proposed a modified version of utilitarianism in a classic book entitled *A Theory of Justice*, published in 1971. Rawls says that, taking all the costs of income transfers into account, the fair distribution of the economic pie is the one that makes the poorest person as well off as possible. The incomes of rich people should be taxed and, after paying the costs of administering the tax and transfer system, what is left should be transferred to the poor. But the taxes must not be so high that they make the economic pie shrink to the point that the poorest person ends up with a smaller piece of pie. A bigger share of a smaller pie can be less than a smaller share of a bigger pie. The goal is to make the piece of pie enjoyed by the poorest person as big as possible. Most likely this piece will not be an equal share.

The "fair results" ideas require a change in the results after the game is over. Some economists say these changes are themselves unfair and propose a different way of thinking about fairness.

It's Not Fair If the *Rules* Aren't Fair

The idea that it's not fair if the rules aren't fair is based on a fundamental principle that seems to be hard wired into the human brain. It is the symmetry principle. The **symmetry principle** is the requirement that people in similar situations be treated similarly. It is the moral principle that lies at the centre of all the big religions and that says, in some form or other, "behave towards other people in the way you expect them to behave towards you."

In economic life, this principle translates into *equality of opportunity*. But equality of opportunity to do what? This question is answered by another Harvard philosopher, Robert Nozick, in a book entitled *Anarchy, State, and Utopia*, published in 1974.

Nozick argues that the idea of fairness as an outcome or result cannot work and that fairness must be based on the fairness of the rules. He suggests that fairness obeys two rules:

1. The state must enforce laws that establish and protect private property.
2. Private property may be transferred from one person to another only by voluntary exchange.

The first rule says that everything that is valuable must be owned by individuals and that the state must ensure that theft is prevented. The second rule says that the only legitimate way a person can acquire property is to buy it in exchange for something else that the person owns. If these rules, which are the only fair rules, are followed, the result is fair. It doesn't matter how unequally the economic pie is shared provided it is baked by people each one of whom voluntarily provides services in exchange for the share of the pie offered in compensation.

These rules satisfy the symmetry principle. And if these rules are not followed, the symmetry principle is broken. You can see these facts by imagining a world in which the laws are not followed.

First, suppose that some resources or goods are not owned. They are common property. Then everyone is free to participate in a grab to use these resources or goods. The strongest will prevail. But when the strongest prevails, the strongest effectively *owns* the resources or goods in question and prevents others from enjoying them.

Second, suppose that we do not insist on voluntary exchange for transferring ownership of resources from one person to another. The alternative is *involuntary transfer*. In simple language, the alternative is theft.

Both of these situations violate the symmetry principle. Only the strong get to acquire what they want. The weak end up with only the resources and goods that the strong don't want.

In contrast, if the two rules of fairness are followed, everyone, strong and weak, is treated in a similar way. Individuals are free to use their resources and human skills to create things that are valued by themselves and others and to exchange the fruits of their efforts with each other. This is the only set of arrangements that obeys the symmetry principle.

Fairness and Efficiency If private property rights are enforced and if voluntary exchange takes place in a competitive market, resources will be allocated efficiently if there are no:

- Price ceilings and price floors
- Taxes, subsidies, and quotas
- Monopolies
- Public goods
- External costs and external benefits

According to the Nozick rules, the resulting distribution of income and wealth will be fair. Let's study a concrete example to examine the claim that if resources are allocated efficiently, they are also allocated fairly.

A Price Hike in a Natural Disaster An earthquake has broken the pipes that deliver drinking water to a city. The price of bottled water jumps from $1 to $8 a bottle in the 30 or so shops that have water for sale.

First, let's agree that the water is being used *efficiently*. There is a fixed amount of bottled water in the city and given the quantity available, some people are willing to pay $8 to get a bottle. The water goes to the people who value it most highly. Consumer surplus and producer surplus are maximized.

So the water resources are being used efficiently. But are they being used fairly? Shouldn't people who can't afford to pay $8 a bottle get some of the available water for a lower price that they can afford? Isn't the fair solution for the shops to sell the water for a lower price that people can afford? Or perhaps it might be fairer if the government bought the water and then made it available to people through a government store at a "reasonable" price. Let's think about these alternative solutions to the water problem of this city.

The first answer that jumps into your mind is that the water should somehow be made available at a more reasonable price. But is this the correct answer?

Shop Offers Water for $5   Suppose that Chip, a shop owner, offers water at $5 a bottle. Who will buy it? There are two types of buyers. Chuck is an example of one type. He values water at $8—is willing to pay $8 a bottle. Recall that given the quantity of water available, the equilibrium price is $8 a bottle. If Chuck buys the water for $5, he consumes it. Chuck ends up with a consumer surplus of $3 on the bottle and Chip receives $3 *less* of producer surplus.

Mitch is an example of the second type of buyer. Mitch would not pay $8 for a bottle. In fact, he wouldn't even pay $5 to consume a bottle of water. But he buys a bottle for $5. Why? He plans to sell the water to someone who is willing to pay $8 to consume it. When Mitch buys the water, Chip again receives a producer surplus of $3 *less* than he would receive if he charged the going market price. Mitch now becomes a water dealer. He sells the water for the going price of $8 and earns a producer surplus of $3.

So by being public spirited and offering water for less than the market price, Chip ends up $3 a bottle worse off and the buyers end up $3 a bottle better off. In both situations, the same people consume the water—those who value it at $8 a bottle. But the distribution of consumer surplus and producer surplus is different in the two cases. When Chip sells water for $5 a bottle, he gets a smaller producer surplus, Chuck gets a larger consumer surplus, and Mitch gets a larger producer surplus.

So which arrangement is fair? The one that favours Chip or the one that favours Chuck and Mitch? The fair-rules view is that both arrangements are fair. Chip voluntarily sells the water for $5, so in effect, he is helping the community to cope with its water problem. It is fair that he should help. But the choice is his. He owns the water. It is not fair that he should be compelled to help.

Government Buys Water   Now suppose instead that the government buys all the water. The going price is $8 a bottle, so that's what the government pays. Now they offer the water for sale for $1 a bottle, its "normal" price. The quantity of water supplied is exactly the same as before. But now, at $1 a bottle, the quantity demanded is much larger than the quantity supplied. There is a shortage of water.

Because there is a large water shortage, the government decides to ration the amount that anyone may buy to one bottle. So everyone lines up to collect his or her bottle. Two of these people are Chuck and Mitch. Chuck, you'll recall, is willing to pay $8 a

bottle. Mitch is willing to pay less than $5. But they both get a bargain. Chuck drinks his $1 bottle and enjoys a $7 consumer surplus. What does Mitch do? Does he drink his bottle? He does not. He sells it to someone who values the water at $8. And he enjoys a $7 producer surplus from his temporary water trading business.

So the people who value the water most highly consume it. But the consumer and producer surpluses are distributed in a different way from what the free market would have delivered. Again, the question arises, which arrangement is fair?

The main difference between the government scheme and Chip's private charitable contributions lies in the fact that to buy the water for $8 and sell it for $1, the government must tax someone $7 for each bottle sold. So whether this arrangement is fair depends on whether the taxes are fair.

Taxes are an involuntary transfer of private property, so according to the fair-rules view, they are unfair. But most economists, and most other people, think that there is such a thing as a fair tax. So it seems that the fair-rules view needs to be weakened a bit. Agreeing that there is such a thing as a fair tax is the easy part. Agreeing on what is a fair tax brings endless disagreement and debate.

R E V I E W   Q U I Z

- What are the two big approaches to fairness?
- Explain the utilitarian idea of fairness and what is wrong with it.
- Explain the big tradeoff and the idea of fairness developed to deal with it.
- What is the main idea of fairness based on fair rules? Explain your answer.

◆ You've now studied the two biggest issues that run right through the whole of economics: efficiency and equity, or fairness. In the next chapter, we study some sources of inefficiency and unfairness. And at many points throughout this book—and in your life—you will return to and use the ideas about efficiency and equity that you've learned in this chapter. *Reading Between the Lines* on pp. 124–125 looks at an example of an inefficiency, and some would argue an inequity, in our economy today.

Inefficiency in Software

THE FINANCIAL POST, JANUARY 18, 1997

Microsoft earnings beat predictions

SEATTLE—Microsoft Corp. said Friday it earned US$741 million in its latest quarter, up sharply from year-before results, but the software giant warned of slower earnings growth in the next fiscal year.

The second-quarter earnings, equal to US57¢ a share, compared with US$575 million (US45¢ a share) in the year-ago quarter.

The results for the quarter ended Dec. 31 beat analysts' forcasts. Wall Street on average had expected Microsoft to report earnings equal to US51¢ a share for the quarter, with estimates ranging from US47¢ to US55¢.

Analysts had said results in that range would be impressive considering that Microsoft had no major new products in the quarter and was up against difficult comparisons with the year-earlier period, which was the first full quarter that its Windows 95 operating system was available. …

"The company performed solidly in all of our businesses, including operating systems, desktop applications, enterprise software, tools, hardware and content," Microsoft chief financial officer Mike Brown said. …

Essence of the Story

■ In January 1997, Microsoft reported earnings for the quarter ended December 31, 1996, that exceeded Wall Street analysts' expectations.

■ Profits were also up on the same quarter of the previous year.

■ Microsoft earned solid profits on all its lines of business.

Economic Analysis

■ Figure 1 shows the demand curve for Windows 95, labelled *D*. The demand curve is also the marginal benefit curve, so it is also labelled *MB*. It tells us the value to users of one more copy of Windows 95.

■ Figure 1 also shows Microsoft's marginal cost curve, *MC*, for producing Windows 95. The curve has a gentle slope, which reflects the assumption that the marginal cost of software does not increase by much as the quantity produced increases.

■ If Windows 95 was produced in a competitive market, the marginal cost curve would also be a supply curve. In this case, equilibrium would occur at point *a*, where the demand curve and the supply curve intersect.

■ At point *a*, production is efficient—marginal benefit equals marginal cost.

■ The consumer surplus arising from Windows 95 is shown by the green area. The producer surplus arising from Windows 95 is shown by the blue area.

■ But Microsoft does not produce at point *a*. Instead, it produces at point *b* in Fig. 2.

■ Microsoft knows that it can make a bigger profit by reducing its output and charging a higher price.

■ By reducing output to Q_b, Microsoft can raise the price of Windows 95 to $90 per unit.

■ Point *b* is good for Microsoft but it is inefficient. Marginal benefit exceeds marginal cost and a deadweight loss arises, as shown by the grey area.

■ With the higher price and smaller quantity at point *b*, Microsoft's producer surplus is greater than at point *a*. But consumer surplus is smaller. And the decrease in consumer surplus is larger than the increase in producer surplus by the size of the deadweight loss.

■ The reason why Microsoft's earnings were greater than expected is that the demand for Windows 95 was greater than Wall Street analysts expected. The demand was greater than expected because the marginal benefit from Windows 95 exceeded expectations.

■ The increase in the marginal benefit arose most likely from the lower cost of computers and the availability of more highly valued applications.

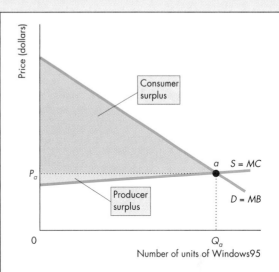

Figure 1 Efficient quantity

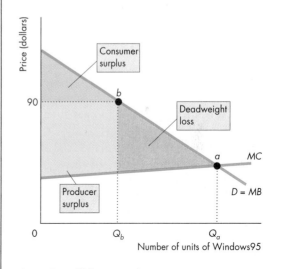

Figure 2 Inefficient quantity

SUMMARY

Key Points

Efficiency: A Refresher (pp. 110–111)

- The marginal benefit received from a good or service—the benefit of consuming one additional unit—is the *value* of the good or service to its consumers.
- The marginal cost of a good or service—the cost of producing one additional unit—is the *opportunity cost* of one more unit to its producers.
- Resources allocation is efficient when marginal benefit equals marginal cost.
- If marginal benefit exceeds marginal cost, an increase in production uses resources more efficiently.
- If marginal cost exceeds marginal benefit, a decrease in production uses resources more efficiently.

Value, Price, and Consumer Surplus (pp. 112–113)

- Marginal benefit is measured by the maximum price that consumers are willing to pay for a good or service.
- Marginal benefit determines demand, and a demand curve is a marginal benefit curve.
- Value is what people are *willing to* pay; price is what people *must* pay.
- Consumer surplus equals value minus price, summed over the quantity consumed.

Cost, Price, and Producer Surplus (pp. 114–115)

- Marginal cost is measured by the minimum price producers must be offered to increase production by one unit.
- Marginal cost determines supply, and a supply curve is a marginal cost curve.
- Opportunity cost is what producers pay; price is what producers receive.
- Producer surplus equals price minus opportunity cost, summed over the quantity produced.

Is the Competitive Market Efficient? (pp. 116–117)

- In a competitive equilibrium, marginal benefit equals marginal cost and resource allocation is efficient.

Obstacles to Efficiency (pp. 117–119)

- Monopoly restricts production and creates deadweight loss.
- A competitive market provides too small a quantity of public goods because of the free-rider problem.
- A competitive market provides too large a quantity of goods and services that have external costs and too small a quantity of goods and services that have external benefits.

Is the Competitive Market Fair? (pp. 120–123)

- Ideas about fairness divide into two groups: fair *results* or fair *rules*.
- Fair-results ideas require income transfers from the rich to the poor.
- Fair-rules ideas require property rights and voluntary exchange.

Key Figures

Key Terms

Price (dollars per sandwich)	Quantity demanded (sandwiches per hour)	Quantity supplied (sandwiches per hour)
0	400	0
1	350	50
2	300	100
3	250	150
4	200	200
5	150	250
6	100	300
7	50	350
8	0	400

PROBLEMS

*1. The figure shows the demand for and supply of floppy disks.

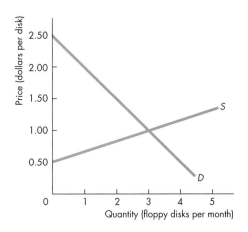

a. What are the equilibrium price and equilibrium quantity of floppy disks?
b. What is the consumer surplus?
c. What is the producer surplus?
d. What is the efficient quantity of floppy disks?

2. The figure shows the demand for and supply of cans of beans.

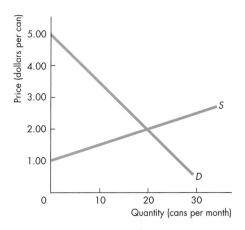

a. What are the equilibrium price and equilibrium quantity of cans of beans?
b. What is the consumer surplus?
c. What is the producer surplus?
d. What is the efficient quantity of beans?

☐ *3. The table gives the demand and supply schedules for sandwiches.

a. What is the maximum price that consumers are willing to pay for the 250th sandwich?
b. What is the minimum price that producers are willing to accept for the 250th sandwich?
c. Are 250 sandwiches an hour less than or greater than the efficient quantity?
d. What is the consumer surplus if the efficient quantity of sandwiches is produced?
e. What is the producer surplus if the efficient quantity of sandwiches is produced?
f. What is the deadweight loss if 250 sandwiches are produced?

4. The table gives the demand and supply schedules for spring water.

Price (dollars per bottle)	Quantity demanded (bottles per day)	Quantity supplied (bottles per day)
0	80	0
0.50	70	10
1.00	60	20
1.50	50	30
2.00	40	40
2.50	30	50
3.00	20	60
3.50	10	70
4.00	0	80

a. What is the maximum price that consumers are willing to pay for the 30th bottle?
b. What is the minimum price that producers are willing to accept for the 30th bottle?
c. Are 30 bottles a day less than or greater than the efficient quantity?
d. What is the consumer surplus if the efficient quantity of spring water is produced?

e. What is the producer surplus if the efficient quantity of spring water is produced?
f. What is the deadweight loss if 30 bottles are produced?

*5. The table gives the demand and supply schedules for train travel for Ben, Beth, and Bo.

Price (cents per passenger kilometre)	Quantity demanded (passenger kilometres)		
	Ben	**Beth**	**Bo**
10	500	300	60
20	450	250	50
30	400	200	40
40	350	150	30
50	300	100	20
60	250	50	10
70	200	0	0

a. If the price of train travel is 40 cents a passenger kilometre, what is the consumer surplus of each traveller?
b. Which traveller has the largest consumer surplus? Explain why.
c. If the price of train travel rises to 50 cents a passenger kilometre, what is the change in consumer surplus of each traveller?

6. The table gives the demand and supply schedules for bus travel for Joe, Jean, and Joy.

Price (cents per passenger kilometre)	Quantity demanded (passenger kilometres)		
	Joe	**Jean**	**Joy**
10	50	600	300
20	45	500	250
30	40	400	200
40	35	300	150
50	30	200	100
60	25	100	50
70	20	0	0

a. If the price of train travel is 50 cents a passenger kilometre, what is the consumer surplus of each passenger?
b. Which passenger has the largest consumer surplus? Explain why.
c. If the price of train travel falls to 30 cents a passenger kilometre, what is the change in consumer surplus of each passenger?

CRITICAL THINKING

1. Study *Reading Between the Lines* on pp. 124–125 on Microsoft and then answer the following questions:
   a. Is the quantity of Microsoft software greater than, less than, or equal to the efficient quantity? Explain your answer by using the concepts of marginal benefit, marginal cost, price, consumer surplus, and producer surplus.
   b. What, if anything, do you think could be done to increase the quantity of software and decrease its price?
   c. Microsoft sells copies of its programs in campus software stores at a huge educational discount. Does this practice increase or decrease consumer surplus? Does it increase or decrease Microsoft's producer surplus? Does it bring the quantity of software closer to the efficient quantity? Explain your answer by using the concepts of marginal benefit, marginal cost, price, consumer surplus, and producer surplus.
   d. Chinese software producers have been accused of making illegal copies of Microsoft products and selling them at much lower prices than Microsoft's own price. Does this practice increase or decrease consumer surplus? Does it increase or decrease Microsoft's producer surplus? Does it bring the quantity of software closer to the efficient quantity? Explain your answer by using the concepts of marginal benefit, marginal cost, price, consumer surplus, and producer surplus.

2. Use the link on the Parkin-Bade Web site to visit Agriculture and Agri-Food Canada and obtain information on the Agricultural Income Disaster Assistance (AIDA) program. Describe the main provisions of the program and explain why you think the program is efficient or inefficient, and fair or unfair.

3. How would you set about determining whether the allocation of your time between studying different subjects is efficient? In what units would you measure marginal benefit and marginal cost? Explain your answer by using the concepts of marginal benefit, marginal cost, price, consumer surplus, and producer surplus.

Chapter 7

Markets in Action

In 1906, San Francisco suffered a devastating earthquake that destroyed more than half the city's homes but killed few people. How did the people of San Francisco cope with this enormous shock? Did rents have to be controlled to keep housing affordable? Were scarce housing resources allocated to their highest-valued uses? ◆ Almost every day, a new machine is invented that saves labour and increases productivity. How do labour markets cope with labour-saving technological change? Does decreasing demand for low-skilled labour drive wages lower and lower? Do we need minimum wage laws to prevent wages from falling?

Turbulent Times

Do minimum wages enable us to use labour efficiently? ◆ Almost everything we buy is taxed. How do taxes affect the prices? Do they increase by the full amount of the tax so that we, the buyers, pay all the tax? Or does the seller pay part of the tax? Do taxes help or hinder the market in its attempt to move resources to where they are valued most highly? ◆ Trade in items such as drugs, automatic firearms, and enriched uranium is illegal. What are the effects of laws that make trading in a good or service illegal on the amounts of such items consumed? And how do such laws affect the prices paid by those who trade illegally? ◆ In 1991, ideal conditions brought high grain yields. But in 1996, crops were devastated by drought and grain yields were low. How do farm prices and revenues react to such output fluctuations? And how do the actions of speculators and farm marketing boards influence farm revenues?

◆ In this chapter, we study a variety of markets. We use the theory of demand and supply (Chapter 4) and the concepts of elasticity (Chapter 5) and efficiency (Chapter 6) to answer the questions just posed. We're going to begin by studying two markets that have the biggest impacts on our lives: the housing market and the labour market. Because these markets are so vital to the economic welfare of everyone, governments often intervene in them to try to control prices. They impose rent ceilings and minimum wages. To set the scene for each, we're going to see how a market responds to turbulent events.

After studying this chapter, you will be able to:

- Explain how housing markets work and how price ceilings create housing shortages and inefficiency

- Explain how labour markets work and how minimum wage laws create unemployment and inefficiency

- Explain the effects of the sales tax

- Explain how markets for illegal goods work

- Explain why farm prices and revenues fluctuate

- Explain how speculation limits price fluctuations

- Explain how farm marketing boards influence prices, quantities produced, and farm revenues

Housing Markets and Rent Ceilings

To SEE HOW A MARKET COPES WITH A SUPPLY shock, let's transport ourselves to San Francisco in April 1906, as the city is suffering from a massive earthquake and fire. You can sense the enormity of San Francisco's problems by reading a headline from the *New York Times* on the first days of the crisis. On April 19, 1906:

Over 500 Dead, $200,000,000 Lost in San Francisco Earthquake
Nearly Half the City Is in Ruins and 50,000 Are Homeless

The commander of federal troops in charge of the emergency described the magnitude of the problem:

> Not a hotel of note or importance was left standing. The great apartment houses had vanished . . . two hundred-and-twenty-five thousand people were . . . homeless.[1]

Almost overnight, more than half the people in a city of 400,000 had lost their homes. Temporary shelters and camps alleviated some of the problem, but it was also necessary to utilize the apartment buildings and houses left standing. As a consequence, they had to accommodate 40 percent more people than they had before the earthquake.

The *San Francisco Chronicle* was not published for more than a month after the earthquake. When the newspaper reappeared on May 24, 1906, the city's housing shortage—what would seem to be a major news item that would still be of grave importance—was not mentioned. Milton Friedman and George Stigler describe the situation:

> *There is not a single mention of a housing shortage!* The classified advertisements listed sixty-four offers of flats and houses for rent, and nineteen of houses for sale, against five advertisements of flats or houses wanted. Then and thereafter a considerable number of all types of accommodation except hotel rooms were offered for rent.[2]

How did San Francisco cope with such a devastating reduction in the supply of housing?

---

[1]Reported in Milton Friedman and George J. Stigler, "Roofs or Ceilings? The Current Housing Problem," in *Popular Essays on Current Problems*, vol. 1, no. 2 (New York: Foundation for Economic Education, 1946), 3–159.
[2]*Ibid*, 3.

The Market Response to a Decrease in Supply

Figure 7.1 shows the market for housing in San Francisco. The demand curve for housing is *D*. There is a short-run supply curve, labelled *SS*, and a long-run supply curve, labelled *LS*.

The short-run supply curve shows the change in the quantity of housing supplied as the rent changes while the number of houses and apartment buildings remains constant. The short-run supply response arises from changes in the intensity with which existing buildings are used. The quantity of housing supplied increases if families rent out rooms that they previously used themselves, and it decreases if families use rooms that they previously rented out to others.

The long-run supply curve shows how the quantity of housing supplied responds to a change in price after enough time has elapsed for new apartment buildings and houses to be erected or for existing ones to be destroyed. In Fig. 7.1, the long-run supply curve is *perfectly elastic*. We do not actually know that the long-run supply curve is perfectly elastic, but it is a reasonable assumption. It implies that the cost of building an apartment is pretty much the same regardless of whether there are 50,000 or 150,000 apartments in existence.

The equilibrium price (rent) and quantity are determined at the point of intersection of the *short-run* supply curve and the demand curve. Before the earthquake, the equilibrium rent is $16 a month and the quantity is 100,000 units of housing.

Figure 7.1(a) shows the situation immediately after the earthquake. The destruction of buildings decreases the supply of housing and shifts the short-run supply curve *SS* leftward to *SS_A*. If the rent remains at $16 a month, only 44,000 units of housing are available. But with only 44,000 units of housing available, the maximum rent that someone is willing to pay for the last available apartment is $24 a month. So rents rise. In Fig. 7.1(a), the rent rises to $20 a month.

As the rent rises, the quantity of housing demanded decreases and the quantity supplied increases to 72,000 units. These changes occur because people economize on their use of space and make spare rooms, attics, and basements available to others. The higher rent allocates the scarce housing to those people who value it most highly and are willing to pay most for it.

But the higher rent has other, long-run effects. Let's look at these long-run effects.

FIGURE 7.1

The San Francisco
Housing Market in 1906

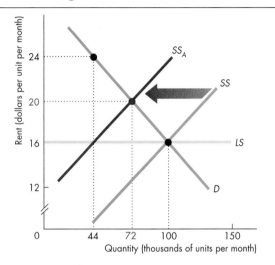

(a) After earthquake

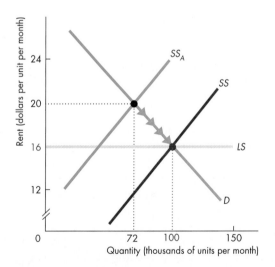

(b) Long-run adjustment

Part (a) shows that before the earthquake 100,000 housing units were rented at $16 a month. After the earthquake, the short-run supply curve shifts from SS to SS_A. The rent rises to $20 a month, and the quantity of housing decreases to 72,000 units. With rent at $20 a month, there is profit in building new apartments and houses. As the building program proceeds, the short-run supply curve shifts rightward (part b). The rent gradually falls to $16 a month, and the quantity of housing increases to 100,000 units—as the arrowed line shows.

Long-Run Adjustments With sufficient time for new apartments and houses to be constructed, supply increases. The long-run supply curve tells us that in the long run, housing is supplied at a rent of $16 a month. Because the rent of $20 a month exceeds the long-run supply price, there is a building boom. Apartments and houses are built, and the short-run supply curve shifts gradually rightward.

Figure 7.1(b) shows the long-run adjustment. As more housing is built, the short-run supply curve shifts rightward and intersects the demand curve at lower rents and larger quantities. The market equilibrium follows the arrows down the demand curve. When the process ends, there is no further profit in building. The rent is back at $16 a month, and 100,000 units of housing are available.

We've just seen how a housing market responds to a decrease in supply. And we've seen that a key part of the adjustment process is a rise in the rent. Suppose the government passes a law to stop the rent from rising. What happens then?

A Regulated Housing Market

We're now going to study the effects of a price ceiling in the housing market. A **price ceiling** is a regulation that makes it illegal to charge a price higher than a specified level. When a price ceiling is applied to housing markets, it is called a **rent ceiling**. How does a rent ceiling affect the housing market?

The effect of a price (rent) ceiling depends on whether it is imposed at a level that is above or below the equilibrium price (rent). A price ceiling set above the equilibrium price has no effect. The reason is that the price ceiling does not constrain the market forces. The force of the law and the market forces are not in conflict. But a price ceiling below the equilibrium price has powerful effects on a market. The reason is that it attempts to prevent the price from regulating the quantities demanded and supplied. The force of the law and the market forces are in conflict, and one (or both) of these forces must yield to some degree. Let's study the effects of a price ceiling set below the equilibrium price by returning to San Francisco. What would have happened in San Francisco if a rent ceiling of $16 a month—the rent before the earthquake—had been imposed?

Figure 7.2 enables us to answer this question. At a rent of $16 a month, the quantity of housing supplied is 44,000 units and the quantity demanded is

FIGURE 7.2

A Rent Ceiling

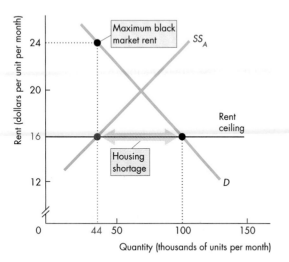

If there had been a rent ceiling of $16 a month, then the quantity of housing supplied after the earthquake would have been stuck at 44,000 units. People would willingly have paid $24 a month for the 44,000th unit. Because the last unit of housing available is worth more than the rent ceiling, frustrated renters will spend time searching for housing and frustrated renters and landlords will make deals in a black market.

100,000 units. So there is a shortage of 56,000 units of housing.

But the story does not end here. Somehow, the 44,000 units of available housing must be allocated among people who demand 100,000 units. How is this allocation achieved? When a rent ceiling creates a housing shortage, two developments occur. They are:

■ Search activity
■ Black markets

Search Activity

The time spent looking for someone with whom to do business is called **search activity**. We spend some time in search activity almost every time we buy something. You want the latest hot CD, and you know four stores that stock it. But which store has the best deal? You need to spend a few minutes on the telephone finding out. In some markets, we

spend a lot of time searching. An example is the used car market. People spend a lot of time checking out alternative dealers and cars.

But when a price is regulated and there is a shortage, search activity increases. In the case of rent-controlled housing markets, frustrated would-be renters scan the newspapers, not only for housing ads but also for death notices! Any information about newly available housing is useful. And they race to be first on the scene when news of a possible supplier breaks.

The *opportunity cost* of a good is equal not only to its price but also to the value of the search time spent finding the good. So the opportunity cost of housing is equal to the rent (a regulated price) plus the time and other resources spent searching for the restricted quantity available. Search activity is costly. It uses time and other resources, such as telephones, cars, and gasoline that could have been used in other productive ways. A rent ceiling controls the rent portion of the cost of housing, but it does not control the opportunity cost, which might even be *higher* than the rent would be if the market were unregulated.

Black Markets

A **black market** is an illegal market in which the price exceeds the legally imposed price ceiling. Black markets occur in rent-controlled housing and scalpers run black markets in tickets for big sporting events and rock concerts.

When rent ceilings are in force, frustrated renters and landlords constantly seek ways of increasing rents. One common way is for a new tenant to pay a high price for worthless fittings, such as $2,000 for threadbare drapes. Another is for the tenant to pay an exorbitant price for new locks and keys—called "key money."

The level of a black market rent depends on how tightly the rent ceiling is enforced. With loose enforcement, the black market rent is close to the unregulated rent. But with strict enforcement, the black market rent is equal to the maximum price that renters are willing to pay.

With strict enforcement of the rent ceiling in the San Francisco example shown in Fig. 7.2, the quantity of housing available remains at 44,000 units. A small number of people offer housing for rent at $24 a month—the highest rent that someone is willing to pay—and the government detects and punishes some of these black market traders.

Inefficiency of Rent Ceilings

In an unregulated market, resources are allocated efficiently. The sum of *consumer surplus* and *producer surplus* is maximized (see Chapter 6, p. 116).

Figure 7.3 shows the inefficiency of a rent ceiling. If the rent is fixed at $16 per unit per month, 44,000 units are supplied. The producer surplus is shown by the blue triangle above the supply curve and below the rent line. Because the quantity of housing is less than the competitive quantity, there is a deadweight loss shown by the grey triangle. This loss is borne by the consumers who can't find housing and by producers who can't supply housing at the new lower price. Consumers who do find housing at the controlled rent gain. If no one incurs search cost, consumer surplus could be as large as the sum of the green triangle and the red rectangle. But consumer surplus can be smaller than this amount because in a regulated housing market, there is no guarantee that the people who find housing are those who value it most highly. The worst case outcome is that in the struggle to find homes people incur search costs that eat up the entire consumer surplus.

Equity? So rent ceilings prevent scarce resources from flowing to their highest-valued use. But don't rent ceilings ensure that scarce housing goes to the people whose need is greatest and make the allocation of scarce housing fair?

The complex ideas about fairness are explored in Chapter 6 (pp. 120–123). Blocking rent adjustments that bring the quantity of housing demanded into equality with the quantity supplied don't end scarcity. So when the law prevents rents from adjusting and blocks the price mechanism from allocating scarce housing, some other allocation mechanism must be used. One of these factors is discrimination on the basis of race, ethnicity, or sex.

Paris, New York, and Toronto are three examples of cities that have rent ceilings but the best example is New York. One consequence of New York's rent ceilings is that families that have lived in the city for a long time—including some rich and famous ones—enjoy low rents, while newcomers pay high rents for hard-to-find apartments. At the same time, landlords in rent-controlled Harlem abandon entire city blocks to rats and drug dealers.

The effects of rent ceilings have led Swedish economist Assar Lindbeck to suggest that rent ceilings are the most effective means yet for destroying cities, even more effective than the hydrogen bomb.

FIGURE 7.3
The Inefficiency of a Rent Ceiling

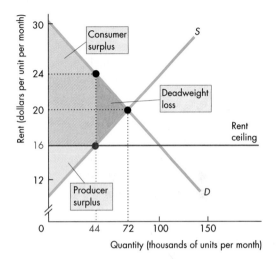

A rent ceiling of $16 a month decreases the quantity of housing supplied to 44,000 units. Producer surplus shrinks to the blue triangle and a deadweight loss (the grey triangle) arises. If people use no resources in search activity, the green triangle plus the red rectangle show consumer surplus. But people might use resources in search activity equal to the amount that they are willing to pay for available housing, the red rectangle.

REVIEW QUIZ

- How does a decrease in the supply of housing change the equilibrium rent in the short run? Who gets to consume the scarce housing resources?
- What are the long-run effects of higher rents following a decrease in the supply of housing?
- What is a rent ceiling and what are the effects of a rent ceiling set above the equilibrium rent?
- What are the effects of a rent ceiling set below the equilibrium rent?
- How do scarce housing resources get allocated when a rent ceiling is in place? Is the allocation fair?

You now know how a price ceiling (rent ceiling) works. Next, we'll learn about the effects of a price floor by studying minimum wages in the labour market.

The Labour Market and the Minimum Wage

FOR EACH ONE OF US, THE LABOUR MARKET IS the market that influences the jobs we get and the wages we earn. Firms decide how much labour to demand, and the lower the wage rate, the greater is the quantity of labour demanded. Households decide how much labour to supply, and the higher the wage rate, the greater is the quantity of labour supplied. The wage rate adjusts to make the quantity of labour demanded equal to the quantity supplied.

But the labour market is constantly hit by shocks, and wages and employment prospects constantly change. The most pervasive source of these shocks is the advance of technology.

New labour-saving technologies become available every year. As a result, the demand for some types of labour, usually the least skilled types, decreases. During the 1980s and 1990s, for example, the demand for telephone operators and television repair persons decreased. Throughout the past 200 years, the demand for low-skilled farm labourers has steadily decreased.

How does the labour market cope with this continuous decrease in the demand for low-skilled labour? Doesn't it mean that the wages of the low-skilled workers are constantly falling?

To answer these questions, we must study the market for low-skilled labour. And just like we did when we studied the housing market, we must look at both the short run and the long run.

In the short run, there are a given number of people who have a given skill, training, and experience. Short-run supply of labour describes how the number of hours of labour supplied by this given number of workers changes as the wage rate changes. To get workers to work more hours, they must be offered a higher wage rate.

In the long run, people can acquire new skills and find new types of jobs. The number of people in the low-skilled labour market depends on the wage rate in this market compared with other opportunities. If the wage rate of low-skilled labour is high enough, people will enter this market. If the wage rate is too low, people will leave it. Some will seek training to enter higher-skilled labour markets, and others will stop working and stay at home or retire.

Long-run supply of labour is the relationship between the quantity of labour supplied and the wage rate after enough time has passed for people to enter or leave the low-skilled labour market. If people can freely enter and leave the low-skilled labour market, the long-run supply of labour is *perfectly elastic*.

Figure 7.4 shows the market for low-skilled labour. Other things remaining the same, the lower the wage rate, the greater is the quantity of labour demanded by firms. The demand curve for labour, D in part (a), shows this relationship between the wage rate and the quantity of labour demanded. Other things remaining the same, the higher the wage rate, the greater is the quantity of labour supplied by households. But the longer the period of adjustment, the greater is the *elasticity of supply* of labour. The short-run supply curve is SS, and a long-run supply curve is LS. In the figure, long-run supply is assumed to be perfectly elastic (the LS curve is horizontal). This market is in equilibrium at a wage rate of $5 an hour and with 22 million hours of labour employed.

What happens if a labour-saving invention decreases the demand for low-skilled labour? Figure 7.4(a) shows the short-run effects of such a change. The demand curve before the new technology is introduced is the curve labelled D. After the introduction of the new technology, the demand curve shifts leftward to D_A. The wage rate falls to $4 an hour, and the quantity of labour employed decreases to 21 million hours. This short-run effect on the wage rate and employment is not the end of the story.

People who are now earning only $4 an hour look around for other opportunities. They see many other jobs (in markets for other types of skills) that pay more than $4 an hour. One by one, workers decide to go back to school or take jobs that pay less but offer on-the-job training. As a result, the short-run supply curve begins to shift leftward.

Figure 7.4(b) shows the long-run adjustment. As the short-run supply curve shifts leftward, it intersects the demand curve D_A at higher wage rates and lower levels of employment. The process ends when workers have no incentive to leave the market for low-skilled labour and the short-run supply curve has shifted all the way to SS_A. At this point, the wage rate has returned to $5 an hour and employment has decreased to 20 million hours a year.

Sometimes, the adjustment process that we've just described is rapid. At other times, it is slow and wages remain low for a long period. To boost the incomes of the lowest paid workers, the government intervenes in the labour market and sets the minimum wage that employers are required to pay. Let's look at the effects of the minimum wage.

FIGURE 7.4

A Market for Low-skilled Labour

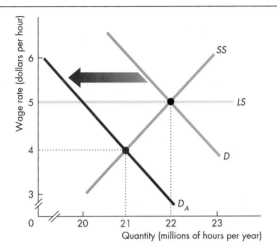

(a) After invention

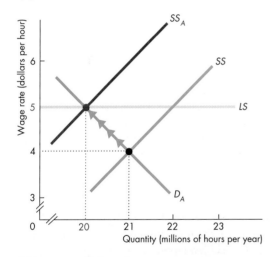

(b) Long-run adjustment

Part (a) shows the immediate effect of a labour-saving invention on the market for low-skilled labour. Initially, the wage rate is $5 an hour and 22 million hours of labour a year are employed. A labour-saving invention shifts the demand curve from D to D_A. The wage rate falls to $4 an hour, and employment decreases to 21 million hours a year. With the lower wage rate, some workers leave this market, and the short-run supply curve starts to shift gradually to SS_A (part b). The wage rate gradually increases, and the employment level decreases. In the long run, the wage rate returns to $5 an hour, and employment decreases to 20 million hours a year.

The Minimum Wage

A **price floor** is a regulation that makes it illegal to trade at a price lower than a specified level. When a price floor is applied to labour markets, it is called a **minimum wage**. If the minimum wage is set *below* the equilibrium wage, the minimum wage has no effect. The minimum wage law and market forces are not in conflict. But if a minimum wage is set *above* the equilibrium wage, the minimum wage is in conflict with the market forces and does have some effects on the labour market. Let's study these effects by returning to the market for low-skilled labour.

Suppose that with an equilibrium wage of $4 an hour (Fig. 7.4a), the government imposes a minimum wage of $5 an hour. What are the effects of this law? Figure 7.5 answers this question. It shows the minimum wage as the horizontal red line labelled "Minimum wage." At this minimum wage, 20 million hours of labour are demanded (point *a*) and 22 million hours of labour are supplied (point *b*), so 2 million hours of available labour go unemployed.

FIGURE 7.5

Minimum Wage and Unemployment

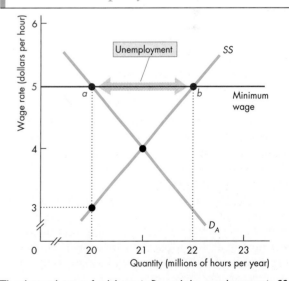

The demand curve for labour is D_A, and the supply curve is SS. In an unregulated market, the wage rate is $4 an hour and 21 million hours of labour a year are employed. If a minimum wage of $5 an hour is imposed, only 20 million hours are hired but 22 million hours are available. Unemployment—*ab*— of 2 million hours a year is created.

The Minimum Wage in Practice

The provincial governments set minimum wages in Canada. In 1999, the minimum wage rates ranged from a low of $5.25 an hour in Newfoundland to a high of $7.20 an hour in Yukon.

Figure 7.5 shows that the minimum wage brings unemployment. But how much unemployment does it bring? Economists do not agree on the answer to this question. Until recently, most economists believed that the minimum wage was a big contributor to high unemployment among low-skilled young workers. But recently this view has been challenged and the challenge rebutted.

David Card, a Canadian economist who works at the University of California at Berkeley, and Alan Krueger of Princeton University say that increases in the minimum wage have not decreased employment and created unemployment. Studying minimum wages in the United States, they say that in California, New Jersey, and Texas, the employment rate of low-income workers increased following an increase in the minimum wage. Card and Krueger suggest three reasons why higher wages might increase employment. First, workers become more conscientious and productive. Second, workers are less likely to quit, so labour turnover, which is costly, is reduced. Third, managers make a firm's operations more efficient.

Most economists are skeptical about the suggestions by Card and Krueger. They ask two questions. First, if higher wages make workers more productive and reduce labour turnover, why don't firms freely pay wage rates above the equilibrium wage to encourage more productive work habits? Second, are there other explanations for the employment responses that Card and Krueger have found?

According to Daniel Hamermesh of the University of Texas at Austin, Card and Krueger got the timing wrong and fell into the trap of the *post hoc* fallacy (described on p. 15). Hamermesh says that firms cut employment *before* the minimum wage is increased in anticipation of the increase. If he is correct, looking for the effects of an increase in the minimum wage *after* the minimum wage rate has increased misses its main effects.

Finis Welch of Texas A&M University and Kevin Murphy of the University of Chicago say the employment effects that Card and Krueger found are caused by regional differences in economic growth, not changes in the minimum wage.

One effect of the minimum wage, according to Fig. 7.5, is an increase in the quantity of labour supplied. If this effect occurs, it might show up as an increase in the number of people who quit school before completing high school. Some economists say that this response does occur.

Inefficiency of the Minimum Wage

An unregulated labour market allocates scarce labour resources to the jobs in which they are valued most highly. The minimum wage frustrates the market mechanism and results in unemployment—wasted labour resources—and an inefficient amount of job search.

In Fig. 7.5, with firms employing only 20 million hours of labour at the minimum wage, many people who are willing to supply labour are unable to get hired. You can see that the 20 millionth hour of labour is available for $3. That is, the lowest wage at which someone is willing to supply the 20 millionth hour—read off from the supply curve—is $3. Someone who manages to find a job earns $5 an hour—$2 an hour more than the lowest wage rate at which someone is willing to work. So it pays unemployed people to spend time and effort searching for one of the hard-to-find jobs.

R E V I E W   Q U I Z

- How does a decrease in the demand for low-skilled labour change the wage rate in the short run?
- What are the long-run effects of a lower wage rate for low-skilled labour?
- What is a minimum wage and what is the effect of a minimum wage that is set above the equilibrium wage?
- What is the effect of a minimum wage that is set below the equilibrium wage?

Next we're going to study a more widespread government intervention in markets: taxes, such as the provincial sales tax. We'll see how taxes change prices and quantities. We'll discover that the sales tax is not paid entirely by the consumer. And we'll see that usually a tax creates a deadweight loss.

Taxes

ALMOST EVERYTHING YOU BUY IS TAXED. BUT who really pays the tax? Because the sales tax is added to the price of a good or service when it is sold, isn't it obvious that *you*, the buyer, pay the tax? Isn't the price higher than it otherwise would be by an amount equal to the tax? It can be, but usually it isn't. And it is even possible that you actually pay none of the tax! Let's see how we can make sense of these apparently absurd statements.

Who Pays the Sales Tax?

Suppose the government puts a $10 sales tax on CD players. What are the effects of the sales tax on the price and quantity of CD players? To answer this question, we need to work out what happens to demand and supply in the market for CD players.

Figure 7.6 shows this market. The demand curve is *D*, and the supply curve is S. With no sales tax, the equilibrium price is $100 per CD player and 5,000 players are bought and sold each week.

When a good is taxed, it has two prices: a price that excludes the tax and a price that *includes* the tax. Buyers respond only to the price that includes the tax, because that is the price they pay. Sellers respond only to the price that excludes the tax, because that is the price they receive. The tax is like a wedge between these two prices.

Think of the price on the vertical axis of Fig. 7.6 as the price paid by buyers—the price that *includes* the tax. When a tax is imposed and the price changes, there is a change in the quantity demanded but no change in demand. That is, there is a movement along the demand curve and no shift of the demand curve.

But the supply changes and the supply curve shifts. The sales tax is like an increase in cost, so supply decreases and the supply curve shifts leftward to *S + tax*. To determine the position of this new supply curve, we add the tax to the minimum price that sellers are willing to accept for each quantity sold. For example, with no tax, sellers are willing to offer 5,000 players a week for $100 a player. So with a $10 tax, they will supply 5,000 players a week for $110—a price that includes the tax. The curve *S + tax* describes the terms on which sellers are willing to offer players for sale now that there is a $10 tax.

Equilibrium occurs where the new supply curve intersects the demand curve—at a price of $105 and

FIGURE 7.6

The Sales Tax

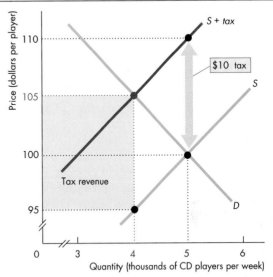

With no sales tax, 5,000 CD players a week are bought and sold at $100 each. A sales tax of $10 a CD player is imposed, and the supply curve shifts leftward to *S + tax*. In the new equilibrium, the price rises to $105 a player and the quantity decreases to 4,000 CD players a week. The sales tax raises the price by less than the tax, lowers the price received by the seller, and decreases the quantity. The sales tax brings in revenue to the government equal to the blue rectangle.

a quantity of 4,000 CD players a week. The $10 sales tax increases the price paid by the buyer by $5 a player. And it decreases the price received by the seller by $5 a player. So the buyer and the seller pay the $10 tax equally.

The tax brings in tax revenue to the government equal to the tax per item multiplied by the number of items sold. The blue area in Fig. 7.6 illustrates the tax revenue. The $10 tax on CD players brings in a tax revenue of $40,000 a week.

In this example, the buyer and the seller split the tax equally: The buyer pays $5 a player and so does the seller. This equal sharing of the tax is a special case and does not usually occur. But some sharing of the tax between the buyer and seller is usual. Also, there are other special cases in which either the buyer or the seller pays the entire tax. The division of the tax between the buyer and the seller depends on the elasticities of demand and supply.

Tax Division and Elasticity of Demand

The division of the tax between the buyer and the seller depends, in part, on the elasticity of demand. There are two extreme cases:

- Perfectly inelastic demand—buyer pays.
- Perfectly elastic demand—seller pays.

Perfectly Inelastic Demand Figure 7.7(a) shows the market for insulin, a vital daily medication of diabetics. Demand is perfectly inelastic at 100,000 doses a day, regardless of the price, as shown by the vertical curve *D*. That is, a diabetic would sacrifice all other goods and services rather than not consume the insulin dose that provides good health. The supply curve of insulin is *S*. With no tax, the price is $2 a dose and the quantity is 100,000 doses a day.

If insulin is taxed at 20¢ a dose, we must add the tax to the minimum price at which drug companies are willing to sell insulin. The result is a new supply curve *S* + *tax*. The price rises to $2.20 a dose, but the quantity does not change. The buyer pays the entire sales tax of 20¢ a dose.

Perfectly Elastic Demand Figure 7.7(b) shows the market for pink marker pens. Demand is perfectly elastic at $1 a pen as shown by the horizontal curve *D*. If pink pens are less expensive than the others, everyone uses pink. If pink pens are more expensive than the others, no one uses them. The supply curve of pink pens is *S*. With no tax, the price of a pink marker is $1, and the quantity is 4,000 pens a week.

If a sales tax of 10¢ a pen is imposed on pink marker pens, we add the tax to the minimum price at which sellers are willing to offer them for sale and the new supply curve is *S* + *tax*. The price remains at $1 a pen, and the quantity decreases to 1,000 a week. The 10¢ sales tax leaves the price paid by the buyer unchanged but lowers the amount received by the seller by the full amount of the sales tax. As a result, sellers decrease the quantity offered for sale.

We've seen that when demand is perfectly inelastic, the buyer pays the entire tax, and when demand is perfectly elastic, the seller pays it. In the usual case, demand is neither perfectly inelastic nor perfectly elastic, and the tax is split between the buyer and the seller. But the division depends on the elasticity of demand. The more inelastic the demand, the larger is the amount of the tax paid by the buyer.

FIGURE 7.7
Sales Tax and the Elasticity of Demand

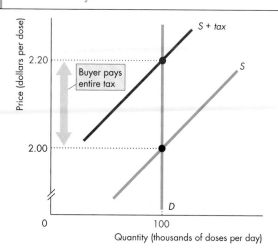

(a) Inelastic demand

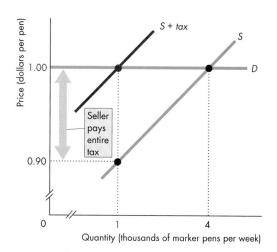

(b) Elastic demand

Part (a) shows the market for insulin, where demand is perfectly inelastic. With no tax, the price is $2 a dose and the quantity is 100,000 doses a day. A sales tax of 20¢ a dose shifts the supply curve to *S* + *tax*. The price rises to $2.20 a dose, but the quantity bought does not change. Buyers pay the entire tax. Part (b) shows the market for pink marker pens. The demand for pink pens is perfectly elastic. With no tax, the price is $1 a pen and the quantity is 4,000 pens a week. A sales tax of 10¢ a pink pen shifts the supply curve to *S* + *tax*. The price remains at $1 a pen, and the quantity of pink pens sold decreases to 1,000 a week. Sellers pay the entire tax.

Tax Division and Elasticity of Supply

The division of the tax between the buyer and the seller also depends, in part, on the elasticity of supply. Again, there are two extreme cases:

■ Perfectly inelastic supply—seller pays.
■ Perfectly elastic supply—buyer pays.

Perfectly Inelastic Supply Figure 7.8(a) shows the market for water from a spring that flows at a constant rate that can't be controlled. Supply is perfectly inelastic at 100,000 bottles a week as shown by the supply curve S. The demand curve for this spring water is D. With no tax, the price is 50¢ a bottle and the 100,000 bottles that flow from the spring are sold.

Suppose this spring water is taxed at 5¢ a bottle. The supply curve does not change because the spring owners still produce 100,000 bottles a week even though the price they receive falls. But buyers are willing to buy the 100,000 bottles only if the price is 50¢ a bottle. So the price remains at 50¢ a bottle, and the seller pays the entire tax. The sales tax reduces the price received by sellers to 45¢ a bottle.

Perfectly Elastic Supply Figure 7.8(b) shows the market for sand from which computer-chip makers extract silicon. Supply of this sand is perfectly elastic at a price of 10¢ a kilogram as shown by the supply curve S. The demand curve for sand is D. With no tax, the price is 10¢ a kilogram and 5,000 kilograms a week are bought.

If this sand is taxed at 1¢ a kilogram, we must add the tax to the minimum supply price. Sellers are now willing to offer any quantity at 11¢ a kilogram along the curve S + tax. A new equilibrium is determined where the new supply curve intersects the demand curve—at a price of 11¢ a kilogram and a quantity of 3,000 kilograms a week. The sales tax has increased the price paid by the buyer by the full amount of the tax—1¢ a kilogram—and decreased the quantity sold.

We've seen that when supply is perfectly inelastic, the seller pays the entire tax, and when supply is perfectly elastic, the buyer pays it. In the usual case, supply is neither perfectly inelastic nor perfectly elastic and the tax is split between the buyer and the seller. But the division between the buyer and the seller depends on the elasticity of supply. The more elastic the supply, the larger is the amount of the tax paid by the buyer.

FIGURE 7.8

Sales Tax and the
Elasticity of Supply

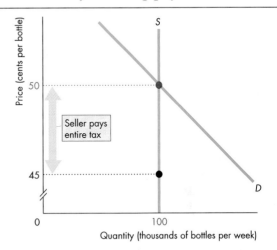

(a) Inelastic supply

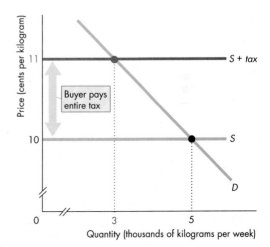

(b) Elastic supply

Part (a) shows the market for water from a mineral spring. Supply is perfectly inelastic. With no tax, the price is 50¢ a bottle. With a sales tax of 5¢ a bottle, the price remains at 50¢ a bottle. The number of bottles bought remains the same, but the price received by the seller decreases to 45¢ a bottle. The seller pays the entire tax. Part (b) shows the market for sand. Supply is perfectly elastic. With no tax, the price is 10¢ a kilogram and 5,000 kilograms a week are bought. The sales tax of 1¢ a kilogram increases the minimum supply price to 11¢ a kilogram. The supply curve shifts to S + tax. The price increases to 11¢ a kilogram. The buyer pays the entire tax.

Sales Taxes in Practice

We've looked at the range of possible effects of a sales tax by studying the extreme cases. In practice, supply and demand are rarely perfectly elastic or perfectly inelastic. They lie somewhere in between. But some items tend towards one of the extremes. For example, a heavily taxed item such as alcohol, tobacco, or gasoline has a low elasticity of demand. Consequently, the buyer pays most of the tax. Also, because demand is inelastic, the quantity bought does not decrease much and the government collects a large tax revenue. It is unusual to heavily tax an item if its demand is elastic. Such a good or service has close substitutes. If a tax is levied on such a good or service, people will reduce their purchases of the taxed good and increase their purchases of an untaxed substitute. That is, the quantity of the taxed good bought decreases by a large amount and the government will not collect much tax revenue. This explains why the items that are taxed are those that have inelastic demands and why, in practice, buyers pay most of the taxes.

Taxes and Efficiency

You've seen that a sales tax places a wedge between the price paid by buyers and the price received by sellers. The price paid by buyers is also the buyers' willingness to pay, which measures marginal benefit. And the price received by sellers is the sellers' minimum supply price, which equals marginal cost.

So, because a tax places a wedge between the buyers' price and the sellers' price, it also puts a wedge between marginal benefit and marginal cost and creates inefficiency. With a higher buying price and a lower selling price, the tax decreases the quantity produced and consumed and a deadweight loss arises. Figure 7.9 shows the inefficiency of taxes. Both the consumer surplus and producer surplus shrink. Part of each surplus goes to the government in tax revenue—the light blue area in the figure. And part of each surplus becomes a deadweight loss—the grey area.

In the extreme cases of perfectly inelastic demand and perfectly inelastic supply, the quantity does not change and there is no deadweight loss. The more inelastic is either demand or supply, the smaller is the decrease in quantity and the smaller is the deadweight loss. When demand or supply is perfectly inelastic, the quantity remains constant and there is no deadweight loss.

FIGURE 7.9
Taxes and Efficiency

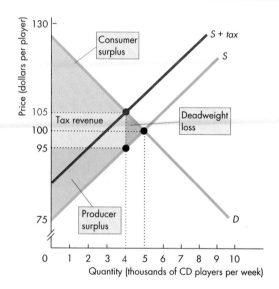

With no sales tax, 5,000 players a week are bought and sold at $100 each. With a sales tax of $10 a player, the buyers' price rises to $105 a player, the sellers' price falls to $95, and the quantity decreases to 4,000 CD players a week. Consumer surplus shrinks to the green area and producer surplus shrinks to the dark blue area. Part of the loss of consumer surplus and producer surplus goes to the government as tax revenue, which is shown as the light blue area. A deadweight loss also arises, which is shown by the grey area.

REVIEW QUIZ

■ How does the elasticity of demand influence the effect of a sales tax on the price paid by the buyer, the price received by the seller, the quantity, the tax revenue, and the deadweight loss?

■ How does the elasticity of supply influence the effect of a sales tax on the price paid by the buyer, the price received by the seller, the quantity, the tax revenue, and the deadweight loss?

■ Why do taxes create a deadweight loss?

Governments make some types of goods such as drugs illegal. Let's see how the market works when trade in an illegal good takes place.

Markets for Illegal Goods

THE MARKETS FOR MANY GOODS AND SERVICES are regulated, but buying and selling some goods is illegal. The best known examples of illegal goods are drugs, such as marijuana, cocaine, and heroin.

Despite the fact that these drugs are illegal, trade in them is a multibillion-dollar business. This trade can be understood by using the same economic model and principles that explain trade in legal goods. To study the market for illegal goods, we're first going to examine the prices and quantities that would prevail if these goods were not illegal. Next, we'll see how prohibition works. Then we'll see how a tax might be used to limit the consumption of these goods.

A Free Market for Drugs

Figure 7.10 shows the market for drugs. The demand curve, D, shows that, other things remaining the same, the lower the price of drugs, the larger is the quantity of drugs demanded. The supply curve, S, shows that, other things remaining the same, the lower the price of drugs, the smaller is the quantity supplied. If drugs were not illegal, the quantity bought and sold would be Q_c and the price would be P_c.

A Market for Illegal Drugs

When a good is illegal, the cost of trading in the good increases. By how much the cost increases and on whom the cost falls depend on the penalties for violating the law and the effectiveness with which the law is enforced. The larger the penalties and the more effective the policing, the higher are the costs. Penalties might be imposed on sellers, buyers, or both.

Penalties on Sellers Drug dealers in Canada face large penalties if their activities are detected. For example, a marijuana dealer could pay a $200,000 fine and serve a 15-year prison term. A heroin dealer could pay a $500,000 fine and serve a 20-year prison term. These penalties are part of the cost of supplying illegal drugs, and they bring a decrease in supply—a leftward shift in the supply curve. To determine the new supply curve, we add the cost of breaking the law to the minimum price that drug dealers are willing to accept. In Fig. 7.10, the cost of breaking the law by selling drugs (*CBL*) is added to the minimum

FIGURE 7.10

A Market for an Illegal Good

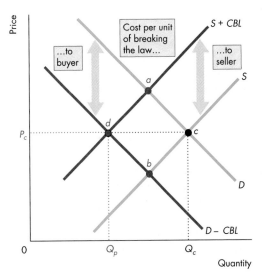

The demand curve for drugs is D, and the supply curve is S. If drugs are not illegal, the quantity bought and sold is Q_c at a price of P_c—point c. If selling drugs is illegal, the cost of breaking the law by selling drugs (*CBL*) is added to the minimum supply price and supply decreases to $S + CBL$. The price rises and the quantity bought decreases—point a. If buying drugs is illegal, the cost of breaking the law is subtracted from the maximum price that buyers are willing to pay, and demand decreases to $D - CBL$. The price falls, and the quantity bought decreases—point b. If both buying and selling are illegal, both the supply and demand curves shift and the quantity bought decreases even more, but (in this example) the price remains at its unregulated level—point d.

price that dealers will accept, and the supply curve shifts leftward to $S + CBL$. If penalties are imposed only on sellers, the market moves from point c to point a. The price increases, and the quantity bought decreases.

Penalties on Buyers In Canada, it is illegal to *possess* drugs such as marijuana, cocaine, and heroin. For example, possession of marijuana can bring a prison term of 1 year and possession of heroin can bring a prison term of 2 years. Penalties fall on buyers and the cost of breaking the law must be subtracted from the value of the good to determine the maximum price buyers are willing to pay for the drugs. Demand decreases, and the demand curve shifts leftward. In Fig. 7.10, the demand curve shifts to $D - CBL$. With penalties imposed on only buyers, the market moves from point c to point b. The price and the quantity bought decrease.

Penalties on Both Sellers and Buyers If penalties are imposed on sellers *and* buyers, both supply and demand decrease and both the supply curve and the demand curve shift. In Fig. 7.10, the costs of breaking the law are the same for both buyers and sellers, so both curves shift leftward by the same amounts. The market moves to point d. The price remains at the competitive market price P_c but the quantity bought decreases to Q_p.

The larger the penalties and the greater the degree of law enforcement, the larger is the decrease in demand and/or supply and the greater is the shift of the demand and/or supply curve. If the penalties are heavier on sellers, the supply curve shifts farther than the demand curve and the price rises above P_c. If the penalties are heavier on buyers, the demand curve shifts farther than the supply curve and the price falls below P_c. In Canada, the penalties on sellers are larger than on buyers so the quantity of drugs traded decreases and the price increases compared with an unregulated market.

With high enough penalties and effective law enforcement, it is possible to decrease demand and/or supply to the point at which the quantity bought is zero. But in reality, such an outcome is unusual. It does not happen in the case of illegal drugs. The key reason is the high cost of law enforcement and insufficient resources for the police to achieve effective enforcement. Because of this situation, some people suggest that drugs (and other illegal goods) should be legalized and sold openly but also be taxed at a high rate in the same way that legal drugs such as alcohol are taxed. How would such an arrangement work?

Legalizing and Taxing Drugs

From your study of the effects of taxes, it is easy to see that the quantity of drugs bought could be decreased if drugs were legalized and taxed. A sufficiently high tax could be imposed to decrease supply, raise the price, and achieve the same decrease in the quantity bought as with a prohibition on drugs. The government would collect a large tax revenue.

Illegal Trading to Evade the Tax It is likely that an extremely high tax rate would be needed to cut the quantity of drugs bought to the level prevailing with a prohibition. It is also likely that many drug dealers and consumers would try to cover up their activities to evade the tax. If they did act in this way, they would face the cost of breaking the law—the tax law. If the penalty for tax law violation is as severe and as effectively policed as drug-dealing laws, the analysis we've already conducted applies also to this case. The quantity of drugs bought would depend on the penalties for law breaking and on the way in which the penalties were assigned to buyers and sellers.

Taxes Versus Prohibition: Some Pros and Cons
So which works more effectively: making drugs illegal and imposing penalties on people who trade in drugs, or legalizing drugs and taxing them?

In favour of taxes and against making drug trading an offence is the fact that the tax revenue can be used to make law enforcement more effective. It can also be used to run a more effective education campaign against addictive drugs.

In favour of prohibition and against taxes is the fact that a prohibition sends a signal that might influence preferences, decreasing the demand for drugs. Also, some people dislike the idea of the government profiting from trade in harmful substances.

R E V I E W Q U I Z

- How does the imposition of a penalty for selling a drug influence demand, supply, price, and the quantity of the drug consumed?
- How does the imposition of a penalty for buying a drug influence demand, supply, price, and the quantity of the drug consumed?
- How does the imposition of a penalty for selling *or* buying a drug influence demand, supply, price, and the quantity of the drug consumed?
- Is there any case for legalizing drugs?

You've seen how price ceilings, price floors, and taxes limit the quantity and create inefficient resource use. You've also seen how in a market for an illegal good, the quantity can be decreased by imposing penalties on either buyers or sellers or by legalizing and taxing the good. In the next and final section of this chapter, we look at agricultural markets and see how governments try to stabilize farm revenues.

Stabilizing Farm Revenues

EARLY FROST, DROUGHT, HEAVY RAIN AND FLOOD, all contribute to fill the lives of farmers with uncertainty. Fluctuations in the weather bring big fluctuations in farm output. How do changes in farm output affect farm prices and farm revenues? And how might farm revenues be stabilized? Let's begin to answer these questions by looking at an agricultural market.

An Unregulated Agricultural Market

Figure 7.11 shows the market for wheat. In both parts, the demand curve for wheat is *D*. Once farmers have harvested their crop, they have no control over the quantity supplied, and supply is inelastic along a *momentary supply curve*. In normal climate conditions, the momentary supply curve is MS_0 (in both parts of the figure).

The price is determined at the point of intersection of the momentary supply curve and the demand curve. In normal conditions, the price is $200 a tonne. The quantity of wheat produced is 20 million tonnes, and farm revenue is $4 billion. Suppose the opportunity cost to farmers of producing wheat is also $4 billion. Then in normal conditions, farmers just cover their opportunity cost.

Poor Harvest Suppose there is a bad growing season, resulting in a poor harvest. What happens to the price of wheat and the revenue of farmers? These questions are answered in Fig. 7.11(a). Supply decreases, and the momentary supply curve shifts leftward to MS_1, where 15 million tonnes of wheat are produced. With a decrease in supply, the price increases to $300 a tonne.

What happens to total farm revenue? It *increases* to $4.5 billion. A decrease in supply has brought an increase in price and an increase in farm revenue. It does so because the demand for wheat is *inelastic*. The percentage decrease in the quantity demanded is less than the percentage increase in price. You can verify this fact by noticing in Fig. 7.11(a) that the increase in revenue from the higher price ($1.5 billion light blue area) exceeds the decrease in revenue from the smaller quantity ($1.0 billion red area). Farmers are now making a revenue in excess of their opportunity cost.

FIGURE 7.11

Harvests, Farm Prices, and Farm Revenue

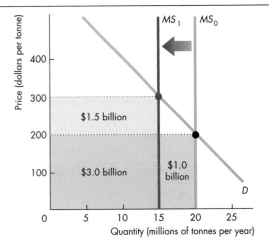

(a) Poor harvest: revenue increases

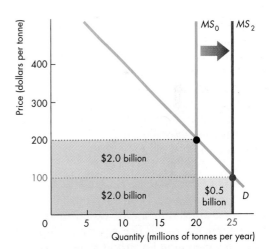

(b) Bumper harvest: revenue decreases

The demand curve for wheat is *D*. In normal times, the supply curve is MS_0 and 20 million tonnes are sold for $200 a tonne. In part (a), a poor harvest decreases supply to MS_1. The price rises to $300 a tonne, and farm revenue increases to $4.5 billion—the $1.5 billion increase from the higher price (light blue area) exceeds the $1.0 billion decrease from the smaller quantity (red area). In part (b), a bumper harvest increases supply to MS_2. The price falls to $100 a tonne, and farm revenue decreases to $2.5 billion—the $2.0 billion decrease from the lower price (red area) exceeds the $0.5 billion increase from the increase in the quantity sold (light blue area).

Although total farm revenue increases when there is a poor harvest, some farmers, whose entire crop is wiped out, suffer a decrease in revenue. Others, whose crop is unaffected, make an enormous gain.

Bumper Harvest Figure 7.11(b) shows what happens in the opposite situation, when there is a bumper harvest. Now supply increases to 25 million tonnes, and the momentary supply curve shifts rightward to MS_2. With the increased quantity supplied, the price falls to $100 a tonne. Farm revenue decreases to $2.5 billion. It does so because the demand for wheat is inelastic. To see this fact, notice in Fig. 7.11(b) that the decrease in revenue from the lower price ($2.0 billion red area) exceeds the increase in revenue from the increase in the quantity sold ($0.5 billion light blue area).

Elasticity of Demand In the example we've just worked through, demand is inelastic. If demand is elastic, the price fluctuations go in the same directions as those we've worked out, but revenue fluctuates in the opposite direction. Bumper harvests increase revenue, and poor harvests decrease it. But the demand for most agricultural products is inelastic, and the case we've studied is the relevant one.

Because farm prices fluctuate, two types of institutions have evolved to stabilize them:

■ Speculative markets in inventories
■ Farm marketing boards

Speculative Markets in Inventories

Many goods, including a wide variety of agricultural products, can be stored. These inventories provide a cushion between production and consumption. If production decreases, goods can be sold from inventory; if production increases, goods can be put into inventory.

In a market that has inventories, we must distinguish production from supply. The quantity produced is not the same as the quantity supplied. The quantity supplied exceeds the quantity produced when goods are sold from inventory. And the quantity supplied is less than the quantity produced when goods are put into inventory. Supply therefore depends on the behaviour of inventory holders.

The Behaviour of Inventory Holders Inventory holders speculate. They hope to buy at a low price

and sell at a high price. That is, they hope to buy goods and put them into inventory when the price is low and sell them from inventory when the price is high. They make a profit or incur a loss equal to their selling price minus their buying price and minus the cost of storage.

But how do inventory holders know when to buy and when to sell? How do they know whether the price is high or low? To decide whether a price is high or low, inventory holders forecast the future price. If the current price is above the forecasted future price, inventory holders sell goods from inventory. If the current price is below the forecasted future price, inventory holders buy goods to put into inventory. This behaviour by inventory holders makes the supply perfectly elastic at the price forecasted by inventory holders.

Let's work out what happens to price and quantity in a market in which inventories are held when production fluctuates. Let's look again at the wheat market.

Fluctuations in Production In Fig. 7.12, the demand curve for wheat is D. Inventory holders expect the future price to be $200 a tonne. The supply curve is S—supply is perfectly elastic at the price expected by inventory holders. Production fluctuates between Q_1 and Q_2.

When production fluctuates and there are no inventories, the price and the quantity fluctuate. We saw this result in Fig. 7.11. But if there are inventories, the price does not fluctuate. When production decreases to Q_1 or 15 million tonnes, inventory holders sell 5 million tonnes from inventory and the quantity bought by consumers is 20 million tonnes. The price remains at $200 a tonne. When production increases to Q_2 or 25 million tonnes, inventory holders buy 5 million tonnes and consumers continue to buy 20 million tonnes. The price remains at $200 a tonne. Inventories reduce price fluctuations. In Fig. 7.12, price fluctuations are entirely eliminated. When there are costs of carrying inventories and when inventories become almost depleted, some price fluctuations do occur, but they are smaller than those occurring in a market without inventories.

Farm Revenue Even if inventory speculation succeeds in stabilizing prices, it does not stabilize farm revenue. With the price stabilized, farm revenue fluctuates as production fluctuates. But now bumper harvests bring larger revenues than poor harvests. The reason is that now farmers, in effect, face a perfectly elastic demand for their output.

■ Price floor
■ Quota
■ Subsidy

FIGURE 7.12

How Inventories Limit Price Changes

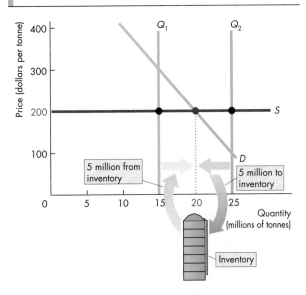

Inventory holders sell wheat from inventory if a poor harvest causes the price to rise above $200 a tonne and buy wheat to hold in inventory if a bumper harvest causes the price to fall below $200 a tonne. So supply (S) is perfectly elastic. When production decreases to Q_1, 5 million tonnes are sold from inventory; when production increases to Q_2, 5 million tonnes are added to inventory. The price remains at $200 a tonne.

Farm Marketing Boards

Most governments intervene in agricultural markets. The most extensive such intervention occurs in the European Union. But intervention also occurs in Canada and the United States, where it is designed to stabilize the prices of agricultural products that include grains, milk, eggs, tobacco, rice, peanuts, cotton, and poultry meats. In Canada, more than 100 farm marketing boards operate and influence more than one-half of total farm sales. A **farm marketing board** is a regulatory agency that intervenes in an agricultural market to stabilize the price of an agricultural product. Farm marketing boards are often supported by governments. How do agricultural markets work when a stabilization program is in place? The answer depends on which type of intervention takes place. There are three types of intervention:

■ Price floor
■ Quota
■ Subsidy

Price Floor   A price floor operates in an agricultural market in much the same way that it operates in other markets. Earlier in this chapter we examined a price floor in the labour market when we studied the effect of minimum wages. The principles are the same in the case of agricultural markets.

Figure 7.13 shows how a price floor works in the market for skim milk powder. The competitive equilibrium price of skim milk powder is $3 a tonne, and 16 million tonnes are produced and bought. If the Canadian Dairy Commission imposes a price floor of $4 a tonne, then the price increases to $4 a tonne and

FIGURE 7.13

A Price Floor

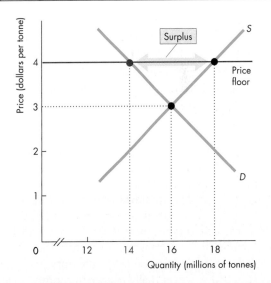

The competitive equilibrium price is $3 a tonne and the equilibrium quantity produced and bought is 16 million tonnes. A price floor of $4 a tonne increases the price to $4 a tonne, decreases the quantity sold to 14 million tonnes, and increases the quantity produced to 18 million tonnes. The price floor creates a surplus of 4 million tonnes. If the Canadian Dairy Commission does not buy the surplus and allows farmers to find their own market, the price will return to its competitive level of $3 a tonne.

the quantity demanded decreases to 14 million tonnes. The quantity supplied increases to 18 million tonnes. Farmers produce a surplus of 4 million tonnes.

This method of supporting the price of an agricultural product will fail unless there is some method of taking up the surplus produced. If farmers are left to find a market for their surplus, then the price will fall below the price floor to the competitive price—$3 a tonne. If, on the other hand, the Canadian Dairy Commission purchases the surplus at the support price, then the price will remain at the price floor. If the marketing board systematically buys more than it sells, then it will end up with a large inventory. Such has been the outcome in the European Union where stabilization agencies have mountains of butter and lakes of wine! The cost of buying and storing the inventory falls on taxpayers, and the main gainers from the support price are the large, efficient farms.

Quota A **quota** is a restriction on the quantity of a good that a farm is permitted to produce. If a quota restricts farm production, then the supply curve becomes perfectly inelastic at the quota quantity.

Figure 7.14 illustrates how a quota works in the market for skim milk. The competitive price is $3 a tonne and the competitive quantity is 16 million tonnes. If the Canadian Dairy Commission imposes a quota that restricts total production to 14 million tonnes, the supply curve becomes the vertical line labelled "Quota." With output restricted by the quota, the quantity produced is now 14 million tonnes and the price increases to $4 a tonne.

But this might not be the end of the story. Farmers are willing to produce skim milk at $2 a tonne, so at a market price of $4 a tonne, they will want to increase their output. If the Canadian Dairy Commission does not prevent quotas from being exceeded, a gradual increase in the quantity of skim milk supplied will eventually restore the competitive equilibrium.

Subsidy A **subsidy** is a payment made by the government to the producer. A subsidy is like a tax—a payment made by a producer to the government— but it goes in the reverse direction. Therefore a subsidy works in a similar way to a tax, but instead of adding something to the price paid by the consumer, a subsidy lowers the price to below what it would be in the absence of a subsidy.

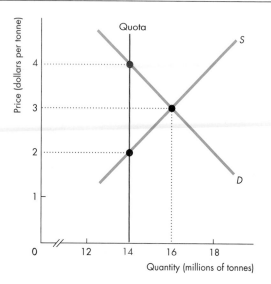

FIGURE 7.14
A Quota

The competitive equilibrium price is $3 a tonne and the equilibrium quantity produced and bought is 16 million tonnes. A quota is set at 14 million tonnes. As a result, the price rises to $4 a tonne and the quantity sold decreases to 14 million tonnes. Producers are willing to supply 14 million tonnes at $2 a tonne, so they will want to increase the quantity that they supply. If the regulatory agency cannot control the quantity produced, then the quantity produced will increase and the price will fall to its competitive level of $3 a tonne.

Figure 7.15 illustrates how a subsidy works in the market for (liquid) milk. The competitive equilibrium is at 30¢ a litre with 16 billion litres produced and bought. The Canadian Dairy Commission then offers a subsidy of 10¢ a litre. The subsidy increases the supply of milk and shifts the supply curve rightward. The magnitude of the shift depends on the size of the subsidy. In this case, farmers are willing to sell each litre for 10¢ less than they would be willing to accept in the absence of a subsidy. The equilibrium price falls to 25¢ a litre, and the quantity produced and bought increases to 17 billion litres. Farmers receive 35¢ a litre, which is the market price of 25¢ a litre plus the subsidy of 10¢ a litre. Thus farmers gain, but taxpayers pay the subsidy. The total subsidy paid is $1.7 billion, which is the 10¢ a litre subsidy multiplied by the 17 billion litres of milk produced.

FIGURE 7.15
A Subsidy

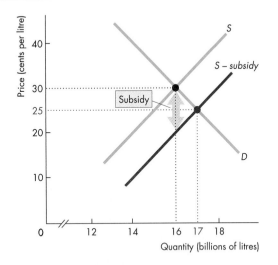

The competitive equilibrium price is 30¢ a litre and the equilibrium quantity produced and bought is 16 billion litres. The Canadian Dairy Commission introduces a subsidy of 10¢ a litre. As a result, producers are now willing to supply each quantity at 10¢ a litre less. The supply curve shifts rightward such that the vertical distance between the supply curve S and the supply curve S – subsidy is 10¢ a litre. The price falls to 25¢ a litre, and the quantity produced and sold increases to 17 billion litres. Producers receive 35¢ a litre, which is the market price of 25¢ a litre plus the subsidy of 10¢ a litre. The total subsidy paid is $1.7 billion, which taxpayers will have to pay.

This method of agricultural support can impose major costs on taxpayers.

Efficiency and Equity in Farm Markets

Are farm marketing boards efficient and are they fair? It is easy to answer the first question. They are generally inefficient. It is harder to answer the second question.

Inefficiency of Farm Marketing Boards   You can see that farm marketing boards are inefficient by looking at what they do to the relationship between marginal cost and marginal benefit. A price floor that exceeds the competitive equilibrium price decreases the quantity demanded and results in a price that equals marginal benefit but that exceeds marginal cost. So both consumer surplus and producer surplus shrink and there is a deadweight loss.

A quota restricts output below the quantity that maximizes the sum of consumer surplus and producer surplus. So it, too, creates deadweight loss.

A subsidy increases production above the competitive level. So it results in marginal cost exceeding marginal benefit and creates deadweight loss.

All the methods of intervention, then, are inefficient. But are they fair?

Equity of Farm Marketing Boards   Farm marketing boards increase the incomes of farmers and decrease the incomes of taxpayers and consumers of farm products compared with what the unregulated market would provide. Because the actions of farm marketing boards create deadweight loss, the gains by farmers are smaller than the losses borne by everyone else.

Whether this redistribution of economic wellbeing towards farmers is fair is a controversial matter. Most farmers probably think it perfectly fair and most other people probably have their doubts. Whatever the merits of either view, it is a curious and perhaps surprising fact that farmers throughout the world manage to persuade the non-farming majority that redistribution towards the farmers is necessary.

R E V I E W   Q U I Z

- Can you explain how poor harvests and bumper harvests influence farm prices and farm revenues?
- Can you explain how the existence of inventories and speculation influence farm prices and farm revenues?
- What are the main actions that farm marketing boards take and how do these actions influence farm prices and farm revenues?

◆ You now know how to use the demand and supply model to predict prices, to study government intervention in markets, and to study the sources and costs of inefficiency. Before you leave this topic, take a look at *Reading Between the Lines* on pp. 148–149 and see what is happening in the illegal market for pirated software today.

POLICY WATCH

The Illegal Market for Pirated Software

GLOBE AND MAIL, JUNE 22, 1998

Stealing programs on Canada's campuses

Steve, a student at Ryerson Polytechnic University in Toronto, keeps his computer humming with the latest games, sophisticated business applications and expensive graphics programs.

The array of software at his disposal would cost several thousand dollars to buy in stores. But for Steve, 20, it's simply a matter of copying borrowed programs onto a blank, recordable CD. Total cost? About $2.50.

Sure, it's illegal, Steve said, but the economics outweigh the legal constraints. ... "We're students. We don't have any money. Can each of us afford to spend $400 for a program like Office 97?"

Software piracy in Canada—counterfeiting and illegal copying of software—costs manufacturers and the Canadian economy an estimated $500-million a year, according to the Canadian Alliance Against Software Theft. CAAST is a coalition of Canadian software makers...

CAAST, formed in 1990 to battle software piracy, said that about four out of every 10 software programs now in use in Canada were not purchased. ...

But tougher legislation to combat piracy is on the way and software firms are hoping

that the threat of penalties of up to $20,000—plus antipiracy hot lines and an ongoing campaign to educate the public—will help to cut the hefty losses this year. ...

"We know that there is definitely a higher rate of piracy on university campuses than there is in Canada in general," said CAAST spokesperson Kimberley Lauder, ...

Popular with students, she said, are so-called compilation CDs that contain an array of programs. ...

For about $50, students can buy a compilation CD that might contain up to $40,000 worth of programs—everything from costly new operating systems and graphics programs, worth hundreds of dollars each, to the newest games that sell for $60 each in stores. ...

Under changes to copyright legislation that are expected to take effect in the fall, software makers will be able to pursue statutory damages... Firms will need to simply show that a loss occurred, and a judge could then set a penalty of $500 to $20,000 for each violation.

Tougher laws and penalties in the United States have helped keep the software piracy rate there down to about half of what it is in Canada, so firms are optimistic that they can significantly reduce piracy here, ...

Essence of the Story

- Software piracy in Canada costs an estimated $500 million per year.

- Tougher legislation to fight software piracy by increasing penalties up to $20,000 is anticipated.

- Currently, students can buy a compilation CD for $50 that contains up to $40,000 worth of pirated programs.

- Tougher laws and penalties in the United States have kept the piracy rate at half the Canadian level.

Economic Analysis

- On university campuses, students can buy illegal CDs that contain numerous software programs.

- Because an illegal CD is cheap to make, the minimum price that software pirates are willing to accept for an illegal CD is low.

- Figure 1 illustrates the campus market for illegal CDs. In this example, the price is $50 a CD and 12,500 CDs are bought each year—at point *a*.

- If each CD contains software worth $40,000, the software industry loses $500 million a year.

- If the sellers of illegal CDs are penalized $100 for each CD sold, then the minimum price that sellers will accept increases and the supply of illegal CDs decreases.

- Figure 2 shows the new supply curve, *S + CBL*. The vertical distance between the supply curve, *S*, and the supply curve, *S + CBL*, equals the $100 penalty on sellers.

- With the penalty on sellers, the price of a CD rises to $100 and the quantity decreases to 7,500 CDs—at point *b*.

- But if a penalty of $50 per CD is also imposed on buyers, then the maximum price that buyers are willing to pay falls and demand decreases.

- Figure 3 shows the new demand curve, *D – CBL*. The vertical distance between the demand curve, *D*, and the demand curve, *D – CBL*, equals the $50 penalty imposed on buyers.

- With penalties on both sellers and buyers, the price rises to $75 a CD and the quantity decreases to 5,000 CDs—at point *c*.

- By imposing penalties on sellers and buyers of illegal CDs, software piracy on Canadian campuses will decrease.

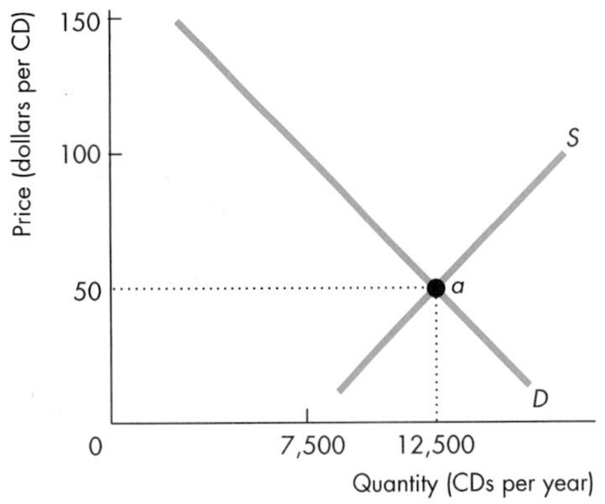

Figure 1 Illegal market for pirated software

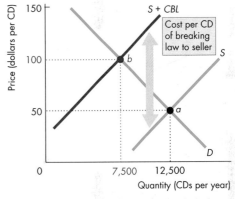

Figure 2 Software market with copyright law enforced on sellers

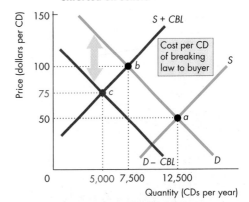

Figure 3 Software market with copyright law enforced on buyers and sellers

You're The Voter

- Would you support legislation that imposes penalties on sellers of pirated software but not on buyers?

- Would you support legislation that imposes penalties on buyers of pirated software but not on sellers?

- List all policy actions you can think of that would decrease the amount of software piracy.

SUMMARY

Key Points

Housing Markets and Rent Ceilings (pp. 130–133)

- A decrease in the supply of housing decreases short-run supply and raises the equilibrium rent.
- Higher rents stimulate building and, in the long run, the quantity of housing increases and rents fall.
- A rent ceiling set below the equilibrium rent creates a housing shortage, wasteful search, and a black market.

The Labour Market and the Minimum Wage (pp. 134–136)

- A decrease in the demand for low-skilled labour lowers the wage rate and reduces employment.
- The lower wage rate encourages people with low skill to acquire more skill, which decreases the supply of low-skilled labour and, in the long run, raises their wage rate.
- A minimum wage set above the equilibrium wage creates unemployment and increases the amount of time people spend searching for jobs.
- Minimum wages hit low-skilled young people hardest.

Taxes (pp. 137–140)

- When a good or service is taxed, usually the price increases and the quantity bought decreases but the price increases by less than the tax. The buyer pays part of the tax, and the seller pays part of the tax.
- The share of a tax paid by the buyer and by the seller depends on the elasticity of demand and the elasticity of supply.
- The less elastic the demand and the more elastic the supply, the greater is the price increase, the smaller is the quantity decrease, and the larger is the share of the tax paid by the buyer.
- If demand is perfectly elastic or supply is perfectly inelastic, the seller pays the entire tax. And if demand is perfectly inelastic or supply is perfectly elastic, the buyer pays the entire tax.

Markets for Illegal Goods (pp. 141–142)

- Penalties on sellers of an illegal good increase the cost of selling the good and decrease its supply. Penalties on buyers decrease their willingness to pay and decrease the demand for the good.
- The higher the penalties and the more effective the law enforcement, the smaller is the quantity bought. The price is higher or lower than the unregulated price, depending on whether the penalties on sellers or buyers are higher.
- A tax set at a sufficiently high rate will decrease the quantity of a drug consumed, but there will be a tendency for the tax to be evaded.

Stabilizing Farm Revenues (pp. 143–147)

- Farm revenues fluctuate because supply fluctuates.
- The demand for most farm products is inelastic, so a decrease in supply increases the price and increases farm revenues, while an increase in supply decreases price and decreases farm revenues.
- Inventory holders and government agencies act to stabilize farm prices and revenues.
- Farm marketing boards use price floors, quotas, and subsidies to increase farm prices and revenues.

Key Figures ◆

Key Terms

PROBLEMS

*1. The figure below shows the demand for and supply of rental housing in the Village:

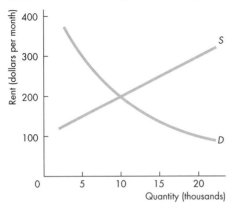

a. What are the equilibrium rent and the equilibrium quantity of rented housing?

If a rent ceiling is set at $150 a month, what is:

b. The quantity of housing rented?
c. The shortage of housing?
d. The maximum price that someone is willing to pay for the last unit of housing available?

2. The figure below shows the demand for and supply of rental housing in Township:

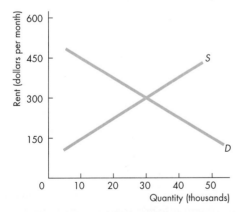

a. What is the equilibrium rent and equilibrium quantity of rented housing?

If a rent ceiling is set at $150 a month, what is:

b. The quantity of housing rented?
c. The shortage of housing?
d. The maximum price that someone is willing to pay for the last unit available?

*3. The table gives the demand for and supply of teenage labour.

Wage rate (dollars per hour)	Quantity demanded	Quantity supplied
	(hours per month)	
2	3,000	1,000
3	2,500	1,500
4	2,000	2,000
5	1,500	2,500
6	1,000	3,000

a. What are the equilibrium wage rate and level of employment?
b. What is the quantity of unemployment?
c. If a minimum wage of $3 an hour is set for teenagers, how many hours do they work?
d. If a minimum wage of $3 an hour is set for teenagers, how many hours of their labour are unemployed?
e. If a minimum wage is set at $5 an hour for teenagers, how many hours of their labour are employed and unemployed?
f. If a minimum wage is set at $5 an hour and demand increases by 500 hours a month, what is the wage rate paid to teenagers and how many hours of their labour are unemployed?

4. The table gives the demand for and supply of high-school graduates.

Wage rate (dollars per hour)	Quantity demanded	Quantity supplied
	(hours per month)	
6	9,000	4,000
7	8,000	5,000
8	7,000	6,000
9	6,000	7,000
10	5,000	8,000

a. What are the equilibrium wage rate and level of employment?
b. What is the level of unemployment?
c. If a minimum wage is set at $7 an hour, how many hours do high-school graduates work?
d. If a minimum wage is set at $7 an hour, how many hours of labour are unemployed?
e. If a minimum wage is set at $9 an hour, how many hours of their labour are employed and unemployed?
f. If the minimum wage is $9 an hour and demand increases by 500 hours a month, what is the wage rate paid to high-school graduates and how many hours of their labour are unemployed?

□ *5. The table gives the demand and supply schedules for chocolate brownies:

Price (cents per brownie)	Quantity demanded	Quantity supplied
	(millions per day)	
50	5	3
60	4	4
70	3	5
80	2	6
90	1	7

a. If brownies are not taxed, what is the price of a brownie and how many are consumed?

b. If brownies are taxed at 20¢ each, what is the price and how many brownies are consumed? Who pays the tax?

6. The table gives the demand and supply schedules for coffee.

Price (dollars per cup)	Quantity demanded	Quantity supplied
	(cups per hour)	
1.50	90	30
1.75	70	40
2.00	50	50
2.25	30	60
2.75	10	70

a. If there is no tax on coffee, what is the price and how much coffee is consumed?

b. If a tax of 75¢ a cup is introduced, what is the price, how much coffee is consumed, and who pays the tax?

□ *7. The demand for and supply of eggs on Turtle Island is:

Price (dollars per dozen)	Quantity demanded	Quantity supplied
	(dozens per week)	
1.20	3,000	500
1.30	2,750	1,500
1.40	2,500	2,500
1.50	2,250	3,500
1.60	2,000	4,500

If the government sets a floor price of $1.50 a dozen, what is the market price, the quantity sold, farm revenue, and surplus of eggs?

8. If in the Turtle Island egg market of problem 7, the government sets a quota of 1,500 dozen eggs a week but sets no floor price, what is the market price, the quantity sold, farm revenues, and shortage of eggs?

CRITICAL THINKING

1. Study *Reading Between the Lines* on the market for illegal pirated software on pp. 148-149 and answer the following questions:

a. Draw the diagrams using a $50 penalty on the sellers and a $100 penalty on the buyers. What changes occur in the quantity of CDs bought and sold each year and in the price?

b. What size of penalty would be required to eliminate software piracy?

c. If the price elasticity of demand is greater than estimated in the diagrams, would the quantity of CDs bought and sold decrease or increase when a $100 penalty on sellers is imposed?

d. Would possible incarceration change the positions of the shifted supply and demand curves?

2. Rent ceilings exist in many Canadian cities. What impact do you think rent ceilings have on the rent that students have to pay for rented accommodation and the amount and quality of that accommodation?

3. Use the links on the Parkin-Bade Web site to obtain information on the minimum wage rates across the provinces. In which province do you think the minimum wage might be causing the most unemployment and why?

4. Use the links on the Parkin-Bade Web site to obtain information and views on taxes on cigarettes. For many years, the provinces have increased the tax on cigarettes. But recently, Quebec and Ontario cut this tax. What do you think will be the change in the price of cigarettes, the quantity of cigarettes sold, and provincial tax revenue? Who will gain from the tax cut—buyers or sellers of cigarettes?

5. Use the links on the Parkin-Bade Web site to obtain information about markets in grain. Some grain growers in Western Canada would like to sell their grain on the world market. Under Canadian law, such action is prohibited. The Wheat Board is the sole seller of these grains. What would be the change in the farm revenues if the law were changed and farmers were allowed to market their own grain?

Understanding How Markets Work

T he four chapters that you've just studied explain how markets work. The market is an amazing instrument. It enables people who have never met and who know nothing about each other to interact and do business. It also enables us to allocate our scarce resources to the uses that we value most highly. Markets can be very simple or highly organized. ◆ A simple market is one that the American historian Daniel J. Boorstin describes in *The Discoverers* (p. 161). In the late 14th century,

The Amazing Market

The Muslim caravans that went southward from Morocco across the Atlas Mountains arrived after twenty days at the shores of the Senegal River. There the Moroccan traders laid out separate piles of salt, of beads from Ceutan coral, and cheap manufactured goods. Then they retreated out of sight. The local tribesmen, who lived in the strip mines where they dug their gold, came to the shore and put a heap of gold beside each pile of Moroccan goods. Then they, in turn, went out of view, leaving the Moroccan traders either to take the gold offered for a particular pile or to reduce the pile of their merchandise to suit the offered price in gold. Once again the Moroccan traders withdrew, and the process went on. By this system of commercial etiquette, the Moroccans collected their gold.

Organized markets are the Toronto Exchange that trades many millions of stocks each day and monthly auctions at which governments sell bonds to finance their debts. ◆ Whether simple, or highly organized, all of these markets determine the prices at which exchanges take place and enable both buyers and sellers to benefit. ◆ Everything and anything that can be exchanged is traded in markets. There are markets for goods and services; for resources such as labour, capital, and raw materials; for dollars, pounds, and yen; for goods to be delivered now and for goods to be delivered in the future. Only the imagination places limits on what can be traded in markets. ◆ You began your study of markets in Chapter 4, by learning about the laws of demand and supply. There, you discovered the forces that make prices adjust to coordinate buying plans and selling plans. In Chapter 5, you learned how to calculate and use the concept of elasticity to predict the responsiveness of prices and quantities to changes in supply and demand. In Chapter 6, you studied efficiency and discovered the conditions under which a market sends resources to uses in which they are valued most highly. And finally, in Chapter 7, you studied markets in action. There, you learned how markets cope with change and discovered how they operate when governments intervene to fix prices, impose taxes, or make some goods illegal.

◇ The laws of demand and supply were discovered during the nineteenth century by some remarkable economists. We conclude our study of demand and supply and markets by looking at the lives and times of some of these economists. We also talk with Richard Harris, one of Canada's most influential economists today.

Probing the Ideas

Discovering the Laws of Demand and Supply

Alfred Marshall

(1842–1924) grew up in an England that was being transformed by the railroad and by the expansion of manufacturing. Mary Paley was one of Marshall's students at Cambridge and when Alfred and Mary married, in 1877, celibacy rules barred Marshall from continuing to teach at Cambridge. By 1884, with more liberal rules, the Marshalls returned to Cambridge where Alfred became Professor of Political Economy.

Many others had a hand in refining the theory of demand and supply, but the first thorough and complete statement of the theory as we know it today was set out by Alfred Marshall, with the acknowledged help of Mary. Published in 1890, the monumental treatise, Principles of Economics, *became the textbook on economics on both sides of the Atlantic for almost half a century. Marshall was an outstanding mathematician, but he kept mathematics and even diagrams in the background. His supply and demand diagram appears only in a footnote.*

> *"The forces to be dealt with are … so numerous, that it is best to take a few at a time. … Thus we begin by isolating the primary relations of supply, demand, and price…"*
>
> ALFRED MARSHALL,
> THE PRINCIPLES OF
> ECONOMICS

The Issues

The laws of demand and supply that you studied in Chapter 4 were discovered during the 1830s by Antoine-Augustin Cournot (1801–1877), a professor of mathematics at the University of Lyon, France. Although

Cournot was the first to use demand and supply, it was the development and expansion of the railroads during the 1850s that gave the newly emerging theory its first practical applications. Railroads then were at the cutting edge of technology just as airlines are today. And as in the airline industry today, competition among the railroads was fierce.

Dionysius Lardner (1793–1859), an Irish professor of philosophy at the University of London, used demand and supply to show railroad companies how they could increase their profits by cutting rates on long-distance business on which competition was fiercest and by raising rates on short-haul business on which they had less to fear from other transportation suppliers. Today, economists use the principles that Lardner worked out during the 1850s to calculate the freight rates and passenger fares that will give airlines the largest possible profit. And the rates calculated have a lot in common with the railroad rates of the nineteenth century. On local routes on which there is little competition, fares per kilometre are highest, and on long-distance routes on which the airlines compete fiercely, fares per kilometre are lowest.

Known satirically among scientists of the day as "Dionysius Diddler," Lardner worked on an amazing range of problems from astronomy to railway engineering to economics. A colourful character, he would have been a regular guest on late-night TV talk shows had they been around in the 1850s. Lardner visited the École des Ponts et Chaussées (the School of Bridges and Roads) in Paris and must have learned a great deal from Jules Dupuit.

In France, Jules Dupuit (1804–1866), a French engineer/economist, used demand to calculate the benefits from building a bridge and, once the bridge was built, for calculating the toll to charge for its use. His work was the forerunner of what is today called *cost-benefit analysis*. Working with the principles invented by Dupuit, economists today calculate the costs and benefits of highways and airports, dams, and power stations.

... and Now

Today, using the same principles that Dupuit devised, economists calculate whether the benefits of expanding airports and air-traffic control facilities are sufficient to cover their costs. Airline companies use the principles developed by Lardner to set their prices and to decide when to offer "seat sales." Like the railroads before them, the airlines charge a high price per kilometre on short flights, for which they face little competition, and a low price per kilometre on long flights, for which competition is fierce.

Then ...

Dupuit used the law of demand to determine whether a bridge or canal would be valued enough by its users to justify the cost of building it. Lardner first worked out the relationship between the cost of production and supply and used demand and supply theory to explain the costs, prices, and profits of railroad operations. He also used the theory to discover ways of increasing revenue by raising rates on short-haul business and lowering them on long-distance freight.

Markets do an amazing job. And the laws of demand and supply help us to understand how markets work. But in some situations, a market must be designed and institutions must be created to enable the market to operate. In recent years, economists have begun to use their tools to design and create markets. One of Canada's leading economists who has studied how markets work in many different contexts is Richard Harris, whom you can meet on the following pages.

Talking with
Richard Harris

Richard G. Harris *is the B.C. Telephone*
Professor of Economics at Simon Fraser University,
and Fellow of the Canadian Institute for Advanced
Research. He began his academic career at Queen's
University, where he became Director of the John
Deutsch Institute for the Study of Economic Policy,
and held visiting appointments at the University of
California at Berkeley, MIT, and the University of
New South Wales. Professor Harris specializes in
international economics and was a special advisor
to the Canadian government during the negotia-
tions that lead to the Canada–U.S. Free Trade
Agreement. He has served as consultant to the
World Bank and the OECD.

Professor Harris has published many books and
articles on Canadian international trade, economic
growth, and Canadian economic policy as well as
on more technical topics. A recently published vol-
ume entitled The Asia-Pacific Region in the
Global Economy: A Canadian Perspective

summarizes the results of a two-year research pro-
gram that he headed.

Robin Bade and Michael Parkin talked with
Professor Harris about his work and the contribu-
tion that he and other economists are making to try
to improve economic policy in Canada.

Professor Harris, what first attracted you to economics?
I was an undergraduate at Queen's University studying mathematics and philosophy and became a bit
disenchanted with the level of abstraction in both
those disciplines. In my introductory economics
course, I was fascinated by the idea that the organization of society could be studied in a scientific way
using a few basic principles that had universal applicability—a concept that was completely novel to me
at the time. I also was very much of the view, which
was typical of most in my generation, that governments effectively controlled all aspects of the economy. The idea that markets were social institutions
that promoted the productive use of resources was a
fairly radical idea for an undergraduate to be exposed
to in the 1960s. While quite critical of the pure free
market view at the time, it was a major intellectual
challenge to think systematically about the issues
rather than to simply express an opinion.

**When Alfred Marshall first described the laws of
demand and supply, he said that "the forces to be dealt
with are ... so numerous, that it is best to take a few at
a time ... [and] ... begin by isolating the primary relations of *demand, supply,* and *price.*" Was Marshall correct? Do the laws of demand and supply have the same
force and relevance today that they did when Marshall
first explained them?**
Absolutely. I don't think one could prove that the laws
of supply and demand are of more or less force or rele-

vance today than in the past—these are universal laws. Occasionally, they are pushed into the background during periods of great social or political upheaval, but they are as inevitable in their relevance to human affairs just as the laws of electromagnetics are to the functioning of your computer. Marshall's emphasis on isolating a few critical channels of influence on supply or demand is good advice and absolutely necessary if a theory is to be of any practical use. In looking at the Canada–U.S. Free Trade Agreement, for example, I found that economies of scale were one of the few factors that figured importantly on the anticipated supply response of industry to the agreement; although people were convinced that large numbers of other influences would matter—such as who owned the firms, what city they were located in, and so forth. Keep your theories simple!

Do the laws of demand and supply apply to the international economy?

Yes, but with some interesting twists. At the international level, an increase in the supply of a good in one country (say Canada) can have important ramifications on the prices of goods consumed or produced in countries that are far removed from Canada. The connection, of course, is that international trade links countries directly and indirectly. If there is discovery of a diamond mine in the Yukon Territory in Canada (which happened recently), this will ultimately impact on wages and incomes in South Africa. Why? Because South Africa is a major world supplier of diamonds and the Yukon mine is a source of competitive supply to the global market of diamonds. This new supply will put downward pressure on the price of diamonds throughout the world and, in particular, will affect the major diamond-producing country—South Africa. International trade allows the laws of supply and demand to have global applicability. If South Africa did not export or import any diamonds, then the Yukon diamond discovery would have had no effect on South Africa.

You've recently studied Canada's place in the Asia–Pacific economy. Can Canadians compete with low-cost Asian producers? Would we be better off if we taxed cheap foreign-produced goods so that Canadian producers could compete more effectively?

Absolutely not. The notion that providing "protection" for domestic producers will lead to an improve-

ment in national well-being is one of the oldest and most discredited ideas in economics. Almost all economists agree that policies, which improve international trade or move the economy towards "freer trade" on average, tend to lead to increases in national income. The Asian example comes up often because the very low wages in Asia suggest that Canadian producers would be wiped out if Asian exporters had free access to the Canadian market. Let's suppose for the moment that Asian clothing producers pay wages much lower than is the case in Canada. Most people recognize that the Canadian consumer would be better off if we allowed cheaper clothing imports from Asia. But many fail to recognize the very important benefits that would come about from having valuable resources —capital and labour—that are being utilized in the clothing industry move to other industries where they are more productive—for example, the automobile industry. This is the law of comparative advantage and it is arguably the most important principle that economics has to teach after opportunity cost.

> *The notion that providing "protection" for domestic producers will lead to an improvement in national well-being is one of the oldest and most discredited ideas in economics.*

You attracted a lot of attention in 1999 by suggesting that the market for the Canadian dollar does not work well and that we would be better off if we closed it down and started using the U.S. dollar. What is wrong with letting the Canadian dollar find its equilibrium price on the foreign exchange market?

There are two basic problems with the current Canadian dollar regime. First, from the point of view of promoting trade and investment between Canada and other countries and, in particular, the United States, there would be enormous benefits from having a single currency—for many of the same reasons that we all benefit from working in a single language. The costs of writing contracts, organizing exchange, managing accounting systems, and so forth are enormously complicated by the use of multiple currencies. Think of anybody organizing an e-commerce business in Canada. The hassle of having to deal with currency exchange for U.S. customers is a tremendous barrier to Canadian entry in that business. Practically speaking, we are not yet ready for a "world money" and Canada trades predominantly with the United States, so that harmonizing on a currency obviously means in this case the U.S. dollar.

> *…from the point of view of promoting trade and investment between Canada and other countries and, in particular, the United States, there would be enormous benefits from having a single currency*

The second reason is that the foreign exchange market is an asset market, analogous to the stock market for example, which is extremely forward looking but whose outcome has immediate and important effects on goods and labour markets in Canada. For example, the depreciation of the Canadian dollar has had an enormous impact in terms of increasing the cost of imported information technology in the last few years. A "floating" or market-determined exchange rate is necessary if a country wishes to set its own monetary policy and inflation rates. But offset against this potential "benefit" are the costs imposed on the economy by the rapid up-and-down movements of the exchange rate. In my opinion, these costs now substantially outweigh the benefits of an independent monetary policy. Small trading countries, such as the Netherlands, gave up using the exchange rate as an instrument of national economic policy a long time ago. It's now time for Canada to do the same.

The world is a long way from achieving free trade in agricultural products. Why can't we let supply and demand work in agricultural markets? What reforms in Canadian and global markets for farm products do you think are needed?

That unfortunately is not an easy question to answer simply because all countries have tended to intervene heavily in their agricultural markets. While the WTO has made some progress in getting commitments to lower agricultural trade barriers, particularly subsidies, remarkably little has been achieved. I think the politics of trade policy is such that it is reasonable to ask a sector such as agriculture to accept lower domestic trade barriers if our trading partners do likewise. But in the absence of a willingness of Europe and the United States to reduce their subsidies, politically why should Canada move first? The problem is compounded because the current agricultural "trade wars" between the European Union and United States have severely depressed the price of a number of products that Canada exports, such as wheat, which in turn has increased the demands for the government to do "something." Agricultural trade policy is more like "disaster relief" these days. Perhaps in the future we can make some progress analogous to that made in the case of industrial products.

Do you think that economics is a good subject in which to major? Why? What else should be studied alongside economics?

Economics is a great major for those who are interested in the forces behind the newspaper headlines, but with an inclination to think systematically about an issue both in terms of looking at the facts and in the application of basic theories to what may appear as a novel problem. It is also extremely useful to anyone interested in a career in business or government. Business, because understanding your market and where it might be going is crucial. Government, for the obvious reason that virtually every government policy must be examined in light of it's economic consequences. If you are interested ultimately in being a professional economist it is very important to get a firm foundation in mathematics and statistics. However, a general knowledge of history and politics is very important—I strongly recommend courses in those areas as well.

Chapter **8**

Utility and Demand

We need water to live. We don't need diamonds for much besides decoration. If the benefits of water far outweigh the benefits of diamonds, why does water cost practically nothing while diamonds are expensive? ◆ When a winter storm cuts off the power supply, the prices of alternative sources of heat, such as firewood, and alternative sources of light, such as candles, rise dramatically. But people buy as much firewood and as many candles as they can get their hands on. Our demand for goods that provide heat and light is price inelastic. But why? ◆ When the CD player was introduced in 1983, it cost more than $1,000, and consumers didn't buy very many. Since then, the price has decreased dramatically, and people are buying CD players in enormous quantities. Our demand for CD players is price elastic. What makes the demand for some things price elastic while the demand for others is price inelastic? ◆ Over the past 20 years, after the effects of inflation are removed, incomes in Canada have increased by 40 percent. Over that same period, expenditure on electricity has increased by more than 60 percent, while expenditure on transportation has increased by less than 20 percent. Thus the proportion of income spent on electricity has increased, and the proportion spent on transportation has decreased. Why, as incomes rise, does the proportion of income spent on some goods rise and that spent on others fall?

◆ In the preceding four chapters, we saw that demand has an important effect on the price of a good. But we did not analyse what exactly shapes a person's demand. This chapter examines household behaviour and its influence on demand. It explains why demand for some goods is elastic and demand for other goods is inelastic. It also explains why the prices of some things, such as diamonds and water, are so out of proportion to their total benefits.

Water, Water, Everywhere

After studying this chapter, you will be able to:

- Explain the household's budget constraint
- Define total utility and marginal utility
- Explain the marginal utility theory of consumer choice
- Use marginal utility theory to predict the effects of changing prices and incomes
- Explain the connection between individual demand and market demand
- Explain the paradox of value

Household Consumption Choices

A HOUSEHOLD'S CONSUMPTION CHOICES ARE determined by many factors, but we can summarize all of these factors under two concepts:

■ Budget constraint
■ Preferences

Budget Constraint

A household's consumption choices are constrained by the household's income and by the prices of the goods and services it buys. The household has a given amount of income to spend and cannot influence the prices of the goods and services it buys.

A household's *budget line* describes the limits to its consumption choices. Let's consider Lisa's household. Lisa has an income of $30 a month and she plans to buy only two goods—movies and pop. Movies cost $6 each; pop costs $3 a six-pack. If Lisa spends all her income, she will reach the limits to her consumption of movies and pop.

Figure 8.1 illustrates Lisa's possible consumption of movies and pop. Rows *a* through *f* in the table show six possible ways of allocating $30 to these two goods. For example, Lisa can see 2 movies for $12 and buy 6 six-packs for $18 (row *c*). Points *a* through *f* in the figure illustrate the possibilities presented in the table. The line passing through these points is Lisa's budget line.

Lisa's budget line is a constraint on her choices. It marks the boundary between what she can afford and what she cannot afford. She can afford all the points on the line and inside it. She cannot afford the points outside the line. The constraint on her consumption depends on prices of movies and pop and on her income. The constraint changes when the price of movies or pop changes or her income changes.

Preferences

How does Lisa divide her $30 between these two goods? The answer depends on her likes and dislikes—her *preferences*. Economists use the concept of utility to describe preferences. The benefit or satisfaction that a person gets from the consumption of a good or service is called **utility**. Let's now see how we can use the concept of utility to describe preferences.

FIGURE 8.1

Consumption Possibilities

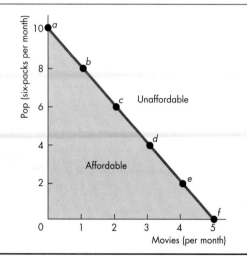

Possibility	Movies		Pop	
	Quantity	Expenditure (dollars)	Six-packs	Expenditure (dollars)
a	0	0	10	30
b	1	6	8	24
c	2	12	6	18
d	3	18	4	12
e	4	24	2	6
f	5	30	0	0

Rows *a* through *f* in the table show six possible ways that Lisa can allocate $30 to movies and pop. For example, Lisa can buy 2 movies and 6 six-packs (row *c*). The combination in each row costs $30. These possibilities are points *a* through *f* in the figure. The line through those points is a boundary between what Lisa can afford and what she cannot afford. Her choices must lie along the line *af* or inside the orange area.

Total Utility

Total utility is the total benefit that a person gets from the consumption of goods and services. The units in which we measure utility are arbitrary, like the units in which we measure temperature. Total utility depends on the level of consumption—more consumption generally gives more total utility. Table 8.1 shows Lisa's total utility from movies and pop. If she sees no movies, she gets no utility from movies. If

TABLE 8.1

Lisa's Total Utility from Movies and Pop

Movies		Pop	
Quantity per month	Total utility	Six-packs per month	Total utility
0	0	0	0
1	50	1	75
2	88	2	117
3	121	3	153
4	150	4	181
5	175	5	206
6	196	6	225
7	214	7	243
8	229	8	260
9	241	9	276
10	250	10	291
11	256	11	305
12	259	12	318
13	261	13	330
14	262	14	341

she sees 1 movie in a month, she gets 50 units of utility. As the number of movies she sees in a month increases, her total utility increases; if she sees 10 movies a month, she gets 250 units of total utility. The other part of the table shows Lisa's total utility from pop. If she drinks no pop, she gets no utility from pop. As the amount of pop she drinks increases, her total utility increases.

Marginal Utility

Marginal utility is the change in total utility that results from a one-unit increase in the quantity of a good consumed. When the number of six-packs Lisa buys increases from 4 to 5 a month, her total utility from pop increases from 181 units to 206 units. Thus for Lisa, the marginal utility of consuming a fifth six-pack each month is 25 units. The table in Fig. 8.2 shows Lisa's marginal utility for pop. Notice that in the table, marginal utility appears midway between the quantities of pop. It does so because it is the *change* in consumption from 4 to 5 packs that produces the *marginal* utility of 25 units. The table dis-

plays calculations of marginal utility for each number of six-packs that Lisa buys from 1 to 5.

Figure 8.2(a) illustrates the total utility that Lisa gets from pop. The more pop Lisa drinks in a month, the more total utility she gets. Part (b) illustrates her marginal utility. This graph tells us that as Lisa drinks more pop, the marginal utility that she gets from pop decreases. For example, her marginal utility decreases from 75 units for the first six-pack to 42 units from the second and 36 units from the third. We call this decrease in marginal utility as the quantity of the good consumed increases the principle of **diminishing marginal utility**.

Marginal utility is positive but diminishes as the consumption of a good increases. Why does marginal utility have these two features? In Lisa's case, she likes pop, and the more she drinks the better. That's why marginal utility is positive. The benefit that Lisa gets from the last six-pack consumed is her marginal utility. To see why marginal utility diminishes, think about the following two situations: In one, you've been studying all through the day and evening and you've been too busy finishing an assignment to go shopping. A friend drops by with a six-pack of pop. The utility you get from that pop is the marginal utility from one six-pack. In the second situation, you've been on a pop binge. You've been working on an assignment all day but you've guzzled three six-packs while doing so. You are up to your eyeballs in pop. You are happy enough to have one more can. But the thrill that you get from it is not very large. It is the marginal utility of the nineteenth can in a day.

Temperature—An Analogy

Utility is similar to temperature. Both are abstract concepts, and both have units of measurement that are arbitrary. You know when you feel hot, and you know when you feel cold. But you can't *observe* temperature. You can observe water turning to steam if it is hot enough or turning to ice if it is cold enough. And you can construct an instrument, called a thermometer, which can help you to predict when such changes will occur. The scale on the thermometer is what we call temperature. But the units in which we measure temperature are arbitrary. For example, we can accurately predict that when a Celsius thermometer shows a temperature of 0, water will turn to ice. But the units of measurement do not matter because this same event also occurs when a Fahrenheit thermometer shows a temperature of 32.

FIGURE 8.2

Total Utility and Marginal Utility

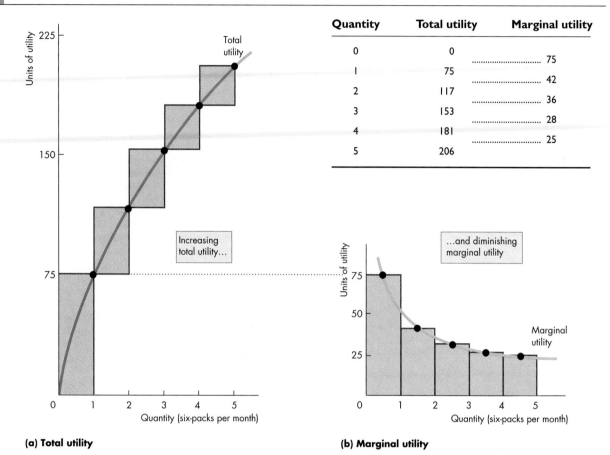

Quantity	Total utility	Marginal utility
0	0	
		75
1	75	
		42
2	117	
		36
3	153	
		28
4	181	
		25
5	206	

(a) Total utility

The table shows that as Lisa drinks more pop her total utility from pop increases. The table also shows her marginal utility—the change in total utility resulting from the last six-pack that she consumes. Marginal utility declines as consumption increases. The figure graphs Lisa's total utility and marginal

(b) Marginal utility

utility from pop. Part (a) shows her total utility. It also shows as a bar the extra total utility she gains from each additional six-pack—her marginal utility. Part (b) shows how Lisa's marginal utility from pop diminishes by placing the bars shown in part (a) side by side as a series of declining steps.

The concept of utility helps us make predictions about consumption choices in much the same way that the concept of temperature helps us make predictions about physical phenomena.

Admittedly marginal utility theory does not enable us to predict how buying plans change with the same precision that a thermometer enables us to predict when water will turn to ice or steam. But the theory provides important insights into buying plans and has some powerful implications, as you are about to discover.

R E V I E W   Q U I Z

- Explain how a consumer's income and the prices of goods limit consumption possibilities.
- What is utility and how do we use the concept of utility to describe a consumer's preferences?
- What is the distinction between total utility and marginal utility?
- What is the key assumption about marginal utility?

Maximizing Utility

A HOUSEHOLD'S INCOME AND THE PRICES THAT it faces limit the household's consumption choices and the household's preferences determine the utility that it can obtain from each consumption possibility. Marginal utility theory assumes that the household chooses the consumption possibility that maximizes its total utility. This assumption of utility maximization is a way of expressing the fundamental economic problem—scarcity. People's wants exceed the resources available to satisfy those wants, so they must make hard choices. In making choices, they try to get the maximum attainable benefit—they try to maximize total utility.

Let's see how Lisa allocates $30 a month between movies and pop to maximize her total utility. We'll continue to assume that movies cost $6 each and pop costs $3 a six-pack.

The Utility-Maximizing Choice

The most direct way to calculate how Lisa spends her income to maximize her total utility is by making a table like Table 8.2. The rows of this table show the affordable combinations of movies and pop that lie along her budget line in Fig. 8.1. The table records three things: first, the number of movies seen and the total utility derived from them (the left-side of the table); second, the number of six-packs consumed and the total utility derived from them (the right-side of the table); and third, the total utility derived from both movies and pop (the centre column).

The first row of Table 8.2 records the situation when Lisa watches no movies and buys 10 six-packs. In this case, Lisa gets no utility from movies and 291 units of total utility from pop. Her total utility from movies and pop (the centre column) is 291 units. The rest of the table is constructed in the same way.

The consumption of movies and pop that maximizes Lisa's total utility is highlighted in the table. When Lisa sees 2 movies and buys 6 six-packs of pop, she gets 313 units of total utility. This is the best Lisa can do, given that she has only $30 to spend and given the prices of movies and six-packs. If she buys 8 six-packs of pop, she can see only 1 movie. She gets 310 units of total utility, 3 less than the maximum attainable. If she sees 3 movies, she can drink only 4 six-packs. She gets 302 units of total utility, 11 less than the maximum attainable.

TABLE 8.2

Lisa's Utility-Maximizing Combination

	Movies		Total utility	Pop	
	Quantity per month	Total utility	from movies and pop	Total utility	Six-packs per month
a	0	0	291	291	10
b	1	50	310	260	8
c	2	88	313	225	6
d	3	121	302	181	4
e	4	150	267	117	2
f	5	175	175	0	0

We've just described Lisa's consumer equilibrium. A **consumer equilibrium** is a situation in which a consumer has allocated all his or her available income in the way that, given the prices of goods and services, maximizes his or her total utility. Lisa's consumer equilibrium is 2 movies and 6 six-packs.

In finding Lisa's consumer equilibrium, we measured her *total* utility from movies and pop. But there is a better way of determining a consumer equilibrium—one that does not involve measuring total utility at all. Let's look at this alternative.

Equalizing Marginal Utility per Dollar Spent

Another way to find out the allocation that maximizes a consumer's total utility is to make the marginal utility per dollar spent on each good equal for all goods. The **marginal utility per dollar spent** is the marginal utility obtained from the last unit of a good consumed divided by the price of the good. For example, Lisa's marginal utility from seeing the first movie is 50 units of utility. The price of a movie is $6, which means that the marginal utility per dollar spent on movies is 50 units divided by $6, or 8.33 units of utility per dollar.

Total utility is maximized when all the consumer's available income is spent and when the marginal utility per dollar spent is equal for all goods.

Lisa maximizes total utility when she spends all her income and consumes movies and pop such that

$$\frac{\text{Marginal utility from movies}}{\text{Price of a movie}} = \frac{\text{Marginal utility from pop}}{\text{Price of pop}}.$$

Call the marginal utility from movies MU_m, the marginal utility from pop MU_p, the price of a movie P_m, and the price of pop P_p. Then Lisa maximizes her utility when she spends all her income and when

$$\frac{MU_m}{P_m} = \frac{MU_p}{P_p}.$$

Let's use this formula to find Lisa's utility-maximizing consumption choice. Table 8.3 sets out Lisa's marginal utilities (which are calculated from Table 8.1) and her marginal utility per dollar spent on each good. For example, in row *b*, Lisa's marginal utility from movies is 50 units, and because movies cost $6 each, her marginal utility per dollar spent on movies is 8.33 units per dollar (50 units divided by $6). Each row exhausts Lisa's income of $30. You can see that Lisa's marginal utility per dollar spent on each good, like marginal utility itself, decreases as more of the good is consumed.

Lisa maximizes her total utility when the marginal utility per dollar spent on movies is equal to the marginal utility per dollar spent on pop—possibility *c*. Lisa consumes 2 movies and 6 six-packs.

Figure 8.3 shows why the rule "equalize marginal utility per dollar spent on all goods" works. Suppose that instead of consuming 2 movies and 6 six-packs (possibility *c*), Lisa consumes 1 movie and 8 six-packs (possibility *b*). She then gets 8.33 units of utility per dollar spent on movies and 5.67 units per dollar spent on pop. Lisa can increase her total utility by buying less pop and seeing more movies. If she spends less on pop and more on movies, her total utility from pop decreases by 5.67 units per dollar and her total utility from movies increases by 8.33 units per dollar. Her total utility increases by 2.66 units per dollar.

Equalizing Marginal Utilities per Dollar Spent

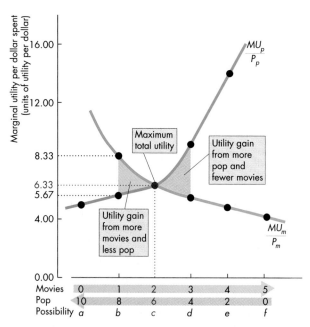

If Lisa consumes 1 movie and 8 six-packs (possibility *b*), she gets 8.33 units of utility from the last dollar spent on movies and 5.67 units of utility from the last dollar spent on pop. She can get more total utility by seeing one more movie. If she consumes 4 six-packs and 3 movies (possibility *d*), she gets 5.50 units of utility from the last dollar spent on movies and 9.33 units of utility from the last dollar spent on pop. She can increase her total utility by seeing one fewer movie. When Lisa's marginal utility per dollar spent on both goods is equal, her total utility is maximized.

TABLE 8.3

Equalizing Marginal Utilities per Dollar Spent

	Movies ($6 each)			Pop ($3 per six-pack)		
	Quantity	Marginal utility	Marginal utility per dollar spent	Six-packs	Marginal utility	Marginal utility per dollar spent
a	0	0		10	15	5.00
b	1	50	8.33	8	17	5.67
c	2	38	6.33	6	19	6.33
d	3	33	5.50	4	28	9.33
e	4	29	4.83	2	42	14.00
f	5	25	4.17	0	0	

Or suppose that Lisa consumes 3 movies and 4 six-packs (possibility *d*). In this situation, her marginal utility per dollar spent on movies (5.50) is less than her marginal utility per dollar spent on pop (9.33). Lisa can now increase her total utility by spending less on movies and more on pop.

The Power of Marginal Analysis The method we've just used to find Lisa's utility-maximizing choice of movies and pop is an example of the power of marginal analysis. By comparing the marginal gain from having more of one good with the marginal loss from having less of another good, Lisa is able to ensure that she gets the maximum attainable utility.

In the example, Lisa consumes at the point at which the marginal utility per dollar spent on movies and pop are equal. Because we buy goods and services in indivisible lumps, the numbers don't always work out so precisely. But the basic approach always works.

The rule to follow is very simple: If the marginal utility per dollar spent on movies exceeds the marginal utility per dollar spent on pop, see more movies and buy less pop; if the marginal utility per dollar spent on pop exceeds the marginal utility per dollar spent on movies, buy more pop and see fewer movies.

More generally, if the marginal gain from an action exceeds the marginal loss, take the action. You have met this principle before and you will meet it time and again in your study of economics. And you will find yourself using it when you make your own economic choices, especially when you must make a big decision.

Units of Utility In calculating Lisa's utility-maximizing choice in Table 8.3 and Fig. 8.3, we have not used the concept of total utility at all. All our calculations use marginal utility and price. By making the marginal utility per dollar spent equal for both goods, we know that Lisa maximizes her total utility.

This way of viewing maximum utility is important; it means that the units in which utility is measured do not matter. We could double or halve all the numbers measuring utility, or multiply them by any other positive number, or square them, or take their square roots. None of these transformations of the units used to measure utility makes any difference to the outcome. It is in this respect that utility is analogous to temperature. Our prediction about the freezing of water does not depend on the temperature scale; our prediction about the household's consumption choice does not depend on the units of utility.

REVIEW QUIZ

■ What is Lisa's goal when she chooses the quantities of movies and pop to consume?
■ What are the two conditions that are met if a consumer is maximizing utility?
■ Explain why equalizing the marginal utility of each good does *not* maximize utility.
■ Explain why equalizing the marginal utility per dollar spent on each good *does* maximize utility.

Predictions of Marginal Utility Theory

LET'S NOW USE MARGINAL UTILITY THEORY TO make some predictions. What happens to Lisa's consumption of movies and pop when their prices change and when her income changes?

To work out the effect of a change in price or income on the consumption choice: First, determine the combinations of movies and pop that just exhaust the new income at the new prices. Second, calculate the new marginal utilities per dollar spent. Third, determine the combinations that make the marginal utilities per dollar spent on movies and pop equal.

A Fall in the Price of Movies

Suppose that the price of a movie falls from $6 to $3. The rows of Table 8.4 show the combinations of movies and pop that exactly exhaust Lisa's $30 of income when movies cost $3 each and pop costs $3 a six-pack. Lisa's preferences do not change when prices change, so her marginal utility schedule remains the same as before. Now divide her marginal utility from movies by $3 to get the marginal utility per dollar spent on movies.

To find how Lisa responds to the fall in the price of a movie compare her new utility-maximizing choice (Table 8.4) with her original choice (Table 8.3). Lisa sees more movies (up from 2 to 5 a month) and drinks less pop (down from 6 to 5 six-packs a month). That is, Lisa *substitutes* movies for pop. Figure 8.4 shows these effects. The fall in the price of a movie produces a movement along Lisa's demand curve for movies (part a) and shifts her demand curve for pop (part b).

TABLE 8.4

How a Change in Price of Movies Affects Lisa's Choices

Movies ($3 each)		Pop ($3 per six-pack)	
Quantity	Marginal utility per dollar spent	Six-packs	Marginal utility per dollar spent
0		10	5.00
1	16.67	9	5.33
2	12.67	8	5.67
3	11.00	7	6.00
4	9.67	6	6.33
5	8.33	5	8.33
6	7.00	4	9.33
7	6.00	3	12.00
8	5.00	2	14.00
9	4.00	1	25.00
10	3.00	0	

A Rise in the Price of Pop

Now suppose that the price of pop rises from $3 to $6 a six-pack. The rows of Table 8.5 show the combinations of movies and pop that exactly exhaust Lisa's $30 of income when movies cost $3 each and pop costs $6 a six-pack. Lisa's preferences don't change when the price of pop changes. Now divide Lisa's marginal utility from pop by $6 to get her marginal utility per dollar spent on pop.

To find the effect of the rise in the price of pop on Lisa's utility-maximizing choice compare her new choice (Table 8.5) with her previous choice (Table 8.4). When the price of pop increases, Lisa drinks less pop (down from 5 to 2 six-packs a month) and sees more movies (up from 5 to 6 a month). That is, Lisa *substitutes* movies for pop. Figure 8.5 shows these effects. The rise in the price of pop produces a movement along Lisa's demand curve for pop (part a) and shifts her demand curve for movies (part b).

FIGURE 8.4

A Fall in the Price of Movies

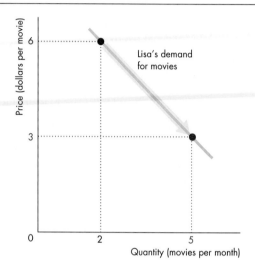

(a) Movies

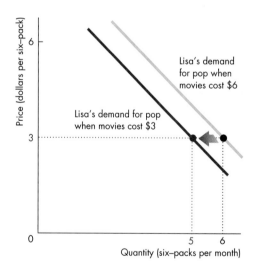

(b) Pop

When the price of a movie falls and the price of pop remains the same, the quantity of movies demanded by Lisa increases and, in part (a), Lisa moves along her demand curve for movies. Also, Lisa decreases her demand for pop and, in part (b), her demand curve for pop shifts leftward.

TABLE 8.5

How a Change in Price of Pop Affects Lisa's Choices

Movies ($3 each)		Pop ($6 per six-pack)	
Quantity	Marginal utility per dollar spent	Six-packs	Marginal utility per dollar spent
0		5	4.17
2	12.67	4	4.67
4	9.67	3	6.00
6	**7.00**	2	**7.00**
8	5.00	1	12.50
10	3.00	0	

Marginal utility theory predicts these two results:

1. When the price of a good rises, the quantity demanded of that good decreases.
2. If the price of one good rises, the demand for another good that can serve as a substitute increases.

Does this sound familiar? It should. These predictions of marginal utility theory correspond to the assumptions that we made about demand in Chapter 4. There we *assumed* that the demand curve for a good sloped downward, and we *assumed* that a rise in the price of a substitute increases demand.

You've now seen that marginal utility theory predicts how the quantities demanded respond to price changes. The theory helps us to understand the shape and the position of a demand curve and how the demand curve for one good shifts when the price of another good changes.

Marginal utility theory also helps us to understand how demand changes when income changes. Let's study the effects of a change in income on demand.

FIGURE 8.5

A Rise in the Price of Pop

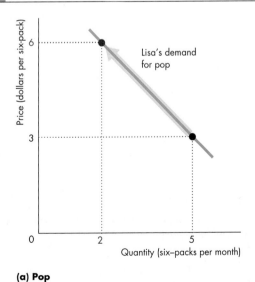

(a) Pop

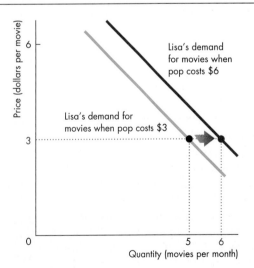

(b) Movies

When the price of pop rises and the price of a movie remains the same, the quantity of pop demanded by Lisa decreases and, in part (a), Lisa moves along her demand curve for pop.

Also, Lisa's demand for movies increases and, in part (b), her demand curve for movies shifts rightward.

A Rise in Income

Let's suppose that Lisa's income increases to $42 a month and that a movie costs $3 and a six-pack costs $3. We saw in Table 8.4 that with these prices and with an income of $30 a month, Lisa sees 5 movies and drinks 5 six-packs a month. We want to compare this choice of movies and pop with Lisa's choice when her income is $42. Table 8.6 shows the calculations needed to make the comparison. With $42, Lisa can see 14 movies a month and buy no pop or buy 14 six-packs a month and see no movies or choose any combination of the two goods in the rows of the table. We calculate the marginal utility per dollar spent in exactly the same way as we did before

and find the quantities at which the marginal utilities per dollar spent on movies and on pop are equal. With an income of $42, the marginal utility per dollar spent on each good is equal when Lisa sees 7 movies and drinks 7 six-packs of pop a month.

By comparing this situation with that in Table 8.4, we see that with an additional $12 a month, Lisa buys 2 more six-packs and sees 2 more movies a month. Lisa's response arises from her preferences, as described by her marginal utilities. Different preferences would produce different quantitative responses. With a larger income, the consumer always buys more of a *normal* good and less of an *inferior* good. For Lisa, pop and movies are normal goods. When her income increases, Lisa buys more of both goods.

You have now completed your study of the marginal utility theory of a household's consumption choices. Table 8.7 summarizes the key assumptions, implications, and predictions of the theory.

TABLE 8.6

Lisa's Choices with an Income of $42 a Month

Movies ($3 each)		Pop ($3 per six-pack)	
Quantity	Marginal utility per dollar spent	Six-packs	Marginal utility per dollar spent
0		14	3.67
1	16.67	13	4.00
2	12.67	12	4.33
3	11.00	11	4.67
4	9.67	10	5.00
5	8.33	9	5.33
6	7.00	8	5.67
7	6.00	7	6.00
8	5.00	6	6.33
9	4.00	5	8.33
10	3.00	4	9.33
11	2.00	3	12.00
12	1.00	2	14.00
13	0.67	1	25.00
14	0.33	0	

TABLE 8.7

Marginal Utility Theory

Assumptions

▪ A consumer derives utility from the goods consumed.

▪ Each additional unit of consumption yields additional total utility; marginal utility is positive.

▪ As the quantity of a good consumed increases, marginal utility decreases.

▪ A consumer's aim is to maximize total utility.

Implication

▪ Total utility is maximized when all the available income is spent and when the marginal utility per dollar spent is equal for all goods.

Predictions

▪ Other things remaining the same, the higher the price of a good, the smaller is the quantity bought (the law of demand).

▪ The higher the price of a good, the greater is the quantity bought of substitutes for that good.

▪ The larger the consumer's income, the greater is the quantity demanded of normal goods.

Individual Demand and Market Demand

Marginal utility theory explains how an individual household spends its income and enables us to derive an individual household's demand curve. In earlier chapters, we have been using *market* demand curves. We can derive a *market* demand curve from individual demand curves. Let's see how.

The relationship between the total quantity demanded of a good and its price is called **market demand**. The market demand curve is what you studied in Chapter 4. The relationship between the quantity demanded of a good by a single individual and its price is called *individual demand*.

Figure 8.6 illustrates the relationship between individual demand and market demand. In this example, Lisa and Chuck are the only people. The market demand is the total demand of Lisa and Chuck. At $3 a movie, Lisa demands 5 movies a month and Chuck demands 2, so the total quantity demanded by the market is 7 movies a month. Lisa's demand curve for movies in part (a) and Chuck's in part (b) sum *horizontally* to give the market demand curve in part (c).

The market demand curve is the horizontal sum of the individual demand curves and is formed by adding the quantities demanded by each individual at each price.

Because marginal utility theory predicts that individual demand curves slope downward, it also predicts that market demand curves slope downward.

FIGURE 8.6

Individual and Market Demand Curves

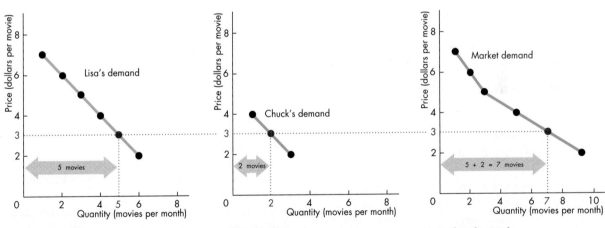

(a) Lisa's demand   **(b) Chuck's demand**   **(c) Market demand**

Price	Quantity of movies demanded		
(dollars per movie)	Lisa	Chuck	Market
7	1	0	1
6	2	0	2
5	3	0	3
4	4	1	5
3	5	2	7
2	6	3	9

The table and figure illustrate how the quantity of movies demanded varies as the price of a movie varies. In the table, the market demand is the sum of the individual demands. For example, at a price of $3, Lisa demands 5 movies and Chuck demands 2 movies, so the total quantity demanded in the market is 7 movies. In the figure, the market demand curve is the horizontal sum of the individual demand curves. Thus when the price is $3, the market demand curve shows that the quantity demanded is 7 movies, the sum of the quantities demanded by Lisa and Chuck.

Marginal Utility and the Real World

Marginal utility theory can be used to answer a wide range of questions about the real world. The theory sheds light on why the demand for CD players is price elastic while the demand for oil is price inelastic and why the demand for electricity is income elastic while the demand for transportation is income inelastic. Elasticities are determined by preferences. The feature of our preferences that determines elasticity is the step size with which marginal utility declines—the steepness of the marginal utility steps in Fig. 8.2(b).

If marginal utility declines in big steps, a small change in the quantity bought brings a big change in the marginal utility per dollar spent. So it takes a big change in price or income to bring a small change in the quantity demanded—demand is inelastic. Conversely, if marginal utility diminishes slowly, even a large change in the quantity bought brings a small change in the marginal utility per dollar spent. So it takes only a small price change to bring a large quantity change—demand is elastic.

But marginal utility theory can do much more than explain households' *consumption* choices. It can be used to explain *all* the choices made by households. One of these choices, the allocation of time between work in the home, office, or factory and leisure, is the theme of Probing the Ideas on pp. 196–197.

R E V I E W   Q U I Z

■ When the price of a good falls and the prices of other goods and a consumer's income remain the same, explain what happens to the consumption of the good whose price has fallen and to the consumption of other goods.

■ Elaborate your answer to the previous question by using demand curves. For which good is there a change in demand and for which is there a change in the quantity demanded?

■ If a consumer's income increases and if all goods are normal goods, how does the quantity bought of each good change?

We're going to end this chapter by returning to a recurring theme throughout your study of economics: the concept of efficiency and the distinction between price and value.

Efficiency, Price, and Value

MARGINAL UTILITY THEORY HELPS US TO DEEPEN our understanding of the concept of efficiency and also helps us to see more clearly the distinction between *value* and *price*. Let's see how.

Consumer Efficiency and Consumer Surplus

When Lisa allocates her limited budget to maximize utility, she is using her resources efficiently. Any other allocation of her budget wastes some resources.

But when Lisa has allocated her limited budget to maximize utility, she is *on* her demand curve for each good. A demand curve is a description of the quantity demanded at each price when utility is maximized. When we studied efficiency in Chapter 6, we learned that value equals marginal benefit and that a demand curve is also a willingness-to-pay curve. It tells us a consumer's *marginal benefit*—the benefit from consuming an additional unit of a good. You can now give the idea of marginal benefit a deeper meaning:

Marginal benefit is the maximum price a consumer is willing to pay for an extra unit of a good or service when utility is maximized.

The Paradox of Value

For centuries, philosophers have been puzzled by a paradox that we raised at the start of this chapter. Water, which is essential to life itself, costs little, but diamonds, which are useless compared to water, are expensive. Why? Adam Smith tried to solve this paradox. But not until the theory of marginal utility had been developed could anyone give a satisfactory answer.

You can solve this puzzle by distinguishing between *total* utility and *marginal* utility. The total utility that we get from water is enormous. But remember, the more we consume of something, the smaller is its marginal utility. We use so much water that its marginal utility—the benefit we get from one more glass of water—diminishes to a small value. Diamonds, on the other hand, have a small total utility relative to water, but because we buy few diamonds, they have a high marginal utility. When a household has maximized its total utility, it has allocated its budget in the way that makes the marginal utility per dollar spent equal for all goods.

FIGURE 8.7
The Paradox of Value

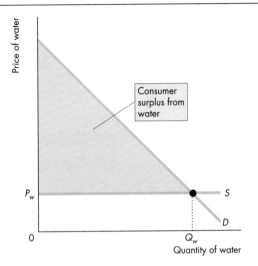

Consumer surplus from water

P_W

S

D

0

Q_W

Quantity of water

(a) Water

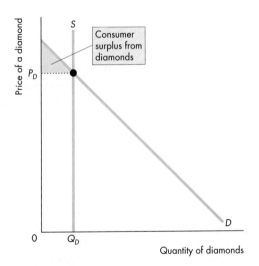

Consumer surplus from diamonds

S

P_D

D

0

Q_D

Quantity of diamonds

(b) Diamonds

Part (a) shows the demand for water, D, and the supply of water, S. The supply is (assumed to be) perfectly elastic at the price P_W. At this price, the quantity of water consumed is Q_W and the consumer surplus from water is the large green triangle. Part (b) shows the demand for diamonds, D, and the supply of diamonds, S. The supply is (assumed to be) perfectly inelastic at the quantity Q_D. At this quantity, the price of diamonds is P_D and the consumer surplus from diamonds is the small green triangle. Water is valuable—has a large consumer surplus—but cheap. Diamonds are less valuable than water—have a smaller consumer surplus—but are expensive.

That is, the marginal utility from a good divided by the price of the good is equal for all goods. This equality of marginal utilities per dollar spent holds true for diamonds and water: Diamonds have a high price and a high marginal utility. Water has a low price and a low marginal utility. When the high marginal utility of diamonds is divided by the high price of diamonds, the result is a number that equals the low marginal utility of water divided by the low price of water. The marginal utility per dollar spent is the same for diamonds as for water.

Another way to think about the paradox of value uses *consumer surplus*. Figure 8.7 explains the paradox of value by using this idea. The supply of water (part a) is perfectly elastic at price P_W, so the quantity of water consumed is Q_W and the consumer surplus from water is the large green area. The supply of diamonds (part b) is perfectly inelastic at quantity Q_D, so the price of diamonds is P_D and the consumer surplus from diamonds is the small green area. Water is cheap but brings a large consumer surplus, while diamonds are expensive but bring a small consumer surplus.

REVIEW QUIZ

- Explain why, along a demand curve, a consumer's choices are efficient.
- Explain the paradox of value and provide an example (different from diamonds and water).
- Does water or diamonds have the greater marginal utility? Does water or diamonds have the greater total utility? Does water or diamonds have the greater consumer surplus?

◆ You have now completed your study of the marginal utility theory. And you've seen how the theory can be used to explain our real-world consumption choices. You can see the theory in action once again in *Reading Between the Lines* on pp. 172–173, where it is used to interpret some recent trends in choices about coffee consumption.

The next chapter presents an alternative theory of household behaviour. To help you see the connection between the two theories of consumer behaviour, we'll continue with the same example. We'll meet Lisa again and discover another way of understanding how she gets the most out of her $30 a month.

POLICY WATCH

The Utility of Coffee

VANCOUVER SUN, JULY 25, 1998

Cashing in on coffee craze

As a rule, Jerry Wennes starts his day at Bean Around the World Coffees on West 10th in Point Grey with a steaming double cafe mocha—two shots of espresso, chocolate syrup and steamed milk, topped with a dollop of foam and garnished with chocolate sprinkles—a bowlful of pleasure for $3.10.

"I call it my energy stop," says the owner of Tap-Roots Ltd., a plumbing company in the Dunbar area. "I don't take coffee at home. The coffee shop is my neighborhood pub where I meet people."

Wennes, who drinks decaffeinated coffee on doctor's orders, can easily spend $10 a day on his favourite brew for an annual total of $3,650, including weekends and holidays.

Based on that figure, going out for coffee is the fifth largest household expense after taxes, shelter, food and transportation, according to Statistics Canada data.

Wennes is not alone in his passion for premium-priced coffee. A growing number of coffee lovers seems willing to shell out $3 and more for specialty coffees and companion confections, creating a market estimated to be worth at least $100 million in the Greater Vancouver area.

And this lucrative and expanding pool of coffee consumers has drawn giant Starbucks Coffee Co. of Seattle, with 80 outlets in the region, into pitched battle with more than 150 independent coffee houses scattered hither and yon. ...

The success of speciality coffee houses is due partly to people treating themselves to small indulgences despite money being tight, said Peter Hume of Hume Consulting.

"After the extravagant spending of the late 1980s followed by the recession in 1991, consumers became more price conscious, as evidenced by the success of big-box retailers," Hume says.

"But people are now prepared to go into Starbucks with a friend and drop $10 on a couple of cappuccinos and a biscotti. It's become very social."...

Essence of the Story

■ For some people, going out for coffee is the fifth highest household expense after taxes, shelter, food, and transportation.

■ The price of a cup of specialty coffee is approximately $3.

■ Drinking coffee in a coffee house has become a popular outing.

Economic Analysis

■ Jerry Wennes spends $10 a day on coffee. Assume that a coffee costs $2.50 and that Jerry drinks 4 cups a day. (Some coffee costs more than $2.50 and some less, but $2.50 is an average price.)

■ Figure 1 shows Jerry's total utility and Fig. 2 shows his marginal utility of coffee and of meals. His marginal utility of meals is greater than his marginal utility of coffee for small quantities but diminishes more quickly. Beyond three meals a day, Jerry is more interested in coffee than in food.

■ Suppose that Jerry has $20 a day to spend on coffee and meals and that meals cost $5 each.

■ Jerry maximized utility by equalizing the marginal utility per dollar spent on coffee and meals. The table (top half) shows that he consumes 4 coffees and 2 meals a day. Figure 3 shows Jerry's marginal utility per dollar spent and his utility-maximizing decision.

■ But Jerry's liking for coffee doesn't mean that he's not sensitive to prices. Suppose the price of an average cup of coffee increases to $5.

■ The table (bottom half) shows that Jerry now decreases his consumption of coffee to 1 cup a day and consumes 3 meals a day.

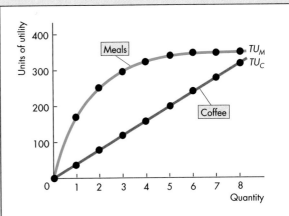

Figure 1 Total utility

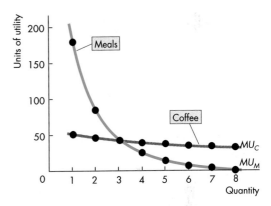

Figure 2 Marginal utility

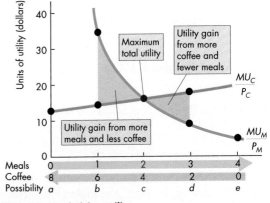

Figure 3 Maximizing utility

Jerry Wennes' Consumption Choices

	Meals ($5 each)			Coffee ($2.50 per cup)		
	Quantity	Marginal utility	Marginal utility per dollar	Cups	Marginal utility	Marginal utility per dollar
a	0			8	32	12.8
b	1	175	35	6	36	14.4
c	2	80	16	4	40	16.0
d	3	45	9	2	45	18.0
e	4	25	5	0		

	Meals ($5 each)			Coffee ($5.00 per cup)		
	Quantity	Marginal utility	Marginal utility per dollar	Cups	Marginal utility	Marginal utility per dollar
a'	0			4	38	7.6
b'	1	175	35	3	40	8.0
c'	2	80	16	2	42	8.4
d'	3	45	9	1	45	9.0
e'	4	25	5	0	50	10.0

SUMMARY

Key Points

Household Consumption Choices (pp. 160–162)

■ A household's choices are determined by its consumption possibilities and preferences.

■ A household's consumption possibilities are constrained by its income and by prices. Some combinations of goods are affordable, and some are not affordable.

■ A household's preferences can be described by marginal utility.

■ The key assumption of marginal utility theory is that the marginal utility of a good or service decreases as consumption of the good or service increases.

Maximizing Utility (pp. 163–165)

■ Marginal utility theory assumes that people buy the affordable combination of goods and services that maximizes total utility.

■ Total utility is maximized when all the available income is spent and when the marginal utility per dollar spent on each good is equal.

■ If the marginal utility per dollar spent on good *A* exceeds that on good *B*, the consumer can increase total utility by buying more of good *A* and less of good *B*.

Predictions of Marginal Utility Theory
(pp. 165–170)

■ Marginal utility theory predicts the law of demand. That is, other things remaining the same, the higher the price of a good, the smaller is the quantity demanded of that good.

■ Marginal utility theory also predicts that other things remaining the same, the higher the income of a consumer, the larger is the quantity demanded of a normal good.

■ Market demand is the sum of all individual demands, and the market demand curve is found by summing horizontally all the individual demand curves.

Efficiency, Price, and Value (pp. 170–171)

■ When a consumer maximizes utility, he or she is using resources efficiently.

■ Marginal utility theory resolves the paradox of the relative value of water and diamonds.

■ When we talk loosely about value, we are thinking of *total* utility or consumer surplus. But price is related to *marginal* utility.

■ Water, which we consume in large amounts, has a high total utility and a large consumer surplus but a low marginal utility and a low price.

■ Diamonds, which we consume in small amounts, have a low total utility and a small consumer surplus but a high marginal utility and a high price.

Key Figures and Table

Key Terms

PROBLEMS

*1. Jason enjoys rock CDs and spy novels and spends $60 a month on them. The following table shows the utility he gets from each good:

Quantity per month	Utility from rock CDs	Utility from spy novels
1	60	20
2	110	38
3	150	53
4	180	64
5	200	70
6	206	75

a. Draw graphs showing Jason's utility from rock CDs and from spy novels.
b. Compare the two utility graphs. Can you say anything about Jason's preferences?
c. Draw graphs that show Jason's marginal utility from rock CDs and from spy novels.
d. What do the two marginal utility graphs tell you about Jason's preferences?
e. If rock CDs and spy novels both cost $10 each, how does Jason spend the $60?

2. Mary enjoys classical CDs and travel books and spends $50 a month on them. The following table shows the utility she gets from each good:

Quantity per month	Utility from classical CDs	Utility from travel books
1	30	30
2	40	38
3	48	44
4	54	46
5	58	47

a. Draw graphs showing Mary's utility from classical CDs and from travel books.
b. Compare the two utility graphs. Can you say anything about Mary's preferences?
c. Draw graphs that show Mary's marginal utility from classical CDs and from travel books.
d. What do the two marginal utility graphs tell you about Mary's preferences?
e. If a classical CD and a travel book cost $10 each, how does Mary spend the $50 a month?

*3. Max enjoys windsurfing and snorkelling. He obtains the following utility from each of these sports:

Hours per day	Utility from windsurfing	Utility from snorkelling
1	120	40
2	220	76
3	300	106
4	360	128
5	400	140
6	412	150
7	422	158

Max has $35 to spend and he can spend as much time as he likes on his leisure pursuits. Windsurfing equipment rents for $10 an hour, and snorkelling equipment rents for $5 an hour.
a. Draw a graph that shows Max's budget line.
b. How long does he spend windsurfing and how long does he spend snorkelling?

4. Rob enjoys rock concerts and the opera. The table shows the utility he gets from each activity:

Concerts per month	Utility from rock concerts	Utility from operas
1	100	60
2	180	110
3	240	150
4	280	180
5	300	200
6	310	210

Rob has $100 a month to spend on concerts. A rock concert ticket is $20, and an opera ticket is $10.
a. Draw a graph that shows Rob's budget line.
b. How many rock concerts and how many operas does he attend?

*5. In problem 3, Max's sister gives him $20 to spend on his leisure pursuits, so he now has $55.
a. Draw a graph that shows Max's budget line.
b. How many hours does Max choose to windsurf and how many hours does he choose to snorkel now that he has $55 to spend?

6. In problem 4, if Rob's uncle gives him $30 to spend on concert tickets, he now has $130.
   a. Draw a graph that shows Rob's budget line.
   b. How many rock concerts and how many operas does he now attend?

*7. In problem 5, if windsurfing equipment now rents for $5 an hour, how long does Max windsurf and how long does he snorkel?

8. In problem 4, if the price of a rock concert decreases to $10, how many rock concerts and operas will Rob attend?

*9. Max takes a Club Med vacation, the cost of which includes unlimited sports activities. There is no extra charge for equipment. If Max windsurfs and snorkels for 6 hours a day, how many hours does he windsurf and how many hours does he snorkel?

10. Rob wins a lottery and has more than enough money to satisfy his desires for rock concerts and opera. He decides that he would like to see 5 concerts each month. How many rock concerts and how many operas does he now attend?

*11. Shirley's and Dan's demand schedules for popcorn are:

Price	Quantity demanded by	
(cents per carton)	Shirley	Dan
	(cartons per week)	
10	12	6
30	9	5
50	6	4
70	3	3
90	1	2

If Shirley and Dan are the only two individuals, what is the market demand for popcorn?

12. Ben's and Jerry's demand schedules for ice cream cones are:

Price	Quantity demanded by	
(dollars per cone)	Ben	Jerry
	(cones per week)	
1.00	8	10
1.30	7	8
1.50	6	6
1.70	5	4
1.90	4	2

If Ben and Jerry are the only two individuals, what is the market demand for ice cream cones?

CRITICAL THINKING

1. Study *Reading Between the Lines* on pp. 172–173 on coffee consumption in Canada and then answer the following questions:
   a. What are the facts about coffee consumption reported in the news article?
   b. How can we account for the consumption of a large quantity of coffee using marginal utility theory?
   c. What does marginal utility theory predict will happen to coffee consumption if the price of coffee rises sharply?
   d. What does marginal utility theory predict will happen to coffee consumption as people's incomes rise?
   e. Why do you think special coffee varieties have become more popular in recent years? Can marginal utility theory account for this trend?

2. In recent years, bottled water, fruit drinks, and sports drinks—new age drinks—have become popular. Use the marginal utility theory you have learned in this chapter to explain the rise in popularity of new age drinks.

3. Use the links on the Parkin-Bade Web site and read what Henry Schimberg, CEO of Coca-Cola Enterprises, says about the market for bottled water in North America. Use the marginal utility theory you have learned in this chapter to interpret and explain Mr. Schimberg's remarks about the bottled water market.

4. Smoking is banned on all airline flights in Canada and on most international flights. Use marginal utility theory to explain:
   a. What effect this ban has on the utility of smokers.
   b. How you expect the ban to influence the decisions of smokers.
   c. What effect this ban has on the utility of non-smokers.
   d. How you expect the ban to influence the decisions of non-smokers.

In your answer to this question, consider decisions about smoking, flying, and the willingness to pay for a flight.

Chapter 9

Possibilities, Preferences, and Choices

Like the continents floating on the earth's mantle, our spending patterns change steadily over time. On such subterranean movements, business empires rise and fall. Goods such as home videos and microwave popcorn now appear on our shopping lists, while 78 rpm phonograph records and horse-drawn carriages have disappeared. Miniskirts appear, disappear, and reappear in cycles of fashion.

Subterranean Movements

◆ But the glittering surface of our consumption obscures deeper and slower changes in how we spend. In the last few years, we've seen a proliferation of gourmet food shops and designer clothing boutiques. Yet we spend a smaller percentage of our income today on food and clothing than we did in 1950. At the same time, the percentage of our income spent on housing, transportation, and recreation has grown steadily. Why does consumer spending change over the years? How do people react to changes in income and changes in the prices of the things they buy? ◆ Similar subterranean movements govern the way we spend our time. For example, the average workweek has fallen steadily from 70 hours a week in the nineteenth century to 35 hours a week today. Although the average workweek is now much shorter than it once was, far more people now have jobs. This change has been especially dramatic for women, who are much more likely to work outside the home than they were in previous generations. Why has the average workweek declined? And why do more women work?

◆ We're going to study a model of choice that predicts the effects of changes in prices and incomes on what people buy and how much work they do.

After studying this chapter, you will be able to:

- Calculate and graph a household's budget line
- Work out how the budget line changes when prices or income changes
- Make a map of preferences by using indifference curves
- Explain the choices that households make
- Predict the effects of price and income changes on consumption choices
- Predict the effects of wage changes on work-leisure choices

Consumption Possibilities

CONSUMPTION CHOICES ARE LIMITED BY INCOME and by prices. A household has a given amount of income to spend and cannot influence the prices of the goods and services it buys. A household's **budget line** describes the limits to its consumption choices.

Let's look at Lisa's budget line.[1] Lisa has an income of $30 a month to spend. She buys two goods—movies and pop. Movies cost $6 each; pop costs $3 for a six-pack. Figure 9.1 shows alternative affordable ways for Lisa to consume movies and pop. Row *a* says that she can buy 10 six-packs of pop and see no movies, a combination of movies and pop that exhausts her monthly income of $30. Row *f* says that Lisa can watch 5 movies and drink no pop—another combination that exhausts the $30 available. Each of the other rows in the table also exhausts Lisa's income. (Check that each of the other rows costs exactly $30.) The numbers in the table define Lisa's consumption possibilities. We can graph Lisa's consumption possibilities as points *a* through *f* in Fig. 9.1.

Divisible and Indivisible Goods Some goods—called divisible goods—can be bought in any quantity desired. Examples are gasoline and electricity. We can best understand household choice if we suppose that all goods and services are divisible. For example, Lisa can consume a half a movie a month *on the average* by seeing one movie every two months. When we think of goods as being divisible, the consumption possibilities are not just the points *a* through *f* shown in Fig. 9.1, but those points plus all the intermediate points that form the line running from *a* to *f*. Such a line is a budget line.

Lisa's budget line is a constraint on her choices. It marks the boundary between what is affordable and what is unaffordable. She can afford any point on the line and inside it. She cannot afford any point outside the line. The constraint on her consumption depends on prices and her income, and the constraint changes when prices or her income changes. Let's see how by studying the budget equation.

---

[1]If you have studied Chapter 8 on marginal utility theory, you have already met Lisa. This tale of her thirst for pop and zeal for movies will sound familiar to you—up to a point. But in this chapter, we're going to use a different method for representing preferences—one that does not require us to resort to the idea of utility.

FIGURE 9.1

The Budget Line

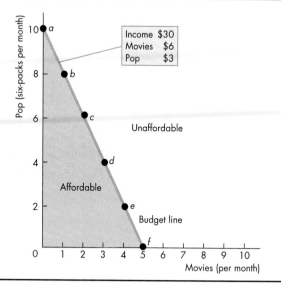

Consumption possibility	Movies (per month)	Pop (six-packs per month)
a	0	10
b	1	8
c	2	6
d	3	4
e	4	2
f	5	0

Lisa's budget line shows the boundary between what she can and cannot afford. The rows of the table list Lisa's affordable combinations of movies and pop when her income is $30, the price of pop is $3 a six-pack, and the price of a movie is $6. For example, row *a* tells us that Lisa exhausts her $30 income when she buys 10 six-packs and sees no movies. The figure graphs Lisa's budget line. Points *a* through *f* on the graph represent the rows of the table. For divisible goods, the budget line is the continuous line *af*. To calculate the equation for Lisa's budget line, start with expenditure equal to income:

$$\$3Q_p + \$6Q_m = \$30.$$

Divide by $3 to obtain

$$Q_p + \$2Q_m = 10.$$

Subtract $2Q_m$ from both sides to obtain

$$Q_p = 10 - 2Q_m.$$

The Budget Equation

We can describe the budget line by using a *budget equation*. The budget equation starts with the fact that

$$\text{Expenditure} = \text{Income}.$$

Expenditure is equal to the sum of the price of each good multiplied by the quantity bought. For Lisa,

Expenditure = (Price of pop × Quantity of pop)
      + (Price of movie × Quantity of movies).

Call the price of pop P_p, the quantity of pop Q_p, the price of a movie P_m, the quantity of movies Q_m, and income y. Using these symbols, Lisa's budget equation is

$$P_p Q_p + P_m Q_m = y.$$

Or, using the prices Lisa faces, $3 for a six-pack and $6 for a movie, and Lisa's income, $30, we get

$$\$3 Q_p + \$6 Q_m = \$30.$$

Lisa can choose any quantities of pop (Q_p) and movies (Q_m) that satisfy this equation. To find the relationship between these quantities, first divide both sides of the equation by the price of pop (P_p) to get

$$Q_p + \frac{P_m}{P_p} \times Q_m = \frac{y}{P_p}.$$

Now subtract the term $(P_m/P_p) \times Q_m$ from both sides of this equation to give

$$Q_p = \frac{y}{P_p} - \frac{P_m}{P_p} \times Q_m.$$

For Lisa, income (y) is $30, the price of a movie (P_m) is $6, and the price of a six-pack (P_p) is $3. So Lisa must choose the quantities of movies and pop to satisfy the equation

$$Q_p = \frac{\$30}{\$3} - \frac{\$6}{\$3} \times Q_m.$$

or

$$Q_p = 10 - 2Q_m.$$

To interpret the equation, go back to the budget line of Fig. 9.1 and check that the equation delivers that budget line. First set Q_m equal to zero. In this case, the budget equation tells us that Q_p, the quantity of pop, is y/P_p, which is 10 six-packs. This combination of Q_m and Q_p is the same as that shown in row *a* of the table in Fig. 9.1. Next set Q_m equal to 5. Q_s is now equal to zero (row *f* of the table). Check that you can derive the other rows.

The budget equation contains two variables chosen by the household (Q_m and Q_p) and two variables (y/P_p and P_m/P_p) that the household takes as given. Let's look more closely at these variables.

Real Income A household's **real income** is the household's income expressed not as money but as a quantity of goods the household can afford to buy. Expressed in terms of pop, Lisa's real income is y/P_p. This quantity is the maximum number of six-packs that she can buy. It is equal to her money income divided by the price of pop. Lisa's income is $30 and the price of pop is $3 a six-pack, so her real income in terms of pop is 10 six-packs, which is shown in Fig. 9.1 as the point at which the budget line intersects the y-axis.

Relative Price A **relative price** is the price of one good divided by the price of another good. In Lisa's budget equation, the variable P_m/P_p is the relative price of a movie in terms of pop. For Lisa, P_m is $6 a movie and P_p is $3 a six-pack, so P_m/P_p is equal to 2 six-packs per movie. That is, to see one more movie, Lisa must give up 2 six-packs.

You've just calculated Lisa's opportunity cost of a movie. Recall that the opportunity cost of an action is the best alternative forgone. For Lisa to see 1 more movie a month, she must forgo 2 six-packs. You've also calculated Lisa's opportunity cost of pop. For Lisa to consume 2 more six-packs a month, she must give up seeing 1 movie. So her opportunity cost of 2 six-packs is 1 movie.

The relative price of a movie in terms of pop is the magnitude of the slope of Lisa's budget line. To calculate the slope of the budget line, recall the formula for slope (Chapter 2): Slope equals the change in the variable measured on the y-axis divided by the change in the variable measured on the x-axis as we move along the line. In Lisa's case (Fig. 9.1), the variable measured on the y-axis is the quantity of pop, and the variable measured on the x-axis is the quantity of movies. Along Lisa's budget line, as pop decreases from 10 to 0 six-packs, movies increase from 0 to 5. Therefore the magnitude of the slope of the budget line is 10 six-packs divided by 5 movies, or 2 six-packs per movie. The magnitude of this slope is exactly the same as the relative price we've just calculated. It is also the opportunity cost of a movie.

A Change in Prices When prices change, so does the budget line. The lower the price of the good measured on the horizontal axis, other things

FIGURE 9.2

Changes in Prices
and Income

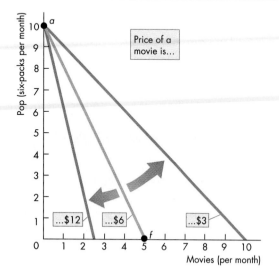

(a) A change in price

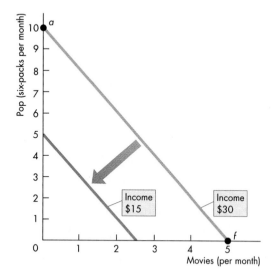

(b) A change in income

In part (a), the price of a movie changes. A fall in the price from $6 to $3 rotates the budget line outward and makes it flatter. A rise in the price from $6 to $12 rotates the budget line inward and makes it steeper.

In part (b), income falls from $30 to $15 while the prices of movies and pop remain constant. The budget line shifts leftward, but its slope does not change.

remaining the same, the flatter is the budget line. For example, if the price of a movie falls from $6 to $3, real income in terms of pop does not change but the relative price of a movie falls. The budget line rotates outward and becomes flatter, as shown in Fig. 9.2(a). The higher the price of the good measured on the horizontal axis, other things remaining the same, the steeper is the budget line. For example, if the price of a movie rises from $6 to $12, the relative price of a movie increases. The budget line rotates inward and becomes steeper as shown in Fig. 9.2(a).

A Change in Income A change in *money income* changes real income but does not change relative prices. The budget line shifts, but its slope does not change. The bigger a household's money income, the bigger is real income and the farther to the right is the budget line. The smaller a household's money income, the smaller is real income and the farther to the left is the budget line. Figure 9.2(b) shows the effect of a change in money income on Lisa's budget line. The initial budget line is the same one that we began with in Fig. 9.1 when Lisa's income is $30. The new budget line shows how much Lisa can consume if her income falls to $15 a month. The two budget lines have the same slope because they have the same relative price. The new budget line is closer to the origin than the initial one because Lisa's real income has decreased.

REVIEW QUIZ

- What does Lisa's budget line show?
- What is Lisa's real income in terms of movies?
- What is Lisa's opportunity cost of pop?
- If a household has an income of $40 and consumes only bus rides at $4 each and magazines of $2 each, what is the equation that describes its budget line?
- If the price of one good changes, what happens to the relative price and to the slope of the budget line?
- If a household's money income changes and no prices change, what happens to the household's real income and its budget line?

We've studied the limits to what a household can consume. Let's now learn how we can describe preferences and make a map that contains a lot of information about a household's preferences.

Preferences and Indifference Curves

YOU ARE GOING TO DISCOVER A VERY NEAT IDEA— that of drawing a map of a person's preferences. A preference map is based on the intuitively appealing assumption that people can sort all the possible combinations of goods into three groups: preferred, not preferred, and indifferent. To make this idea more concrete, let's ask Lisa to tell us how she ranks various combinations of movies and pop.

Figure 9.3(a) shows part of Lisa's answer. She tells us that she currently consumes 2 movies and 6 six-packs a month at point c. She then lists all the combinations of movies and pop that she says are equally acceptable to her as her current consumption. When we plot these combinations of movies and pop we get the green curve in Fig. 9.3(a). This curve is the key element in a map of preferences and is called an indifference curve.

An **indifference curve** is a line that shows combinations of goods among which a consumer is *indifferent*. The indifference curve in Fig. 9.3(a) tells us that Lisa is just as happy to consume 2 movies and 6 six-packs a month at point c as to consume the combination of movies and pop at point g or at any other point along the curve.

Lisa also says that she prefers all the combinations of movies and pop in the yellow area above the indifference curve in Fig. 9.3(a) to any combination on the indifference curve. And she prefers any combination on the indifference curve to any combination in the grey area below the indifference curve.

The indifference curve in Fig. 9.3(a) is just one of a whole family of such curves. This indifference curve appears again in Fig. 9.3(b) labelled I_1. The curves labelled I_0 and I_2 are two other indifference curves. Lisa prefers any point on indifference curve I_2 to any point on indifference curve I_1, and she prefers any point on I_1 to any point on I_0. We refer to I_2 as being a higher indifference curve than I_1, and I_1 as being higher than I_0.

A preference map is a series of indifference curves that resemble the contour lines on a map. By looking at the shape of the contour lines on a map, we can draw conclusions about the terrain. Similarly, by looking at the shape of indifference curves, we can draw conclusions about a person's preferences.

Let's learn how to "read" a preference map.

FIGURE **9.3**

FIGURE **9.3**
A Preference Map

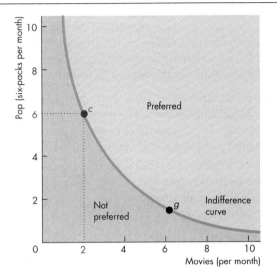

(a) An indifference curve

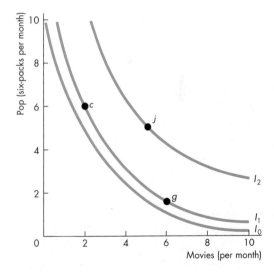

(b) Lisa's preference map

In part (a), Lisa consumes 6 six-packs of pop and 2 movies a month at point c. She is indifferent between all the points on the green indifference curve such as c and g. She prefers any point above the indifference curve (yellow area) to any point on it, and she prefers any point on the indifference curve to any point below it (grey area). A preference map is a number of indifference curves. Part (b) shows three—I_0, I_1, and I_2—that are part of Lisa's preference map. She prefers point j to point c or g, so she prefers any point on I_2 to any point on I_1.

Marginal Rate of Substitution

The **marginal rate of substitution** (*MRS*) is the rate at which a person will give up good y (the good measured on the y-axis) to get one additional unit of good x (the good measured on the x-axis) and at the same time remain indifferent (remain on the same indifference curve). The marginal rate of substitution is measured by the magnitude of the slope of an indifference curve.

■ If the indifference curve is *steep*, the marginal rate of substitution is *high*. The person is willing to give up a large quantity of good y to get a small quantity of good x while remaining indifferent.

■ If the indifference curve is *flat*, the marginal rate of substitution is *low*. The person is willing to give up only a small amount of good y to get a large amount of good x to remain indifferent.

Figure 9.4 shows you how to calculate the marginal rate of substitution. Suppose that Lisa consumes 6 six-packs and 2 movies at point c on indifference curve I_1. Her marginal rate of substitution is calculated by measuring the magnitude of the slope of the indifference curve at point c. To measure this magnitude, place a straight line against, or tangent to, the indifference curve at point c. Along that line, as pop consumption decreases by 10 six-packs, movie consumption increases by 5. So at point c, Lisa is willing to give up pop for movies at the rate of 2 six-packs per movie. Her marginal rate of substitution is 2.

Now, suppose that Lisa consumes 6 movies and 1.5 six-packs at point g in Fig. 9.4. Her marginal rate of substitution is now measured by the slope of the indifference curve at point g. That slope is the same as the slope of the tangent to the indifference curve at point g. Here, as pop consumption decreases by 4.5 six-packs, movie consumption increases by 9. So at point g, Lisa is willing to give up pop for movies at the rate of 1/2 six-pack per movie. Her marginal rate of substitution is 1/2.

As Lisa's consumption of movies increases and her consumption of pop decreases, her marginal rate of substitution diminishes. Diminishing marginal rate of substitution is the key assumption of consumer theory. The assumption of **diminishing marginal rate of substitution** is a general tendency for the marginal rate of substitution to diminish as the consumer moves along an indifference curve, increasing consumption of the good measured on the x-axis and decreasing consumption of the good measured on the y-axis.

FIGURE 9.4
The Marginal Rate of Substitution

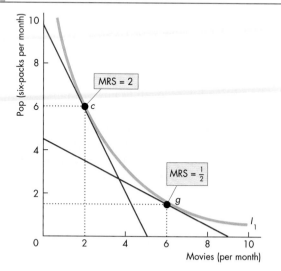

The magnitude of the slope of an indifference curve is called the marginal rate of substitution (MRS). The red line at point c tells us that Lisa is willing to give up 10 six-packs to see 5 movies. Her marginal rate of substitution at c is 10 divided by 5, which equals 2. The red line at point g tells us that Lisa is willing to give up 4.5 six-packs to see 9 movies. Her marginal rate of substitution at g is 4.5 divided by 9, which equals 1/2.

Your Own Diminishing Marginal Rate of Substitution You may be able to appreciate why we assume the principle of a diminishing marginal rate of substitution by thinking about your own preferences. Imagine that in a week, you consume 10 six-packs of pop and no movies. Most likely you are willing to give up a lot of pop so that you can go to the movies just once. But now imagine that in a week, you consume 1 six-pack and 6 movies. Most likely you will now not be willing to give up much pop to see a seventh movie. As a general rule, the greater the number of movies you see, the smaller is the quantity of pop you are willing to give up to see one additional movie.

The shape of a person's indifference curves incorporates the principle of the diminishing marginal rate of substitution because the curves are bowed towards the origin. The tightness of the bend of an indifference curve tells us how willing a person is to substitute one good for another while remaining indifferent. Let's look at some examples that make this point clear.

Degree of Substitutability

Most of us would not regard movies and pop as being close substitutes for each other. We probably have some fairly clear ideas about how many movies we want to see each month and how many cans of pop we want to drink. Nevertheless, to some degree, we are willing to substitute between these two goods. No matter how big a pop freak you are, there is surely some increase in the number of movies you can see that will compensate you for being deprived of a can of pop. Similarly, no matter how addicted you are to the movies, surely some number of cans of pop will compensate you for being deprived of seeing one movie. A person's indifference curves for movies and pop might look something like those shown in Fig. 9.5(a).

Close Substitutes Some goods substitute so easily for each other that most of us do not even notice which we are consuming. The different brands of personal computers are an example. So long as it has an "Intel inside" and runs Windows, most of us don't care whether our PC is a Dell, a Compaq, a Toshiba, or any of a dozen other brands. The same holds true for marker pens. Most of us don't care whether we use a marker pen from the campus bookstore or the local supermarket. When two goods are perfect substitutes for each other, their indifference curves are straight lines that slope downward, as Fig. 9.5(b) illustrates. The marginal rate of substitution is constant.

Complements Some goods cannot substitute for each other at all. Instead they are complements. The complements in Fig. 9.5(c) are left and right running shoes. Indifference curves of perfect complements are L-shaped. One left running shoe and one right running shoe are as good as one left shoe and two right ones. Having two of each is preferred to having one of each, but having two of one and one of the other is no better than having one of each.

The extreme cases of perfect substitutes and perfect complements shown here don't often happen in reality. They do, however, illustrate that the shape of the indifference curve shows the degree of substitutability between two goods. The more perfectly

---

FIGURE 9.5

The Degree of Substitutability

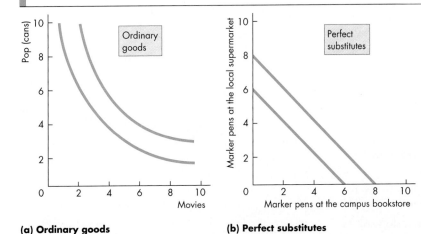

(a) Ordinary goods

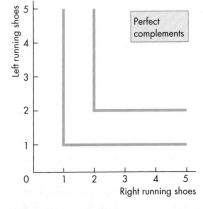

(c) Perfect complements

(b) Perfect substitutes

The shape of the indifference curves reveals the degree of substitutability between two goods. Part (a) shows the indifference curves for two ordinary goods: movies and pop. To consume less pop and remain indifferent, one must see more movies. The number of movies that compensates for a reduction in pop increases as less pop is consumed. Part (b) shows the indifference curves for two perfect substitutes. For the consumer to remain indifferent, one fewer marker pen from the local supermarket must be replaced by one extra marker pen from the campus bookstore. Part (c) shows two perfect complements—goods that cannot be substituted for each other at all. Having two left running shoes with one right running shoe is no better than having one of each. But having two of each is preferred to having one of each.

"With the pork I'd recommend an Alsatian white or a Coke."

substitutable the two goods, the more nearly are their indifference curves straight lines and the less quickly does the marginal rate of substitution fall. Poor substitutes for each other have tightly curved indifference curves, approaching the shape of those shown in Fig. 9.5(c).

As you can see in the cartoon, according to the waiter's preferences, Coke and Alsatian white wine are perfect substitutes and each is a complement with pork. We hope the customers agree with him.

R E V I E W   Q U I Z

- What is an indifference curve and how does an indifference map show preferences?
- Why does an indifference curve slope downward and why is it bowed towards the origin?
- What do we call the magnitude of the slope of an indifference curve?
- What is the key assumption about a consumer's marginal rate of substitution?

The two components of the model of household choice are now in place: the budget line and the preference map. We will now use these components to work out the household's choice and to predict how choices change when prices and income change.

Predicting Consumer Behaviour

WE ARE NOW GOING TO PREDICT THE QUANTITIES of movies and pop that Lisa *chooses* to buy. Figure 9.6 shows Lisa's budget line from Fig. 9.1 and her indifference curves from Fig. 9.3(b). We assume that Lisa consumes at her best affordable point, which is 2 movies and 6 six-packs—at point *c*. Here, Lisa

- Is on her budget line
- Is on her highest attainable indifference curve
- Has a marginal rate of substitution between movies and pop equal to the relative price of movies and pop.

For every point inside the budget line, such as point *i*, there are points *on* the budget line that Lisa

FIGURE   9.6

The Best Affordable Point

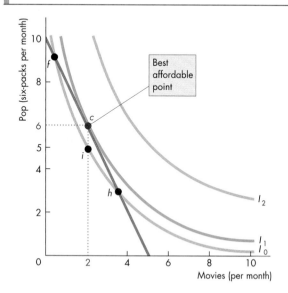

Lisa's best affordable point is *c*. At that point, she is on her budget line and also on the highest attainable indifference curve. At a point such as *h*, Lisa is willing to give up more movies in exchange for pop than she has to. She can move to point *i*, which is just as good as point *h* and have some unspent income. She can spend that income and move to *c*, a point that she prefers to point *i*.

prefers. For example, she prefers all the points on the budget line between *f* and *h* to point *i*. So she chooses a point on the budget line.

Every point on the budget line lies on an indifference curve. For example, point *h* lies on the indifference curve I_0. At point *h*, Lisa's marginal rate of substitution is less than the relative price. Lisa is willing to give up more movies in exchange for pop than the budget line says she must give up. So she moves along her budget line from *h* towards *c*. As she does so, she passes through a number of indifference curves (not shown in the figure) located between indifference curves I_0 and I_1. All of these indifference curves are higher than I_0, and therefore Lisa prefers any point on them to point *h*. But when Lisa gets to point *c*, she is on the highest attainable indifference curve. If she keeps moving along the budget line, she starts to encounter indifference curves that are lower than I_1. So Lisa chooses point *c*.

At the chosen point, the marginal rate of substitution (the magnitude of the slope of the indifference curve) equals the relative price (the magnitude of the slope of the budget line).

Let's use this model of household choice to predict the effects on consumption of changes in prices and income. We'll begin by studying the effect of a change in price.

A Change in Price

The effect of a change in price on the quantity of a good consumed is called the **price effect**. We will use Fig. 9.7(a) to work out the price effect of a fall in the price of a movie. We start with movies costing $6 each, pop costing $3 a six-pack, and Lisa's income at $30 a month. In this situation, she consumes 6 six-packs and 2 movies a month at point *c*.

Now suppose that the price of a movie falls to $3. With a lower price of a movie, the budget line rotates outward and becomes flatter. (Check back with Fig. 9.2 (a) for a refresher on how a price change affects the budget line.) The new budget line is the dark orange one in Fig. 9.7(a).

Lisa's best affordable point is now point *j*, where she consumes 5 movies and 5 six-packs of pop. Lisa drinks less pop and watches more movies now that movies cost less. She cuts her pop consumption from 6 to 5 six-packs and increases the number of movies she sees from 2 to 5 a month. Lisa substitutes movies for pop when the price of a movie falls and the price of pop and her income remain constant.

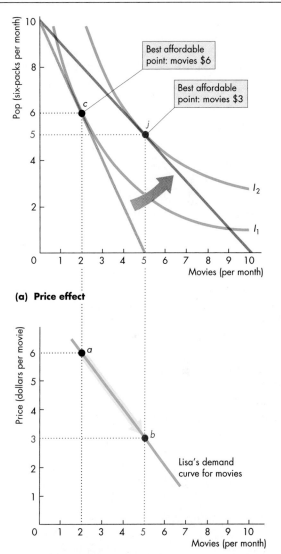

FIGURE 9.7

Price Effect and Demand Curve

(a) Price effect

(b) Demand curve

Initially, Lisa consumes at point *c* (part a). If the price of a movie falls from $6 to $3, she consumes at point *j*. The move from *c* to *j* is the price effect.

Part (b) shows Lisa's demand curve for movies. At a price of $6 a movie, Lisa sees 2 movies a month, at point *a*. At a price of $3 a movie, she sees 5 movies a month, at point *b*. Lisa's demand curve traces out her best affordable quantity of movies as the price of a movie varies.

The Demand Curve In Chapter 4, we asserted that the demand curve slopes downward. We can now derive a demand curve from a consumer's budget line and indifference curves. By doing so, we can see that the law of demand and the downward-sloping demand curve are consequences of the consumer's choosing his or her best affordable combination of goods.

To derive Lisa's demand curve for movies, lower the price of a movie and find her best affordable point at different prices. We've just done this for two movie prices in Fig. 9.7(a). Figure 9.7(b) highlights these two prices and two points that lie on Lisa's demand curve for movies. When the price of a movie is $6, Lisa sees 2 movies a month at point a. When the price falls to $3, she increases the number of movies she sees to 5 a month at point b. The demand curve is made up of these two points plus all the other points that tell us Lisa's best affordable consumption of movies at each movie price, given the price of pop and Lisa's income. As you can see, Lisa's demand curve for movies slopes downward. The lower the price of a movie, the more movies she watches each month. This is the law of demand.

Next, let's examine how Lisa changes her consumption of movies and pop when her income changes.

A Change in Income

The effect of a change in income on consumption is called the **income effect**. Let's work out the income effect by examining how consumption changes when income changes and prices remain constant. Figure 9.8(a) shows the income effect when Lisa's income falls. With an income of $30 and with a movie costing $3 and pop $3 a six-pack, she consumes at point j—5 movies and 5 six-packs. If her income falls to $21, she consumes at point k—consuming 4 movies and 3 six-packs. When Lisa's income falls, she consumes less of both goods. Movies and pop are normal goods.

The Demand Curve and the Income Effect

A change in income leads to a shift in the demand curve, as shown in Fig. 9.8(b). With an income of $30 and a movie costing $3, Lisa's demand curve is D_0, the same curve as in Fig. 9.7. But when her income falls to $21, Lisa sees only 4 movies at point c. With less income, she plans to see fewer movies at each price, so her demand curve shifts leftward to D_1.

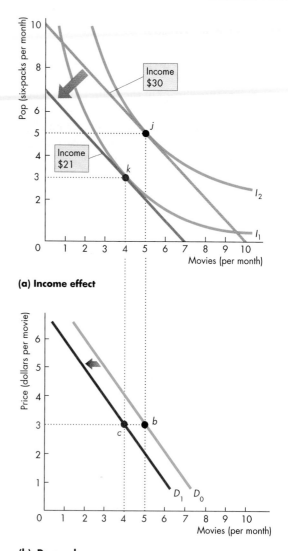

FIGURE 9.8

Income Effect and Change in Demand

(a) Income effect

(b) Demand curve

A change in income shifts the budget line and changes the best affordable point and changes consumption. In part (a), when Lisa's income decreases from $30 to $21, she consumes less of both movies and pop. In part (b), Lisa's demand curve for movies when her income is $30 is D_0. When Lisa's income decreases to $21, her demand curve for movies shifts leftward to D_1. Lisa's demand for movies decreases because she now sees fewer movies at each price.

Substitution Effect and Income Effect

For a normal good, a fall in price *always* increases the quantity bought. We can prove this assertion by dividing the price effect into two parts:

■ Substitution effect
■ Income effect.

Figure 9.9(a) shows the price effect, and Fig. 9.9(b) divides the price effect into its two parts.

Substitution Effect   The **substitution effect** is the effect of a change in price on the quantity bought when the consumer (hypothetically) remains indifferent between the original and the new situation. To work out Lisa's substitution effect, we imagine that when the price of a movie falls, Lisa's income also falls by an amount that leaves her on the same indifference curve as before.

Figure 9.9 shows the substitution effect. When the price of a movie falls from $6 to $3, suppose (hypothetically) that Lisa's income falls to $21. What's special about $21? It is the income that is just enough, at the new price of a movie, to keep Lisa's best affordable point on the *same* indifference curve as her original consumption point *c*. Lisa's budget line in this situation is the light orange line shown in Fig. 9.9(b). With the new price of a movie and the new smaller income, Lisa's best affordable point is *k* on indifference curve I_1. The move from *c* to *k* isolates the substitution effect of the price change. The substitution effect of the fall in the price of a movie is an increase in the consumption of movies from 2 to 4. The direction of the substitution effect never varies: When the relative price of a good falls, the consumer substitutes more of that good for the other good.

Income Effect   To calculate the substitution effect, we gave Lisa a $9 pay cut. Now let's give Lisa her $9 back. The $9 increase in income shifts Lisa's budget line outward, as shown in Fig. 9.9(b). The slope of the budget line does not change because both prices remain constant. This change in Lisa's budget line is similar to the one illustrated in Fig. 9.8. As Lisa's budget line shifts outward, her best affordable point becomes *j* on indifference curve I_2. The move from *k* to *j* isolates the income effect of the price change. The income effect of the fall in the price of a movie is the increase in the quantity of movies seen from 4 to 5. As Lisa's income increases, she increases her consumption of movies. For

FIGURE   9.9

Substitution Effect and Income Effect

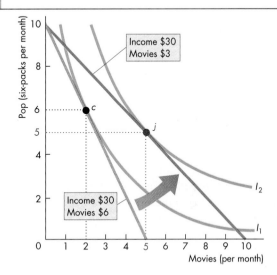

(a) Price effect

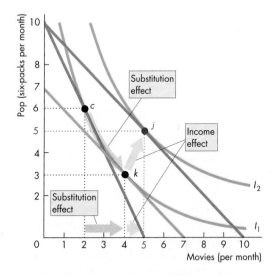

(b) Substitution effect and income effect

The price effect in part (a) can be separated into a substitution effect and an income effect in part (b). To isolate the substitution effect, we confront Lisa with the new price but keep her on her original indifference curve, I_1. The substitution effect is the move from *c* to *k*. To isolate the income effect, we confront Lisa with the new price of movies but increase her income so that she can move from the original indifference curve, I_1, to the new one, I_2. The income effect is the move from *k* to *j*.

Lisa, a movie is a normal good. For a normal good, the income effect reinforces the substitution effect.

Inferior Goods   The example that we have just studied is that of a change in the price of a normal good. The effect of a change in the price of an inferior good is different. Recall that an inferior good is one whose consumption decreases as income increases. For an inferior good, the income effect is negative. Thus for an inferior good, a lower price does not always lead to an increase in the quantity demanded. The lower price has a substitution effect that increases the quantity demanded. But the lower price also has a negative income effect that reduces the demand for the inferior good. Thus the income effect offsets the substitution effect to some degree. If the negative income effect exceeded the positive substitution effect, the demand curve would slope upward. This case does not appear to occur in the real world.

Back to the Facts

We started this chapter by observing how consumer spending has changed over the years. The indifference curve model explains those changes. Spending patterns are determined by best affordable choices. Changes in prices and incomes change the best affordable choice and change consumption patterns.

R E V I E W   Q U I Z

- When a consumer chooses the combination of goods and services to buy, what is she or he trying to achieve?
- Can you explain the conditions that are met when a consumer has found the best affordable combination of goods to buy? (Use the terms "budget line," "marginal rate of substitution," and "relative price" in your explanation.)
- If the price of a normal good falls, what happens to the quantity demanded of that good?
- Into what two effects can we divide the effect of a price change?
- For a normal good, does the income effect reinforce the substitution effect or does it partly offset the substitution effect?

The model of household choice can explain many other household choices. Let's look at one of them.

Work-Leisure Choices

HOUSEHOLDS MAKE MANY CHOICES OTHER THAN those about how to spend their income on the various goods and services available. We can use the model of consumer choice to understand many other household choices. Some of these choices are discussed on pp. 158–159. Here we'll study a key choice: How much labour to supply.

Labour Supply

Every week, we allocate our 168 hours between paid work—called *labour*—and all other activities—called *leisure*. How do we decide how to allocate our time between labour and leisure? We can answer this question by using the theory of household choice.

The more hours we spend on *leisure*, the smaller is our income. The relationship between leisure and income is described by an *income-time budget line*. Figure 9.10(a) shows Lisa's income-time budget line. If Lisa devotes the entire week to leisure—168 hours—she has no income and is at point z. By supplying labour in exchange for a wage, she can convert hours into income along the income-time budget line. The slope of that line is determined by the hourly wage rate. If the wage rate is $5 an hour, Lisa faces the flattest budget line. If the wage rate is $10 an hour, she faces the middle budget line. And if the wage rate is $15 an hour, she faces the steepest budget line.

Lisa buys leisure by not supplying labour and by forgoing income. The opportunity cost of an hour of leisure is the hourly wage rate forgone.

Figure 9.10(a) also shows Lisa's indifference curves for income and leisure. Lisa chooses her best attainable point. This choice of income and time allocation is just like her choice of movies and pop. She gets onto the highest possible indifference curve by making her marginal rate of substitution between income and leisure equal to her wage rate. Lisa's choice depends on the wage rate she can earn. At a wage rate of $5 an hour, Lisa chooses point a and works 20 hours a week (168 minus 148) for an income of $100 a week. At a wage rate of $10 an hour, she chooses point b and works 35 hours a week (168 minus 133) for an income of $350 a week. And at a wage rate of $15 an hour, she chooses point c and works 30 hours a week (168 minus 138) for an income of $450 a week.

FIGURE 9.10
The Supply of Labour

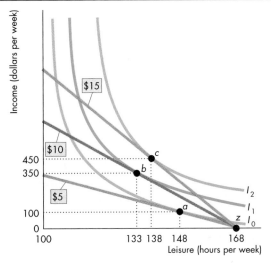

(a) Time allocation decision

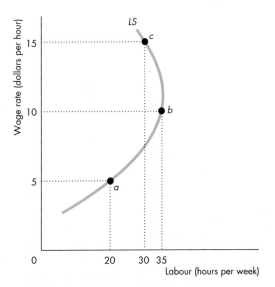

(b) Labour supply curve

In part (a), at a wage rate of $5 an hour, Lisa takes 148 hours of leisure and works 20 hours a week at point *a*. If the wage rate increases from $5 to $10, she decreases her leisure to 133 hours and increases her work to 35 hours a week at point *b*. But if the wage rate increases from $10 to $15, Lisa *increases* her leisure to 138 hours and *decreases* her work to 30 hours a week at point *c*. Part (b) shows Lisa's labour supply curve. Points *a*, *b*, and *c* on the supply curve correspond to Lisa's choices on her income-time budget line in part (a).

The Labour Supply Curve

Figure 9.10(b) shows Lisa's labour supply curve. This curve shows that as the wage rate increases from $5 an hour to $10 an hour, Lisa increases the quantity of labour supplied from 20 hours a week to 35 hours a week. But when the wage rate increases to $15 an hour, she decreases her quantity of labour supplied to 30 hours a week.

Lisa's supply of labour is similar to that described for the economy as a whole at the beginning of this chapter. As wage rates have increased, work hours have decreased. At first, this pattern seems puzzling. We've seen that the hourly wage rate is the opportunity cost of leisure. So a higher wage rate means a higher opportunity cost of leisure. This fact on its own leads to a decrease in leisure and an increase in work hours. But instead, we've cut our work hours. Why? Because our incomes have increased. As the wage rate increases, incomes increase, so people demand more of all normal goods. Leisure is a normal good, so as incomes increase, people demand more leisure.

The higher wage rate has both a *substitution effect* and an *income effect*. The higher wage rate increases the opportunity cost of leisure and so leads to a substitution effect away from leisure. And the higher wage rate increases income and so leads to an income effect towards more leisure.

This theory of household choice can explain the facts about work patterns described at the beginning of this chapter. First, it can explain why the average workweek has fallen steadily from 70 hours in the nineteenth century to 35 hours today. The reason is that as wage rates have increased, although people have substituted work for leisure, they have also decided to use their higher incomes in part to consume more leisure. Second, the theory can explain why more women now have jobs in the labour market. The reason is that increases in their wage rates and improvements in their job opportunities have led to a substitution effect away from working at home and towards working in the labour market.

◇ This theory of household choice can also explain trends in the furniture industry, as you can see in *Reading Between the Lines* on pp. 190–191. In the chapters that follow, we're going to study the choices made by firms. We'll see how, in the pursuit of profit, firms make choices that determine the supply of goods and services and the demand for productive resources.

Indifference Curves for Furniture

THE CALGARY HERALD, JULY 25, 1998

Inflatable furniture returns with a BANG!

It's back. It's bold. And it's blown up.

"It" is inflatable furniture and home fashions made from this heavy-duty PVC vinyl are one of the hottest retro decorating crazes around these days. "It's an exciting product to have," says Maureen Reid, of Reid Stationers, which is selling plenty of these perky plastics. ...

People apparently have an instant reaction to the inflatable furniture when they see the Day-Glo decorating pieces.

"They notice and comment on it right away," says Seabird Urtasun, owner of the Land and Sea store in Eau Claire Market. "Everybody want(s) to interact with it—squeezing it, sitting and bouncing on it. And you can't miss it, because of the colors."...

"We have the sofas and chairs, which are the bigger pieces, but also lots of other things to go with them," says Urtasun. "There are love seats, side tables, pillows, a chaise, and even a mirror." ...

This fun and funky furniture trend is taking furniture sales by storm with local retailers saying they can't stock it fast enough because it interests such a wide segment of the population. ...

Of course, it...has a lot of appeal to the younger set. ...

"The new generation is really taking to it," says Reid. "People are buying it for teens' rooms as gifts and young adults like the look of it and the fact it's affordable as a first furniture purchase. It's also practical if you move a lot."

Prices for inflatable furniture range from about $100 to $150 for a sofa, while chairs, which can pack down to the size of a large book and weigh less than a pound, can be found for around $65 to $100. ...

They're tough, but comfy, say air furniture aficionados, while also being easy to move around. ...

So if you're looking for lots of quirkiness and comfort, and want a piece that's super-in right now, inflatable furniture is in your future. Just add air.

Essence of the Story

■ Teens and young adults like the look and the price of inflatable furniture.

■ Retailers say that inflatable furniture also appeals to other segments of the population.

■ Many types of traditional furniture such as sofas, chairs, and tables are available as inflatable furniture.

■ Lisa, a student, is furnishing her first apartment. She can choose traditional furniture or inflatable furniture.

■ Figure 1 shows Lisa's indifference curves for inflatable furniture and conventional furniture.

■ The magnitude of the slope of an indifference curve is the marginal rate of substitution (*MRS*).

■ The marginal rate of substitution tells how many units of conventional furniture Lisa is willing to give up to gain more inflatable furniture while remaining on the same indifference curve.

■ If Lisa consumes on indifference curve I_0, at point *a*, she is willing to give up one unit of conventional furniture to get one additional unit of inflatable furniture—the move from *a* to *b*.

■ If Lisa consumes on indifference curve I_1, at point *c*, she is willing to give up less than one unit of conventional furniture to get one additional unit of inflatable furniture—the move from *c* to *d*.

■ And if Lisa consumes on indifference curve I_2, at point *e*, she is willing to give up almost no conventional furniture to get one additional unit of inflatable furniture—the move from *e* to *f*.

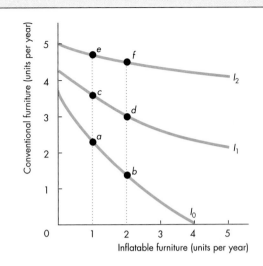

Figure 1 Preferences for furniture

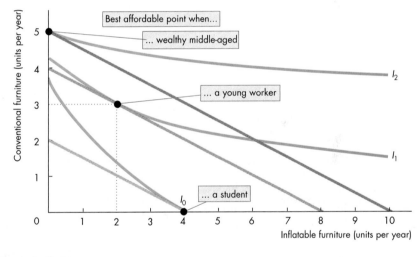

Figure 2 Choices

■ Figure 2 shows Lisa's choices.

■ While she is a student, she has a low income and the highest indifference curve she can reach is I_0. Her best affordable point is at 4 units of inflatable furniture and no conventional furniture.

■ But Lisa knows that when she is a twenty-

something–year-old worker, she will have an income that enables her to reach indifference curve I_1. Her preferences don't change but her best affordable point will then be at 2 units of inflatable furniture and 3 units of conventional furniture.

■ And Lisa knows that when she is a wealthy middle-aged woman, she

will have an income that enables her to reach indifference curve I_2. Her best affordable point will then be at no units of inflatable furniture and 5 units of conventional furniture.

■ For Lisa, inflatable furniture is an *inferior good*. As her income increases, her consumption of inflatable furniture decreases.

SUMMARY

Key Points

Consumption Possibilities (pp. 178–180)

- The budget line is the boundary between what the household can and cannot afford given its income and the prices of goods.
- The point at which the budget line intersects the y-axis is the household's real income in terms of the good measured on that axis.
- The magnitude of the slope of the budget line is the relative price of the good measured on the x-axis in terms of the good measured on the y-axis.
- A change in price changes the slope of the budget line. A change in income shifts the budget line but does not change its slope.

Preferences and Indifference Curves (pp. 181–184)

- A consumer's preferences can be represented by indifference curves. An indifference curve joins all the combinations of goods among which the consumer is indifferent.
- A consumer prefers any point above an indifference curve to any point on it and any point on an indifference curve to any point below it.
- The magnitude of the slope of an indifference curve is called the marginal rate of substitution.
- The marginal rate of substitution diminishes as consumption of the good measured on the y-axis decreases and consumption of the good measured on the x-axis increases.

Predicting Consumer Behaviour (pp. 184–188)

- A household consumes at its best affordable point. This point is on the budget line and on the highest attainable indifference curve and has a marginal rate of substitution equal to relative price.
- The effect of a price change (the price effect) can be divided into a substitution effect and an income effect.
- The substitution effect is the effect of a change in price on the quantity bought when the consumer (hypothetically) remains indifferent between the original and the new situation.

- The substitution effect always results in an increase in consumption of the good whose relative price has fallen.
- The income effect is the effect of a change in income on consumption.
- For a normal good, the income effect reinforces the substitution effect. For an inferior good, the income effect works in the opposite direction to the substitution effect.

Work-Leisure Choices (pp. 188–189)

- The indifference curve model of household choice enables us to understand how a household allocates its time between work and leisure.
- Work hours have decreased and leisure hours have increased because the income effect on the demand for leisure has been greater than the substitution effect.

Key Figures ◆

Key Terms

PROBLEMS

*1. Sara has an income of $12 a week. Popcorn costs $3 a bag, and cola costs $3 a can.
   a. What is Sara's real income in terms of cola?
   b. What is her real income in terms of popcorn?
   c. What is the relative price of cola in terms of popcorn?
   d. What is the opportunity cost of a can of cola?
   e. Calculate the equation for Sara's budget line (placing bags of popcorn on the left side).
   f. Draw a graph of Sara's budget line with cola on the x-axis.
   g. In part (f), what is the slope of Sara's budget line? What does it represent?

2. Marc has an income of $20 per week. CDs cost $10 each and root beer costs $5 a can.
   a. What is Marc's real income in terms of root beer?
   b. What is his real income in terms of CDs?
   c. What is the relative price of root beer in terms of CDs?
   d. What is the opportunity cost of a can of root beer?
   e. Calculate the equation for Marc's budget line (placing cans of root beer on the left side).
   f. Draw a graph of Marc's budget line with CDs on the x-axis.
   g. In part (f), what is the slope of Marc's budget line? What does it represent?

*3. Sara's income and the prices she faces are the same as in problem 1. The figure illustrates Sara's preferences.

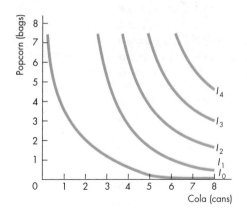

a. What are the quantities of popcorn and cola that Sara buys?
b. What is Sara's marginal rate of substitution of popcorn for cola at the point at which she consumes?

4. Marc's income and the prices he faces are the same as in problem 2. The figure illustrates his preferences.

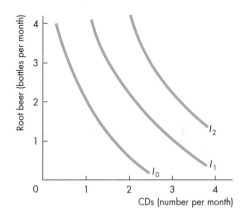

a. What are the quantities of root beer and CDs that Marc buys?
b. What is Marc's marginal rate of substitution of CDs for root beer at the point at which he consumes?

*5. Now suppose that in the situation described in problem 3, the price of cola falls to $1.50 per can and the price of popcorn and Sara's income remain constant.
   a. Find the new quantities of cola and popcorn that Sara buys.
   b. Find two points on Sara's demand curve for cola.
   c. Find the substitution effect of the price change.
   d. Find the income effect of the price change.
   e. Is cola a normal good or an inferior good for Sara?
   f. Is popcorn a normal good or an inferior good for Sara?

6. Now suppose that in problem 4, the price of a CD falls to $5 and the price of root beer and income remain constant.
   a. Find the new quantities of root beer and CDs that Marc buys.
   b. Find two points on Marc's demand curve for CDs.

c. Find the substitution effect of the price change.

d. Find the income effect of the price change.

e. Are CDs a normal good or an inferior good for Marc?

f. Is root beer a normal good or an inferior good for Marc?

*7. Pam buys cookies and comic books. The price of a cookie is $1 and the price of a comic book is $2. Each month, Pam spends all of her income and buys 30 cookies and 5 comic books. Next month, the price of a cookie will fall to 50¢ and the price of a comic book will rise to $5. Assume that Pam's preference map is similar to that in Fig. 9.3(b).

a. Will Pam be able to buy 30 cookies and 5 comic books next month?

b. Will Pam want to buy 30 cookies and 5 comic books?

c. Which situation does Pam prefer: cookies at $1 and comic books at $2 or cookies at 50¢ and comic books at $3?

d. If Pam changes the quantities that she buys, which good will she buy more of and which less of?

e. When the prices change next month, will there be an income effect and a substitution effect at work or just one of them?

8. Pete buys tuna and golf balls. The price of tuna is $2 a can, and the price of golf balls is $1 each. Each month, Pete spends all of his income and buys 20 cans of tuna and 40 golf balls. Next month, the price of tuna will rise to $3 a can and the price of golf balls will fall to 50¢ each. Assume that Pete's preference map is similar to that in Fig. 9.3(b).

a. Will Pete be able to buy 20 cans of tuna and 40 golf balls next month?

b. Will Pete want to buy 20 cans of tuna and 40 golf balls?

c. Which situation does Pete prefer: tuna at $2 a can and golf balls at $1 each or tuna at $3 a can and golf balls at 50¢ each?

d. If Pete changes the quantities that he buys, which good will he buy more of and which less of?

e. When the prices change next month, will there be an income effect and a substitution effect at work or just one of them?

CRITICAL THINKING

 1. Study *Reading Between the Lines* about inflatable furniture on pp. 190–191, and then answer the following questions.

a. What types of people buy inflatable furniture?

b. Do the people who buy inflatable furniture have different preferences from the people who buy conventional furniture?

c. Use the indifference curve model to explain the buying patterns that we observe in the markets for inflatable and conventional furniture.

d. What do you predict would happen to the quantity of inflatable furniture bought if its price fell with the price of conventional furniture remaining the same?

2. The GST is a tax on goods and services. It replaced a federal sales tax on goods only. When we replaced the federal sales tax with the GST:

a. What happened to the relative price of CDs and haircuts?

b. What happened to the budget line showing the quantities of CDs and haircuts you can afford to buy?

c. How would you change your purchases of CDs and haircuts?

d. Which type of tax is best for the consumer and why?

e. Show in a figure the changes and show the substitution effect and the income effect.

3. Jim spends his income on apartment rent, food, clothing, and vacations. He gets a pay raise from $3,000 a month to $4,000 a month. At the same time, airfares and other vacation-related costs increase by 50 percent while other prices remain the same.

a. How do you think Jim will change his spending pattern as a result of the changes in his income and prices?

b. Can you say whether Jim is better off or worse off in his new situation?

c. If *all* prices rise by 50 percent, how does Jim change his purchases? Is he better off or worse off? Why?

d. Show in a figure the changes in Jim's choices that the change in income and changes in prices induce.

Understanding Households' Choices

The powerful forces of demand and supply shape the fortunes of families, businesses, nations, and empires in the same unrelenting way that the tides and winds shape rocks and coastlines. You saw in Chapters 4 through 7 how these forces raise and lower prices, increase and decrease quantities bought and sold, cause revenues to fluctuate, and send resources to their most valuable uses. ◆ These powerful forces begin quietly and privately with the choices that each one of us makes. Chapters 8 and 9 probe these individual choices. In Chapter 8, you learned about the marginal utility theory of human decisions. This theory explains people's consumption plans. It also explains people's consumption of leisure time and its flip side, the supply of work time. Marginal utility theory can even be used to explain "non-economic" choices, such as whether to marry and how many children to have. In a sense, there are no non-economic choices.

Making the Most of Life

If there is scarcity, there must be choice. And economics studies all such choices. Chapter 9 describes a tool that enables us to make a map of people's likes and dislikes, a tool called an *indifference curve*. Indifference curves are considered an advanced topic, so this chapter is *strictly optional*. But the presentation of indifference curves in Chapter 9 is the clearest and most straightforward available, so if you want to learn about this tool, this chapter is the place to do so.

◇ The earliest economists (Adam Smith and his contemporaries) did not have a very deep understanding of households' choices. It was not until the nineteenth century that progress was made in this area. On the following pages, you can spend some time with Jeremy Bentham, the person who pioneered the use of the concept of utility to study human choices, and with Martin Dooley of McMaster University, who is one of Canada's most influential students of human behaviour.

Probing the Ideas

People as Rational Decision Makers

Jeremy Bentham

(1748–1832), who lived in London, was the son and grandson of a lawyer and was himself trained as a barrister. But he rejected the opportunity to maintain the family tradition and instead, spent his life as a writer, activist, and Member of Parliament, in the pursuit of rational laws that would bring the greatest happiness to the greatest number.

Bentham, whose embalmed body is preserved to this day in a glass cabinet in the University of London, was the first person to use the concept of utility to explain human choices. But in Bentham's day, the distinction between explaining and prescribing was not a sharp one, and Bentham was ready to use his ideas to tell people how they ought to behave. He was one of the first to propose pensions for the retired, guaranteed employment, minimum wages, and social benefits such as free education and free medical care.

"... it is the greatest happiness of the greatest number that is the measure of right and wrong."

JEREMY BENTHAM,
FRAGMENT ON GOVERNMENT

The Issues

The economic analysis of human behaviour in the family, the workplace, the markets for goods and services, the markets for labour services, and financial markets is based on the idea that our behaviour can be understood as a response to scarcity. Everything we do can be understood as a choice that maximizes total benefit subject to the constraints imposed by our limited resources and technology. If people's preferences are stable in the face of changing constraints, then we have a chance of predicting how they will respond to an evolving environment.

The economic approach explains the incredible change that has occurred during the past 100 years in the way women allocate their time as the consequence of changing constraints, not of changing attitudes. Technological advances have equipped the nation's farms and factories with machines that have increased the productivity of both women and men, thereby raising the wages they can earn. The increasingly technological world has increased the return to education for both women and men and has led to a large increase in high school and college graduates of both sexes. And equipped with an ever-widening array of gadgets and appliances that cut the time taken to do household jobs, an increasing proportion of women have joined the labour force.

The economic explanation might not be correct, but it is a powerful one. And if it is correct, the changing attitudes are a consequence, not a cause, of the economic advancement of women.

By 1997, more than 60 percent of women were in the labour force, and although many had low-paying jobs, increasingly women were found in the professions and in executive positions. What brought about this dramatic change compared with 100 years earlier? Was it a change in preferences or a change in the constraints that women face?

Then ...

Economists explain people's actions as the consequences of choices that maximize total utility subject to constraints. In the 1890s, fewer than 20 percent of women chose market employment, and most of those who did had low-paying and unattractive jobs. The other 80 percent of women chose non-market work in the home. What were the constraints that led to these choices?

Many economists stand on the shoulders of Jeremy Bentham and study the choices of individuals and families. One of these is Martin Dooley of McMaster University. Professor Dooley's work shows the power of viewing human choices as being rational ones that respond to incentives. You can meet him on the following pages.

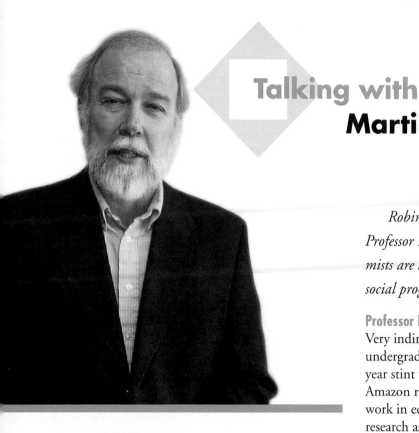

Talking with
Martin Dooley

Martin D. Dooley *is Professor of Economics at McMaster University. Born in South Bend, Indiana in 1947, Professor Dooley was an undergraduate at Indiana University, a graduate student at the University of Wisconsin, and a Postdoctoral Fellow at the University of Chicago. He received his Ph.D. in 1977 and has been on the faculty of McMaster University since 1981. Professor Dooley studies labour economics, health economics, and the economics of the family. He is currently working on the social and economic determinants of child health and development, welfare use, and the stability of marriages.*

Professor Dooley's work is a good example of how the theory of consumer choice has been extended and applied to choices that are broader than those about how to spend a fixed budget, and of how economic incentives influence a wide range of decisions.

Robin Bade and Michael Parkin talked with Professor Dooley about his work and how economists are attempting to improve the effectiveness of social programs.

Professor Dooley, how did you get into economics?
Very indirectly. I only minored in economics as an undergraduate but my interest grew during a two-year stint working for the (U.S.) Peace Corps in the Amazon region of Brazil. I initially pursued graduate work in economic development but a summer research assistantship shifted my focus to my current interests.

What is the connection between the three major areas in which you currently work: labour economics, health economics, and the economics of the family?
There are many connections. The character of our lives and work influence our health status and our health influences our lives and work. An important factor linking all three areas is the fact that we spend most of our lives either residing in a family unit or at least in close contact with relatives. We care for our relations and are cared for by them. We share with them both our personal income and personal services such as health care, childcare, and others. That family members share time and money is, I am sure, more than obvious to the reader, but discussions of both labour market policy and health policy often ignore this fact, at least when it is convenient to do so. For example, the beneficiaries of efforts to raise female earnings include the male family members with whom women share their pay cheques. The "cost savings" achieved by shortening hospital stays may be partially or even fully offset by increased money and time burdens on the family. These examples and many others show that a necessary ingredient for good policy analysis is a full accounting of

the benefits and costs, including the less obvious effects that work through the family.

What exactly is health economics? Isn't health care so vital that it stands above economics?

One is strongly tempted to think that economic factors have little impact on health-care decisions because "your good health is everything." A bit of reflection indicates that we do indeed care about our health, but much else besides. I routinely drive on four-lane highways at (legal) speeds that pose a minor risk to my health in order to economize on time. I enjoy my trips to the food court even though my doctor tells me it would be better for my health to go to the squash court.

Health economists deal with many issues. One is how to deliver health-care services in an efficient and fair manner. This requires the study of how health-care consumers and providers react to incentives. What would be, for example, the impact on preventative health care of a fee for routine physical examinations? What is the superior way to reimburse physicians—fee-for-service or a salary? The health economics question with which I am involved is how socioeconomic factors influence child health and development. The data clearly show that children from poor families have more psychiatric disorders and schooling problems than do children from non-poor families. But what should we infer from this finding?

One interpretation is that the problems are directly attributable to low income, that is, due either to inadequate levels of consumption or the stress brought on by economic insecurity. This suggests that providing better cash transfers to poor parents will directly improve outcomes for their children. An alternative interpretation, however, is that some other variable, such as poor parental health or education, is responsible for both low income and poor child health. This interpretation suggests that greater cash transfers might not be an effective way to improve the well-being of the children concerned and that alternatives should be considered. Both interpretations will likely have some merit but we are just beginning to understand the key policy issue of the relative importance of each interpretation.

What issues in the economics of the family are you working on?

One issue is the way in which economic factors influence marital stability. Research shows that wives suffer much greater income loss after separation and divorce than do husbands even after accounting for alimony and child support payments. One implication is that wives who have higher personal earnings relative to the earnings of their husbands have less to lose economically from a split and less need to stick with a bad marriage for fear of the economic consequences of single life. My work with Pierre Lefebvre and Phil Merrigan of UQAM confirms that marriages in which the wife's earnings more closely approximate (or exceed) those of her husband are less stable—other things being equal.

People on welfare face some hard choices. Does welfare keep them from getting jobs and developing human capital?

The disincentives are strong. "Welfare taxes" result from the fact that benefit cheques are reduced when income from virtually any other source is increased. And the rate of taxation is commonly equal to or

Health economists deal with many issues. One is how to deliver health care services in an efficient and fair manner.

close to 100 percent. As a result, most welfare clients perform little paid work. Of course, some earnings are not reported but the evidence indicates that this is not a major issue. The welfare tax clearly makes paid-work not pay!

So why don't we lower this tax rate?

Some provinces have done so but only to 75–80 percent. This means that an $8 an hour job, not uncommon among welfare clients, still only pays $2 an hour once the welfare reduction is taken into account— an offer that is easy to refuse.

So why not lower the welfare tax to 25 percent or less?

The main reason is that this step will be very costly for governments at least in the foreseeable future. Some existing welfare clients may get jobs and see their benefit cheques shrink. But the lower tax rate means that clients can earn a lot more without exhausting their welfare cheque and leaving the welfare rolls.

Can you give us an example to show the effects of lowering the tax rate?

If the monthly welfare benefit for non-workers is $1,000 and the tax rate is 100 percent, then monthly earnings of $1,000 will reduce the actual welfare payment to zero and cause an exit from the welfare rolls. At a tax rate of 25 percent, however, it will take $4,000 of monthly earnings to fully "tax away" this same benefit (because $1,000 is 25 percent of $4,000). Hence, many more families will potentially qualify for a welfare benefit—possibly all those earning between $1,000 and $4,000 per month. The effect might be to increase total welfare expenditures greatly. Furthermore, the work incentives of any new clients will worsen because the welfare tax they face has risen from zero percent (not on welfare) to 25 percent (on welfare). Lowering the welfare tax rate improves the work incentive for existing clients but lowers it for any newly attracted or retained clients—and there is no easy way around this dilemma.

I believe that few corners of human behaviour are untouched by economic factors ...

Why do you think so many lone mothers are on welfare?

The work incentives for lone mothers on welfare are especially weak. Paid work means high child-care costs and leaving the welfare rolls also means the loss of valuable subsidies for drugs, dental care, and housing. My research shows that the response of lone mothers to the incentives is strong. Over the last 25 years, for example, Canadian lone mothers under age 35 increased their welfare participation and decreased their labour force participation, but that just the opposite was true of lone mothers age 35 and over. An important reason for this was that, relative to welfare benefits, the typical labour market earnings of young, unskilled workers fell substantially during this period but the earnings of older workers did not.

Can we hope to design an economic policy program towards the family that brings genuinely equal opportunities for all and that does not confront the poorest people with disincentives to work?

For lone-mother families at least, it is very hard to do so in a way that is both inexpensive and does not penalize poor children. As I indicated above, simply lowering the welfare tax is likely to be expensive. Mandatory work requirements for mothers on welfare bring the day-care problem to the fore. Government could pay for child care, which would increase public expenditures, or force the lone mothers to pay for it, which would lower further the well-being of Canada's least fortunate children.

One suggestion, which is currently being implemented, is to "take kids off welfare." The federal child tax benefit for low-income families is being enriched to the point where welfare benefits for children can and will be eliminated in all provinces without lowering the disposable income of families with children on welfare. This policy is not without drawbacks but it will lower the incentive, especially for larger families, to leave the labour market, where pay cheques do not depend on the number of dependents, and go on welfare, where benefit cheques do depend on this factor.

Is there any way in which economists can measure the disincentives experimentally?

Yes. An interesting idea is being tested in a social experiment now underway in New Brunswick and British Columbia. A randomly selected group of lone mothers on welfare have been permitted to keep an unusually large portion of their welfare benefits after entering the labour market but only if they take a full-time job. The goal is to attract more lone mothers into employment that offers advancement opportunities sufficient to escape what for some is a recurring cycle of welfare and dead-end jobs.

Do you think that economics is a good subject in which to major? Why? What else should be studied alongside it?

I believe that few corners of human behaviour are untouched by economic factors and that equally few are untouched by non-economic factors. The insights one gets from the study of economics are widely applicable. And the study of every other social science complements and enriches the insights provided by economics.

Chapter **10**

Organizing Production

In the fall of 1990, a British scientist named Tim Berners-Lee invented the World Wide Web. This remarkable idea paved the way for the creation and growth of thousands of profitable businesses. One of these businesses is CANOE—Canadian Online Explorer—founded by Sun Media, one of Canada's largest news organizations, and BCE Media. ◆ How do CANOE and the other 2 million firms that operate in Canada make their business decisions? How do they operate efficiently? ◆ Businesses range from multinational giants, such as Microsoft, to small family restaurants and local Internet service providers. Three-quarters of all firms are operated by their owners. But corporations like CANOE and Microsoft account for 90 percent of all business sales. What are the different types a firm can take? Why do some remain small while others become giants? Why are most firms owner-operated? ◆ Many businesses operate in a highly competitive environment and struggle to earn their profits. Others, like Microsoft, seem to have cornered the market on their products and earn large profits. What are the different types of market in which firms operate and why is it harder to make a profit in some markets than in others? ◆ Most of the components of an IBM personal computer are made by other firms. Microsoft created its Windows operating system and Intel makes its processor chip. Other firms make hard drives and modems, and yet others make CD drives, sound cards, and so on. Why doesn't IBM make all its own computer components? Why does it leave these activities to other firms and buy from them in markets? How do firms decide what to make themselves and what to buy in the marketplace from other firms?

Spinning a Web

◆ In this chapter, we are going to learn about firms and the choices they make to cope with scarcity. We begin by studying the economic problems and choices that *all* firms face.

After studying this chapter, you will be able to:

- Explain what a firm is and describe the economic problems that *all* firms face
- Distinguish between technological efficiency and economic efficiency
- Define and explain the principal–agent problem
- Describe and distinguish between different types of business organization
- Describe and distinguish between different types of markets in which firms operate
- Explain why firms coordinate some economic activities and markets coordinate others

The Firm and Its Economic Problem

THE 2 MILLION FIRMS IN CANADA DIFFER IN SIZE and in the scope of what they do. But they all perform the same basic economic functions. Each **firm** is an institution that hires productive resources and that organizes those resources to produce and sell goods and services.

Our goal is to predict firm behaviour. To do so, we need to know a firm's goals and the constraints it faces. We begin with the goals.

The Firm's Goal

If you asked a group of entrepreneurs what they are trying to achieve, you would get many different answers. Some would talk about making a quality product, others about business growth, others about market share, and others about the job satisfaction of their work force. All of these goals might be pursued, but they are not the fundamental goal. They are means to a deeper goal.

A firm's goal is to *maximize profit*. A firm that does not seek to maximize profit is either eliminated or bought out by firms that do seek to maximize profit.

What exactly is the profit that a firm seeks to maximize? To answer this question, let's look at Sidney's Sweaters.

Measuring a Firm's Profit

Sidney runs a successful business that makes sweaters. Sidney's Sweaters receives $400,000 a year for the sweaters it sells. Its expenses are $80,000 a year for wool, $20,000 for utilities, $120,000 for labour, and $10,000 in interest on a bank loan. With receipts of $400,000 and expenses of $230,000, Sidney's Sweaters' annual surplus is $170,000.

Sidney's accountant lowers this number by $20,000, which he says is the depreciation (fall in value) of the firm's buildings and knitting machines during the year. (Accountants use Revenue Canada rules based on standards established by the accounting profession to calculate the depreciation.) So the accountant reports that the profit of Sidney's Sweaters is $150,000 a year.

Sidney's accountant measures cost and profit to ensure that the firm pays the correct amount of

income tax and to show the bank how its loan has been used. But we want to predict the decisions that a firm makes. These decisions respond to *opportunity cost* and *economic profit*.

Opportunity Cost

The **opportunity cost** of any action is the highest-valued alternative forgone. The action that you choose not to do—the highest-valued alternative forgone—is the cost of the action that you choose to do. For a firm, the opportunity cost of production is the value of the firm's best alternative use of its resources.

Opportunity cost is a real alternative forgone. But so that we can compare the cost of one action with that of another action, we express opportunity cost in money units. A firm's opportunity costs are:

■ Explicit costs
■ Implicit costs

Explicit Costs   Explicit costs are paid in money. The amount paid for a resource could have been spent on something else, so it is the opportunity cost of using the resource. For Sidney, his expenditures on wool, utilities, wages, and bank interest are explicit costs.

Implicit Costs   A firm incurs implicit costs when it forgoes an alternative action but does not make a payment. A firm incurs implicit costs when it:

1. Uses its own capital.
2. Uses its owner's time or financial resources.

The cost of using its own capital is an implicit cost—and an opportunity cost—because the firm could rent the capital to another firm. The rental income forgone is the firm's opportunity cost of using its own capital. This opportunity cost is called the **implicit rental rate** of capital.

People rent houses, apartments, cars, telephones, and videotapes. And firms rent photocopiers, earth-moving equipment, satellite launching services, and so on. If a firm rents capital, it incurs an *explicit* cost. If a firm buys the capital it uses, it incurs an *implicit* cost. The implicit rental rate of capital is made up of:

1. Economic depreciation
2. Interest forgone

Economic depreciation is change in the *market* value of capital over a given period. It is calculated as the market price of the capital at the beginning of the period minus its market price at the end of the period. For example, suppose that Sidney could have sold his buildings and knitting machines on December 31, 1998, for $400,000. If he can sell the same capital on December 31, 1999, for $375,000, his economic depreciation during 1999 is $25,000—the fall in the market value of the machines. This $25,000 is an implicit cost of using the capital during 1999.

The funds used to buy capital could have been used for some other purpose. And in their next best use, they would have yielded a return—an interest income. This forgone interest is part of the opportunity cost of using the capital. For example, Sidney's Sweaters could have bought government bonds instead of a knitting factory. The interest forgone on the government bonds is an implicit cost of operating the knitting factory.

Cost of Owner's Resources   A firm's owner often supplies *entrepreneurial ability*—the productive resource that organizes the business, makes business decisions, innovates, and bears the risk of running the business. The return to entrepreneurship is profit and the *average* return for supplying entrepreneurial ability is called **normal profit**. Normal profit is part of a firm's opportunity cost, because it is the cost of a forgone alternative—running another firm. If normal profit in the textile business is $50,000 a year, this amount must be added to Sidney's costs to determine his opportunity cost.

The owner of a firm also can supply labour (in addition to entrepreneurship). The return to labour is a wage. And the opportunity cost of the owner's time spent working for the firm is the wage income forgone by not working in the best alternative job. Suppose that Sidney could take another job that pays $40,000 a year. By working for his knitting business and forgoing this income, Sidney incurs an opportunity cost of $40,000 a year.

Economic Profit

What is the bottom line—the profit or loss of the firm? A firm's **economic profit** is equal to its total revenue minus its opportunity cost. The firm's opportunity cost is the sum of its explicit costs and implicit costs. And the implicit costs, remember, include *normal profit*. The return to entrepreneurial ability is greater than normal in a firm that makes a positive economic profit. And the return to entrepreneurial

ability is less than normal in a firm that makes a negative economic profit—a firm that incurs an economic loss.

Economic Accounting: A Summary

Table 10.1 summarizes the economic accounting concepts that you've just studied. Sidney's Sweaters' total revenue is $400,000. Its opportunity cost (explicit costs plus its implicit costs) is $365,000. And its economic profit is $35,000.

To achieve the objective of maximum profit—maximum economic profit—a firm must make five basic decisions:

1. What goods and services to produce and in what quantities
2. How to produce—the techniques of production to use
3. How to organize and compensate its managers and workers
4. How to market and price its products
5. What to produce itself and what to buy from other firms

In all these decisions, a firm's actions are limited by the constraints that it faces. Our next task is to learn about these constraints.

TABLE 10.1

Economic Accounting

Item		Amount
Total Revenue		**$400,000**
Opportunity Costs		
Wool	$ 80,000	
Utilities	20,000	
Wages paid	120,000	
Bank interest paid	10,000	
Total Explicit Costs		$ 230,000
Sidney's wages forgone	40,000	
Sidney's interest forgone	20,000	
Economic depreciation	25,000	
Normal profit	50,000	
Total Implicit Costs		$ 135,000
Total Cost		**$365,000**
Economic Profit		$ 35,000

The Firm's Constraints

Three features of its environment limit the maximum profit a firm can make. They are:

- Technology constraints
- Information constraints
- Market constraints

Technology Constraints   Economists define technology broadly. A **technology** is any method of producing a good or service. Technology includes the detailed designs of machines. It also includes the layout of the workplace. And it includes the organization of the firm. For example, the shopping mall is a technology for producing retail services. It is a different technology from the catalogue store, which in turn is different from the downtown store.

It might seem surprising that a firm's profits are limited by technology. For it seems that technological advances are constantly increasing profit opportunities. Almost every day, we learn about some new technological advance that amazes us. With computers that speak and recognize our own speech and cars that can find the address we need in a city we've never visited before, we are able to accomplish ever more.

Technology is advancing. But at each point in time, to produce more output and gain more revenue, a firm must hire more resources and incur greater costs. The increase in profit that the firm can achieve is limited by the technology available for transforming resources into output. For example, using its current plant and work force, Ford can produce some maximum number of cars per day. To produce more cars per day, Ford must hire more resources and incur greater costs, which limits the increase in profit that Ford can make by selling the additional cars.

Information Constraints   We never possess all the information we would like to make decisions. We lack information about both the future and the present. For example, suppose you plan to buy a new computer. When should you buy it? The answer depends on how the price is going to change in the future. Where should you buy it? The answer depends on the prices at hundreds of different computer shops. To get the best deal, you must compare the quality and prices in every shop. But the opportunity cost of this comparison exceeds the cost of the computer!

Similarly, a firm is constrained by limited information about the quality and effort of its work force,

the current and future buying plans of its customers, and the plans of its competitors. Workers slacken off when managers believe they are working hard. Customers switch to competing suppliers. Firms must compete against competition from a new firm.

Firms try to create incentive systems for workers to ensure they work hard even when no one is monitoring their efforts. And firms spend millions of dollars on market research. But none of these efforts and expenditures eliminates the problems of incomplete information and uncertainty. And the cost of coping with limited information itself limits profit.

Market Constraints   What each firm can sell and the price it can obtain is constrained by the willingness to pay of its customers and by the prices and marketing efforts of other firms. Similarly, the resources that each firm can buy and the prices it must pay are limited by the willingness of people to work for and invest in the firm. Firms spend billions of dollars a year marketing and selling their products. Some of the most creative minds strive to find the right message that will produce a knockout television advertisement. Market constraints and the expenditures firms make to overcome them limit the profit a firm can make.

R E V I E W   Q U I Z

- Why do firms seek to maximize profit? What happens to firms that don't pursue this goal?
- Why do accountants and economists calculate a firm's cost and profit in different ways?
- What are the items that make opportunity cost depart from the accountants' measure of cost?
- Why is normal profit an opportunity cost?
- What are the three types of constraint that firms face? How does each constraint limit the profit that a firm can make?

In the rest of this chapter and in Chapters 11 through 14, we study the decisions that firms make. We're going to learn how we can predict a firm's behaviour as the response to the constraints that it faces and to changes in those constraints. We begin by taking a closer look at the technology constraints, information constraints, and market constraints that firms face.

Technology and Economic Efficiency

MICROSOFT EMPLOYS A LARGE WORK FORCE. And most Microsoft workers possess a large amount of human capital. But the firm uses a small amount of physical capital. In contrast, a coal mining company employs a huge amount of mining equipment (physical capital) and almost no labour. Why? The answer lies in the concept of efficiency. There are two concepts of production efficiency: technological efficiency and economic efficiency. **Technological efficiency** occurs when the firm produces a given output by using the least inputs. **Economic efficiency** occurs when the firm produces a given output at least cost. Let's explore the two concepts of efficiency by studying an example.

Suppose that there are four alternative techniques for making TV sets:

a. *Robot production*. One person monitors the entire computer-driven process.

b. *Production line*. Workers specialize in a small part of the job as the emerging TV set passes them on a production line.

c. *Bench production*. Workers specialize in a small part of the job but walk from bench to bench to perform their tasks.

d. *Hand-tool production*. A single worker uses a few hand tools to make a TV set.

Table 10.2 sets out the amounts of labour and capital required by each of these four methods to make 10 TV sets a day.

Which of these alternative methods are technologically efficient?

Technological Efficiency

Recall that technological efficiency occurs when the firm produces *a* given output by using the least inputs. Inspect the numbers in the table and notice that method *a* uses the most capital but the least labour. Method *d* uses the most labour but the least capital. Methods *b* and *c* lie between the two extremes. They use less capital but more labour than method *a* and less labour but more capital than method *d*. Compare methods *b* and *c*. Method *c* requires 100 workers and 10 units of capital to pro-

duce 10 TV sets. Those same 10 TV sets can be produced by method *b* with 10 workers and the same 10 units of capital. Because method *c* uses the same amount of capital and more labour than method *b*, method *c* is not technologically efficient.

Are any of the other methods not technologically efficient? The answer is no. Each of the others is technologically efficient. Method *a* uses more capital but less labour than method *b*, and method *d* uses more labour but less capital than method *b*.

Which of the methods are economically efficient?

Economic Efficiency

Recall that economic efficiency occurs when the firm produces a given output at least cost. Suppose that labour costs $75 per person-day and that capital costs $250 per machine-day. Table 10.3(a) calculates the costs of using the different methods. By inspecting the table, you can see that method *b* has the lowest cost. Although method *a* uses less labour, it uses too much expensive capital. And although method *d* uses less capital, it uses too much expensive labour.

Method *c*, which is technologically inefficient, is also economically inefficient. It uses the same amount of capital as method *b* but 10 times as much labour, so it costs more. A technologically inefficient method is never economically efficient.

Although *b* is the economically efficient method in this example, method *a* or *d* could be economically efficient with different input prices.

First, suppose that labour costs $150 a person-day and capital costs only $1 a machine-day. Table 10.3(b) now shows the costs of making a TV set. In this case,

TABLE 10.2

Four Ways of Making 10 TV Sets a Day

| Method | Quantities of inputs | |
	Labour	Capital
a Robot production	1	1,000
b Production line	10	10
c Bench production	100	10
d Hand-tool production	1,000	1

TABLE 10.3

The Costs of Different Ways of Making 10 TV Sets a Day

(a) Four ways of making TVs

Method	Labour cost ($75 per day)		Capital cost ($250 per day)		Total cost	Cost per TV set
a	$75	+	$250,000	=	$250,075	$25,007.50
b	750	+	2,500	=	3,250	325.00
c	7,500	+	2,500	=	10,000	1,000.00
d	75,000	+	250	=	75,250	7,525.00

(b) Three ways of making TVs: High Labour Costs

Method	Labour cost ($150 per day)		Capital cost ($1 per day)		Total cost	Cost per TV set
a	$150	+	$1,000	=	$1,150	$115.00
b	1,500	+	10	=	1,510	151.00
d	150,000	+	1	=	150,001	15,000.10

(c) Three ways of making TVs: High Capital Costs

Method	Labour cost ($1 per day)		Capital cost ($1000 per day)		Total cost	Cost per TV set
a	$1	+	$1,000,000	=	$1,000,001	$100,000.10
b	10	+	10,000	=	10,010	1,001.00
d	1,000	+	1,000	=	2,000	200.00

---

method *a* is economically efficient. Capital is now so cheap relative to labour that the method that uses the most capital is the economically efficient method.

Second, suppose that labour costs only $1 a person-day while capital costs $1,000 a machine-day. Table 10.3(c) shows the costs in this case. Method *d*, which uses a lot of labour and little capital, is now the least-cost method and economically efficient method.

From these examples, you can see that while technological efficiency depends only on what is feasible, economic efficiency depends on the relative costs of resources. The economically efficient method is the one that uses the smaller amount of a more expensive resource and a larger amount of a less expensive resource.

A firm that is not economically efficient does not maximize profit. Natural selection favours efficient firms and opposes inefficient firms. Inefficient firms go out of business or are taken over by firms that lower costs. Profit-maximizing firms are better able to survive temporary adversity than inefficient ones.

REVIEW QUIZ

■ How do we define technological efficiency ? Is a firm technologically efficient if it uses the latest technology? Why?

■ How do we define economic efficiency? Is a firm economically inefficient if it can cut costs by producing less? Why?

■ Explain the key distinction between technological efficiency and economic efficiency.

■ Why do some firms use large amounts of capital and small amounts of labour while others use small amounts of capital and large amounts of labour?

You have now seen how the technology constraints that a firm faces influence the amounts of capital and labour that it employs. Next we study information constraints and the diversity of *organization structures* they generate.

Information and Organization

EACH FIRM ORGANIZES THE PRODUCTION OF goods and services by combining and coordinating the productive resources it hires. But there is variety across firms in how they organize production. Firms use a mixture of two systems:

■ Command systems
■ Incentive systems

Command Systems

A **command system** is a method of organizing production that uses a managerial hierarchy. Commands pass downward through the managerial hierarchy and information passes upward. Managers spend most of their time collecting and processing information about the performance of the people under their control and making decisions about commands to issue and how best to get those commands implemented.

The military uses the purest form of command system. A commander-in-chief makes the big decisions about strategic objectives. Beneath this highest level, generals organize their military resources. Beneath the generals, successively lower ranks organize smaller and smaller units but pay attention to ever increasing degrees of detail. At the bottom of the managerial hierarchy are the people who operate weapons systems.

Command systems in firms are not as rigid as they are in the military. But they share some similar features. A chief executive officer (CEO) sits at the top of a firm's command system. Senior executives who report to and receive commands from the CEO specialize in managing production, marketing, finance, personnel, and perhaps other aspects of the firm's operations. Beneath these senior managers might be several tiers of middle management ranks that stretch downward to the managers that supervise the day-to-day operations of the business. Beneath these managers are the people who operate the firm's machines and who make and sell goods and services.

Small firms have one or two layers of managers while large firms have several layers. As production processes have become ever more complex, management ranks have swollen. Today, more people have management jobs than ever before. But the information revolution of the 1990s slowed the growth of management and, in some industries, it decreased the number of layers of managers and brought a shakeout of middle managers.

Managers make enormous efforts to be well informed. And they try hard to make good decisions and issue commands that end up using resources efficiently. But managers always have incomplete information about what is happening in the divisions of the firm for which they are responsible. It is for this reason that firms use incentive systems as well as command systems to organize production.

Incentive Systems

An **incentive system** is a method of organizing production that uses a market-like mechanism inside the firm. Instead of issuing commands, senior managers create compensation schemes that will induce workers to perform in ways that maximize the firm's profit.

Selling organizations use incentive systems most extensively. Sales representatives who spend most of their working time alone and unsupervised are induced to work hard by being paid a small salary and a large performance-related bonus.

But incentive systems operate at all levels in a firm. A CEO's compensation plan includes a share in the firm's profit, and factory floor workers sometimes receive compensation based on the quantity they produce.

Mixing the Systems

Firms use a mixture of commands and incentives. And they choose the mixture to maximize profit. They use commands when it is easy to monitor performance or when a small deviation from an ideal performance is very costly. They use incentives when monitoring performance is either not possible or too costly to be worth doing.

For example, it is easy and not very costly to monitor the performance of workers on a production line. And if one person works too slowly, the entire line slows. So a production line is organized with a command system.

In contrast, it is costly to monitor a CEO. What, for example, did Matthew Barrett (a former president of the Bank of Montreal) contribute to the success in the global market of that bank? This question cannot be answered with certainty, yet a big bank must put someone in charge of operations and provide this person the *incentive* to be efficient. Incentives and the contracts that create them are an attempt to cope with a general problem called the principal–agent problem.

The Principal–Agent Problem

The **principal–agent problem** is the problem of devising compensation rules that induce an *agent* to act in the best interest of a *principal*. For example, the stockholders of the Royal Bank are *principals* and the bank's managers are *agents*. The stockholders (the principals) must induce the managers (agents) to act in the stockholders' best interest. Similarly, Bill Gates, (a principal) must induce the programmers working on Windows 2000 (agents) to work efficiently.

Agents, whether they are managers or workers, pursue their own goals and often impose costs on a principal. For example, the goal of a stockholder of the Royal Bank (a principal) is to maximize the bank's profit. But the bank's profit depends on the actions of its managers (agents), who have their own goals. Perhaps a manager takes a customer to a ball game on the pretence that she is building customer loyalty, when in fact she is simply taking on-the-job leisure. This same manager is also a principal and her tellers are agents. The manager wants the tellers to work hard and attract new customers so she can meet her operating targets. But the tellers enjoy conversations with each other and keep customers waiting in line. Nonetheless, the bank constantly strives to find ways of improving performance and increasing profits.

Coping with the Principal–Agent Problem

Issuing commands does not address the principal–agent problem. In most firms, the shareholders can't monitor the managers and often the managers can't monitor the workers. Each principal must create incentives that induce each agent to work in the interests of the principal. Three ways of attempting to cope with the principal–agent problem are:

■ Ownership
■ Incentive pay
■ Long-term contracts

Ownership By assigning to a manager or worker ownership (or part-ownership) of a business, the principal can sometimes induce a job performance that increases a firm's profits. Part-ownership schemes

for senior managers are quite common, and they are less common but not unknown for workers. For example, in 1995 Canadian Pacific Ltd. sold off CP Express and Transport, a coast-to-coast trucking operation, to its 3,500 employees.

Incentive Pay Incentive pay schemes—pay related to performance—are very common. They are based on a variety of performance criteria such as profits or production or sales targets. Promoting an employee for good performance is another example of an incentive pay scheme.

Long-Term Contracts Long-term contracts tie the long-term fortunes of managers and workers (agents) to the success of the principal(s)—the owner(s) of the firm. For example, a multi-year employment contract for a CEO encourages that person to take a long-term view and devise strategies that achieve maximum profit over a sustained period.

These three ways of coping with the principal–agent problem give rise to different types of business organization. Each type of business organization is a different response to the principal–agent problem. It uses ownership, incentives, and long-term contracts in different ways. Let's look at the main types of business organization.

Types of Business Organization

The three main types of business organization are:

■ Sole proprietorship
■ Partnership
■ Corporation

Sole Proprietorship A *sole proprietorship* is a firm with a single owner—a proprietor—who has unlimited liability. *Unlimited liability* is the legal responsibility for all the debts of a firm up to an amount equal to the entire wealth of the owner. If a sole proprietorship cannot pay its debts, those to whom the firm owes money can claim the personal property of the owner. Corner stores, computer programmers, and artists are all examples of sole proprietorships.

The proprietor makes management decisions, receives the firm's profits, and is responsible for its losses. Profits from a sole proprietorship are taxed at the same rate as other sources of the proprietor's personal income.

Partnership A *partnership* is a firm with two or more owners who have unlimited liability. Partners must agree on an appropriate management structure and on how to divide the firm's profits among themselves. The profits of a partnership are taxed as the personal income of the owners. But each partner is legally liable for all the debts of the partnership (limited only by the wealth of an individual partner). Liability for the full debts of the partnership is called *joint unlimited liability*. Most law firms are partnerships.

Corporation A *corporation* is a firm owned by one or more limited liability stockholders. *Limited liability* means that the owners have legal liability only for the value of their initial investment. This limitation of liability means that if the corporation becomes bankrupt, its owners are not required to use their personal wealth to pay the corporation's debts.

Corporation profits are taxed independently of stockholders' incomes. Because stockholders pay taxes on the income they receive as dividends on stocks,

corporate profits are taxed twice. The stockholders also pay capital gains tax on the profit they earn by selling a stock for a higher price than they paid for it. Corporate stocks generate capital gains when a corporation retains some of its profit and reinvests it in profitable activities. So even retained earnings are taxed twice because the capital gains they generate are taxed.

Pros and Cons of Different Types of Firms

The different types of business organization arise as different ways of trying to cope with the principal–agent problem. Each has advantages in particular situations. And because of its special advantages, each type continues to exist. Each type also has its disadvantages, which explains why it has not driven out the other two.

Table 10.4 summarizes these pros and cons of the different types of firm.

TABLE 10.4

The Pros and Cons of Different Types of Firms

Type of Firm	Pros	Cons
Sole Proprietorship	▪ Easy to set up ▪ Simple decision making ▪ Profits taxed only once as owner's income	▪ Bad decisions not checked by need for consensus ▪ Owner's entire wealth at risk ▪ Firm dies with owner ▪ Capital is expensive ▪ Labour is expensive
Partnership	▪ Easy to set up ▪ Diversified decision making ▪ Can survive withdrawal of partner ▪ Profits taxed only once as owners' incomes	▪ Achieving consensus may be slow and expensive ▪ Owners' entire wealth at risk ▪ Withdrawal of partner may create capital shortage ▪ Capital is expensive
Corporation	▪ Owners have limited liability ▪ Large-scale, low-cost capital available ▪ Professional management not restricted by ability of owners ▪ Perpetual life ▪ Long-term labour contracts cut labour costs	▪ Complex management structure can make decisions slow and expensive ▪ Profits taxed twice as company profit and as stockholders' income

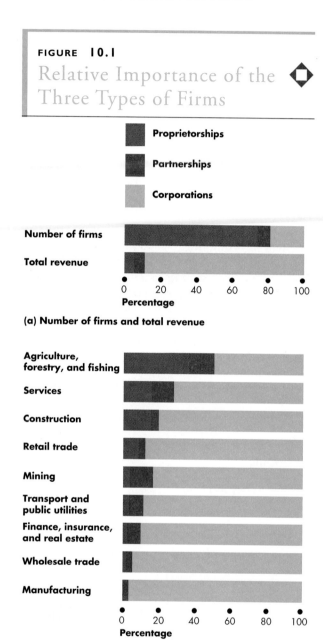

FIGURE 10.1

Relative Importance of the Three Types of Firms

(a) Number of firms and total revenue

(b) Total revenue in various industries

The data shown are for the United States because we do not have comparable data for Canada. In the United States, three-quarters of all firms are sole proprietorships, almost one-fifth are corporations, and only a twentieth are partnerships. Corporations account for 86 percent of business revenue (part a). But sole proprietorships and partnerships account for a significant percentage of business revenue in some industries (part b).

Source: U.S. Bureau of the Census, *Statistical Abstract of the United States:* 1998, 118th ed. CD-ROM.(Washington, DC: 1998): 855, 856, and 1103.

The Relative Importance of Different Types of Firms

Figure 10.1(a) shows the relative importance of the three main types of firms in the U.S. economy. The figure also shows that the revenue of corporations is much larger than that of the other types of firms. Although only 18 percent of all firms are corporations, they generate 86 percent of revenue.

Figure 10.1(b) shows the percentage of revenue generated by the different types of firms in various industries. Sole proprietorships in agriculture, forestry, and fishing generate about 36 percent of the total revenue in those sectors. Sole proprietorships in the service sector, construction, and retail trades also generate a large percentage of total revenue. Partnerships in agriculture, forestry, and fishing generate about 14 percent of total revenue. Partnerships are more prominent in services; mining; and finance, insurance, and real estate than in other sectors. Corporations are important in all sectors and in manufacturing have the field almost to themselves.

Why do corporations dominate the business scene? Why do the other types of business survive? And why are sole proprietorships and partnerships more prominent in some sectors? The answer to these questions lies in the pros and cons of the different types of business organization that are summarized in Table 10.4 above. Corporations dominate where a large amount of capital is used. But sole proprietorships dominate where flexibility in decision making is critical.

REVIEW QUIZ

■ Explain the distinction between a command system and an incentive system.

■ What is the principal–agent problem and what are the three ways in which firms try to cope with it?

■ What are the three types of firm? Explain the major advantages and disadvantages of each type.

■ Why do all three types of firm survive and in which sectors are the three types most prominent?

You've now seen how technology constraints influence a firm's use of capital and labour and how information constraints influence a firm's organization. We'll now look at market constraints and see how they influence the environment in which firms compete for business.

Markets and the Competitive Environment

THE MARKETS IN WHICH FIRMS OPERATE VARY A great deal. Some are highly competitive and profits are hard to come by. Some appear to be almost free from competition and firms earn large profits. Some markets are dominated by fierce advertising campaigns in which each firm seeks to persuade buyers that it has the best products. And some markets display a war-like character.

Economists identify four market types:

1. Perfect competition
2. Monopolistic competition
3. Oligopoly
4. Monopoly

Perfect competition arises when there are many firms each selling an identical product; many buyers; and no restrictions on the entry of new firms into the industry. The many firms and buyers are all well informed about the prices of the products of each firm in the industry. The worldwide markets for corn, rice, and other grain crops are examples of perfect competition.

Monopolistic competition is a market structure in which a large number of firms compete by making similar but slightly different products. Making a product slightly different from the product of a competing firm is called **product differentiation**. Product differentiation gives a monopolistically competitive firm an element of monopoly power. The firm is the sole producer of the particular version of the good in question. For example, in the market for running shoes, Nike, Reebok, Fila, and Asics all make their own version of the perfect shoe. Each of these firms has a monopoly on a particular brand of shoe. Differentiated products are not necessarily different products. What matters is that consumers *perceive* them to be different. For example, different brands of aspirin are chemically identical (salicylic acid) and differ only in their packaging.

Oligopoly is a market structure in which a small number of firms compete. Computer software, airplane manufacture, and international air transportation are examples of oligopolistic industries. Oligopolies might produce almost identical products, such as the colas produced by Coke and Pepsi. Or they might produce differentiated products such as Chevrolet's Lumina and Ford's Taurus.

A **monopoly** is an industry that produces a good or service for which no close substitute exists and in which there is one supplier that is protected from competition by a barrier preventing the entry of new firms. In some places, the phone, gas, electricity, and water suppliers are local monopolies—monopolies restricted to a given location. Microsoft Corp., the software developer that created Windows, the operating system used by PCs, is an example of a global monopoly.

Perfect competition is the most extreme form of competition. Monopoly is the most extreme absence of competition. The other two market types fall between these extremes.

Many factors must be taken into account to determine which market structure describes a particular real-world market. One of these factors is the extent to which the market is dominated by a small number of firms. To measure this feature of markets, economists use indexes called measures of concentration. Let's look at these measures.

Measures of Concentration

Economists use two measures of concentration:

■ The four-firm concentration ratio

■ The Herfindahl-Hirschman Index

The Four-Firm Concentration Ratio   The **four-firm concentration ratio** is the percentage of the value of sales accounted for by the four largest firms in an industry. The range of the concentration ratio is from almost zero for perfect competition to 100 percent for monopoly. This ratio is the main measure used to assess market structure.

Table 10.5 shows two calculations of the four-firm concentration ratio, one for tires and one for printing. In this example, 14 firms produce tires. The largest four have 80 percent of the sales, so the four-firm concentration ratio is 80 percent. In the printing industry, with 1,004 firms, the largest four firms have only 0.5 percent of the sales, so the four-firm concentration ratio is 0.5 percent.

A low concentration ratio indicates a high degree of competition, and a high concentration ratio indicates an absence of competition. A monopoly has a concentration ratio of 100 percent—the largest (and only) firm has 100 percent of the sales. A four-firm concentration ratio that exceeds 60 percent is regarded as an indication of a market that is highly concentrated and dominated by a few firms in an oligopoly. A ratio of less than 40 percent is regarded as an indication of a competitive market.

The Herfindahl-Hirschman Index   The **Herfindahl-Hirschman Index**—also called the HHI—is the square of the percentage market share of each firm summed over the largest 50 firms (or summed over all the firms if there are fewer than 50) in a market. For example, if there are four firms in a market and the market shares of the firms are 50 percent, 25 percent, 15 percent, and 10 percent, the Herfindahl-Hirschman Index is

$$HHI = 50^2 + 25^2 + 15^2 + 10^2 = 3,450.$$

In perfect competition, the HHI is small. For

TABLE 10.5

Concentration Ratio Calculations

Tiremakers		Printers	
Firm	**Sales** (millions of dollars)	**Firm**	**Sales** (millions of dollars)
Top, Inc.	200	Fran's	2.5
ABC, Inc.	250	Ned's	2.0
Big, Inc.	150	Tom's	1.8
XYZ, Inc.	100	Jill's	1.7
Largest 4 firms	700	Largest 4 firms	8.0
Other 10 firms	175	Other 1,000 firms	1,592.0
Industry	**875**	Industry	**1,600.0**

Four-firm concentration ratios:

Tiremakers: $\dfrac{700}{875} \times 100 = 80\%$

Printers: $\dfrac{8}{1,600} \times 100 = 0.5\%$

example, if each of the largest 50 firms in an industry has a market share of 0.1 percent, the HHI is $0.1^2 \times 50 = 0.5$. In a monopoly, the HHI is 10,000—the firm has 100 percent of the market: $100^2 = 10,000$.

The HHI can be used to classify markets across the spectrum of types. A market in which the HHI is less than 1,000 is regarded as being competitive and the smaller the number, the greater is the degree of competition. A market in which the HHI lies between 1,000 and 1,800 is regarded as being moderately competitive—a form of monopolistic competition. Although the HHI of 10,000 is needed for a pure monopoly, a market in which the HHI exceeds 1,800 is regarded as being uncompetitive and a potential matter for concern by competition regulators.

Concentration Measures for the Canadian Economy

Figure 10.2 shows a selection of concentration ratios calculated by Statistics Canada.

Industries that produce tobacco products, petroleum and coal products, transport equipment, communications, and beverages have a high degree of concentration and are oligopolies. Services, clothing, furniture, retail trade, and knitting mills have low concentration measures and are highly competitive. Industries that produce food and electrical products are moderately concentrated. These industries are examples of monopolistic competition.

Concentration measures are a useful indicator of the degree of competition in a market. But they must be supplemented by other information to determine a market's structure. Table 10.6 summarizes the range of other information along with the measures of concentration that determine which market structure describes a particular real-world market.

Limitations of Concentration Measures

The three main limitations of concentration measures alone as determinants of market structure are their failure to take proper account of:

■ The geographical scope of the market
■ Barriers to entry and firm turnover
■ The correspondence between a market and an industry

FIGURE 10.2

Concentration Measures in Canada

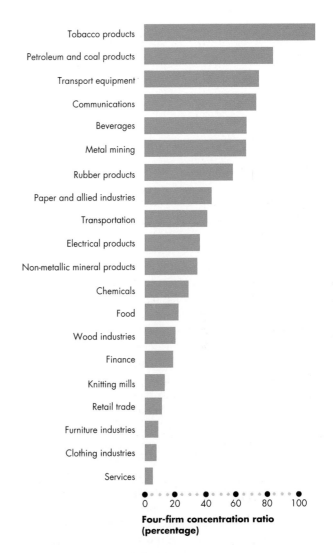

Four-firm concentration ratio (percentage)

The industries that produce tobacco products, petroleum and coal products, transport equipment, communications, and beverages are highly concentrated, while those that produce services, clothing, furniture, retail trade services, and knitware are highly competitive. The industries that produce food and electrical products have an intermediate degree of concentration.

Source: Statistics Canada, *StatCan: CANSIM Disc*, March 1999.

TABLE 10.6

Market Structure

Characteristics	Perfect competition	Monopolistic competition	Oligopoly	Monopoly
Number of firms in industry	Many	Many	Few	One
Product	Identical	Differentiated	Either identical or differentiated	No close substitutes
Barriers to entry	None	None	Moderate	High
Firm's control over price	None	Some	Considerable	Considerable or regulated
Concentration ratio	0	Low	High	100
HHI (approx. ranges)	Less than 100	101 to 999	More than 1,000	10,000
Examples	Wheat, corn	Food, clothing	Automobiles, cereals	Local water supply

Geographical Scope of Market   Concentration measures take a *national* view of the market. Many goods are sold in a national market, but some are sold in a *regional* market and some in a *global* one. The newspaper industry consists of local markets. The concentration measures for newspapers are low, but there is a high degree of concentration in the newspaper industry in most cities. The auto industry is a global market. The big three North American car makers don't have much domestic competition, either in Canada or in the United States. But they face tough competition from foreign producers both here and more especially in foreign markets.

Barriers to Entry and Turnover   Concentration measures don't measure barriers to entry. Some industries are highly concentrated but have easy entry and an enormous amount of turnover of firms. For example, many small towns have few restaurants but there are no restrictions on opening a restaurant and many firms attempt to do so.

Also, an industry might be competitive because of *potential entry*—because a few firms in a market face competition from many firms that can easily enter the market and will do so if economic profits are available.

Market and Industry   To calculate concentration ratios, Statistics Canada classifies each firm as being in a particular industry. But markets do not always correspond closely to industries for three reasons.

First, markets are often narrower than industries. For example, the pharmaceutical industry, which has a low concentration ratio, operates in many separate markets for individual products—for example, measles vaccine and AIDS fighting drugs. These drugs do not compete with each other, so this industry, which looks competitive, includes firms that are monopolies (or near monopolies) in markets for individual drugs.

Second, most firms make several or even many products. For example, Labatt produces beer and milk, among many other items. So this one firm operates in several separate markets. But Statistics Canada classifies Labatt as being in the brewing industry. The fact that Labatt competes with other producers of milk does not show up in the concentration ratios for the milk market.

Third, firms switch from one market to another depending on profit opportunities. For example, Canadian Pacific Ltd., which today provides hotel services, forest products, coal and petroleum products, as well as rail services, has diversified from being just a railroad company. Publishers of newspapers and magazines are today diversifying into Internet and multimedia products. These switches among industries show that there is much scope for entering and exiting an industry and so measures of concentration have limited usefulness.

Despite their limitations, concentration measures do provide a basis for determining the degree of competition in an industry when they are combined with information about the geographical scope of the market, barriers to entry, and the extent to which large, multiproduct firms straddle a variety of markets.

FIGURE 10.3
The Market Structure of the North American Economy

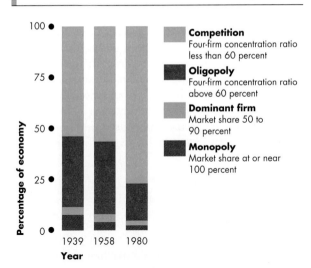

Three-quarters of the North American economy is effectively competitive (perfect competition or monopolistic competition), one fifth is oligopoly, and the rest is monopoly. The economy became more competitive between 1939 and 1980. (Professor Shepherd, whose 1982 study remains the latest word on this topic, suspects that although some industries have become more concentrated, others have become less concentrated, so the net picture has probably not changed much since 1980.)

Source: William G. Shepherd, "Causes of Increased Competition in the U.S. Economy, 1939–1980," *Review of Economics and Statistics*, November 1982, pp. 613–626.

Market Structures in the North American Economy

How competitive are the markets of North America? Do most firms operate in competitive markets or in markets with monopoly elements?

Figure 10.3 provides part of the answer to these questions. It shows the market structure of the U.S. economy and the trends in market structure between 1939 and 1980. (Unfortunately, comparable data for Canada alone and data for the 1980s and 1990s are not available.)

In 1980, three-quarters of the value of goods and services bought and sold in the United States was traded in markets that are essentially competitive—markets that have almost perfect competition or monopolistic competition. Monopoly and the dominance of a single firm accounted for about 5 percent of sales. Oligopoly, which is found mainly in manufacturing, accounted for about 18 percent of sales.

Over the period covered by the data in Fig. 10.3, the U.S. economy became increasingly competitive. You can see that the competitive markets have expanded most (the blue areas) and the oligopoly markets have shrunk most (the red areas).

But also, during the past decade, the U.S. economy has become much more exposed to competition from the rest of the world. Figure 10.3 does not capture this international competition.

REVIEW QUIZ

- What are the four market types? Explain the distinguishing characteristics of each.
- What are the two measures of concentration? Explain how each measure is calculated.
- Under what conditions do the measures of concentration give a good indication of the degree of competition in a market?
- Is our economy competitive? Is it becoming more competitive or less competitive?

You now know the variety of market types and the way we classify firms and industries into the different market types. Our final question in this chapter is what determines the items that firms decide to buy from other firms rather than produce for themselves?

Firms and Markets

AT THE BEGINNING OF THIS CHAPTER, WE defined a firm as an institution that hires productive resources and organizes them to produce and sell goods and services. To organize production, firms coordinate the economic decisions and activities of many individuals. But firms are not the only co-ordinators of economic decisions. You learned in Chapter 4 that markets also coordinate decisions. By adjusting prices, markets make the decisions of buy-ers and sellers consistent—make the quantities demanded equal to the quantities supplied for differ-ent goods and services.

Markets can coordinate production. An example of market coordination versus firm coordination is the production of a rock concert. A promoter hires a stadium, some stage equipment, audio and video recording engineers and technicians, some rock groups, a superstar, a publicity agent, and a ticket agent—all market transactions—and sells tickets to thousands of rock fans, audio rights to a recording company, and video and broadcasting rights to a tele-vision network—another set of market transactions. If rock concerts were produced like corn flakes, the firm producing them would own all the capital used (stadiums, stage, sound and video equipment) and would employ all the labour needed (singers, engi-neers, sales people, and so on).

Another example of market coordination versus firm coordination is *outsourcing*. A firm uses out-sourcing when it buys parts or products from another firm rather than making them itself. The major automakers use outsourcing for windshields and win-dows, gearboxes, tires, and many other car parts.

What determines whether a firm or markets coordinate a particular set of activities? How do firms decide whether to buy from another firm or manu-facture an item themselves? The answer is cost. Taking account of the opportunity cost of time as well as the costs of the other inputs, people use the method that costs least. In other words, they use the economically efficient method.

Firms coordinate economic activity when they can perform a task more efficiently than markets. In such a situation, it is profitable to set up a firm. If markets can perform a task more efficiently than a firm can, people will use markets, and any attempt to set up a firm to replace such market coordination will be doomed to failure.

Why Firms?

There are four key reasons why, in many instances, firms are more efficient than markets as coordinators of economic activity. Firms can achieve:

- Lower transactions costs
- Economies of scale
- Economies of scope
- Economies of team production

Transactions Costs   The idea that firms exist because there are activities in which they are more effi-cient than markets was first suggested by University of Chicago economist and Nobel Laureate Ronald Coase. Coase focused on the firm's ability to reduce or elimi-nate transactions costs. **Transactions costs** are the costs arising from finding someone with whom to do business, of reaching an agreement about the price and other aspects of the exchange, and of ensuring that the terms of the agreement are fulfilled. *Market* transac-tions require buyers and sellers to get together and to negotiate the terms and conditions of their trading. Sometimes, lawyers have to be hired to draw up con-tracts. A broken contract leads to still more expenses. A *firm* can lower such transactions costs by reducing the number of individual transactions undertaken.

Consider, for example, two ways of getting your creaking car fixed.

Firm coordination: You take the car to the garage. The garage owner coordinates parts and tools as well as the mechanic's time, and your car gets fixed. You pay one bill for the entire job.

Market coordination: You hire a mechanic who diag-noses the problems and makes a list of the parts and tools needed to fix them. You buy the parts from the local wrecker's yard and rent the tools from ABC Rentals. You hire the mechanic again to fix the prob-lems. You return the tools and pay your bills—wages to the mechanic, rental to ABC, and the cost of the parts used to the wrecker.

What determines the method that you use? The answer is cost. Taking account of the opportunity cost of your own time as well as the costs of the other inputs that you would have to buy, you will use the method that costs least. In other words, you will use the economically efficient method.

The first method requires that you undertake only one transaction with one firm. It's true that the firm has to undertake several transactions—hiring the labour and buying the parts and tools required to do the job. But the firm doesn't have to undertake those transactions simply to fix your car. One set of such transactions enables the firm to fix hundreds of cars. Thus there is an enormous reduction in the number of individual transactions that take place if people get their cars fixed at the garage rather than going through an elaborate sequence of market transactions.

Economies of Scale   When the cost of producing a unit of a good falls as its output rate increases, economies of scale exist. Automakers, for example, experience economies of scale because as the scale of production increases, the firm can use cost saving equipment and highly specialized labour. An automaker that produces only a few cars a year must use hand-tool methods that are costly. Economies of scale arise from specialization and the division of labour that can be reaped more effectively by firm coordination rather than market coordination.

Economies of Scope   A firm experiences **economies of scope** when it uses specialized (and often expensive) resources to produce *a range of goods and services*. For example, Microsoft hires specialist programmers, designers, and marketing experts, and uses their skills across a range of software products. As a result, Microsoft coordinates the resources that produce software at a lower cost than an individual can who buys all these services in markets.

Economies of Team Production   A production process in which the individuals in a group specialize in mutually supportive tasks is *team production*. Sport provides the best example of team activity. Some team members specialize in pitching and some in batting, some in defence and some in offence. The production of goods and services offers many examples of team activity. For example, production lines in automobile and TV manufacturing plants work most efficiently when individual activity is organized in teams, each specializing in a small task. You can also think of an entire firm as being a team. The team has buyers of raw material and other inputs, production workers, and salespeople. There are even specialists within these various groups. Each individual member of the team specializes, but the value of the output of the team and the profit that it earns depend on the coordinated activities of all the team's members. The idea that firms arise as a consequence of the economies of team production was first suggested by

Armen Alchian and Harold Demsetz of the University of California at Los Angeles.

Because firms can economize on transactions costs, reap economies of scale, and organize efficient team production, it is firms rather than markets that coordinate most of our economic activity. But there are limits to the economic efficiency of firms. If a firm becomes too big or too diversified in the things that it seeks to do, the cost of management and monitoring per unit of output begins to rise, and at some point, the market becomes more efficient at coordinating the use of resources. IBM is an example of a firm that became too big to be efficient. In an attempt to restore efficient operations, IBM split up its large organization into a number of "Baby Blues," each of which specializes in a segment of the computer market.

Sometimes firms enter into long-term relationships with each other that effectively cut out ordinary market transactions and make it difficult to see where one firm ends and another begins. For example, GM has long-term relationships with suppliers of windows, tires, and other parts. Wal-Mart has long-term relationships with suppliers of the goods it sells in its stores. Such relationships make transactions costs lower than they would be if GM or Wal-Mart went shopping on the open market each time it wanted new supplies.

REVIEW QUIZ

- What are the two ways in which economic activity can be coordinated?
- What determines whether a firm or markets coordinate production?
- What are the main reasons why firms can often coordinate production at a lower cost than markets?

◆ *Reading Between the Lines* on pp. 218–219 explores the economic problem faced by Levi Strauss, the firm that produces denim jeans. We continue to study firms and their decisions in the next four chapters. In Chapter 11, we learn about the relationships between cost and output at different output levels. These cost-output relationships are common to all types of firms in all types of markets. We then turn to problems that are special to firms in different types of markets—perfect competition in Chapter 12, monopoly in Chapter 13, and monopolistic competition and oligopoly in Chapter 14.

Levi Strauss's Economic Problem

WALL STREET JOURNAL, FEBRUARY 23, 1999

Levi Strauss to close one-half of plants in North America, cut staff in area

BY REBECCA QUICK

Taking the ax to its operations for the second time in just over a year, Levi Strauss and Co. said it will close half of its 22 manufacturing plants in North America, laying off about 5,900 employees, or 30% of its total in the U.S. and Canada. …

The … denim empire has seen sales of its pioneering jeans shrink, caught in a market squeeze between trendy, expensive jeans from designers like Ralph Lauren, and cheaper brands from department stores like J.C. Penney. Since 1990, Levi's market share of men's jeans dropped to 25% from 48%, according to Tactical Retail Solutions, a market-research firm in New York. And last week, Levi Strauss said its sales slumped 13% in 1998, to $6 billion from $6.9 billion a year earlier. …

But the company said the latest round of closings wouldn't lower its production because it intends to shift much of the work to independent contractors in other countries. Many of Levi Strauss's competitors, including Guess and Tommy Hilfiger, have most if not all of their jeans produced overseas. There, labor costs are frequently much lower than the $10.12 an hour in wages and benefits paid to the average U.S. garment worker.

Aside from chopping its labor bills, Levi Strauss said it will also be able to reduce the time it takes to get apparel into stores. "The drawback to owning your own plant is that changing the line a plant produces is very time- and cost-consuming," said Clarence Grebey, a spokesman for Levi Strauss. "If we go to contractors to do that, we can get our consumers into the product more quickly." …

Essence of the Story

■ Since 1990, Levi Strauss and Company's share of the market for men's jeans has shrunk from 48 percent to 25 percent as the market shares of designer and department store brands have expanded.

■ Most of Levi's competitors produce their jeans overseas where labour costs are lower than those in North America.

■ Levi plans to cut production in North America and transfer the work to independent contractors in other countries.

■ Besides cutting labour costs, Levi says it can get its products into stores more quickly from contractors than from its own plants.

■ Figure 1 shows how Levi Strauss's market share has shrunk from **48** percent to **25** percent, squeezed by designer brands (like Calvin Klein, Tommy Hilfiger, Mossimo, Ralph Lauren, and Donna Karan) and other brands (like Lee and Wrangler, and The Gap) and store brands (like J.C. Penney and Sears).

■ The predicament faced by Levi Strauss illustrates all the aspects of the firm and its economic problem described in this chapter.

■ Levi Strauss and Company is in business to maximize profit. The firm might engage in philanthropic acts but to do so, it must first maximize profit.

■ During the 1990s, the market for jeans has become more competitive and the company's profit has been squeezed.

■ Most large suppliers of jeans are publicly-owned companies with many stockholders. Levi Strauss is a privately-owned company that remains under the control of the descendants of Levi Strauss, who created the firm more than 100 years ago.

■ Jeans can be supplied to the consumer at the lowest possible cost if some firms specialize in *designing* jeans, some in *manufacturing* jeans, some in *marketing*, and some in *information* services.

■ The technology for *designing* and *marketing* jeans is sophisticated and uses the latest information systems. Firms link computers to retailers to manage inventories and use the Internet to obtain customers' measurements.

■ The technology for *manufacturing* jeans involves a small number of operations and basic parts. It uses simple machines and relatively low-skilled labour.

■ Because of the technology for manufacturing jeans, they can be made at least cost in countries that have low labour costs and by achieving economies from long production runs of one particular type of jean.

■ By closing some of its factories in North America and buying jeans from specialist manufacturers, Levi Strauss is capturing these cost savings and economies.

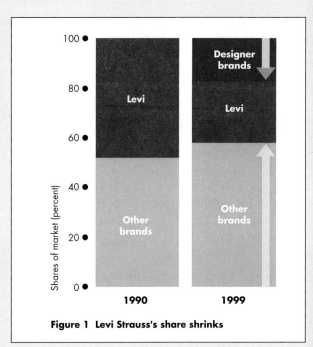

Figure 1 Levi Strauss's share shrinks

SUMMARY

Key Points

The Firm and Its Economic Problem (pp. 202–204)

- Firms hire and organize resources to produce and sell goods and services.
- Firms seek to maximize economic profit, which is total revenue minus opportunity cost.
- Technology, information, and markets limit a firm's profit.

Technology and Economic Efficiency (pp. 205–206)

- A method of production is technologically efficient when it is not possible to increase output without using more inputs.
- A method of production is economically efficient when the cost of producing a given output is as low as possible.

Information and Organization (pp. 207–210)

- Firms use a combination of command systems and incentive systems to organize production.
- Faced with incomplete information and uncertainty, firms induce managers and workers to perform in ways consistent with the firm's goals.
- Sole proprietorships, partnerships, and corporations use ownership, incentives, and long-term contracts to cope with the principal–agent problem.

Markets and the Competitive Environment (pp. 211–215)

- Perfect competition occurs when there are many buyers and sellers of an identical product and when new firms can easily enter a market.
- Monopolistic competition occurs when a large number of firms compete with each other by making slightly different products.
- Oligopoly is a situation in which a small number of producers compete with each other.

- Monopoly is a firm that produces a good or service for which there are no close substitutes and that is protected by a barrier that prevents the entry of competitors.

Firms and Markets (pp. 216–217)

- Firms coordinate economic activities when they can perform a task more efficiently—at lower cost—than markets.
- Firms economize on transactions costs and achieve the benefits of economies of scale, economies of scope, and economies of team production.

Key Figure and Tables

Key Terms

P R O B L E M S

*1. One year ago, Jack and Jill set up a vinegar bottling firm (called JJVB). Use the following information to calculate JJVB's explicit costs and implicit costs during its first year of operation:
  a. Jack and Jill put $50,000 of their own money into the firm.
  b. They bought equipment for $30,000.
  c. They hired one employee to help them for an annual wage of $20,000.
  d. Jack gave up his previous job, at which he earned $30,000, and spent all his time working for JJVB.
  e. Jill kept her old job, which paid $30 an hour, but gave up 10 hours of leisure each week (for 50 weeks) to work for JJVB.
  f. JJVB bought $10,000 of goods and services from other firms.
  g. The market value of the equipment at the end of the year was $28,000.

2. One year ago, Ms. Moffat and Mr. Spieder opened a cheese firm (called MSCF). Use the following information to calculate MSCF's explicit costs and implicit costs during its first year of operation:
  a. Moffat and Spieder put $70,000 of their own money into the firm.
  b. They bought equipment for $40,000.
  c. They hired one employee to help them for an annual wage of $18,000.
  d. Moffat gave up her previous job, at which she earned $22,000, and spent all her time working for MSCF.
  e. Spieder kept his old job, which paid $20 an hour, but gave up 20 hours of leisure each week (for 50 weeks) to work for MSCF.
  f. MSCF bought $5,000 of goods from other firms.
  g. The market value of the equipment at the end of the year was $37,000.

*3. Four methods for doing a tax return are: personal computer, pocket calculator, pocket calculator with pencil and paper, pencil and paper. With a PC, the job takes an hour; with a pocket calculator, it takes 12 hours; with a pocket calculator and pencil and paper, it takes 12 hours; and with a pencil and paper,

it takes 16 hours. The PC and its software cost $1,000, the pocket calculator costs $10, and the pencil and paper cost $1.
  a. Which, if any, of the methods is technologically efficient?
  b. Which method is economically efficient if the wage rate is
    i) $5 an hour?
    ii) $50 an hour?
    iii) $500 an hour?

4. Sue can do her accounting assignment by using: a personal computer; a pocket calculator; a pocket calculator and a pencil and paper; or a pencil and paper. With a PC, Sue completes the job in half an hour; with a pocket calculator, it takes 4 hours; with a pocket calculator and with a pencil and paper, it takes 5 hours; and with a pencil and paper, it takes 14 hours. The PC and its software cost $2,000, the pocket calculator costs $15, and the pencil and paper cost $3.
  a. Which, if any, of the methods is technologically efficient?
  b. Which method is economically efficient if Sue's wage rate is
    i) $10 an hour?
    ii) $20 an hour?
    iii) $50 an hour?

*5. Alternative ways of laundering 100 shirts are:

Method	Labour (hours)	Capital (machines)
a	1	10
b	5	8
c	20	4
d	50	1

  a. Which methods are technologically efficient?
  b. Which method is economically efficient if the hourly wage rate and rental rate are:
    i) Wage rate $1, rental rate $100?
    ii) Wage rate $5, rental rate $50?
    iii) Wage rate $50, rental rate $5?

6. Alternative ways of making 100 shirts a day are:

Method	Labour (hours)	Capital (machines)
a	10	50
b	20	40
c	50	20
d	100	10

a. Which methods are technologically efficient?
b. Which method is economically efficient if the hourly wage rate and rental rate are:
    i) Wage rate $1, rental rate $100?
    ii) Wage rate $5, rental rate $50?
    iii) Wage rate $50, rental rate $5?

*7. Sales of the firms in the tattoo industry are:

Firm	Sales (dollars)
Bright Spots	450
Freckles	325
Love Galore	250
Native Birds	200
Other 15 firms	800

a. Calculate the four-firm concentration ratio.
b. What is the structure of the tattoo industry?

8. Sales of the firms in the pet food industry are:

Firm	Sales (thousands of dollars)
Big Collar, Inc.	50
Shiny Coat, Inc.	75
Friendly Pet, Inc.	60
Nature's Way, Inc.	65
Other 8 firms	400

a. Calculate the four-firm concentration ratio.
b. What is the structure of the industry?

*9. Market shares of chocolate makers are:

Firm	Market share (percent)
Mayfair, Inc.	15
Bond, Inc.	10
Magic, Inc.	20
All Natural, Inc.	15
Truffles, Inc.	25
Gold, Inc.	15

a. Calculate the Herfindahl-Hirschman Index.
b. What is the structure of the industry?

10. Market shares of mat makers are:

Firm	Market share (percent)
Made-to-Last, Inc.	20
Big Wheel, Inc.	17
Magic Carpet, Inc.	22
Supreme, Inc.	17
Copra, Inc.	24

a. Calculate the Herfindahl-Hirschman Index.
b. What is the structure of the industry?

CRITICAL THINKING

 1. Study the news article about Levi Strauss and Company in *Reading Between the Lines* on pp. 218–219 and then:
a. Describe the economic problem that the firm faced in 1998.
b. Use the links on the Parkin-Bade Web site to find information about some of Levi Strauss's main competitors. What do you think the economic problems of these competitors are?
c. Consider the market share of Levi Strauss in 1990 and 1998. Do you think the market for blue jeans is an example of monopoly, oligopoly, monopolistic competition, or perfect competition? Explain your answer.
d. Use the links on the Parkin-Bade Web site to find information about *where* Levi Strauss and Co. is closing factories. Which Canadian plant closed, and what special problems do you think arose?
e. Compare and contrast how Levi Strauss achieves technological efficiency and economic efficiency.
f. If more and more manufacturing leaves Canada and goes to other countries, what do you think the effect will be on the Canadian economy? [Hint: Think about the *PPF* and efficiency.]

 2. Use the links on the Parkin-Bade Web site to obtain information about the auto industry.
a. What are the main economic problems faced by auto producers?
b. Why are auto producers merging?

 3. Use the links on the Parkin-Bade Web site to obtain information about the steel industry.
a. What are the main economic problems faced by steel producers?
b. Why are steel producers seeking protection from international competition?
c. Is the number of steel producers likely to increase or decrease during the next few years? Why?

Output and Costs

Size does not guarantee survival in business. True, the Hudson's Bay Company has been around a long time and has grown pretty large. But most of the giants of fifty years ago don't even exist today. Remaining small does not guarantee survival either. Every year, millions of small businesses close down. Call a random selection of restaurants and fashion boutiques from *last* year's yellow pages and see how many have vanished. What does a firm have to do to be one of the survivors? ◆ Firms differ in lots of ways—from Mom-and-Pop's convenience store to multinational giants producing hi-tech goods. But regardless of their size or what they produce, all firms must decide how much to produce and how to produce it. How do firms make these decisions? ◆ Most automakers in North America could produce more cars than they can sell. Why do automakers have expensive equipment lying around that isn't fully used? Many electric utilities don't have enough production equipment on hand to meet demand on the coldest and hottest days and must buy power from other producers. Why don't these firms install more equipment so that they can supply the market themselves?

Survival of the Fittest

◇ We are going to answer these questions in this chapter. To do so, we are going to study the economic decisions of a small, imaginary firm—Sidney's Sweaters Inc., a producer of knitted sweaters. The firm is owned and operated by Sidney. By studying the economic problems of Sidney's Sweaters and the way Sidney copes with them, we will be able to get a clear view of the problems that face *all* firms—small ones like Sidney's Sweaters as well as the giants. We're going to begin by setting the scene and describing the time frames in which Sidney makes his business decisions.

After studying this chapter, you will be able to:

■ Distinguish between the short run and the long run

■ Explain the relationship between a firm's output and labour employed in the short run

■ Explain the relationship between a firm's output and costs in the short run

■ Derive and explain a firm's short-run cost curves

■ Explain the relationship between a firm's output and costs in the long run

■ Derive and explain a firm's long-run average cost curve

Decision Time Frames

PEOPLE WHO OPERATE FIRMS MAKE MANY decisions. And all of the decisions are aimed at one overriding objective: maximum attainable profit. But the decisions are not all equally critical. Some of the decisions are big ones. Once made, they are costly (or impossible) to reverse. If such a decision turns out to be incorrect, it might lead to the failure of the firm. Some of the decisions are small ones. They are easily changed. If one of these decisions turns out to be incorrect, the firm can change its actions and survive.

The biggest decision that any firm makes is what industry to enter. For most entrepreneurs, their background knowledge and interests drive this decision. But the decision also depends on profit prospects. No one sets up a firm without believing it will be profitable. And profit depends on total revenue and opportunity cost (see Chapter 10, pp. 202–203).

The firm that we study has already chosen the industry in which to operate. It has also chosen its most effective method of organization. But it has not decided the quantity to produce, the quantities of resources to hire, or the price at which to sell its output.

Decisions about the quantity to produce and the price to charge depend on the type of market in which the firm operates. Perfect competition, monopolistic competition, oligopoly, and monopoly all confront the firm with their own special problems.

But decisions about how to produce a given output do not depend on the type of market in which the firm operates. These decisions are similar for *all* types of firms in *all* types of markets.

The actions that a firm can take to influence the relationship between output and cost depend on how soon the firm wants to act. A firm that plans to change its output rate tomorrow has fewer options than one that plans to change its output rate six months from now.

To study the relationship between a firm's output decision and its costs, we distinguish two decision time frames:

- The short run
- The long run

The Short Run

The **short run** is a time frame in which the quantities of some resources are fixed. For most firms, the fixed resources are the firm's technology, buildings, and capital. The management organization is also fixed in the short run. We call the collection of fixed resources the firm's *plant*. So in the short run, a firm's plant is fixed.

For Sidney's Sweaters, the fixed plant is its factory building and its knitting machines. For an electric power utility, the fixed plant is its buildings, generators, computers, and control systems. For an airport, the fixed plant is the runways, terminal buildings, and traffic control facilities.

To increase output in the short run, a firm must increase the quantity of variable inputs it uses. Labour is usually the variable input. So to produce more output, Sidney's Sweaters must hire more labour and operate its knitting machines for more hours per day. Similarly, an electric power utility must hire more labour and operate its generators for more hours per day. And an airport must hire more labour and operate its runways, terminals, and traffic control facilities for more hours per day.

Short-run decisions are easily reversed. The firm can increase or decrease output in the short run by increasing or decreasing the labour hours it hires.

The Long Run

The **long run** is a time frame in which the quantities of *all* resources can be varied. That is, the long run is a period in which the firm can change its *plant*.

To increase output in the long run, a firm is able to choose whether to change its plant as well as whether to increase the quantity of labour it hires. Sidney's Sweaters can decide whether to install some additional knitting machines, use a new type of machine, reorganize its management, or hire more labour. An electric power utility can decide whether to install more generators. And an airport can decide whether to build more runways, terminals, and traffic-control facilities.

Long-run decisions are *not* easily reversed. Once a plant decision is made, the firm must live with it for some time. To emphasize this fact, we call the *past* cost of buying a new plant a **sunk cost**. A sunk cost is irrelevant to the firm's decisions. The only costs that influence its decisions are the short-run cost of changing its labour inputs and the long-run cost of changing its plant in the future.

We're going to study costs in the short run and the long run. We begin with the short run and describe the technology constraint the firm faces.

Short-Run Technology Constraint

TO INCREASE OUTPUT IN THE SHORT RUN, A FIRM must increase the quantity of labour employed. We describe the relationship between output and the quantity of labour employed by using three related concepts:

■ Total product
■ Marginal product
■ Average product

These product concepts can be illustrated either by product schedules or by product curves. Let's look first at the product schedules.

TABLE 11.1

Total Product, Marginal Product, and Average Product

	Labour (workers per day)	Total product (sweaters per day)	Marginal product (sweaters per additional worker)	Average product (sweaters per worker)
a	0	0		
			4	
b	1	4		4.00
			6	
c	2	10		5.00
			3	
d	3	13		4.33
			2	
e	4	15		3.75
			1	
f	5	16		3.20

Total product is the total amount produced. Marginal product is the change in total product that results from a one-unit increase in labour. For example, when labour increases from 2 to 3 workers a day (row *c* to row *d*), total product increases from 10 to 13 sweaters. (Marginal product is shown between the rows to emphasize that it is the result of *changing* the quantity of labour.) The marginal product of going from 2 to 3 workers is 3 sweaters. Average product is total product divided by the quantity of labour employed. For example, the average product of 3 workers is 4.33 sweaters per worker (13 sweaters a day divided by 3 workers).

Product Schedules

Table 11.1 shows some data that describe Sidney's Sweaters' total product, marginal product, and average product. The numbers tell us how Sidney's Sweaters' production changes as more workers are employed. They also tell us about the productivity of Sidney's Sweaters' labour force.

Focus first on the columns headed "Labour" and "Total product." **Total product** is the total output produced. You can see from the numbers in these columns that as Sidney employs more labour, total product increases. For example, when Sidney employs 1 worker, total product is 4 sweaters a day and when he employs 2 workers, total product is 10 sweaters a day. Each increase in employment brings an increase in total product.

Marginal product tells us by how much total product increases when employment increases. The **marginal product** of labour is the change in total product that results from a one-unit increase in the quantity of labour employed. For example, in Table 11.1, when Sidney increases employment from 2 to 3 workers, the marginal product of the third worker is 3 sweaters—total product goes from 10 to 13 sweaters.

Average product tells how productive workers are on the average. The **average product** of labour is equal to total product divided by the quantity of labour employed. For example, in Table 11.1, the average product of 3 workers is 4.33 sweaters per worker—13 sweaters a day divided by 3 workers.

If you look closely at the numbers in Table 11.1, you can see some patterns. For example, as employment increases, marginal product at first increases and then begins to decrease. For example, marginal product increases from 4 sweaters a day when the first worker is hired to 6 sweaters a day when the second worker is hired. It then decreases to 3 sweaters a day when the third worker is hired. Average product also at first increases and then decreases. The relationships between employment and the three product concepts can be seen more clearly by looking at the product curves.

Product Curves

The product curves are graphs of the relationships between employment and the product concepts you've just studied. They show how total product, marginal product, and average product change as employment changes. They also show the relationships among the three concepts. Let's look at the product curves.

Total Product Curve

Figure 11.1 shows Sidney's Sweaters' total product curve, *TP*. As employment increases, so does the number of sweaters knitted. Points *a* through *f* on the curve correspond to the same rows in Table 11.1.

The total product curve is similar to the *production possibility frontier* (explained in Chapter 3). It separates the attainable output levels from those that are unattainable. All the points that lie above the curve are unattainable. Points that lie below the curve, in the orange area, are attainable. But they are inefficient—they use more labour than is necessary to produce a given output. Only the points *on* the total product curve are technologically efficient.

Notice especially the shape of the total product curve. As employment increases from zero to 1 worker per day, the curve becomes steeper. Then, as employment continues to increase to 3, 4, and 5 workers a day, the curve becomes less steep. The steeper the slope of the total product curve, the greater is marginal product, as you are about to see.

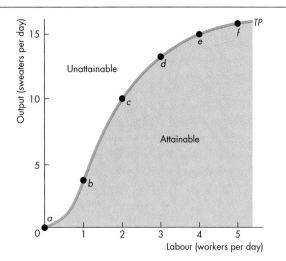

FIGURE 11.1

Total Product Curve

The total product curve (*TP*), based on the data in Table 11.1, shows how the quantity of sweaters produced changes as the quantity of labour employed changes. For example, 2 workers can produce 10 sweaters a day (point *c*). Points *a* through *f* on the curve correspond to the rows of Table 11.1. The total product curve separates attainable outputs from unattainable outputs. Points below the *TP* curve are inefficient.

Marginal Product Curve

Figure 11.2 shows the marginal product of labour. Part (a) reproduces the total product curve, which is the same as the total product curve in Fig. 11.1. Part (b) shows the marginal product curve, *MP*.

In part (a), the orange bars illustrate the marginal product of labour. The height of each bar measures marginal product. Marginal product is also measured by the slope of the total product curve. Recall that the slope of a curve is the change in the value of the variable measured on the *y*-axis—output—divided by the change in the variable measured on the *x*-axis—labour input—as we move along the curve. A one-unit increase in labour input, from 2 to 3 workers, increases output from 10 to 13 sweaters, so the slope from point *c* to point *d* is 3, the same as the marginal product that we've just calculated.

We've calculated the marginal product of labour for a series of unit increases in the quantity of labour. But labour is divisible into smaller units than one person. It is divisible into hours and even minutes. By varying the amount of labour in the smallest imaginable units, we can draw the marginal product curve shown in Fig. 11.2(b). The *height* of this curve measures the *slope* of the total product curve at a point. Part (a) shows that an increase in employment from 2 to 3 workers increases output from 10 to 13 sweaters (an increase of 3). The increase in output of 3 sweaters appears on the vertical axis of part (b) as the marginal product of going from 2 to 3 workers. We plot that marginal product at the midpoint between 2 and 3 workers. Notice that marginal product shown in Fig. 11.2(b) reaches a peak at 1.5 workers, and at that point, marginal product is more than 6. The peak occurs at 1.5 workers because the total product curve is steepest when employment increases from 1 worker to 2 workers.

The total product and marginal product curves are different for different firms and different types of goods. Ford Motor Company's product curves are different from those of Jim's Burger Stand, which in turn are different from those of Sidney's sweater factory. But the shapes of the product curves are similar, because almost every production process has two features:

- Increasing marginal returns initially
- Diminishing marginal returns eventually

Increasing Marginal Returns Increasing marginal returns occur when the marginal product of an additional worker exceeds the marginal product of the

FIGURE 11.2

Marginal Product

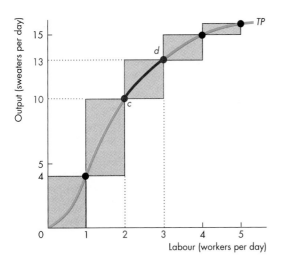

(a) Total product

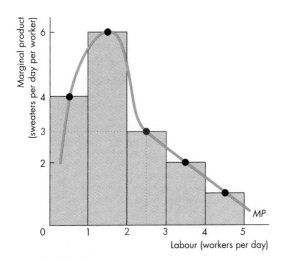

(b) Marginal product

Marginal product is illustrated by the orange bars. For example, when labour increases from 2 to 3, marginal product is the orange bar whose height is 3 sweaters. (Marginal product is shown midway between the labour inputs to emphasize that it is the result of *changing* inputs.) The steeper the slope of the total product curve (*TP*) in part (a), the larger is marginal product (*MP*) in part (b). Marginal product increases to a maximum in this example when the second worker is employed and then declines—diminishing marginal product.

previous worker. Increasing marginal returns arise from increased specialization and division of labour in the production process.

For example, if Sidney employs just one worker, that person must learn all the aspects of sweater production: running the knitting machines, fixing breakdowns, packaging and mailing sweaters, buying and checking the type and colour of the wool. That one person must perform all these tasks.

If Sidney hires a second person, the two workers can specialize in different parts of the production process. As a result, two workers produce more than twice as much as one. The marginal product of the second worker is greater than the marginal product of the first worker. Marginal returns are increasing.

Diminishing Marginal Returns Most production processes experience increasing marginal returns initially. But all production processes eventually reach a point of *diminishing* marginal returns. **Diminishing marginal returns** occur when the marginal product of an additional worker is less than the marginal product of the previous worker.

Diminishing marginal returns arise from the fact that more and more workers are using the same capital and working in the same space. As more workers are added, there is less and less for the additional workers to do that is productive. For example, if Sidney hires a third worker, output increases but not by as much as it did when he added the second worker. In this case, after two workers are hired, all gains from specialization and the division of labour have been exhausted. By hiring a third worker, the factory produces more sweaters, but the equipment is being operated closer to its limits. There are even times when the third worker has nothing to do because the machines are running without the need for further attention. Adding yet more and more workers continues to increase output but by successively smaller amounts. Marginal returns are diminishing. This phenomenon is such a pervasive one that it is called a "law"—"the law of diminishing returns." The **law of diminishing returns** states that

As a firm uses more of a variable input, with a given quantity of fixed inputs, the marginal product of the variable input eventually diminishes.

You are going to return to the law of diminishing returns when we study a firm's costs. But before we do that, let's look at the average product of labour and the average product curve.

Average Product Curve

Figure 11.3 illustrates Sidney's Sweaters' average product of labour, *AP*. It also shows the relationship between average product and marginal product. Points *b* through *f* on the average product curve correspond to those same rows in Table 11.1. Average product increases from 1 to 2 workers (its maximum value at point *c*) but then decreases as yet more workers are employed. Notice also that average product is largest when average product and marginal product are equal. That is, the marginal product curve cuts the average product curve at the point of maximum average product. For employment levels at which marginal product exceeds average product, average product is increasing. For employment levels at which marginal product is less than average product, average product is decreasing.

The relationship between the average and marginal product curves is a general feature of the relationship between the average and marginal values of any variable. Let's look at a familiar example.

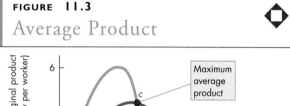

FIGURE 11.3
Average Product

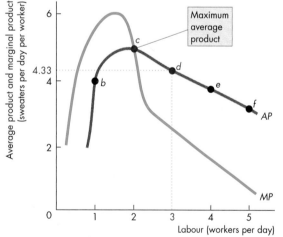

The figure shows the average product of labour and the connection between the average product and marginal product. With 1 worker, marginal product exceeds average product, so average product is increasing. With 2 workers, marginal product equals average product, so average product is at its maximum. With more than 2 workers, marginal product is less than average product, so average product is decreasing.

Marginal Grade and Grade Point Average

To see the relationship between average product and marginal product, think about the similar relationship between Sidney's average grade and marginal grade over five semesters. (Suppose Sidney is a part-time student who takes just one course each semester.) In the first semester, Sidney takes calculus and his grade is a 2. This grade is his marginal grade. It is also his average grade—his GPA. In the next semester, Sidney takes French and gets a 3. French is Sidney's marginal course and his marginal grade is 3. His GPA rises to 2.5. Because his marginal grade exceeds his average grade, it pulls his average up. In the third semester, Sidney takes economics and gets a 4—his new marginal grade. Because his marginal grade exceeds his GPA, it again pulls his average up. Sidney's GPA is now 3, the average of 2, 3, and 4. The fourth semester, he takes history and gets a 3. Because his marginal grade is equal to his average, his GPA does not change. In the fifth semester, Sidney takes English and gets a 2. Because his marginal grade, a 2, is below his GPA of 3, his GPA falls.

This everyday relationship between marginal and average values agrees with that between marginal and average product. Sidney's GPA increases when his marginal grade exceeds his GPA. His GPA falls when his marginal grade is below his GPA. And his GPA is constant when his marginal grade equals his GPA. The relationship between marginal product and average product is exactly the same as that between Sidney's marginal and average grades.

REVIEW QUIZ

- Explain how the marginal product of labour and the average product of labour change as the quantity of labour employed increases (a) initially and (b) eventually.
- What is the law of diminishing returns? Why does marginal product eventually diminish?
- Explain the relationship between marginal product and average product. How does average product change when marginal product exceeds average product? How does average product change when average product exceeds marginal product? Why?

Sidney cares about his product curves because they influence his costs. Let's look at Sidney's costs.

Short-Run Cost

TO PRODUCE MORE OUTPUT IN THE SHORT RUN, a firm must employ more labour, which means it must increase its costs. We describe the relationship between output and cost by using three cost concepts:

- Total cost
- Marginal cost
- Average cost

Total Cost

A firm's **total cost** (TC) is the cost of the productive resources it uses. Total cost includes the cost of land, capital, and labour. It also includes the cost of entrepreneurship, which is *normal profit* (see Chapter 10, p. 203). We divide total cost into total fixed cost and total variable cost.

Total fixed cost (TFC) is the cost of the firm's fixed inputs. Because the quantity of a fixed input does not change as output changes, fixed cost does not change as output changes.

Total variable cost (TVC) is the cost of the firm's variable inputs. Because to change its output, a firm must change the quantity of variable inputs, total variable cost changes as output changes.

Total cost is the sum of total fixed cost and total variable cost. That is,

$$TC = TFC + TVC.$$

The table in Fig. 11.4 shows Sidney's total costs. With one knitting machine that costs $25 a day, TFC is $25. To produce more sweaters, Sidney hires more labour, which costs $25 a day. TVC, which increases as output increases, is the number of workers multiplied by $25. For example, to produce 13 sweaters a day, Sidney hires 3 workers and TVC is $75. TC is the sum of TFC and TVC, so to produce 13 sweaters a day, Sidney's total cost, TC, is $100. Check the calculation in each row of the table.

Figure 11.4 graphs Sidney's total cost curves. These curves graph total cost against total product. The green total fixed cost curve (TFC) is horizontal because total fixed cost does not change when output changes. It is a constant at $25. The purple total variable cost curve (TVC) and the blue total cost curve (TC) both increase as output increases. The vertical distance between the TVC and TC curve is total fixed cost as shown by the arrows.

Let's now look at Sidney's Sweaters' marginal cost.

FIGURE 11.4
Total Cost Curves

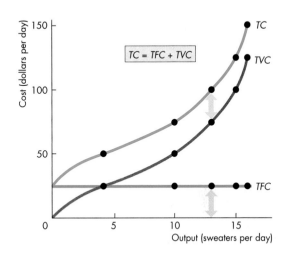

Labour (workers per day)	Output (sweaters per day)	Total fixed cost (TFC)	Total variable cost (TVC)	Total cost (TC)
			(dollars per day)	
a	0	0	25	0	25
b	1	4	25	25	50
c	2	10	25	50	75
d	3	13	25	75	100
e	4	15	25	100	125
f	5	16	25	125	150

Sidney rents a knitting machine for $25 a day. This amount is Sidney's Sweaters' total fixed cost. Sidney hires workers at a wage rate of $25 a day, and this cost is Sidney's Sweaters' total variable cost. For example, if Sidney employs 3 workers, total variable cost is (3 × $25), which equals $75. Total cost is the sum of total fixed cost and total variable cost. For example, when Sidney employs 3 workers, total cost is $100—total fixed cost of $25 plus total variable cost of $75. The graph shows Sidney's Sweaters' total cost curves. Total fixed cost (TFC) is constant—it graphs as a horizontal line—and total variable cost (TVC) increases as output increases. Total cost (TC) also increases as output increases. The vertical distance between the total cost curve and the total variable cost curve is total fixed cost, as illustrated by the two arrows.

Marginal Cost

In Fig. 11.4, total variable cost and total cost increase at a decreasing rate at small levels of output and begin to increase at an increasing rate as output increases. To understand these patterns in the changes in total cost, we need to use the concept of *marginal cost*.

A firm's **marginal cost** is the change in total cost that results from a one-unit increase in output. We calculate marginal cost (MC) as the change in total cost (ΔTC) divided by the change in output (ΔQ). That is:

$$MC = \frac{\Delta TC}{\Delta Q}.$$

The table in Fig. 11.5 shows this calculation. When, for example, output increases from 10 sweaters to 13 sweaters, total cost increases from $75 to $100. The change in output is 3 sweaters, and the change in total cost is $25. The marginal cost of one of those 3 sweaters is ($25 ÷ 3), which equals $8.33.

Figure 11.5 graphs the marginal cost data in the table as the red marginal cost curve, MC. This curve is U-shaped because, when Sidney hires a second worker, marginal cost decreases, but when he hires a third, a fourth, and a fifth worker, marginal cost successively increases.

Marginal cost decreases at low outputs because of economies from greater specialization. It eventually increases because of *the law of diminishing returns*. The law of diminishing returns means that each additional worker produces a successively smaller addition to output. So to get an additional unit of output, ever more workers are required. Because more workers are required to produce one additional unit of output, the cost of the additional output—marginal cost—must eventually increase.

Marginal cost tells us how total cost changes as output changes. The final cost concept tells us what it costs, on the average, to produce a unit of output. Let's now look at Sidney's Sweaters' average costs.

Average Cost

There are three average costs:

1. Average fixed cost
2. Average variable cost
3. Average total cost

Average fixed cost (AFC) is total fixed cost per unit of output. **Average variable cost** (AVC) is total variable cost per unit of output. **Average total cost** (ATC) is total cost per unit of output. To calculate the average cost concepts, begin with total cost:

$$TC = TFC + TVC.$$

Divide each total cost term by the quantity produced, Q, to give

$$\frac{TC}{Q} = \frac{TFC}{Q} + \frac{TVC}{Q}$$

or,

$$ATC = AFC + AVC.$$

The table in Fig. 11.5 shows the calculation of average total cost. For example, when output is 10 sweaters, average fixed cost is ($25 ÷ 10), which equals $2.50, average variable cost is ($50 ÷ 10), which equals $5.00, and average total cost is ($75 ÷ 10), which equals $7.50. Note that average total cost is equal to average fixed cost ($2.50) plus average variable cost ($5.00).

Figure 11.5 shows the average cost curves. The green average fixed cost curve (AFC) slopes downward. As output increases, the same constant fixed cost is spread over a larger output. The blue average total cost curve (ATC) and the purple average variable cost curve (AVC) are U-shaped. The vertical distance between the average total cost and average variable cost curves is equal to average fixed cost—as indicated by the two arrows. That distance shrinks as output increases because average fixed cost declines with increasing output.

The marginal cost curve intersects the average variable cost curve and the average total cost curve at their minimum points. That is, when marginal cost is less than average cost, average cost is decreasing, and when marginal cost exceeds average cost, average cost is increasing. This relationship holds for both the ATC curve and the AVC curve and is another example of the relationship you saw in Fig. 11.3 for average product and marginal product and for course grades.

Why the Average Total Cost Curve Is U-Shaped

Average total cost, ATC, is the sum of average fixed cost, AFC, and average variable cost, AVC. So the shape of the ATC curve combines the shapes of the

FIGURE 11.5
Marginal Cost and Average Costs

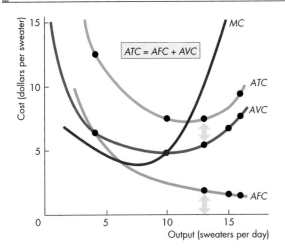

Marginal cost is calculated as the change in total cost divided by the change in output. When output increases from 4 to 10, an increase of 6, total cost increases by $25 and marginal cost is $25 ÷ 6, which equals $4.17. Each average cost concept is calculated by dividing the related total cost by output. When 10 sweaters are produced, AFC is $2.50 ($25 ÷ 10), AVC is $5 ($50 ÷ 10), and ATC is $7.50 ($75 ÷ 10).

The figure shows the marginal cost curve and the average cost curves. The marginal cost curve (MC) is U-shaped and intersects the average variable cost curve and the average total cost curve at their minimum points. Average fixed cost (AFC) decreases as output increases. The average total cost curve (ATC) and average variable cost curve (AVC) are U-shaped. The vertical distance between these two curves is equal to average fixed cost, as illustrated by the two arrows.

	Labour (workers per day)	Output (sweaters per day)	Total fixed cost (TFC)	Total variable cost (TVC)	Total cost (TC)	Marginal cost (MC) (dollars per additional sweater)	Average fixed cost (AFC)	Average variable cost (AVC)	Average total cost (ATC)
				(dollars per day)				(dollars per sweater)	
a	0	0	25	0	25		—	—	—
						.... 6.25			
b	1	4	25	25	50		6.25	6.25	12.50
						.... 4.17			
c	2	10	25	50	75		2.50	5.00	7.50
						.... 8.33			
d	3	13	25	75	100		1.92	5.77	7.69
						.... 12.50			
e	4	15	25	100	125		1.67	6.67	8.33
						.... 25.00			
f	5	16	25	125	150		1.56	7.81	9.38

AFC and *AVC* curves. The U-shape of the *ATC* curve arises from two opposing forces:

- Spreading fixed cost over a larger output
- Eventually diminishing returns

When output increases, the firm spreads its fixed costs over a larger output and its average fixed cost decreases—its average fixed cost curve slopes downward.

Diminishing returns means that as output increases, ever-larger amounts of labour are needed to produce an additional unit of output. So average

variable cost eventually increases, and the *AVC* curve eventually slopes upward.

The shape of the average total cost curve combines these two effects. Initially, as output increases, both average fixed cost and average variable cost decrease, so average total cost decreases and the *ATC* curve slopes downward. But as output increases further and diminishing returns set in, average variable cost begins to increase. Eventually, average variable cost increases more quickly than average fixed cost decreases, so average total cost increases and the *ATC* curve slopes upward.

Cost Curves and Product Curves

The technology that a firm uses determines its costs. Figure 11.6 shows the links between the firm's technology constraint (its product curves) and its cost curves. The upper part of the figure shows the average product curve and the marginal product curve—like those in Fig. 11.3. The lower part of the figure shows the average variable cost curve and the marginal cost curve—like those in Fig. 11.5.

The figure highlights the links between technology and costs. As labour increases initially, marginal product and average product rise and marginal cost and average variable cost fall. Then, at the point of maximum marginal product, marginal cost is a minimum. As labour increases further, marginal product diminishes and marginal cost increases. But average product continues to rise and average variable cost continues to fall. Then, at the point of maximum average product, average variable cost is a minimum. As labour increases further, average product diminishes and average variable cost increases.

Shifts in the Cost Curves

The position of a firm's short-run cost curves depends on two factors:

■ Technology
■ Prices of productive resources

Technology A technological change that increases productivity shifts the total product curve upward. It also shifts the marginal product curve and the average product curve upward. Because with a better technology, the same inputs can produce more output, technological change lowers costs and shifts the cost curves downward.

For example, advances in robot production techniques have increased productivity in the automobile industry. As a result, the product curves of Chrysler, Ford, and GM have shifted upward, and their cost curves have shifted downward. But the relationships between their product curves and cost curves have not changed. The curves are still linked in the way shown in Fig. 11.6.

Often a technological advance results in a firm using more capital (a fixed input) and less labour (a variable input). For example, today the telephone

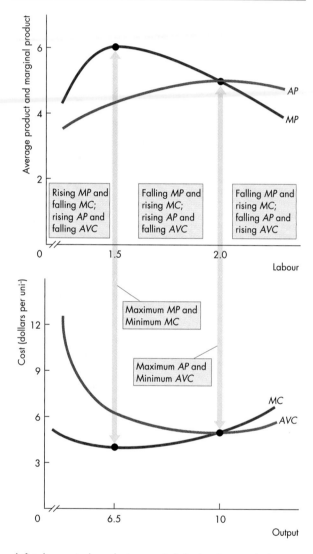

A firm's marginal product curve is linked to its marginal cost curve. If marginal product rises, marginal cost falls. If marginal product is a maximum, marginal cost is a minimum. If marginal product diminishes, marginal cost rises. A firm's average product curve is linked to its average variable cost curve. If average product rises, average variable cost falls. If average product is a maximum, average variable cost is a minimum. If average product diminishes, average variable cost rises.

TABLE 11.2

A Compact Glossary of Costs

Term	Symbol	Definition	Equation
Fixed cost		Cost that is independent of the output level; cost of a fixed input	
Variable cost		Cost that varies with the output level; cost of a variable input	
Total fixed cost	TFC	Cost of the fixed inputs	
Total variable cost	TVC	Cost of the variable inputs	
Total cost	TC	Cost of all inputs	$TC = TFC + TVC$
Total product (output)	TP	Total quantity produced (output Q)	
Marginal cost	MC	Change in total cost resulting from a one-unit increase in total product	$MC = \Delta TC \div \Delta Q$
Average fixed cost	AFC	Total fixed cost per unit of output	$AFC = TFC \div Q$
Average variable cost	AVC	Total variable cost per unit of output	$AVC = TVC \div Q$
Average total cost	ATC	Total cost per unit of output	$ATC = AFC + AVC$

companies use computers to connect long-distance calls in place of the human operators they used in the 1980s. When such a technological change occurs, costs decrease, but fixed costs increase and variable costs decrease. This change in the mix of fixed cost and variable cost means that at low output levels average total cost might increase, while at high output levels, average total cost decreases.

Prices of Resources An increase in the price of a productive resource increases costs and shifts the cost curves. But how the curves shift depends on which resource price changes. An increase in rent or some other component of *fixed* cost shifts the fixed cost curves (*TFC* and *AFC*) upward and shifts the total cost curve (*TC*) upward but leaves the variable cost curves (*AVC* and *TVC*) and the marginal cost curve (*MC*) unchanged. An increase in the wage rate or some other component of *variable* cost shifts the variable curves (*TVC* and *AVC*) upward and shifts the (*MC*) upward but leaves the fixed cost curves (*AFC* and *TFC*) unchanged. So, for example, if truck drivers' wage rates increase, the variable cost and mar-

ginal cost of transportation services increase. If the interest expense paid by a trucking company increases, the fixed cost of transportation services increases.

You've now completed your study of short-run costs. All the concepts that you've met are summarized in a compact glossary in Table 11.2.

R E V I E W   Q U I Z

- What relationships do a firm's short-run cost curves show?
- How does marginal cost change as output increases (a) initially, and (b) eventually?
- What does the law of *diminishing returns* imply for the shape of the marginal cost curve?
- What is the shape of the average fixed cost curve and why?
- What are the shapes of the average variable cost curve and the average total cost curve and why?

CHAPTER 11 OUTPUT AND COSTS

Long-Run Cost

IN THE SHORT RUN, A FIRM CAN VARY THE
quantity of labour but the quantity of capital is fixed.
In the long run, a firm can vary both the quantity of
labour and the quantity of capital. We are now going
to see how costs vary when the quantities of labour
and capital vary. That is, we are going to study a
firm's long-run costs. *Long-run cost* is the cost of production when a firm uses the economically efficient
quantities of labour and capital.

The behaviour of long-run cost depends on the
firm's *production function*, which is the relationship
between the maximum output attainable and the
quantities of both labour and capital.

The Production Function

Table 11.3 shows Sidney's Sweaters' production function. The table lists total product schedules for four
different quantities of capital. We identify the quantity of capital by the plant size. The numbers for
Plant 1 are for a factory with one knitting machine—
the case we've just studied. The other three plants
have 2, 3, and 4 machines. If Sidney's Sweaters doubles its capital to 2 knitting machines, the various
amounts of labour can produce the outputs shown in
the second column of the table. The other two
columns show the outputs of yet larger quantities of
capital. Each column of the table could be graphed as
a total product curve for each plant.

Diminishing Returns   Diminishing returns occur
at all four quantities of capital as the quantity of
labour increases. You can check that fact by calculating the marginal product of labour in plants with
2, 3, and 4 machines. At each plant size, as the
quantity of labour increases, its marginal product
(eventually) diminishes.

Diminishing Marginal Product of Capital
Diminishing returns also occurs as the quantity of
capital increases. You can check that fact by calculating the marginal product of capital at a given quantity of labour. The *marginal product of capital* is the
change in total product divided by the change in capital when the quantity of labour is constant—equivalently, the change in output resulting from a one-unit
increase in the quantity of capital. For example, if

TABLE 11.3

The Production Function

Labour (workers per day)	Output (sweaters per day)			
	Plant 1	Plant 2	Plant 3	Plant 4
1	4	10	13	15
2	10	15	18	21
3	13	18	22	24
4	15	20	24	26
5	16	21	25	27
Knitting machines (number)	1	2	3	4

The table shows the total product data for four quantities of
capital. The greater the plant size, the larger is the total product for any given quantity of labour. But for a given plant size,
the marginal product of labour diminishes. And for a given
quantity of labour, the marginal product of capital diminishes.

Sidney has 3 workers and increases capital from 1
machine to 2 machines, output increases from 13 to
18 sweaters a day. The marginal product of capital is
5 sweaters per day. If Sidney increases the number of
machines from 2 to 3, output increases from 18 to 22
sweaters per day. The marginal product of the third
machine is 4 sweaters per day, down from 5 sweaters
per day for the second machine.

Let's now see what the production function
implies for long-run costs.

Short-Run Cost and Long-Run Cost

Continue to assume that labour costs $25 per worker
per day and capital costs $25 per machine per day.
Using these input prices and the data in Table 11.3,
we can calculate and graph the average total cost
curves for factories with 1, 2, 3, and 4 knitting
machines. We've already studied the costs of a factory
with 1 machine in Figs. 11.4 and 11.5. In Fig. 11.7,
the average total cost curve for that case is ATC_1.
Figure 11.7 also shows the average total cost curve for
a factory with 2 machines, ATC_2, with 3 machines,
ATC_3, and with 4 machines, ATC_4.

You can see, in Fig. 11.7, that plant size has a big
effect on the firm's average total cost. Two things
stand out:

FIGURE 11.7
Short-Run Costs of Four Different Plants

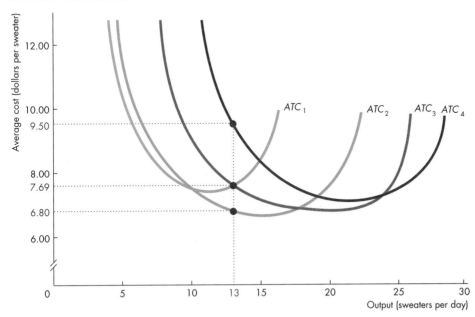

The figure shows short-run average total cost curves for four different quantities of capital. Sidney's Sweaters can produce 13 sweaters a day with 1 knitting machine on ATC_1 or with 3 knitting machines on ATC_3 for an average cost of $7.69 per sweater. Sidney's Sweaters can also produce 13 sweaters by using 2 knitting machines on ATC_2 for $6.80 per sweater or with 4 machines on ATC_4 for $9.50 per sweater. If Sidney's Sweaters produces 13 sweaters a day, the least-cost method of production—the long-run method—is with 2 machines on ATC_2.

- Each short-run average total cost curve is U-shaped.
- For each short-run average total cost curve, the larger the plant, the greater is the output at which average total cost is a minimum.

Each short-run average total cost curve is U-shaped because, as the quantity of labour increases, its marginal product at first increases and then diminishes. And these patterns in the marginal product of labour, which we examined in some detail for the plant with 1 knitting machine on pp. 226–227, occur at all plant sizes.

The minimum average total cost for a larger plant occurs at a greater output than it does for a smaller plant because the larger plant has a higher fixed cost and therefore, for any given output level, a higher average fixed cost.

Which short-run average cost curve Sidney's Sweaters operates on depends on its plant size. But in the long run, Sidney chooses the plant size. And which plant size he chooses depends on the output he plans to produce. The reason is that the average total cost of producing a given output depends on the plant size.

To see why, suppose that Sidney plans to produce 13 sweaters a day. With 1 machine, the average total

cost curve is ATC_1 (in Fig. 11.7) and the average total cost of 13 sweaters a day is $7.69 per sweater. With 2 machines, on ATC_2, average total cost is $6.80 per sweater. With 3 machines on ATC_3, average total cost is $7.69 per sweater, the same as with 1 machine. Finally, with 4 machines, on ATC_4, average total cost is $9.50 per sweater.

The economically efficient plant size for producing a given output is the one that has the lowest average total cost. For Sidney, the economically efficient plant to use to produce 13 sweaters a day is the one with 2 machines.

In the long run, Sidney chooses the plant size that minimizes average total cost. When a firm is producing a given output at the least possible cost, it is operating on its *long-run average cost curve*.

The **long-run average cost curve** is the relationship between the lowest attainable average total cost and output when both the plant size and labour are varied. The long-run average cost curve is a planning curve. It tells the firm the plant size and the quantity of labour to use at each output to minimize cost. Once the plant size is chosen, the firm operates on the short-run cost curves that apply to that plant size.

The Long-Run Average Cost Curve

Figure 11.8 shows Sidney's Sweaters' long-run average cost curve *LRAC*. This long-run average cost curve is derived from the short-run average total cost curves in Fig. 11.7. For output rates up to 10 sweaters a day, average total cost is the lowest on ATC_1. For output rates between 10 and 18 sweaters a day, average total cost is the lowest on ATC_2. For output rates between 18 and 24 sweaters a day, average total cost is the lowest on ATC_3. And for output rates in excess of 24 sweaters a day, average total cost is the lowest on ATC_4. The segment of each of the four average total cost curves along which average total cost is lowest is highlighted in dark blue in Fig. 11.8. The scallop-shaped curve made up of these four segments is the long-run average cost curve.

Economies and Diseconomies of Scale

Economies of scale are features of a firm's technology that lead to falling long-run average cost as output increases. When economies of scale are present, the *LRAC* curve slopes downward. The *LRAC* curve in Fig. 11.8 shows that Sidney's Sweaters experiences economies of scale for outputs up to 15 sweaters a day.

With given input prices, economies of scale occur if the percentage increase in output exceeds the percentage increase in all inputs. For example, if when a firm increases both its labour and capital by 10 percent, output increases by more than 10 percent, its average total cost falls. Economies of scale are present.

The main source of economies of scale is greater specialization of both labour and capital. For example, if GM produces 100 cars a week, each worker must perform many different tasks and the capital must be general-purpose machines and tools. But if GM produces 10,000 cars a week, each worker specializes and becomes highly proficient in a small number of tasks. Also, the capital is specialized and productive.

Diseconomies of scale are features of a firm's technology that lead to rising long-run average cost as output increases. When diseconomies of scale are present, the *LRAC* curve slopes upward. In Fig. 11.8, Sidney's Sweaters experiences diseconomies of scale at outputs greater than 15 sweaters a day.

With given input prices, diseconomies of scale occur if the percentage increase in output is less than

FIGURE 11.8

Long-Run Average Cost Curve

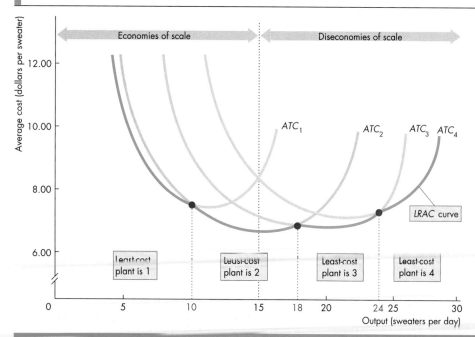

In the long run, Sidney's Sweaters can vary both capital and labour inputs. The long-run average cost curve traces the lowest attainable average total cost of production. Sidney's Sweaters produces on its long-run average cost curve, if it uses 1 machine to produce up to 10 sweaters a day, 2 machines to produce between 10 and 18 sweaters a day, 3 machines to produce between 18 and 24 sweaters a day, and 4 machines to produce more than 24 sweaters a day. Within these ranges, Sidney's Sweaters varies its output by varying its labour input.

the percentage increase in all inputs. For example, if when a firm increases both its labour and capital by 10 percent, output increases by less than 10 percent, its average total costs rises. Diseconomies of scale are present.

The main source of diseconomies of scale is the difficulty of managing a very large enterprise. The larger the firm, the greater is the challenge of organizing it and the greater is the cost of communicating up and down the management ladder and among managers. Eventually, management complexity brings rising average cost. Diseconomies of scale occur in all production processes but perhaps at only a very large output rate.

Constant returns to scale are features of a firm's technology that lead to constant long-run average cost as output increases. When constant returns to scale are present, the *LRAC* curve is horizontal.

With given input prices, constant returns to scale occur if the percentage increase in output equals the percentage increase in inputs. For example, if when a firm increases its labour and capital by 10 percent, output increases by 10 percent, its average total cost is constant. Constant returns to scale are present.

For example, General Motors can double its production of Chevy Cavaliers by doubling its production facility for those cars. It can build an identical production line and hire an identical number of workers. With the two identical production lines, GM produces exactly twice as many cars.

Minimum Efficient Scale A firm experiences economies of scale up to some output level. Beyond that level, it moves into constant returns to scale or diseconomies of scale. A firm's **minimum efficient scale** is the smallest quantity of output at which long-run average cost reaches its lowest level.

The minimum efficient scale plays a role in determining market structure, as you will learn in the next three chapters. The minimum efficient scale also helps to answer some questions about real businesses.

Economies of Scale at Sidney's Sweaters
Sidney's production technology, shown in Table 11.3, illustrates economies of scale and diseconomies of scale. If Sidney's inputs increase from 1 machine and 1 worker to 2 of each, a 100 percent increase in all inputs, output increases by more than 100 percent from 4 sweaters to 15 sweaters a day. Sidney experiences economies of scale and his long-run average cost decreases. But if Sidney's inputs increase to 3 machines and 3 workers, a 50 percent increase, out-

put increases by less than 50 percent from 15 sweaters to 22 sweaters a day. Now Sidney's experiences diseconomies of scale and its long-run average cost increases. Sidney's minimum efficient scale is at 15 sweaters a day.

Producing Cars and Generating Electric Power
At the beginning of this chapter, we posed the question: Why do automakers have expensive equipment lying around that isn't fully used? You can now answer this question. An automaker uses the plant that minimizes the average total cost of producing the output that it can sell. But it operates below the efficient minimum scale. Its short-run average total cost curve looks like ATC_1. If it could sell more cars, it would produce more cars and its average total cost would fall.

We also noted that many electric utilities don't have enough production equipment to meet demand on the coldest and hottest days and have to buy power from other producers. You can now see why this happens and why an electric utility doesn't build more generating capacity. A power producer uses the plant size that minimizes the average total cost of producing the output that it can sell on a normal day. But it produces above the minimum efficient scale and experiences diseconomies of scale. Its short-run average total cost curve looks like ATC_3. With a larger plant size, its average total costs of producing its normal output would be higher.

R E V I E W   Q U I Z

- What does a firm's production show and how is it related to a total product curve?
- Does the law of diminishing returns apply to capital as well as labour? Explain why.
- What does a firm's long-run average cost curve show? How is it related to the firm's short-run average cost curves?
- What are economies of scale and diseconomies of scale? How do they arise? And what do they imply for the shape of the long-run average cost curve?
- How is a firm's minimum efficient scale determined?

◆ *Reading Between the Lines* on pp. 238–239 applies what you've learned about a firm's product curves and cost curves. It looks at the total product curves and cost curves of some big aluminum producers.

Lowering the Cost of Aluminum

GLOBE AND MAIL, AUGUST 12, 1999

Merger to save Alcan and partners $600-million a year

BY ALAN FREEMAN

The mega-merger of aluminum producers Alcan Aluminium Ltd., Pechiney SA and Alusuisse Lonza Group AG (Algroup) will lead to annual cost savings of $600-million (U.S.) and the loss of as many as 4,500 jobs worldwide. ...

After 3½ months of secret talks, the chiefs of Montreal-based Alcan, France's Pechiney and Switzerland's Algroup yesterday announced details of the complex transaction that will create the world's largest aluminum company, with combined 1998 revenue of $21.6-billion and 91,000 employees in 59 countries. ...

The $600-million in savings are expected to come within two years... As much as 5 per cent of the combined company's 91,000 employees are to be eliminated.

"We will be eliminating overheads, we will be saving on the sales side because of overlapping of our sales organizations and there will be streamlining of our production facilities," Mr. Rodier said. "Whether this results in plant closures or not has yet to be seen. We may have some closures but we don't know exactly and we don't know when."

Not only will head office functions be merged but there will be a combination of research facilities, technical services and information technology functions. ...

DEAL HIGHLIGHTS

- The new company will be temporarily referred to as Alcan-Pechiney-Algroup or APA.
- APA will be a Canadian corporation with legal headquarters in Montreal and regional headquarters in Europe. The office of the CEO will be in New York City.
- Deals should lead to annual cost savings of $600-million (U.S.) within two years.
- Five per cent of APA's employees or about 4,500 people will be let go.

Reprinted with permission from *The Globe and Mail*.
Further reproduction prohibited.

Essence of the Story

■ Alcan Aluminium Ltd., Pechiney SA, and Alusuisse Lonza Group AG plan to merge.

■ The goal of the merger is to achieve cost savings, and the companies say that with the merger, costs can be cut by $600 million within two years.

■ The labour force of the merged company would be 4,500 workers fewer than the existing combined labour forces of the three companies.

■ Alcan Aluminium Ltd., Pechiney SA, and Alusuisse Lonza Group AG are huge firms that operate bauxite mines, aluminum refiners, and 27 smelters on six continents.

■ These firms are large because there are economies of scale in many of their production activities.

■ Figure 1 shows the technology these firms face in the form of a total product curve for aluminum production. Alcan, Pechiney, and Alusuisse operate on total product curve TP_0.

■ Alcan employs 36,000 people and produces 4.5 million tonnes of aluminum a year.* Pechiney employs 11,550 people and produces 2.5 million tonnes of aluminum a year. Alusuisse employs 10,300 employees and produces 1.5 million tonnes of aluminum a year.

■ If Alcan, Alusuisse, and Pechiney merge into a single very large firm, they will be able to operate on a new total product curve. The new curve is TP_1 in Fig. 1.

*The numbers of persons employed in aluminum production and the number of tonnes of aluminum produced are based on data from Alcan, Pechiney, and Alusuisse and the authors' calculations and assumptions.

■ You can interpret the statement, "We will be eliminating overheads, we will be saving on the sales side because of overlapping of our sales organizations and there will be streamlining of our production facilities," as meaning that the combined firm does not move along the existing total product curve but jumps to a new higher total product curve TP_1 and increases productivity.

■ Figure 2 shows the effect of the merger on average total cost.

■ The average total cost curve on which the three firms operate before the merger is ATC_0. This curve uses an average of fixed costs for the three firms. Given the assumed total product curve in Fig. 1, Alusuisse and Pechiney operate in the region of falling average total cost and Alcan operates in the region of rising average total cost.

■ After the merger, the average total cost curve shifts to ATC_1. The bigger merged firm has greater fixed costs than the three separate firms, so at small output rates, average total cost is higher in the new firm than in the existing firms.

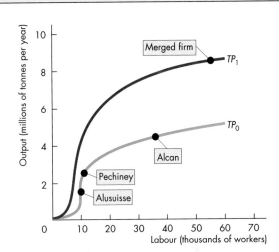

Figure 1 Total product

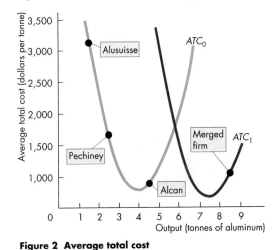

Figure 2 Average total cost

■ But at the large output rate at which the combined firm will operate, average total cost is lower for the merged firm than it was for Alusuisse and Pechiney, but slightly higher than it was for Alcan.

■ Notice that the new combined firm might operate on the upward-sloping portion of its new ATC curve, as in this example, even though it has benefited from economies of scale.

SUMMARY

Key Points

Decision Time Frames (p. 224)

- In the short run, the quantity of one resource is fixed and the quantities of the other resources can be varied.
- In the long run, the quantities of all resources can be varied.

Short-Run Technology Constraint (pp. 225–228)

- A total product curve shows the output a firm can produce with a given quantity of capital and different quantities of labour.
- Initially, the marginal product of labour increases as the quantity of labour increases, but eventually marginal product diminishes—the law of diminishing returns.
- Average product also increases initially and eventually diminishes.

Short-Run Cost (pp. 229–233)

- As output increases, total fixed cost is constant and total variable cost and total cost increase.
- As output increases, average fixed cost decreases; average variable cost, average total cost, and marginal cost decrease at small outputs and increase at large outputs. These cost curves are U-shaped.

Long-Run Cost (pp. 234–237)

- Long-run cost is the cost of production when all inputs—labour and capital—have been adjusted to their economically efficient levels.
- There is a set of short-run cost curves for each different plant size. There is one least-cost plant size for each output. The larger the output, the larger is the plant size that will minimize average total cost.
- The long-run average cost curve traces out the lowest attainable average total cost at each output when both capital and labour inputs can be varied.

- With economies of scale, the long-run average cost curve slopes downward. With diseconomies of scale, the long-run average cost curve slopes upward.

Key Figures and Table

Key Terms

PROBLEMS

*1. Rubber Duckies' total product schedule is:

Labour (workers per week)	Output (rubber boats per week)
1	1
2	3
3	6
4	10
5	15
6	21
7	26
8	30
9	33
10	35

a. Draw the total product curve.
b. Calculate the average product of labour and draw the average product curve.
c. Calculate the marginal product of labour and draw the marginal product curve.
d. What is the relationship between average product and marginal product when Rubber Duckies produces (i) fewer than 30 boats a week and (ii) more than 30 boats a week?

2. Charlie's Chocolates' total product schedule is:

Labour (workers per day)	Output (boxes per day)
1	12
2	24
3	48
4	84
5	132
6	192
7	240
8	276
9	300
10	312

a. Draw the total product curve.
b. Calculate the average product of labour and draw the average product curve.
c. Calculate the marginal product of labour and draw the marginal product curve.
d. What is the relationship between the average product and marginal product when Charlie's Chocolates produces (i) fewer than 276 boxes a day and (ii) more than 276 boxes a day?

*3. In problem 1, the price of labour is $400 a week and total fixed cost is $1,000 a week.
a. Calculate total cost, total variable cost, and total fixed cost for each output in the table and draw the short-run total cost curves.
b. Calculate average total cost, average fixed cost, average variable cost, and marginal cost at each output in the table and draw the short-run average and marginal cost curves.

4. In problem 2, the price of labour is $50 per day and total fixed costs are $50 per day.
a. Calculate total cost, total variable cost, and total fixed costs for each output in the table and draw the short-run total cost curves.
b. Calculate average total cost, average fixed cost, average variable cost, and marginal cost at each output in the table and draw the short-run average and marginal cost curves.

*5. In problem 3, suppose that Rubber Duckies' total fixed cost increases to $1,100 a week. Explain what changes occur to the short-run average and marginal cost curves.

6. In problem 4, suppose that the price of labour increases to $70 per day. Explain what changes occur to the short-run average and marginal cost curves.

*7. In problem 3, Rubber Duckies buys a second plant and now the total product of each quantity of labour doubles. The total fixed cost of operating each plant is $1,000 a week. The wage rate is $400 a week.
a. Set out the average total cost schedule when Rubber Duckies operates two plants.
b. Draw the long-run average cost curve.
c. Over what output range is it efficient to operate one plant and two plants?

8. In problem 4, Charlie's Chocolates buys a second plant and now the total product of each quantity of labour doubles. The total fixed cost of operating each plant is $50 a day. The wage rate is $50 a day.
a. Set out the average total cost curve when Charlie's operates two plants.
b. Draw the long-run average cost curve.
c. Over what output range is it efficient to operate one plant and two plants?

*9. The table shows the production function of Bonnie's Balloon Rides.

Labour	Output (rides per day)			
(workers per day)	Plant 1	Plant 2	Plant 3	Plant 4
1	4	10	13	15
2	10	15	18	21
3	13	18	22	24
4	15	20	24	26
5	16	21	25	27
Balloons (number)	1	2	3	4

Bonnie must pay $500 a day for each balloon she rents and $250 a day for each balloon operator she hires.
a. Find and graph the average total cost curve for each plant size.
b. Draw Bonnie's long-run average cost curve.
c. What is Bonnie's minimum efficient scale?
d. Explain how Bonnie uses her long-run average cost curve to decide how many balloons to rent.

10. The table shows the production function of Mario's Pizza-to-Go.

Labour	Output (pizzas per day)			
(workers per day)	Plant 1	Plant 2	Plant 3	Plant 4
1	4	8	11	13
2	8	12	15	17
3	11	15	18	20
4	13	17	20	22
Ovens (number)	1	2	3	4

Mario must pay $100 a day for each oven he rents and $75 a day for each kitchen hand he hires.
a. Find and graph the average total cost curve for each plant size.
b. Draw Mario's long-run average cost curve.
c. Over what output range does Mario experience economies of scale?
d. Explain how Mario uses his long-run average cost curve to decide how many ovens to rent.

 CRITICAL THINKING

1. Study *Reading Between the Lines* on pp. 238–239 and then answer the following questions:
   a. Sketch the average product curve and the marginal product curve that correspond to the total product curve TP_0.
   b. Sketch the average product curve and the marginal product curve that correspond to the total product curve TP_1.
   c. Why does Fig. 2 show Alusuisse and Pechiney operating on the downward-sloping portion of the ATC curve and Alcan operating on the upward-sloping portion?
   d. Use the links on the Parkin-Bade Web site to obtain information about the labour force, revenue, and cost of other big aluminum companies.
   e. Using the size of the labour force and total cost data, how does the merged Alcan-Alusuisse-Pechiney compare with the other big aluminum companies?
   f. Which of the big aluminum companies do you think is the most efficient and why?

 2. A telecommunication company is considering replacing human telephone operators with computers. This change will increase total fixed cost and decrease total variable cost. Either use the spreadsheet on the Parkin-Bade Web site or create your own example and sketch:
   a. The total cost curves for the original technology that uses human operators.
   b. The average cost curves for the original technology that uses human operators.
   c. The marginal cost curves for the original technology that uses human operators.
   d. The total cost curves for the new technology that uses computers.
   e. The average cost curves for the new technology that uses computers.
   f. The marginal cost curves for the new technology that uses computers.

 3. A spreadsheet on the Parkin-Bade Web site provides information about the cost of operating an ATM. Use this data to work out the average cost curves for an ATM. Under what conditions might a bank *not* install an ATM but use a human teller instead?

Chapter 12

Perfect Competition

It is morning rush hour and a six-vehicle pile-up snarls the traffic on Toronto's busiest section of Highway 401. Human injuries are light, but the toll in dented car bodies, buckled wheels and damaged tires, and crushed mufflers is huge. Competition to clean up the mess begins. Fifty towing companies compete for the initial clean-up. Several hundred body shops and repair shops battle for a place in a crowded market. How does competition affect prices and profits? ◆ Whether you want your car fixed or a pizza delivered, you have lots of choice. Just look in the Yellow Pages if you're not

Collision Course in Car Repairs

convinced! In this competitive environment, new firms enter and try their luck while other firms are squeezed out of business. ◆ In August 1995, almost 1.5 million people were unemployed. Of these, 900,000 were unemployed because they had lost their jobs or were laid off by firms seeking to trim their costs and avoid bankruptcy. Retailers, computer manufacturers, and firms in almost every sector of the economy laid workers off even though the economy was expanding and the total number of jobs was growing. Why do firms lay off workers? When will a firm temporarily shut down and lay off its workers? ◆ The price of a personal computer keeps falling. A slow computer cost $5,000 a few years ago, and a fast one costs only $2,000 today. What goes on in an industry when the price of its output falls sharply? What happens to the profits of the firms producing such goods?

◆ Car repairs, computers, and most other goods are produced by more than one firm, and these firms compete with each other for sales. To study competitive markets, we are going to build a model of a market in which competition is as fierce and extreme as possible—more extreme than in the examples we've just considered. We call this situation "perfect competition."

After studying this chapter, you will be able to:

- **Define perfect competition**
- **Explain how price and output are determined in a competitive industry**
- **Explain why firms sometimes shut down temporarily and lay off workers**
- **Explain why firms enter and leave an industry**
- **Predict the effects of a change in demand and of a technological advance**
- **Explain why perfect competition is efficient**

Competition

THE FIRMS THAT YOU STUDY IN THIS CHAPTER face the force of raw competition. We call this extreme form of competition perfect competition. **Perfect competition** is an industry in which

- Many firms sell identical products to many buyers.
- There are no restrictions on entry into the industry.
- Established firms have no advantage over new ones.
- Sellers and buyers are well informed about prices.

Farming, fishing, wood pulping and paper milling, the manufacture of paper cups and plastic shopping bags, grocery retailing, photo finishing, lawn service, plumbing, painting, dry cleaning, and the provision of laundry services are all examples of highly competitive industries.

How Perfect Competition Arises

First, perfect competition arises if the minimum efficient scale of a single producer is small relative to the demand for a good or service (see Chapter 11, p. 237). The **minimum efficient scale** is the smallest quantity of output at which long-run average cost reaches its lowest level. Where the minimum efficient scale of a firm is small relative to the demand, there is room for many firms in an industry.

Second, perfect competition arises if each firm is perceived to produce a good or service that has no unique characteristics so that consumers don't care which firm they buy from.

Price Takers

Firms in perfect competition must make many decisions. But one thing they do *not* decide is the price at which to sell their output. Firms in perfect competition are price takers. A **price taker** is a firm that cannot influence the price of the good or service that it sells.

The reason why a perfectly competitive firm is a price taker is that it produces a tiny proportion of the total output of a particular good and buyers are well informed about the prices of other firms.

Imagine that you are a farmer in Saskatchewan. You have 500 hectares of wheat under cultivation—which sounds like a lot. But then you go on a drive.

Westward towards the Rocky Mountains, eastward through Manitoba, and southward through the Dakotas you find unbroken stretches of wheat. You would find similar scenes in Argentina, Australia, and Ukraine. Your 500 hectares is a drop in the ocean.

Nothing makes your wheat any better than any other farmer's, and all the buyers of wheat know the price at which they can do business. If everybody else sells their wheat for $300 a tonne and you want $310, why would people buy from you? They can simply go to the next farmer, and the one after that, and the next and buy all they need for $300. This price is determined in the market for wheat, and you are a *price taker*.

The *market* demand for wheat is not perfectly elastic. The market demand curve is downward sloping, and its elasticity depends on the substitutability of wheat for other grains such as barley, rye, corn, and rice. But the demand for wheat from farm *A* is perfectly elastic because wheat from farm *B* is a *perfect substitute* for wheat from farm *A*. A price taker faces a perfectly elastic demand curve.

Economic Profit and Revenue

A firm's goal is to maximize **economic profit**, which is equal to total revenue minus total cost. Total cost is the *opportunity cost* of production, which includes the firm's **normal profit**, the return that the firm's entrepreneur can obtain in the best alternative business.

A firm's **total revenue** equals the price of its output multiplied by the number of units of output sold (price × quantity). **Marginal revenue** is the change in total revenue that results from a one-unit increase in the quantity sold. Marginal revenue is calculated by dividing the change in total revenue by the change in the quantity sold.

Figure 12.1 illustrates these revenue concepts. Sidney's Sweaters is one of a thousand similar small firms. In Fig. 12.1(a), demand and supply in the sweater market determine the price, which is $25 a sweater. Sidney must take this price. He cannot influence it by changing the quantity of sweaters he produces.

The table shows three different quantities of sweaters produced. As the quantity varies, the price remains constant—in this example at $25 a sweater. Total revenue is equal to the price multiplied by the quantity sold. For example, if Sidney sells 8 sweaters, his total revenue is 8 × $25, which equals $200.

FIGURE 12.1

Demand, Price, and Revenue in Perfect Competition

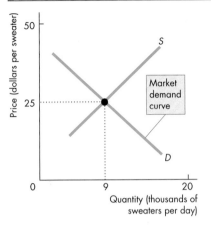

(a) Sweater market

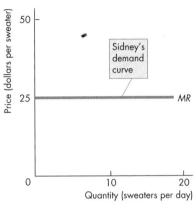

(b) Sidney's demand and
marginal revenue

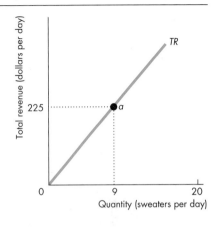

(c) Sidney's total revenue

Quantity sold (Q) (sweaters per day)	Price (P) (dollars per sweater)	Total revenue (TR = P × Q) (dollars)	Marginal revenue (MR = ΔTR/ΔQ) (dollars per additional sweater)
8	25	200	
			·························· 25
9	25	225	
			·························· 25
10	25	250	

Market demand and supply determine the market price. In part (a), the market price is $25 a sweater and 9,000 sweaters are bought and sold. Sidney faces a perfectly elastic demand at the market price of $25 a sweater. The table calculates total revenue and marginal revenue. Part (b) of the figure shows Sidney's demand curve, which is also its marginal revenue curve (MR). Part (c) shows Sidney's total revenue curve (TR). Point a corresponds to the second row of the table.

Marginal revenue is the change in total revenue that results from a one-unit increase in quantity. For example, when the quantity sold increases from 8 to 9, total revenue increases from $200 to $225, so marginal revenue is $25 a sweater. (Notice that in the table, marginal revenue appears *between* the lines for the quantities sold to remind you that marginal revenue results from the *change* in the quantity sold.)

Because the price remains constant when the quantity sold changes, the change in total revenue resulting from a one-unit increase in the quantity sold equals price. Therefore in perfect competition, marginal revenue equals price.

Figure 12.1(b) shows Sidney's marginal revenue curve (MR). This curve tells us the change in total revenue that results from selling one more sweater. This same curve is also the firm's demand curve. The firm, being a price taker, can sell any quantity it chooses at this price. The firm faces a perfectly elastic demand for its output.

The total revenue curve (TR), in part (c), shows the total revenue at each quantity sold. For example, if Sidney sells 9 sweaters, total revenue is $225 (point a). Because each additional sweater sold brings in a constant amount—$25—the total revenue curve is an upward-sloping straight line.

REVIEW QUIZ

- Explain why a firm in perfect competition is a price taker.
- In perfect competition, what is the relationship between a firm's demand curve and the market demand curve?
- In perfect competition, why is a firm's demand curve also its marginal revenue curve?
- Why is the total revenue curve in perfect competition an upward-sloping straight line?

The Firm's Decisions in Perfect Competition

FIRMS IN A PERFECTLY COMPETITIVE INDUSTRY face a given market price and have the revenue curves that you've studied. These revenue curves summarize the market constraint faced by a perfectly competitive firm.

Firms also face a technology constraint, which is described by the product curves (total product, average product, and marginal product) that you studied in Chapter 11. The technology available to the firm determines its costs, which are described by the cost curves (total cost, average cost, and marginal cost) that you also studied in Chapter 11.

The task of the competitive firm is to make the maximum economic profit possible, given the constraints it faces. To achieve this objective, a firm must make four key decisions: two in the short run and two in the long run.

Short-Run Decisions The short run is a time frame in which each firm has a given plant and the number of firms in the industry is fixed. But many things can change in the short run and the firm must react to these changes. For example, the price for which the firm can sell its output might have seasonal fluctuations, or it might fluctuate with general business fluctuations. The firm must react to short-run price fluctuations and decide:

1. Whether to produce or to shut down

2. If the decision is to produce, what quantity to produce

Long-Run Decisions The long run is a time frame in which each firm can change the size of its plant and decide whether to leave the industry. Other firms can decide to enter the industry. So in the long run, both the plant size of each firm and the number of firms in the industry can change. Also in the long run, the constraints facing firms can change. For example, the demand for the good can permanently decrease, or technological advance can change the industry's costs. The firm must react to such long-run changes and decide:

1. Whether to increase or decrease its plant size

2. Whether to remain in an industry or leave it

The Firm and the Industry in the Short Run and the Long Run To study a competitive industry, we begin by looking at an individual firm's short-run decisions. We then see how the short-run decisions of all firms in a competitive industry combine to determine the industry price, output, and economic profit. Then we turn to the long run and study the effects of long-run decisions on the industry price, output, and economic profit. All the decisions that we study are driven by a single objective: to maximize economic profit.

Profit-Maximizing Output

A perfectly competitive firm maximizes economic profit by choosing its output level. One way of finding the profit-maximizing output is to study a firm's total revenue and total cost curves and to find the output level at which total revenue exceeds total cost by the largest amount. Figure 12.2 shows how to do this for Sidney's Sweaters. The table lists Sidney's total revenue and total cost at different outputs, and part (a) of the figure shows Sidney's total revenue and total cost curves. These curves are graphs of the numbers shown in the first three columns of the table. The total revenue curve (TR) is the same as that in Fig. 12.1(c). The total cost curve (TC) is similar to the one that you met in Chapter 11. As output increases, so does total cost.

Economic profit equals total revenue minus total cost. The fourth column of the table in Fig. 12.2 shows Sidney's economic profit, and part (b) of the figure illustrates these numbers as Sidney's profit curve. This curve shows that Sidney makes an economic profit at outputs between 4 and 12 sweaters a day. At outputs less than 4 sweaters a day, Sidney incurs an economic loss. Sidney also incurs an economic loss if output exceeds 12 sweaters a day. At outputs of 4 sweaters and 12 sweaters a day, total cost equals total revenue and Sidney's economic profit is zero. An output at which total cost equals total revenue is called a *break-even point*. The firm's economic profit is zero but because normal profit is part of total cost, a firm makes normal profit at a break-even point. That is, at the break-even point, the entrepreneur makes an income equal to the best alternative return forgone.

Notice the relationship between the total revenue, total cost, and profit curves. The vertical distance between the total revenue and total cost curves measures economic profit. When the total revenue

FIGURE 12.2
Total Revenue, Total Cost, and Economic Profit

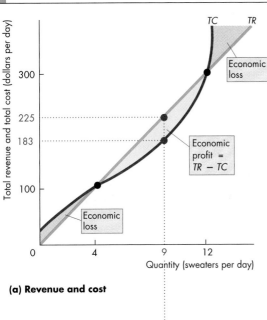

(a) Revenue and cost

(b) Economic profit and loss

Quantity (Q) (sweaters per day)	Total revenue (TR) (dollars)	Total cost (TC) (dollars)	Economic profit (TR – TC) (dollars)
0	0	22	−22
1	25	45	−20
2	50	66	−16
3	75	85	−10
4	100	100	0
5	125	114	11
6	150	126	24
7	175	141	34
8	200	160	40
9	225	183	42
10	250	210	40
11	275	245	30
12	300	300	0
13	325	360	−35

The table lists Sidney's total revenue, total cost, and economic profit. Part (a) graphs the total revenue and total cost curves. Economic profit, in part (a), is the height of the blue area between the total cost and total revenue curves. Sidney's makes maximum economic profit, $42 a day ($225 – $183), when it produces 9 sweaters—the output at which the vertical distance between the total revenue and total cost curves is at its largest. At outputs of 4 sweaters a day and 12 sweaters a day, Sidney makes zero economic profit—these are break-even points. At outputs less than 4 and greater than 12 sweaters a day, Sidney incurs an economic loss. Part (b) of the figure shows Sidney's profit curve. The profit curve is at its highest when economic profit is at a maximum and cuts the horizontal axis at the break-even points.

curve in part (a) is above the total cost curve, between 4 and 12 sweaters, the firm is making an economic profit, and the profit curve in part (b) is above the horizontal axis. At the break-even point, where the total cost and total revenue curves inter-

sect, the profit curve intersects the horizontal axis. The profit curve is at its highest when TR exceeds TC by the largest amount. In this example, profit maximization occurs at an output of 9 sweaters a day. At this output, Sidney's economic profit is $42 a day.

Marginal Analysis

Another way of finding the profit-maximizing output is to use *marginal analysis* and compare marginal revenue, *MR*, with marginal cost, *MC*. As output increases, marginal revenue remains constant but marginal cost changes. At low output levels, marginal cost decreases, but it eventually increases. So where the marginal cost curve intersects the marginal revenue curve, marginal cost is rising.

If marginal revenue exceeds marginal cost (if *MR* > *MC*), then the extra revenue from selling one more unit exceeds the extra cost incurred to produce it. The firm makes an economic profit on the marginal unit, so its economic profit increases if output *increases*.

If marginal revenue is less than marginal cost (if *MR* < *MC*), then the extra revenue from selling one more unit is less than the extra cost incurred to produce it. The firm incurs an economic loss on the marginal unit, so its economic profit decreases if output increases and its economic profit increases if output *decreases*.

Economic profit is maximized when the firm produces the quantity at which marginal revenue equals marginal cost (*MR* = *MC*).

The rule *MR* = *MC* is a prime example of marginal analysis. To check that the rule works, look at Fig. 12.3. The table lists Sidney's marginal revenue and marginal cost and the figure shows the marginal revenue and marginal cost curves. Marginal revenue is a constant $25 a sweater. Over the range of outputs shown in the table, marginal cost increases from $19 a sweater to $35 a sweater.

Focus on the highlighted rows of the table. If Sidney increases output from 8 sweaters to 9 sweaters, marginal revenue is $25 and marginal cost is $23. Because marginal revenue exceeds marginal cost, economic profit increases. The last column of the table shows that economic profit increases from $40 to $42, an increase of $2. This economic profit from the ninth sweater is shown as the blue area in the figure.

If Sidney increases output from 9 sweaters to 10 sweaters, marginal revenue is still $25, but marginal cost is $27. Because marginal revenue is less than marginal cost, economic profit decreases. The last column of the table shows that economic profit decreases from $42 to $40. This loss from the tenth sweater is shown as the red area in the figure.

Sidney maximizes economic profit by producing 9 sweaters a day, the quantity at which marginal revenue equals marginal cost.

FIGURE 12.3
Profit-Maximizing Output

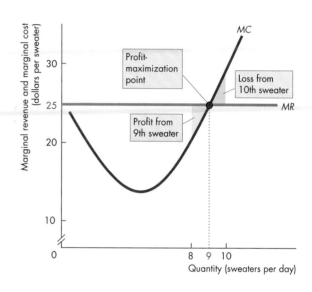

Quantity (Q) (sweaters per day)	Total revenue (TR) (dollars)	Marginal revenue (MR) (dollars per additional sweater)	Total cost (TC) (dollars)	Marginal cost (MC) (dollars per additional sweater)	Economic profit (TR – TC) (dollars)
7	175		141		34
		25		19	
8	200		160		40
		25		23	
9	225		183		42
		25		27	
10	250		210		40
		25		35	
11	275		245		30

Another way of finding the profit-maximizing output is to determine the output at which marginal revenue equals marginal cost. The table shows that if output increases from 8 to 9 sweaters, marginal cost is $23, which is less than the marginal revenue of $25. If output increases from 9 to 10 sweaters, marginal cost is $27, which exceeds the marginal revenue of $25. The figure shows that marginal cost and marginal revenue are equal when Sidney produces 9 sweaters a day. If marginal revenue exceeds marginal cost, an increase in output increases economic profit. If marginal revenue is less than marginal cost, an increase in output decreases economic profit. If marginal revenue equals marginal cost, economic profit is maximized.

Profits and Losses in the Short Run

In the short run, although the firm produces the profit-maximizing output, it does not necessarily end up making an economic profit. It might do so, but it might alternatively break even (with a normal profit), or incur an economic loss. To determine which of these outcomes occurs, we compare the firm's total revenue and total cost or, equivalently, we compare price with average total cost. If price equals average total cost, the firm breaks even—makes normal profit. If price exceeds average total cost, the firm makes an economic profit. If price is less than average total cost, the firm incurs an economic loss. Figure 12.4 shows these three possible short-run profit outcomes.

Three Possible Profit Outcomes In part (a), the price of a sweater is $20. Sidney produces 8 sweaters a day. Average total cost is also $20 a sweater, so Sidney makes normal profit and zero economic profit. Sidney breaks even.

In part (b), the price of a sweater is $25. Profit is maximized when output is 9 sweaters a day. Here, price exceeds average total cost (*ATC*), so Sidney

makes an economic profit. This economic profit is $42 a day. It is made up of $4.67 per sweater ($25.00 – $20.33), multiplied by the number of sweaters ($4.67 × 9 = $42). The blue rectangle shows this economic profit. The height of that rectangle is profit per sweater, $4.67, and the length is the quantity of sweaters produced, 9 a day, so the area of the rectangle measures Sidney's economic profit of $42 a day.

In part (c), the price of a sweater is $17. Here, price is less than average total cost and Sidney incurs an economic loss. Price and marginal revenue are $17 a sweater, and the profit-maximizing (in this case, loss-minimizing) output is 7 sweaters a day. Sidney's total revenue is $119 a day (7 × $17). Average total cost is $20.14 a sweater so the economic loss is $3.14 per sweater ($20.14 – $17.00). This loss per sweater multiplied by the number of sweaters is $22 ($3.14 × 7 = $22). The red rectangle shows this economic loss. The height of that rectangle is economic loss per sweater, $3.14, and the length is the quantity of sweaters produced, 7 a day, so the area of the rectangle measures Sidney's economic loss of $22 a day.

FIGURE 12.4

Three Possible Profit Outcomes in the Short Run

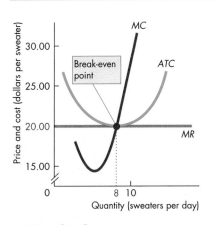

(a) Normal profit

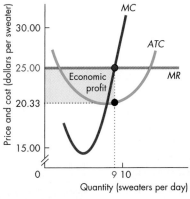

(b) Economic profit

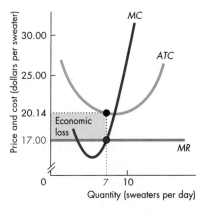

(c) Economic loss

In the short run, the firm might break even (making a normal profit), make an economic profit, or incur an economic loss. If the price equals minimum average total cost, the firm breaks even and makes a normal profit (part a). If the price exceeds

the average total cost of producing the profit-maximizing output, the firm makes an economic profit (the blue rectangle in part b). If the price is below minimum average total cost, the firm incurs an economic loss (the red rectangle in part c).

The Firm's Short-Run Supply Curve

A perfectly competitive firm's short-run supply curve shows how its profit-maximizing output varies as the market price varies, other things remaining the same. Figure 12.5 (a) shows Sidney's marginal cost and average variable cost curves, and part (b) shows the firm's supply curve. There is a direct link between the marginal cost and average variable cost curves and the supply curve. Let's see what that link is.

Temporary Plant Shutdown In the short run, a firm cannot avoid incurring its fixed cost. But the firm can avoid variable costs by temporarily laying off its workers and shutting down. If a firm shuts down, it produces no output and it incurs a loss equal to total fixed cost. This loss is the largest that a firm need incur. A firm shuts down if price falls below the minimum of average variable cost. The **shutdown point** is the output and price at which the firm just covers its total variable cost—point s in Fig. 12.5(a). If the price is $17, the marginal revenue curve is MR_0 and the profit-maximizing output is 7 sweaters a day at point s. But both price and average variable cost equal $17, so Sidney's total revenue equals its total variable cost. Sidney incurs an economic loss equal to total fixed cost. At a price below $17, no matter what quantity Sidney produces, average *variable* cost exceeds price and the firm's loss exceeds total fixed cost. At a price below $17, Sidney shuts down.

The Short-Run Supply Curve If the price is above minimum average variable cost, Sidney maximizes profit by producing the output at which marginal cost equals price. We can determine the quantity produced at each price from the marginal cost curve. At a price of $25, the marginal revenue curve is MR_1 and Sidney maximizes profit by producing 9 sweaters. At a price of $31, the marginal revenue curve is MR_2 and Sidney produces 10 sweaters.

Sidney's short-run supply curve, shown in Fig. 12.5(b), has two separate parts: First, at prices that exceed minimum average variable cost, the supply curve is the same as the marginal cost curve above the shutdown point (s). Second, at prices below minimum average variable cost, Sidney shuts down and produces nothing. Its supply curve runs along the vertical axis. At a price of $17, Sidney is indifferent between shutting down and producing 7 sweaters a day. Either way, Sidney incurs a loss of $22 a day

FIGURE 12.5

A Firm's Supply Curve

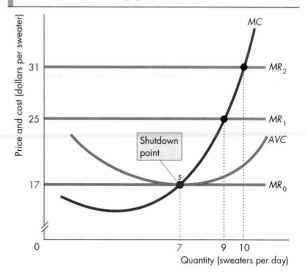

(a) Marginal cost and average variable cost

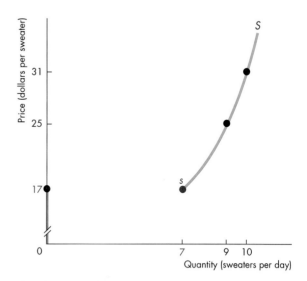

(b) Sidney's supply curve

Part (a) shows Sidney's profit-maximizing output at various market prices. At $25 a sweater, Sidney produces 9 sweaters. At $17 a sweater, Sidney produces 7 sweaters. At any price below $17 a sweater, Sidney produces nothing. Sidney's shutdown point is s. Part (b) shows Sidney's supply curve—the number of sweaters Sidney will produce at each price. It is made up of its marginal cost curve (part a) at all points above its average variable cost curve and the vertical axis at all prices below minimum average variable cost.

Short-Run Industry Supply Curve

The **short-run industry supply curve** shows the quantity supplied by the industry at each price when the plant size of each firm and the number of firms remain constant. The quantity supplied by the industry at a given price is the sum of the quantities supplied by all firms in the industry at that price.

Figure 12.6 shows the supply curve for the competitive sweater industry. In this example, the industry consists of 1,000 firms exactly like Sidney's Sweaters. At each price, the quantity supplied by the industry is 1,000 times the quantity supplied by a single firm.

The table in Fig. 12.6 shows the firm's and the industry's supply schedule and how the industry supply curve is constructed. At prices below $17, every firm in the industry shuts down; the quantity supplied by the industry is zero. At a price of $17, each firm is indifferent between shutting down and producing nothing or operating and producing 7 sweaters a day. Some firms will shut down and others will supply 7 sweaters a day. The quantity supplied by each firm is *either* 0 *or* 7 sweaters, but the quantity supplied by the industry is *between* 0 (all firms shut down) and 7,000 (all firms produce 7 sweaters a day each).

To construct the industry supply curve, we sum the quantities supplied by the individual firms at each price. Each of the 1,000 firms in the industry has a supply schedule like Sidney's. At prices below $17, the industry supply curve runs along the price axis. At a price of $17, the industry supply curve is horizontal—supply is perfectly elastic. As the price rises above $17, each firm increases its quantity supplied and the quantity supplied by the industry increases by 1,000 times that of each firm.

R E V I E W   Q U I Z

- Why does a firm in perfect competition produce the quantity at which marginal cost equals price?
- What is the lowest price at which a firm will produce an output? Explain why.
- What is the largest economic loss that a firm incurs in the short run and why?
- What is the relation among a firm's supply curve, its marginal cost curve, and its average variable cost curve?
- How do we derive an industry supply curve?

FIGURE 12.6

Industry Supply Curve

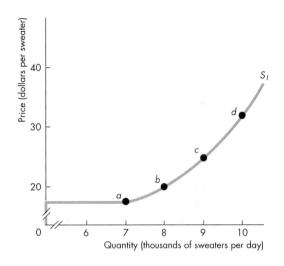

	Price (dollars per sweater)	Quantity supplied by Sidney's Sweaters (sweaters per day)	Quantity supplied by industry (sweaters per day)
a	17	0 or 7	0 to 7,000
b	20	8	8,000
c	25	9	9,000
d	31	10	10,000

The industry supply schedule is the sum of the supply schedules of all individual firms. An industry that consists of 1,000 identical firms has a supply schedule similar to that of the individual firm but the quantity supplied by the industry is 1,000 times as large as that of the individual firm (see table). The industry supply curve is S_I. Points $a, b, c,$ and d correspond to the rows of the table. At the shutdown price of $17, each firm produces either 0 or 7 sweaters per day. The industry supply curve is perfectly elastic at the shutdown price.

So far, we have studied a single firm in isolation. We have seen that the firm's profit-maximizing actions depend on the market price, which the firm takes as given. But how is the market price determined? Let's find out.

Output, Price, and Profit in Perfect Competition

To DETERMINE THE MARKET PRICE AND THE quantity bought and sold in a perfectly competitive market, we need to study how market demand and market supply interact. We begin by studying a perfectly competitive market in the short run when the number of firms is fixed and each firm has a given plant size.

Short-Run Equilibrium

Industry demand and industry supply determine the market price and industry output. Figure 12.7(a) shows a short-run equilibrium. The supply curve S is the same as S_I in Fig. 12.6. If the demand curve D_1 illustrates the industry demand, then the equilibrium price is $20. Although industry demand and supply determines this price, each firm takes the price as given and produces its profit-maximizing output, which is 8 sweaters a day. Because the industry has 1,000 firms, industry output is 8,000 sweaters a day.

A Change in Demand

Changes in demand bring changes to short-run industry equilibrium. Figure 12.7(b) shows these changes.

If demand increases and the demand curve shifts rightward to D_2, the price rises to $25. At this price, each firm maximizes profit by increasing output. The new output level is 9 sweaters a day for each firm and 9,000 sweaters a day for the industry.

If demand decreases and the demand curve shifts leftward to D_3, the price now falls to $17. At this price, each firm maximizes profit by decreasing its output. The new output level is 7 sweaters a day for each firm and 7,000 sweaters a day for the industry.

If the demand curve shifts farther leftward than D_3, the price remains constant at $17. Some firms continue to produce 7 sweaters a day, and others temporarily shut down. Firms are indifferent between these two activities, and, whichever they choose, they incur an economic loss equal to total fixed cost. The number of firms continuing to produce is just enough to satisfy the market demand at a price of $17.

Let's now look at the profits that firms make and losses they can incur in a short-run equilibrium.

FIGURE 12.7

Short-Run Equilibrium

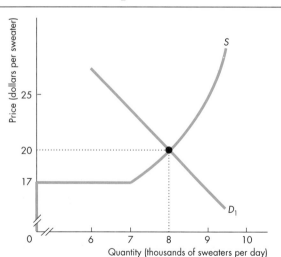

(a) Equilibrium

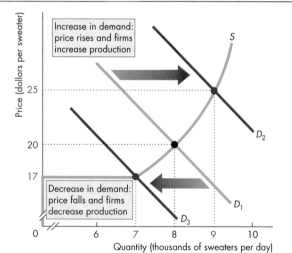

(b) Change in equilibrium

In part (a), the industry supply curve is S. Demand is D_1 and the price is $20. At this price, each firm produces 8 sweaters a day and the industry produces 8,000 sweaters a day. In part (b), when demand increases to D_2, the price rises to $25 and

each firm increases its output to 9 sweaters a day. Industry output is 9,000 sweaters a day. When demand decreases to D_3, the price falls to $17 and each firm decreases its output to 7 sweaters a day. Industry output is 7,000 sweaters a day.

Long-Run Adjustments

In short-run equilibrium, a firm might make an economic profit, incur an economic loss, or break even (make normal profit). Although each of these three situations is a short-run equilibrium, only one of them is a long-run equilibrium. To see why, we need to examine the forces at work in a competitive industry in the long run.

In the long run, an industry adjusts in two ways:

- Entry and exit
- Changes in plant size

Let's look first at entry and exit.

Entry and Exit

In the long run, firms respond to economic profit and economic loss by either entering or exiting an industry. Firms enter an industry in which firms are making an economic profit and they exit an industry in which firms are incurring an economic loss. Temporary economic profit and temporary economic loss like the win or loss at a casino do not trigger entry and exit. But the prospect of persistent economic profit or loss does.

Entry and exit influence price, the quantity produced, and economic profit. The immediate effect of these decisions is to shift the industry supply curve. If more firms enter an industry, supply increases and the industry supply curve shifts rightward. If firms exit an industry, supply decreases and the industry supply curve shifts leftward.

Let's see what happens when new firms enter an industry.

The Effects of Entry Figure 12.8 shows the effects of entry. Suppose that all the firms in this industry have cost curves like those in Fig. 12.4. At any price greater than $20, firms make an economic profit. At any price less than $20, firms incur an economic loss. And at a price of $20, firms make zero economic profit. Also suppose that the demand curve for sweaters is D. If the industry supply curve is S_1, sweaters sell for $23, and 7,000 sweaters a day are produced. Firms in the industry make an economic profit. This economic profit is a signal for new firms to enter the industry. As these events unfold, supply increases and the industry supply curve shifts rightward to S_0. With the greater supply and unchanged demand, the market price falls from $23 to $20 a

sweater and the quantity produced by the industry increases from 7,000 to 8,000 sweaters a day.

Industry output increases but Sidney's Sweaters and the other firms in the industry *decrease* output! Because the price falls, each firm produces less. But because the number of firms in the industry increases, the industry as a whole produces more.

Because price falls, each firm's economic profit decreases. When the price falls to $20, economic profit disappears and each firm makes a normal profit.

You have just discovered a key proposition:

As new firms enter an industry, the price falls and the economic profit of each existing firm decreases.

An example of this process occurred in recent years in the personal computer industry. When IBM introduced its first PC in the early 1980s, there was little competition and the price of PCs gave IBM a big profit. But new firms such as Compaq, NEC, Dell, and a host of others entered the industry with

FIGURE 12.8

Entry and Exit

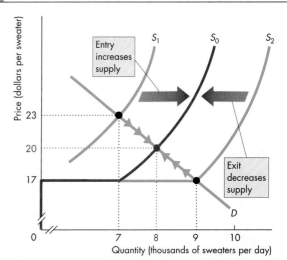

When new firms enter the sweater industry, the industry supply curve shifts rightward, from S_1 to S_0. The equilibrium price falls from $23 to $20, and the quantity produced increases from 7,000 to 8,000 sweaters. When firms exit the sweater industry, the industry supply curve shifts leftward, from S_2 to S_0. The equilibrium price rises from $17 to $20, and the quantity produced decreases from 9,000 to 8,000 sweaters.

machines that were technologically identical to IBM's. In fact, they were so similar that they came to be called "clones." The massive wave of entry into the personal computer industry shifted the supply curve rightward and lowered the price and the economic profit for all firms.

Let's now look at the effects of exit.

The Effects of Exit   Figure 12.8 shows the effects of exit. Suppose that firm's costs and market demand are the same as before. But now suppose the supply curve is S_2. The market price is $17 and 9,000 sweaters a day are produced. Firms now incur an economic loss. This economic loss is a signal for some firms to exit the industry. As firms exit, the supply curve shifts leftward to S_0. With the decrease in supply, industry output decreases from 9,000 to 8,000 sweaters and the price rises from $17 to $20.

As the price rises, Sidney's Sweaters, like each other firm in the industry, moves up along its supply curve and increases output. That is, for each firm that remains in the industry, the profit-maximizing output increases. Because the price rises and each firm sells more, economic loss decreases. When the price rises to $20, each firm makes a normal profit.

You have just discovered a second key proposition:

As firms leave an industry, the price rises and the economic loss of each remaining firm decreases.

An example of a firm leaving an industry is International Harvester, a manufacturer of farm equipment. For decades, people associated the name "International Harvester" with tractors, combines, and other farm machines. But International Harvester wasn't the only maker of farm equipment. The industry became intensely competitive, and the firm began losing money. Now the company has a new name, Navistar International, and it doesn't make tractors any more. After years of losses and shrinking revenues, it got out of the farm business in 1985 and started to make trucks.

International Harvester exited because it was incurring an economic loss. Its exit decreased supply and made it possible for the remaining firms in the industry to break even.

You've now seen how economic profits induce entry, which in turn lowers profits and how economic losses induce exit, which in turn eliminates losses. Let's now look at changes in plant size.

Changes in Plant Size

A firm changes its plant size if, by doing so, it can lower its costs and increase its economic profit. You can probably think of lots of examples of firms changing their plant size.

One example that has almost certainly happened near your campus in recent years is a change in the plant size of Kinko or similar copy shops. Another is the number of FedEx vans that you see on the streets and highways. And another is the number of square metres of retail space devoted to selling computers and video games. These are examples of firms increasing their plant size to seek larger profits.

There are also many examples of firms decreasing their plant size to avoid economic losses. One of these is Eaton's, the department store company, before it finally closed down. As competition from other retailers become tougher, Eaton's closed some lines of business. Many firms have scaled back in a process called *downsizing* in recent years.

Figure 12.9 shows a situation in which Sidney's Sweaters can increase its profit by increasing its plant size. With its current plant, Sidney's marginal cost curve is MC_0, and its short-run average total cost curve is $SRAC_0$. The market price is $25 a sweater, so Sidney's marginal revenue curve is MR_0, and Sidney maximizes profit by producing 6 sweaters a day.

Sidney's Sweaters' long-run average cost curve is $LRAC$. By increasing its plant size—installing more machines—Sidney can move along its long-run average cost curve. As Sidney's Sweaters increases its plant size, its short-run marginal cost curve shifts rightward.

Recall that a firm's short-run supply curve is linked to its marginal cost curve. As Sidney's marginal cost curve shifts rightward, so does its supply curve. If Sidney's Sweaters and the other firms in the industry increase their plants, the short-run industry supply curve shifts rightward and the market price falls. The fall in the market price limits the extent to which Sidney can profit from an increase in plant size.

Figure 12.9 also shows Sidney's Sweaters in a long-run competitive equilibrium. This situation arises when the market price has fallen to $20 a sweater. Marginal revenue is MR_1, and Sidney maximizes profit by producing 8 sweaters a day. In this situation, Sidney's Sweaters cannot increase its profit by changing its plant size. Sidney's Sweaters is producing at minimum long-run average cost (point m on $LRAC$).

Because Sidney's Sweaters is producing a mini-

FIGURE 12.9
Plant Size and Long-Run Equilibrium

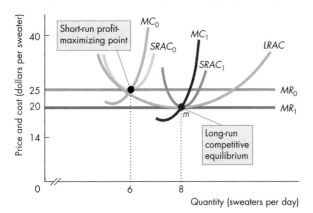

Initially, Sidney's plant has marginal cost curve MC_0 and short-run average total cost curve $SRAC_0$. The market price is $25 a sweater, and Sidney's marginal revenue is MR_0. The short-run profit-maximizing quantity is 6 sweaters a day. Sidney can increase his profit by increasing the plant size. If all firms in the sweater industry increase their plant sizes, the short-run industry supply increases and the market price falls. In long-run equilibrium, a firm operates with the plant size that minimizes its average cost. Here, Sidney operates the plant with short-run marginal cost MC_1 and short-run average cost $SRAC_1$. Sidney is also on the long-run average cost curve $LRAC$ and produces at point m. Output is 8 sweaters a day, and its average total cost equals the price of a sweater—$20.

mum long-run average cost, it has no incentive to change its plant size. Either a bigger plant or a smaller plant has a higher long-run average cost. If Fig. 12.9 describes the situation of all firms in the sweater industry, the industry is in long-run equilibrium. No firm has an incentive to change its plant size. Also, because each firm is making zero economic profit (normal profit), no firm has an incentive to enter the industry or to leave it.

Long-Run Equilibrium

Long-run equilibrium occurs in a competitive industry when economic profit is zero (when firms earn normal profit). If the firms in a competitive industry are making an economic profit, new firms enter the

industry. If firms can lower their costs by increasing their plant size, they expand. Each of these actions increases industry supply, shifts the industry supply curve rightward, lowers the price, and decreases economic profit.

Firms continue to enter and economic profit continues to decrease as long as firms in the industry are earning positive economic profits. When economic profit has been eliminated, firms stop entering the industry. And when firms are operating with the least-cost plant size, they stop expanding.

If the firms in a competitive industry are incurring an economic loss, some firms exit the industry. If firms can lower their costs by decreasing their plant size, they downsize. Each of these actions decreases industry supply, shifts the industry supply curve leftward, raises the price, and decreases economic loss.

Firms continue to exit and economic loss continues to decrease as long as firms in the industry are incurring economic losses. When economic loss has been eliminated, firms stop exiting the industry. And when firms are operating with the least-cost plant size, they stop downsizing.

So in long-run equilibrium in a competitive industry, firms neither enter nor exit the industry and neither expand nor downsize. Each firm earns normal profit.

REVIEW QUIZ

▪ When a firm in perfect competition produces the quantity that maximizes profit, what is the relationship between the firm's marginal cost, marginal revenue, and price?

▪ If the firms in a competitive industry earn an economic profit, what happens to supply, price, output, and economic profit?

▪ If the firms in a competitive industry incur an economic loss, what happens to supply, price, output, and economic profit?

You've seen how a competitive industry adjusts towards its long-run equilibrium. But a competitive industry is rarely *in* a state of long-run equilibrium. It is constantly and restlessly evolving towards such an equilibrium. But the constraints that firms in the industry face are constantly changing. Two persistent sources of change are in tastes and technology. Let's see how a competitive industry reacts to such changes.

Changing Tastes and Advancing Technology

INCREASED AWARENESS OF THE HEALTH HAZARD of smoking has caused a decrease in the demand for tobacco and cigarettes. The development of inexpensive car and air transportation has caused a huge decrease in the demand for long-distance trains and buses. Solid-state electronics have caused a large decrease in the demand for TV and radio repair. The development of good-quality inexpensive clothing has decreased the demand for sewing machines. What happens in a competitive industry when there is a permanent decrease in the demand for its products?

The development of the microwave oven has produced an enormous increase in demand for paper, glass, and plastic cooking utensils and for plastic wrap. The widespread use of the personal computer has brought a huge increase in the demand for floppy disks. What happens in a competitive industry when the demand for its output increases?

Advances in technology are constantly lowering the costs of production. New biotechnologies have dramatically lowered the costs of producing many food and pharmaceutical products. New electronic technologies have lowered the cost of producing just about every good and service. What happens in a competitive industry when technological change lowers its production costs?

Let's use the theory of perfect competition to answer these questions.

A Permanent Change in Demand

Figure 12.10(a) shows a competitive industry that initially is in long-run equilibrium. The demand curve is D_0, the supply curve is S_0, the market price is P_0, and industry output is Q_0. Figure 12.10(b) shows a single firm in this initial long-run equilibrium. The firm produces q_0 and makes a normal profit and zero economic profit.

Now suppose that demand decreases and the demand curve shifts leftward to D_1, as shown in part (a). The price falls to P_1, and the quantity supplied by the industry decreases from Q_0 to Q_1 as the industry slides down its short-run supply curve S_0. Part (b) shows the situation facing a firm. Price is now below the firm's minimum average total cost, so the firm incurs an economic loss. But to keep its loss to a

minimum, the firm adjusts its output to keep marginal cost equal to price. At a price of P_1, each firm produces an output of q_1.

The industry is now in short-run equilibrium but not long-run equilibrium. It is in short-run equilibrium because each firm is maximizing profit. But it is not in long-run equilibrium because each firm is incurring an economic loss—its average total cost exceeds the price.

The economic loss is a signal for some firms to leave the industry. As they do so, short-run industry supply decreases and the supply curve gradually shifts leftward. As industry supply decreases, the price rises. At each higher price, a firm's profit-maximizing output is greater, so the firms remaining in the industry increase their output as the price rises. Each firm slides up its marginal cost or supply curve (part b). That is, as firms exit the industry, industry output decreases but the output of the firms that remain in the industry increases. Eventually, enough firms leave the industry for the industry supply curve to have shifted to S_1 (part a). At this time, the price has returned to its original level, P_0. At this price, the firms remaining in the industry produce q_0, the same quantity that they produced before the decrease in demand. Because firms are now making normal profits and zero economic profit, no firm wants to enter or exit the industry. The industry supply curve remains at S_1, and industry output is Q_2. The industry is again in long-run equilibrium.

The difference between the initial long-run equilibrium and the final long-run equilibrium is the number of firms in the industry. A permanent decrease in demand has decreased the number of firms. Each remaining firm produces the same output in the new long-run equilibrium as it did initially and earns a normal profit. In the process of moving from the initial equilibrium to the new one, firms incur economic losses.

We've just worked out how a competitive industry responds to a permanent *decrease* in demand. A permanent increase in demand triggers a similar response, except in the opposite direction. The increase in demand brings a higher price, economic profit, and entry. Entry increases industry supply and eventually lowers the price to its original level.

The demand for airline travel in the world economy has increased permanently in recent years and the deregulation of the airlines has freed up firms to seek profit opportunities in this industry. The result has been a massive rate of entry of new airlines. The

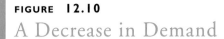

FIGURE 12.10

A Decrease in Demand

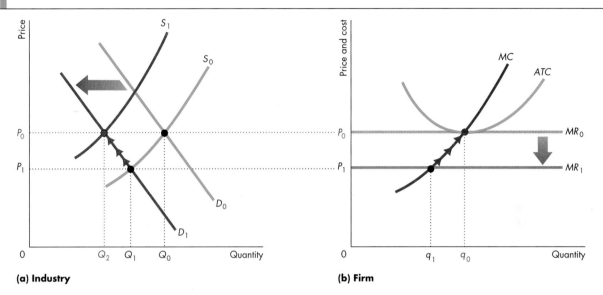

(a) Industry

An industry starts out in long-run competitive equilibrium. Part (a) shows the industry demand curve D_0, the industry supply curve S_0, the equilibrium quantity Q_0, and the market price P_0. Each firm sells its output at price P_0, so its marginal revenue curve is MR_0 in part (b). Each firm produces q_0 and makes a normal profit. Demand decreases permanently from D_0 to D_1 (part a). The equilibrium price falls to P_1, each firm decreases its output to q_1 (part b), and industry output decreases to Q_1 (part a).

(b) Firm

In this new situation, firms incur economic losses and some firms leave the industry. As they do so, the industry supply curve gradually shifts leftward, from S_0 to S_1. This shift gradually raises the market price from P_1 back to P_0. While the price is below P_0, firms incur economic losses and some firms leave the industry. Once the price has returned to P_0, each firm makes a normal profit. Firms have no further incentive to leave the industry. Each firm produces q_0, and industry output is Q_2.

process of competition and change in the airline industry is similar to what we have just studied (but with an increase in demand rather than a decrease in demand).

We've now studied the effects of a permanent change in demand for a good. To study these effects, we began and ended in a long-run equilibrium and examined the process that takes a market from one equilibrium to another. It is this process, not the equilibrium points, that describes the real world.

One feature of the predictions that we have just generated seems odd: In the long run, regardless of whether demand increases or decreases, the price returns to its original level. Is this outcome inevitable? In fact, it is not. It is possible for the long-run equilibrium price to remain the same, rise, or fall.

External Economies and Diseconomies

The change in the long-run equilibrium price depends on external economies and external diseconomies. **External economies** are factors beyond the control of an individual firm that lower its costs as the *industry* output increases. **External diseconomies** are factors outside the control of a firm that raise the firm's costs as *industry* output increases. With no external economies or external diseconomies, a firm's costs remain constant as the industry output changes.

Figure 12.11 illustrates these three cases and introduces a new supply concept: the long-run industry supply curve.

A **long-run industry supply curve** shows how the quantity supplied by an industry varies as the market price varies after all the possible adjustments have been made, including changes in plant size and the number of firms in the industry.

Part (a) shows the case we have just studied—no external economies or diseconomies. The long-run industry supply curve (LS_A) is perfectly elastic. In this case, a permanent increase in demand from D_0 to D_1 has no effect on the price in the long run. The increase in demand brings a temporary increase in price to P_S and a short-run quantity increase from Q_0 to Q_S. Entry increases short-run supply from S_0 to S_1, which lowers the price to its original level, P_0, and increases the quantity to Q_1.

Part (b) shows the case of external diseconomies. The long-run supply industry curve (LS_B) slopes upward. A permanent increase in demand from D_0 to D_1 increases the price in both the short run and the long run. As in the previous case, the increase in demand brings a temporary increase in price to P_S and a short-run quantity increase from Q_0 to Q_S. Entry increases short-run supply from S_0 to S_2, which lowers the price to P_2 and increases the quantity to Q_2.

One source of external diseconomies is congestion. The airline industry provides a good example. With bigger airline industry output, there is more congestion of airports and airspace, which results in longer delays and extra waiting time for passengers and airplanes. These external diseconomies mean that as the output of air transportation services increases (in the absence of technological advances), average cost increases. As a result, the long-run supply curve is upward sloping. So a permanent increase in demand brings an increase in quantity and a rise in the price. (Industries with external diseconomies might nonetheless have a falling price because technological advances shift the long-run supply curve downward.)

Part (c) shows the case of external economies. In this case, the long-run industry supply curve (LS_C) slopes downward. A permanent increase in demand from D_0 to D_1 increases the price in the short run and lowers it in the long run. Again, the increase in demand brings a temporary increase in price to P_S, and a short-run quantity increase from Q_0 to Q_S. Entry increases short-run supply from S_0 to S_3, which lowers the price to P_3 and increases the quantity to Q_3.

FIGURE 12.11

Long-Run Changes in Price and Quantity

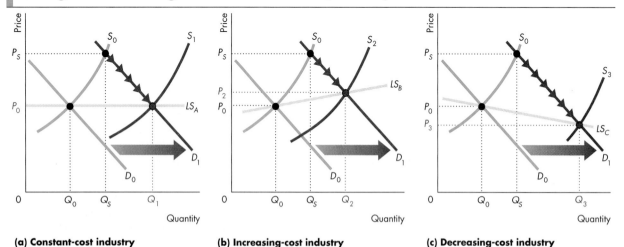

(a) Constant-cost industry   **(b) Increasing-cost industry**   **(c) Decreasing-cost industry**

Three possible changes in price and quantity occur in the long run. When demand increases from D_0 to D_1, entry occurs and the industry supply curve shifts from S_0 to S_1. In part (a), the long-run supply curve, LS_A, is horizontal. The quantity increases from Q_0 to Q_1 and the price remains constant at P_0. In part (b), the long-run supply curve is LS_B; the price rises to P_2, and the quantity increases to Q_2. This case occurs in an industry with external diseconomies. In part (c), the long-run supply curve is LS_C; the price falls to P_3, and the quantity increases to Q_3. This case occurs in an industry with external economies.

One of the best examples of external economies is the growth of specialist support services for an industry as it expands. As farm output increased in the nineteenth and early twentieth centuries, the services available to farmers expanded and average farm costs fell. For example, new firms specialized in the development and marketing of farm machinery and fertilizers. As a result, average farm costs decreased. Farms enjoyed the benefits of external economies. As a consequence, as the demand for farm products increased, the output increased but the price fell.

Over the long term, the prices of many goods and services have fallen, not because of external economies but because of technological change. Let's now study this influence on a competitive market.

Technological Change

Industries are constantly discovering lower-cost techniques of production. Most cost-saving production techniques cannot be implemented, however, without investing in new plant and equipment. As a consequence, it takes time for a technological advance to spread through an industry. Some firms whose plants are on the verge of being replaced will be quick to adopt the new technology, while other firms whose plants have recently been replaced will continue to operate with an old technology until they can no longer cover their average variable cost. Once average variable cost cannot be covered, a firm will scrap even a relatively new plant (embodying an old technology) in favour of a plant with a new technology.

New technology allows firms to produce at a lower cost. As a result, as firms adopt a new technology, their cost curves shift downward. With lower costs, firms are willing to supply a given quantity at a lower price, or, equivalently, they are willing to supply a larger quantity at a given price. In other words, industry supply increases, and the industry supply curve shifts rightward. With a given demand, the quantity produced increases and the price falls.

Two forces are at work in an industry undergoing technological change. Firms that adopt the new technology make an economic profit. So there is entry by new-technology firms. Firms that stick with the old technology incur economic losses. They either exit the industry or switch to the new technology.

As old-technology firms disappear and new-technology firms enter, the price falls and the quantity produced increases. Eventually, the industry arrives at a long-run equilibrium in which all the firms use the new technology and make a zero economic profit (a normal profit). Because in the long run competition eliminates economic profit, technological change brings only temporary gains to producers. But the lower prices and better products that technological advances bring are permanent gains for consumers.

The process that we've just described is one in which some firms experience economic profits and others experience economic losses. It is a period of dynamic change for an industry. Some firms do well, and others do badly. Often, the process has a geographical dimension—the expanding new technology firms bring prosperity to what was once the boondocks and traditional industrial regions decline. Sometimes, the new-technology firms are in a foreign country, while the old-technology firms are in the domestic economy. The information revolution of the 1990s has produced many examples of changes like these. The computer programming industry, traditionally concentrated in the United States, now flourishes in Canada, Britain, and India. Television shows and movies, traditionally made in Los Angeles and New York, are now made in large numbers in Toronto and Vancouver.

Technological advances are not confined to the information and entertainment industry. Even milk production is undergoing a major technological change because of genetic engineering.

R E V I E W   Q U I Z

- Describe the course of events in a competitive industry that follow a decrease in demand. What happens to output, price, and economic profit in the short run and in the long run? Explain how the presence of external economies and diseconomies influences the outcome.

- Describe the course of events in a competitive industry following an increase in demand. What happens to output, price, and economic profit in the short run and in the long run? Explain how the presence of external economies and diseconomies influences the outcome.

- Describe the course of events in a competitive industry following the adoption of a new technology. What happens to output, price, and economic profit in the short run and in the long run?

Competition and Efficiency

A COMPETITIVE INDUSTRY CAN ACHIEVE AN efficient use of resources. You studied efficiency in Chapter 6 using only the concepts of demand, supply, consumer surplus, and producer surplus. But now that you have learned what lies behind the demand and supply curves of a competitive market, you can gain a deeper understanding of how the competitive market achieves efficiency.

Efficient Use of Resources

Recall that resource use is efficient when we produce the goods and services that people value most highly (see Chapter 6, pp. 110–111). If someone can become better off without anyone else becoming worse off, resources are *not* being used efficiently. For example, suppose we produce a computer that no one uses and that no one will ever use. Suppose also that some people are clamouring for more video games. If we produce one less computer and reallocate the unused resources to produce more video games, some people will become better off and no one will be worse off. So the initial resource allocation was inefficient.

In the more technical language that you have learned, resource use is efficient when marginal benefit equals marginal cost. In the computer and video games example, the marginal benefit of video games exceeds the marginal cost. And the marginal cost of a computer exceeds its marginal benefit. So by producing fewer computers and more video games, we move resources towards a higher-value use.

Choices, Equilibrium, and Efficiency

We can use what you have learned about the decisions made by consumers and competitive firms and market equilibrium to describe an efficient use of resources.

Choices Consumers allocate their budgets to get the most value possible out of them. And we derive a consumer's demand curve by finding how the best budget allocation changes as the price of a good changes. So consumers get the most value out of their resources at all points along their demand curves, which are also their marginal benefit curves.

Competitive firms produce the quantity that maximizes profit. And we derive the firm's supply curve by finding the profit-maximizing quantities at each price. So firms get the most value out of their resources at all points along their supply curves, which are also their marginal cost curves. (On their supply curves, firms are *technologically efficient*—they get the maximum possible output from given inputs—and *economically efficient*—they combine resources to minimize cost. See Chapter 10, pp. 205–206.)

Equilibrium In competitive equilibrium, the quantity demanded equals the quantity supplied. So the price equals the consumers' marginal benefit and the producers' marginal cost. In this situation, the gains from trade between consumers and producers are maximized. These gains from trade are the consumer surplus plus the producer surplus.

The gains from trade for consumers are measured by *consumer surplus*, which is the area between the demand curve and the price paid. (See Chapter 6, p. 113.) The gains from trade for producers are measured by *producer surplus*, which is the area between the marginal cost curve and the price received. The total gains from trade are the sum of consumer surplus and producer surplus.

Efficiency If the people who consume and produce a good or service are the only ones affected by it, and if the market for the good or service is in equilibrium, then resources are being used efficiently. They cannot be reallocated to increase their value.

In such a situation, there are no *external benefits* or *external costs*. **External benefits** are benefits that accrue to people other than the buyer of a good. For example, you might get a benefit from your neighbour's expenditure on her garden. Your neighbour buys the quantities of garden plants that make her as well off as possible, not her plus you.

In the absence of external benefits, the market demand curve measures marginal *social* benefit—the value that *everyone* places on one more unit of a good or service.

External costs are costs not borne by the producer of a good or service but by someone else. For example, a firm might lower its costs by polluting. The cost of pollution is an external cost. Firms produce the output level that maximizes their own profit and they do not count the cost of pollution as a charge against their profit.

In the absence of external costs, the market supply curve measures marginal *social* cost—the entire marginal cost that *anyone* bears to produce one more unit of a good or service.

An Efficient Allocation   Figure 12.12 shows an efficient allocation. Consumers are efficient at all points on the demand curve, D (which is also the marginal benefit curve MB). Producers are efficient at all points on the supply curve, S (which is also the marginal cost curve MC). Resources are used efficiently at the quantity Q^* and price P^*. Marginal benefit equals marginal cost, and the sum of producer surplus (blue area) and consumer surplus (green area) is maximized.

If output is Q_0, marginal cost is C_0 and marginal benefit is B_0. Producers can supply more of the good for a cost lower than the price consumers are willing to pay and everyone gains by increasing the quantity produced. If output is greater than Q^*, marginal cost exceeds marginal benefit. It costs producers more to supply the good than the price consumers are willing to pay and everyone gains by decreasing the quantity produced.

Efficiency of Perfect Competition

Perfect competition achieves efficiency if there are no external benefits and external costs. In such a case, the benefits accrue to the buyers of the good and the costs are borne by its producer. In Fig. 12.12, the equilibrium quantity Q^* at the price P^* is efficient.

There are three main obstacles to efficiency:

1. Monopoly
2. Public goods
3. External costs and external benefits

Monopoly   Monopoly (Chapter 13) restricts output below its competitive level to raise price and increase profit. Government policies (Chapter 19) arise to limit such use of monopoly power.

Public goods   Goods such as national defence, the enforcement of law and order, the provision of clean drinking water, and the disposal of sewage and garbage are examples of public goods. Left to competitive markets, too small a quantity of them would be produced. Government institutions and policies (Chapter 18) help to overcome the problem of providing an efficient quantity of public goods.

External Costs and External Benefits   The production of steel and chemicals can generate air and water pollution and perfect competition might produce too large a quantity of these goods. Government policies (Chapter 20) attempt to cope with external costs and benefits.

◇ You've now completed your study of perfect competition. And *Reading Between the Lines* on pp. 262–263 gives you an opportunity to use what you have learned to understand recent events in the highly competitive Canadian retail services market with the exit from that market of Eaton's.

Although many markets approximate the model of perfect competition, many do not. Your next task is to study markets at the opposite extreme of market power—monopoly. Then, in Chapter 14, we'll study markets that lie between perfect competition and monopoly—monopolistic competition (competition with monopoly elements) and oligopoly (competition among a few producers). When you have completed this study, you'll have a toolkit that enables you to understand the variety of real-world markets.

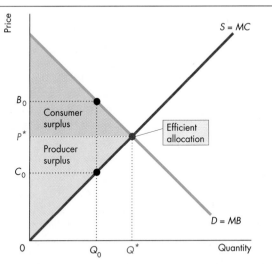

FIGURE 12.12

Efficiency of Competition

The efficient use of resources requires: consumers to be efficient, which occurs when they are on their demand curves; firms to be efficient, which occurs when they are on their supply curves; and the market to be in equilibrium with no external benefits or external costs. Resources are used efficiently at the quantity Q^* and the price P^*. With no external benefits or external costs, perfect competition achieves an efficient use of resources. If output is Q_0, the cost of producing one more unit, C_0, is less than its marginal benefit, B_0, and resources are not used efficiently.

Competition in Canadian Retailing

NATIONAL POST, AUGUST 21, 1999

130-year-old retailer winding down operations

BY ZENA OLIJNYK

After a long and agonizing death watch, the once mighty department store retailer T. Eaton Co. Ltd. announced late last night that the end has come...

As a result, the livelihood of 13,000 employees—many who have made their life's career at the department store chain built by Irish immigrant Timothy Eaton in 1869—is threatened. ...

Trading in the retailer's shares was halted yesterday, having closed Thursday at 71 cents, a far cry from the $15 a share the company got when it went public in June, 1998. ...

But retail consultant Len Kubas said that the end of Eaton's is not all doom and gloom. "The $1-billion in sales rung up at Eaton's stores won't just disappear. That money will go to other retailers, who might end up stronger as a result," he said. "As for the workers, there is always a need for good, well-trained retail staff in the industry."

Essence of the Story

■ Eaton's, founded in 1869 by Irish immigrant Timothy Eaton, announced August 20, 1999, that it was closing down.

■ About 13,000 employees would lose their jobs.

■ Eaton's shares had fallen from $15 a share in June 1998 to 71 cents a share on August 19, 1999.

■ A retail consultant noted that Eaton's business will go to other retailers and most of Eaton's workers will find other jobs in the industry.

Economic Analysis

■ The retail market is highly competitive and we will assume that it is perfectly competitive.

■ Figure 1 shows the market in August 1999. The market in part (a) determines the price of retail services, which is Eaton's marginal revenue in part (b).

■ In part (b), Eaton's produces the quantity of services at which marginal revenue equals marginal cost, but incurs an economic loss shown by the red rectangle.

■ In Fig. 2, Eaton's liquidates its stock. Marginal cost falls from MC_0 to MC_1 because Eaton's does not now incur costs of buying new inventory to replace what it sells.

■ With a lower marginal cost at Eaton's, the industry supply increases and the price falls. Eaton's sells more, but during this period the profits of other retailers are squeezed.

■ Figure 3 shows the situation after Eaton's is gone. Another firm buys Eaton's assets, reorganizes them, and operates at a normal profit (zero economic profit). The retail market is now again in long-run equilibrium.

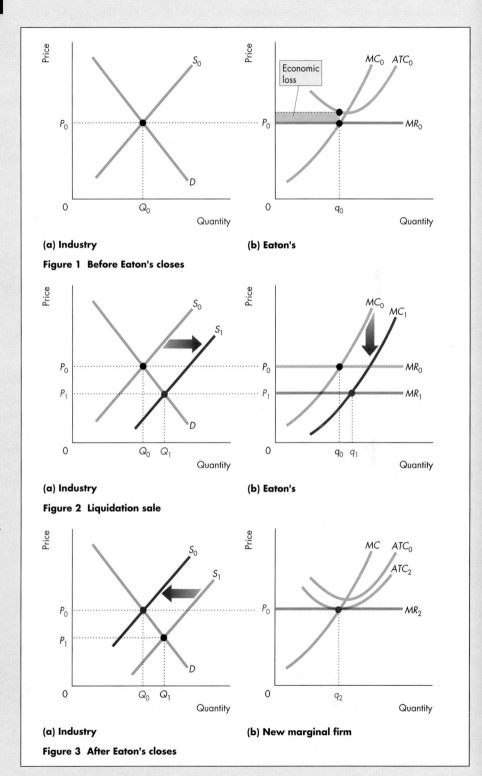

(a) Industry

Figure 1 Before Eaton's closes

(b) Eaton's

(a) Industry

Figure 2 Liquidation sale

(b) Eaton's

(a) Industry

Figure 3 After Eaton's closes

(b) New marginal firm

SUMMARY

Key Points

Competition (pp. 244–245)

- Perfect competition arises when demand is large relative to the efficient scale of production and when firms produce identical products.
- A perfectly competitive firm is a price taker.

The Firm's Decisions in Perfect Competition (pp. 246–251)

- The firm produces the output at which marginal revenue (price) equals marginal cost.
- In the short run, a firm can make an economic profit, incur an economic loss, or break even.
- If price is less than minimum average variable cost, the firm temporarily shuts down.
- A firm's supply curve is the upward-sloping part of its marginal cost curve above minimum average variable cost.
- An industry supply curve shows the sum of the quantities supplied by each firm at each price.

Output, Price, and Profit in Perfect Competition (pp. 252–255)

- Market demand and supply determine price.
- The firm produces the output at which price equals marginal cost.
- Economic profit induces entry. Economic loss induces exit.
- Entry and plant expansion increase supply and lower price and profit. Exit and plant contraction decrease supply and raise price and profit.
- In long-run equilibrium, economic profit is zero. There is no entry, exit, or change in plant size.

Changing Tastes and Advancing Technology (pp. 256–259)

- A permanent decrease in demand leads to a smaller industry output and a smaller number of firms.
- A permanent increase in demand leads to a larger industry output and a larger number of firms.

- The long-run effect of a change in demand on price depends on whether there are external economies (price falls) or external diseconomies (price rises) or neither (price remains constant).
- New technologies increase supply and in the long run lower the price and increase the quantity.

Competition and Efficiency (pp. 260–261)

- Resources are used efficiently when we produce goods and services in the quantities that people value most highly.
- When there are no external benefits and external costs, perfect competition achieves an efficient allocation. Marginal benefit equals marginal cost and the sum of consumer surplus and producer surplus is maximized.
- The existence of monopoly, public goods, and external costs and external benefits presents obstacles to efficiency.

Key Figures

Key Terms

PROBLEMS

*1. Quick Copy is one of the many copy shops near the campus. The figure shows Quick Copy's cost curves.

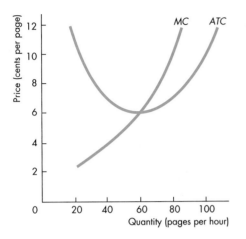

a. If the market price of copying one page is 10 cents, what is Quick Copy's profit-maximizing output?

b. Calculate Quick Copy's profit.

c. With no change in demand or technology, how will the price change in the long run?

2. Bob's is one of many burger stands along the beach. The figure shows Bob's cost curves.

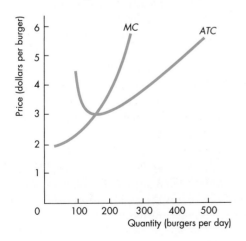

a. If the market price of a burger is $4, what is Bob's profit-maximizing output?

b. Calculate the profit that Bob's makes.

c. With no change in demand or technology, how will the price change in the long run?

*3. Pat's Pizza Kitchen is a price taker. Pat's cost of producing pizza is:

Output (pizzas per hour)	Total cost (dollars per hour)
0	10
1	21
2	30
3	41
4	54
5	69

a. If a pizza sells for $14, what is Pat's profit-maximizing output?

b. What is Pat's shutdown point?

c. Derive Pat's supply curve.

d. Over what price range will Pat leave the pizza industry?

e. Over what price range will other firms with costs identical to Pat's enter the industry?

f. What is the price of a pizza in the long run?

4. Lucy's Lasagna is a price taker. Lucy's cost of producing lasagna is:

Output (plates per hour)	Total cost (dollars per hour)
0	5
1	20
2	26
3	35
4	46
5	59

a. If lasagna sells for $7.50 a plate, what is Lucy's profit-maximizing output?

b. What is Lucy's shutdown point?

c. Over what price range will Lucy leave the lasagna industry?

d. Over what price range will other firms with costs identical to Lucy's enter the industry?

e. What is the price of lasagna in the long run?

*5. The market demand schedule for cassettes is:

Price (dollars per cassette)	Quantity demanded (thousands of cassettes per week)
3.65	500
5.20	450
6.80	400
8.40	350
10.00	300
11.60	250
13.20	200
14.80	150

The market is perfectly competitive, and each firm has the following cost structure:

Output (cassettes per week)	Marginal cost (dollars per additional cassette)	Average variable cost (dollars per cassette)	Average total cost
150	6.00	8.80	15.47
200	6.40	7.80	12.80
250	7.00	7.00	11.00
300	7.65	7.10	10.43
350	8.40	7.20	10.06
400	10.00	7.50	10.00
450	12.40	8.00	10.22
500	12.70	9.00	11.00

There are 1,000 firms in the industry.
a. What is the market price?
b. What is the industry's output?
c. What is the output produced by each firm?
d. What is the economic profit made by each firm?
e. Do firms enter or exit the industry?
f. What is the number of firms in the long run?

6. The same demand conditions as those in problem 5 prevail, and there are 1,000 firms in the industry, but fixed costs increase by $980. What now are your answers to the questions in problem 5?

*7. In problem 5, the price of a compact disc decreases the demand for cassettes and the demand schedule becomes:

Price (dollars per cassette)	Quantity demanded (thousands of cassettes per week)
2.95	500
4.13	450
5.30	400
6.48	350
7.65	300
8.83	250
10.00	200
11.18	150

What now are your answers to the questions in problem 5?

8. In problem 6, the price of a compact disc decreases the demand for cassettes and the demand schedule becomes that given in the table in problem 7. What now are your answers to the questions in problem 6?

CRITICAL THINKING

 1. After you have studied *Reading Between the Lines* on pp. 262–263, answer the following questions.
   a. Why is it reasonable to assume that retailing is a highly competitive (and perhaps perfectly competitive) industry?
   b. What exactly do retailers produce? [Hint: Think about the services that they provide to you over and above the merchandise that you buy from them.]
   c. What is the economic problem that Eaton's faced in the summer of 1999?
   d. Use the link on the Parkin-Bade Web site and obtain information on Eaton's revenues and costs during 1998 and 1999.
   e. What trends can you see in the company's revenues and costs?
   f. How do you think the disappearance of Eaton's affects other retailers in Canada in both the short run and the long run?
   g. What do you think will happen to Eaton's employees in the short run and in the long run? Use what you know about demand and supply to answer this question.
   h. Can you think of some major changes in retailing technology that might have harmed Eaton's during the past few years?
   i. Who are the winners and who are the losers from the exit of Eaton's?
   j. Was the Canadian retail market efficient before the exit of Eaton's? Is it efficient now that Eaton's is gone?

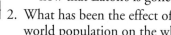 2. What has been the effect of an increase in world population on the wheat market and the individual wheat farmer? Explain your answer.

3. Visit the Parkin-Bade Web site and study the Web *Reading Between the Lines*, "Dumping Steel." Then answer the following questions.
   a. What is the argument in the news article about limiting steel imports?
   b. Do you agree with the argument? Why or why not?
   c. Why do Canada and the United States claim that foreign steel is being dumped in North America?

Chapter 13

Monopoly

You have been reading a lot in this book about firms that want to maximize profit. But perhaps you've been looking around at some of the places where you do business and wondering whether they are really so intent on profit. After all, don't you get a student's discount when you get a haircut? Don't museums and movie theatres give discounts to students, too? And what about the airline that gives a discount for buying a ticket in advance? Are your barber and movie theatre owner, as well as the museum and airline opera-

The Profits of Generosity

tors, simply generous folks to whom the model of profit-maximizing firms does not apply? Aren't they simply throwing profit away by cutting ticket prices and offering discounts? ◆ When you buy electric power, you don't shop around. You buy from your electric power utility, which is your only available supplier. If you live in the north of London, Ontario, and want cable TV service, you only have one option: buy from Rogers Cablesystems. These are examples of a single producer of a good or service controlling its supply. Such firms are obviously not like firms in perfectly competitive industries. They don't face a market-determined price. In practice, most monopolies are regulated. But to understand why they are regulated, we need to understand how an unregulated firm behaves. How does it choose the quantity to produce and the price at which to sell it? How does its behaviour compare with firms in perfectly competitive industries? Do such firms charge prices that are too high and that damage the interests of consumers? Do such firms bring any benefits? Finally, how are monopolies regulated?

◆ In this chapter, we study markets in which an individual firm can influence the quantity supplied and exert an influence on price. We also examine whether monopoly is as efficient as competition.

After studying this chapter, you will be able to:

- Explain how monopoly arises and distinguish between single-price monopoly and price-discriminating monopoly

- Explain how a single-price monopoly determines its output and price

- Compare the performance and efficiency of single-price monopoly and competition

- Define rent seeking and explain why it arises

- Explain how price discrimination increases profit

- Explain how monopoly regulation influences output, price, economic profit, and efficiency

Market Power

MARKET POWER AND COMPETITION ARE THE TWO forces that operate in most markets. **Market power** is the ability to influence the market, and in particular the market price, by influencing the total quantity offered for sale.

The firms in perfect competition that you studied in Chapter 12 have no market power. They face the force of raw competition and are price takers. The firms that we study in this chapter operate at the opposite extreme. They face no competition and exercise raw market power. We call this extreme *monopoly*. A **monopoly** is an industry that produces a good or service for which no close substitute exists and in which there is one supplier that is protected from competition by a barrier preventing the entry of new firms.

Examples of monopoly include natural gas distribution and the delivery of first-class mail, as well as DeBeers, the South African diamond producer, and Microsoft Corp., the software developer that created your computer's operating system.

How Monopoly Arises

Monopoly has two key features:

■ No close substitutes
■ Barriers to entry

No Close Substitutes   If a good has a close substitute, even though only one firm produces it, that firm effectively faces competition from the producers of substitutes. Water supplied by a local public utility is an example of a good that does not have close substitutes. While it does have a close substitute for drinking—bottled spring water—it has no effective substitutes for showering or washing a car.

Monopolies are constantly under attack from new products and ideas that substitute for products produced by monopolies. For example, Federal Express, Purolator, and the fax machine have weakened the monopoly of Canada Post. Similarly, the satellite dish has weakened the monopoly of cable television companies.

But new products also are constantly creating monopolies. An example is Microsoft's monopoly in DOS during the 1980s and in the Windows operating system today.

Barriers to Entry   Legal or natural constraints that protect a firm from potential competitors are called **barriers to entry**. A firm can sometimes create its own barrier to entry by acquiring a significant portion of a key resource. DeBeers, for example, controls more than 80 percent of the world's supply of natural diamonds. But most monopolies arise from two other types of barrier: legal barriers and natural barriers.

Legal Barriers to Entry   Legal barriers to entry create legal monopoly. A **legal monopoly** is a market in which competition and entry are restricted by the granting of a public franchise, government licence, patent, or copyright.

A *public franchise* is an exclusive right granted to a firm to supply a good or service. An example is Canada Post, which has the exclusive right to carry first-class mail. A *government licence* controls entry into particular occupations, professions, and industries. Examples of this type of barrier to entry are medicine, law, dentistry, schoolteaching, architecture, and many other professional services. Licensing does not always create monopoly, but it does restrict competition.

A *patent* is an exclusive right granted to the inventor of a product or service. A *copyright* is an exclusive right granted to the author or composer of a literary, musical, dramatic, or artistic work. Patents and copyrights are valid for a limited time period that varies from country to country. In Canada, a patent is valid for 20 years. Patents encourage the *invention* of new products and production methods. They also stimulate *innovation*—the use of new inventions—by encouraging inventors to publicize their discoveries and offer them for use under licence. Patents have stimulated innovations in areas as diverse as soybean seeds, pharmaceuticals, memory chips, and video games.

Natural Barriers to Entry   Natural barriers to entry create **natural monopoly**, which is an industry in which one firm can supply the entire market at a lower price than two or more firms can.

Figure 13.1 shows a natural monopoly in the distribution of electric power. Here, the demand curve for electric power is D and the average total cost curve is ATC. Because average total cost decreases as output increases, economies of scale prevail over the entire length of the ATC curve. One firm can produce 4 million kilowatt-hours at 5 cents a kilowatt-hour. At this price, the quantity demanded is 4 million kilowatt-hours. So if the price was 5 cents, one firm could supply the entire market. If two firms shared the market, it would cost each of them 10 cents a kilowatt-hour to produce a total of 4 million kilowatt-hours. If four firms shared the market, it would cost each of them 15 cents a kilowatt-hour to produce a total of 4 million kilowatt-hours. So in conditions like those shown in Fig. 13.1, one firm can supply the entire market at a lower cost than two or more firms can. The distribution of electric power is an example of natural monopoly. So is the distribution of water and gas.

Most monopolies are regulated in some way by government agencies. We will study such regulation at the end of this chapter. But for two reasons we'll first study unregulated monopoly. First, we can better understand why governments regulate monopolies and the effects of regulation if we also know how an unregulated monopoly behaves. Second, even in industries with more than one producer, firms often have a degree of monopoly power, and the theory of monopoly sheds light on the behaviour of such firms and industries.

A major difference between monopoly and competition is that a monopoly sets its own price. But in doing so, it faces a market constraint. Let's see how the market limits a monopoly's pricing choices.

Monopoly Price-Setting Strategies

All monopolies face a tradeoff between price and the quantity sold. To sell a larger quantity, the monopolist must charge a lower price. But there are two broad monopoly situations that create different tradeoffs. They are:

- Single price
- Price discrimination

Single Price   DeBeers sells diamonds (of a given size and quality) for the same price to all its customers. If it tried to sell at a low price to some customers and at a higher price to others, only the low-price customers would buy from DeBeers. Others would buy from DeBeers' low-price customers.

DeBeers is a *single-price* monopoly. A **single-price monopoly** is a firm that must sell each unit of its output for the same price to all its customers.

Price Discrimination   Many firms price discriminate, and most are *not* monopolies. Airlines offer a dizzying array of different prices for the same trip. Pizza producers charge one price for a single pizza and almost give away a second pizza. These are examples of *price discrimination*. **Price discrimination** is the practice of selling different units of a good or service for different prices. Different customers might pay different prices (like airline passengers) or one customer might pay different prices for different quantities bought (like the bargain price for a second pizza).

When a firm price discriminates, it looks as if it is doing its customers a favour. In fact, it is charging the highest possible price for each unit sold and making the largest possible profit.

Not all monopolies can price discriminate. The main obstacle to price discrimination is resale by customers who buy for a low price. Because of resale possibilities, price discrimination is limited to monopolies that sell services that cannot be resold.

We'll look first at single-price monopoly.

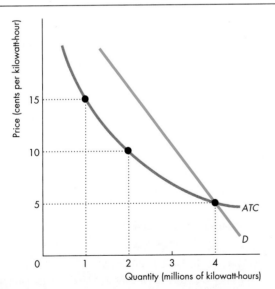

FIGURE   13.1

Natural Monopoly

The demand curve for electric power is *D* and the average total cost curve is *ATC*. Economies of scale exist over the entire *ATC* curve. One firm can distribute 4 million kilowatt-hours at a cost of 5 cents a kilowatt-hour. This same total output costs 10 cents a kilowatt-hour with two firms and 15 cents a kilowatt-hour with four firms. So one firm can meet the market demand at a lower cost than two or more firms can, and the market is a natural monopoly.

A Single-Price Monopoly's Output and Price Decision

To understand how a single-price monopoly makes its output and price decision, we must first study the link between price and marginal revenue.

Price and Marginal Revenue

Because in a monopoly there is only one firm, the firm's demand curve is the market demand curve. Let's look at Bobbie's Barbershop, the only barbershop in Trout River, Newfoundland. The table in Fig. 13.2 shows the market demand schedule for haircuts in Trout River. At $20, Bobbie sells no haircuts. The lower the price, the more haircuts Bobbie can sell. For example, at $12 a haircut, consumers demand 4 haircuts per hour (row *e*).

Total revenue (*TR*) is the price (*P*) multiplied by the quantity sold (*Q*). For example, in row *d*, Bobbie sells 3 haircuts at $14 each, so total revenue is $42. *Marginal revenue* (*MR*) is the change in total revenue (*TR*) resulting from a one-unit increase in the quantity sold. For example, if the price falls from $16 (row *c*) to $14 (row *d*), the quantity sold increases from 2 to 3 haircuts. Total revenue rises from $32 to $42, so the change in total revenue is $10. Because the quantity sold increases by 1 haircut, marginal revenue equals the change in total revenue and is $10. Marginal revenue is placed between the two rows to emphasize that marginal revenue relates to the *change* in the quantity sold.

Figure 13.2 shows the market demand curve (*D*) and the marginal revenue curve (*MR*). It also illustrates the calculation we've just made. Notice that at each output, marginal revenue is less than price—the marginal revenue curve lies below the demand curve. Why is marginal revenue less than price? It is because when the price is lowered to sell one more unit, two opposing forces affect total revenue. The lower price results in a revenue loss, and the increased quantity sold results in a revenue gain. For example, at a price of $16, Bobbie sells 2 haircuts (point *c*). If she lowers the price to $14, she sells 3 haircuts and has a revenue gain of $14 on the third haircut. But she now receives only $14 on the first two—$2 less than before. As a result, she loses $4 of revenue on the first 2 haircuts. To calculate marginal revenue, she must deduct this amount from the revenue gain of $14. So her marginal revenue is $10, which is less than the price.

FIGURE 13.2

Demand and Marginal Revenue

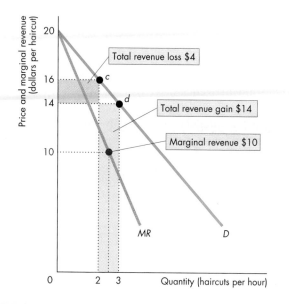

The table shows the demand schedule for haircuts. Total revenue (*TR*) is price multiplied by quantity sold. For example, in row *c* the price is $16 a haircut, Bobbie sells 2 haircuts and total revenue is $32. Marginal revenue (*MR*) is the change in total revenue that results from a one-unit increase in the quantity sold. For example, when the price falls from $16 to $14 a haircut, the quantity sold increases by 1 haircut and total revenue increases by $10. Marginal revenue is $10. The demand curve, *D*, and the marginal revenue curve, *MR*, are based on the numbers in the table and illustrate the calculation of marginal revenue when the price falls from $16 to $14.

	Price (P)	Quantity demanded (Q)	Total revenue (TR = P × Q)	Marginal revenue (MR = ΔTR/ΔQ)
	(dollars per haircut)	(haircuts per hour)	(dollars)	(dollars per haircut)
a	20	0	0	
				18
b	18	1	18	
				14
c	16	2	32	
				10
d	14	3	42	
				6
e	12	4	48	
				2
f	10	5	50	

Marginal Revenue and Elasticity

A single-price monopoly's marginal revenue is related to the *elasticity of demand* for its good. The demand for a good can be *elastic* (the elasticity of demand is greater than 1), *inelastic* (the elasticity of demand is less than 1), or *unit elastic* (the elasticity of demand is equal to 1). You know that a monopoly produces a good or service for which there is no close substitute. And you perhaps recall (see Chapter 5, p. 95 for a refresher) that the *closer* the substitutes for a good or service, the *more* elastic is the demand for it. So you might expect that the demand for what a monopoly produces is inelastic. It turns out that this conclusion is incorrect. A monopoly always operates where demand is elastic! Let's find out why.

If demand is elastic, a fall in price brings an increase in total revenue—the increase in revenue from the increase in quantity sold outweighs the decrease in revenue from the lower price—and marginal revenue is positive. If demand is inelastic, a fall in price brings a decrease in total revenue—the increase in revenue from the increase in quantity sold is outweighed by the decrease in revenue from the lower price—and marginal revenue is negative. If demand is unit elastic, total revenue does not change—the increase in revenue from the increase in quantity sold offsets the decrease in revenue from the lower price—and marginal revenue is zero (see Chapter 5, pp. 94–95).

Figure 13.3 illustrates the relationship between marginal revenue, total revenue, and elasticity. As the price of a haircut gradually falls from $20 to $10, the quantity of haircuts demanded increases from 0 to 5 an hour. Over this output range, marginal revenue is positive (part a), total revenue increases (part b), and the demand for haircuts is elastic. As the price falls from $10 to $0 a haircut, the quantity of haircuts demanded increases from 5 to 10 an hour. Over this output range, marginal revenue is negative (part a), total revenue decreases (part b), and the demand for haircuts is inelastic. When the price is $10 a haircut, marginal revenue is zero, total revenue is a maximum, and the demand for haircuts is unit elastic.

Monopoly Demand Is Always Elastic   The relationship between marginal revenue and elasticity that you've just discovered implies that a profit-maximizing monopoly never produces an output in the inelastic range of its demand curve. If it did so, it could charge a higher price, produce a smaller quantity, and increase its profit. Let's now look more closely at a monopoly's output and price decision.

FIGURE 13.3
Marginal Revenue and Elasticity

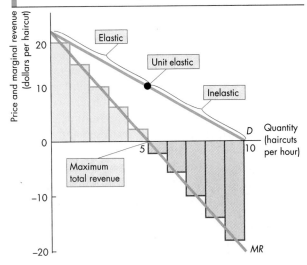

(a) Demand and marginal revenue curves

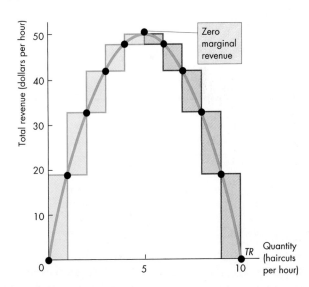

(b) Total revenue curve

In part (a), the demand curve is *D* and the marginal revenue curve is *MR*. In part (b), the total revenue curve is *TR*. Over the range from 0 to 5 haircuts an hour, a price cut increases total revenue so marginal revenue is positive, as shown by the blue bars. Demand is elastic. Over the range 5 to 10 haircuts an hour, a price cut decreases total revenue so marginal revenue is negative, as shown by the red bars. Demand is inelastic. At 5 haircuts an hour, total revenue is maximized, and marginal revenue is zero. Demand is unit elastic.

272

Output and Price Decision

To determine the output level and price that maximize a monopoly's profit, we need to study the behaviour of both revenue and costs as output varies. A monopoly and a competitive firm face the same types of technology and cost constraints. But they face different market constraints. The competitive firm is a price taker, whereas the monopoly's output decision influences the price it receives. Let's see how.

Bobbie's revenue, which we studied in Fig. 13.2, is shown again in Table 13.1. The table also contains information on Bobbie's costs and economic profit. Total cost (TC) rises as output increases, and so does total revenue (TR). Economic profit equals total revenue minus total cost. As you can see in the table, the maximum profit ($12) occurs when Bobbie sells 3 haircuts for $14 each. If she sells 2 haircuts for $16 each or 4 haircuts for $12 each, her economic profit will be only $8.

You can see why 3 haircuts is Bobbie's profit-maximizing output by looking at the marginal revenue and marginal cost columns. When Bobbie increases output from 2 to 3 haircuts, her marginal revenue is $10 and her marginal cost is $6. Profit increases by the difference—$4 an hour. If Bobbie increases output yet further, from 3 to 4 haircuts, her

marginal revenue is $6 and her marginal cost is $10. In this case, marginal cost exceeds marginal revenue by $4, so profit decreases by $4 an hour. When marginal revenue exceeds marginal cost, profit increases if output increases. When marginal cost exceeds marginal revenue, profit increases if output decreases. When marginal cost and marginal revenue are equal, profit is maximized.

The information set out in Table 13.1 is shown graphically in Fig. 13.4. Part (a) shows Bobbie's total revenue curve (TR) and total cost curve (TC). Economic profit is the vertical distance between TR and TC. Bobbie maximizes her profit at 3 haircuts an hour—economic profit is $42 minus $30, or $12.

A monopoly, like a competitive firm, maximizes profit by producing the output at which marginal cost equals marginal revenue. Figure 13.4(b) shows Bobbie's demand curve (D) and marginal revenue curve (MR) along with her marginal cost curve (MC) and average total cost curve (ATC). Bobbie maximizes her profit by doing 3 haircuts an hour. But what price does she charge for a haircut? To set the price, the monopolist uses the demand curve and finds the highest price at which it can sell the profit-maximizing output. In Bobbie's case, the highest price at which she can sell 3 haircuts an hour is $14.

TABLE 13.1

A Monopoly's Output and Price Decision

Price (P) (dollars per haircut)	Quantity demanded (Q) (haircuts per hour)	Total revenue (TR = P × Q) (dollars)	Marginal revenue (MR = ΔTR/ΔQ) (dollars per haircut)	Total cost (TC) (dollars)	Marginal cost (MC = ΔTC/ΔQ) (dollars per haircut)	Profit (TR − TC) (dollars)
20	0	0		20		−20
			18		1	
18	1	18		21		−3
			14		3	
16	2	32		24		+8
			10		6	
14	3	42		30		+12
			6		10	
12	4	48		40		+8
			2		15	
10	5	50		55		−5

This table gives the information needed to find the profit-maximizing output and price. Total revenue (TR) equals price multiplied by the quantity sold. Profit equals total revenue minus total cost (TC). Profit is maximized when the price is $14 and 3 haircuts are sold. Total revenue is $42, total cost is $30, and economic profit is $12 ($42 − $30).

FIGURE 13.4

A Monopoly's Output and Price

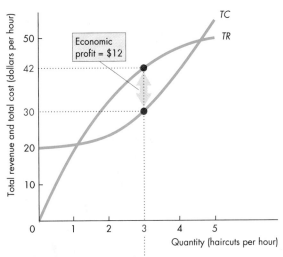

(a) Total revenue and total cost curves

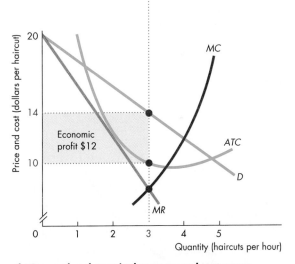

(b) Demand and marginal revenue and cost curves

In part (a), economic profit is the vertical distance between total revenue (*TR*) minus total cost (*TC*), and it is maximized at 3 haircuts an hour. In part (b), economic profit is maximized when marginal cost (*MC*) equals marginal revenue (*MR*). The price is determined by the demand curve (*D*) and is $14. Economic profit, the blue rectangle, is $12—the profit per haircut ($4) multiplied by 3 haircuts.

All firms maximize profit by producing the output at which marginal revenue equals marginal cost. For a competitive firm, price equals marginal revenue, so price also equals marginal cost. For a monopoly, price exceeds marginal revenue, so price also exceeds marginal cost.

A monopoly charges a price that exceeds marginal cost, but does it always make an economic profit? In Bobbie's case, when she produces 3 haircuts an hour, her average total cost is $10 (read from the *ATC* curve) and her price is $14 (read from the *D* curve). Her profit per haircut is $4 ($14 minus $10). Bobbie's economic profit is shown by the blue rectangle, which equals the profit per haircut ($4) multiplied by the number of haircuts (3), for a total of $12.

If firms in a perfectly competitive industry make a positive economic profit, new firms enter. That does not happen in monopoly. Barriers to entry prevent new firms from entering an industry in which there is a monopoly. So a monopoly can make a positive economic profit and continue to do so indefinitely. Sometimes that profit is large, as in the international diamond business.

Bobbie makes a positive economic profit. But suppose that the owner of the shop that Bobbie rents increases Bobbie's rent. If Bobbie pays an additional $12 an hour, her fixed cost increases by $12 an hour. Her marginal cost and marginal revenue don't change, so her profit-maximizing output remains at 3 haircuts an hour. Her profit decreases by $12 an hour to zero. If Bobbie pays more than an additional $12 an hour for her shop rent, she incurs an economic loss. If this situation were permanent, Bobbie would go out of business. But entrepreneurs are a hardy lot, and Bobbie might find another shop where the rent is less.

R E V I E W   Q U I Z

- What is the relationship between marginal cost and marginal revenue when a single-price monopoly maximizes profit?
- How does a single-price monopoly determine the price it will charge its customers?
- What is the relationship among price, marginal revenue, and marginal cost when a single-price monopoly is maximizing profit?
- Why can a monopoly make a positive economic profit even in the long run?

Single-Price Monopoly and Competition Compared

IMAGINE AN INDUSTRY THAT IS MADE UP OF MANY small firms operating in perfect competition. Then imagine that a single firm buys out all these small firms and creates a monopoly.

What will happen in this industry? Will the price rise or fall? Will the quantity produced increase or decrease? Will economic profit increase or decrease? Will either the original competitive situation or the new monopoly situation be efficient?

These are the questions we're now going to answer. First, we look at the effects of monopoly on the price and quantity produced. Then we turn to the questions about efficiency.

Comparing Output and Price

Figure 13.5 shows the market we'll study. The market demand curve is D. The demand curve is the same regardless of how the industry is organized. But the supply side and the equilibrium are different in monopoly and competition. First, let's look at the case of perfect competition.

Perfect Competition   Initially, with many small perfectly competitive firms in the market, the market supply curve is S. This supply curve is obtained by summing the supply curves of all the individual firms in the market.

In perfect competition, equilibrium occurs where the supply curve and the demand curve intersect. The quantity produced by the industry is Q_C, and the price is P_C. Each firm takes the price P_C and maximizes its profit by producing the output at which its own marginal cost equals the price. Because each firm is a small part of the total industry, there is no incentive for any firm to try to manipulate the price by varying its output.

Monopoly   Now suppose that this industry is taken over by a single firm. Consumers do not change so the market demand curve remains the same as in the case of perfect competition. But now, the monopoly recognizes this demand curve as a constraint on its sales. And the monopoly is confronted with the marginal revenue curve, MR.

The monopoly maximizes profit by producing the quantity at which marginal revenue equals marginal

cost. To find the monopoly's marginal cost curve, first recall that in perfect competition, the industry supply curve is the sum of the supply curves of the firms in the industry. Also recall that each firm's supply curve is its marginal cost curve (see Chapter 12, p. 250). So when the industry is taken over by a single firm, the competitive industry's supply curve becomes the monopoly's marginal cost curve. To remind you of this fact, the supply curve is also labelled MC.

The output at which marginal revenue equals marginal cost is Q_M. This output is smaller than the competitive output Q_C. And the monopoly charges the price P_M, which is higher than P_C. We have established that:

Compared to a perfectly competitive industry, a single-price monopoly restricts its output and charges a higher price.

We've seen how the output and price of a monopoly compare with those in a competitive industry. Let's now compare the efficiency of the two types of market.

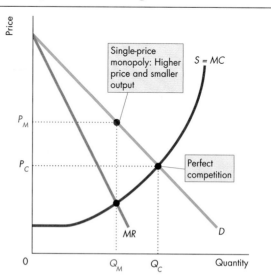

FIGURE 13.5

Monopoly's Smaller Output and Higher Price

A competitive industry produces the quantity Q_C at price P_C. A single-price monopoly produces the quantity Q_M at which marginal revenue equals marginal cost and sells that quantity for the price P_M. Compared to perfect competition, a single-price monopoly restricts output and raises the price.

Efficiency Comparison

When we studied efficiency in perfect competition, (see Chapter 12, pp. 260–261), we discovered that if there are no external costs and benefits, perfect competition results in an efficient use of resources. Along the demand curve, consumers are efficient. Along the supply curve, producers are efficient. And where the curves intersect—the competitive equilibrium—both consumers and producers are efficient. Price equals marginal cost and the sum of consumer surplus and producer surplus is maximized.

Monopoly restricts output below the competitive level and is inefficient. If a monopoly's output was increased, marginal benefit would exceed marginal cost and resources would be used more efficiently.

Figure 13.6 illustrates the inefficiency of monopoly and shows the loss of consumer and producer surpluses in a monopoly. In perfect competition (part a), consumers pay P_C for each unit. The demand curve ($D = MB$) shows the maximum price that consumers are willing to pay for each unit. This price measures the value of the good to the consumer. Value minus price equals *consumer surplus*. (See Chapter 6, p. 113.) In Fig. 13.6(a), consumer surplus is shown by the green triangle.

The marginal cost of production (opportunity cost) in perfect competition is shown by the supply curve ($S = MC$). The amount received by the producer in excess of this marginal cost is *producer surplus*. In Fig. 13.6(a), the blue area shows producer surplus.

At the competitive equilibrium, the sum of consumer surplus and producer surplus is maximized and resources are used efficiently.

In Fig. 13.6(b), a monopoly restricts output to Q_M and sells that output for P_M. Consumer surplus decreases to the smaller green triangle. Consumers lose partly by having to pay more for the good and partly by getting less of it. Part of the original producer surplus is also lost. The total loss resulting from the smaller monopoly output (Q_M) is the grey triangle. The part of the grey triangle above P_C is the loss of consumer surplus, and the part of the triangle below P_C is a loss of producer surplus. The entire grey triangle measures the loss of consumer surplus plus producer surplus. This loss is called the *deadweight loss*. The smaller output and higher price drive a wedge between marginal benefit and marginal cost and eliminate the producer surplus and the consumer surplus on the output that a competitive industry would have produced but that the monopoly does not.

FIGURE 13.6
Inefficiency of Monopoly

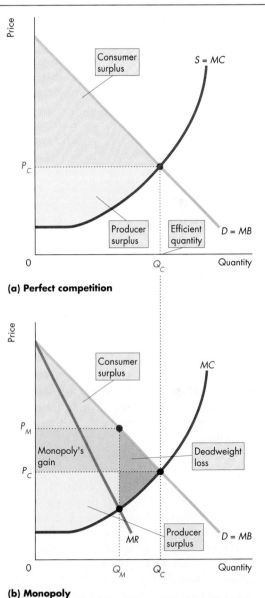

(a) Perfect competition

(b) Monopoly

In perfect competition (part a), the quantity Q_C is sold at the price P_C. Consumer surplus is shown by the green triangle, and producer surplus is shown by the blue area. In long-run equilibrium, the sum of consumer surplus and producer surplus is maximized. A single-price monopoly (part b) restricts output to Q_M and increases the price to P_M. Consumer surplus is the smaller green triangle. The monopoly takes the blue rectangle and creates a deadweight loss (the grey triangle).

Redistribution of Surpluses

You've seen that monopoly is inefficient. The sum of consumer surplus and producer surplus is smaller with monopoly than with competition. There is a social loss. But monopoly also brings a *redistribution* of surpluses.

Some of the loss in consumer surplus goes to the monopoly. In Fig. 13.6, the monopoly gets the difference between the higher price, P_M, and the competitive price, P_C, on the quantity sold, Q_M. So the monopoly takes the part of the consumer surplus shown by the blue rectangle. This portion of the loss of consumer surplus is not a loss to society. It is redistribution from consumers to the monopoly producer.

Rent Seeking

You've seen that monopoly creates a deadweight loss and so is inefficient. But the social cost of monopoly exceeds the deadweight loss because of an activity called rent seeking. **Rent seeking** is the attempt to capture a consumer surplus, a producer surplus, or an economic profit. The activity is not confined to monopoly. But the attempt to make an economic profit is a major form of rent seeking.

You've seen that a monopoly makes its economic profit by diverting part of consumer surplus to itself. Thus the pursuit of an economic profit by a monopoly is rent seeking. It is the attempt to capture consumer surplus.

Rent seekers pursue their goals in two main ways. They might

- Buy a monopoly
- Create a monopoly

Buy a Monopoly To rent seek by buying a monopoly, a person searches for a monopoly that is for sale at a lower price than the monopoly's economic profit. Trading taxicab licences is an example of this type of rent seeking. In some cities, taxicabs are regulated. The city restricts both the fares and the number of taxis that can operate so operating a taxi results in economic profit or rent. A person who wants to operate a taxi must buy a licence from someone who already has one. This type of rent seeking transfers rents from the buyer to the seller of the monopoly. The only person who ends up with rent is the one who created the monopoly in the first place. Even so, people rationally devote their time and effort to seeking out profitable

monopoly businesses to buy. In the process, they use up scarce resources that could otherwise have been employed producing goods and services.

Create a Monopoly Rent seeking by creating a monopoly is mainly a political activity. It takes the form of lobbying and trying to influence the political process. Such influence might be sought by making campaign contributions in exchange for legislative support or by indirectly seeking to influence political outcomes through publicity in the media or more direct contacts with politicians and bureaucrats. An example of a monopoly right created in this way is the cable television monopoly created and regulated by the Canadian Radio-television and Telecommunications Commission (CRTC). Another is a regulation that restricts "split-run" magazines. These are regulations that restrict output and increase price.

This type of rent seeking is a costly activity that uses up scarce resources. Taken together, firms spend billions of dollars lobbying MPs, MPPs, and bureaucrats in the pursuit of licences and laws that create barriers to entry and establish a monopoly right. Everyone has an incentive to rent seek, and because there are no barriers to entry into the rent-seeking activity, there is a great deal of competition for new monopoly rights.

Rent-Seeking Equilibrium

Barriers to entry create monopoly. But there is no barrier to entry into rent seeking. Rent seeking is like perfect competition. If an economic profit is available, a new rent seeker will try to get some of it. And competition among rent seekers pushes up the price that must be paid for a monopoly right to the point at which only a normal profit can be made by operating the monopoly. For example, competition for the right to operate a taxi in Toronto leads to a price of more than $80,000 for a taxi licence, which is sufficiently high to eliminate economic profit for taxi operators and leave them with normal profit.

Figure 13.7 shows a rent-seeking equilibrium. The cost of rent seeking is a fixed cost that must be added to a monopoly's other costs. Rent seeking and rent-seeking costs increase to the point at which no economic profit is made. The average total cost curve, which includes the fixed cost of rent seeking, shifts upward until it just touches the demand curve. Economic profit (and producer surplus) are zero.

FIGURE 13.7
Rent-Seeking Equilibrium

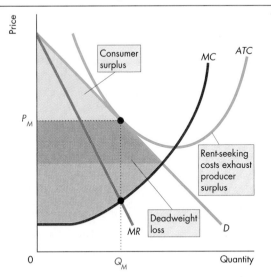

With competitive rent seeking, a monopoly uses all its economic profit to prevent another firm from taking its economic rent. The firm's rent-seeking costs are fixed costs. They add to total fixed cost and to average total cost. The *ATC* curve shifts upward until, at the profit-maximizing price, the firm breaks even.

They have been lost in rent seeking. Consumer surplus is unaffected. But the deadweight loss of monopoly now includes the original deadweight loss triangle plus the lost producer surplus, shown by the enlarged grey area in the figure.

R E V I E W   Q U I Z

- Why does a single-price monopoly produce a smaller output and charge a higher price than what would prevail if the industry were perfectly competitive?
- Why is a single-price monopoly inefficient?
- What is rent seeking and how does it influence the inefficiency of monopoly?

So far, we've considered only a single-price monopoly. But many monopolies do not operate with a single price. Instead, they price discriminate. Let's now see how price-discriminating monopoly works.

Price Discrimination

PRICE DISCRIMINATION—SELLING A GOOD OR service at a number of different prices—is widespread. You encounter it when you travel, go to the movies, get your hair cut, buy pizza, or visit an art museum. Most price discriminators are *not* monopolies, but monopolies price discriminate when they can do so. To be able to price discriminate a monopoly must:

1. Identify and separate different buyer types
2. Sell a product that cannot be resold.

Price discrimination is charging different prices for a single good or service because of differences in buyers' willingness to pay and not because of differences in production costs. So not all price *differences* are price *discrimination*. Some goods that are similar but not identical have different prices because they have different production costs. For example, the cost of producing electricity depends on time of day. If an electric power company charges a higher price for consumption between 7:00 and 9:00 in the morning and between 4:00 and 7:00 in the evening than at other times of the day, it is not price discriminating.

At first sight, it appears that price discrimination contradicts the assumption of profit maximization. Why would a movie operator allow children to see movies at half price? Why would a hairdresser charge students and senior citizens less? Aren't these firms losing profit by being nice to their customers?

Deeper investigation shows that far from losing profit, price discriminators make a bigger profit than they would otherwise. So a monopoly has an incentive to find ways of discriminating and charging each buyer the highest possible price. Some people pay less with price discrimination, but others pay more.

Price Discrimination and Consumer Surplus

The key idea behind price discrimination is to convert consumer surplus into economic profit. Demand curves slope down because the value that people place on any good decreases as the quantity consumed of that good increases. When all the units consumed are sold for a single price, consumers benefit. The benefit is the value the consumers get from each unit of the good minus the price actually paid for it. We call this benefit *consumer surplus*. (If you need to refresh your understanding of consumer surplus, flip back to Chapter 6, page 113.) Price discrimination is an attempt by a monopoly to capture as much of the consumer surplus as possible for itself.

To extract every dollar of consumer surplus from every buyer, the monopoly would have to offer each individual customer a separate price schedule based on that customer's own willingness to pay. Clearly, such price discrimination cannot be carried out in practice because a firm does not have enough information about each consumer's demand curve.

But firms try to extract as much consumer surplus as possible and, to do so, they discriminate in two broad ways:

■ Among units of a good
■ Among groups of buyers

Discriminating Among Units of a Good   One method of price discrimination charges each buyer a different price on each unit of a good bought. A discount for bulk buying is an example of this type of discrimination. The larger the order, the larger is the discount—and the lower is the price. (Note that some discounts for bulk arise from lower costs of production for greater bulk. In these cases, such discounts are not price discrimination.)

Discriminating Among Groups of Buyers   Price discrimination often takes the form of discriminating between different groups of consumers on the basis of age, employment status, or some other easily distinguished characteristic. This type of price discrimination works when each group has a different average willingness to pay for the good or service.

For example, a face-to-face sales meeting with a customer might bring a large and profitable order. For salespeople and other business travellers, the marginal benefit from a trip is large and the price that such a traveller will pay for a trip is high. In contrast, for a vacation traveller, any of several different trips or even no vacation trip are options. So for vacation travellers, the marginal benefit of a trip is small and the price that such a traveller will pay for a trip is low. Because business travellers are willing to pay more than vacation travellers are, it is possible for an airline to profit by price discriminating between these two groups. Similarly, because students have a lower willingness to pay for a haircut than a working person does, it is possible for a hairdresser to profit by price discriminating between these two groups.

Let's see how an airline exploits the differences in demand by business and vacation travellers and increases its profit by price discriminating.

Profiting by Price Discriminating

Global Air has a monopoly on an exotic route. Figure 13.8 shows the demand curve (*D*) and the marginal revenue curve (*MR*) for travel on this route. It also shows Global Air's marginal cost curve (*MC*) and average total cost curve (*ATC*).

Initially, Global is a single-price monopoly and maximizes its profit by producing 8,000 trips a year (the quantity at which *MR* equals *MC*). The price is $1,200 per trip. The average total cost of a trip is $600, so economic profit is $600 a trip. On 8,000 trips, Global's economic profit is $4.8 million a year, shown by the blue rectangle. Global's customers enjoy a consumer surplus shown by the green triangle.

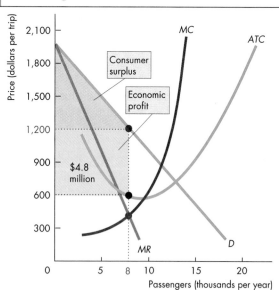

FIGURE 13.8

A Single Price of Air Travel

Global Air has a monopoly on an air route. The market demand curve is *D* and the marginal revenue curve is *MR*. Global Air's marginal cost curve is *MC* and its average total cost curve is *ATC*. As a single-price monopoly, Global maximizes profit by selling 8,000 trips a year at $1,200 a trip. Its profit is $4.8 million a year—the blue rectangle. Global's customers enjoy a consumer surplus—the green triangle.

Global is struck by the fact that many of its customers are business travellers and Global suspects they are willing to pay more than $1,200 a trip. So Global does some market research, which tells Global that some business travellers are willing to pay as much as $1,800 a trip. Also, these customers almost always change their travel plans at the last moment. Another group of business travellers is willing to pay $1,600. These customers know a week ahead when they will travel and they never want to stay over a weekend. Yet another group would pay up to $1,400 and these travellers know two weeks ahead when they will travel and don't want to stay away over a weekend.

So Global announces a new fare schedule. No restrictions, $1,800; 7-days advance purchase, no cancellation, $1,600; 14-days advance purchase, no cancellation, $1,400; 14-days advance purchase, must stay over weekend, $1,200.

Figure 13.9 shows the outcome with this new fare structure and also shows why Global is pleased

with its new fares. It sells 2,000 seats at each of its four prices. Global's economic profit increases by the blue steps in Fig. 13.9. Its economic profit is now its original $4.8 million a year plus an additional $2.4 million from its new higher fares. Consumer surplus has shrunk to the smaller green area.

Perfect Price Discrimination

But Global reckons it can do even better. It plans to achieve **perfect price discrimination**, which extracts the entire consumer surplus. To do so, Global must come up with a host of additional fares ranging between $1,200 and $2,000, each one of which appeals to a small market segment of the business market and that extracts the entire consumer surplus from the business travellers.

With perfect price discrimination, something special happens to marginal revenue. For the perfect price discriminator, the demand curve becomes the marginal revenue curve. The reason is that when the price is cut to sell a larger quantity, the firm sells only the marginal unit at the lower price. All the other units continue to be sold for the highest price the buyers are willing to pay.

With marginal cost equal to price, Global can obtain yet greater profit by increasing output up to the point at which price (and marginal revenue) is equal to marginal cost.

So, Global now seeks additional travellers who will not pay as much as $1,200 a trip but who will pay more than marginal cost. More creative pricing comes up with vacation specials and other fares that have combinations of advance reservation, minimum-stay, and other restrictions that make these fares unattractive to its existing customers but attractive to a further group of travellers. With all these fares and specials, Global increases sales, extracts the entire consumer surplus, and maximizes economic profit.

Figure 13.10 shows the outcome with perfect price discrimination. The dozens of fares paid by the original travellers who are willing to pay between $1,200 and $2,000 has extracted the entire consumer surplus from this group and converted it into economic profit for Global.

The new fares between $900 and $1,200 have attracted 3,000 additional travellers but taken their entire consumer surplus also. Global is earning an economic profit of more than $9 million.

Real-world airlines are just as creative as Global as you can see in the cartoon!

FIGURE 13.9

Price Discrimination

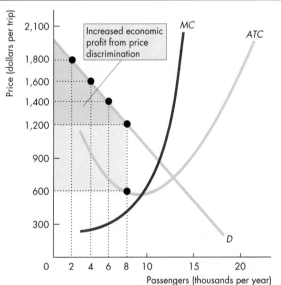

Global revises its fare structure. No restrictions at $1,800; 7-days advance purchase at $1,600; 14-days advance purchase at $1,400; and must stay over weekend at $1,200. Global sells 2,000 units at each of its four new fares. Its economic profit increases by $2.4 million a year to $7.2 million a year, which is shown by the original blue rectangle plus the blue steps. Global's customers' consumer surplus shrinks.

FIGURE 13.10
Perfect Price Discrimination

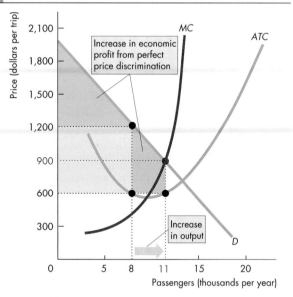

Dozens of fares discriminate among different types of business traveller, and many new low fares with restrictions appeal to vacation travellers. With perfect price discrimination, the demand curve becomes Global's marginal revenue curve. Economic profit is maximized when the lowest price equals marginal cost. Global sells 11,000 tickets between $2,000 and $900 each and makes an economic profit of $9.35 million a year.

Would it bother you to hear how little I paid for this flight?

From William Hamilton, "Voodoo Economics," ©1992 by The Chronicle Publishing Company, p. 3. Reprinted with permission of Chronicle Books.

Efficiency and Rent Seeking with Price Discrimination

With perfect price discrimination, output increases to the point at which price equals marginal cost—where the marginal cost curve intersects the demand curve. This output is identical to that of perfect competition. Perfect price discrimination pushes consumer surplus to zero but increases producer surplus to equal the sum of consumer surplus and producer surplus in perfect competition. Deadweight loss with perfect price discrimination is zero. So perfect price discrimination achieves efficiency.

The more perfectly the monopoly can price discriminate, the closer its output gets to the competitive output and the more efficient is the outcome.

But there are two differences between perfect competition and perfect price discrimination. First, the distribution of the surplus is different. It is shared by consumers and producers in perfect competition while the producer gets it all with perfect price discrimination. Second, because the producer grabs the surplus, rent seeking becomes profitable.

People use resources in pursuit of rents and the bigger the rents, the more resources get used pursuing them. With free entry into rent seeking, the long-run equilibrium outcome is that rent seekers use up the entire producer surplus.

R E V I E W   Q U I Z

- What is price discrimination and how is it used to increase a monopoly's profit?
- What happens to consumer surplus when a monopoly price discriminates?
- What happens to consumer surplus, economic profit, and output if a monopoly perfectly price discriminates?
- What are some of the ways that real-world airlines use to price discriminate?

You've seen that monopoly is profitable for the producer but costly for other people. It results in inefficiency. Because of these features of monopoly, it is subject to policy debate and regulation. We'll now study the key monopoly policy issues.

Monopoly Policy Issues

THE COMPARISON OF MONOPOLY AND competition makes monopoly look bad. Monopoly is inefficient and it captures consumer surplus and converts it into producer surplus or pure waste in the form of rent-seeking costs. If monopoly is so bad, why do we put up with it? Why don't we have laws that crack down on monopoly so hard that it never rears its head? We do indeed have laws that limit monopoly power and regulate the prices that monopolies are permitted to charge. But monopoly also brings some benefits. We begin this review of monopoly policy issues by looking at the benefits of monopoly. We then look at monopoly regulation.

Gains from Monopoly

The main reason why monopoly exists is that it has potential advantages over a competitive alternative. These advantages arise from:

- Economies of scale and economies of scope
- Incentives to innovation

Economies of Scale and Scope   Economies of scale and scope can lead to *natural monopoly*. And as you saw at the beginning of this chapter, in a natural monopoly, a single firm can produce at a lower average cost than a larger number of smaller firms can.

A firm experiences *economies of scale* when an increase in its output of a good or service brings a decrease in the average total cost of producing it—see Chapter 11, p. 236. A firm experiences *economies of scope* when an increase in the *range of goods produced* brings a decrease in average total cost—see Chapter 10, p. 217. Economies of scope occur when different goods can share specialized (and usually costly) capital resources. For example, McDonald's can produce both hamburgers and french fries at a lower average total cost than can two separate firms—a burger firm and a french fries firm—because at McDonald's hamburgers and french fries share the use of specialized food storage and preparation facilities. A firm that produces a wide range of products can hire specialist computer programmers, designers, and marketing experts whose skills can be used across the product range, thereby spreading their costs and lowering the average total cost of production of each of the goods.

Large-scale firms that have control over supply and can influence price—and that therefore behave like the monopoly firm that you've studied in this chapter—can reap these economies of scale and scope. Small, competitive firms cannot. Consequently there are situations in which the comparison of monopoly and competition that we made earlier in this chapter is not valid. Recall that we imagined the takeover of a large number of competitive firms by a monopoly firm. But we also assumed that the monopoly would use exactly the same technology as the small firms and have the same costs. If one large firm can reap economies of scale and scope, its marginal cost curve will lie below the supply curve of a competitive industry made up of many small firms. It is possible for such economies of scale and scope to be so large as to result in a larger output and lower price under monopoly than a competitive industry would achieve.

Examples of industries in which economies of scale are so significant that they lead to a natural monopoly are becoming more rare. Public utilities such as gas, electric power, local telephone service, and garbage collection once were natural monopolies. But technological advances now enable us to separate the *production* of electric power and natural gas from their *distribution*. The provision of water, though, remains a natural monopoly. There are many examples in which a combination of economies of scale and economies of scope arise. Some examples are the brewing of beer, the manufacture of refrigerators and other household appliances, the manufacture of pharmaceuticals, and the refining of petroleum.

Where significant economies of scale and scope exist, it is usually worth putting up with monopoly and regulating its prices.

Incentives to Promote Innovation   Invention leads to a wave of innovation as new knowledge is applied to the production process. Innovation may take the form of developing a new product or a lower-cost way of making an existing product. Controversy rages over whether large firms with monopoly power or small competitive firms lacking such monopoly power are the most innovative. It is clear that some temporary monopoly power arises from innovation. A firm that develops a new product or process and patents it obtains an exclusive right to that product or process for the term of the patent.

But does the granting of a monopoly, even a temporary one, to an innovator increase the pace of innovation? One line of reasoning suggests that it does. Without protection, an innovator is not able to enjoy the profits from innovation for very long. Thus the incentive to innovate is weakened. A contrary argument is that monopolies can afford to be lazy while competitive firms cannot. Competitive firms must strive to innovate and cut costs even though they know that they cannot hang on to the benefits of their innovation for long. But that knowledge spurs them on to greater and faster innovation.

The evidence on whether monopoly leads to greater innovation than competition is mixed. Large firms do more research and development than do small firms. But measuring research and development is measuring the volume of inputs into the process of innovation. What matters is not input but output. Two measures of the output of research and development are the number of patents and the rate of productivity growth. On these measures, there is no clear evidence that big is better. But there is a clear pattern in the process of diffusion of technological knowledge. After innovation, a new process or product spreads gradually through the industry, with large firms jumping on the bandwagon more quickly than the remaining small firms. Thus large firms speed the process of diffusion of technological advances.

Regulating Natural Monopoly

Where demand and cost conditions create a natural monopoly, a government agency usually regulates the prices of the monopoly. By regulating a monopoly, some of the worst aspects of monopoly can be avoided, or at least made more moderate. One such natural monopoly is in the distribution of natural gas. Let's look at the regulation of this activity.

Fig. 13.11 shows the market demand curve D and the marginal revenue curve, MR, the average total cost curve ATC, and the marginal cost curve MC for a gas distribution company that is a natural monopoly.

The firm's marginal cost is constant at 10 cents per cubic metre. But average total cost decreases as output increases. The reason is that the natural gas company has a large investment in pipelines and so has high fixed costs. These fixed costs are part of the company's average total cost and so appear in the ATC curve. The average total cost curve slopes downward because as the number of cubic metres sold increases, the fixed cost is spread over a larger number of units. (If you need to refresh your memory on how the average total cost curve is calculated, take a quick look back at Chapter 11, pp. 230–231.)

This one firm can supply the entire market at a lower cost than two firms can because average total cost is falling even when the entire market is supplied. (Refer back to pp. 268–269 if you need a quick refresher on natural monopoly.)

Profit Maximization   First, suppose the natural gas company is not regulated and instead maximizes profit. Fig. 13.11 shows the outcome in this case. The company produces 2 million cubic metres a day, the quantity at which marginal cost equals marginal revenue. It prices this gas at 20 cents a cubic metre and makes an economic profit of 2 cents a cubic metre, or $40,000 a day.

This outcome is fine for the gas company, but it is inefficient. Price or marginal benefit is 20 cents a cubic metre when marginal cost is 10 cents a cubic metre. Also, the gas company is making a big profit. What can regulation do to improve this outcome?

The Efficient Regulation   If the monopoly regulator wants to achieve an efficient use of resources, it must require the gas monopoly to produce the quantity of gas that brings marginal benefit into equality with marginal cost. Marginal benefit is what the consumer is willing to pay and is shown by the market demand curve. Marginal cost is shown by the firm's marginal cost curve. You can see in Fig. 13.11 that this outcome occurs if the price is regulated at 10 cents per cubic metre and if 4 million cubic metres per day are produced. The regulation that produces this outcome is called a marginal cost pricing rule. A **marginal cost pricing rule** sets price equal to marginal cost. It maximizes total surplus in the regulated industry. In this example, that surplus is all consumer surplus and is the area of the triangle under the demand curve and above the marginal cost curve.

The marginal cost pricing rule is efficient. But it leaves the natural monopoly incurring an economic loss. Because average total cost is falling as output increases, marginal cost is below average total cost. And because price equals marginal cost, price is below average total cost. Average total cost minus price is the loss per unit produced. It's pretty obvious that a natural gas company that is required to use a marginal cost pricing rule will not stay in business for long. How can a company cover its costs and, at the same time, obey a marginal cost pricing rule?

One possibility is price discrimination. The company might charge a higher price to some customers but marginal cost to the customers who pay least. Another possibility is to use a two part price (called a

FIGURE 13.11

Regulating a Natural Monopoly

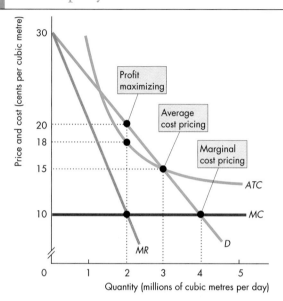

A natural monopoly is an industry in which average total cost is falling even when the entire market demand is satisfied. A natural gas producer faces the market demand curve *D*. The firm's marginal cost is constant at 10 cents per cubic metre, as shown by the curve labelled *MC*. Fixed costs are large, and the average total cost curve, which includes average fixed cost, is shown as *ATC*. A marginal cost pricing rule sets the price at 10 cents per cubic metre. The monopoly produces 4 million cubic metres per day and incurs an economic loss. An average cost pricing rule sets the price at 15 cents per cubic metre. The monopoly produces 3 million cubic metres a day and makes normal profit.

two-part tariff). For example, the gas company might charge a monthly fixed fee that covers its fixed cost and then charge for gas consumed at marginal cost.

But a natural monopoly cannot always cover its costs in these ways. If a natural monopoly cannot cover its total cost from its customers, and if the government wants it to follow a marginal cost pricing rule, the government must give the firm a subsidy. In such a case, the government raises the revenue for the subsidy by taxing some other activity. But as we saw in Chapter 7, taxes themselves generate deadweight loss. Thus the deadweight loss resulting from additional taxes must be subtracted from the efficiency

gained by forcing the natural monopoly to adopt a marginal cost pricing rule.

Average Cost Pricing Regulators almost never impose efficient pricing because of its consequences for the firm's profit. Instead, they compromise by permitting the firm to cover all its costs and to earn a normal profit. Normal profit, recall, is a cost of production and we include it along with the firm's other fixed costs in the average total cost curve. So pricing to cover cost and normal profit means setting price equal to average total cost—called an **average cost pricing rule**.

Figure 13.11 shows the average cost pricing outcome. The natural gas company charges 15 cents a cubic metre and sells 3 million cubic metres per day. This outcome is better for consumers than the unregulated profit-maximizing outcome. The price is 5 cents a cubic metre lower and the quantity consumed is 1 million cubic metres per day more. And the outcome is better for the producer than the marginal cost pricing rule outcome. The firm earns normal profit. The outcome is inefficient, but less so than the unregulated profit-maximizing outcome.

REVIEW QUIZ

- What are the two main reasons why monopoly is worth tolerating?
- Can you provide some examples of economies of scale and economies of scope?
- Why might a monopoly have a greater incentive to innovate than a small competitive firm?
- What is the price that achieves an efficient outcome for a regulated monopoly? And what is the problem with this price?
- Compare the consumer surplus, producer surplus, and deadweight loss that arise from average cost pricing with those of profit-maximization pricing and marginal cost pricing.

You've now studied two market structures: perfect competition and monopoly. *Reading Between the Lines* on pp. 284–285 looks at monopoly in action. In the next chapter, we're going to study the ground between monopoly and perfect competition. But you'll discover that the lessons you've learned from these two extreme market types are still relevant and help to understand how real-world markets work.

Telephone Monopoly

FINANCIAL POST, OCTOBER 2, 1998

Cheaper calls likely as Teleglobe loses monopoly

Average overseas calling rates could be halved with the end yesterday of Teleglobe Inc.'s monopoly over the routing of Canada's international phone traffic.

"A call to Europe that costs 90¢ a minute today could be 30¢ within a year or two," said Bernard Courtois, Bell Canada's group vice-president for regulatory issues.

Carriers including Bell and AT&T Long Distance Services Co. welcomed the end to Teleglobe's long-standing monopoly, and said regulations enacted yesterday to govern the overseas market are in line with expectations.

AT&T said eliminating all routing restrictions for Canadian telecom traffic will allow carriers to choose the cheapest and most efficient channels, with savings ultimately passed on to customers. ...

"International rates had been exceedingly high," said David Colville, vice-chairman of the Canadian Radio-television & Telecommunications Commission, which regulates telephone companies in Canada.

"I think you'll see dramatic reductions in the short term."

For more than 40 years, Montreal-based Teleglobe and its predecessor companies enjoyed a monopoly over facilities linking Canada to overseas destinations. All traffic had to move over Teleglobe's Canadian network. The business today is worth $1 billion a year to Teleglobe.

The monopoly came to a formal end yesterday as a result of international agreements, signed by more than 80 countries, aimed at increasing competition in global telecommunications services. Legislative and regulatory changes to open up Canada's international phone market also came into effect.

With Canada's domestic and international telecom markets now fully open, the CRTC said it expects to see a flurry of new entrants to the international calling business. ...

Essence of the Story

- Teleglobe Inc.'s monopoly over the routing of Canadian international phone traffic has ended.

- New entrants are expected in the international calling market.

- David Colville, vice-chairman of the CRTC, says that while the monopoly existed, prices were exceedingly high.

- Prices are now expected to fall.

- A call to Europe that cost 90¢ per minute under the monopoly could fall to 30¢ per minute within two years.

Economic Analysis

■ When Teleglobe Inc. has a monopoly over Canadian international phone traffic, the price of a call to Europe is 90¢ per minute.

■ When the international phone market becomes competitive, the price of a call to Europe is expected to fall.

■ Figure 1 compares the monopoly and a competitive market.

■ When Teleglobe Inc. is a monopoly, it maximizes profit by producing the quantity at which marginal revenue equals marginal cost. This quantity is Q_m in Fig. 1.

■ Teleglobe charges the highest price for which output Q_m can be sold. That price is 90¢ per minute, as seen on the demand curve, D, at point a.

■ In October 1998, Teleglobe's monopoly ended.

■ Initially, there is no change in cost. The industry supply curve, S, is the same as Teleglobe's marginal cost curve, MC.

■ The quantity produced by the industry and the price are determined by the intersection of the supply curve, S, and the demand curve, D, at point b.

■ The quantity bought and sold increases from Q_m under the monopoly to Q_c and the price falls from 90¢ per minute to 50¢ per minute.

■ When Teleglobe is a monopoly, output is restricted and the price is higher than in a competitive market.

■ In the long run, new entrants are expected in the international calling market.

■ Figure 2 shows that as supply increases, the supply curve shifts rightward from S_0 to S_1, the price falls further to 30¢ per minute, and the quantity of phone calls increases from Q_c to Q_1.

■ As the number of firms increases, the quantity of phone calls becomes even larger than in the monopoly market and the price falls even further.

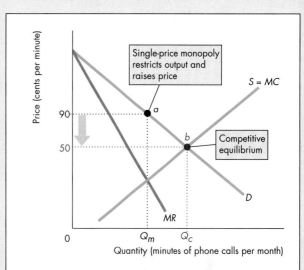

Figure 1 Market becomes competitive

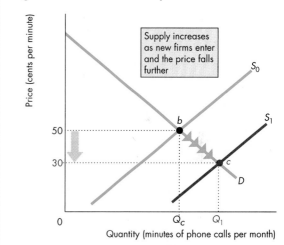

Figure 2 New firms enter the market

SUMMARY

Key Points

Market Power (pp. 268–269)

- A monopoly is an industry with a single supplier of a good or service that has no close substitutes and in which barriers to entry prevent competition.
- Barriers to entry may be legal (public franchise, licence, patent, copyright, firm owns control of a resource) or natural (created by economies of scale).
- A monopoly might be able to price discriminate when there is no resale possibility.
- Where resale is possible, a firm charges one price.

A Single-Price Monopoly's Output and Price Decision (pp. 270–273)

- The demand for a monopoly's output is the market demand curve and a single-price monopoly's marginal revenue is less than price.
- A monopoly maximizes profit by producing the output at which marginal revenue equals marginal cost and by charging the maximum price that consumers are willing to pay for that output.

Single-Price Monopoly and Competition Compared (pp. 274–277)

- A single-price monopoly charges a higher price and produces a smaller quantity than a perfectly competitive industry.
- A single-price monopoly restricts output and creates a deadweight loss.
- Monopoly imposes costs that equal its deadweight loss plus the cost of the resources devoted to rent seeking.

Price Discrimination (pp. 277–280)

- Price discrimination is an attempt by the monopoly to convert consumer surplus into economic profit.
- Perfect price discrimination extracts all the consumer surplus. Such a monopoly charges a different price for each unit sold and obtains the maximum price that each consumer is willing to pay for each unit bought.

- With perfect price discrimination, the monopoly produces the same output as would a perfectly competitive industry.
- Rent seeking with perfect price discrimination might eliminate the entire consumer surplus and producer surplus.

Monopoly Policy Issues (pp. 281–283)

- Monopolies with large economies of scale and scope can produce a larger quantity at a lower price than a competitive industry can achieve and monopoly might be more innovative than competition.
- Efficient regulation requires a monopoly to charge a price equal to marginal cost, but for a natural monopoly such a price is less than average total cost.
- Average cost pricing is a compromise pricing rule that covers a firm's costs and provides a normal profit but is not efficient. It is more efficient than unregulated profit maximization.

Key Figures and Table

Key Terms

P R O B L E M S

*1. Minnie's Mineral Springs, a single-price monopoly, faces the market demand schedule:

Price (dollars per bottle)	Quantity demanded (bottles)
10	0
8	1
6	2
4	3
2	4
0	5

a. Calculate Minnie's total revenue schedule.
b. Calculate its marginal revenue schedule.

2. Dolly's Diamond Mines, a single-price monopoly, faces the market demand schedule:

Price (dollars per kilogram)	Quantity demanded (kilograms per day)
2,200	5
2,000	6
1,800	7
1,600	8
1,400	9
1,200	10

a. Calculate Dolly's total revenue schedule.
b. Calculate its marginal revenue schedule.

*3. Minnie's Mineral Springs in problem 1 has the following total cost:

Quantity produced (bottles)	Total cost (dollars)
0	1
1	3
2	7
3	13
4	21
5	31

Use a graph to calculate the profit-maximizing
a. Output
b. Price
c. Marginal cost
d. Marginal revenue
e. Economic profit
f. Does Minnie's use resources efficiently? Explain your answer.

4. Dolly's Diamond Mines in problem 2 has the following total cost:

Quantity produced (kilograms per day)	Total cost (dollars)
5	8,000
6	9,000
7	10,200
8	11,600
9	13,200
10	15,000

Use a graph to calculate the profit-maximizing
a. Output
b. Price
c. Marginal cost
d. Marginal revenue
e. Economic profit
f. Does Dolly's Mines use resources efficiently? Explain your answer.

*5. The figure illustrates the situation facing the publisher of the only newspaper containing local news in an isolated community.

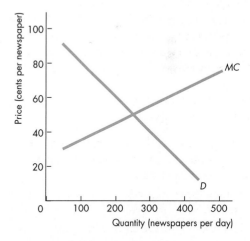

a. What quantity of newspapers will maximize the publisher's profit?
b. What price will the publisher charge?
c. What is the publisher's daily total revenue?
d. At the price charged for a newspaper, is the demand elastic or inelastic? Why?

6. In problem 5, the publisher installs a new printing press that makes the marginal cost constant at 20 cents per copy.
a. What quantity of newspapers will maximize the publisher's profit?

b. What price will the publisher charge?

c. What is the publisher's daily total revenue?

d. At the price charged for a newspaper, is the demand elastic or inelastic? Why?

*7. In problem 5, what is:

a. The efficient quantity of newspapers to print each day? Explain your answer.

b. Consumer surplus?

c. Deadweight loss created by the publisher?

8. In problem 6, what is:

a. The efficient quantity of newspapers to print each day? Explain your answer.

b. Consumer surplus?

c. Deadweight loss created by the publisher?

*9. In problem 3, what is the maximum value of resources that will be used in rent seeking to acquire Minnie's monopoly? Considering this loss, what is the total social cost of Minnie's monopoly?

10. In problem 4, what is the maximum value of resources that will be used in rent seeking to acquire Dolly's monopoly? Considering this loss, what is the total social cost of Dolly's monopoly?

*11. The figure illustrates the situation facing a natural monopoly.

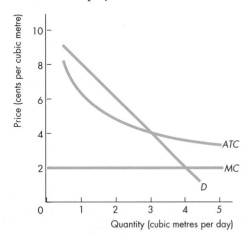

What quantity will be produced and what will the deadweight loss be if the firm is:

a. An unregulated profit-maximizer?

b. Regulated to earn only normal profit?

c. Regulated to be efficient?

12. What are the answers to the three questions in problem 11, if marginal cost falls by 50 percent?

CRITICAL THINKING

1. Study *Reading Between the Lines* on pp. 284–285 and then answer the following questions.

a. Was Teleglobe a natural monopoly or a legal monopoly?

b. Did Teleglobe operate efficiently? Explain.

c. With the end of Teleglobe's monopoly, what do you predict will happen to the price of international phone calls originating in Canada? What will happen to producer surplus, consumer surplus, and deadweight loss?

d. Is it necessary for the CRTC to regulate the providers of international telephone services? Why or why not?

e. If the market for international phone calls becomes competitive, will it then be efficient?

f. Suppose that some foreign firms enter the market for Canadian international phone calls. Will the market then be efficient or inefficient? Explain.

2. Use the links on the Parkin-Bade Web site to study the market for computer chips.

a. Is it correct to call Intel a monopoly? Why or why not?

b. How does Intel try to raise barriers to entry in this market?

3. Use the links on the Parkin-Bade Web site to obtain information about Microsoft. Then answer the following questions.

a. Is it correct to call Microsoft a monopoly?

b. How do you think Microsoft sets the price of Windows 98 and decides how many copies of the program to sell?

c. How would the arrival of a viable alternative operating system to Windows affect Microsoft?

d. How would you regulate the software industry to ensure that resources are used efficiently?

e. "Anyone is free to buy stock in Microsoft, so everyone is free to share in Microsoft's economic profit and the bigger that economic profit, the better for all." Evaluate this statement.

Chapter 14

Monopolistic Competition and Oligopoly

Every week, we receive a newspaper stuffed with supermarket flyers describing this week's "specials," providing coupons and other enticements, all designed to grab our attention and persuade us that A&P, Zehr's, Safeway, Loblaws, and Miracle Mart have the best deals in town. One claims the lowest price, another the best brands, yet another the best value for money even if its prices are not the lowest. How do firms locked in fierce competition with other firms set their prices, pick their products, and choose the quantities to produce? How are the profits of such firms affected by the actions of other firms?

◆ Before 1994, only one firm made the chips that drive IBM and compatible PCs: Intel Corporation. During 1994, the prices of powerful personal computers based on Intel's fast Pentium chips collapsed. The reason: Intel suddenly faced competition from new chip producers such as Advanced Micro Devices Inc. and Cyrix Corp. The price of Intel's Pentium processor, set at more than $1,000 when it was launched in 1993, fell to less than $200 by spring 1996, and today you can buy a Pentium-based computer for less than $1,000. How did competition among a small number of chip makers bring such a rapid fall in the price of chips and computers?

◇ The theories of monopoly and perfect competition do not predict the kind of behaviour that we've just described. There are no flyers and coupons, best brands, or price wars in perfect competition because each firm produces an identical product and is a price taker. And there are none in monopoly because each monopoly firm has the entire market to itself. To understand coupons, flyers, and price wars, we need the richer models explained in this chapter.

Flyers and War Games

After studying this chapter, you will be able to:

- Explain how output and price are determined in a monopolistically competitive industry
- Explain why advertising costs are high in a monopolistically competitive industry
- Explain why the price might be sticky in an oligopoly industry
- Explain how price and output are determined when an industry has one dominant firm and several small firms
- Use game theory to make predictions about price wars and competition among a small number of firms

Monopolistic Competition

YOU HAVE STUDIED TWO TYPES OF MARKET structure: perfect competition and monopoly. In perfect competition, a large number of firms produce identical goods, there are no barriers to entry, and each firm is a price taker. In the long run, there is no economic profit. In monopoly, a single firm is protected from competition by barriers to entry and can make an economic profit, even in the long run.

Many real-world markets are competitive, but not as fiercely so as perfect competition. Firms in these markets possess some power to set their prices like monopolies do. We call this type of market *monopolistic competition*.

Monopolistic competition is a market structure in which:

- A large number of firms compete
- Each firm produces a differentiated product
- Firms compete on product quality, price, and marketing
- Firms are free to enter and exit.

Large Number of Firms

In monopolistic competition, as in perfect competition, the industry consists of a large number of firms. The presence of a large number of firms has three implications for the firms in the industry.

Small Market Share In monopolistic competition, each firm supplies a small part of the total industry output. Consequently, each firm has only limited power to influence the price of its product. Each firm's price can deviate from the average price of other firms by a relatively small amount.

Ignore Other Firms A firm in monopolistic competition must be sensitive to the average market price of the product. But it does not pay attention to any one individual competitor. Because all the firms are relatively small, no one firm can dictate market conditions so no one firm's actions directly affect the actions of the other firms.

Collusion Impossible Firms in monopolistic competition would like to be able to conspire to fix a higher price—called collusion. But because there are many firms, collusion is not possible.

Product Differentiation

A firm practises **product differentiation** if it makes a product that is slightly different from the products of competing firms. A differentiated product is one that is a close substitute but not a perfect substitute for the products of the other firms. Some people will pay more for one variety of the product, so when its price rises, the quantity demanded falls but it does not (necessarily) fall to zero. For example, Adidas, Asics, Diadora, Etonic, Fila, New Balance, Nike, Puma, and Reebok all make differentiated running shoes. Other things remaining the same, if the price of Adidas running shoes rises and the prices of the other shoes remain constant, Adidas sells fewer shoes and the other producers sell more. But Adidas shoes don't disappear unless the price rises by a large enough amount.

Competing on Quality, Price, and Marketing

Product differentiation enables a firm to compete with other firms in three areas: product quality, price, and marketing.

Quality The quality of a product is the physical attributes that make it different from the products of other firms. Quality includes design, reliability, the service provided to the buyer, and the buyer's ease of access to the product. Quality lies on a spectrum that runs from high to low. Some firms—Dell Computers is an example—offer high-quality products. They are well designed and reliable and the customer receives quick and efficient service. Other firms offer lower-quality products. These are less well designed and might not work perfectly, and the buyer might have to travel some distance to obtain them.

Price Because of product differentiation, a firm in monopolistic competition faces a downward-sloping demand curve. So, like a monopoly, the firm can set both its price and its output. But there is a tradeoff between the product's quality and price. A firm that makes a high-quality product can charge a higher price than a firm that makes a low-quality product.

Marketing Because of product differentiation, a firm in monopolistic competition must market its product. Marketing takes two main forms: advertising and packaging. A firm that produces a high-quality product wants to sell it for a suitably high price. To be able to do so, it must advertise and package its product in a way that convinces buyers that they are getting the higher quality for which they are paying a higher price. For example, drug companies advertise and package their brand-name drugs to persuade buyers that these items are superior to the lower-priced generic alternatives. Similarly, a low-quality producer uses advertising and packaging to persuade buyers that although the quality is low, the low price more than compensates for this fact.

Entry and Exit

In monopolistic competition, there is free entry and free exit. Consequently, a firm cannot make an economic profit in the long run. When firms make an economic profit, new firms enter the industry. This entry lowers prices and eventually eliminates economic profit. When economic losses are incurred, some firms leave the industry. This exit increases prices and profits and eventually eliminates the economic loss. In long-run equilibrium, firms neither enter nor leave the industry and the firms in the industry make zero economic profit.

Examples of Monopolistic Competition

Monopolistic competition is visible just about everywhere you look. Figure 14.1 shows eleven industries that are good examples. Even in the most concentrated of these industries, finance, the largest four firms receive less than 20 percent of industry total revenue. In the least concentrated, clothing, the largest four firms receive only 7 percent of industry total revenue. So these industries are very competitive, but the firms in them produce differentiated products.

R E V I E W   Q U I Z

- What are the distinguishing characteristics of monopolistic competition?
- How do firms in monopolistic competition compete?
- Provide some examples of industries located near your school that operate in monopolistic competition (other than the examples just given).

FIGURE 14.1
Examples of Monopolistic Competition

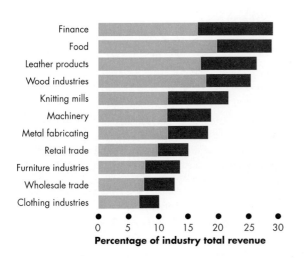

These industries operate in monopolistic competition. The blue bars show the percentage of industry total revenue received by the largest 4 firms. The red bars show the percentage of industry total revenue received by the next 4 firms. So the entire length of the red and blue bars combined shows the percentage of industry total revenue received by the largest 8 firms.

Source: Annual Report of the Ministry of Industry, Science and Technology Under the Corporations and Labour Unions Returns Act, March 1990, p. 94.

Output and Price in Monopolistic Competition

WE ARE NOW GOING TO LEARN HOW OUTPUT AND price are determined in monopolistic competition. First, we will suppose that the firm has already decided on the quality of its product and on its marketing program. For a given product and a given amount of marketing activity, the firm faces given costs and market conditions.

Figure 14.2 shows how a firm in monopolistic competition determines its price and output. Part (a) deals with the short run, and part (b) deals with the long run. We'll concentrate first on the short run.

Short Run: Economic Profit

The demand curve *D* shows the demand for the

firm's product. It is the demand curve for Nautica jackets, not jackets in general. The curve labelled *MR* is the marginal revenue curve associated with the demand curve. It is derived just like the marginal revenue curve of a single-price monopoly that you studied in Chapter 13. The figure also shows the firm's average total cost (*ATC*) and marginal cost (*MC*). These curves are similar to the cost curves that you first encountered in Chapter 11.

Nautica maximizes profit by producing the output at which marginal revenue equals marginal cost. In Fig. 14.2, this output is 150 jackets a day. Nautica charges the maximum price that buyers are willing to pay for this quantity, which is determined by the demand curve. This price is $190 a jacket. When Nautica produces 150 jackets a day, the firm's average total cost is $140 a jacket, so it makes a short-run economic profit of $7,500 a day ($50 a jacket multiplied by 150 jackets a day). The blue rectangle shows this economic profit.

FIGURE 14.2

Output and Price in Monopolistic Competition

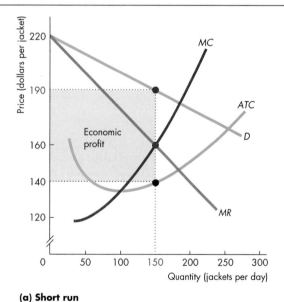

(a) Short run

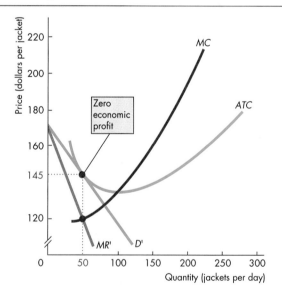

(b) Long run

Part (a) shows the short-run outcome. Profit is maximized by producing 150 jackets per day and selling them for $190 per jacket. Average total cost is $140 per jacket, and the firm makes an economic profit (the blue rectangle) of $7,500 a day.

Economic profit encourages new entrants in the long run, and part (b) shows the long-run outcome. The entry of new

firms decreases each firm's demand and shifts the demand curve and marginal revenue curve leftward. When the demand curve has shifted to *D'*, the marginal revenue curve is *MR'* and the firm is in long-run equilibrium. The output that maximizes profit is 50 jackets a day and the price is $145 per jacket. Average total cost is also $145 per jacket, so economic profit is zero.

So far, the firm in monopolistic competition looks just like a single-price monopoly. It produces the quantity at which marginal revenue equals marginal cost and then charges the highest price that buyers are willing to pay for that quantity, determined by the demand curve. The key difference between monopoly and monopolistic competition lies in what happens in the long run.

Long Run: Zero Economic Profit

There is no restriction on entry in monopolistic competition, so economic profit attracts new entrants. As new firms enter the industry, the firm's demand curve and marginal revenue curve start to shift leftward. At each point in time, the firm maximizes its short-run profit by producing the quantity at which marginal revenue equals marginal cost and by charging the highest price that buyers are willing to pay for this quantity. But as the demand curve shifts leftward, the profit-maximizing quantity and price fall.

Figure 14.2(b) shows the long-run equilibrium. Nautica's demand curve has shifted leftward to D', and its marginal revenue curve has shifted leftward to MR'. Nautica produces 50 jackets a day and sells them at a price of $145 each. At this output level, the firm's average total cost is also $145 a jacket. So Nautica is making zero economic profit.

When all the firms are making zero economic profit, there is no incentive for new firms to enter the industry.

If demand is so low relative to costs that firms are incurring economic losses, exit will occur. As firms leave an industry, the demand for the remaining firm's products increases and their demand curves shift rightward. The exit process ends when all the firms are making zero economic profit.

Monopolistic Competition and Efficiency

When we studied a perfectly competitive industry, we discovered that in some circumstances, such an industry allocates resources efficiently. A key feature of efficiency is that marginal benefit equals marginal cost. Price measures marginal benefit, so efficiency requires price to equal marginal cost. When we studied monopoly, we discovered that such a firm creates an inefficient use of resources because it restricts output to a level at which price exceeds marginal cost. In such

a situation, the marginal benefit exceeds marginal cost and production is less than its efficient level.

Monopolistic competition shares this feature of monopoly. Even though there is zero economic profit in long-run equilibrium, the monopolistically competitive industry produces an output at which price equals average total cost but exceeds marginal cost. This outcome means that firms in monopolistic competition always have excess capacity in long-run equilibrium.

Excess Capacity A firm's **capacity output** is the output at which average total cost is a minimum—the output at the minimum of the U-shaped ATC curve. This output is 100 jackets a day in Fig. 14.3. Firms in monopolistic competition always have *excess capacity*, in the long run. In Fig. 14.3, Nautica produces 50 jackets a day and has excess capacity of 50 jackets a day. That is, Nautica produces a smaller out-

FIGURE 14.3

Excess Capacity

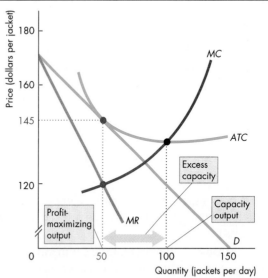

In the long run, entry decreases demand to the point at which the firm makes zero economic profit. Here the firm produces 50 jackets a day. The firm's capacity is the output at which average total cost is a minimum. Here, capacity output is 100 jackets a day. Because the demand curve in monopolistic competition slopes downward, the output that maximizes profit is always less than capacity output in long-run equilibrium. The firm operates with excess capacity in long-run equilibrium.

put than that which minimizes average total cost. Consequently, the consumer pays a price that exceeds minimum average total cost. This result arises from the fact that Nautica faces a downward-sloping demand curve. The demand curve slopes down because of product differentiation, so product differentiation creates excess capacity.

You can see the excess capacity in monopolistic competition all around you. Family restaurants (except for the truly outstanding ones) almost always have some empty tables. You can always get a pizza delivered in less than 30 minutes. It is rare that every pump at a gas station is in use with customers waiting in line. There is always an abundance of realtors ready to help find or sell a home.

These industries are all examples of monopolistic competition. The firms have excess capacity. They could sell more by cutting their prices. But they would then incur economic losses.

Because in monopolistic competition, price exceeds marginal cost, this market structure, like monopoly, is inefficient. The marginal cost of producing one more unit of output is less than the marginal benefit to the consumer, determined by the price the consumer is willing to pay. But the inefficiency of monopolistic competition arises from product differentiation—from product variety. Consumers value variety, but it is achievable only if firms make differentiated products. So the loss in efficiency that occurs in monopolistic competition must be weighed against the gain of greater product variety.

REVIEW QUIZ

▧ How does a firm in monopolistic competition decide how much to produce and at what price to offer its product for sale?
▧ Why can a firm in monopolistic competition earn an economic profit only in the short run?
▧ Is monopolistic competition efficient?
▧ Why do firms in monopolistic competition operate with excess capacity?

You've seen how the firm in monopolistic competition determines its output and price in the short run and the long run when it produces a given product and undertakes a *given* marketing effort. But how does the firm choose its product quality and marketing effort? We'll now study these decisions.

Product Development and Marketing

WHEN WE STUDIED A FIRM'S OUTPUT AND PRICE decision, we supposed that it had already made its product and marketing decisions. We're now going to study these decisions and the impact they have on the firm's output, price, and economic profit.

Innovation and Product Development

To enjoy economic profits, firms in monopolistic competition must be in a state of continuous product development. The reason is that wherever economic profits are earned, imitators emerge and set up business. So to maintain its economic profit, a firm must seek out new products that will provide it with a competitive edge, even if only temporarily. A firm that manages to introduce a new and differentiated variety will temporarily increase the demand for its product and will be able to temporarily increase its price. It will make an economic profit. Eventually, new firms that make close substitutes for the new product will enter and compete away the economic profit arising from this initial advantage. So to restore economic profit, the firm must again innovate.

The decision to innovate is based on the same type of profit-maximizing calculation that you've already studied. Innovation and product development are costly activities but they also bring in additional revenues. The firm must balance the cost and benefit at the margin. At a low level of product development, the marginal revenue from a better product exceeds the marginal cost. When the marginal dollar spent on product development brings in a dollar of revenue, the firm is spending the profit-maximizing amount on product development.

For example, when Eidos Interactive released Tomb Raider III, it was probably not the best game that Eidos could have created. Rather, it was the game that balanced the marginal benefit and willingness of the consumer to pay for further game enhancements against the marginal cost of these enhancements.

Efficiency and Product Innovation Is product innovation an efficient activity? Does it benefit the consumer? There are two views about these questions. One view is that monopolistic competition brings to market many improved products that bring great benefits to the consumer. Clothing, kitchen and other household appliances, computers, computer programs, cars, and many other products keep getting better every year and the consumer benefits from these improved products.

But many so-called improvements amount to little more than changing the appearance of a product. And sometimes, the improvement is restricted to a different look in the packaging. In these cases, there is little objective benefit to the consumer.

But regardless of whether a product improvement is real or imagined, its value to the consumer is its marginal benefit, which equals the amount the consumer is willing to pay. In other words, the value of product improvements is the increase in price that the consumer is willing to pay. The marginal benefit to the producer is marginal revenue, which equals marginal cost. Because price exceeds marginal cost in monopolistic competition, product development is not pushed to its efficient level.

Marketing

Some product differentiation is achieved by designing and developing products that are actually different from those of the other firms. But firms also attempt to create a consumer perception of product differentiation even when actual differences are small. Advertising and packaging are the principal means used by firms to achieve this end. An American Express card is a different product from a Visa card. But the actual differences are not the main ones that American Express emphasizes in its marketing. The deeper message is that if you use an American Express card, you can be like Tiger Woods (or some other high-profile successful person).

Marketing Expenditures   Firms in monopolistic competition incur huge costs in order to persuade buyers to appreciate and value the differences between their own products and those of their competitors. So a large proportion of the prices that we pay cover the cost of selling a good. And this proportion is increasing. Advertising in newspapers and magazines and on radio and television is the main selling cost. But it is not the only one. Selling costs include the cost of shopping malls that look like movie sets; glossy catalogues and brochures; and the salaries, airfares, and hotel bills of salespeople.

A survey conducted by a commercial agency suggests that for cleaning supplies and toys, around 15 percent of the price of an item is spent on advertising. Figure 14.4 shows some estimates for other industries.

For the North American economy as a whole, there are more than 20,000 advertising agencies that employ more than 200,000 people and have sales of $45 billion. But these numbers are only part of the total cost of advertising because firms have their own internal advertising departments, the cost of which can only be guessed.

Advertising expenditures and other selling costs affect the profits of firms in two ways. They increase costs and they change demand. Let's look at these effects.

Selling Costs and Total Costs   Selling costs such as advertising expenditures increase the costs of a monopolistically competitive firm above those of a competitive firm or a monopoly. Advertising costs and other selling costs are fixed costs. They do not vary as total output varies. So, just like fixed produc-

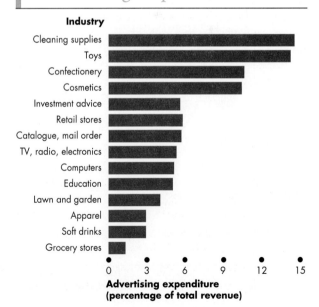

FIGURE 14.4

Advertising Expenditures

Advertising expenditures are a large part of total revenue for producers of cleaning supplies, toys, confectionery, and cosmetics.

Source: Schoenfeld & Associates, Lincolnwood, Illinois, reported at http://www.toolkit.cch.com/text/p03_7006.stm

tion costs, advertising costs per unit decrease as production increases.

Figure 14.5 shows how selling costs and advertising expenditures change a firm's average total cost. The blue curve shows the average total cost of production. The red curve shows the firm's average total cost of production plus advertising. The height of the red area between the two curves shows the average fixed cost of advertising. The *total* cost of advertising is fixed. But the *average* cost of advertising decreases as output increases.

The figure shows that if advertising increases the quantity sold by a large enough amount, it can lower average total cost. For example, if the quantity sold increases from 25 jackets a day with no advertising to 130 jackets a day with advertising, average total cost falls from $170 a jacket to $160 a jacket. The reason is that although the *total* fixed cost has increased, the greater fixed cost is spread over a greater output, so average total cost decreases.

FIGURE 14.5
Selling Costs and Total Cost

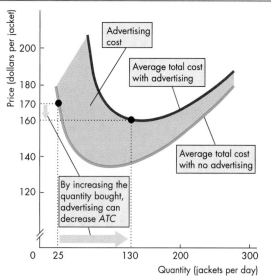

Selling costs such as the cost of advertising are fixed costs. When added to the average total cost of production, these costs increase average total cost (*ATC*) by a greater amount at small outputs than at large outputs. If advertising enables the quantity sold to increase from 25 jackets to 130 jackets a day, it *lowers* average total cost from $170 to $160 a jacket.

Selling Costs and Demand Advertising and other selling efforts change the demand for a firm's product. But how? Does demand increase or does it decrease? The most natural answer is that advertising increases demand. By informing people about the quality of its products or by persuading people to switch from the products of other firms, a firm might expect to increase the demand for its own products.

But all firms in monopolistic competition advertise. And all seek to persuade customers that they have the best deal around. If advertising enables a firm to survive, it might increase the number of firms. And to the extent that it increases the number of firms, it *decreases* the demand faced by any one firm.

Efficiency: The Bottom Line To the extent that selling costs provide consumers with services that they value and with information about the precise nature of the differentiation of products, they enable the consumer to make a better choice. But the opportunity cost of the additional services and information must be weighed against the gain to the consumer.

The bottom line on the question of efficiency of monopolistic competition is ambiguous. In some cases, the gains from extra product variety unquestionably offset the selling costs and the extra cost arising from excess capacity. The tremendous varieties of books and magazines, clothing, food, and drinks are examples of such gains. It is less easy to see the gains from being able to buy brand-name drugs that have a chemical composition identical to that of a generic alternative. But some people do willingly pay more for the brand-name alternative.

REVIEW QUIZ

- What are the two main ways other than by adjusting price in which a firm in monopolistic competition competes with other firms?
- Why might product innovation and development be efficient and why might it be inefficient?
- How do advertising expenditures influence a firm's cost curves? Do they increase or decrease average total cost?
- How do advertising expenditures influence a firm's demand curve? Do they increase or decrease demand?
- Why is it difficult to determine whether monopolistic competition is efficient or inefficient? What is your opinion about the bottom line and why?

Oligopoly

ANOTHER TYPE OF MARKET THAT STANDS between the extremes of perfect competition and monopoly is oligopoly. **Oligopoly** is a market structure in which a small number of firms compete.

In oligopoly, the quantity sold by any one firm depends on that firm's price *and* on the other firms' prices and quantities sold. To see why, suppose you run one of the three gas stations in a small town. If you cut your price and your two competitors don't cut theirs, your sales increase and the sales of the other two firms decrease. With lower sales, the other firms most likely cut their prices too. If they do cut their prices, your sales and profits take a tumble. So before deciding to cut your price, you must predict how the other firms will react and attempt to calculate the effects of those reactions on your own profit.

Several models have been developed to explain the prices and quantities in oligopoly. But no one theory has been found that can explain all the different types of behaviour that we observe in such markets. The models fall into two broad groups: traditional models and game theory models. We'll look at both types, starting with two traditional models.

The Kinked Demand Curve Model

The kinked demand curve model of oligopoly is based on the assumption that each firm believes that:

1. If it raises its price, others will not follow.
2. If it cuts its price, so will the other firms.

Figure 14.6 shows the demand curve (D) that a firm believes describes the demand for its product. The demand curve has a kink at the current price, P, and quantity, Q. A small price rise above P brings a big decrease in the quantity sold. The other firms hold their current price and the firm has the highest price, so it loses market share. Even a large price cut below P brings only a small increase in the quantity demanded. In this case, other firms match the price cut, so the firm gets no price advantage over its competitors.

The kink in the demand curve creates a break in the marginal revenue curve (*MR*). To maximize profit, the firm produces the quantity Q where the marginal cost curve passes through the gap *ab* in the marginal revenue curve. If marginal cost fluctuates between *a* and *b*, like the marginal cost curves MC_0 and MC_1,

FIGURE 14.6

The Kinked Demand Curve Model

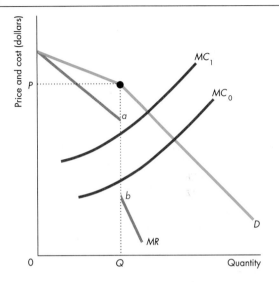

The price in an oligopoly market is P. Each firm believes the demand curve for its product is D. A small price rise above P brings a big decrease in the quantity sold because other firms do not raise their prices. Even a big price cut below P brings only a small increase in the quantity sold because other firms also cut their prices. Because the demand curve is kinked, the marginal revenue curve, MR, has a break *ab*. Profit is maximized by producing Q. The marginal cost curve passes through the break in the marginal revenue curve. Marginal cost changes inside the range *ab* leave the price and quantity unchanged.

the firm does not change its price or its output. Only if marginal cost fluctuates outside the range *ab* does the firm change its price and output. So the kinked demand curve model predicts that price and quantity are insensitive to small cost changes.

A problem with the kinked demand curve model is that the firms' beliefs about the demand curve are not always correct and firms can figure out that they are not correct. If marginal cost increases by enough to cause the firm to increase its price and if all firms experience the same increase in marginal cost, they all increase their prices together. The firm's beliefs that others will not join it in a price rise is incorrect. A firm that bases its actions on beliefs that are wrong does not maximize profit and might even end up incurring an economic loss.

Dominant Firm Oligopoly

A second traditional model explains a dominant firm oligopoly, which arises when one firm—the dominant firm—has a big cost advantage over the other firms and produces a large part of the industry output. The dominant firm sets the market price and the other firms are price takers. Examples of dominant firm oligopoly are a large gasoline retailer or a big video rental store that dominates its local market.

To see how a dominant firm oligopoly works, suppose that 11 firms operate gas stations in a city. Big-G is the dominant firm. Figure 14.7 shows the market for gas in this city. In part (a), the demand curve D tells us the total quantity of gas demanded in the city at each price. The supply curve S_{10} is the supply curve of the 10 small suppliers.

Part (b) shows the situation facing Big-G. Its marginal cost curve is MC. Big-G's demand curve is XD

and its marginal revenue curve is MR. Big-G's demand curve shows the excess demand not met by the 10 small firms. For example, at a price of $1 a litre, the quantity demanded is 20,000 litres, the quantity supplied by the 10 small firms is 10,000 litres, and the excess quantity demanded is 10,000, measured by the distance ab in both parts of the figure.

To maximize profit, Big-G operates like a monopoly. It sells 10,000 litres a week for a price of $1 a litre (point b). The 10 small firms take the price of $1 a litre. They behave just like firms in perfect competition. The quantity of gas demanded in the entire city at $1 a litre is 20,000 litres, as shown in part (a). Of this amount, Big-G sells 10,000 litres and the 10 small firms each sell 1,000 litres.

The traditional theories of oligopoly do not enable us to understand all oligopoly markets and, in recent years, economists have developed new models based on game theory. Let's now learn about game theory.

FIGURE 14.7

A Dominant Firm Oligopoly

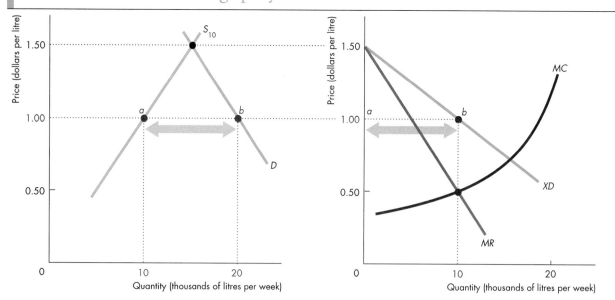

(a) Ten small firms and market demand

(b) Big-G's price and output decision

The demand curve for gas in a city is D in part (a). There are 10 small competitive firms that together have a supply curve of S_{10}. In addition, there is 1 large firm, Big-G, shown in part (b). Big-G faces the demand curve XD, determined as market demand D minus the supply of the other 10 firms S_{10}—the demand that is not satisfied by the small firms. Big-G's mar-

ginal revenue is MR, and marginal cost is MC. Big-G sets its output to maximize profit by equating marginal cost, MC, and marginal revenue, MR. This output is 10,000 litres per week. Big-G can sell this quantity at a price of $1 a litre (point b on XD). The other 10 firms take this price, and each firm sells 1,000 litres per week, point a in part (a).

Game Theory

THE MAIN TOOL THAT ECONOMISTS USE TO analyze *strategic behaviour*—behaviour that takes into account the expected behaviour of others and the mutual recognition of interdependence—is called **game theory**. Game theory was invented by John von Neumann in 1937 and extended by von Neumann and Oskar Morgenstern in 1944. Today, it is one of the major research fields in economics.

Game theory seeks to understand oligopoly as well all other forms of economic, political, social, and even biological rivalries by using a method of analysis specifically designed to understand games of all types, including the familiar games of everyday life. We will begin our study of game theory, and its application to the behaviour of firms, by thinking about familiar games.

What Is a Game?

What is a game? At first thought, the question seems silly. After all, there are many different games. There are ball games and parlour games, games of chance and games of skill. But what is it about all these different activities that make them games? What do all these games have in common? They share three features:

■ Rules
■ Strategies
■ Payoffs

Let's see how these common features of games apply to a game called "the prisoners' dilemma." This game, it turns out, captures some of the essential features of oligopoly, and it gives a good illustration of how game theory works and how it generates predictions.

The Prisoners' Dilemma

Art and Bob have been caught red-handed, stealing a car. Facing airtight cases, they will receive a sentence of 2 years each for their crime. During his interviews with the two prisoners, the Crown attorney begins to suspect that he has stumbled on the two people who were responsible for a multimillion-dollar bank robbery some months earlier. But this is just a suspicion. The Crown attorney has no evidence on which he can convict them of the greater crime unless he can get them to confess. The Crown attorney decides to make the prisoners play a game with the following rules.

Rules Each prisoner (player) is placed in a separate room and cannot communicate with the other player. Each is told that he is suspected of having carried out the bank robbery and that:

If both of them confess to the larger crime, each will receive a sentence of 3 years for both crimes.

If he alone confesses and his accomplice does not, he will receive an even shorter sentence of 1 year while his accomplice will receive a 10-year sentence.

Strategies In game theory, **strategies** are all the possible actions of each player. Art and Bob each have two possible actions:

1. Confess to the bank robbery.
2. Deny having committed the bank robbery.

Payoffs Because there are two players, each with two strategies, there are four possible outcomes:

1. Both confess.
2. Both deny.
3. Art confesses and Bob denies.
4. Bob confesses and Art denies.

Each prisoner can work out exactly what happens to him—his *payoff*—in each of these four situations. We can tabulate the four possible payoffs for each of the prisoners in what is called a payoff matrix for the game. A **payoff matrix** is a table that shows the payoffs for every possible action by each player for every possible action by each other player.

Table 14.1 shows a payoff matrix for Art and Bob. The squares show the payoffs for each prisoner—the red triangle in each square shows Art's and the blue triangle shows Bob's. If both prisoners confess (top left), each gets a prison term of 3 years. If Bob confesses but Art denies (top right), Art gets a 10-year sentence and Bob gets a 1-year sentence. If Art confesses and Bob denies (bottom left), Art gets a 1-year sentence and Bob gets a 10-year sentence. Finally, if both of them deny (bottom right), neither can be convicted of the bank robbery charge but both are sentenced for the car theft—a 2-year sentence.

Equilibrium The equilibrium of a game occurs when each player takes the best possible action given the action of the other players. In the case of the prisoners' dilemma, the equilibrium occurs when Art makes his best choice given Bob's choice and when Bob makes his best choice given Art's choice. Let's find the equilibrium of the prisoners' dilemma game.

First, look at the situation from Art's point of view. If Bob confesses, it pays Art to confess because in that case, he is sentenced to 3 years rather than 10 years. If Bob does not confess, it still pays Art to confess because in that case he receives 1 year rather than 2 years. So Art's best action is to confess.

Second, look at the situation from Bob's point of view. If Art confesses, it pays Bob to confess because in that case, he is sentenced to 3 years rather than 10 years. If Art does not confess, it still pays Bob to confess because in that case he receives 1 year rather than 2 years. So Bob's best action is to confess.

Because each player's best action is to confess, each does confess, each gets a 3-year prison term, and the Crown attorney has solved the bank robbery. This is the equilibrium of the game.

Nash Equilibrium   The equilibrium concept that we have used is called a **Nash equilibrium**; it is so named because it was first proposed by John Nash of Princeton University, who received the Nobel Prize for Economic Science in 1994.

The prisoners' dilemma has a special kind of Nash equilibrium called a dominant strategy equilibrium. A *dominant strategy* is a strategy that is the same regardless of the action taken by the other player. In other words, each player has a unique best action regardless of what the other player does. A **dominant strategy equilibrium** occurs when there is a dominant strategy for each player.

The Dilemma   Now that you have found the outcome to the prisoners' dilemma, you can better see the dilemma. The dilemma arises as each prisoner contemplates the consequences of denying. Each prisoner knows that if both of them deny, they will receive only a 2-year sentence for stealing the car. But neither has any way of knowing that his accomplice will deny. Each poses the following questions: Should I deny and rely on my accomplice to deny so that we will both get only 2 years? Or should I confess in the hope of getting just 1 year (provided that my accomplice denies) knowing that if my accomplice does confess, we will both get 3 years in prison? The dilemma is resolved by finding the equilibrium of the game.

TABLE 14.1

Prisoners' Dilemma Payoff Matrix

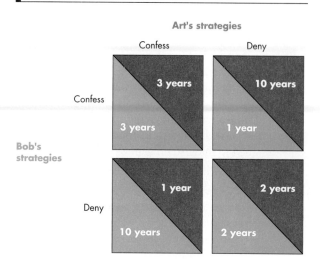

Each square shows the payoffs for the two players, Art and Bob, for each possible pair of actions. In each square, the red triangle shows Art's payoff and the blue triangle shows Bob's. For example, if both confess, the payoffs are in the top left square. The equilibrium of the game is for both players to confess and each gets a 3-year sentence.

A Bad Outcome   For the prisoners, the equilibrium of the game, with each confessing, is not the best outcome. If neither of them confesses, each gets only 2 years for the lesser crime. Isn't there some way in which this better outcome can be achieved? It seems that there is not, because the players cannot communicate with each other. Each player can put himself in the other player's place, and so each player can figure out that there is a dominant strategy for each of them. The prisoners are indeed in a dilemma. Each knows that he can serve 2 years only if he can trust the other to deny. But each prisoner also knows that it is not in the best interest of the other to deny. So each prisoner knows that he must confess, thereby delivering a bad outcome for both.

Let's now see how we can use the ideas we've just developed to understand a host of economic situations such as price fixing, price wars, and other aspects of the behaviour of firms in oligopoly.

An Oligopoly Price-Fixing Game

To UNDERSTAND HOW OLIGOPOLIES FIX PRICES, we're going to study a special case of oligopoly called duopoly. **Duopoly** is a market structure in which only two producers compete. You can probably find some examples of duopoly in your city. Many cities have only two local newspapers, two taxi companies, two car rental firms, two copy centres, or two campus bookstores. But the main reason for studying duopoly is not its realism. We study duopoly because it captures the essence of oligopoly and yet is more revealing.

Our goal is to predict the prices charged and the quantities produced by the two firms. To pursue that goal, we're going to study the duopoly game.

We will suppose that the two firms, Trick and Gear, enter into a collusive agreement. A **collusive agreement** is an agreement between two (or more) producers to restrict output in order to raise prices and profits. Such an agreement is illegal and is undertaken in secret. A group of firms that has entered into a collusive agreement to restrict output and increase prices and profits is called a **cartel**. The strategies that firms in a cartel can pursue are to:

- Comply
- Cheat

Complying simply means sticking to the agreement. Cheating means breaking the agreement in a manner designed to benefit the cheating firm.

Because each firm has two strategies, there are four possible combinations of actions for the two firms:

- Both firms comply.
- Both firms cheat.
- Trick complies and Gear cheats.
- Gear complies and Trick cheats.

We'll begin by describing the cost and demand conditions in a duopoly industry.

Cost and Demand Conditions

Trick and Gear face identical costs and Fig. 14.8(a) shows their average total cost curve (*ATC*) and marginal cost curve (*MC*). Figure 14.8(b) shows the market demand curve for switchgears (*D*). Each firm produces an identical product, so one firm's switchgear is a perfect substitute for the other's. The price of each firm's product, therefore, is identical. And the higher the price, the smaller is the quantity demanded.

This industry is a natural duopoly. Two firms can produce this good at a lower cost than either one firm or three firms can. For each firm, average total cost is at its minimum when production is 3,000 units a week. And when price equals minimum average total cost, the total quantity demanded is 6,000 units a week. So two firms can just supply that quantity.

FIGURE 14.8

Costs and Demand

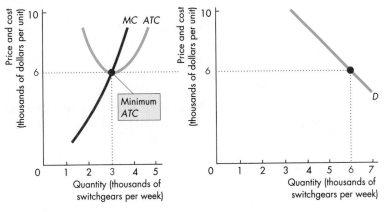

(a) Individual firm   **(b) Industry**

The average total cost curve for each firm is *ATC*, and the marginal cost curve is *MC* (part a). Minimum average total cost is at $6,000 a unit and it occurs at a production of 3,000 units a week. Part (b) shows the industry demand curve. At a price of $6,000, the quantity demanded is 6,000 units per week. The two firms can produce this output at the lowest possible average cost. If the market had one firm, it would be profitable for another to enter. If the market had three firms, one would exit. There is room for just two firms in this industry. It is a natural duopoly.

Colluding to Maximize Profits

Let's begin by working out the payoffs to the two firms if they collude to make the maximum industry profit by acting like a monopoly. The calculations that the two firms will perform are exactly the same calculations that a monopoly performs. (You can refresh your memory of these calculations by looking at Chapter 13, pp. 272–273.) The only thing that the duopolies must do that is additional to what a monopolist must do is to agree on how much of the total output each of them will produce.

Figure 14.9 shows the price and quantity that maximize industry profit for the duopolies. Part (a) shows the situation for each firm, and part (b) shows the situation for the industry as a whole. The curve labelled MR is the industry marginal revenue curve. This marginal revenue curve is exactly like that of a single-price monopoly. The curve labelled MC_I is the industry marginal cost curve if each firm produces the same level of output. That curve is constructed by adding together the outputs of the two firms at each level of marginal cost. That is, at each level of marginal cost, industry output is twice as much as the output of each individual firm. Thus the curve MC_I in part (b) is twice as far to the right as the curve MC in part (a).

To maximize industry profit, the duopolists agree to restrict output to the rate that makes the industry marginal cost and marginal revenue equal. That output rate, as shown in part (b), is 4,000 units a week.

The highest price for which the 4,000 switchgears can be sold is $9,000 each. This is the price that Trick and Gear agree to charge.

To hold the price at $9,000 a unit, production must be not exceed 4,000 units a week. So Trick and Gear must agree on production levels for each of them that totals 4,000 units a week. Let's suppose that they agree to split the market equally so that each firm produces 2,000 switchgears a week. Because the firms are identical, this division is the most likely.

The average total cost (ATC) of producing 2,000 switchgears a week is $8,000, so the profit per unit is $1,000 and economic profit is $2 million (2,000 units × $1,000 per unit). The economic profit of each firm is represented by the blue rectangle in Fig. 14.9(a).

We have just described one possible outcome for a duopoly game: The two firms collude to produce the monopoly profit-maximizing output and divide that output equally between themselves. From the industry point of view, this solution is identical to a monopoly. A duopoly that operates in this way is indistinguishable from a monopoly. The economic profit that is made by a monopoly is the maximum total profit that can be made by colluding duopolies.

But with price greater than marginal cost, either firm might think of trying to increase profit by cheating on the agreement and producing more than the agreed amount. Let's see what happens if one of the firms does cheat in this way.

FIGURE 14.9

Colluding to Make Monopoly Profits

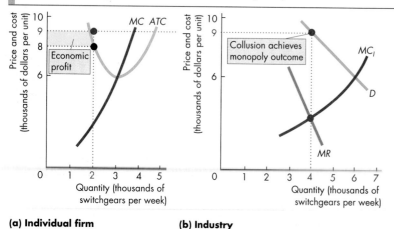

(a) Individual firm   **(b) Industry**

The industry marginal cost curve, MC_I (part b) is the horizontal sum of the two firms' marginal cost curves, MC (part a). The industry marginal revenue curve is MR. To maximize profit, the firms produce 4,000 units a week (the quantity at which marginal revenue equals marginal cost). They sell that output for $9,000 a unit. Each firm produces 2,000 units a week. Average total cost is $8,000 a unit, so each firm makes an economic profit of $2 million (blue rectangle)— 2,000 units multiplied by $1,000 profit a unit.

One Firm Cheats on a Collusive Agreement

To set the stage for cheating on their agreement, Trick convinces Gear that demand has decreased and that it cannot sell 2,000 units a week. Trick tells Gear that it plans to cut its price in order to sell the agreed 2,000 units each week. Because the two firms produce an identical product, Gear matches Trick's price cut but still produces only 2,000 units a week.

In fact, there has been no decrease in demand. Trick plans to increase output, which it knows will lower the price, and Trick wants to ensure that Gear's output remains at the agreed level.

Figure 14.10 illustrates the consequences of Trick cheating. Suppose that Trick, the cheat, increases output to 3,000 units a week (part b). If Gear, the complier, sticks to the agreement to produce only 2,000 units a week (part a), total output is 5,000 a week, and given demand (part c), the price falls to $7,500 a unit.

Gear continues to produce 2,000 units a week at a cost of $8,000 a unit and incurs a loss of $500 a unit or $1 million a week. This economic loss is represented by the red rectangle in part (a). Trick produces 3,000 units a week at an average total cost of

$6,000. With a price of $7,500, Trick makes a profit of $1,500 a unit and therefore an economic profit of $4.5 million. This economic profit is the blue rectangle in part (b).

We've now described a second possible outcome for the duopoly game: One of the firms cheats on the collusive agreement. In this case, the industry output is larger than the monopoly output and the industry price is lower than the monopoly price. The total economic profit made by the industry is less than the monopoly's economic profit. Trick (the cheat) makes an economic profit of $4.5 million, and Gear (the complier) incurs an economic loss of $1 million. The industry makes an economic profit of $3.5 million, which is $0.5 million less than the economic profit a monopoly would make. But the profit is distributed unevenly. Trick makes a bigger economic profit while Gear incurs an economic loss.

A similar outcome would arise if Gear cheated and Trick complied with the agreement. The industry profit and price would be the same, but in this case Gear (the cheat) would make an economic profit of $4.5 million and Trick (the complier) would incur an economic loss of $1 million.

Let's next see what happens if both firms cheat.

FIGURE 14.10

One Firm Cheats

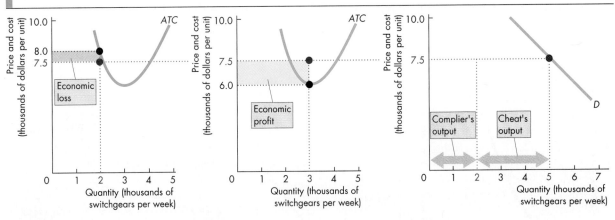

(a) Complier

(b) Cheat

(c) Industry

One firm, shown in part (a), complies with the agreement and produces 2,000 units. The other firm, shown in part (b), cheats on the agreement and increases its output to 3,000 units. Given the market demand curve, shown in part (c), and with a total production of 5,000 units a week, the price falls to

$7,500. At this price, the complier in part (a) incurs an economic loss of $1 million ($500 per unit × 2,000 units) shown by the red rectangle. In part (b), the cheat makes an economic profit of $4.5 million ($1,500 per unit × 3,000 units), shown as the blue rectangle.

Both Firms Cheat

Suppose that instead of just one firm cheating on the collusive agreement, both firms cheat. In particular, suppose that each firm behaves in exactly the same way as the cheating firm that we have just analyzed. Each tells the other that it is unable to sell its output at the going price and that it plans to cut its price. But because both firms cheat, each will propose a successively lower price. As long as price exceeds marginal cost, each firm has an incentive to increase its production—to cheat. Only when price equals marginal cost is there no further incentive to cheat. This situation arises when the price has reached $6,000. At this price, marginal cost equals price. Also, price equals minimum average total cost. At a price less than $6,000, each firm incurs an economic loss. At a price of $6,000, each firm covers all its costs and makes zero economic profit (makes normal profit). Also, at a price of $6,000, each firm wants to produce 3,000 units a week, so the industry output is 6,000 units a week. Given the demand conditions, 6,000 units can be sold at a price of $6,000 each.

Figure 14.11 illustrates the situation just described. Each firm, shown in part (a), produces 3,000 units a week, and at this output level average total cost is a minimum ($6,000 per unit). The market as a whole, shown in part (b), operates at the point at which the demand curve (D) intersects the industry marginal cost curve. This marginal cost curve is constructed as the horizontal sum of the

marginal cost curves of the two firms. Each firm has lowered its price and increased its output to try to gain an advantage over the other firm. Each has pushed this process as far as it can without incurring an economic loss.

We have now described a third possible outcome of this duopoly game: Both firms cheat. If both firms cheat on the collusive agreement, the output of each firm is 3,000 units a week and the price is $6,000. Each firm makes zero economic profit.

The Payoff Matrix

Now that we have described the strategies and payoffs in the duopoly game, let's summarize the strategies and the payoffs in the form of the game's payoff matrix and then calculate the equilibrium.

Table 14.2 sets out the payoff matrix for this game. It is constructed in exactly the same way as the payoff matrix for the prisoners' dilemma in Table 14.1. The squares show the payoffs for the two firms—Gear and Trick. In this case, the payoffs are profits. (In the case of the prisoners' dilemma, the payoffs were losses.)

The table shows that if both firms cheat (top left), they achieve the perfectly competitive outcome—each firm makes zero economic profit. If both firms comply (bottom right), the industry makes the monopoly profit and each firm earns an economic profit of $2 million. The top right and bottom left squares show what happens if one firm

---

FIGURE 14.11

Both Firms Cheat

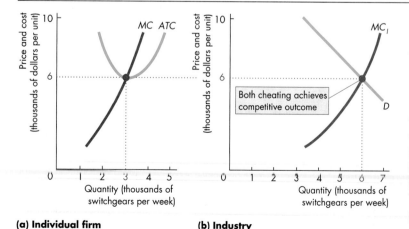

(a) Individual firm　　　　**(b) Industry**

If both firms cheat by increasing production, the collusive agreement collapses. The limit to the collapse is the competitive equilibrium. Neither firm will cut price below $6,000, (minimum average total cost) for to do so results in losses. In part (a), both firms produce 3,000 units a week at an average total cost of $6,000 a unit. In part (b), with a total production of 6,000 units, the price falls to $6,000. Each firm now makes zero economic profit because price equals average total cost. This output and price are the ones that would prevail in a competitive industry.

TABLE 14.2
Duopoly Payoff Matrix

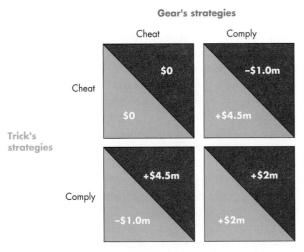

Each square shows the payoffs from a pair of actions. For example, if both firms comply with the collusive agreement, the payoffs are recorded in the bottom right square. The red triangle shows Gear's payoff, and the blue triangle shows Trick's. The equilibrium is a Nash equilibrium in which both firms cheat.

cheats while the other complies. The firm that cheats makes an economic profit of $4.5 million, and the firm that complies incurs a loss of $1 million.

This duopoly game is like the prisoners' dilemma that we examined earlier in this chapter; it is a duopolists' dilemma.

Equilibrium of the Duopolists' Dilemma

What do the firms do? Do they comply or cheat? To answer these questions, we must find the equilibrium of the duopoly dilemma.

Look at things from Gear's point of view. Gear reasons as follows: Suppose that Trick cheats. If I comply, I will incur an economic loss of $1 million. If I also cheat, I will make zero economic profit. Zero is better than *minus* $1 million, so I'm better off if I cheat. Now suppose Trick complies. If I cheat, I will make an economic profit of $4.5 million, and if I comply, I will make an economic profit of $2 mil-

lion. A $4.5 million profit is better than a $2 million profit, so I'm better off if I cheat. So regardless of whether Trick cheats or complies, it pays Gear to cheat. Cheating is Gear's dominant strategy.

Trick comes to the same conclusion as Gear because the two firms face an identical situation. So both firms cheat. The equilibrium of the duopoly game is that both firms cheat. And although the industry has only two firms, the price and quantity are the same as in a competitive industry and each firm makes zero economic profit.

Although we have done this analysis for only two firms, it would not make any difference (other than to increase the amount of arithmetic) if we were to play the game with three, four, or more firms. In other words, although we have analyzed duopoly, the game theory approach can also be used to analyze oligopoly. The analysis of oligopoly is much harder, but the essential ideas that we have learned also apply to oligopoly.

Repeated Games

The games we've studied are played just once. In contrast, most real-world games get played repeatedly. This fact suggests that real-world duopolies might find some way of learning to cooperate so that their efforts to collude are more effective.

If a game is played repeatedly, one player has the opportunity to penalize the other player for previous "bad" behaviour. If Gear cheats this week, perhaps Trick will cheat next week. Before Gear cheats this week, won't it take account of the possibility of Trick cheating next week? What is the equilibrium of this more complicated prisoners' dilemma game when it is repeated indefinitely?

Actually, there is more than one possibility. One is the Nash equilibrium that we have just analyzed. Both players cheat and each makes zero economic profit forever. In such a situation, it will never pay one of the players to start complying unilaterally; because to do so would result in a loss for that player and a profit for the other. The price and quantity remain at the competitive levels forever. But another equilibrium, called a cooperative equilibrium, is possible. A **cooperative equilibrium** is an equilibrium in which the players make and share the monopoly profit.

A cooperative equilibrium may occur if each player knows that the other player will punish cheating. There are two extremes of punishment. The smallest penalty that one player can impose on the other is what is called "tit for tat." A *tit-for-tat strategy* is one in which a player cooperates in the current period if the other player cooperated in the previous period but cheats in the current period if the other player cheated in the previous period. The most severe form of punishment that one player can impose on the other arises in what is called a trigger strategy. A *trigger strategy* is one in which a player cooperates if the other player cooperates but plays the Nash equilibrium strategy forever thereafter if the other player cheats.

In the duopoly game between Gear and Trick, a tit-for-tat strategy keeps both players cooperating and earning monopoly profits. Let's see why.

If both firms stick to the collusive agreement in period 1, each makes an economic profit of $2 million. Suppose that Trick contemplates cheating in period 2. The cheating produces a quick $4.5 million economic profit and inflicts a $1 million economic loss on Gear. Adding up the profits over two periods of play, Trick comes out ahead by cheating ($6.5 million compared with $4 million if it did not cheat). The next period, Gear punishes Trick with its tit-for-tat response and cheats. But Trick must cooperate to induce Gear to cooperate again in period 4. Gear now makes an economic profit of $4.5 million and Trick incurs an economic loss of $1 million. Adding up the profits over three periods of play, Trick would have made more profit by cooperating. In that case, its economic profit would have been $6 million compared with $5.5 million from cheating and generating Gear's tit-for-tat response.

What is true for Trick is also true for Gear. Because each firm makes a larger profit by sticking with the collusive agreement, both firms do so and the monopoly price, quantity, and profit prevail.

In reality, whether a cartel works like a one-play game or a repeated game depends primarily on the number of players and the ease of detecting and punishing cheating. The larger the number of players, the harder it is to maintain a cartel.

Games and Price Wars

The theory of price and output determination under duopoly can help us understand real-world behaviour and, in particular, price wars. Some price wars can be interpreted as the implementation of a tit-for-tat strategy. We've seen that with a tit-for-tat strategy in place, firms have an incentive to stick to the monop-

oly price. But fluctuations in demand lead to fluctuations in the monopoly price, and sometimes, when the price changes, it might seem to one of the firms that the price has fallen because the other has cheated. In this case, a price war will break out. The price war will end only when each firm has satisfied itself that the other is ready to cooperate again. There will be cycles of price wars and the restoration of collusive agreements. Fluctuations in the world price of oil can be interpreted in this way.

Some price wars arise from the entry of a small number of firms into an industry that had previously been a monopoly. Although the industry has a small number of firms, the firms are in a prisoners' dilemma, and they cannot impose effective penalties for price cutting. The behaviour of prices and outputs in the computer chip industry during 1995 and 1996 can be explained in this way. Until 1995, the market for Pentium chips for IBM-compatible computers was dominated by one firm, Intel Corporation, which was able to make maximum economic profit by producing the quantity of chips at which marginal cost equalled marginal revenue. The price of Intel's chips was set to ensure that the quantity demanded equalled the quantity produced. Then in 1995 and 1996, with the entry of a small number of new firms, the industry became an oligopoly. If the firms had maintained Intel's price and shared the market, together they could have made economic profits equal to Intel's profit. But the firms were in a prisoners' dilemma. So prices tumbled closer to competitive levels.

R E V I E W   Q U I Z

■ Why does a collusive agreement to restrict output and raise price create a game like the prisoners' dilemma?

■ What creates an incentive for firms in a collusive agreement to cheat and increase production?

■ What is the equilibrium strategy for each firm in a prisoners' dilemma and why do the firms not collude?

■ If a prisoners' dilemma game is played repeatedly, what punishment strategies might the players employ and how does playing the game repeatedly change the equilibrium?

The game theory approach can be extended to deal with a much wider range of choices that firms face. Let's look at some other oligopoly games.

Other Oligopoly Games

FIRMS MUST DECIDE WHETHER TO MOUNT expensive advertising campaigns; whether to modify their product; whether to make their product more reliable (the more reliable a product, usually, the more expensive it is to produce but the more are people willing to pay for it); whether to price discriminate and, if so, among which groups of customers and to what degree; whether to undertake a large research and development (R&D) effort aimed at lowering production costs; or whether to enter or leave an industry. All of these choices can be analyzed by using game theory. The basic method that you have studied can be applied to these problems by working out the payoff for each of the alternative strategies and then finding the equilibrium of the game.

We'll look at two examples: first an R&D game and second an entry-deterrence game.

An R&D Game

Disposable diapers were first marketed in 1966. The two market leaders from the start of this industry have been Procter & Gamble (maker of Pampers) and Kimberly-Clark (maker of Huggies). Procter & Gamble has about 40 percent of the total market, and Kimberly-Clark has about 33 percent. When the disposable diaper was first introduced in 1966, it had to be cost-effective in competition with reusable, laundered diapers. A costly research and development effort resulted in the development of machines that could make disposable diapers at a low enough cost to achieve that initial competitive edge. But as the industry has matured, a large number of firms have tried to get into the business and take market share away from the two industry leaders, and the industry leaders themselves have battled each other to maintain or increase their own market share.

During the early 1990s, Kimberly-Clark was the first to introduce Velcro closures. And in 1996, Procter & Gamble was the first to introduce "breathable" diapers into the North American market. The key to success in this industry (in any industry) is designing products that people value highly relative to the cost of producing them. The firm that develops the most highly valued product and also develops the least-cost technology for producing it gains a competitive edge, undercutting the rest of the market, increasing its market share, and increasing its

profit. But the research and development effort that must be undertaken to achieve product improvements and cost reductions is itself costly. This cost of research and development must be deducted from the profit resulting from the increased market share that lower costs achieve. If no firm does R&D, every firm can be better off, but if one firm initiates the R&D activity, all must follow.

Each firm is in a research and development dilemma situation that is similar to the game played by Art and Bob. Although the two firms play an ongoing game against each other, it has more in common with the one-play game than a repeated game. The reason is that research and development is a long-term process. Effort is repeated, but payoffs occur only infrequently and with uncertainty.

Table 14.3 illustrates the dilemma (with hypothetical numbers) for the R&D game that Kimberly-Clark and Procter & Gamble are playing. Each firm

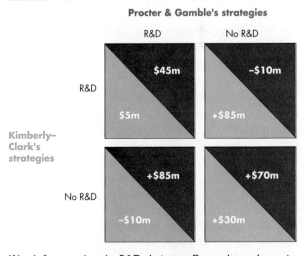

Procter & Gamble's strategies

	R&D	No R&D
R&D	$45m / $5m	−$10m / +$85m
No R&D	+$85m / −$10m	+$70m / +$30m

Kimberly-Clark's strategies

If both firms undertake R&D, their payoffs are those shown in the top left square. If neither firm undertakes R&D, their payoffs are in the bottom right square. When one firm undertakes R&D and the other one does not, their payoffs are in the top right and bottom left squares. The red triangle shows Procter & Gamble's payoff, and the blue triangle shows Kimberly-Clark's. The dominant strategy equilibrium for this game is for both firms to undertake R&D. The structure of this game is the same as that of the prisoners' dilemma.

has two strategies: to spend $25 million a year on R&D or to spend nothing on R&D. If neither firm spends on R&D, they make a joint profit of $100 million: $30 million for Kimberly-Clark and $70 million for Procter & Gamble (bottom right square of the payoff matrix). If each firm conducts R&D, market shares are maintained but each firm's profit is lower by the amount spent on R&D (top left square of the payoff matrix). If Kimberly-Clark pays for R&D but Procter & Gamble does not, Kimberly-Clark gains a large part of Procter & Gamble's market. Kimberly-Clark profits, and Procter & Gamble loses (top right square of the payoff matrix). Finally, if Procter & Gamble conducts R&D and Kimberly-Clark does not, Procter & Gamble gains market share from Kimberly-Clark, increasing its profit, while Kimberly-Clark incurs a loss (bottom left square).

Confronted with the payoff matrix in Table 14.3, the two firms calculate their best strategies. Kimberly-Clark reasons as follows: If Procter & Gamble does not undertake R&D, we will make $85 million if we do and $30 million if we do not; so it pays us to do R&D. If Procter & Gamble conducts R&D, we will lose $10 million if we don't and make $5 million if we do. Again, R&D pays off. Thus conducting R&D is a dominant strategy for Kimberly-Clark. It pays, regardless of Procter & Gamble's decision.

Procter & Gamble reasons similarly: If Kimberly-Clark does not undertake R&D, we will make $70 million if we follow suit and $85 million if we conduct R&D. It therefore pays to conduct R&D. If Kimberly-Clark does undertake R&D, we will make $45 million by doing the same and lose $10 million by not doing R&D. Again, it pays us to conduct R&D. So for Procter & Gamble, R&D is also a dominant strategy.

Because R&D is a dominant strategy for both players, it is the Nash equilibrium. The outcome of this game is that both firms conduct R&D. They make less profit than they would if they could collude to achieve the cooperative outcome of no R&D.

The real-world situation has more players than Kimberly-Clark and Procter & Gamble. There are a large number of other firms sharing a small portion of the market, all of them ready to eat into the market share of Procter & Gamble and Kimberly-Clark. So the R&D effort by these two firms not only serves the purpose of maintaining shares in their own battle, but also helps to keep barriers to entry high enough to preserve their joint market share.

Let's now study an entry deterrence game in which a firm tries to prevent other firms from entering an industry. Such a game is played in a type of market called a contestable market.

Contestable Markets

A **contestable market** is a market in which one firm (or a small number of firms) operates but in which both entry and exit are free, so that the firm (or firms) in the market faces competition from *potential* entrants. Examples of contestable markets are routes served by airlines and by barge companies that operate on the major waterways. These markets are contestable because even though only one or a few firms actually operate on a particular air route or river, other firms could enter those markets if an opportunity for economic profit arose and could exit those markets if the opportunity for economic profit disappeared. The potential entrance prevents the firm (or few firms) from making an economic profit.

If the concentration ratio is used to determine the degree of competition, a contestable market appears to be uncompetitive. But a contestable market behaves as if it were perfectly competitive. To see why, let's look at a game that we'll call an entry-deterrence game.

Entry-Deterrence Game

In the entry-deterrence game we'll study, there are two players. One player is Agile Air, the only firm operating on a particular route. The other player is Wanabe Inc., a potential entrant that is making a normal profit in its current business. Agile Air must play first and can't react to Wanabe. Agile may set its price at the monopoly level or at the competitive level. When Agile has made its price decision, Wanabe decides whether to enter and undercut Agile's price or not to enter.

Table 14.4 shows the payoffs for the two firms. If Agile sets the monopoly price and Wanabe enters and undercuts Agile's price, Wanabe makes an economic profit and Agile incurs an economic loss. If Agile sets the monopoly price and Wanabe does not enter, Agile makes a monopoly profit and Wanabe earns normal profit. So if Agile sets a monopoly price, Wanabe enters. If Agile sets a competitive price and Wanabe enters and undercuts Agile's price, both firms incur an economic loss. But if Agile sets a competitive price and Wanabe does not enter, both firms earn a normal profit.

TABLE 14.4

TABLE 14.4
Agile Versus Wanabe: An Entry-Deterrence Game

Agile's Only Play
(Agile must set its price before Wanabe plays and cannot react to Wanabe.)

Agile is the only firm in a contestable market. Agile must play first and can't react to Wanabe. If Agile sets the monopoly price, Wanabe earns an economic profit by entering and undercutting Agile's price or a normal profit by not entering. So if Agile sets the price at the monopoly level, Wanabe enters. If Agile sets the competitive price, Wanabe earns a normal profit if it does not enter or incurs an economic loss if it does enter. In this case, Wanabe will not enter. The Nash equilibrium of this game is for Agile to set the competitive price, for Wanabe not to enter, and for both firms to make normal profit.

The Nash equilibrium for this game is a competitive price at which Agile Air earns a normal profit and Wanabe does not enter. If Agile raised the price to the monopoly level, Wanabe would enter and by undercutting Agile's price would take all the business, leaving Agile with an economic loss equal to total cost. Agile avoids this outcome by setting a competitive price and deterring Wanabe from entering.

Limit Pricing The practice of charging a price below the monopoly profit-maximizing price and producing a quantity greater than that at which marginal revenue equals marginal cost in order to deter entry is called **limit pricing**. The game that we've just studied

is an example of limit pricing but the practice is more general. For example, a firm can use limit pricing to try to convince potential entrants that its own costs are so low that new entrants will incur an economic loss if they enter the industry. To see how this works, let's go back to Agile and Wanabe.

Wanabe knows the current market price but does not know Agile's costs and profit. It can infer those costs though. Suppose Wanabe believes that marginal revenue is 50 percent of price. If the price is $100, then Wanabe estimates that marginal revenue is $50. Wanabe might assume that Agile is maximizing profit by setting marginal revenue equal to marginal cost. Given this assumption, Wanabe estimates Agile's marginal cost to be $50. If Wanabe's marginal cost is greater than $50, it can't compete with Agile, so it will drop the idea of entering this industry. But if its marginal cost is less than $50, it might be able to enter the industry and also to drive Agile out.

Recognizing that Wanabe (and other potential entrants) reason in this way, Agile might decide to use limit pricing to send a false but possibly believable signal to them. It might cut its price to (say) $80 to make Wanabe believe that its marginal cost is only $40 (50 percent of $80). The lower Wanabe believes Agile's marginal cost to be, the less likely is Wanabe to enter. The strategic use of limit pricing makes it possible, in some situations, for a firm (or group of firms) to maintain a monopoly or collusive oligopoly and limit entry.

◆ The two market structures you've studied in this chapter—monopolistic competition and oligopoly—are the most common ones you encounter in real-world markets. *Reading Between the Lines* on pp. 310–311 shows you monopolistic competition in action in the Canadian vacation travel market.

A key element in our study of markets for goods and services is the behaviour of firms' costs. Costs are determined by technology and by the prices of productive resources. We have treated resource prices as given. We are now going to see how resource prices are themselves determined. Resource prices interact with the goods market that we have just studied in two ways. First, they determine the firm's production costs. Second, they determine household incomes and therefore influence the demand for goods and services. Resource prices also affect the distribution of income. We study each of these interactions in the next three chapters.

Monopolistic Competition in the Vacation Travel Market

NATIONAL POST, AUGUST 18, 1999

Tour companies hit by overcapacity in Canada

By SCHEHERAZADE DANESHKHU
AND EDWARD ALDEN

The cold climes of Canada have left Airtours and First Choice, the British-based package-holiday companies, hot and bothered recently.

Airtours said late last week it was looking at all the options for its North American operations after deepening losses in Canada. First Choice also recently reported losses in Canada for the first time in many years after one of the worst winters in the Canadian tour operating industry.

"It's a simple problem," said Tim Byrne, Airtours' finance director. "There is too much capacity."

Winter is high season in Canada, when people fly south to escape the chill, and the attractions of this counter-cyclical market for British tour operators are clear.

They can base some of their aircraft in Canada instead of leaving them idle in the winter. Peter Long, managing-director of First Choice, says that because Canadians travel in the winter, British tour operators can contract beds with

hotels year round and not just during the summer, thereby securing more favourable terms. ...

In 1995, for example, First Choice made an operating profit of £7.9-million ($18.7-million) in Canada and losses of £19.9-million in Britain.

First Choice, which entered the market before Airtours, says its Canadian operation is core to the company and it has no intention of selling it. ...

Airline overcapacity in the Canadian market last winter led to deep discounting on flights to such traditional holiday destinations as Florida, Hawaii and California.

The three largest charter operators are Air Transat, which also operates its own package tour company, Canada 3000 and Royal Aviation. ...

The problem of overcapacity is being addressed for this winter. Air Transat has taken two aircraft from its fleet; First Choice says it will take out its three aircraft and Skyservice, a smaller charter that flies exclusively for Airtours' Sunquest, has taken out another.

Essence of the Story

■ Airtours and First Choice are participants in the Canadian winter tour market providing holidays in southern climates.

■ Both companies recorded losses in Canada in 1998.

■ This was the first loss in many years for First Choice.

■ Prices in 1998 for flights to Florida, Hawaii, and California were lower than in previous years.

■ Several tour companies will be flying fewer planes in 1999.

Economic Analysis

- The tour industry in Canada is an example of monopolistic competition.

- Figure 1 shows the average total cost curve, *ATC*, marginal cost curve, *MC*, demand curve, *D*, and marginal revenue curve, *MR*, of First Choice in 1995.

- First Choice maximizes profit by selling Q_0 vacations at a price of P_0. Its average total cost is C_0 and the blue rectangle shows First Choice's economic profit.

- Because First Choice and other firms were profitable, entry occurred.

- By 1998, the demand curve for First Choice vacations had shifted leftward to D' and the marginal revenue curve had shifted to MR' in Fig. 2.

- When the demand for First Choice vacations decreases, there is no change in the firm's cost. First Choice now maximizes profit by selling Q_1 vacations at a price of P_1. Its average total cost is C_1.

- But because C_1 exceeds P_1, First Choice now incurs an economic loss.

- First Choice now cuts costs by decreasing the size of its fleet of aircraft.

- Figure 3 shows the effects of the new smaller aircraft fleet on cost, output, price, and profit.

- The average total cost curve shifts downward to ATC_1 and the marginal cost curve shifts downward to MC_1. With lower costs but no change in demand, First Choice expands output to Q_2 vacations a year. Average total cost and price are equal ($C_2 = P_2$) and the firm makes normal profit.

- The industry is in long-run equilibrium.

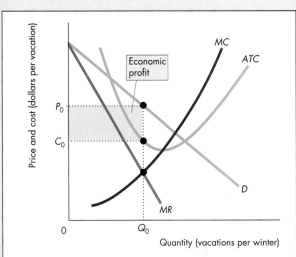

Figure 1 First Choice in 1995

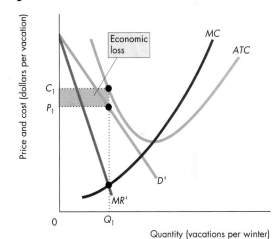

Figure 2 First Choice in 1998

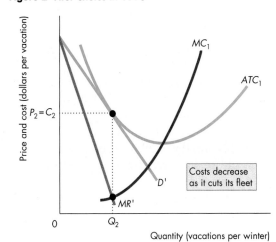

Figure 3 First Choice grounds some aircraft

311

SUMMARY

Key Points

Monopolistic Competition (pp. 290–291)

▨ Monopolistic competition occurs when a large number of firms compete with each other on product quality, price, and marketing.

Output and Price in Monopolistic Competition (pp. 292–294)

▨ Firms in monopolistic competition face downward-sloping demand curves and produce the quantity at which marginal revenue equals marginal cost.

▨ Entry and exit result in zero economic profit and excess capacity in long-run equilibrium.

Product Development and Marketing (pp. 294–296)

▨ Firms in monopolistic competition innovate and develop new products to maintain economic profit.

▨ Advertising expenditures increase total cost but they might lower average total cost if they increase the quantity sold by enough.

▨ Advertising expenditures might increase demand but they might also decrease the demand facing a firm by increasing competition.

▨ Whether monopolistic competition is inefficient depends on the value we place on product variety.

Oligopoly (pp. 297–298)

▨ If rivals match price cuts but do not match price hikes, they face a kinked demand curve and change prices only when large cost changes occur.

▨ If one firm dominates a market, it acts like a monopoly and the small firms take its price as given and act like perfectly competitive firms.

Game Theory (pp. 299–300)

▨ Game theory is a method of analyzing strategic behaviour.

▨ In a prisoners' dilemma, two prisoners acting in their own interest harm their joint interest.

An Oligopoly Price-Fixing Game (pp. 301–306)

▨ An oligopoly (duopoly) price-fixing game is a prisoners' dilemma.

▨ The firms might collude, one firm might cheat, or both firms might cheat.

▨ In a one-play game, both firms cheat and output and price are the same as in perfect competition.

▨ In a repeated game, a punishment strategy can produce a cooperative equilibrium in which price and output are the same as in a monopoly.

Other Oligopoly Games (pp. 307–309)

▨ Firms' decisions about whether to enter or leave an industry; how much to spend selling the product; whether to modify the product; whether to undertake research and development can be studied by using game theory.

Key Figures and Table

Key Terms

PROBLEMS

*1. The figure shows the situation facing Lite and Kool Inc., a producer of running shoes.

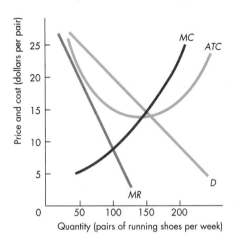

a. What quantity does Lite and Kool produce?
b. What does it charge?
c. How much profit does Lite and Kool make?

2. The figure shows the situation facing Well Done Inc., a producer of steak sauce.

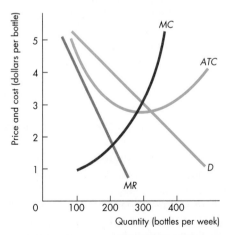

a. What quantity does Well Done produce?
b. What does it charge?
c. How much profit does Well Done make?

*3. A firm in monopolistic competition produces running shoes. If it spends nothing on advertising, it can sell no shoes at $100 a pair and, for each $10 cut in price, the quantity of shoes it can sell increases by 25 pairs a day so that at $20 a pair, it can sell 200 pairs a day. The firm's total fixed cost is $4,000 a day. Its average variable cost and marginal cost is a constant $20 per pair. If the firm spends $3,000 a day on advertising, it can double the quantity of shoes sold at each price.

a. If the firm doesn't advertise, what is the quantity of shoes produced and what is the price per pair?
b. What is the firm's economic profit or economic loss?
c. If the firm does advertise, what is the quantity of shoes produced and what is the price per pair?
d. What is the firm's economic profit or economic loss?
e. Will the firm advertise or not? Why?

4. The firm in problem 3 has the same demand and costs as before if it does not advertise. But it hires a new advertising agency. If the firm spends $3,000 a day on advertising with the new agency, it can double the amount that consumers are willing to pay at each quantity demanded.

a. If the firm hires the new agency, what is the quantity of shoes produced and what is the price per pair?
b. What is the firm's economic profit or economic loss?
c. Will the firm advertise or not? Why?
d. What is the firm's economic profit in the long run?

*5. A firm with a kinked demand curve experiences an increase in its fixed costs. Explain the effects on the firm's price, output, and economic profit/loss.

6. A firm with a kinked demand curve experiences an increase in its variable cost. Explain the effects on the firm's price, output, and economic profit/loss.

*7. An industry with one very large firm and 100 very small firms experiences an increase in the demand for its product. Use the dominant firm model to explain the effects on the price, output, and economic profit of
a. The large firm
b. A typical small firm

8. An industry with one very large firm and 100 very small firms experiences an increase in total variable cost. Use the dominant firm

model to explain the effects on the price, output, and economic profit of

a. The large firm

b. A typical small firm

*9. Consider the following game: The game has two players, and each player is asked a question. The players can answer the question honestly or they can lie. If both answer honestly, each receives a payoff of $100. If one answers honestly and the other lies, the liar gains at the expense of the honest player. In that event, the liar receives a payoff of $500 and the honest player gets nothing. If both lie, then each receives a payoff of $50.

a. Describe this game in terms of its players, strategies, and payoffs.

b. Construct the payoff matrix.

c. What is the equilibrium for this game?

10. Describe the game known as the prisoners' dilemma. In describing the game:

a. Make up a story that motivates the game.

b. Work out a payoff matrix.

c. Describe how the equilibrium of the game is arrived at.

*11. Two firms, Soapy and Sudsies Inc., are the only producers of soap powder. They collude and agree to share the market equally. If neither firm cheats on the agreement, each makes $1 million economic profit. If either firm cheats, the cheater increases its economic profit to $1.5 million while the firm that abides by the agreement incurs an economic loss of $0.5 million. Neither firm has any way of policing the other's actions.

a. Describe the best strategy for each firm in a game that is played once.

b. What is the economic profit for each firm if both cheat?

c. Construct the payoff matrix of a game that is played just once.

d. What is the equilibrium if the game is played once?

e. If this duopoly game can be played many times, describe some of the strategies that each firm might adopt.

12. Two firms, Faster and Quicker, are the only two producers of sports cars on an island that has no contact with the outside world. The firms collude and agree to share the market equally. If neither firm cheats on the agree-

ment, each firm makes $3 million economic profit. If either firm cheats, the cheater can increase its economic profit to $4.5 million, while the firm that abides by the agreement incurs an economic loss of $1 million. Neither firm has any way of policing the actions of the other.

a. What is the economic profit for each firm if they both cheat?

b. What is the payoff matrix of a game that is played just once?

c. What is the best strategy for each firm in a game that is played once?

d. What is the equilibrium if the game is played once?

e. If this game can be played many times, what are two strategies that could be adopted?

CRITICAL THINKING

1. After you have studied *Reading Between the Lines* on pp. 310–311, answer the following questions.

a. How would you characterize the Canadian tour industry in 1995: in long-run equilibrium, making economic profit, or incurring economic loss? What evidence enables you to reach your conclusion?

b. If the tour companies continue to incur economic losses through 2000, what do you predict will happen in the industry? Be specific about the quantity of companies, prices, and economic profits.

c. Suppose that people in Canada decide that during 2000 driving to their holiday destinations and making their own hotel reservations is better than using a tour company. What will happen to the price of a tour holiday and the number of tour companies?

d. Suppose that the decision made by the people of Canada in part (c) is permanent. Now what will happen to the price of a tour holiday and the number of tour companies?

2. Why do Molson and Labatt's spend huge amounts on advertising? Do they benefit? Does the consumer benefit? Explain your answer.

Understanding Firms and Markets

Our economy is constantly changing. Every year, new goods appear and old ones disappear. New firms are born and old ones die. This process of change is initiated and managed by firms operating in markets. When a new product is invented, just one or two firms sell it initially. For example, when the personal computer first became available, there was an Apple or an IBM. The IBM-PC had just one operating system, DOS, made by Microsoft. One firm, Intel, made the chip that ran the IBM-PC. These are examples of industries in which the producer has market power to determine the price of the product and the quantity produced. The extreme case of a single producer that cannot be challenged by new competitors is *monopoly*, which Chapter 13 explains. ◆ But not all industries with just one producer are monopolies. In many cases, the firm that is first to produce a new good faces severe competition from new rivals. One firm facing potential competition is the case of a *contestable market*. If demand increases and makes space for more than one firm, an industry becomes increasingly competitive. Even with just two rivals, the industry changes its face in a dramatic way. *Duopoly*—the case of just two producers—illustrates this dramatic change. The two firms must pay close attention to each other's production and prices and must predict the effects of their own actions on the actions of the other firm. We call this situation one of *strategic interdependence*. As the number of rivals grows, the industry becomes an *oligopoly*, a market in which a small number of firms devise strategies and pay close attention to the strategies of their competitors. ◆ With the continued arrival of new firms in an industry, the market eventually becomes competitive. Competition might be limited because each firm produces its own special version or brand of a good. This case is called *monopolistic competition* because it has elements of both monopoly and competition. Chapter 14 explores the behaviour of firms in all of these types of markets that lie between monopoly at one extreme and perfect competition at the other. ◆ When competition is extreme—the case that we call *perfect competition*—the market changes again in a dramatic way. Now the firm is unable to influence price. Chapter 12 explains this case. ◆ Often, an industry that is competitive becomes less so as the bigger and more successful firms in the industry begin to swallow up the smaller firms, either by driving them out of business or by acquiring their assets. Through this process, an industry might return to oligopoly or even monopoly. You can see such a movement in the auto and banking industries today. ◆ By studying firms and markets, we gain a deeper understanding of the forces that allocate scarce resources and begin to see the anatomy of the invisible hand.

◇ Many economists have advanced our understanding of these forces and we'll now meet two of them: John von Neumann, who pioneered the idea of game theory, and Nancy Gallini, one of today's leading students of strategic behaviour.

Managing Change

Probing the Ideas

Market Power

John von Neumann *was one of the great minds of the twentieth century. Born in Budapest, Hungary, in 1903, Johnny, as he was known, showed early mathematical brilliance. His first mathematical publication was an article that grew out of a lesson with his tutor, which he wrote at the age of 18! But it was at the age of 25, in 1928, that von Neumann published the article that began a flood of research on game theory—a flood that has still not subsided today. In that article, he proved that in a zero-sum game (like sharing a pie), there exists a best strategy for each player.*

Von Neumann invented the computer and built the first modern practical computer, and he worked on the "Manhattan Project," which developed the atomic bomb at Los Alamos, New Mexico, during World War II.

Von Neumann believed that the social sciences would progress only if they used mathematical tools. But he believed they needed different tools from those developed from the physical sciences.

"Real life consists of bluffing, of little tactics of deception, of asking yourself what is the other man going to think I mean to do."

JOHN VON NEUMANN, TOLD TO JACOB BRONOWSKI (IN A LONDON TAXI) AND REPORTED IN *THE ASCENT OF MAN*

The Issues

It is not surprising that firms with market power will charge higher prices than those charged by competitive firms. But how much higher?

This question has puzzled generations of economists. Adam Smith said,

"The price of a monopoly is upon every occasion the highest which can be got." But he was wrong. Antoine-Augustin Cournot (see p. 154) first worked out the price a monopoly will charge. It is not the "highest which can be got" but the price that maximizes profit. Cournot's work was not appreciated until almost a century later when Joan Robinson explained how a monopoly sets its price.

Questions about monopoly became urgent and practical during the 1870s, a time when rapid technological change and falling transportation costs enabled huge monopolies to emerge. Monopolies dominated oil, steel, railroads, tobacco, and even sugar. Industrial empires grew ever larger.

The success of the nineteenth century monopolies led to the creation of our anti-combine laws—laws that limit the use of monopoly power. Those laws have been used to prevent monopolies from being set up and to break up existing monopolies. They were used in the United States during the 1960s to end a conspiracy between General Electric, Westinghouse, and other firms when they colluded to fix their prices instead of competing with each other. The laws were used during the 1980s to bring greater competition to long-distance telecommunication. But in spite of anti-combine laws, near monopolies still exist. Among the most prominent today are those in computer chips and operating systems. Like their forerunners, today's near monopolies make huge profits. But unlike the situation in the nineteenth century, the technological change taking place today is strengthening the forces of competition. Today's information technologies are creating substitutes for services that previously had none. Direct satellite TV is competing with cable and new phone companies are competing with the traditional phone monopolies.

In spite of anti-combine laws that regulate monopolies, they still exist. One is the monopoly in cable television. In many cities, one firm decides which channels viewers will receive and the price they will pay. During the 1980s, with the advent of satellite technology and specialist cable program producers such as CNN and HBO, the cable companies expanded their offerings. At the same time, they steadily increased prices and their businesses became very profitable. But the very technologies that made cable television profitable are now challenging its market position. Direct satellite TV services are eroding cable's monopoly and bringing greater competition to this market.

Then ...

Ruthless greed, exploitation of both workers and customers—these are the traditional images of monopolies and the effects of their power. These images appeared to be an accurate description during the 1880s, when monopolies were at their peak of power and influence. One monopolist, John D. Rockefeller, Sr., built his giant Standard Oil Company, which, by 1879, was refining 90 percent of the nation's oil and controlling its entire pipeline capacity.

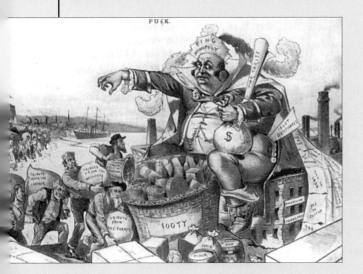

Today, many economists who work on microeconomics use the ideas that John von Neumann pioneered. Game theory is the tool of choice. One economist who has made good use of this tool is Nancy Gallini of the University of Toronto, whom you can meet on the following pages.

Talking with
Nancy Gallini

Nancy T. Gallini *is Professor of Economics at the University of Toronto. Born in 1952, Professor Gallini was an undergraduate at the University of Missouri at Columbia and a graduate student at the University of California, Berkeley. She completed her Ph.D. and began her academic career at the University of Toronto in 1979. Professor Gallini studies the strategic behaviour of firms. Her work has covered a wide range of issues including the effects of patent laws on the efficiency of technological change and the reasons why in some markets a firm operates its own outlets and franchises others. Professor Gallini's work is an outstanding example of how technical (mathematical) economics helps us to understand the strategies that we see firms using in the marketplace.*

Robin Bade and Michael Parkin talked with Professor Gallini about her work and how economists are trying to better understand the complex world of competition and monopoly.

Why were you attracted to economics?

If you were to ask a random group of sixth graders about their career aspirations, chances are that "becoming an economist" would not appear on their top 10 list. This should come as no surprise. While many high schools have now introduced economics into their curriculum, the first encounter with this fascinating discipline for many is introductory economics in first-year university. For me, economics arrived even later, but when it did, I was instantly hooked. For three rather undirected years at university I had been taking 7:30 a.m. classes in mathematics and, while fascinated with these eye-opening sessions, I couldn't quite see myself proving mathematical theorems the rest of my life. So, I had one of those "What should I be when I grow up" conversations with a teaching assistant who was also a graduate student in economics. Next thing I knew I was working in a summer job as a research assistant for an economics prof, John Kuhlman. When Professor Kuhlman was not performing on stage for thousands of introductory economics students, he was performing on the stand as an expert witness in antitrust cases. With his latest price-fixing case as a backdrop, I learned how mathematics could be used to evaluate problems in game theory—in this case, rival firms devising ingenious methods for jointly agreeing to raise prices to consumers. Watching powerful companies succumb to the elegance of economic reasoning was the hook that turned my attention towards graduate school in economics. It didn't take long to find out that price fixing only touched the surface of the amazing world of economics.

Why is game theory a central tool for studying the wide range of economic questions that you work on?

The price-fixing case I just mentioned was analysed with game theory tools because it involved economic agents (firms in this case) whose actions (setting prices) affected the payoffs or profits to other agents (competing firms).

Sounds like that applies to a lot of real-world situations?

Absolutely. Game theory is a remarkably useful tool for analysing and predicting outcomes in any situation in which agents (consumers, firms, governments, countries) interact with each other. Their interaction may be as common as selling products to customers or as complex as negotiating trade agreements or nuclear disarmament policies between countries.

Antitrust, one of my areas of research, studies the law and economics of the behaviour of firms that can reduce or deter competition in markets. This area involves heavy use of game theory. Many students will have heard about the recent Microsoft cases. Over the past years, Microsoft has engaged in a variety of practices that have attracted the attention of antitrust authorities—for example, "bundling" their operating system with an Internet browser or charging a royalty on each computer sold by retailers whether or not it included Microsoft's Windows system. We can use game theory models to analyse incentives for firms to engage in practices like this, asking whether they are anticompetitive with the effect of lessening competition or simply efficient ways of conducting business.

Do our current patent laws encourage the efficient amount and direction of innovation?

This is a very interesting question. It's the focus of lively debates in domestic and international arenas, especially regarding new complex technologies in the computer and biotechnology industries. Patents are property rights on inventions that give the inventor the exclusive right to use, make, or license her new product or process. By preventing the widespread copying of new inventions, patents give inventors the incentive to develop new technologies and to disclose information on those inventions so that others may build upon them after the patent has expired.

The downside of the patent system is that, because the owner has a monopoly on its invention, the use of the invention will not be efficient. This tradeoff between the dynamic benefits of innovation vs. the allocative costs in the use of the innovation is at the heart of the patent system. While the costs from suboptimal use of inventions is a concern, it is

now widely recognized that dynamic benefits from technological progress are at least as important to social welfare as is the elimination of the costs from non-competitive prices. The patent system may be only a second-best solution but it is a reasonably effective mechanism for encouraging the creation and diffusion of innovation.

Do patents create too much or too little temporary monopoly power?

The hardest part about implementing a patent system is getting the patent scope right. Patent scope refers to the extent of the patent coverage, the set of products or processes over which the patentee has exclusive rights. Patents that are weak will be easy to invent around; patents that are strong may deter others from developing subsequent improvements or related inventions. With the advent of new complex technologies, the debate on whether patents are too weak or strong has greatly intensified.

The downside of the patent system is that, because the owner has a monopoly on its invention, the use of the invention will not be efficient.

Some scholars and practitioners worry that patents are too strong in at least two situations. The first occurs when innovations build upon each other. That is, a pioneer invention may be the foundation for later improvements or applications of the invention. For example, if patents are awarded on genetic material, then innovators of new drugs requiring that genetic material may have to pay large royalties for the right to bring the drug to market. If these royalties are large, then future research may be discouraged.

A second concern, especially among competition authorities, is awarding patents on inventions for which network externalities are important. Network externalities are present when the value of a particular invention depends on the number of users. A Macintosh computer may be more useful to you if more students with whom you work and share files also use that operating system. If an incumbent firm has amassed a large base of captured customers, then other customers will be less willing to sign on with a new entrant. Hence, strong patent protection in the presence of network externalities may be a significant barrier to entry.

These two features have the common result that early innovators may capture a secure hold on the market by blocking subsequent research or because network externalities tipped the customer base in their favour. While strong patents may delay subse-

---

Many clever practices for increasing profits are price discrimination schemes in disguise.

---

quent innovation, one should not jump to conclusions that patents, therefore, should be weak in these instances. If they were, then the pioneer may not have the incentive to create the initial invention or disclose information on it in the first place! Moreover, vigorous competition may constrain the innovator's market power in these situations. There is no consensus on the level of protection that strikes the "right" balance between incentives to early and later inventors. What is clear, however, is that economic analysis can contribute immensely to this debate.

What are some of the truly clever ways in which firms try to extract consumer surplus, other than by standard price discrimination? How do they work?

Many clever practices for increasing profits are price discrimination schemes in disguise. For example, offering coupons on selected items, "tying" computer hardware with software and offering "no name" cereal brands are all ways for a single firm to extract surplus when consumers value the product differently. Firms may also work in concert with each other to extract surplus through clever devices, for example, the "most-favoured customer" (MFC) clause. You may have participated in an MFC arrangement if you pur-

chased a product from a retailer who guaranteed you a rebate if the price fell over some specified period of time, for example, the next six months. You may have thought such an offer sounded like a good deal. In fact, you may have been agreeing to a mechanism for the retailer to commit *not* to lower its prices! Think about what would happen if the firm were to lower its price. Under the MFC, it has committed to paying rebates to past customers. So, even if a rival lowers its prices, the retailer may not because the MFC makes price reductions very costly. That is, the MFC ties the retailer's hands from competing with its rival. This "good deal" to consumers may in fact be a clever scheme by firms to raise prices.

What is the case for majoring in economics today? What are the main benefits of an economic degree?

At a recent job-training session for our undergraduate students, Halina Kalita, who is a Ph.D. graduate from our department and now a successful economist at the Royal Bank, gave a superb presentation on how to prepare for the job market. She emphasized the importance of a solid training in economics. Essential to the job, she noted, is the ability to think through a wide range of complex problems, to simplify these problems to their most relevant features, and to be able to adjust to rapid changes in financial and international markets. Those are precisely the skills that a student of economics learns.

Just how much in demand are these skills? We set out to provide an informed response to the most frequently asked question from our prospective undergraduates: "What can I do with an economics degree?" We surveyed recently graduated students and their replies were encouraging: Nearly 80 percent had jobs within only a couple of months after graduating. They found jobs as economic analysts, accounting trainees, banking officers, and financial officers in a wide range of private and public sector organizations that include the large banks, consulting firms, accounting firms, and departments in the Ontario and federal governments. Of course, another fascinating career path for an economics student is graduate school. With a Ph.D. not only will you be able to push forward the frontiers of economic research but you will also have the opportunity to teach other bright students like yourself the wonders of this marvelous discipline.

Chapter 15

Demand and Supply in Resource Markets

It may not be your birthday, and even if it is, chances are you are spending most of it working. But at the end of the week or month (or, if you're devoting all your time to university, when you graduate), you will receive the returns from your labour. Those *returns* vary a lot. Ed Jones, who spends his chilly winter days in a small container suspended from the top of Toronto's Bank of Montreal cleaning windows, makes a happy return of $12 an hour.

Many Happy Returns

Damon Stoudamire, who plays no more than 82 basketball games a year, makes a very happy return of $4.6 million over three years—including the gift of a Mercedes-Benz to his mother. Students working at what have been called McJobs—serving fast food or labouring in the fields of the Niagara Peninsula—earn just a few dollars an hour. Why aren't *all* jobs well paid? ◆ Most of us have little trouble spending our pay. But most of us do manage to save some of what we earn. What determines the amount of saving that people do and the returns they make on that saving? How do the returns on saving influence the allocation of savings across the many industries and activities that use our capital resources? ◆ Some people receive income from supplying land, but the amount earned varies enormously with the land's location and quality. For example, a hectare of farmland in Manitoba rents for about $1,000 a year, while a block in Toronto's Yorkville rents for several million dollars a year. What determines the rent that people are willing to pay for different blocks of land? Why are rents so enormously high in big cities and so relatively low in the great farming regions of the nation?

◆ In this chapter, we study the markets for productive resources— labour, capital, land, and entrepreneurship—and learn how their prices and people's incomes are determined.

After studying this chapter, you will be able to:

- Explain how firms choose the quantities of labour, capital, and natural resources to employ

- Explain how people choose the quantities of labour, capital, and natural resources to supply

- Explain how wages, interest, and natural resource prices are determined in competitive resource markets

- Explain the concept of economic rent and distinguish between economic rent and opportunity cost

Resource Prices and Incomes

GOODS AND SERVICES ARE PRODUCED BY USING the four economic resources—*labour, capital, land,* and *entrepreneurship*. (These resources are defined in Chapter 3, p. 38.) Incomes are determined by *resource prices*—the *wage* rate for labour, the *interest* rate for capital, the *rental* rate for land, and the rate of *normal profit* for entrepreneurship—and the quantities of resources used.

In addition to the four resource incomes, a residual income, *economic profit* (or *economic loss*) is paid to (or borne by) firms' owners. For a small firm, the owner is usually the entrepreneur. For a large corporation, the owners are the stockholders who supply capital.

An Overview of a Competitive Resource Market

We're going to learn how competitive resource markets determine the prices, quantities used, and incomes of productive resources. The tool that we use is the demand and supply model. The quantity demanded of a resource depends on its price, and the law of demand applies to resources just as it does to goods and services. The lower the price of a resource, other things remaining the same, the greater is the quantity demanded. Figure 15.1 shows the demand curve for a resource as the curve labelled *D*.

The quantity supplied of a resource also depends on its price. With a possible exception that we'll identify later in this chapter, the law of supply applies to resources. The higher the price of a resource, other things remaining the same, the greater is the quantity supplied of the resource. Figure 15.1 shows the supply curve of a resource as the curve labelled *S*.

The equilibrium is at the point of intersection of the demand and supply curves. In Fig. 15.1, the price is *PR* and the quantity used is *QR*.

The income earned by the resource is its price multiplied by the quantity used. In Fig. 15.1, the resource income equals the area of the blue rectangle. This income is the total income received by the resource. Each person who supplies the resource receives the resource price multiplied by the quantity supplied by that person. Changes in demand and supply change the equilibrium price and quantity and change income.

An increase in demand shifts the demand curve rightward and increases price, quantity, and income. An increase in supply shifts the supply curve rightward and decreases price. The quantity used increases, and the income of the resource can increase, decrease, or remain constant. The change in income that results from a change in supply depends on the elasticity of demand for the resource. If demand is elastic, income rises; if demand is inelastic, income falls; and if demand is unit elastic, income remains constant (see Chapter 5, pp. 94–95).

The rest of this chapter explores the influences on the demand for and supply of productive resources. It also studies the influences on the elasticities of supply and demand for resources. These elasticities have major effects on resource prices, quantities used, and incomes.

We begin with the market for labour. But most of what we learn about the labour market also applies to the other resource markets that we study later in the chapter.

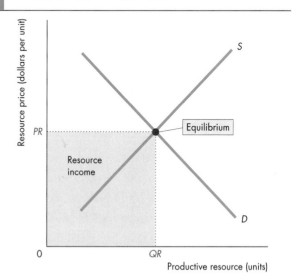

FIGURE 15.1

Demand and Supply in a Resource Market

The demand curve for a productive resource (*D*) slopes downward, and the supply curve (*S*) slopes upward. Where the demand and supply curves intersect, the resource price (*PR*) and the quantity of a resource used (*QR*) are determined. The resource income is the product of the resource price and the quantity of the resource, as represented by the blue rectangle.

Labour Markets

FOR MOST OF US, THE LABOUR MARKET IS OUR only source of income. And in recent years, many people have had a tough time. But over the years, both wage rates and the quantity of labour have moved steadily upward. Figure 15.2(a) shows the record since 1960. Using 1992 dollars to remove the effects of inflation, total compensation per hour of work almost doubled from $9 in 1960 to $17.50 in 1998. Over the same period, the quantity of labour employed exactly doubled from 12.5 billion hours in 1960 to 25 billion hours in 1998.

Figure 15.2(b) shows why these trends occurred. The demand increased from LD_{60} to LD_{98} and this increase was much larger than the increase in supply from LS_{60} to LS_{98}.

A lot of diversity lies behind the average wage rate and the aggregate quantity of labour. During the 1980s and 1990s, some wage rates have grown more rapidly than the average and others have fallen. To understand the trends in the labour market, we must probe the forces that influence the demand for labour and the supply of labour. This chapter studies these forces (and Chapter 16 takes a deeper look at them). We begin on the demand side of the labour market.

The Demand for Labour

The demand for labour is a derived demand. A **derived demand** is a demand for a productive resource, which is *derived* from the demand for the goods and services produced by the resource. The derived demand for labour (and the other resources demanded by firms) is driven by the firm's objective, which is to maximize profit.

You learned in Chapters 12, 13, and 14 that a profit-maximizing firm produces the output at which marginal cost equals marginal revenue. This principle holds true for all firms regardless of whether they operate in perfect competition, monopolistic competition, oligopoly, or monopoly.

A firm that maximizes profit hires the quantity of labour that can produce the profit-maximizing output. What is that quantity of labour? And how does it change as the wage rate changes? We can answer these questions by comparing the *marginal* revenue earned by hiring one more worker with the *marginal* cost of that worker. Let's look first at the marginal revenue side of this comparison.

FIGURE 15.2

Labour Market Trends in Canada

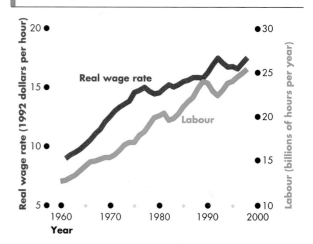

(a) Labour and wage rate

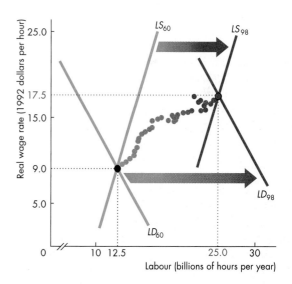

(b) Changes in demand and supply in the labour market

Between 1960 and 1998, the wage rate doubled and the quantity of labour employed almost doubled (part a). The demand for labour increased from LD_{60} to LD_{98} and the supply of labour increased from LS_{60} to LS_{98}. Demand increased by more than supply, so both the wage rate and the quantity of labour employed increased (part b).

Source: Statistics Canada, *StatCan: CANSIM Disc*, 1999, and authors' assumptions and calculations.

Marginal Revenue Product

The change in total revenue that results from employing one more unit of labour is called the **marginal revenue product** of labour. Table 15.1 shows you how to calculate marginal revenue product for a perfectly competitive firm.

The first two columns show the total product schedule for Max's Wash 'n' Wax car wash service. The numbers tell us how the number of car washes per hour varies as the quantity of labour varies. The third column shows the *marginal product of labour*—the change in total product that results from a one-unit increase in the quantity of labour employed. (Look back at p. 225 for a quick refresher on these concepts.)

The car wash market in which Max operates is perfectly competitive and he can sell as many washes as he chooses at $4 a wash, the (assumed) market price. So Max's *marginal revenue* is $4 a wash.

Given this information, we can now calculate *marginal revenue product* (fourth column). It equals marginal product multiplied by marginal revenue. For example, the marginal product of hiring a second worker is 4 car washes an hour and because marginal revenue is $4 a wash, the marginal revenue product of the second worker is $16 (4 washes at $4 each).

The last two columns of Table 15.1 show an alternative way to calculate the marginal revenue product of labour. Total revenue is equal to total product multiplied by price. For example, two workers produce 9 washes per hour and generate a total revenue of $36 (9 washes at $4 each). One worker produces 5 washes per hour and generates a total revenue of $20 (5 washes at $4 each). Marginal revenue product, in the sixth column, is the change in total revenue from hiring one more worker. When the second worker is hired, total revenue increases from $20 to $36, an increase of $16. So the marginal revenue product of the second worker is $16, which agrees with our previous calculation.

Diminishing Marginal Revenue Product As the quantity of labour increases, marginal revenue product diminishes. For a firm in perfect competition, marginal revenue product diminishes because marginal product diminishes. In monopoly (or in monopolistic competition) marginal revenue product diminishes for a second reason. When more labour is hired and total product increases, the firm must cut its price to sell the extra product. So marginal product *and* marginal revenue decrease, both of which bring decreasing marginal revenue product.

TABLE 15.1

Marginal Revenue Product at Max's Wash 'n' Wax

	Quantity of labour (L) (workers)	Total product (TP) (car washes per hour)	Marginal product (MP = $\Delta TP/\Delta L$) (washes per worker)	Marginal revenue product (MRP = MR × MP) (dollars per worker)	Total revenue (TR = P × TP) (dollars)	Marginal revenue product (MRP = $\Delta TR/\Delta L$) (dollars per worker)
a	0	0			0	
			5	20		20
b	1	5			20	
			4	16		16
c	2	9			36	
			3	12		12
d	3	12			48	
			2	8		8
e	4	14			56	
			1	4		4
f	5	15			60	

The car wash market is perfectly competitive and the price is $4 a wash. Marginal revenue is also $4 a wash. Marginal revenue product equals marginal product (column 3) multiplied by marginal revenue. For example, the marginal product of the second worker is 4 washes and marginal revenue is $4 a wash. So the marginal revenue product of the second worker

(in column 4) is $16. Alternatively, if Max hires 1 worker (row b), total product is 5 washes an hour and total revenue is $20 (column 5). If he hires 2 workers (row c), total product is 9 washes an hour and total revenue is $36. By hiring the second worker, total revenue rises by $16—the marginal revenue product of labour is $16.

The Labour Demand Curve

Figure 15.3 shows how the labour demand curve is derived from the marginal revenue product curve. The *marginal revenue product curve* graphs the marginal revenue product of a resource at each quantity of the resource hired. Figure 15.3(a) illustrates the marginal revenue product curve for workers employed by Max. The horizontal axis measures the number of workers that Max hires, and the vertical axis measures the marginal revenue product of labour. The blue bars show the marginal revenue product of labour as Max employs more workers. These bars correspond to the numbers in Table 15.1. The curve labelled *MRP* is Max's marginal revenue product curve.

A firm's marginal revenue product curve is also its demand for labour curve. Figure 15.3(b) shows Max's demand for labour curve (*D*). The horizontal axis measures the number of workers hired—the same as in part (a). The vertical axis measures the wage rate in dollars per hour. In Fig. 15.3(a), when Max increases the quantity of labour employed from 2 workers an hour to 3 workers an hour, his marginal revenue product is $12 an hour. In Fig. 15.3(b), at a wage rate of $12 an hour, Max hires 3 workers an hour.

The marginal revenue product curve is also the demand for labour curve because the firm hires the profit-maximizing quantity of labour. If the wage rate is less than marginal revenue product, the firm can increase its profit by employing one more worker. Conversely, if the wage rate is greater than marginal revenue product, the firm can increase its profit by employing one fewer worker. But if the wage rate equals marginal revenue product, then the firm cannot increase its profit by changing the number of workers it employs. The firm is making the maximum possible profit. Thus the quantity of labour demanded by the firm is such that the wage rate equals the marginal revenue product of labour.

Because the marginal revenue product curve is also the demand curve, and because marginal revenue product diminishes as the quantity of labour employed increases, the demand for labour curve slopes downward. The lower the wage rate, other things remaining the same, the more workers a firm hires.

When we studied firms' output decisions, we discovered that a condition for maximum profit is that marginal revenue equals marginal cost. We've now discovered another condition for maximum profit: Marginal revenue product of a resource equals the resource's price. Let's study the connection between these two conditions.

FIGURE 15.3

The Demand for Labour at Max's Wash 'n' Wax

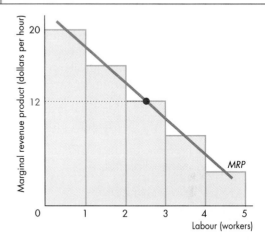

(a) Marginal revenue product

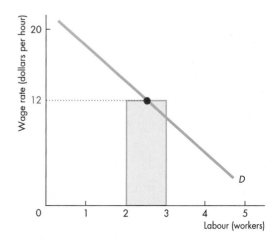

(b) Demand for labour

Max's Wash 'n' Wax operates in a perfectly competitive car wash market and can sell any quantity of washes at $4 a wash. The blue bars in part (a) represent the firm's marginal revenue product of labour. They are based on the numbers in Table 15.1. The orange line is the firm's marginal revenue product of labour curve. Part (b) shows Max's demand for labour curve. This curve is identical to Max's marginal revenue product curve. Max demands the quantity of labour that makes the wage rate equal to the marginal revenue product of labour. The demand for labour curve slopes downward because marginal revenue product diminishes as the quantity of labour employed increases.

Equivalence of Two Conditions for Profit Maximization

Profit is maximized when at the quantity of labour hired, *marginal revenue product* equals the wage rate and when, at the quantity produced, *marginal revenue* equals *marginal cost*. These two conditions for maximum profit are equivalent. The quantity of labour that maximizes profit produces the output that maximizes profit. To see the equivalence of the two conditions for maximum profit, first recall that

Marginal revenue product = Marginal revenue × Marginal product.

If we call marginal revenue product *MRP*, marginal revenue *MR*, and marginal product *MP*,

$$MRP = MR \times MP.$$

If we call the wage rate *W*, the first condition for maximum profit is

$$MRP = W.$$

But *MRP = MR × MP*, so

$$MR \times MP = W.$$

This equation tells us that when profit is maximized, marginal revenue multiplied by marginal product equals the wage rate.

Divide the last equation by marginal product, *MP*, to obtain

$$MR = W \div MP.$$

This equation states that when profit is maximized, marginal revenue equals the wage rate divided by the marginal product of labour. The wage rate divided by the marginal product of labour equals marginal cost. It costs the firm *W* to hire one more hour of labour. But the labour produces *MP* units of output. So the cost of producing one of those units of output, which is marginal cost, is *W* divided by *MP*. If we call marginal cost *MC*, then

$$MR = MC,$$

which is the second condition for maximum profit.

Because the first condition for maximum profit implies the second condition, these two conditions are equivalent.

Table 15.2 summarizes the reasoning and calculations that show the equivalence between the two conditions for maximum profit.

TABLE 15.2

Two Conditions for Maximum Profit

Symbols

Marginal product	**MP**
Marginal revenue	**MR**
Marginal cost	**MC**
Marginal revenue product	**MRP**
Resource price	**PR**

Two Conditions for Maximum Profit

1.   **MR = MC**   2.   **MRP = PR**

Equivalence of Conditions

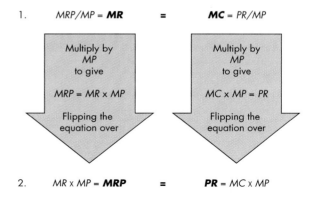

1.   MRP/MP = **MR**   =   **MC** = PR/MP

Multiply by MP to give

MRP = MR × MP

Flipping the equation over

Multiply by MP to give

MC × MP = PR

Flipping the equation over

2.   MR × MP = **MRP**   =   **PR** = MC × MP

The two conditions for maximum profit are marginal revenue (*MR*) equals marginal cost (*MC*) and marginal revenue product (*MRP*) equals the price of the resource (*PR*). These two conditions are equivalent because marginal revenue product (*MRP*) equals marginal revenue (*MR*) multiplied by marginal product (*MP*), and the resource price (*PR*) equals marginal cost (*MC*) multiplied by marginal product (*MP*).

Max's Numbers Check the numbers for Max's Wash 'n' Wax and confirm that the conditions you've just examined work. Max's profit-maximizing labour decision is to hire 3 workers if the wage rate is $12 an hour. When Max hires 3 hours of labour, marginal product is 3 washes per hour. Max sells the 3 washes an hour for a marginal revenue of $4 a wash. So marginal revenue product is 3 washes multiplied by $4 a wash, which equals $12 per hour. At a wage rate of $12 an hour, Max is maximizing profit.

Equivalently, Max's marginal cost is $12 an hour divided by 3 washes per hour, which equals $4 per wash. At a marginal revenue of $4 a wash, Max is maximizing profit.

You've discovered that the law of demand applies for labour just as it does for goods and services. Other things remaining the same, the lower the wage rate (the price of labour), the greater is the quantity of labour demanded.

Let's now study the influences that change the demand for labour and shift the demand for labour curve.

Changes in the Demand for Labour

The demand for labour depends on three factors:

1. The price of the firm's output
2. The prices of other productive resources
3. Technology

The higher the price of a firm's output, the greater is its demand for labour. The price of output affects the demand for labour through its influence on marginal revenue product. A higher price for the firm's output increases marginal revenue, which, in turn, increases the marginal revenue product of labour. A change in the price of a firm's output leads to a shift in the firm's demand for labour curve. If the price of the firm's output increases, the demand for labour increases, and the demand for labour curve shifts rightward.

The other two influences affect the *long-run demand for labour*, which is the relationship between the wage rate and the quantity of labour demanded when all resources can be varied. In contrast, the *short-run demand for labour* is the relationship between the wage rate and the quantity of labour demanded when the quantities of the other resources are fixed and labour is the only variable resource. A change in the relative price of productive resources— such as the relative price of labour and capital—leads to a substitution away from the resource whose relative price has increased and towards the resource whose relative price has decreased. So if the price of using capital decreases relative to that of using labour,

the firm substitutes capital for labour and increases the quantity of capital demanded.

But the demand for labour might increase or decrease. If the lower price of capital increases the scale of production by enough, the demand for labour increases. Otherwise the demand for labour decreases.

Finally, a new technology that changes the marginal product of labour changes the demand for labour. For example, the electronic telephone exchange has decreased the demand for telephone operators. This same new technology has increased the demand for telephone engineers. Again, these effects are felt in the long run when the firm adjusts all its resources and incorporates new technologies into its production process. Table 15.3 summarizes the influences on a firm's demand for labour.

We saw in Fig. 15.3 that the demand for labour has increased over time and the demand curve has shifted rightward. We can now give some of the reasons for this increase in demand. Advances in technology and investment in new capital increase the marginal product of labour and increase the demand for labour.

TABLE 15.3

A Firm's Demand for Labour

The Law of Demand

(Movements along the demand curve for labour)

The quantity of labour demanded by a firm

Decreases if:	*Increases if:*
■ The wage rate increases	■ The wage rate decreases

Changes in Demand

(Shifts in the demand curve for labour)

A firm's demand for labour

Decreases if:	*Increases if:*
■ The firm's output price decreases	■ The firm's output price increases
■ A new technology decreases the marginal product of labour	■ A new technology increases the marginal product of labour

(Changes in the prices of other resources have an ambiguous effect on the demand for labour.)

Market Demand

So far, we've studied the demand for labour by an individual firm. The market demand for labour is the total demand by all firms. By adding together the quantities demanded by all firms at each wage rate, we find the market demand for labour curve (just as we find the market demand curve for any good or service). Because a firm's demand for labour curve slopes downward, so does the market demand curve.

Elasticity of Demand for Labour

The demand for labour, on the average, is estimated to be about 3. This number means that the demand for labour is elastic. This fact is important because it means that an increase in the supply of labour, other things remaining the same, lowers the wage rate but increases labour income. If the demand for labour were inelastic, an increase in the supply of labour would decrease labour income. And if the demand for labour were unit elastic, an increase in the supply of labour would leave labour income unchanged.

Although the demand for labour is elastic on the average, there is variation across different types of labour. And the demand for labour is less elastic in the short run, when only labour can be varied, than in the long run, when labour and other resources can be varied. The elasticity of demand for a specific type of labour depends on:

■ The labour intensity of the production process
■ The elasticity of demand for the product
■ The substitutability of capital for labour

Labour Intensity   A labour-intensive production process is one that uses a lot of labour and little capital. Home building is an example. The greater the degree of labour intensity, the more elastic is the demand for labour. To see why, first suppose wages are 90 percent of total cost. A 10 percent increase in the wage rate increases total cost by 9 percent. Firms will be sensitive to such a large change in total cost, so if wages increase, firms will decrease the quantity of labour demanded by a relatively large amount. But if wages are 10 percent of total cost, a 10 percent increase in the wage rate increases total cost by only 1 percent. Firms will be less sensitive to this increase in cost, so if wages increase in this case, firms will decrease the quantity of labour demanded by a relatively small amount.

The Elasticity of Demand for the Product   The greater the elasticity of demand for the good, the larger is the elasticity of demand for the labour used to produce it. An increase in the wage rate increases marginal cost and decreases the supply of the good. The decrease in the supply of the good increases the price of the good and decreases the quantity demanded of the good and the quantities of the resources used to produce it. The greater the elasticity of demand for the good, the larger is the decrease in the quantity demanded of the good and so the larger is the decrease in the quantities of the productive resources used to produce it.

The Substitutability of Capital for Labour   The more easily capital can be used instead of labour in production, the more elastic is the long-run demand for labour. For example, it is easy to use robots rather than assembly line workers in car factories and grape-picking machines for labour in vineyards. So the long-run demand for these types of labour is elastic. At the other extreme, it is difficult (but possible) to substitute computers for newspaper reporters, bank loan officers, and teachers. So the long-run demand for these types of labour is less elastic.

Let's now turn from the demand side of the labour market to the supply side and examine the decisions that people make about how to allocate time between working and other activities.

The Supply of Labour

People can allocate their time to two broad activities—labour supply and leisure. (Leisure is a catch-all. It includes all activities other than supplying labour.) For most people, leisure is more enjoyable than supplying labour. We'll look at the labour supply decision of Amy, who is like most people. She enjoys her leisure time, and she would be pleased if she didn't have to spend her weekends working a supermarket checkout line.

But Amy has chosen to work weekends. The reason is that she is offered a wage rate that exceeds her *reservation wage*. Amy's reservation wage is the lowest wage at which she is willing to supply labour. If the wage rate exceeds her reservation wage, she supplies some labour. But how much labour does she supply? The quantity of labour that Amy is willing to supply depends on the wage rate.

Substitution Effect Other things remaining the same, the higher the wage rate Amy is offered, at least over a range, the greater is the quantity of labour that she supplies. The reason is that Amy's wage rate is her *opportunity cost of leisure*. If she quits work an hour early to catch a movie, the cost of that extra hour of leisure is the wage rate that Amy forgoes. The higher the wage rate, the less willing is Amy to forgo the income and take the extra leisure time. This tendency for a higher wage rate to induce Amy to work longer hours is a *substitution effect*.

But there is also an *income effect* that works in the opposite direction to the substitution effect.

Income Effect The higher Amy's wage rate, the higher is her income. A higher income, other things remaining the same, induces Amy to increase her demand for most goods. Leisure is one of those goods. Because an increase in income creates an increase in the demand for leisure, it also creates a decrease in the quantity of labour supplied.

Backward-Bending Supply of Labour Curve As the wage rate rises, the substitution effect brings an increase in the quantity of labour supplied, while the income effect brings a decrease in the quantity of labour supplied. At low wage rates, the substitution

effect is larger than the income effect, so as the wage rate rises, people supply more labour. But as the wage rate continues to rise, the income effect eventually becomes larger than the substitution effect and the quantity of labour supplied decreases. The labour supply curve is *backward bending*.

Figure 15.4(a) shows the labour supply curves, for Amy, Jack, and Lisa. Each labour supply curve is backward bending but the three people have different reservation wage rates.

Market Supply The market supply of labour curve is the sum of the individual supply curves. Figure 15.4(b) shows the market supply curve (S_M) derived from the supply curves of Amy, Jack, and Lisa (S_A, S_B, S_C) in Fig. 15.4(a). At wage rates of less than $1 an hour, no one supplies any labour. At a wage rate of $1 an hour, Amy works but Jack and Lisa don't. As the wage rate increases and reaches $7 an hour, all three of them work. The market supply curve S_M eventually bends backward but it has a long upward-sloping section.

Changes in the Supply of Labour The supply of labour changes when influences other than the wage rate change. The key factors that change the supply of labour and that over the years have increased it are:

FIGURE 15.4

The Supply of Labour

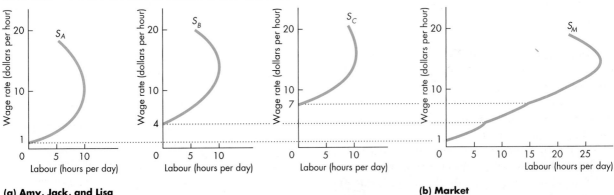

(a) Amy, Jack, and Lisa

(b) Market

Part (a) shows the labour supply curves of Amy (S_A), Jack (S_B), and Lisa (S_C). Each person has a reservation wage below which he or she will supply no labour. As the wage rises, the quantity of labour supplied increases to a maximum. If the wage continues to rise, the quantity of labour supplied begins to decrease.

Each person's supply curve eventually bends backward. Part (b) shows how, by adding the quantities of labour supplied by each person at each wage rate, we derive the market supply curve of labour (S_M). The market supply curve has a long upward-sloping region before it bends backward.

1. Adult population
2. Technological change and capital accumulation

An increase in the adult population increases the supply of labour. Also, an increase in capital in home production (of meals, laundry services, and cleaning services) increases the supply of labour. These factors that have increased the supply of labour have shifted the labour supply curve rightward.

Let's now build on what we've learned about the demand for labour and the supply of labour and study labour market equilibrium and the trends in wage rates and employment.

Labour Market Equilibrium

Wages and employment are determined by equilibrium in the labour market. You saw, in Fig. 15.2, that the wage rate and employment have both increased over the years. You can now explain why.

Trends in the Demand for Labour   The demand for labour has *increased* because of technological change and the accumulation of capital and the demand for labour curve has shifted rightward.

Many people are surprised that technological change and capital accumulation *increase* the demand for labour. They see new technologies *destroying jobs*, not creating them. Downsizing has become a catch-word of the 1990s as the computer and information age has taken hold and eliminated millions of "good" jobs, even of managers. So how can it be that technological change *creates* jobs and increases the demand for labour?

Technological change destroys some jobs and creates others. But it creates more jobs than it destroys, and *on the average* the new jobs pay more than the old ones did. But to benefit from the advances in technology, people must acquire new skills and change their jobs. For example, during the past 15 years, the demand for typists has fallen almost to zero. But the demand for people who can type (on a computer rather than a typewriter) and do other things as well has increased. And the output of these people is worth more that that of a typist. So the demand for people with typing (and other) skills has increased.

Trends in the Supply of Labour   The supply of labour has increased because of population growth and technological change and capital accumulation in the home. The mechanization of home production of fast-food preparation services (the freezer and the microwave oven) and laundry services (the automatic washer and dryer and drip dry clothing) has decreased the time spent on activities that once were full-time jobs and has led to a large increase in the supply of labour. As a result, the supply of labour curve has shifted steadily rightward, but at a slower pace than the shift in the demand curve.

Trends in Equilibrium   Because technological advances and capital accumulation have increased demand by more than population growth and technological change in home production has increased supply, both wages and employment have increased. But not everyone has shared in the advancing prosperity that comes from higher wage rates. Some groups have been left behind and some have even seen their wage rates fall. Why?

Two key reasons can be identified. First, technological change affects the marginal productivity of different groups in different ways. High-skilled computer-literate workers have benefited from the information revolution while low-skilled workers have suffered. The demand for the services of the first group has increased and the demand for the services of the second group has decreased. (Draw a supply and demand figure and you will see that these changes widen the wage difference between the two groups). Second, international competition has lowered the marginal revenue product of low-skilled workers and so decreased the demand for their labour. We look further at skill differences in Chapter 16 and at trends in the distribution of income in Chapter 17.

R E V I E W   Q U I Z

- Describe and explain the trends in wage rates and employment.
- Why do we call the demand for labour a *derived* demand? From what is it derived?
- What is the distinction between marginal revenue product and marginal revenue? Provide an example that illustrates the distinction.
- When a firm's marginal revenue product equals the wage rate, marginal revenue also equals marginal cost. Why? Provide a numerical example different from that in the text.
- What determines the amount of labour that households plan to supply?

Capital Markets

CAPITAL MARKETS ARE THE CHANNELS THROUGH which firms obtain *financial* resources to buy *physical* capital resources. These financial resources come from saving.

For most of us, the capital market is where we make our biggest ticket transactions. We borrow in the capital market to buy a home. And we lend in the capital market to build up a fund on which to live when we retire. Do the rates of return on capital increase like wage rates of labour increase?

Figure 15.5(a) answers this question by showing the record since 1965. We measure the rate of return on capital as the interest rate adjusted for the loss in the value of money that arises from inflation—the real interest rate. The real interest rate has fluctuated. It ranged between 2 percent a year and 3 percent a year during the late 1960s, became negative during the 1970s, climbed to 9 percent during the 1980s, and fell to average 5 percent a year during the 1990s. The quantity of capital employed increased steadily. In 1998, it stood at around $3.2 trillion (1992 dollars), 3 times its 1965 level.

Figure 15.5(b) shows why these trends occurred. Demand increased from KD_{65} to KD_{98} and this increase was similar to the increase in supply from KS_{65} to KS_{98}. To understand the trends in the capital market, we must again probe the forces of demand and supply. Many of the ideas you've already met in your study of demand and supply in the labour market apply to the capital market as well. But there are some special features of capital. Its main special feature is that when people buy capital, they must compare *present* costs with *future* benefits. Let's discover how these comparisons are made by studying the demand for capital.

The Demand for Capital

A firm's demand for *financial* capital stems from its demand for *physical* capital, and the amount that a firm plans to borrow in a given time period is determined by its planned investment—purchases of new capital. This decision is driven by its attempt to maximize profit. As a firm increases the quantity of capital employed, other things remaining the same, the marginal revenue product of capital eventually diminishes. To maximize profit, a firm increases its plant size and uses more capital if the marginal

FIGURE 15.5

Capital Market Trends in Canada

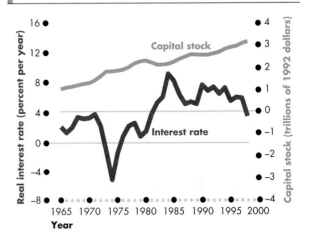

(a) Capital stock and interest rate

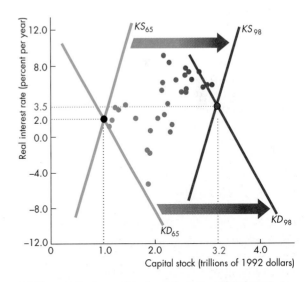

(b) Changes in demand and supply in the capital market

Between 1960 and 1998, the real interest rate fluctuated between *minus* 5 percent a year (in 1974) and 9 percent a year (in 1984). During the same period, the quantity of capital employed increased by 300 percent. The demand for capital increased from KD_{65} to KD_{98} and the supply of capital increased from KS_{65} to KS_{98}.

Source: Statistics Canada, StatCan: *CANSIM Disc*, 1999, and authors' assumptions and calculations.

revenue product of capital exceeds the cost of capital. But the marginal revenue product comes in the future and capital must be paid for in the present. So the firm must convert *future* marginal revenue products into a *present value* so that it can be compared with the price of a new piece of capital equipment.

To make this conversion, we use the technique of discounting.

Discounting and Present Value

Discounting is converting a future amount of money to a present value. And the **present value** of a future amount of money is the amount that, if invested today, will grow to be as large as that future amount when the interest that it will earn is taken into account.

The easiest way to understand discounting and present value is to begin with the relationship between an amount invested today, the interest that it earns, and the amount that it will grow to in the future. The future amount is equal to the present amount (present value) plus the interest it will accumulate in the future. That is:

Future amount = Present value + Interest income

The interest income is equal to the present value multiplied by the interest rate, *r*, so

Future amount = Present value + (*r* × Present value)

or

Future amount = Present value × (1 + *r*).

If you have $100 today and the interest rate is 10 percent a year ($r = 0.1$), one year from today you will have $110—the original $100 plus $10 interest. Check that the above formula delivers that answer: $100 × 1.1 = $110.

The formula that we have just used calculates a future amount one year from today from the present value and an interest rate. To calculate the present value, we just work backward. Instead of multiplying the present value by (1 + *r*), we divide the future amount by (1 + *r*). That is,

$$\text{Present value} = \frac{\text{Future amount}}{(1 + r)}.$$

You can use this formula to calculate present value. This calculation of present value is called discounting. Let's check that we can use the present value

formula by calculating the present value of $110 one year from now when the interest rate is 10 percent a year. You'll be able to guess that the answer is $100 because we just calculated that $100 invested today at 10 percent a year becomes $110 in one year. Thus it follows immediately that the present value of $110 in one year's time is $100. But let's use the formula. Putting the numbers into the above formula, we have

$$\text{Present value} = \frac{\$110}{(1 + 0.1)}$$

$$= \frac{\$110}{1.1} = \$100.$$

Calculating the present value of an amount of money one year from now is the easiest case. But we can also calculate the present value of an amount any number of years in the future. As an example, let's see how we calculate the present value of an amount of money that will be available two years from now.

Suppose that you invest $100 today for two years at an interest rate of 10 percent a year. The money will earn $10 in the first year, which means that by the end of the first year, you will have $110. If the interest of $10 is invested, then the interest earned in the second year will be a further $10 on the original $100 plus $1 on the $10 interest. Thus the total interest earned in the second year will be $11. The total interest earned overall will be $21 ($10 in the first year and $11 in the second year). After two years, you will have $121. From the definition of present value, you can see that the present value of $121 two years hence is $100. That is, $100 is the present amount that, if invested at an interest rate of 10 percent a year, will grow to $121 two years from now.

To calculate the present value of an amount of money two years in the future, we use the formula

$$\text{Present value} = \frac{\substack{\text{Amount of money} \\ \text{two years in future}}}{(1 + r)^2}.$$

Use this formula to calculate the present value of $121 two years from now at an interest rate of 10 percent a year. With these numbers the formula gives

$$\text{Present value} = \frac{\$121}{(1 + 0.1)^2}$$

$$= \frac{\$121}{(1.1)^2}$$

$$= \frac{\$121}{1.21}$$

$$= \$100.$$

We can calculate the present value of an amount of money any number of years in the future by using a formula based on the two that we've already used. The general formula is

$$\text{Present value} = \frac{\text{Amount of money } n \text{ in future}}{(1 + r)^n}.$$

For example, if the interest rate is 10 percent a year, $100 to be received 10 years from now has a present value of $38.55. That is, if $38.55 is invested today at an interest rate of 10 percent, it will accumulate to $100 in 10 years. (You might check that calculation on your pocket calculator.)

You've seen how to calculate the present value of an amount of money one year in the future, two years in the future, and n years in the future. Most practical applications of present value calculate the present value of a sequence of future amounts of money that spread over several years. To calculate the present value of a sequence of amounts over several years, we use the formula you have learned and apply it to each year. We then sum the present values for each year to find the present value of the sequence of amounts.

For example, suppose that a firm expects to receive $100 a year for each of the next five years. And suppose that the interest rate is 10 percent per year (0.1 per year). The present value of these five payments of $100 each is calculated by using the following formula:

$$PV = \frac{\$100}{1.1} + \frac{\$100}{1.1^2} + \frac{\$100}{1.1^3} + \frac{\$100}{1.1^4} + \frac{\$100}{1.1^5}$$

which equals:

$$PV = \$90.91 + \$82.64 + \$75.13 + \$68.30 + \$62.09$$

$$= \$397.07.$$

You can see that the firm receives $500 over five years. But because the money arrives in the future, it is not worth $500 today. Its present value is only $397.07.

And the farther in the future it arrives, the smaller is its present value. The $100 received one year in the future is worth $90.91 today. And the $100 received five years in the future is worth only $68.30 today.

Let's now see how a firm uses the concept of present value to achieve an efficient use of capital.

The Present Value of a Computer We'll see how a firm decides how much capital to buy by calculating the present value of a new computer.

Tina runs Taxfile, Inc., a firm that sells advice to taxpayers. Tina is considering buying a new computer that costs $10,000. The computer has a life of two years, after which it will be worthless. If Tina buys the computer, she will pay $10,000 now and she expects to generate business that will bring in an additional $5,900 at the end of each of the next two years.

To calculate the present value, PV, of the marginal revenue product of a new computer, Tina calculates

$$PV = \frac{MRP_1}{(1 + r)} + \frac{MRP_2}{(1 + r)^2}.$$

Here, MRP_1 is the marginal revenue product received by Tina at the end of the first year. It is converted to a present value by dividing it by $(1 + r)$, where r is the interest rate (expressed as a proportion). The term MRP_2 is the marginal revenue product received at the end of the second year. It is converted to a present value by dividing it by $(1 + r)^2$.

If Tina can borrow or lend at an interest rate of 4 percent a year, the present value of her marginal revenue product is given by

$$PV = \frac{\$5,900}{(1 + 0.04)} + \frac{\$5,900}{(1 + 0.04)^2}$$

$$PV = \$5,673 + \$5,455$$

$$PV = \$11,128.$$

The present value of $5,900 one year in the future is $5,900 divided by 1.04 (4 percent as a proportion is 0.04). The present value of $5,900 two years in the future is $5,900 divided by $(1.04)^2$. Tina works out those two present values and then adds them to get the present value of the future flow of marginal revenue product, which is $11,128.

Table 15.4, parts (a) and (b), summarizes the data and the calculations we've just made. Review these calculations and make sure you understand them.

TABLE 15.4

Net Present Value of an Investment—Taxfile, Inc.

(a) Data

Price of computer	$10,000
Life of computer	2 years
Marginal revenue product	$5,900 at end of each year
Interest rate	4% a year

(b) Present value of the flow of marginal revenue product

$$PV = \frac{MRP_1}{(1 + r)} + \frac{MRP_2}{(1 + r)^2}$$

$$= \frac{\$5,900}{1.04} + \frac{\$5,900}{(1.04)^2}$$

$$= \$5,673 + \$5,455$$

$$= \$11,128$$

(c) Net present value of investment

$$NPV = PV \text{ of Marginal revenue product}$$
$$- \text{ Cost of computer}$$

$$= \$11,128 - \$10,000$$

$$= \$1,128$$

Tina's Decision to Buy Tina decides whether to buy the computer by comparing the present value of its future flow of marginal revenue product with its purchase price. She makes this comparison by calculating the net present value (*NPV*) of the computer. **Net present value** is the present value of the future flow of marginal revenue product generated by the capital minus the cost of the capital. If net present value is positive, the firm buys additional capital. If the net present value is negative, the firm does not buy additional capital. Table 15.4(c) shows the calculation of Tina's net present value of a computer. The net present value is $1,128—greater than zero—so Tina buys the computer.

Tina can buy any number of computers that cost $10,000 and have a life of two years. But like all other productive resources, capital is subject to diminishing

marginal returns. The greater the amount of capital employed, the smaller is its marginal revenue product. So if Tina buys a second computer or a third one, she gets successively smaller marginal revenue products from the additional machines.

Table 15.5(a) sets out Tina's marginal revenue products for one, two, and three computers. The marginal revenue product of one computer (the case just reviewed) is $5,900 a year. The marginal revenue product of a second computer is $5,600 a year, and the marginal revenue product of a third computer is $5,300 a year. Table 15.5(b) shows the calculations of the present values of the marginal revenue products of the first, second, and third computers.

You've seen that with an interest rate of 4 percent a year, the net present value of one computer is positive. At an interest rate of 4 percent a year, the present value of the marginal revenue product of a second computer is $10,562, which exceeds its price by $562. So Tina buys a second computer. But at an interest rate of 4 percent a year, the present value of the marginal revenue product of a third computer is $9,996, which is $4 less than the price of the computer. So Tina does not buy a third computer.

A Change in the Interest Rate We've seen that at an interest rate of 4 percent a year, Tina buys two computers but not three. Suppose that the interest rate is 8 percent a year. In this case, the present value of the first computer is $10,521 (see Table 15.5b), so Tina still buys one machine because it has a positive net present value. At an interest rate of 8 percent a year, the net present value of the second computer is $9,986, which is less than $10,000, the price of the computer. So, at an interest rate of 8 percent a year, Tina buys only one computer.

Suppose that the interest rate is even higher, at 12 percent a year. In this case, the present value of the marginal revenue product of one computer is $9,971 (see Table 15.5b). At this interest rate, Tina buys no computers.

These calculations trace Taxfile's demand schedule for capital, which shows the value of computers demanded by Taxfile at each interest rate. Other things remaining the same, as the interest rate rises, the quantity of capital demanded decreases. The higher the interest rate, the smaller is the quantity of *physical* capital demanded. But to finance the purchase of *physical* capital, firms demand *financial* capital. So the higher the interest rate, the smaller is the quantity of *financial* capital demanded.

TABLE 15.5

Taxfile's Investment Decision

(a) Data

Price of computer	$10,000
Life of computer	2 years
Marginal revenue product:	
Using 1 computer	$5,900 a year
Using 2 computers	$5,600 a year
Using 3 computers	$5,300 a year

(b) Present value of the flow of marginal revenue product

If r = 0.04 (4% a year):

Using 1 computer: $PV = \dfrac{\$5,900}{1.04} + \dfrac{\$5,900}{(1.04)^2} = \$11,128.$

Using 2 computers: $PV = \dfrac{\$5,600}{1.04} + \dfrac{\$5,600}{(1.04)^2} = \$10,562.$

Using 3 computers: $PV = \dfrac{\$5,300}{1.04} + \dfrac{\$5,300}{(1.04)^2} = \$9,996.$

If r = 0.08 (8% a year):

Using 1 computer: $PV = \dfrac{\$5,900}{1.08} + \dfrac{\$5,900}{(1.08)^2} = \$10,521.$

Using 2 computers: $PV = \dfrac{\$5,600}{1.08} + \dfrac{\$5,600}{(1.08)^2} = \$9,986.$

If r = 0.12 (12% a year):

Using 1 computer: $PV = \dfrac{\$5,900}{1.12} + \dfrac{\$5,900}{(1.12)^2} = \$9,971.$

Demand Curve for Capital

The quantity of capital demanded by a firm depends on the marginal revenue product of capital and the interest rate. A firm's demand curve for capital shows the relationship between the quantity of capital demanded by the firm and the interest rate, other things remaining the same. The market demand curve (as in Fig. 15.5) shows the relationship between the total quantity of capital demanded and the interest rate, other things remaining the same.

Changes in the Demand for Capital Figure 15.5 shows that the demand for capital has increased steadily over the years. The demand for capital changes when expectations about the future marginal revenue product of capital change. An increase in the expected marginal revenue product of capital increases the demand of capital. Two main factors that change the marginal revenue product of capital and bring changes in the demand for capital are:

1. Population growth
2. Technological change

An increase in the population increases the demand for all goods and services and so increases the demand for the capital that produces them. Advances in technology increase the demand for some types of capital and decrease the demand for other types. For example, the development of diesel engines for railroad transportation decreased the demand for steam engines and increased the demand for diesel engines. In this case, the railroad industry's overall demand for capital did not change much. In contrast, the development of desktop computers increased the demand for office computing equipment, decreased the demand for electric typewriters, and increased the overall demand for capital in the office.

Let's now turn to the supply side of the capital market.

The Supply of Capital

The quantity of capital supplied results from people's saving decisions. The main factors that determine saving are:

■ Income
■ Expected future income
■ Interest rate

Income Saving is the act of converting *current* income into *future* consumption. Usually, the higher a person's income, the more he or she plans to consume both in the present and in the future. But to increase *future* consumption, the person must save. So, other things remaining the same, the higher a person's income, the more he or she saves. The relationship between saving and income is remarkably stable. Most people save a constant proportion of their income.

Expected Future Income Because a major reason for saving is to increase future consumption, the amount that a person saves depends not only on current income but also on *expected future income*. If a person's current income is high and expected future income is low, he or she will have a high level of saving. But if a person's current income is low and expected future income is high, he or she will have a low (perhaps even negative) level of saving.

Young people (especially students) usually have low current incomes compared with their expected future income. To smooth out consumption over their lifetime, young people consume more than they earn and incur debts. Such people have a negative amount of saving. In middle age, most people's incomes reach their peak. At this stage in life, saving is at its maximum. After retirement, people spend part of the wealth they have accumulated during their working lives.

Interest Rate A dollar saved today grows into a dollar plus interest tomorrow. The higher the interest rate, the greater is the amount that a dollar saved today becomes in the future. Thus the higher the interest rate, the greater is the opportunity cost of current consumption. With a higher opportunity cost of current consumption, people cut their consumption and increase their saving.

Supply Curve of Capital

The supply curve of capital (like that in Fig. 15.5) shows the relationship between the quantity of capital supplied and the interest rate, other things remaining the same. An increase in the interest rate brings an increase in the quantity of capital supplied and a movement along the supply curve. The supply curve is inelastic in the short run but probably quite elastic in the long run. The reason is that in any given year, the total amount of saving is small relative to the stock of capital in existence. So even a large change in the saving rate brings only a small change in the quantity of capital supplied.

Changes in the Supply of Capital The main influences on the supply of capital are the size and age distribution of the population and the level of income.

Other things remaining the same, an increase in the population or an increase in income brings an increase in the supply of capital. Also, other things

remaining the same, the larger the proportion of middle-aged people, the higher is the saving rate. The reason is that middle-aged people do most of the saving as they build up a pension fund to provide a retirement income. Any one of the factors that increases the supply of capital shifts the supply curve of capital rightward.

Let's now use what we've learned about the demand for and supply of capital and see how the interest rate is determined.

The Interest Rate

Saving plans and investment plans are co-ordinated through capital markets and the interest rate adjusts to make these plans compatible.

Figure 15.6 shows the capital market. Initially, the demand for capital is KD_0 and the supply of capital is KS_0. The equilibrium interest rate is 6 percent a year and the quantity of capital is $2 trillion. If the interest rate exceeds 6 percent a year, the quantity of capital supplied exceeds the quantity of capital demanded and the interest rate falls. And if the interest rate is less than 6 percent a year, the quantity of capital demanded exceeds the quantity of capital supplied and the interest rate rises.

Over time, both the demand for capital and the supply of capital increase. The demand curve shifts rightward to KD_1 and the supply curve also shifts rightward to KS_1. Both curves shift because the same forces influence both. Population growth increases both demand and supply. Technological advances increase demand and bring higher incomes, which in turn increase supply. Because both demand and supply increase over time the quantity of capital trends upward and the interest rate has no trend.

Although the interest rate does not follow a rising or falling trend, it does fluctuate, as you can see in Fig. 15.5(a). The reason is that the demand for capital and the supply of capital do not change in lockstep. Sometimes rapid technological change brings an increase in the demand for capital *before* it brings rising incomes that increase the supply of capital. When this sequence of events occurs, the interest rate rises. The early 1980s appear to be such a time, as you can see in Fig. 15.5(a).

At other times, the demand for capital grows slowly or even decreases temporarily. In this situation, supply outgrows demand and the interest rate falls. Figure 15.5(a) shows that 1975 was one of these times.

FIGURE 15.6
Capital Market Equilibrium

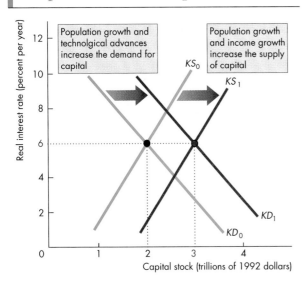

Initially, the demand for capital is KD_0 and the supply of capital is KS_0. The equilibrium interest rate is 6 percent a year and the capital stock is $2 trillion. Over time, both demand and supply increase to KD_1 and KS_1. The capital stock increases but the interest rate is constant. Demand and supply increase because they are influenced by common factors.

R E V I E W   Q U I Z

- What have been the main trends in the capital stock and interest rates since 1965?
- What is discounting and how is it used to calculate a present value? When might you want to calculate a present value to make a decision?
- How does a firm compare the future marginal revenue product of capital with the current cost of capital?
- What are the main influences on a firm's demand for capital?
- What are the main influences on the supply of capital?
- How can we explain the trends in the capital stock and interest rates?

The lessons that we've just learned about capital markets can be used to understand the prices of exhaustible natural resource prices. Let's see how.

Land and Exhaustible Natural Resource Markets

LAND IS THE QUANTITY OF NATURAL RESOURCES. All natural resources are called land and they fall into two categories:

- Nonexhaustible
- Exhaustible

A **nonexhaustible natural resource** is a natural resource that can be used repeatedly. Examples are land (in its everyday sense), rivers, lakes, rain, and sunshine.

An **exhaustible natural resource** is a natural resource that can be used only once and that cannot be replaced once it has been used. Examples are coal, natural gas, and oil—the so-called hydrocarbon fuels.

The demand for natural resources as inputs into production is based on the same principle of marginal revenue product as the demand for labour (and the demand for capital). But the supply of natural resources is special. Let's look first at the supply of nonexhaustible natural resources.

The Supply of Land (Nonexhaustible Natural Resource)

The quantity of land and other nonexhaustible natural resources available is fixed. The quantity supplied cannot be changed by individual decisions. People can vary the amount of land they own. But when one person buys some land, another person sells it. The aggregate quantity of land supplied of any particular type and in any particular location is fixed, regardless of the decisions of any individual. This fact means that the supply of each particular piece of land is perfectly inelastic. Figure 15.7 illustrates such a supply. Regardless of the rent available, the quantity of land supplied in Toronto's Yorkville is a fixed number of square metres.

Because the supply of land is fixed regardless of its price, price is determined by demand. The greater the demand for a specific block of land, the higher is its price.

Expensive land can be, and is, used more intensively than inexpensive land. For example, high-rise buildings enable land to be used more intensively. However, to use land more intensively, it has to be combined with another productive resource—capital.

FIGURE 15.7

The Supply of Land

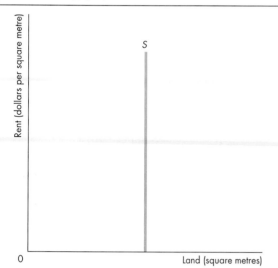

The supply of a given block of land is perfectly inelastic. No matter what the rent, no more land than the quantity that exists can be supplied.

An increase in the amount of capital on a block of land does not change the quantity of land itself.

Although the supply of each type of land is fixed and its supply is perfectly inelastic, each individual firm, operating in competitive land markets, faces an elastic supply of land. For example, Bloor Street in Toronto has a fixed amount of land, but Chapters, the bookstore, could rent some space from The Bay, the department store. Each firm can rent the quantity of land that it demands at the going rent, as determined in the marketplace. Thus provided that land markets are competitive, firms are price takers in these markets, just as they are in the markets for other productive resources.

The Supply of an Exhaustible Natural Resource

The *stock* of a natural resource is the quantity in existence at a given time. This quantity is fixed and is independent of the price of the resource. The *known* stock of a natural resource is the quantity that has been discovered. This quantity increases over time because advances in technology enable ever less accessible sources to be discovered. Both of these *stock* concepts influence the price of a natural resource. But the influence is indirect. The direct influence on price is the rate at which the resource is supplied for use in production—called the *flow* supply.

The flow supply of an exhaustible natural resource is *perfectly elastic* at a price that equals the present value of the expected price next period.

To see why, think about the economic choices of Saudi Arabia, a country that possesses a large inventory of oil. Saudi Arabia can sell an additional billion barrels of oil right now and use the income it receives to buy Canadian bonds. Or it can keep the billion barrels in the ground and sell them next year. If it sells the oil and buys Canadian bonds, it earns the interest rate on the bonds. If it keeps the oil and sells it next year, it earns the price increase or loses the price decrease between now and next year.

If Saudi Arabia expects the price to rise next year by a percentage that equals the current interest rate, the price that it expects next year equals $(1 + r)$ multiplied by this year's price. For example, if this year's price is $12 a barrel and the interest rate is 5 percent $(r = 0.5)$, then next year's expected price is $1.05 \times \$12$, which equals $12.60 a barrel.

With the price expected to rise to $12.60 next year, Saudi Arabia is indifferent between selling now for $12 and not selling now but waiting until next year and selling for $12.60. It expects to make the same return either way. So, at $12 a barrel, Saudi Arabia will sell whatever quantity is demanded.

But if Saudi Arabia expects the price to rise next year by a percentage that exceeds the current interest rate, it expects to make a bigger return by hanging on to the oil than it can make from selling the oil and buying bonds. So it keeps the oil and sells none. And if it expects the price to rise next year by a percentage that is less than the current interest rate, the bond gives a bigger return than the oil so it sells as much oil as it can.

Recall the idea of discounting and present value. The minimum price at which Saudi Arabia is willing to sell oil is the present value of the expected future price. At this price, it will sell as much oil as buyers demand. So its supply is perfectly elastic.

Price and the Hotelling Principle

Figure 15.8 shows the equilibrium in a natural resource market. Because supply is perfectly elastic at the present value of next period's expected price, the

FIGURE 15.8

An Exhaustible Natural Resource Market

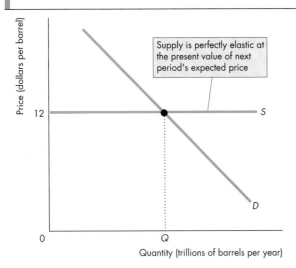

Supply is perfectly elastic at the present value of next period's expected price

The supply of an exhaustible natural resource is perfectly elastic at the *present value* of next period's expected price. The demand for an exhaustible natural resource is determined by its marginal revenue product. The price is determined by supply and equals the *present value* of next period's expected price.

FIGURE 15.9

Falling Resource Prices

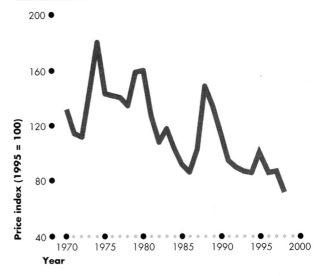

The prices of metals (here an average of the prices of aluminium, copper, iron ore, lead, manganese, nickel, silver, tin, and zinc) have tended to fall over time, not rise as predicted by the Hotelling Principle. The reason is that unanticipated advances in technology have decreased the cost of extracting resources and greatly increased the exploitable known reserves.

Source: International Financial Statistics, International Monetary Fund, Washington, D.C. (various issues).

actual price of the natural resource equals the present value of next period's expected price. Also, because the current price is the present value of the expected future price, the price of the resource is expected to rise at a rate equal to the interest rate.

The proposition that the price of a resource is expected to rise at a rate equal to the interest rate is called the *Hotelling Principle*. It was first realized by Harold Hotelling, a mathematician and economist at Columbia University. But as Fig. 15.9 shows, *actual* prices do not follow the path of *expected* prices predicted by the Hotelling Principle. Why do natural resource prices sometimes fall rather than follow their expected path and increase over time?

The key reason is that the future is unpredictable. Expected technological change is reflected in the price of a natural resource. But a previously unexpected new technology that leads to the discovery or the more efficient use of an exhaustible natural resource causes its price to fall. Over the years, as technology has advanced, we have become more efficient in our use of exhaustible resources. And we

haven't just become more efficient. We've become more efficient than we expected to.

REVIEW QUIZ

- Why is the supply of a *nonexhaustible* natural resource such as land perfectly inelastic?
- At what price is the flow supply of an exhaustible natural resource perfectly elastic and why?
- Why is the price of an exhaustible natural resource expected to rise at a rate equal to the interest rate?
- Why do the prices of exhaustible resources not follow the path predicted by the Hotelling Principle?

People supply resources to earn an income. But some people earn enormous incomes. Are such incomes necessary to induce people to work and supply other resources? Let's now answer this question.

Income, Economic Rent, and Opportunity Cost

YOU'VE NOW SEEN HOW RESOURCE PRICES ARE determined by the interaction of demand and supply. And you've seen that demand is determined by marginal productivity and supply is determined by the resources available and by people's choices about their use. The interaction of demand and supply in resource markets determines who receives a large income and who receives a small income.

Large and Small Incomes

An NBA player earns $10 million a year because he has a high marginal revenue product—reflected in the demand for his services—and the supply of people with the combination of talents needed for this kind of job is small—reflected in the supply. Equilibrium occurs at a *high* wage rate and a *small* quantity employed. And if the demand for basketball players increases, their incomes increase by a large amount and the number of players barely changes.

People who do McJobs earn a low wage rate because they have a low marginal revenue product—reflected in the demand—and many people are able and willing to supply their labour for these jobs. Equilibrium occurs at a *low* wage rate and a *large* quantity employed. And if the demand for workers in McJobs increases, the number of people doing these jobs increases by a large amount and the wage rate barely changes.

Another difference between a basketball player and a fast-food cook is that if the basketball player was hit with a pay cut, he would probably still supply his services, but if a fast-food cook was hit with a pay cut, he would probably quit. This difference arises from the interesting distinction between economic rent and opportunity cost.

Economic Rent and Opportunity Cost

The total income of a productive resource is made up of its economic rent and its opportunity cost. **Economic rent** is the income received by the owner of a resource over and above the amount required to induce that owner to offer the resource for use. Any productive resource can receive an economic rent. The income required to induce the supply of a productive

resource is the opportunity cost of using a productive resource—the value of the resource in its next best use.

Figure 15.10(a) illustrates the way in which a resource income has an economic rent and opportunity cost component. The figure shows the market for a productive resource. It could be *any* productive resource—labour, capital, or land—but we'll suppose it is labour. The demand curve is D, and its supply curve is S. The wage rate is W, and the quantity employed is C. The income earned is the sum of the yellow and green areas. The yellow area below the supply curve measures opportunity cost, and the green area above the supply curve but below the resource price measures economic rent.

To see why the area below the supply curve measures opportunity cost, recall that a supply curve can be interpreted in two different ways. It shows the quantity supplied at a given price and it shows the minimum price at which a given quantity is willingly supplied. If suppliers receive only the minimum amount required to induce them to supply each unit of the productive resource, they will be paid a different price for each unit. The prices will trace the supply curve, and the income received is entirely opportunity cost—the yellow area in Fig. 15.10(a).

The concept of economic rent is similar to the concepts of consumer surplus and producer surplus that you met in Chapter 6. Recall that consumer surplus is the maximum price someone is willing to pay, as indicated by the demand curve, minus the price paid. Producer surplus equals price minus opportunity cost. In a parallel sense, economic rent is the price a person receives for the use of a resource minus the minimum price at which a given quantity of the resource is willingly supplied.

Economic rent is not the same thing as the "rent" that a farmer pays for the use of some land or the "rent" that you pay for your apartment. Everyday "rent" is a price paid for the services of land or a building. *Economic rent* is a component of the income received by any productive resource.

The portion of the income of a productive resource that consists of economic rent depends on the elasticity of the supply of the productive resource. When the supply of a productive resource is perfectly inelastic, its entire income is economic rent. Most of Garth Brooks' and Pearl Jam's income is economic rent. Also, a large part of the income of a major league baseball player is economic rent. When the supply of a productive resource is perfectly elastic, none of its income is economic rent. Most of the income of a baby sitter is opportunity cost. In gener-

FIGURE 15.10

Economic Rent and Opportunity Cost

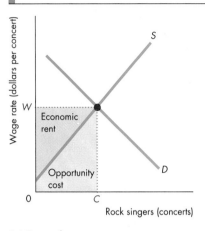

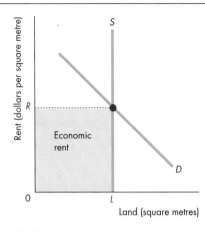

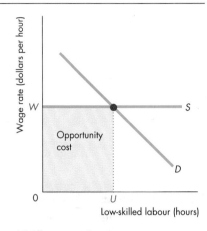

(a) General case   (b) All economic rent   (c) All opportunity cost

When a resource supply curve slopes upward—the general case—as in part (a), part of the resource income is economic rent (green) and part is opportunity cost (yellow).

When the supply of a productive resource is perfectly inelastic (the supply curve is vertical), as in part (b), the entire resource income is economic rent. When the supply of the productive resource is perfectly elastic, as in part (c), the resource's entire income is opportunity cost.

al, when the supply curve is neither perfectly elastic nor perfectly inelastic, like that illustrated in Fig. 15.10(a), some part of the resource income is economic rent and the other part is opportunity cost.

Parts (b) and (c) of Fig. 15.10 show the other two possibilities. Part (b) shows the market for a particular block of land in Toronto. The quantity of land is fixed in size at L square metres. Therefore the supply curve of the land is vertical—perfectly inelastic. No matter what the rent on the land is, there is no way of increasing the quantity that can be supplied. Suppose that the demand curve in Fig. 15.10(b) shows the marginal revenue product of this block of land. Then it commands a rent of R. The entire income accruing to the owner of the land is the green area in the figure. This income is *economic rent*.

Figure 15.10(c) shows the market for a productive resource that is in perfectly elastic supply. An example of such a market might be that for low-skilled labour in a poor country such as India or China. In those countries, large amounts of labour flock to the cities and are available for work at the going wage rate (in this case, W). Thus in these situations, the supply of labour is almost perfectly elastic. The entire income earned by this labour is opportunity cost. They receive no economic rent.

REVIEW QUIZ

- Why do basketball players earn larger incomes than do baby sitters?
- What is the distinction between an economic rent and an opportunity cost?
- Is the income that the Toronto Raptors pays to Charles Oakley an economic rent or compensation for his opportunity cost?
- Is a Big Mac more expensive in Toronto than in Brandon, Manitoba, because rents are higher in Toronto, or are rents higher in Toronto because people in Toronto are willing to pay more for a Big Mac?

Reading Between the Lines on pp. 342–343 looks at the market for hockey players. The next chapter studies labour markets more closely and explains differences in wage rates among high-skilled and low-skilled workers and males and females. Chapter 17 looks at how the market economy distributes income and at efforts by governments to redistribute income and modify the market outcome.

Rents and Opportunity Costs on the Ice

THE GLOBE AND MAIL, JANUARY 19, 1999

NHL average salary climbs to $1.3-million

BY NEIL STEVENS

The return of Pavel Bure to the National Hockey League nudges the average annual player salary toward $1.3-million (U.S.) and lifts the Florida Panthers into the upper echelon of team payrolls.

The average salary was $1.17-million (U.S.) at the end of the 1997-98 season, and it shot up with the dozens of free-agent signings since the summer. With Bure's old $8 million (U.S.) contract with the Vancouver Canucks put into the mix, the average goes up to $1.3-million (U.S.).

But what Bure will make this season isn't precisely known. The Panthers, who acquired Bure in a trade with the Canucks, tore up the Vancouver contract and gave him a new one for the rest of the season, believed to be worth about $3 million (U.S.). ...

Bure, whose $8-million contract with Vancouver had put him fifth on the league-wide list, is expected to make his debut with Florida tomorrow in Uniondale, N.Y., against the Islanders.

Sergei Fedorov of the Detroit Red Wings is the top-paid NHL player this season, at $14-million (U.S.) from a front-loaded deal the Red Wings assumed in matching the free-agent offer Fedorov received from the Carolina Hurricanes last year.

Paul Kariya of the Anaheim Mighty Ducks and Eric Lindros of the Philadelphia Flyers are each receiving $8.5-million (U.S.) this season. Buffalo Sabres goaltender Dominik Hasek is getting $8-million (U.S.).

Bure slides in ahead of Mats Sundin of the Toronto Maple Leafs, whose rate is $6.3-million (U.S.). Wayne Gretzky of the New York Rangers, Doug Gilmour of the Chicago Blackhawks, Peter Forsberg of the Colorado Avalanche and Mark Messier of the Canucks are each getting $6-million (U.S.). ...

While Bure is at the high end of the salary scale, the least-paid of more than 620 players who have appeared in NHL games this season have been Stephen Leach of the Phoenix Coyotes ($150,000 Cdn.), backup Anaheim goalie Dominic Roussel ($160,000 U.S.) and Nashville goalie Tomas Vokoun ($275,000 Cdn.).

Essence of the Story

■ The average NHL salary in 1997–98 was $1.17 million (U.S.). In 1998–99, it was $1.3 million (U.S.).

■ Sergei Fedorov of the Detroit Red Wings is the highest-paid player, receiving $14 million (U.S.) per season.

■ Next on the highest-paid list are Paul Kariya and Eric Lindros at $8.5 million (U.S.) per season, and Dominik Hasek and Pavel Bure at $8 million (U.S.) per season.

■ The lowest-paid NHL player is Stephen Leach of the Phoenix Coyotes who receives $150,000 (Canadian) per season.

■ The marginal revenue product of players of the quality of Sergei Fedorov, Paul Kariya, and Eric Lindros is enormous.

■ These players fill arenas and generate huge revenues for their teams.

■ The supply of top-performing hockey players is limited. At a wage rate below the minimum industrial wage, no one would be willing to work and train to perform at the standard of these players. The quantity supplied would be zero.

■ At a wage rate similar to the average industrial wage, a large number of people are willing to work and train to play competition quality hockey. But few have the talent to perform at the level of a Fedorov, Kariya, or Lindros.

■ No matter by how much the wage rate rises above the average industrial wage, the quantity of top-performing hockey players does not increase. The supply is inelastic.

■ Figure 1 shows the supply of top-performing hockey players as the curve labelled S. The average industrial wage rate is a. As the wage rate for hockey increases above this wage rate, the quantity of star players supplied increases, but up to a maximum of Q_0. This quantity is limited by the available talent pool.

■ The demand for top-performing players is determined by their marginal revenue product and is the curve D.

■ Equilibrium in the market for top-performing hockey players occurs at an average wage rate of $1.3 million (U.S.) a year.

■ Most of their income is economic rent, which is shown as the green area. The rest, shown by the yellow area, is *opportunity cost*.

■ Figure 2 shows the situation facing an individual hockey team. The team faces a perfectly elastic supply of top-performing players shown by the curve S_i. The team's demand curve is D_i, and the team hires Q_i top-performing players.

■ If the teams could collude, they might be able to keep players' wages down. But competition for the best players means that each team must pay the going market wage for its talent.

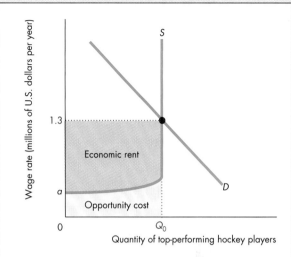

Figure 1 **The market for hockey superstars**

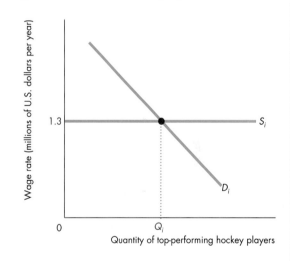

Figure 2 **Florida Panthers**

SUMMARY

Key Points

Resource Prices and Incomes (p. 322)

- An increase in the demand for a productive resource increases the resource's price and total income; a decrease in the demand for a productive resource decreases its price and total income.

- An increase in the supply of a productive resource increases the quantity used but decreases price and might increase or decrease its total income depending on whether demand is elastic or inelastic.

Labour Markets (pp. 323–330)

- The marginal revenue product of labour determines the demand for labour.

- The demand for labour increases if the price of the firm's output rises or if technological change and capital accumulation increase marginal product.

- The elasticity of demand for labour depends on the labour intensity of production, the elasticity of demand for the product, and on the ease with which labour can be substituted for capital.

- The quantity of labour supplied increases as the wage rate increases but, at high wage rates, the supply curve eventually bends backwards.

- An increase in population or an advance in home production technology increases the supply of labour.

- Real wages and employment increase because demand increases by more than supply.

Capital Markets (pp. 331–337)

- To make an investment decision, a firm compares the *present value* of the marginal revenue product of capital with the price of capital.

- Population growth and technological change increase the demand for capital.

- The higher the interest rate, the greater is the level of saving and the quantity of capital supplied.

- The supply of capital increases as incomes increase.

- Capital market equilibrium determines the real interest rate.

Land and Exhaustible Natural Resource Markets (pp. 337–339)

- The demand for natural resources is determined by marginal revenue product.

- The supply of land is inelastic.

- The supply of exhaustible natural resources is perfectly elastic at a price equal to the present value of the expected future price.

- The price of exhaustible natural resources is expected to rise at a rate equal to the interest rate, but it fluctuates and sometimes falls.

Income, Economic Rent, and Opportunity Cost (pp. 340–341)

- Economic rent is the income received by a resource owner over and above the amount needed to induce the owner to supply the productive resource for use.

- The rest of a resource's income is opportunity cost.

- When the supply of a resource is perfectly inelastic, its entire income is economic rent; and when supply is perfectly elastic, the entire income is opportunity cost.

Key Figures and Tables

Key Terms

PROBLEMS

*1. The figure illustrates the market for blueberry pickers:

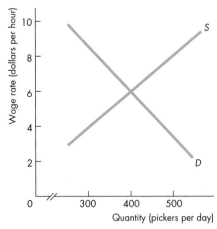

a. What is the wage rate paid to pickers?
b. How many blueberry pickers get hired?
c. What is the income received by pickers?

2. In problem 1, if the demand for blueberry pickers increases by 100 a day,
a. What is the new wage rate paid to the pickers?
b. How many additional pickers get hired?
c. What is the total income paid to pickers?

*3. The fish packing industry is competitive and Wanda owns a fish shop. She employs students to sort and pack the fish. Students can pack the following amounts of fish in an hour:

Number of students	Quantity of fish (kilograms)
1	20
2	50
3	90
4	120
5	145
6	165
7	180
8	190

The market price of fish is 50¢ a kilogram and the wage rate of packers is $7.50 an hour.
a. Calculate the marginal product of the students and draw the marginal product curve.
b. Calculate the marginal revenue product of the students and draw the marginal revenue product curve.
c. Find Wanda's demand for labour curve.
d. How many students does Wanda employ?

4. The party ice market is competitive and Barry makes party ice. He employs workers to bag the ice. The baggers can produce the following quantities in an hour:

Number of workers	Quantity of ice (bags)
1	40
2	100
3	180
4	240
5	290
6	330
7	360
8	380

The market price of ice is 25¢ a bag and the wage rate of a bagger is $5.00 an hour.
a. Calculate the marginal product of the workers and draw the marginal product curve.
b. Calculate the marginal revenue product of the workers and draw the marginal revenue product curve.
c. Find Barry's demand for labour curve.
d. How much ice does Barry sell?

*5. If, in problem 3, the price of fish falls to 33.33¢ a kilogram but fish packers' wages remain at $7.50 an hour, what happens to:
a. Wanda's marginal product?
b. Wanda's marginal revenue product?
c. Wanda's demand for labour curve?
d. the number of students Wanda employs?

6. If, in problem 4, the price of party ice falls to 10¢ a bag but baggers' wages remain at $5.00 an hour, what happens to:
a. Barry's marginal product?
b. Barry's marginal revenue product?
c. Barry's demand for labour curve?
d. the number of students Barry employs?

*7. Back at Wanda's fish shop described in problem 3, packers' wages increase to $10 an hour, but the price of fish remains at 50¢ a kilogram.
a. What happens to marginal revenue product?
b. What happens to Wanda's demand for

labour curve?

c. How many students does Wanda employ?

8. Back at Barry's party ice shop described in problem 4, baggers' wages increase to $10 an hour, but the price of ice remains at 25¢ a bag.

a. What happens to marginal revenue product?

b. What happens to Barry's demand for labour curve?

c. How many baggers does Barry employ?

*9. Using the information in problem 3, calculate Wanda's marginal revenue, marginal cost, and marginal revenue product. Show that when Wanda is making maximum profit, marginal cost equals marginal revenue and marginal revenue product equals the wage rate.

10. Using the information in problem 4, calculate Barry's marginal revenue, marginal cost, and marginal revenue product. Show that when Barry is making maximum profit, marginal cost equals marginal revenue and marginal revenue product equals the wage rate.

*11. Venus makes Firecrackers, which she sells in December each year for New Year's celebrations. She must decide how many firecracker production lines to install. Each production line costs $1 million and operates for only two years, after which it must be replaced. With one production line, Venus expects to sell $590,000 worth of firecrackers a year. With two production lines, she expects to sell $1,150,000 worth of firecrackers each year. And with three production lines, she expects to sell $1,680,000 worth of firecrackers a year. The interest rate is 5 percent a year. How many production lines does Venus install? Explain your answer.

12. Vulcan Balloon Rides must decide how many balloons to operate. Each balloon costs $10,000 and must be replaced after three years of service. With one balloon, Vulcan expects to sell $5,900 worth of rides a year. With two balloons, it expects to sell $11,500 worth of rides each year. And with three balloons, it expects to sell $16,800 worth of rides a year. The interest rate is 8 percent a year. How many balloons does Vulcan operate? Explain your answer.

*13. Greg has found an oil well in his backyard. A geologist estimates that a total of 10 million barrels can be pumped for a pumping cost of a dollar a barrel. The price of oil is $20 a barrel. How much oil does Greg sell each year? If you can't predict how much he will sell, what extra information would you need to be able to do so?

14. Orley has a wine cellar in which he keeps choice wines from around the world. What does Orley expect to happen to the prices of the wines he keeps in his cellar? Explain your answer. How does Orley decide which wine to drink and when to drink it?

*15. Use the figure in problem 1, and show on the figure the blueberry pickers' economic rent and opportunity cost.

16. In the situation described in problem 2, show on the figure the blueberry pickers' economic rent and opportunity cost.

CRITICAL THINKING

1. Study *Reading Between the Lines* on pp. 342–343 and answer the following questions:

a. What determines the demand for hockey players?

b. What determines the supply of hockey players?

c. What do you think Sergei Fedorov, Paul Kariya, and Eric Lindros would do if they didn't play hockey?

d. What does your answer to (c) tell you about the opportunity cost of these players?

e. What does your answer to (c) tell you about the economic rent received by these players?

f. Why don't hockey players have contracts that give them their entire marginal revenue product?

g. Why don't hockey teams negotiate contracts that pay the players their opportunity cost?

2. "We are running out of natural resources and must take urgent action to conserve our precious reserves." Do you agree? Why or why not?

3. Why do we keep finding new reserves of oil? Why don't we do once-and-for-all a big survey that catalogues the earth's entire inventory of natural resources?

Chapter 16

Labour Markets

As you well know, school is not just a party. Those exams and problem sets require a lot of time and effort. Are they worth the sweat that goes into them? What is the payoff? Is it sufficient to make up for the years of tuition, room and board, and lost wages? (You could, after all, be working for pay now instead of slogging through this economics course.) ◆ Many workers belong to labour unions. Usually, union workers earn a higher wage than nonunion workers in comparable jobs. Why? How are unions able to get higher wages for their members than the wages that nonunion workers are

The Sweat of Our Brows

paid? ◆ Among the most visible and persistent differences in earnings are those between men and women. Men, on the average, earn incomes that are one-third higher than the incomes earned by women. Certainly a lot of individuals defy the averages. But why do women so consistently earn less than men? Is it because of discrimination and exploitation? Or is it because of economic factors? Or is it a combination of the two? ◆ Equal pay laws have resulted in programs that try to ensure that jobs of equivalent value receive the same pay regardless of the pay set by the market. Can pay equity laws bring economic help to low-paid women? ◆ We've heard more and more during the past year about a Canadian brain drain—talented and well-educated Canadians migrating south to work in the United States. Is there a brain drain, and if there is, why does it occur?

◆ In this chapter, we answer questions such as these by continuing our study of labour markets. We begin by extending the competitive labour market model developed in Chapter 15 to study the effects of education and training on wages. We then study labour unions and the differences in union and nonunion wage rates. We also study differences in the wage rates of men and women, the effects of pay equity laws, and the source of the Canadian "brain drain."

After studying this chapter, you will be able to:

- ■ Explain why high-skilled workers earn more, on the average, than low-skilled workers
- ■ Explain why university and college graduates earn more, on the average, than high school graduates
- ■ Explain why union workers earn higher wages than nonunion workers
- ■ Explain why, on the average, men earn more than women
- ■ Predict the effects of pay equity laws
- ■ Explain why many well-educated Canadians are moving to the United States to work

Skill Differentials

EVERYONE IS SKILLED BUT THE VALUE THE market places on different types of skills varies a great deal so that differences in skills lead to large differences in earnings. For example, a clerk in a law firm earns less than a tenth of the earnings of the attorney he assists. An operating room assistant earns less than a tenth of the earnings of the surgeon she works with. Differences in skills arise partly from differences in education and partly from differences in on-the-job training. Differences in earnings between workers with varying levels of education and training can be explained by using a model of competitive labour markets. In the real world, there are many different levels and varieties of education and training. To keep our analysis as clear as possible, we'll study a model economy with two different skill levels and two types of labour: high-skilled labour and low-skilled labour. We'll study the demand for and supply of these two types of labour and see why there is a difference in their wages and what determines that difference. Let's begin by looking at the demand for the two types of labour.

The Demand for High-Skilled and Low-Skilled Labour

High-skilled workers can perform a variety of tasks that low-skilled workers would perform badly or perhaps could not even perform at all. Imagine an untrained, inexperienced person performing surgery or piloting an airplane. High-skilled workers have a higher marginal revenue product than do low-skilled workers. As we learned in Chapter 15, a firm's demand for labour curve is the same as the marginal revenue product of labour curve.

Figure 16.1(a) shows the demand curves for high-skilled (D_H) and low-skilled (D_L) labour. At any given level of employment, firms are willing to pay a higher wage rate to a high-skilled worker than to a low-skilled worker. The gap between the two wage rates measures the marginal revenue product of skill—for example, at an employment level of 2,000 hours, firms are willing to pay $12.50 for a high-skilled worker and only $5 for a low-skilled worker, a difference of $7.50 an hour. Thus the marginal revenue product of skill is $7.50 an hour.

The Supply of High-Skilled and Low-Skilled Labour

Skills are costly to acquire. Furthermore, a worker usually pays the cost of acquiring a skill before benefiting from a higher wage. For example, attending college usually leads to a higher income, but the higher income is not earned until after graduation. These facts imply that the acquisition of a skill is an investment. To emphasize the investment nature of acquiring a skill, we call that activity an investment in human capital. **Human capital** is the accumulated skill and knowledge of human beings.

The opportunity cost of acquiring a skill includes actual expenditures on such things as tuition and room and board and also costs in the form of lost or reduced earnings while the skill is being acquired. When a person goes to school full time, that cost is the total earnings forgone. However, some people acquire skills on the job. Such skill acquisition is called on-the-job training. Usually, a worker undergoing on-the-job training is paid a lower wage than one doing a comparable job but not undergoing training. In such a case, the cost of acquiring the skill is the difference between the wage paid to a person not being trained and that paid to a person being trained.

Supply Curves of High-Skilled and Low-Skilled Labour The position of the supply curve of high-skilled workers reflects the cost of acquiring the skill. Figure 16.1(b) shows two supply curves: one for high-skilled workers and the other for low-skilled workers. The supply curve for high-skilled workers is S_H, and that for low-skilled workers is S_L.

The high-skilled workers' supply curve lies above the low-skilled workers' supply curve. The vertical distance between the two supply curves is the compensation that high-skilled workers require for the cost of acquiring the skill. For example, suppose that the quantity of low-skilled labour supplied is 2,000 hours at a wage rate of $5 an hour. This wage rate compensates the low-skilled workers mainly for their time on the job. Consider next the supply of high-skilled workers. To induce 2,000 hours of high-skilled labour to be supplied, firms must pay a wage rate of $8.50 an hour. This wage rate for high-skilled labour is higher than that for low-skilled labour because high-skilled labour must be compensated not only for the time on the job but also for the time and other costs of acquiring the skill.

FIGURE 16.1

FIGURE 16.1
Skill Differentials

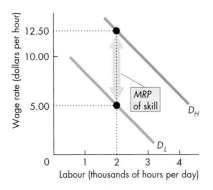

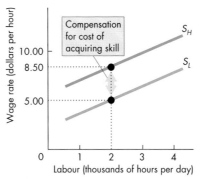

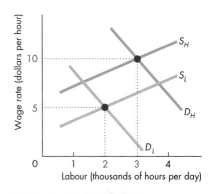

(a) Demand for high-skilled and low-skilled labour

(b) Supply of high-skilled and low-skilled labour

(c) Markets for high-skilled and low-skilled labour

Part (a) illustrates the marginal revenue product of skill. Low-skilled workers have a marginal revenue product that gives rise to the demand curve marked D_L. High-skilled workers have a higher marginal revenue product than low-skilled workers. Therefore the demand curve for high-skilled workers, D_H, lies to the right of D_L. The vertical distance between these two curves is the marginal revenue product of the skill.

Part (b) shows the effects of the cost of acquiring skills on the supply curves of labour. The supply curve for low-

skilled workers is S_L. The supply curve for high-skilled workers is S_H. The vertical distance between these two curves is the required compensation for the cost of acquiring a skill.

Part (c) shows the equilibrium employment and the wage differential. Low-skilled workers earn a wage rate of $5 an hour and 2,000 hours of low-skilled labour are employed. High-skilled workers earn a wage rate of $10 and 3,000 hours of high-skilled labour are employed. The wage rate for high-skilled workers always exceeds that for low-skilled workers.

Wage Rates of High-Skilled and Low-Skilled Labour

To work out the wage rates of high-skilled and low-skilled labour, we have to bring together the effects of skill on the demand and supply of labour.

Figure 16.1(c) shows the demand curves and the supply curves for high-skilled and low-skilled labour. These curves are exactly the same as those plotted in parts (a) and (b). Equilibrium occurs in the market for low-skilled labour where the supply and demand curves for low-skilled labour intersect. The equilibrium wage rate is $5 an hour, and the quantity of low-skilled labour employed is 2,000 hours. Equilibrium in the market for high-skilled workers occurs where the supply and demand curves for high-skilled workers intersect. The equilibrium wage rate is $10 an hour, and the quantity of high-skilled labour employed is 3,000 hours.

As you can see in part (c), the equilibrium wage rate of high-skilled labour is higher than that of low-skilled labour. This outcome occurs for two reasons: First, high-skilled labour has a higher marginal revenue product than low-skilled labour, so at a given wage rate, the quantity of high-skilled labour demanded exceeds that of low-skilled labour. Second, skills are costly to acquire, so at a given wage rate, the quantity of high-skilled labour supplied is less than that of low-skilled labour. The wage differential (in this case, $5 an hour) depends on both the marginal revenue product of the skill and the cost of acquiring it. The higher the marginal revenue product of the skill, the larger is the vertical distance between the demand curves. The more costly it is to acquire a skill, the larger is the vertical distance between the supply curves. The higher the marginal revenue product of the skill and the more costly it is to acquire, the larger is the wage differential between high-skilled and low-skilled workers.

Do Education and Training Pay?

There are large and persistent differences in earnings based on the degree of education and training. An indication of these differences is visible every day in the jobs columns of the newspaper. Take a few minutes and look at today's paper and see if you can find some examples. You'll almost certainly see lots of jobs for programmers and information systems managers that offer incomes greater than $50,000 a year. Look in *The Economist* weekly newsmagazine and you'll see jobs with income tags of $100,000 and more. All of these jobs seek applicants who have completed a university education in a relevant field and often seek relevant previous work experience.

Then look in the local newspaper at the types of jobs on offer for people with no special educational qualifications and limited work experience. You'll see such jobs on offer for incomes not much higher than the minimum wage.

Although the snapshot that you can get from newspaper advertisements is a useful one, it doesn't tell you directly about the lifetime experience of people with different levels of education. To obtain this information, we need to look at the kind of data that Statistics Canada collects. Figure 16.2 shows some of this data. The figure highlights two important sources of earnings differences:

1. Education
2. Work experience

The higher the level of education, other things remaining the same, the higher are a person's earnings. Work experience and the amount of on-the-job training a person has received is strongly correlated with age. Thus as a person gets older, up to middle age, earnings increase.

We can see from Fig. 16.2 that going through high school, postsecondary, and university education leads to higher incomes. But do they pay in the sense of yielding a higher income that compensates for the cost of education and for the delay in the start of earnings? For most people, postsecondary education does indeed pay. Rates of return have been estimated to be in the range of 5 to 10 percent after allowing for inflation, which suggests that a postsecondary degree is a better investment than almost any other that a person can undertake.

Education is an important source of earnings differences. But there are others. We next see how labour unions affect wages and why union wages tend to exceed nonunion wages.

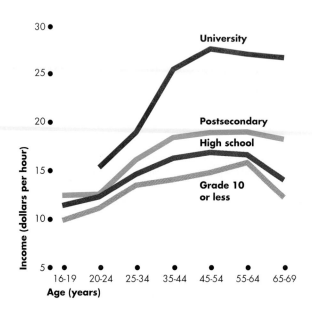

FIGURE 16.2

Education and Earnings

The figure shows the average earnings of employees at various ages and with varying levels of education. Earnings increase with length of education and also with age but only up to the mid-50s. Beyond that age, earnings decrease. These differences show the importance of experience and education in influencing skill differentials.

Source: Statistics Canada, *Survey of Consumer Finances,* 1997.*
*This analysis is based on a Statistics Canada microdata tape. All the computations on these microdata were performed by Audra J. Bowlus at the University of Western Ontario. The responsibility for the use and interpretation of these data is entirely that of the authors.

R E V I E W   Q U I Z

■ Why is the demand for high-skilled labour greater than the demand for low-skilled labour?

■ Why is the supply of high-skilled labour less than the supply of low-skilled labour?

■ How does education influence wage rates? Does education pay?

■ How does work experience influence wage rates?

Let's now look at the influence of labour unions on the labour market.

Union–Nonunion Wage Differentials

WAGE DIFFERENTIALS CAN ARISE FROM monopoly power in the labour market. Just as a monopoly producer can restrict output and raise price, so a monopoly owner of a resource can restrict supply and raise the price of the resource.

The main source of monopoly power in the labour market is the labour union. A **labour union** is an organized group of workers whose purpose it is to increase the wage rate and influence other job conditions for its members. The union seeks to restrict competition and, as a result, increases the price at which labour is traded.

There are two main types of union: craft unions and industrial unions. A **craft union** is a group of workers who have a similar range of skills but work for many different firms in many different industries and regions. An example of a craft union is Glass, Molders, Pottery, Plastics and Allied Workers International Union. An **industrial union** is a group of workers who have a variety of skills and job types but work for the same firm or industry. The United Steelworkers Union and the United Paperworkers Union are examples of industrial unions.

Most unions are members of the Canadian Labour Congress (CLC). The CLC was created in 1956 when two labour organizations combined: the Labour Council of Canada (TLC), which was founded in 1883 to organize craft unions, and the Canadian Congress of Labour (CCL), founded in 1940 to organize industrial unions. The CLC often acts as the national voice of organized labour in the media and in the political arena.

Unions vary enormously in size. Craft unions are the smallest and industrial unions are the biggest. Figure 16.3 shows the six largest unions in Canada as measured by the number of members. Union strength peaked in1983 when 40 percent of the work force belonged to unions. That percentage has fallen slightly since then. Changes in union membership, however, have been uneven in the past several decades. Some unions have declined dramatically while others, especially those in the government sector, have increased in strength.

In some firms or plants where a union operates, all workers are required to be members of the union. Such a situation is known as a *closed shop*. A closed shop is an arrangement in which only union mem-

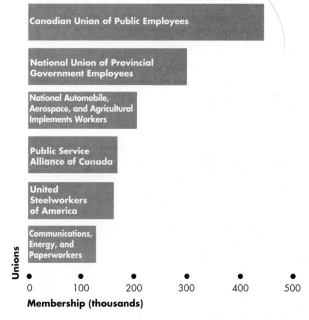

FIGURE 16.3
Unions with the Largest Membership

The labour unions with the largest membership are the two big public service unions. Together, they have almost 1 million members.

Source: Bureau of Labour Organization, *Directory of Labour Organizations*.

bers may be employed by a firm. There are other firms and plants in which a union negotiates the terms and conditions of employment but in which workers are not required to join the union. Nevertheless, in such situations, an arrangement called the Rand formula applies. The **Rand formula** is a rule (set out by Mr. Justice Ivan Rand in 1945) that makes it compulsory for all workers to contribute funds to the union whether or not they belong to the union.

Unions negotiate with employers or their representatives in a process called **collective bargaining**. The main weapons available to the union and the employer in collective bargaining are the strike and the lockout. A *strike* is a group decision to refuse to work under prevailing conditions. A *lockout* is a firm's refusal to operate its plant and employ its workers.

Each party uses the threat of a strike or a lockout to try to get an agreement in its own favour. Sometimes when the two parties in the collective bargaining process cannot agree on the wage rate or other conditions of employment, they agree to submit their disagreement to binding arbitration. *Binding arbitration* is a process in which a third party—an arbitrator—determines the wage rate and other employment conditions on behalf of the negotiating parties.

Although they are not labour unions in a legal sense, professional associations act in ways similar to labour unions. A *professional association* is an organized group of professional workers such as lawyers, dentists, or physicians (an example of which is the Ontario Medical Association—OMA).

The source of all monopoly power is a barrier to entry. Without a barrier to entry, even when there is only one supplier of a resource (or good or service) that supplier does not have monopoly power. Many professional associations know the importance of barriers to entry and they control entry into their professions by a system of licensing. Usually, the licensing takes the form of ensuring that members of the professional association meet some minimum standards of competence. This aspect of licensing brings clear benefits to consumers. But it also brings benefits to the members of the association by raising their level of income above what a competitive market would deliver.

Union's Objectives and Constraints

A union has three broad objectives that it strives to achieve for its members:

1. To increase compensation
2. To improve working conditions
3. To expand job opportunities

Each of these objectives contains a series of more detailed goals. For example, in seeking to increase members' compensation, a union operates on a variety of fronts: wage rates, fringe benefits, retirement pay, and such things as vacation allowances. In seeking to improve working conditions, a union is concerned with occupational health and safety as well as the environmental quality of the workplace. In seeking to expand job opportunities, a union tries to get greater job security for existing union members and to find ways of creating additional jobs for them.

A union's ability to pursue its objectives is restricted by two sets of constraints—one on the supply side of the labour market and the other on the demand side. On the supply side, the union's activities are limited by how well it can restrict nonunion workers from offering their labour in the same market as the union labour. The larger the fraction of the work force controlled by the union, the more effective the union can be in this regard. It is difficult for a union to operate in a market in which there is an abundant supply of willing nonunion labour. For example, the market for part-time checkout clerks is very tough for a union to organize because of the enormous rate of turnover of participants in that market. At the other extreme, unions in the construction industry can better pursue their goals because they can influence the number of people who can obtain skills as electricians, plasterers, and carpenters. The professional associations of dentists and physicians are best able to restrict the supply of dentists and physicians. These groups control the number of qualified workers by controlling either the examinations that new entrants must pass or entrance into professional degree programs.

On the demand side of the labour market, the union faces a tradeoff that arises from firms' profit-maximizing decisions. Because labour demand curves slope downward, anything a union does that increases the wage rate or other employment costs decreases the quantity of labour demanded.

Despite the difficulties they face, unions do operate in competitive labour markets. Let's see how they do so.

Unions in a Competitive Labour Market

When a union operates in an otherwise competitive labour market, it seeks to increase wages and other compensation and to limit employment reductions by increasing demand for the labour of its members. That is, the union tries to take actions that shift the demand curve for its members' labour rightward.

Figure 16.4 illustrates a competitive labour market that a union enters. The demand curve is D_C, and the supply curve is S_C. Before the union enters the market, the wage rate is $7 an hour and 100 hours of labour are employed.

Now suppose that a union is formed to organize the workers in this market. The union can attempt to increase the wage rate in this market in two ways. It

FIGURE 16.4
A Union in a Competitive Labour Market

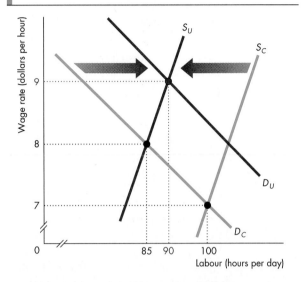

In a competitive labour market, the demand curve is D_C and the supply curve is S_C. Competitive equilibrium occurs at a wage rate of $7 an hour with 100 hours employed. By restricting employment below the competitive level, the union shifts the supply of labour to S_U. If the union can do no more than that, the wage rate will increase to $8 an hour, but employment will decrease to 85 hours. If the union can increase the demand for labour (by increasing the demand for the good produced by union members or by raising the price of substitute labour) and shift the demand curve to D_U, then it can increase the wage rate still higher, to $9 an hour, and achieve employment of 90 hours.

can try to restrict the supply of labour or it can try to stimulate the demand for labour. First, look at what happens if the union has sufficient control over the supply of labour to be able to artificially restrict that supply below its competitive level—to S_U. If that is all the union is able to do, employment falls to 85 hours of labour and the wage rate rises to $8 an hour. The union simply picks its preferred position along the demand curve that defines the tradeoff it faces between employment and the wage rate.

You can see that if the union can only restrict the supply of labour, it raises the wage rate but decreases the number of jobs available. Because of this outcome unions try to increase the demand for labour and

shift the demand curve rightward. Let's see what they might do to achieve this outcome.

How Unions Try to Change the Demand for Labour

Unless a union can take actions that change the demand for the labour that it represents, it has to accept the fact that a higher wage rate can be obtained only at the price of lower employment.

The union tries to operate on the demand for labour in two ways. First, it tries to make the demand for union labour less elastic. Second, it tries to increase the demand for union labour. Making the demand for labour less elastic does not eliminate the tradeoff between employment and wages. But it does make the tradeoff less unfavourable. If a union can make the demand for labour less elastic, it can increase the wage rate at a lower cost in terms of lost employment opportunities. But if the union can increase the demand for labour, it might even be able to increase both the wage rate and the employment opportunities of its members.

Some methods used by unions to change the demand for the labour of its members are to:

- Increase the marginal product of union members
- Encourage import restrictions
- Support minimum wage laws
- Support immigration restrictions
- Increase demand for the good produced

Unions try to increase the marginal product of their members, which in turn increases the demand for their labour, by organizing and sponsoring training schemes, by encouraging apprenticeship and other on-the-job training activities, and by professional certification.

One of the best examples of import restrictions is the support by the Canadian Auto Workers Union (CAW) for import restrictions on foreign cars.

Unions support minimum wage laws to increase the cost of employing low-skilled labour. An increase in the wage rate of low-skilled labour leads to a decrease in the quantity demanded of low-skilled labour and to an increase in demand for high-skilled union labour, a substitute for low-skilled labour.

Restrictive immigration laws decrease the supply and increase the wage rate of low-skilled workers. As a result, the demand for high-skilled union labour increases.

Because the demand for labour is a derived demand, an increase in the demand for the good produced increases the demand for union labour. The best examples of attempts by unions in this activity are in the textile and auto industries. The garment workers' union urges us to buy union-made clothes, and the CAW asks us to buy only North American cars made by union workers.

Figure 16.4 illustrates the effects of an increase in the demand for the labour of a union's members. If the union can also take steps that increase the demand for labour to D_U, it can achieve an even bigger increase in the wage rate with a smaller fall in employment. By maintaining the restricted labour supply at S_U, the union increases the wage rate to $9 an hour and achieves an employment level of 90 hours of labour.

Because a union restricts the supply of labour in the market in which it operates, its actions increase the supply of labour in nonunion markets. Workers who can't get union jobs must look elsewhere for work. This increase in supply in nonunion markets lowers the wage rate in those markets and further widens the union–nonunion differential.

The Scale of Union–Nonunion Wage Differentials

We have seen that unions can influence the wage rate by restricting the supply of labour and increasing the demand for labour. How much of a difference to wage rates do unions make in practice?

Union wage rates are, on the average, 30 percent higher than nonunion wage rates. In mining and financial services, union and nonunion wages are similar. In services, manufacturing, and transportation, the differential is between 11 and 19 percent. In wholesale and retail trades, the differential is 28 percent, and in construction it is 65 percent.

But these union–nonunion wage differentials don't give a true measure of the effects of unions. In some industries, union wages are higher than nonunion wages because union members do jobs that involve greater skill. Even without a union, those workers receive a higher wage. To calculate the effects of unions, we have to examine the wages of unionized and nonunionized workers who do nearly identical work. The evidence suggests that after allowing for skill differentials, the union–nonunion wage differential lies between 10 percent and 25 percent. For example, airline pilots who belong to the Air Line

Pilots' Union earn about 25 percent more than nonunion pilots with the same level of skill.

Let's now turn to the case in which employers have considerable influence in the labour market.

Monopsony

A **monopsony** is a market in which there is a single buyer. This market type is unusual but it does exist. With the growth of large-scale production over the last century, large manufacturing plants such as coal mines, steel and textile mills, and car manufacturers became the major employer in some regions, and in some places a single firm employed almost all the labour. Today, in Canada, the provincial health insurance plans are the major employer of physicians and other health-care professionals. These employers have monopsony power.

In monopsony, the employer determines the wage rate and pays the lowest wage at which it can attract the labour it plans to hire. A monopsony makes a bigger profit than a group of firms that compete with each other for their labour. Let's find out how they achieve this outcome.

Like all firms, a monopsony has a downward-sloping marginal revenue product curve, which is *MRP* in Fig. 16.5. This curve tells us the extra revenue the monopsony receives by selling the output produced by an extra hour of labour. The supply of labour curve is *S*. This curve tells us how many hours are supplied at each wage rate. It also tells us the minimum wage for which a given quantity of labour is willing to work.

A monopsony recognizes that to hire more labour, it must pay a higher wage rate; equivalently, by hiring less labour, it can pay a lower wage rate. Because a monopsony controls the wage rate, the marginal cost of labour exceeds the wage rate. The marginal cost of labour is shown by the curve *MCL*. The relationship between the marginal cost of labour curve and the supply curve is similar to the relationship between the marginal cost and average cost curves that you studied in Chapter 11. The supply curve is like the average cost of labour curve. In Fig. 16.5, the firm can hire 49 hours of labour for a wage rate of just below $4.90 an hour. The firm's total labour cost is $240. But suppose that the firm hires 50 hours of labour. It can hire the 50th hour of labour for $5 an hour. The total cost of labour is now $250 an hour. So, hiring the 50th hour of labour increases the cost of labour from $240 to $250,

FIGURE 16.5

A Monopsony Labour Market

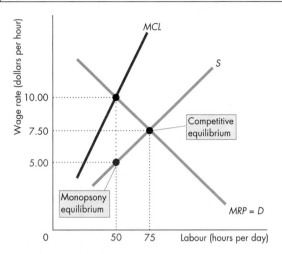

A monopsony is a market structure in which there is a single buyer. A monopsony in the labour market has marginal revenue product curve MRP and faces a labour supply curve S. The marginal cost of labour curve is MCL. Making the marginal cost of labour equal to marginal revenue product maximizes profit. The monopsony hires 50 hours of labour and pays the lowest wage for which that labour will work, which is $5 an hour.

which is a $10 increase. The marginal cost of labour is $10 an hour. The curve MCL shows the $10 marginal cost of hiring the 50th hour of labour.

To calculate the profit-maximizing quantity of labour to hire, the firm sets the marginal cost of labour equal to the marginal revenue product of labour. That is, the firm wants the cost of the last worker hired to equal the extra total revenue brought in. In Fig. 16.5, this outcome occurs when the monopsony employs 50 hours of labour. What is the wage rate that the monopsony pays? To hire 50 hours of labour, the firm must pay $5 an hour, as shown by the supply of labour curve. So each worker is paid $5 an hour. But the marginal revenue product of labour is $10 an hour, which means that the firm makes an economic profit of $5 on the last hour of labour that it hires. Compare this outcome with that in a competitive labour market. If the labour market shown in Fig. 16.5 were competitive, equilibrium would occur at the point of intersection of the demand curve and the supply curve. The wage rate would be $7.50 an hour and 75 hours of labour a day would be

employed. So, compared with a competitive labour market, a monopsony decreases both the wage rate and the level of employment.

The ability of a monopsony to lower the wage rate and employment level and make an economic profit depends on the elasticity of labour supply. The more elastic the supply of labour, the less opportunity a monopsony has to cut the wage rate and employment and make an economic profit.

Monopsony Tendencies   Today, monopsony is rare. Workers can commute long distances to a job, so most people have more than one potential employer. But firms that are dominant employers in isolated communities do face an upward-sloping supply of labour curve and so have a marginal cost of labour that exceeds the wage rate. But in such situations, there is also, usually, a union. Let's see how unions and monopsonies interact.

Monopsony and Unions   When we studied monopoly in Chapter 13, we discovered that a single seller in a market is able to determine the price in that market. We have just studied monopsony—a market with a single buyer—and discovered that in such a market, the buyer is able to determine the price. Suppose that a union starts to operate in a monopsony labour market. A union is like a monopoly. It controls the supply of labour and acts like a single seller of labour. If the union (monopoly seller) faces a monopsony buyer, the situation is one of **bilateral monopoly**. In bilateral monopoly, the wage rate is determined by bargaining between the two sides. Let's study the bargaining process.

In Fig. 16.5, if the monopsony is free to determine the wage rate and the level of employment, it hires 50 hours of labour for a wage rate of $5 an hour. But suppose that a union represents the workers and can, if necessary, call a strike. Also suppose that the union agrees to maintain employment at 50 hours but seeks the highest wage rate the employer can be forced to pay. That wage rate is $10 an hour. That is, the wage rate equals the marginal revenue product of labour. It is unlikely that the union will get the wage rate up to $10 an hour. But it is also unlikely that the firm will keep the wage rate down to $5 an hour. The monopsony firm and the union bargain over the wage rate, and the result is an outcome between $10 an hour (the maximum that the union can achieve) and $5 an hour (the minimum that the firm can achieve).

The actual outcome of the bargaining depends on the costs that each party can inflict on the other as a result of a failure to agree on the wage rate. The firm can shut down the plant and lock out its workers, and the workers can shut down the plant by striking. Each party knows the other's strength and knows what it will lose if it does not agree to the other's demands. If the two parties are equally strong and they realize it, they will split the difference and agree to a wage rate of $7.50 an hour. If one party is stronger than the other—and both parties know that—the agreed wage will favour the stronger party. Usually, an agreement is reached without a strike or a lockout. The threat—knowledge that such an event can occur—is usually enough to bring the bargaining parties to an agreement. But when a strike or lockout does occur, it is often because one party has misjudged the costs each party can inflict on the other.

Minimum wage laws have interesting effects in monopsony labour markets. Let's study these effects.

Monopsony and the Minimum Wage

In a competitive labour market, a minimum wage that exceeds the equilibrium wage decreases employment (see Chapter 7, pp. 135–136). In a monopsony labour market, a minimum wage can *increase* both the wage rate and employment. Let's see how.

Figure 16.6 shows a monopsony labour market in which the wage rate is $5 an hour and 50 hours of labour are employed. A minimum wage law is passed that requires employers to pay at least $7.50 an hour. The monopsony in Fig. 16.6 now faces a perfectly elastic supply of labour at $7.50 an hour up to 75 hours. Above 75 hours, a wage that exceeds $7.50 an hour must be paid to hire additional hours of labour. Because the wage rate is a fixed $7.50 an hour up to 75 hours, the marginal cost of labour is also constant at $7.50 an hour up to 75 hours. Beyond 75 hours, the marginal cost of labour rises above $7.50 an hour. To maximize profit, the monopsony sets the marginal cost of labour equal to its marginal revenue product. That is, the monopsony hires 75 hours of labour at $7.50 an hour. The minimum wage law has made the supply of labour perfectly elastic and made the marginal cost of labour the same as the wage rate up to 75 hours. The law has not affected the supply of labour curve or the marginal cost of labour at employment levels above 75 hours. The minimum wage law has succeeded in raising the wage rate by $2.50 an hour and increasing the amount of labour employed by 25 hours.

FIGURE 16.6
Minimum Wage in Monopsony

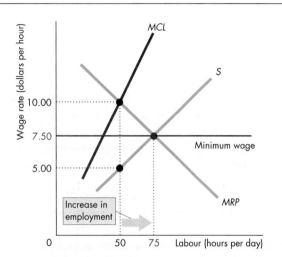

In a monopsony labour market, the wage rate is $5 an hour and 50 hours are hired. If a minimum wage law increases the wage rate to $7.50 an hour, employment increases to 75 hours.

R E V I E W   Q U I Z

- What are the main methods that labour unions use to increase the wage rates of their members above the levels of nonunion wage rates?
- What are the main methods that professional associations use to increase the wage rates of their members above competitive market levels?
- What is a monopsony and why is a monopsony able to pay a lower wage rate than a competitive firm?
- What is the effect of a minimum wage in monopsony? What is the effect of a minimum wage in a competitive labour market? Why are the two effects different?

You now understand two sources of wage differentials: skill differentials and the actions of labour unions. These two sources of wage differentials are easy to see and to analyse. The third source of wage differentials, sex, is harder to explain but it is the most sensitive of the sources of income differentials.

Wage Differentials Between the Sexes

THE OBJECTIVE OF THIS SECTION IS TO SHOW YOU how to use economic analysis to address a controversial and emotionally charged issue: persistent earnings differentials between the sexes. Figure 16.7 gives a snapshot of these differences in 1991. For both part-time and full-time workers, Canadian women, on the average, earned 61.5 percent of Canadian men's earnings. For full-time workers, the earnings of women were 69.6 percent of men's earnings.

Why does this earnings differential exist? Does it arise because there is discrimination against women, or is there some other explanation? This controversial question generates an enormous amount of passion.

It is not our intention to make you angry, but that might happen as an unintended consequence of this discussion.

We are going to examine four possible explanations for earnings differences:

- Job types
- Discrimination
- Differences in human capital
- Differences in the degree of specialization

Job Types

Some of the difference in men's and women's wages arises from the fact that men and women do different jobs and, for the most part, men's jobs are better paid than women's jobs. But there are increasing numbers of women entering areas that were traditionally the preserve of men. This trend is particularly clear in professions such as architecture, medicine, economics, law, accounting, and pharmacology. The percentage of total enrolments in university courses in these subjects for women has increased from less than 20 percent in 1970 to approaching, and in some cases exceeding, 50 percent today. Women are also increasingly seen as bus drivers, police officers, and construction workers, all jobs that traditionally were done mainly by men.

But there are many situations in which women earn less than men, even when they do essentially the same job. One possible reason is that women are discriminated against. Let's see how discrimination might affect wage rates.

Discrimination

To see how discrimination can affect wage rates, let's look at an example—the market for investment advisors. Suppose that there are two groups of investment advisers who are identical in their skills at picking good investments. One group consists of females and the other of males. Figure 16.8 shows the supply curves of females, S_F, (in part a) and of males, S_M (in part b). The marginal revenue product of investment advisors, as shown by the two curves labelled MRP in parts (a) and (b), is the same for both groups.

If everyone is free of prejudice about sex, the market determines a wage rate of $40,000 a year for all investment advisors. But if the customers of investment houses are prejudiced against women, this prejudice is reflected in wage rates and employment.

FIGURE 16.7

Sex Differentials

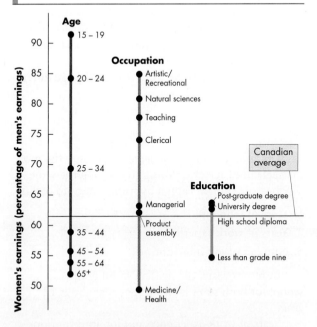

Women on the average earn about 61.5 percent of the amount earned by men. Much of this difference is accounted for by age—the incomes of younger women are much closer to those of men than are those of older women. The difference also arises from the fact that women predominate in lower-paid jobs. Education also plays a role.

Source: Statistics Canada, *Women in the Workplace:* 1993.

FIGURE 16.8

Discrimination

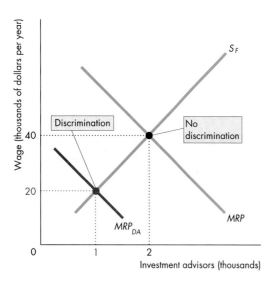

(a) Women

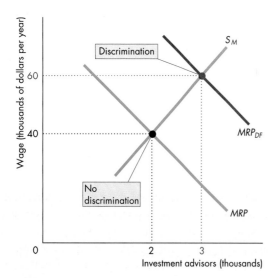

(b) Men

With no discrimination, the wage rate is $40,000 a year and 2,000 of each group are hired. With discrimination against women, the marginal revenue product curve in part (a) is MRP_{DA} and in part (b) MRP_{DF}. The wage rate for women falls to $20,000 a year, and only 1,000 are employed. The wage rate for men rises to $60,000 a year, and 3,000 are employed.

Suppose that the marginal revenue product of the females, when discriminated against, is MRP_{DA}, where *DA* stands for "discriminated against." Suppose that the marginal revenue product for males, the group discriminated in favour of, is MRP_{DF}, where *DF* stands for "discriminated in favour of." With these marginal revenue product curves, females earn $20,000 a year, and only 1,000 will work as investment advisors. Males earn $60,000 a year, and 3,000 of them will work as investment advisors.

Economists disagree about whether prejudice actually causes wage differentials, and one line of reasoning suggests that it does not. In the example you've just studied, customers who buy from men pay a higher service charge for investment advice than the customers who buy from women. This price difference acts as an incentive to encourage people who are prejudiced to buy from the people against whom they are prejudiced. This force could be so strong as to eliminate the effects of discrimination altogether. Suppose, as is true in manufacturing, that a firm's customers never meet its workers. If such a firm discriminates against women, it cannot compete with firms who hire women because its costs are higher than those of the non-prejudiced firms. So only those firms that do not discriminate survive in a competitive industry.

Let's now turn to the third source of wage differentials: human capital.

Differences in Human Capital

The more human capital a person possesses, the more that person earns, other things remaining the same. We measure human capital by using three indicators:

1. Years of schooling
2. Years of work experience
3. Number of job interruptions

In recent years, the median number of years in school for both sexes is almost equal at about 12 years.

Years of work experience and job interruptions are interrelated. For people of a given age and given amount of schooling, a person who has had fewer job interruptions has usually had more years of work experience. But interruptions to a career disrupt and reduce the effectiveness of job experience, slow down the accumulation of human capital, and even sometimes result in the depreciation of human capital through its lack of use. Historically and today, job interruptions are more serious for women than for men. Traditionally, women's careers have been interrupted for bearing and rearing children. This factor is a possible source of lower wages, on the average, for women. But just as education differences are virtually disappearing, so career interruptions for women are becoming less common. Maternity leave and day-care facilities are providing an increasing number of women with uninterrupted employment that makes their human capital accumulation more similar to that of men.

Thus it seems that human capital differences possibly can account for earnings differentials between women and men in the past and for some of the differentials that still remain. The trends, however, suggest that wage differentials from this source will eventually disappear.

There is one final source of wage differences that is likely to affect women's incomes adversely: the relative degree of specialization of women and men.

Differences in the Degree of Specialization

Families must choose how to allocate the time of their members between working for a wage and doing jobs in the home, such as cooking, cleaning, shopping, organizing vacations and, most importantly in terms of the time and commitment that it takes, in the bearing and rearing of children.

Let's look at the choices of Bob and Sue. Bob and Sue are both 35 years old. They both have masters degrees, Bob in programming and Sue in journalism. Both of them developed successful careers in their chosen fields and both earned about the same income until they decided to have children. Bob and Sue now have two pre-school children and they have made some tough choices.

To make these choices, they began by setting out the alternatives. As Bob and Sue saw things, they could organize their lives as parents in any of the following ways:

1. Bob specializes in earning an income and Sue diversifies by working shorter hours at her job and taking time off as needed to care for the children and the home.

2. Sue specializes in earning an income and Bob diversifies by working shorter hours at his job and taking time off as needed to care for the children and the home.

3. Both of them diversify between earning an income and working shorter hours, taking time off as needed to care for the children and the home and sharing household chores in the evenings and at the weekends.

The time allocation they choose depends on their preferences and on the earning potential of each of them. The choice of an increasing number of households is the third one. Each person diversifies between earning an income and doing some home chores.

But in most households, Bob specializes in earning an income and Sue diversifies between earning an income and taking care of the home. It seems likely that with this allocation, Bob will earn more than Sue. If Sue devotes time and effort to ensuring Bob's mental and physical well-being, the quality of Bob's market labour will be higher than if he were diversified. If the roles were reversed, Sue would be able to supply market labour that earns more than Bob.

To test whether the degree of specialization accounts for wage differentials between the sexes, economists have studied two groups: "never married" men and "never married" women. The available evidence suggests that, on the average, when they have the same amount of human capital—measured by years of schooling, work experience, and career interruptions—the wage rates of these two groups are not significantly different.

REVIEW QUIZ

- How important are differences in the types of jobs that men and women do in influencing their relative earnings?

- How important do you think discrimination is in influencing their relative earnings?

- How important are differences in the human capital of men and women in influencing their relative earnings?

- How might differences in the degree of specialization of men and women result in men earning higher wage rates than women?

Pay equity laws are designed to reduce the wage differences between the sexes. Do these laws work?

Pay Equity Laws

THE FEDERAL GOVERNMENT AND ALL PROVINCIAL
governments have passed laws that require *equal pay
for equal work without discrimination on the basis of
sex.* Increasingly, attempts are being made to find ways
of comparing jobs that are essentially different but
require, on some criteria, similar degrees of skill. Such
comparisons lead to a broader concept than "equal
pay for equal work"; they call for equal pay for comparable work. Paying the same wage for different jobs
that are judged to be comparable is called **pay equity**.

Advocates of pay equity laws argue that analysing
the characteristics of jobs and determining their
worth on objective grounds should determine wages.
But such a method of determining wage rates does
not achieve the objectives sought by supporters of
wage equality. Let's see why.

Figure 16.9 shows how pay equity laws work.
Part (a) shows the market for oil rig operators and
part (b) the market for nurses. The marginal revenue
product curves (MRP_R and MRP_N) and the supply
curves (S_R and S_N) are shown for each type of labour.
Competition generates a wage rate W_R for oil rig
operators and W_N for nurses.

Suppose it is decided that these two jobs are
comparable and that the courts enforce a wage rate of
W_C for both groups. What happens? First, there is a
shortage of oil rig operators. Oil rig companies are
able to hire only S_R workers at the wage rate W_C.
They cut back their production or build more expensive labour-saving oil rigs. Also the number of nurses
employed decreases. But this decrease occurs because
hospitals demand fewer nurses. At the higher wage
W_C, hospitals demand only D_N nurses. The quantity
of nurses supplied is S_N, and the difference between
S_N and D_N is the number of unemployed nurses
looking for jobs. These nurses eventually accept non-
nursing jobs (which they don't like as much as nursing jobs), quite likely at a lower rate of pay than that
of nurses.

FIGURE 16.9

The Problem with Pay Equity

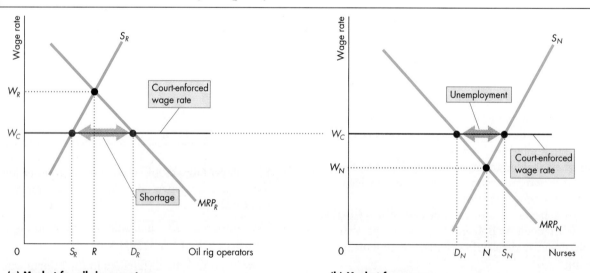

(a) Market for oil rig operators

(b) Market for nurses

Part (a) shows the demand for and supply of oil rig operators,
MRP_R and S_R, and part (b) shows the demand for and supply of
nurses, MRP_N and S_N. The competitive equilibrium wage rate
for oil rig operators is W_R, and that for nurses is W_N. If an
evaluation of the two jobs finds that they are comparable and
pay equity rules that the wage rate W_C be paid to both types

of workers, such a wage creates a shortage of oil rig
operators and a surplus of nurses. Oil producers search for
labour-saving ways of producing oil (that are more expensive),
and nurses search for other jobs (that are less desirable to
them and probably are less well paid)

Although pay equity laws can eliminate wage differences, they can only do so by incurring costly unintended consequences. They limit job opportunities and create unemployment among workers whose wage rate they raise. And they make it hard for employers to hire workers whose wage rate is held down. Only in the rare case of a monopsonistic labour market does equalizing wage rates not create permanent surpluses and shortages of skills. In this situation, a pay equity law works in a similar way to a minimum wage law.

Effective Wage Policies

We have now surveyed the major sources of wage differentials. Of the various possible sources of differences in wage rates, one stands out: the level of education. People with postgraduate degrees earn much more than college graduates, who in turn earn much more than high school graduates, who in turn earn more than people who have not completed high school. This source of wage differences is the main one on which an effective policy can operate.

By pursuing the most effective education available in grade school, high school, and college and university, people can equip themselves with human capital that brings significantly higher earnings. But in today's rapidly changing world, education and human capital accumulation must be an ongoing enterprise. The most successful workers are those who are able to repeatedly retool and actively embrace each new technological advance. The least successful are those who get locked into a particular technology and are unable or unwilling to adapt when that technology becomes redundant. So an effective wage policy is one that emphasizes the importance of ongoing education and training.

R E V I E W   Q U I Z

■ What is a pay equity law and what does it seek to achieve?

■ Do pay equity laws eliminate wage differences? What other effects do pay equity laws have that benefit or harm lower-paid workers?

■ What is the most effective policy that can eliminate wage differentials among men and women?

We're now going to turn to the final topic of this chapter: migration.

Migration

SIXTY MILLION PEOPLE, OR ONE PERCENT OF THE world's current population and twice the population of Canada, have migrated from the country in which they were born. We'll study two questions about migration:

■ How many people migrate into and out of Canada and where do they come from and go to?

■ How does migration affect employment and wage rates of Canadians?

Scale and Origin of Migration Into Canada

About 100,000 immigrants arrive in Canada each year. This number seems large when compared with the population of metropolitan areas like Regina, Saskatchewan (199,000) or Saint John, New Brunswick (129,000). But it represents only one-third of one percent of the Canadian population, or 3 immigrants per 1,000 Canadians.

Figure 16.10 shows some interesting facts about the places of origin of Canadian immigrants. Before 1960, 90 percent of Canadian immigrants came from Europe. Fewer than 5 percent came from the United States and the rest of the American continent (which includes the Caribbean), and only 3 percent came from Asia. But gradually, over the decades, Asia replaced Europe as the main place of origin of new immigrants. By the 1990s, new migrants coming from Europe had fallen to 19 percent of the total and new migrants from Asia had increased to 57 percent of the total. Migration inside the American continent increased between 1960 and the 1970s and then decreased.

Scale and Destination of Migrating Canadians

Despite the enormous amount of publicity that surrounds the idea of a Canadian brain drain, the numbers of Canadians who leave to live in other countries is tiny. The main destination for Canadians is the United States. But the numbers are so small that the U.S. Census Department doesn't report them as a separate category in its summary tables of the origins of U.S. immigrants. The exact number of

FIGURE 16.10

The Scale and Sources of Canadian Immigration

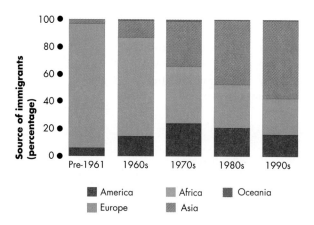

This figure shows that before 1960, almost all Canada's immigrants came from Europe. But over the years, Asia has replaced Europe as the main source of our new immigrants.

Canadians in the United States is not known, but it is fewer that 500,000.

Despite the small numbers, Canadian migration into the United States is significant in a number of highly visible areas. Canadian academics, journalists, movie stars and directors, doctors, musicians, computer scientists, architects, engineers, and business leaders feature prominently among the people who have left Canada over the years. So despite the small numbers involved, Canada does have a "brain drain."

How does migration influence the labour market? Let's study this question.

Immigrants and the Labour Market

Immigration increases the supply of labour. By so doing, it lowers the wage rates of existing workers. At the same time, it decreases the supply of labour and raises wage rates in the country the immigrants are leaving. Figure 16.11 shows these effects in the labour markets of Canada (part a) and Asia (part b). The demand for labour in Canada is LD_{CAN} and in Asia it is LD_A. Before immigration takes place,

25 million workers in Canada earn $15 an hour and 500 million workers in Asia earn $1 an hour. (The numbers are hypothetical.)

If the movement of people between Canada and Asia were entirely unrestricted, Asians would enter Canada, so long as by doing so they could increase their incomes. In this example, the labour force of Canada increases to 150 million and the wage rate falls to $8 an hour. In Asia, the labour force decreases to 375 million and the wage rate rises to $8 an hour. In the world equilibrium, there is no incentive for anyone to migrate between the two regions.

You can apply the analysis in Fig. 16.11 to the situation in Canada and the United States. Suppose the United States is the high-wage country and Canada is the low-wage country. Figure 16.11 can be interpreted as showing what would happen with a free border between Canada and the United States. The wage rate in Canada would rise and that in the United States would fall until wage rates in the two countries became equal.

The economic effects of migration that we've just studied apply not only to the movement of people between nations but also to the movement of people across the regions of a single country.

Again, you can use Fig. 16.11 to analyse migration among regions. Now suppose that Ontario is the high-wage region and Newfoundland is the low-wage region. With a higher wage rate in Toronto than in St. John's, some people decide to migrate from Newfoundland to Ontario. The decrease in the supply of labour in Newfoundland increases the wage rate there and the increase in the supply of labour in Ontario decreases its wage rate.

Does the outcome shown in Fig. 16.11 really occur? And are the effects large ones (like the ones in the example in Fig. 16.11)?

The outcome shown in Fig. 16.11 probably does not occur for at least three reasons. First, people are not willing to vote for an open-border immigration law. Instead, they vote for immigration laws that prevent the free movement of people and so prevent the outcome shown in Fig. 16.11.

Second, immigrants not only add to the supply of labour. They also add to the demand for goods and services and to the supply of capital.

Because immigrants bring a demand for goods and services, firms increase production and the demand for labour increases. This increase in the demand for labour limits the extent to which the wage rate falls.

FIGURE 16.11

Immigration and the Labour Market

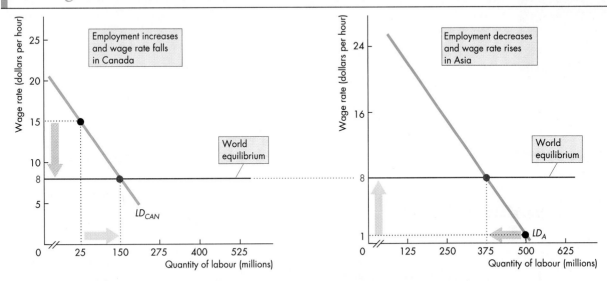

(a) The Canadian labour market

(b) The Asian labour market

Part (a) shows the labour market in Canada. The demand for labour is LD_{CAN} and with 25 million workers, the wage rate is $15 an hour. Part (b) shows the labour market in Asia. The demand for labour is LD_A and with 500 million workers, the wage rate is $1 an hour. With free movement of people between the two regions, people leave Asia and migrate to Canada. Employment increases and the wage rate falls in Canada and employment decreases and the wage rate rises in Asia. The world equilibrium occurs when the wage rate is equal in the two regions, at $8 an hour.

Because some immigrants bring capital with them, the additional capital is invested in businesses and the demand for labour increases.

Third, immigrants are not necessarily *substitutes* for domestic labour. They might be *complements* to it. For example, a shortage of low-skilled labour might cause a firm to close down and lay off its high-skilled workers. Immigration might restore the ability of the firm to operate profitably and enable it to hire again.

For these three reasons, the effects of immigration on wage rates are smaller than those shown in Fig. 16.11 and might even go in the opposite direction.

Immigration is a topic that creates a great deal of passion. It is important when studying its economic effects to stand back from the emotion that often attaches to the topic and try to analyse its effects dispassionately. Much less is known about the effects of immigration than can be supported by the rhetoric about it. And the numbers of people involved are so small that the economic effects are likely to be small.

REVIEW QUIZ

▨ Where do most of the immigrants into Canada come from? How has the number and place of origin of immigrants changed in recent years?

▨ How does immigration influence wage rates? Is the effect likely to be small or large?

◆ *Reading Between the Lines* on pages 364–365 returns to the Canadian labour market and looks at some recent data on the influence of education on jobs and earnings. It presents one more piece of evidence that the hard work that you are now doing will reap its reward.

In the next chapter, we're going to examine the distributions of income and wealth that result from the operation of labour markets and the markets for other productive resources.

POLICY
WATCH

Investing in Human Capital

THE GLOBE AND MAIL, MARCH 1, 1999

The importance of being educated

BY BRUCE LITTLE

Something happened last year that hasn't occurred through the 1990s: Jobs were created in Canada for people who hadn't graduated from high school.

Just a handful, mind you, fewer than 2,000 across the whole country, ...

This is not a figure that should encourage would-be school drop-outs. If they've learned any math at all, they'll realize that 2,000 net new jobs don't go very far, not when there are about 437,000 people with similar qualifications seeking the kind of work that goes to people with little schooling.

When future scholars look back on the 1990s, they may see it as the decade when the labour market divided once and for all into the educational haves and have-nots. The latest annual figures from Statistics Canada's labour-force survey again drive home the brutal lesson that getting an education and getting a job go hand in hand.

All told, 386,000 jobs were added to the economy in 1998, the best showing of the decade. Of those, 298,000 went to people with either a university degree or some other postsecondary diploma or certificate. They accounted for 51 per cent of the labour force but got 77 per cent of the new jobs.

An additional 86,000 jobs went to people with at least a high-school diploma (and perhaps some post-secondary schooling, though no diploma). That group, comprising 30 per cent of the labour force, got 22 per cent of the new jobs.

The final 2,000 jobs (less than 1 per cent of the new jobs created) were picked up by the 19 per cent of the work force who are unschooled and presumably unskilled. ...

Through economic recession, recovery and expansion, this growing link between education and employment has been one of the overarching trends of the 1990s job market. ...

The very young (those 15 to 24) have a better chance to cope with employers' relentless drive to avoid the ill educated. They can look at the figures, examine the charts and come to the obvious conclusion: Stay in school. ...

Essence of the Story

■ One percent of the new jobs created in 1998 went to people with no high-school diploma.

■ Seventy-seven percent of the new jobs created in 1998 went to people with a university degree or a postsecondary diploma.

■ People with a university degree or postsecondary diploma account for 51 percent of the Canadian labour force and 77 percent of new jobs.

■ People without a high-school diploma account for 19 percent of the Canadian labour force and less than 1 percent of new jobs.

Economic Analysis

■ Most people earn their income by working. And the income they earn depends on the demand for and supply of the skills they have to offer.

■ The figure illustrates the market for two types of labour: those with a university degree or post-secondary diploma and those without a high-school diploma. We'll identify the groups as *H* for high education and *L* for low education.

■ The demand for labour with a low education is D_L and the supply of labour with a low education is S_L.

■ Equilibrium in the low-education labour market occurs at a wage rate of $13 an hour and a quantity of 3 million people employed (19 percent of the labour force).

■ People with university degrees earn more than people with no high-school diploma for two reasons: Their marginal productivity is higher, so the demand for their labour is greater. And their training is costly so at a given wage rate, they are willing to supply less of their labour than are people without a high-school diploma.

■ The figure shows the demand curve for high-education labour, D_H, is to the right of the demand curve for low-education labour, D_L.

■ The vertical distance between the two demand curves is the marginal revenue product of the extra skills that university and postsecondary graduates possess.

■ The supply of high-education labour is less than the supply of low-education labour.

■ Education costs time and other resources, and to obtain the supply curve of high-education labour these costs must be added to the wage rate at which a low-education person is willing to work.

■ In the figure, the supply curve of high-education labour, S_H, is to the left of the supply curve of low-education labour, S_L.

■ The vertical distance between the two supply curves is the opportunity cost of education (converted to a rate per hour of work.)

■ Equilibrium in the high-education labour market occurs at a wage rate of $30 an hour and a quantity of 8 million people employed (51 percent of the labour force).

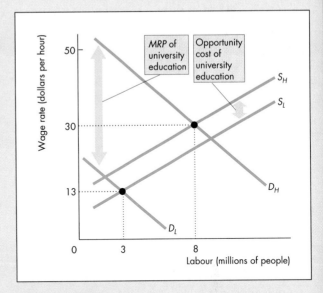

■ Despite the fact that the supply of high-education labour is less than the supply of low-education labour, the productivity differential between the two types of labour is so large that the demand for and equilibrium quantity of high-education labour exceeds that of low-education labour.

You're The Voter

■ Does the big payoff from education mean that the government should spend more on education?

■ Or does it mean that because education leads to a higher income, the government should pay less for education and leave people to make their own choices based on likely personal payoff?

■ Would you vote for more education dollars? Or would you vote for fewer education dollars and lower taxes through deductions for educational expenses?

S U M M A R Y

Key Points

Skill Differentials (pp. 348–350)

▦ Skill differentials arise from differences in marginal revenue products and because skills are costly to acquire.

▦ Wage rates of high-skilled and low-skilled labour are determined by demand and supply in the two labour markets.

Union–Nonunion Wage Differentials (pp. 351–356)

▦ Labour unions influence wages by controlling the supply of labour.

▦ In competitive labour markets, unions obtain higher wage rates only at the expense of lower employment but they try to influence the demand for labour.

▦ In a monopsony, a union can increase the wage rate without sacrificing employment.

▦ Bilateral monopoly occurs when a union confronts a single buyer of labour. The wage rate is determined by bargaining between the two parties.

▦ Union workers earn 10 to 25 percent more than comparable nonunion workers.

Wage Differentials Between the Sexes (pp. 357–359)

▦ Wage differentials between men and women arise from differences in types of jobs, discrimination, differences in human capital, and differences in degree of specialization.

▦ Well-paid jobs are more likely to be held by men than by women. But discrimination is hard to measure objectively.

▦ Historically, men have had more human capital than women, but human capital differences arising from schooling differences have been falling and have almost been eliminated.

▦ Differentials based on work experience have kept women's pay below that for men because women's careers have traditionally been interrupted more frequently than those of men. This difference is smaller today than in the past.

▦ Differentials arising from different degrees of specialization are probably important and might persist. Men have traditionally been more specialized in market activity, on the average, than women.

Pay Equity Laws (pp. 360–361)

▦ Pay equity laws determine wage rates by using objective characteristics rather than what the market will pay to assess the value of different types of jobs.

▦ Determining wage rates through pay equity will result in a decrease in the number of people employed in jobs on which the market places a lower value and a shortage of workers that the market values more highly.

Migration (pp. 361–363)

▦ About 100,000 people a year migrate into Canada and increasingly they come from Asia. Few Canadians leave, and most of those who do so earn high incomes in the United States.

▦ Immigration probably lowers wage rates only slightly.

Key Figures

Key Terms

PROBLEMS

*1. The demand for and supply of low-skilled labour are given by the following figure:

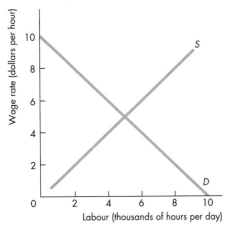

Workers can be trained—can obtain a skill—and their marginal productivity doubles. (The marginal product at each employment level is twice the marginal product of a low-skilled worker.) But the cost of acquiring the skill adds $2 an hour to the wage that must be offered to attract high-skilled labour. What is:
a. The wage rate of low-skilled labour?
b. The quantity of low-skilled labour employed?
c. The wage rate of high-skilled labour?
d. The quantity of high-skilled labour employed?

2. The demand for and supply of low-skilled labour are given by the following figure:

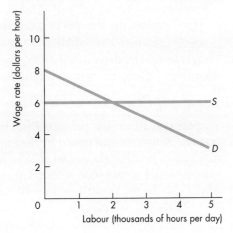

Workers can be trained—can obtain a skill—and their marginal productivity increases by $5 an hour. (The marginal product at each employment level is $5 greater than that of a low-skilled worker.) The cost of acquiring the skill adds $3 an hour to the wage that must be offered to attract high-skilled labour. What is:
a. The wage rate of low-skilled labour?
b. The quantity of low-skilled labour employed?
c. The wage rate of high-skilled labour?
d. The quantity of high-skilled labour employed?
e. Why does the wage rate increase by exactly the cost of acquiring the skill?

*3. Suppose in problem 1 that high-skilled workers become unionized and the union restricts the amount of high-skilled labour to 5,000 hours. What is:
a. The wage rate of high-skilled workers?
b. The wage differential between low- and high-skilled workers?

4. Suppose in problem 2 that high-skilled workers become unionized and the union restricts the amount of high-skilled labour to 2,000 hours. What is:
a. The wage rate of high-skilled workers?
b. The wage differential between low- and high-skilled workers?

*5. If in problem 1, the government introduces a minimum wage rate of $6 an hour for low-skilled workers
a. What is the wage rate paid to low-skilled workers?
b. How many hours of low-skilled labour gets hired each day?

6. If in problem 2, the government introduces a minimum wage rate of $8 an hour for low-skilled workers
a. What is the wage rate paid to low-skilled workers?
b. How many hours of low-skilled labour gets hired each day?

*7. A monopsony gold mining firm operates in an isolated part of the Amazon basin. The following table shows the labour supply schedule (columns 1 and 2) and the firm's total product schedule (columns 2 and 3). The price of gold is $1.40 per grain.

Wage rate (dollars per day)	Workers (number per day)	Quantity of gold produced (grains per day)
5	0	0
6	1	10
7	2	25
8	3	45
9	4	60
10	5	70
11	6	75

a. What wage rate does the company pay?
b. How many workers does the gold mine hire?
c. What is the marginal revenue product at the quantity of labour employed?

8. A monopsony logging firm operates in an isolated part of the Rocky Mountains. The following table shows the firm's labour supply schedule (columns 1 and 2) and total product schedule (columns 2 and 3). The price of logs is $1.50 a tonne.

Wage rate (dollars per day)	Workers (number per day)	Quantity of logs produced (tonnes per day)
2.50	0	0
3.00	1	7
3.50	2	13
4.00	3	18
4.50	4	22
5.00	5	25
5.50	6	27

a. What wage rate does the company pay?
b. How many workers does the firm hire?
c. What is the marginal revenue product at the quantity of labour employed?

*9. In problem 7, explain the effects of a court-enforced wage rate above the equilibrium wage rate on employment and unemployment.

10. In problem 8, explain the effects of the arrival of new immigrants on the demand for labour, the supply of labour, and the wage rate.

CRITICAL THINKING

1. Study *Reading Between the Lines* on pp. 364–365 and then answer the following questions:
   a. What are the broad facts about the job-market prospects of people who don't finish high school?
   b. How does a university degree influence a person's job-market prospects? Explain, using the analysis that you've learned in this chapter.
   c. Why do you think the Canadian economy created jobs for people with no high-school diploma in 1998?
   d. Why do you think the Canadian economy did *not* create jobs for people with no high-school diploma during the earlier 1990s?
   e. How do you think the job prospects of university graduates and high-school dropouts will evolve over the next few years?

2. Use the link on the Parkin-Bade Web site to visit the CLC and look at the "Don't Buy List." Choose an item on this list that interests you and explain why the CLC recommends a boycott of this item. Explain how not buying this item increases either the wage rate or employment of union members.

3. Use the link on the Parkin-Bade Web site to visit the Department of Labour, and obtain data for the past three months on usual weekly earnings and employment.
   a. What has happened to earnings and employment during the past three months?
   b. Try to explain the changes by using the tools of demand and supply.

4. "Wages should be determined on the basis of what is fair." Debate this proposition. Set out the cases for and against. Then determine and explain your verdict.

5. Suppose that all nations permitted free immigration. Which nations would be the biggest suppliers of immigrants and why? Which nations would attract most immigrants and why? Describe the world economy 10 years after the start of this process.

17

Inequality and Redistribution

Ken Thomson's family fortune, earned from the activities of the International Thomson Organization, is estimated as Canada's largest at more than $10 billion. Other billionaire Canadians are Charles Bronfman, owner of the Seagram Company, and Derek A. Price, owner of Starlaw Holdings, a massive Montreal firm that supplies investment and financial services. In stark contrast to these richest Canadians are the poorest, who can be seen any evening on the park benches of our major cities and in the hostels of the Salvation Army. Here are men and women who have no visible wealth at all other than their meagre clothes and a few possessions. ◆ Most Canadians are not as poor as those who seek help from the Salvation Army, but there is a large amount of relative poverty in our nation. One in ten families has an income that is so low that it spends close to half its income on rent. ◆ Why are some people exceedingly rich, while others are very poor and own almost nothing? Are the rich getting richer and the poor getting poorer? Does the information we have about the inequality of income and wealth in Canada paint an accurate picture or a misleading one? How do taxes, social security, and welfare programs influence economic inequality?

Riches and Rags

◆ In this chapter, we study economic inequality—its extent, its sources, and its potential remedies. We look at taxes and government programs that redistribute incomes and study their effects on economic inequality in Canada. Whether the inequality that the market economy generates is fair or unfair is a hard question to answer. We studied this question in Chapter 6 (see pp. 120–123). Here, our focus is on the amount of inequality, the reasons for it, and the effects of programs to reduce it. We'll begin by looking at some facts about economic inequality in Canada today and the recent trends.

After studying this chapter, you will be able to:

- Describe the inequality in income and wealth in Canada
- Explain why wealth inequality is greater than income inequality
- Explain how economic inequality arises
- Explain the effects of taxes, social security, and welfare programs on economic inequality

Economic Inequality in Canada

WE STUDY INEQUALITY BY LOOKING AT THE distribution of income and the distribution of wealth. A family's income is the amount that it receives in a given period. A family's wealth is the value of the things it owns at a point in time.

We measure income as the wages, interest, rent, and profit earned by a family in a year. In 1997, the average Canadian family income was $57,146. But there was considerable inequality around that average. The poorest 20 percent of families received 7.4 percent of total income. The next poorest 20 percent of families received 13.2 percent of total income. But the richest 20 percent of families received 36.4 percent of total income.

We measure wealth as the value of holdings of real estate plus financial assets minus financial liabilities. The most recent data available measure wealth in 1984. The median family wealth in 1984 was a little more than $40,000. The variation around this value was enormous. The distribution of wealth is much more unequal than the distribution of income. The poorest 40 percent of families owned only 2 percent of total wealth. The richest 10 percent owned more than 50 percent of total wealth. And the richest 1 percent owned 24 percent of total wealth.

Lorenz Curves

Figure 17.1 shows the distributions of income and wealth. The table divides families into five groups, called *quintiles*, that range from the lowest income (row *a*) to highest income (row *e*). It shows the percentages of income of each of these groups. For example, row *a* tells us that the lowest quintile of families receives 7.4 percent of total income. The table also shows the *cumulative* percentages of families and income. For example, row *b* tells us that the lowest two quintiles (lowest 40 percent) of families receive 20.6 percent of total income (7.4 percent for the lowest quintile and 13.2 percent for the next lowest). The data on cumulative income shares are illustrated by a Lorenz curve. A **Lorenz curve** graphs the cumulative percentage of income against the cumulative percentage of families.

If income were distributed equally to every family, the cumulative percentages of income received by the cumulative percentages of families would fall along

FIGURE 17.1

Lorenz Curves for Income and Wealth

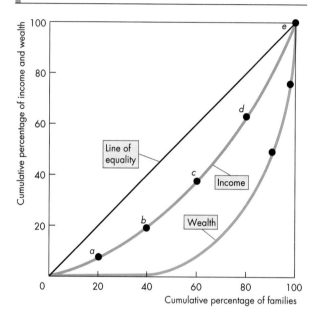

	Families		**Income**	
	Percentage	Cumulative percentage	Percentage	Cumulative percentage
a	Lowest 20	20	7.4	7.4
b	Second 20	40	13.2	20.6
c	Third 20	60	18.1	38.7
d	Fourth 20	80	24.9	63.6
e	Highest 20	100	36.4	100.0

The cumulative percentages of income and wealth are graphed against the cumulative percentage of families. If income and wealth were distributed equally, each 20 percent of families would have 20 percent of the income and wealth—the line of equality. Points *a* through *e* on the Lorenz curve for income correspond to the rows of the table. The Lorenz curve for wealth shows that wealth is more unequally distributed than income.

Sources: Income: Statistics Canada, *Income Distributions by Size in Canada*, 1997. Wealth: James B. Davies, "Distribution of Wealth in Canada," University of Western Ontario, mimeographed, March 1991, and Lars Osberg, "Canada's Economic Performance: Inequality, Poverty, and Growth," in *False Promises, The Failure of Conservative Economics* (Vancouver: New Start Books, 1992).

the straight line labelled "Line of equality." The actual distribution of income is shown by the Lorenz curve labelled "Income." The closer the Lorenz curve is to the line of equality, the more equal is the distribution.

The figure also shows a Lorenz curve for wealth. This curve is based on the distribution described above, in which total wealth is divided approximately equally between the top 1 percent, the next 9 percent, and the bottom 90 percent of families.

You can see from the two Lorenz curves in Fig. 17.1 that the Lorenz curve for wealth is much farther away from the line of equality than the Lorenz curve for income is, so the distribution of wealth is much more unequal than the distribution of income.

Inequality over Time

Figure 17.2 shows how the distribution of income has changed since 1980.

■ The share of income received by the richest 20 percent of families has increased.

■ The share of income received by the second and third poorest groups of families has decreased.

Despite a great deal of research on the topic, economists are still not sure why these trends in the distribution of income have occurred. The most promising explanation is that the highest-income group has gained because rapid technological change has increased the return to education. The lower-income groups have suffered for a variety of reasons. One of them is increased international mobility and competition that are keeping down the wages of low-skilled labour. Another is that the same technological trends that have increased the return to education have decreased the demand for and the wages of low-skilled labour.

Who Are the Poor and the Rich?

What are the characteristics of poor and rich families? The lowest-income family in Canada today is most likely to be a single-parent mother and her children. She is under 24 years old, has no job, and lives in Quebec. The highest-income family is a married couple with two full-time jobs. They are between 45 and 54 years old and live in Ontario.

These snapshot profiles are the extremes in Fig. 17.3. That figure illustrates the importance of source of income, family type, sex of the family head, age of the family head, labour force status, number of chil-

FIGURE **17.2**

Trends in the Distribution of Income: 1980–1997

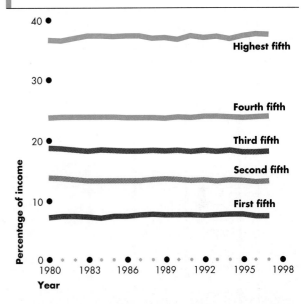

The distribution of income in Canada became less equal in the 1980s and 1990s. The fifth with the highest income gained the most and the fifths with the second and third highest incomes lost the most.

Source: Statistics Canada, *Income Distributions by Size in Canada,* 1997.

dren, education, and region of residence in influencing the likelihood that a family is living in poverty.

Poverty

Families at the low end of the income distribution are so poor that they are considered to be living in poverty. **Poverty** is a state in which a family's income is too low to be able to buy the quantities of food, shelter, and clothing that are deemed necessary. Poverty is a relative concept. Millions of people living in Africa and Asia survive on incomes of less than $400 a year. In Canada, poverty is measured in terms of a low-income cutoff. The **low-income cutoff** is the income level, determined separately for different types of families (for example, single persons, couples, one parent), that is selected such that families with incomes below that limit normally spend

FIGURE 17.3

The Incidence of Low Income by Family Characteristics

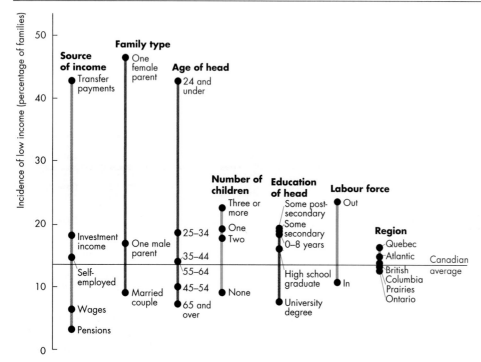

Source: Statistics Canada, *Income Distributions by Size in Canada*, 1997.

The vertical axis shows the incidence of low income—the percentage of families whose income falls below a low-income cutoff (the income level such that 54.7 percent of income is spent on food, shelter, and clothing). For Canada, on the average, in 1997 14 percent of families have incomes below the low-income cutoff. But that percentage varies depending on source of income, family type, sex and age of family head, number of children, education, and region of residence as indicated by the figure. Source of income, family type, and sex and age of family head are by far the most important factors influencing incidence of low income.

54.7 percent or more of their income on food, shelter, and clothing. The low-income cutoffs currently used by Statistics Canada are based on family expenditure data for 1992. Statistics Canada measures the incidence of low income as the percentage of families whose income falls below a low-income cutoff.

Figure 17.3 shows how the incidence of low income is related to other family characteristics. Poverty is heavily influenced by source of income and family status. More than 40 percent of families receiving transfer payments from the government are below the poverty line. About 46 percent of families in which the family head is a female and no husband is present are below the poverty level, while only 9 percent of married couples live in poverty. Almost 43 percent of families with the head 24 years or under live in poverty, while only 14 percent of families with the head 25 to 34 years do. More than 16 percent of families in Quebec live in poverty, while 12 percent of families in Ontario do. Almost 20 percent of

families in which the head has 8 or fewer years of education are below the poverty line, while only 8 percent of families in which the head is a university graduate are.

R E V I E W   Q U I Z

- Which is distributed more unequally: income or wealth?
- Has the distribution of income become more equal or more unequal?
- Which group of families has experienced the largest increase in income share during the past 20 years?
- The influences on a family's income are: age of family head, education of members, number of children, family type, labour force status, source of income, and region of residence. Rank the items in decreasing order of importance.

Comparing Like with Like

To DETERMINE THE DEGREE OF INEQUALITY, WE compare one person's economic situation with another person's. But what is the correct measure of a person's economic situation? Is it income or is it wealth? And is it *annual* income, the measure we've used so far in this chapter, or income over a longer time period—for example, over a family's lifetime?

Wealth Versus Income

Wealth is a stock of assets and income is the flow of earnings that results from the stock of wealth. Suppose that a person owns assets worth $1 million—has a wealth of $1 million. If the rate of return on assets is 5 percent a year, then this person receives an income of $50,000 a year from those assets. We can use either the wealth of $1 million or the income of $50,000 to describe this person's economic condition. When the rate of return is 5 percent a year, $1 million of wealth equals $50,000 of income in perpetuity. Wealth and income are simply different ways of looking at the same thing.

But in Fig. 17.1, the distribution of wealth is much more unequal than the distribution of income. Why? It is because the wealth data measure tangible assets and exclude the value of human capital, while the income data measure income from both tangible assets and human capital.

Table 17.1 illustrates the consequence of omitting human capital from the wealth data. Lee has twice the wealth and twice the income of Peter. But Lee's human capital is less than Peter's—$200,000 compared with $499,000. And Lee's income from human capital of $10,000 is less than Peter's income from human capital of $24,950. Lee's nonhuman capital is larger than Peter's—$800,000 compared with $1,000. And Lee's income from nonhuman capital of $40,000 is larger than Peter's income from nonhuman capital of $50.

The national wealth and income surveys record their incomes of $50,000 and $25,000 respectively, which indicates that Lee is twice as well off as Peter. And they record their tangible assets of $800,000 and $1,000 respectively, which indicates that Lee is 800 times as wealthy as Peter. Because the national survey of wealth excludes human capital, the income distribution is a more accurate measure of economic inequality than is the wealth distribution.

TABLE 17.1

Capital, Wealth, and Income

	Lee		Peter	
	Wealth	**Income**	**Wealth**	**Income**
Human capital	200,000	10,000	499,000	24,950
Nonhuman capital	800,000	40,000	1,000	50
Total	$1,000,000	$50,000	$500,000	$25,000

When wealth is measured to include the value of human capital as well as nonhuman capital, the distribution of income and the distribution of wealth display the same degree of inequality.

Annual or Lifetime Income and Wealth?

A typical family's income changes over time. It starts out low, grows to a peak when the family's workers reach retirement age, and then falls after retirement. Also, a typical family's wealth changes over time. Like income, it starts out low, grows to a peak at the point of retirement, and falls after retirement.

Suppose we look at three families that have identical lifetime incomes. One family is young, one is middle-aged, and one is retired. The middle-aged family has the highest income and wealth, the retired family has the lowest, and the young family falls in the middle. The distributions of annual income and wealth in a given year are unequal but the distributions of lifetime income and wealth are equal. So some of the measured inequality arises from the fact that different families are at different stages in the life cycle. Inequality of annual incomes overstates the degree of lifetime inequality.

R E V I E W   Q U I Z

■ Which is the more accurate indicator of the degree of inequality: the distribution of income or the distribution of wealth? Why is one of these a better measure than the other?

■ Which is the more accurate indicator of the degree of inequality: the distribution of lifetime income or the distribution of annual income? Why is one of these a better measure than the other?

Let's look at the sources of economic inequality.

Resource Prices, Endowments, and Choices

A FAMILY'S INCOME DEPENDS ON THREE THINGS:

- Resource prices
- Resource endowments
- Choices

The distribution of income depends on the distribution of these three things across the population. The first two are outside our individual control and are determined by market forces and by history. From the viewpoint of each one of us, they appear to be determined by luck. The last item is under individual control. We make choices that influence our incomes. Let's look at the three factors that influence incomes.

Resource Prices

Everyone faces the same interest rates in capital markets, but people face differing wage rates in the labour market. And the labour market is the biggest single source of income for most people. To what extent do variations in wage rates account for the unequal distribution of income? The answer is that they do to some extent, but wage differences cannot account for all the inequality. High-skilled workers earn about 4 times as much as low-skilled workers. High-paid professionals earn about 3 times as much as high-skilled workers. So high-paid professionals earn around 12 times what the least skilled earn.

Differences in resource endowments are another.

Resource Endowments

There is a large amount of variety in a family's endowments of capital and of human abilities. Differences in capital make a big contribution to differences in incomes. But so do differences in ability.

Physical and mental differences (some inherited, some learned) have a normal, or bell-shaped, distribution—like the distribution of heights or weights. The distribution of ability across individuals is a major source of inequality in income and wealth. But it is not the only source. If it were, the distributions of income and wealth would look like the bell-shaped curve that describes the distribution of heights. In fact, these distributions are skewed towards high incomes and look like the curve in Fig. 17.4. This

figure shows income on the horizontal axis and the percentage of families receiving each income on the vertical axis. In 1997, the median family income—the income that separates families into two groups of equal size—was $50,361. The most common income—called the mode income—is less than the median income. The mean income—also called the average income—is greater than the median income and in 1997 was $57,146. A skewed distribution like the one shown in Fig. 17.4 is one in which many more people have incomes below the average than above it, a large number of people have low incomes, and a small number of people have high incomes. The distribution of (nonhuman) wealth has a shape similar to that of the distribution of income but is even more skewed.

The skewed shape of the distribution of income cannot be explained by the bell-shaped distribution of individual abilities. It results from the choices that people make.

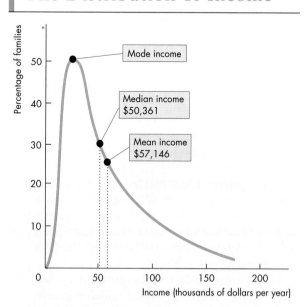

FIGURE 17.4

The Distribution of Income

The distribution of income is unequal and is not symmetric around the mean income. There are many more people with incomes below the mean income than above it. Also, the distribution has a long thin upper tail, which represents a small number of families that earn very large incomes.

Choices

While many poor families feel trapped and do not have many options open to them, a family's income and wealth depend partly on the choices that its members make. You are going to discover that the choices people make exaggerate the differences among them and make the distribution of income more unequal than the distribution of abilities, as well as make the distribution of income skewed.

Wages and the Supply of Labour   Other things remaining the same, the quantity of labour that a person supplies usually increases as that person's wage rate increases. A person who has a low wage rate chooses to work fewer hours than a person who has a high wage rate.

Because the quantity of labour supplied increases as the wage rate increases, the distribution of income is more unequal than the distribution of hourly wages. It is also skewed, like the distribution shown in Fig. 17.4. People whose wage rates are below the average tend to work fewer hours than the average, and their incomes bunch together below the average. People whose wage rates are above the average tend to work more hours than the average, and their incomes stretch out above the average.

Saving and Bequests   Another choice that results in unequal distributions in income and wealth is the decision to save and make bequests. A *bequest* is a gift from one generation to the next. The higher a family's income, the more that family tends to save and accumulate wealth across generations.

Saving and bequests are not inevitably a source of increased inequality. If a family saves to redistribute an uneven income over the life cycle and enable consumption to be constant, the act of saving decreases the degree of inequality. If a lucky generation that has a high income saves a large amount and makes a bequest to a generation that is unlucky, this act of saving also decreases the degree of inequality. But two features of bequests make intergenerational transfers of wealth a source of increased inequality:

■ Debts cannot be bequeathed
■ Mating is assortative

Debts Cannot Be Bequeathed   Although a person may die with debts that exceed assets—with negative wealth—debts cannot be forced onto other family members. Because a zero inheritance is the smallest inheritance that anyone can receive, bequests can only add to future generations' wealth and income potential.

Most people inherit nothing or a very small amount. A few people inherit enormous fortunes. As a result, bequests make the distribution of income persistently more unequal than the distribution of ability and job skills. A family that is poor in one generation is more likely to be poor in the next. A family that is wealthy in one generation is likely to be wealthy in the next. But there is a tendency for income and wealth to converge, across generations, to the average. Although there can be long runs of good luck or bad luck, or good judgment or bad judgment, across the generations, such long runs are uncommon. But a feature of human behaviour that slows the convergence of wealth to the average and makes inequalities persist is assortative mating.

Assortative Mating   *Assortative mating* is the tendency for people to marry within their own socio-economic class. In the vernacular, "like attracts like." Although there is a good deal of folklore that "opposites attract," perhaps such Cinderella tales appeal to us because they are so rare in reality. Marriage partners tend to have similar socioeconomic characteristics. Wealthy individuals seek wealthy partners. The consequence of assortative mating is that inherited wealth becomes more concentrated in a small number of families and the distribution of wealth becomes more unequal.

R E V I E W   Q U I Z

▨ What role do wage rates, endowments, and choices play in creating income inequality?
▨ What is the main reason that wage rates are unequal?
▨ If the distribution of endowments is bell shaped, what makes the distribution of income skewed?
▨ Which choices that people make generate the skew in the distribution of income?
▨ How do bequests and assortative mating make the distribution of wealth more unequal and skewed?

We've now examined why inequality exists. Next, we're going to see how taxes and government programs redistribute income and wealth.

Income Redistribution

THE THREE MAIN WAYS THAT GOVERNMENTS IN Canada redistribute income are:

▪ Income taxes
▪ Income maintenance programs
▪ Subsidized services

Income Taxes

Income taxes may be progressive, regressive, or proportional. A **progressive income tax** is one that taxes income at a marginal rate that increases with the level of income. The term "marginal," applied to income tax rates, refers to the fraction of the last dollar earned that is paid in taxes. A **regressive income tax** is one that taxes income at a marginal rate that decreases with the level of income. A **proportional income tax** (also called a *flat-rate income tax*) is one that taxes income at a constant rate, regardless of the level of income.

The income tax rates that apply in Canada are composed of two parts: federal and provincial taxes. There is variety in the detailed tax arrangements in the individual provinces but the tax system, at both the federal and provincial levels, is progressive. The poorest families pay no income tax. Most Canadians who earn between $10,000 and $30,000 a year, except for those living in Quebec, pay around 25 percent of their taxable income. In Quebec, for the same income range, the marginal tax rates ranged from 30 to almost 40 percent. Canadians with incomes between $30,000 and $60,000 a year pay between 40 and 45 percent and those with incomes above $60,000 pay a marginal tax rate of 45 to 50 percent.

Income Maintenance Programs

Much of the revenue that the government receives from taxes is redistributed to individuals and families through a number of income maintenance programs. Three main government programs redistribute income by making direct payments (in cash, services, or vouchers) to individuals and families. They are:

▪ Social security programs
▪ Employment insurance system
▪ Welfare programs

Social Security   Three programs, Old Age Security (OAS), Guaranteed Income Supplement (GIS), and Spouse Allowance (SPA) ensure a minimum level of income for the elderly. Monthly cash payments to retired or disabled workers or their surviving spouses are paid for by compulsory payroll taxes on both employers and employees. In 1999, the maximum OAS was $410.82 a month, the maximum GIS for a single person was $488.23 and for a married couple was $806.24, and the maximum SPA was $804.64.

Employment Insurance   To provide an income to unemployed workers, the federal government has established an unemployment compensation program. The Employment Insurance program is funded by employee and employer contributions, and after a qualifying period the worker is entitled to receive a benefit if the worker becomes unemployed. The maximum unemployment benefit is $413 a week or 55 percent of gross weekly earnings over the previous 20 weeks.

Welfare Programs   Other federal welfare programs provide income maintenance for families and persons. They are:

1. Canada Assistance Plan, a plan shared equally by the federal and provincial governments that gives financial assistance to families and individuals who are in need, regardless of the cause; the assistance includes food, shelter, fuel, utilities, family supplies, items required to carry on a trade, certain welfare services, and specified health and social services
2. Family Allowance and Child Tax Credit programs, designed to help families who have inadequate financial support
3. Canada/Quebec Pension Plans, funded equally by employee and employer contributions, provide retirement benefits, survivor benefits, disability benefits, and death benefits
4. Workers' Compensation, a provincial program funded by employers, designed to provide financial assistance as well as medical care and rehabilitation of workers injured at work

Subsidized Services

A great deal of redistribution takes place in Canada through the provision of subsidized services, which is the provision of goods and services by the government at prices below the cost of production. The taxpayers who consume these goods and services receive a transfer in kind from the taxpayers who do not consume them. The two most important areas in which this form of redistribution takes place are education—both kindergarten through grade 12 and college and university—and health care.

In 1998, Canadian students enrolled in the universities in Ontario paid annual tuition fees of around $3,500. The cost of one year's education at one of these universities in 1998 was about $17,500. Thus families with a member enrolled in these institutions received a benefit from the government of about $14,000 a year. Those with several college or university students received proportionately higher benefits.

Government provision of health care to all residents has brought high-quality and high-cost health care to millions of people who earn too little to buy such services themselves. As a result, this program has contributed a great deal to reducing inequality.

The Scale of Income Redistribution

A family's income in the absence of government redistribution is called *market income*. One way of measuring the scale of income redistribution is to calculate the percentage of market income paid in taxes and the percentage received in benefits at each income level. Making such a calculation in a way that takes into account the value of the services provided by the government is almost impossible. The only calculations available ignore this aspect of redistribution and focus on taxes and cash benefits.

Figure 17.5 shows how much redistribution in aggregate takes place in Canada. The income distribution that takes account of government policies is called the *distribution after taxes and benefits*. Figure 17.5 illustrates the amount of redistribution that takes place among the five income groups by comparing the Lorenz curves for the market distribution and the distribution after taxes and benefits. As you can see, there is considerable redistribution, especially to boost the incomes of the very poor. The poorest 20 percent of families receive more than 70 percent of their income from the government. The second poorest 20 percent receive 43 percent of their income from the government. In contrast, the richest 20 percent receive almost nothing from the government. But a great deal of inequality remains after the redistribution.

FIGURE 17.5

Income Redistribution

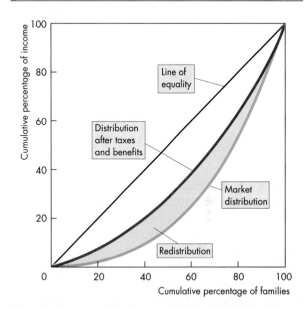

Taxes and income maintenance programs reduce the degree of inequality. In 1997, the 20 percent of families with the lowest incomes received net benefits that increased their share of total income from 1.6 percent to 7.4 percent. The 20 percent of families with the highest incomes paid taxes that decreased their share of total income from 46.4 percent to 36.4 percent of total income.

Source: Statistics Canada, *Income Distributions by Size in Canada*, 1997 and authors' assumptions and calculations.

The Big Tradeoff

The redistribution of income creates what has been called the **big tradeoff**, a tradeoff between equity and efficiency. The big tradeoff arises because redistribution uses scarce resources and weakens incentives.

A dollar collected from a rich person does not translate into a dollar received by a poor person. Some of it gets used up in the process of redistribution. Tax-collecting agencies such as Revenue Canada and welfare-administering agencies (as well as tax accountants and lawyers) use skilled labour, computers, and other scarce resources to do their work. The bigger the scale of redistribution, the greater is the opportunity cost of administering it.

But the cost of collecting taxes and making welfare payments is a small part of the total cost of redistribution. A bigger cost arises from the inefficiency—deadweight loss—of taxes and benefits. Greater equality can be achieved only by taxing productive activities such as work and saving. Taxing people's income from their work and saving lowers the after-tax income they receive. This lower income makes them work and save less, which in turn results in a smaller output and less consumption not only for the rich who pay the taxes but also for the poor who receive the benefits.

Both taxpayers and benefit recipients face weaker incentives. In fact, under our current welfare arrangements, some of the weakest incentives are those faced by families that benefit under programs such as Guaranteed Income Supplement. When a person in one of these families gets a job, benefits are withdrawn and the family in effect pays a tax of 100 percent on its marginal earnings. This marginal tax rate is higher than that paid by the wealthiest Canadians, and it helps lock poor families in a welfare trap.

So the scale and methods of income redistribution must pay close attention to the incentive effects of taxes and benefits.

A Major Welfare Challenge

The poorest people in Canada (see pp. 371–372) are young women who have not completed high school, have a child (or children), and live without a partner. But all single mothers present a major welfare challenge. First, their numbers are large. There are approximately one million single mothers in Canada today. Second, their economic plight and the economic prospects for their children are serious.

Janet Peterson and her four children aged between 3 and 13 are one example. Janet has a serious physical disability. She receives a social assistance cheque each month for $1,286, or $15,432 a year. The low-income cutoff for a family of five is $30,910. So Janet and her children live in severe poverty. She spends $625 a month on rent, $400 on food, and the rest on gas, hydro, the phone, and transportation. To provide Janet Peterson (and the other million single mothers) with an income that matches the low-income cutoff would cost more than $10 billion a year.

Janet Peterson has a physical disability that makes it unlikely that she could work. Many other single mothers are in this situation. But this is not the typical case. Most single mothers are physically fit and are capable of working. And some of them are well educated and therefore can earn a high wage rate. Even those single mothers who have not completed high school are capable of either attending school or getting a job.

For physically fit single mothers, the long-term solution to their problem is education and on-the-job training—acquiring human capital. The short-term solution is welfare. But welfare must be designed to minimize the disincentive to pursue the long-term goal. This is the challenge in designing an adequate welfare program. One possible program is the negative income tax, which we now describe.

Negative Income Tax

Negative income tax is *not* on the political agenda. But it is popular among economists and it is the subject of several real-world experiments.

A **negative income tax** gives every family a *guaranteed minimum annual income* and taxes *all* income above the guaranteed minimum at a fixed *marginal tax rate*. Suppose the guaranteed minimum annual income is $10,000 and the marginal tax rate is 25 percent. A family with no market income receives the $10,000 guaranteed minimum income from the government. This family "pays" income tax of *minus* $10,000, hence the name, *negative* income tax. A family with a market income of $40,000 also receives the $10,000 guaranteed minimum income from the government. But it also pays $10,000—25 percent of its market income—to the government. So this family pays no income tax. It has the break-even income. Families with a market income of between zero and $40,000 "pay" a negative income tax. They receive more than they pay. A family with a market income of $60,000 receives the $10,000 guaranteed minimum income from the government, but it pays $15,000—25 percent of its market income—to the government. So this family pays income tax of $5,000. All families with incomes greater than $40,000 pay income tax to the government.

Figure 17.6 illustrates a negative income tax and compares it with our current arrangements. In both parts of the figure, the horizontal axis measures *market income* and the vertical axis measures income *after* taxes are paid and benefits are received. The 45° line shows the hypothetical case of "no redistribution."

FIGURE 17.6

Comparing Traditional Programs and a Negative Income Tax

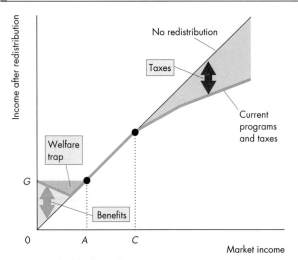

(a) Current redistribution arrangements

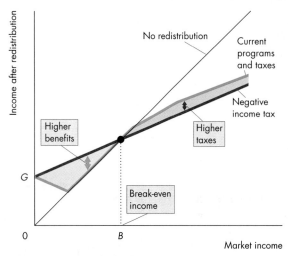

(b) A negative income tax

Part (a) shows traditional redistribution arrangements—the blue curve. Benefits of *G* are paid to those with no income. As incomes increase from zero to *A*, benefits are withdrawn, *lowering* income after redistribution below *G* and creating a welfare trap—the grey triangle. As incomes increase from *A* to *C*, there is no redistribution. As incomes increase above *C*, income taxes are paid at successively higher rates.

In part (b), a negative income tax gives a guaranteed annual income of *G* and decreases benefits at the same rate as the tax rate on incomes. The red line shows how market incomes translate into income after redistribution. Families with market incomes below *B*, the break-even income, receive net benefits. Those with market incomes above *B* pay net taxes.

Part (a) shows traditional redistribution arrangements—the blue curve. Benefits of *G* are paid to those with no income. As incomes increase from zero to *A*, benefits are withdrawn. This arrangement creates a *welfare trap* shown as the grey triangle. It does not pay a person to work if the income he or she can earn is less than *A*. Over the income range *A* to *C*, each additional dollar of market income increases income after redistribution by a dollar. At incomes greater than *C*, income taxes are paid and at successively higher rates, so income after redistribution is smaller than market income.

Part (b) shows the negative income tax. The guaranteed annual income is *G*, and the break-even income is *B*. Families with market incomes below *B* receive a net benefit (blue area), and those with incomes above *B* pay taxes (red area). A negative income tax removes the welfare trap and gives greater encouragement to low-income families to seek more employment, even at low wage rates. It also over-

comes many of the other problems arising from existing income maintenance programs.

REVIEW QUIZ

- What are the methods that governments in Canada use to redistribute income?
- How large is the scale of redistribution in Canada?
- What is the major welfare challenge and how is it being tackled in Canada today?
- What problem is a negative income tax designed to solve? Why don't we have a negative income tax?

◆ *Reading Between the Lines* on pp. 380–381 takes another look at the trends in the distribution of income in Canada in recent years and of the anatomy of the changing distribution.

The Changing Income Distribution

THE GLOBE AND MAIL, MARCH 8, 1999

Poverty is single and she has a child

By Bruce Little

The headlines for the latest study of family incomes from Statistics Canada were predictable: The rich get richer and the poor get poorer. ...

Between 1970 and 1995, the top 30 per cent saw their share of all income increase 1.9 per cent... while the bottom 70 per cent saw their share fall 1.9 points...

What is most striking from the Statistics Canada study are the huge changes in the nature of families, and their income, over a quarter-century. Analyst Abdul Rashid's report appears in the agency's quarterly publication Perspectives on Labour and Income.

Using census data, Mr. Rashid took the total number of families, split them into 10 equal groups (called deciles) and ranked them according to income. In effect, he provides answers to the questions: Who's rich? Who's poor? ...

Begin with age. In 1970, fewer than 12 per cent of Canadians were 65 or older, yet they accounted for more than 26 per cent of the families in the bottom

decile. To a considerable degree, extreme poverty was a problem of the old, ...

By 1995, more than 15 per cent of all families were headed by someone 65 or older, but they constituted a mere 6 per cent of the bottom income group. The old had not grown rich by any stretch, but many had moved up the income scale; they accounted for 30 per cent of those in the third income decile, double their share in 1970.

In 1995, the bottom 10 per cent were still receiving about 1.5 per cent of all income, just as they had in 1970. But if the old have moved up the income ladder, who are today's poor?

Largely, they are single mothers. In 1970, they headed just over 7 per cent of all families; by 1995, the figure topped 12 per cent. ... Single mothers accounted for 24 per cent of those in the bottom decile in 1970 and a staggering 40 per cent in 1995.

What about the top end of the income scale, the best-off 10 per cent? ...

By 1995, both the husbands and wives were working in 81 per cent of those upper-income homes. ...

Essence of the Story

■ Between 1970 and 1995, the rich in Canada became richer and the poor became poorer.

■ The composition of family types in the lowest income decile has changed.

■ In 1970, less than 12 percent of Canadians were 65 or older and they composed 26 percent of the families in the lowest income decile.

■ In 1995, 15 percent of Canadians were 65 or older and they composed 6 percent of the families in the lowest income decile.

■ Between 1970 and 1995, the percentage of families headed by single mothers increased from 7 percent to 12 percent and their inclusion in the lowest income decile increased from 24 percent to 40 percent.

■ 81 percent of upper-income homes contain two wage earners.

Economic Analysis

■ The lowest income decile includes all families that receive the lowest 10 percent of all income.

■ Between 1970 and 1995, the number of families headed by female single parents increased.

■ Because these families generally have low incomes, a disproportionate increase in the incidence of female single-parent families occurred in the lowest income decile.

■ Figure 1 shows the composition of the lowest income decile by the age of the head of the family in 1970 and Fig. 2 shows the composition in 1995.

■ The largest change comes in the 65-and-over age group, but there is also a significant increase in the 25-to-34 age group and the 35-to-44 age group.

■ Changes in social security payments including Old Age Security, the Guaranteed Income Supplement, and Canada and Quebec Pension Plans have helped elderly families move out of the lowest income decile.

■ Although the number of families headed by single mothers in the lowest income decile has increased from 24 percent to 40 percent, the 15-to-24 age group has increased from 9.8 percent to only 10.7 percent. So it appears that the largest percentage increase in single mothers in the lowest income decile is not occurring in the teenage years.

■ Figure 3 compares the composition of the lowest income decile and the highest income decile by family structure in 1995.

■ The female single-parent family, which comprises 40 percent of the lowest income decile, is only 1.4 percent of the highest income decile.

■ The highest income decile is dominated by the two-income family while the lowest income decile is dominated by the female single-parent family.

■ Family structure and spousal work patterns are significant influences on income determination.

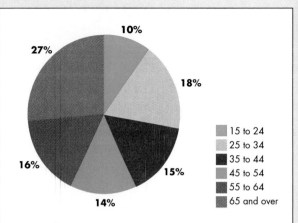

Figure 1 Distribution of family income by age in 1970

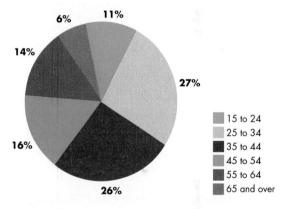

Figure 2 Distribution of family income by age in 1995

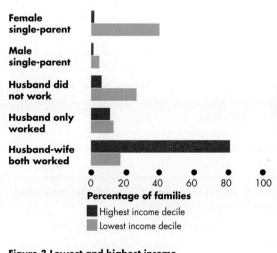

Figure 3 Lowest and highest income deciles by family structure

SUMMARY

Key Points

Economic Inequality in Canada (pp. 370–372)

- The richest 1 percent of Canadians own 24 percent of the total wealth in the country.
- Income is distributed less unevenly than wealth. Throughout the 1970s, 1980s, and 1990s, inequality increased.
- The poorest people in Canada are single mothers with less than eight years of schooling and no job who live in Quebec. The richest people live in Ontario and are middle-aged couples with two full-time jobs.

Comparing Like with Like (p. 373)

- The distribution of wealth exaggerates the degree of inequality because it excludes human capital.
- The distributions of annual income and wealth exaggerate lifetime inequality because they do not take the life cycle into account.

Resource Prices, Endowments, and Choices (pp. 374–375)

- Differences in income and wealth arise from differences in resource prices, endowments, and choices.
- People who earn high wage rates generally work more hours than those who earn low wage rates, so the distribution of income becomes more unequal and more skewed than the distribution of wage rates.

Income Redistribution (pp. 376–379)

- Governments redistribute income through income taxes, income maintenance programs, and provision of subsidized services.
- Income taxes are progressive.
- Redistribution creates a "big tradeoff" between equity and efficiency, which arises because the process of redistribution uses resources and weakens the incentives to work and save.

- Traditional income maintenance programs create a welfare trap that discourages work, so poverty is persistent. Reforms seek to lessen the severity of the welfare trap. A more radical negative income tax reform would encourage those on welfare to find work.

Key Figures

Key Terms

PROBLEMS

*1. You are provided with the following information about income shares in an economy:

Percentage of families	Income shares (percent)
Lowest 20%	5
Second 20%	11
Third 20%	17
Fourth 20%	24
Highest 20%	43

a. Draw the Lorenz curve for income in this economy.

b. Compare the distributions of income in this economy with that in Canada. Is Canadian income distributed more equally or less equally than in the economy described in the table?

2. You are provided with the following information about wealth shares in an economy:

Percentage of families	Wealth shares (percent)
Lowest 20%	0
Second 20%	1
Third 20%	3
Fourth 20%	11
Highest 20%	85

a. Draw the Lorenz curve for wealth in this economy.

b. Compare the distribution of wealth in this economy with that in Canada. Is Canadian wealth distributed more equally or less equally than in the economy described in the table?

c. Explain which of the two variables—income in problem 1 or wealth in problem 2—is more unequally distributed.

*3. Imagine an economy with five people who are identical in all respects. Each lives for 70 years. For the first 14 of those years, they earn no income. For the next 35 years, they work and earn $30,000 a year from their work. For their remaining years, they are retired and have no income from labour. To make the arithmetic easy, let's suppose that the interest rate in this economy is zero; the individuals consume all their income during their lifetime and at a

constant annual rate. What are the distributions of income and wealth in this economy if the individuals have the following ages:

a. All are 45

b. 25, 35, 45, 55, 65

Does case (a) have greater inequality than case (b)?

4. In the economy described in problem 3, there is a "baby boom." Two people who were born in the same year are now 25. One person is 35, one 45, one 55, and no one is 65. What are the distributions of income and wealth:

a. This year?

b. 10 years in the future?

c. 20 years in the future?

d. 30 years in the future?

e. 40 years in the future?

f. Comment on and explain the changes in the distributions of income and wealth in this economy.

*5. An economy consists of 10 people, each of whom has the following labour supply schedule:

Wage rate (dollars per hour)	Hours worked per day
1	1
2	2
3	4
4	6
5	8

The people differ in ability and earn different wage rates. The distribution of *wage rates* is as follows:

Wage rate (dollars per hour)	Number of people
1	1
2	2
3	4
4	2
5	1

a. Calculate the average wage rate.

b. Calculate the ratio of the highest to the lowest wage rate.

c. Calculate the average daily income.

d. Calculate the ratio of the highest to the lowest daily income.

e. Sketch the distribution of hourly wage rates.

f. Sketch the distribution of daily incomes.
g. What important lesson is illustrated by this problem?

6. In the economy described in problem 5, the productivity of low-skilled labour falls and that of high-skilled labour rises. Consequently, the distribution of *wage rates* changes to the following:

Wage rate (dollars per hour)	Number of people
0	1
1	2
3	4
5	2
6	1

The labour supply schedule is the same as in problem 5. For this changed situation:
a. Calculate the average wage rate.
b. Calculate the ratio of the highest to the lowest wage rate.
c. Calculate the average daily income.
d. Calculate the ratio of the highest to the lowest daily income.
e. Sketch the distribution of hourly wage rates.
f. Sketch the distribution of daily incomes.
g. What important lesson is illustrated by comparing the economy in this problem with the one in problem 5?

*7. The table shows the distribution of market income in an economy.

Percentage of families	Income (millions of dollars)
Lowest 20%	5
Second 20%	10
Third 20%	18
Fourth 20%	28
Highest 20%	39

The government redistributes income with the taxes and benefits shown in the following table:

Percentage of families	Income taxes (percent of income)	Benefits (millions of dollars)
Lowest 20%	0	10
Second 20%	10	8
Third 20%	15	3
Fourth 20%	20	0
Highest 20%	30	0

a. Draw the Lorenz curve for this economy after taxes and benefits.
b. Is the scale of redistribution of income in this economy greater or smaller than in Canada?

8. In the economy described in problem 7, the government replaces its existing taxes and benefits with a negative income tax. What changes do you expect to occur in the economy?

CRITICAL THINKING

1. Study *Reading Between the Lines* on pp. 380–381, and then:
   a. Describe the main facts about the distribution of income reported in the news article.
   b. Explain how you think the tax system and the welfare system change the situation described in the news article.
   c. How can we explain the trends reported in this news article? Are the trends inevitable or can we take measures to reverse them? Explain.

2. Use the link on the Parkin-Bade Web site to visit Statistics Canada to obtain information on average family income in the city in which you live. Also find the Statistics Canada data for London, Ontario. Then use the link on the Parkin-Bade Web site to visit the *London Free Press* poverty site. Review the information on poverty that you find there. Then:
   a. Describe the main facts about poverty and the distribution of income in London, Ontario.
   b. Do you think the situation described in London is similar, worse, or not as bad as that in your own home city?
   c. Explain why you think your city is performing better or worse than London, Ontario and better or worse than the country as a whole.

Understanding Resource Markets

For Whom?

During the past 35 years, the rich have been getting richer and the poor poorer. This trend is new. From the end of World War II until 1965, the poor got richer at a faster pace than the rich and the gap between rich and poor narrowed a bit. What are the forces that generate these trends? The answer to this question is the interaction of the forces of supply and demand in resource markets. ◆ The three categories of resources are human, capital, and natural. Human resources include labour, human capital, and entrepreneurship. The income of labour and human capital depends on wage rates and employment levels, which are determined in labour markets. The income from capital depends on interest rates and the amount of capital, which are determined in capital markets. The income from natural resources depends on prices and quantities, which are determined in natural resource markets. Only the return to entrepreneurship is not determined directly in a market. That return is normal profit plus economic profit, and it depends on how successful each entrepreneur is in the business that he or she runs. ◆ The chapters in this part study the forces at play in resource markets and explain how those forces have led to changes in the distribution of income. ◆ In the overview of all the resource markets in Chapter 15, you learned how the demand for resources results from the profit-maximizing decisions of firms. You studied these

decisions from a different angle in Chapters 10–14, where you learned how firms choose their profit-maximizing output. In Chapter 15, you learned how a firm's profit-maximizing output decision determines its demand for productive resources. You also learned how resource supply decisions are made and how equilibrium determines resource prices and the incomes of resource owners. ◆ You discovered that some of the biggest incomes earned by superstars are a surplus that we call *economic rent*. ◆ Chapter 15 uses the labour market as the main example. But you also learned in that chapter some special features of capital markets and natural resource markets. ◆ In Chapter 16, you took a closer look at the labour market and studied the main sources of differences among people's wages. ◆ Then, in Chapter 17, you studied the distribution of income. This chapter took you back to the fundamentals of economics and answered one of the big questions: Who gets to consume the goods and services that are produced?

◇ Many outstanding economists have advanced our understanding of resource markets and the role they play in helping to resolve the conflicts between the demands of humans and the resources available. One of them is Thomas Robert Malthus whom you can meet on the following page. Also, we will talk with Craig Riddell, a professor of economics at the University of British Columbia, who has made important contributions to our understanding of modern labour markets.

The Economist

Thomas Robert Malthus

(1766–1834), an English clergyman and economist, was an extremely influential social scientist. In his best selling Essay on the Principle of Population, *published in 1798, he predicted that population growth would outstrip food production and said that wars, famine, and disease were inevitable unless population growth was held in check by what he called "moral restraint." By "moral restraint" he meant marrying at a late age and living a celibate life. He married at the age of 38 a wife of 27, marriage ages that he recommended for others. Malthus's ideas were regarded as too radical in their day. And they led Thomas Carlyle, a contemporary thinker, to dub economics the "dismal science." But the ideas of Malthus had a profound influence on Charles Darwin, who got the key idea that led him to the theory of natural selection from reading the* Essay on the Principle of Population. *And David Ricardo and the classical economists were strongly influenced by Malthus's ideas.*

"The passion between the sexes has appeared in every age to be so nearly the same, that it may always be considered, in algebraic language as a given quantity."

Thomas Robert Malthus, *An Essay on the Principle of Population*

The Issues

Is there a limit to economic growth, or can we expand production and population without effective limit? Thomas Malthus gave one of the most influential answers to these questions in 1798. He reasoned that population, unchecked, would grow at a geometric rate—1, 2, 4, 8, 16 ...—while the food supply would grow at an arithmetic rate—1, 2, 3, 4, 5 ... To prevent the population from outstripping the available food supply, there would be periodic wars, famines, and plagues. In Malthus's view, only what he called moral restraint could prevent such periodic disasters.

As industrialization proceeded through the nineteenth century, Malthus's idea came to be applied to all natural resources, especially those that are exhaustible.

Modern-day Malthusians believe that his basic idea is correct and that it applies not only to food but also to every natural resource. These prophets of doom believe that in time, we will be reduced to the subsistence level that Malthus predicted. He was a few centuries out in his predictions but not dead wrong.

One modern-day Malthusian is ecologist Paul Ehrlich, who believes that we are sitting on a "population bomb." Governments must limit both population growth and the resources that may be used each year, says Ehrlich.

In 1931, Harold Hotelling developed a theory of natural resources with different predictions from those of Malthus. The Hotelling Principle is that the relative price of an exhaustible natural resource will steadily rise, bringing a decline in the quantity used and an increase in the use of substitute resources.

Julian Simon (who died in 1998) challenged both the Malthusian gloom and the Hotelling Principle. He believed that people are the "ultimate resource" and predicted that a rising population lessens the pressure on natural resources. A bigger population provides a larger number of resourceful people who can work out more efficient ways of using scarce resources. As these solutions are found, the prices of exhaustible resources actually fall. To demonstrate his point, in 1980, Simon bet Ehrlich that the prices of five metals—copper, chrome, nickel, tin, and tungsten—would fall during the 1980s. Simon won the bet!

... and Now

In Tokyo, the pressure on space is so great that in some residential neighbourhoods, a parking space costs $1,700 a month. To economize on this expensive space—and to lower the cost of car ownership and hence boost the sale of cars— Honda, Nissan, and Toyota, three of Japan's big car producers, have developed a parking machine that enables two cars to occupy the space of one. The most basic of these machines costs a mere $10,000—less than 6 months' parking fees.

Then ...

No matter whether it is agricultural land, an exhaustible natural resource, or the space in the centre of Winnipeg, and no matter whether it is 2000, or, as shown here, 1913, there is a limit to what is available, and we persistently push against that limit. Economists see urban congestion as a consequence of the value of doing business in the city centre relative to the cost. They see the price mechanism, bringing ever-higher rents and prices of raw materials, as the means of allocating and rationing scarce natural resources. Malthusians, in contrast, explain congestion as the consequence of population pressure, and they see population control as the solution.

Malthus developed his ideas about population growth in a world in which women played a limited role in the economy. Malthus did not consider the opportunity cost of women's time a factor to be considered in predicting trends in the birth rate and population growth. But today, the opportunity cost of women's time is a crucial factor because of the expanded role that women play in the labour force. One economist who has made significant contributions to our knowledge of labour markets is Craig Riddell. You can meet Professor Riddell on the following pages.

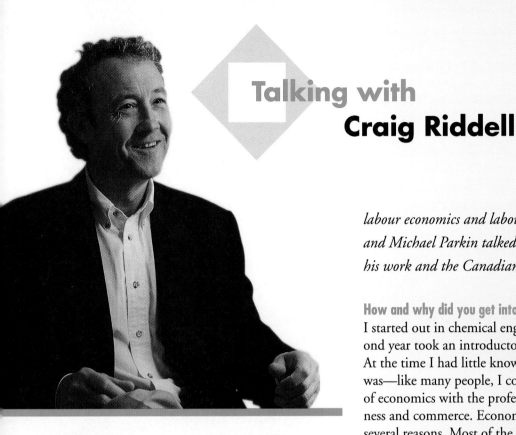

Talking with Craig Riddell

labour economics and labour relations. Robin Bade and Michael Parkin talked to Craig Riddell about his work and the Canadian labour market.

Craig Riddell, *who was born in Toronto in 1946, is a Professor of Economics and former Head of the Department of Economics at the University of British Columbia. He was an undergraduate at the Royal Military College of Canada and a graduate student at Queen's University, where he obtained his Ph.D. in 1977. He began teaching at the University of Alberta in 1975 and moved to the University of British Columbia in 1979. Professor Riddell has acted as economic advisor and consultant to numerous federal and provincial government departments as well as international agencies. He is former Academic Co-Chair of the Canadian Employment Research Forum, an Associate of the Canadian Institute for Advanced Research, and past President of the Canadian Economics Association.*

Professor Riddell is a prolific researcher. In recent years he has examined a variety of issues in

How and why did you get into economics?
I started out in chemical engineering, but in the second year took an introductory course in economics. At the time I had little knowledge of what economics was—like many people, I confused the social science of economics with the professional program of business and commerce. Economics appealed to me for several reasons. Most of the subject matter was of immense social importance: What makes some countries rich and others poor? How should societies allocate their scarce resources in order to achieve the highest level of well-being for their citizens? What causes ups and downs of economics activity with the business cycle? and so on. I also liked the analytical rigour and the fact that the discipline seemed to have developed a set of tools that could be employed to address these "big questions"—as well as many smaller ones. Finally, the policy relevance of the subject was an attractive feature.

You have spent a lot of time in recent years studying unemployment. Why do you find this topic so absorbing?
One reason is the importance of the subject: unemployment may result in the underutilization of people's time and talents, reduce incomes and increase poverty. And persistent high unemployment raises questions in many observers' minds about the ability of the labour market to perform its key function of matching the demands of workers for jobs and of employers for workers. For these reasons, the unemployment rate is one of the most closely followed economic indicators.

Why in recent years has the Canadian unemployment rate remained so high compared with the U.S. unemployment rate?

At the outset, we need to recognize (or admit!) that we still don't fully understand the answer to this question, despite a fair amount of research. However, some important aspects are reasonably clear. First, it is important to distinguish between the 1980s and the 1990s. An unemployment rate gap of about 2 to 3 percentage points emerged beginning in the early 1980s, and this differential widened further in the 1990s. It is tempting to attribute the higher relative Canadian unemployment to weaker economic performance in Canada—that is, that the Canadian economy wasn't growing at a sufficiently rapid rate and wasn't creating enough jobs. This has been the case in the 1990s—both output growth and employment growth were lower in Canada than in the United States. The widening of the unemployment gap in the 1990s can largely be attributed to the weaker economic growth in Canada during the first half of that decade, much of which in turn appears to be due to the much more aggressive anti-inflation policy pursued in Canada during the late 1980s and early 1990s. However, this same story does not apply to the 1980s. During that decade, the performance of the Canadian economy did not deteriorate relative to the United States. Indeed, both overall growth in the production of goods and services and growth in employment were very similar in the two countries. Most of the unemployment gap during the 1980s can be attributed to the change in how Canadians spend their time when not employed relative to Americans, with Canadians becoming more likely to be engaged in job search, whereas Americans became more likely to drop out of the labour force when not employed. Understanding the causes of this change in behaviour is the key to understanding the emergence of the unemployment differential.

How does the Canadian labour market differ from that in the United States?

Relative to the differences that exist between most economies and societies, Canada and the United States are very similar. These similarities are evident in the labour market as well—for example, both countries have highly educated and skilled work forces, and similar industrial and occupational struc-

tures. But there are also a number of differences. Canadian labour market policies generally lie between the extremes of the more *laissez-faire* American approach and the more highly regulated European approach. The principal Canadian income support programs for the working-age population—unemployment insurance and welfare—cover a large fraction of the population and provide higher levels than their U.S. counterparts.

One of the principal conclusions of recent comparative Canada–U.S. labour research is that these differences in labour market and income support policies do influence outcomes and behaviour in the two societies—they are "small differences that matter" (borrowing a phrase that summed up the conclusions of one set of studies).

Can you give an example from your own work that illustrates this "small differences that matter" idea?

The divergence in the importance of unions in the two countries during the past three decades is a good

> *Most of the unemployment gap during the 1980s can be attributed to the change in how Canadians spend their time when not employed relative to Americans, ...*

illustration. The extent of unionization in Canada and the United States was very similar as recently as the mid-1960s, yet now union coverage in Canada is more than double that of the United States. A worker picked at random from either the public or the private sectors is more than twice as likely to be covered by a union contract in Canada than his or her counterpart in the United States.

A number of explanations have been offered for the decline of the unions in the United States and the emergence of a substantial Canada–U.S. unionization differential. These include: (i) changes in economic structure (decline of manufacturing employment, growth of service sector employment, growth of part-time work, growth of small firms, etc.); (ii) differences in social attitudes towards unions; (iii) greater demand for union coverage among Canadian workers; and (iv) differences between the two countries in labour laws relating to unionization and collective bargaining and in the administration and enforcement of these laws. My work on Canada–U.S. unionization finds very little support for the first three of these explanations, and points to the differences in the laws and their administration as the principal source of the differences in union coverage.

Another topic you have worked on is unemployment insurance. This has also been an area of considerable policy debate and reform in Canada. What role has the research played in this debate?

This case is a good illustration of progress in social science. In 1971, Canada made massive changes to its Unemployment Insurance program, including substantially increased coverage of the program, higher benefit levels, lower qualification requirements, and

Economics requires a diverse set of skills ... it's a mistake to concentrate mainly on highly technical and analytical subjects. Having a good "tool kit" is necessary, but not sufficient.

other major changes. At the time relatively little was known about the labour market effects of Unemployment Insurance. Since then a substantial body of research on these effects—in Canada and elsewhere—has been built up. With hindsight, we now recognize that some of the 1971 changes were probably unwise. Recent reforms to the Unemployment Insurance program (now called "Employment Insurance") have had the advantage of a much greater base of information about the likely impacts of changes to the program. Indeed, the 1996 amendments to the Unemployment Insurance program had

more research input than any previous package of reforms.

What type of labour market research do you foresee having the greatest payoff in the future?

International comparative research, an area that has seen some growth recently, seems likely to be able to pay dividends for some time. There are a wide variety of labour market policies and institutions across countries, and this great variation provides much scope for a richer understanding of the impacts of these institutions and policies.

I also believe that there is great potential to learn from social experiments—that is, situations in which there is random assignment into "treatment" and "control" groups. Economics will remain a largely nonexperimental science for a long time, and random assignment is not practical or even feasible in all circumstances. Nonetheless, there are many labour market interventions whose impacts on behaviour could be determined with greater confidence than now exists through the use of social experiments. Policy makers need to take a long-term view—that such experiments add to society's stock of knowledge about the probable effects of policy interventions, thus making it more likely that future policies will achieve their desired effects and making it clearer what the unintended consequences of these policies will be.

What subjects would you advise a student to pursue if he or she wants to become a professional economist today?

Economics requires a diverse set of skills, making it a challenging but also very interesting profession. On the one hand, it's important to have a solid grounding in mathematics and statistics. I would stress the value of good empirical skills—the manipulation and interpretation of data—because I expect economics to continue to become an increasingly empirical science. On the other hand, it's important to have a good knowledge of instituitions and policy issues. Thus I believe it's a mistake to concentrate mainly on highly technical and analytical subjects. Having a good "tool kit" is necessary, but not sufficient. This argues for being exposed to a wide range of subjects father than focusing narrowly.

Chapter **18**

Market Failure and Public Choice

In 1998, the federal, provincial, and municipal governments in Canada employed 1.5 million people and spent 42 cents of every dollar earned by Canadians. Do we need this much government? Is government, as some conservatives and Reform Party members suggest, too big? Is government "the problem"? Or, despite its enormous size, is government too small to do all the things it must attend to? Is government, as some liberals and social democrats suggest, not contributing enough to economic life? ◆ Government touches

Government— the Solution or the Problem?

many aspects of our lives. It is present at our birth, paying for the hospitals in which we are born and training the doctors and nurses who deliver us. It is present throughout our education, paying for schools, colleges, and universities in which we study. It is present throughout our working lives, taxing our incomes, regulating our work environment, and paying us benefits when we are unemployed. It is present throughout our retirement, paying us a pension and, when we die, taxing our bequests. And government provides services such as the enforcement of law and order and the provision of national defence. But the government does not make all our choices. We decide what work to do, how much to save, and what to spend our income on. Why does the government participate in some aspects of our lives but not others? ◆ Almost everyone, from the poor, single mother to the wealthy taxpayer, grumbles about government services. Why is the bureaucracy so unpopular? And what determines the scale on which public services are provided?

◆ We begin our study of governments and markets by describing the government sector and explaining how, in the absence of a government, the market economy fails to achieve an efficient allocation of resources. We also explain how the scale of government is determined.

After studying this chapter, you will be able to:

- Explain how the economic role for government arises from market failure and inequity

- Distinguish between public goods and private goods and explain the free-rider problem

- Explain how the quantity of public goods is determined

- Explain why most of the government's revenue comes from income taxes and why income taxes are progressive

- Explain why some goods are taxed at a much higher rate than others

The Economic Theory of Government

THE ECONOMIC THEORY OF GOVERNMENT SEEKS to predict the economic actions that governments take and the consequences of those actions. Governments exist to help people cope with scarcity and provide a nonmarket mechanism for allocating scarce resources. Four economic problems that governments help people cope with are:

- Public goods
- Monopoly
- Externalities
- Economic inequality

Public Goods

Some goods and services are consumed either by everyone or by no one. Examples are national defence, law and order, and sewage and waste disposal services. National defence systems cannot isolate individuals and refuse to protect them. Airborne diseases from untreated sewage do not favour some people and hit others. A good or service that can be consumed simultaneously by everyone and from which no one can be excluded is called a **public good**.

The market economy fails to deliver the efficient quantity of public goods because of a free-rider problem. Everyone tries to free ride on everyone else because the good is available to all whether they pay for it or not. We'll study public goods and the free-rider problem later in this chapter.

Monopoly

Monopoly and *rent seeking* prevent the allocation of resources from being efficient. Every business tries to maximize profit. And when a monopoly exists, it can increase profit by restricting output and increasing price. Until fairly recently, for example, Bell Canada had a monopoly on long-distance telephone services, and the quantity of long-distance services was much smaller and the price much higher than they are today. Since the end of Bell's monopoly, the quantity of long-distance calls has exploded.

Some monopolies arise from *legal barriers to entry*—barriers to entry created by governments—but

a major activity of government is to regulate monopoly and to enforce laws that prevent cartels and other restrictions on competition. We study these regulations and laws in Chapter 19.

Externalities

An **externality** is a cost or benefit that arises from an economic transaction and that falls on people who do not participate in that transaction. For example, when a chemical factory (legally) dumps its waste into a river and kills the fish, it imposes an external cost on the members of a fishing club who fish downstream. External costs and benefits are not usually taken into account by the people whose actions create them. For example, when the chemical factory decides whether to dump waste into the river, it does not take the fishing club's views into account. When a homeowner fills her garden with spring bulbs, she generates an external benefit for all the passers-by. In deciding how much to spend on this lavish display, she takes into account only the benefits accruing to herself. We study externalities in Chapter 20.

These three problems from which government economic activity arises create an *inefficient* use of resources, a situation called **market failure**. When market failure occurs, the market produces too many of some goods and services and too few of some others. In these cases, the cost of producing a good does not equal the value that people place on it. By reallocating resources, it is possible to make some people better off while making no one worse off. So some government activity is an attempt to modify the market outcome so as to moderate the effects of market failure.

Economic Inequality

Government economic activity also arises because an unregulated market economy delivers what most people regard as an unfair distribution of income. To lessen the degree of inequality, governments tax some people and pay benefits to others. You studied inequality and redistribution in Chapter 17. In this chapter, we'll look further at taxes and try to explain why the income tax is progressive and why some goods are taxed at extremely high rates.

Before we begin to study each of these problems from which government activity arises, let's look at the arena in which governments operate, the "political marketplace."

Public Choice and the Political Marketplace

Government is a complex organization made up of millions of individuals, each with his or her *own* economic objectives. Government policy is the outcome of the choices made by these individuals. To analyse these choices, economists have developed a *public choice theory* of the political marketplace. The actors in the political marketplace are:

■ Voters
■ Politicians
■ Bureaucrats

Figure 18.1 illustrates the choices and interactions of these actors. Let's look at each in turn.

Voters   Voters are the consumers in the political marketplace. In markets for goods and services, people express their preferences by their willingness to pay. In the political marketplace, they express their preferences by their votes, campaign contributions, and lobbying activity. Public choice theory assumes that people support the policies they believe will make them better off and oppose the policies they believe will make them worse off. It is voters' *perceptions* rather than reality that guide their choices.

Politicians   Politicians are the entrepreneurs of the political marketplace. Public choice theory assumes that the objective of a politician is to get elected and to remain in office. Votes to a politician are like economic profit to a firm. To get enough votes, politicians propose policies that they expect will appeal to a majority of voters.

Bureaucrats   Bureaucrats are the hired officials in government departments. They are the producers or firms in the political marketplace. Public choice theory assumes that bureaucrats aim to maximize their own utility and that to achieve this objective, they try to maximize the budget of their department.

The bigger the budget of a department, the greater is the prestige of its chief and the larger is the opportunity for promotion for people farther down the bureaucratic ladder. So all the members of a department have an interest in maximizing the department's budget. To maximize their budgets, bureaucrats devise programs that they expect will appeal to politicians and they help politicians to explain their programs to voters.

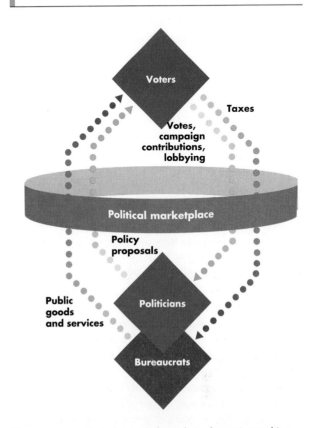

FIGURE 18.1
The Political Marketplace

Voters express their demands for policies by voting, making campaign contributions, and lobbying. Politicians propose policies to appeal to a majority of voters. Bureaucrats try to maximize the budgets of their departments. A political equilibrium emerges in which no group can improve its position by making a different choice.

Political Equilibrium

Voters, politicians, and bureaucrats make choices to best further their own objectives. But each group is constrained by the preferences of the other groups and by what is technologically feasible. The outcome that results from the choices of voters, politicians, and bureaucrats is a **political equilibrium**, which is a situation in which all their choices are compatible and in which no group can improve its position by making a different choice. Let's see how voters, politicians, and bureaucrats interact to determine the quantity of public goods.

Public Goods and the Free-Rider Problem

WHY DOES THE GOVERNMENT PROVIDE GOODS and services such as national defence and public health? Why don't we buy environmental protection from Arctic Ozone, Inc., a private firm that competes for our dollars in the marketplace in the same way that McDonald's and Coca-Cola do? The answer to these questions lies in the free-rider problem created by public goods. Let's explore this problem. We begin by looking at the nature of a public good.

Public Goods

A *public good* is a good or service that can be consumed simultaneously by everyone and from which no one can be excluded. The first feature of a public good is called nonrivalry. A good is *nonrival* if the consumption by one person does not decrease the consumption by another person. An example is watching a television show. The opposite of nonrival is rival. A good is *rival* if the consumption by one person decreases the consumption by another person. An example is eating a hotdog.

The second feature of a public good is that it is nonexcludable. A good is *nonexcludable* if it is impossible, or extremely costly, to prevent someone from benefiting from a good. An example is national defence. It would be difficult to exclude someone from being defended. The opposite of nonexcludable is excludable. A good is *excludable* if it is possible to prevent a person from enjoying the benefits of a good. An example is cable television. Cable companies can ensure that only those people who have paid the fee receive programs.

Figure 18.2 classifies goods according to these two criteria and gives examples of goods in each category. National defence is a *pure* public good. One person's consumption of the security provided by our national defence system does not decrease the security of someone else—defence is nonrival. And the military cannot select those whom it will protect and those whom it will leave exposed to threats—defence is nonexcludable.

Many goods have a public element but are not pure public goods. An example is a highway. A highway is nonrival until it becomes congested. One more car on a highway with plenty of space does not reduce anyone else's consumption of transportation

FIGURE 18.2
Public Goods and Private Goods

	Rival	**Nonrival**
Excludable	**Pure private goods** Food Car House	**Excludable and nonrival** Cable television Bridge Highway
Non-excludable	**Nonexcludable and rival** Fish in the ocean Air	**Pure public goods** Lighthouse National defence

A pure public good (bottom right) is one for which consumption is nonrival and from which it is impossible to exclude a consumer. Pure public goods pose a free-rider problem. A pure private good (top left) is one for which consumption is rival and from which consumers can be excluded. Some goods are nonexcludable but are rival (bottom left), and some goods are nonrival but are excludable (top right).

Source: Adapted from and inspired by E. S. Savas, *Privatizing the Public Sector*, Chatham House Publishers, Inc., Chatham, NJ, 1982, p. 34.

services. But once the highway becomes congested, one extra vehicle lowers the quality of the service available to everyone else—it becomes rival like a private good. Also, users can be excluded from a highway by tollgates. Another example is fish in the ocean. Ocean fish are rival because a fish taken by one person is not available for anyone else. Ocean fish are also nonexcludable because it is difficult to prevent people from catching them.

The Free-Rider Problem

Public goods create a free-rider problem. A **free rider** is a person who consumes a good without paying for it. Public goods create a *free-rider problem* because the quantity of the good that a person is able to consume is not influenced by the amount the person pays for the good. So no one has an incentive to pay enough for a public good. Let's look more closely at the free-rider problem by studying an example.

The Benefit of a Public Good

Suppose that a device has been invented that makes it possible to eliminate acid rain. Let's call this device an acid-rain check. The benefit provided by an acid-rain check is the *value* of its services. The *value* of a *private* good is the maximum amount that a person is willing to pay for one more unit, which is shown by the person's demand curve. The value of a *public* good is the maximum amount that all the *people* are willing to pay for one more unit of it.

Total benefit is the dollar value that a person places on a given level of provision of a public good. The greater the quantity of a public good, the larger is a person's total benefit. *Marginal benefit* is the increase in total benefit that results from a one-unit increase in the quantity of a public good.

Figure 18.3 shows the marginal benefit that arises from acid-rain checks for a society with just two members, Lisa and Max. Lisa's and Max's marginal benefits are graphed as MB_L and MB_M, respectively, in parts (a) and (b) of the figure. The marginal benefit from a public good is similar to the marginal utility from a private good—its magnitude diminishes as the quantity of the good increases. For Lisa, the marginal benefit from the first acid-rain check is $80, and from the second it is $60. By the time 5 acid-rain checks are deployed, Lisa's marginal benefit is zero. For Max, the marginal utility from the first acid-rain check is $50, and from the second it is $40. By the time 5 acid-rain checks are installed, Max perceives only $10 worth of marginal benefit.

Part (c) shows the economy's marginal benefit curve, *MB*. An individual's marginal benefit curve for a public good is similar to the individual's demand curve for a private good. But the economy's marginal benefit curve for a public good is different from the market demand curve for a private good. To obtain the market demand curve for a *private* good, we sum the quantities demanded by all individuals at each price—we sum the individual demand curves *horizontally* (see Chapter 8, p. 169). But to find the economy's marginal benefit curve of a *public* good, we sum the marginal benefits of each individual at each quantity—we sum the individual marginal benefit curves *vertically*. The resulting marginal benefit for the economy made up of Lisa and Max is the economy's marginal benefit curve graphed in part (c)—the curve *MB*. Lisa's marginal benefit from the first acid-rain check gets added to Max's marginal benefit from the first acid-rain check because they *both* consume the first acid-rain check.

FIGURE 18.3

Benefits of a Public Good

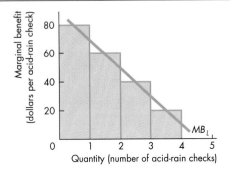

(a) Lisa's marginal benefit

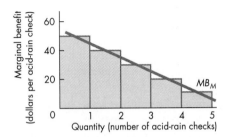

(b) Max's marginal benefit

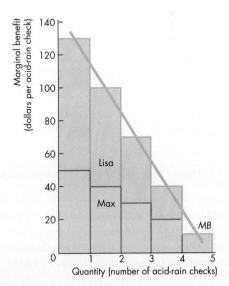

(c) Economy's marginal benefit

The marginal benefit to the economy at each quantity of the public good is the sum of the marginal benefits of all individuals. The marginal benefit curves are MB_L for Lisa, MB_M for Max, and *MB* for the economy.

The Efficient Quantity of a Public Good

An economy with two people would not buy any acid-rain checks—because the total benefit falls far short of the cost. But an economy with 25 million people might. To determine the efficient quantity, we need to take the cost as well as the benefit into account.

The cost of an acid-rain check is based on technology and the prices of the resources used to produce it (see Chapter 11).

Figure 18.4 shows the benefits and costs. The second and third columns of the table show the total and marginal benefits. The next two columns show the total and marginal cost of producing acid-rain checks. The final column shows net benefit. Part (a) graphs total benefit, *TB*, and total cost, *TC*.

The efficient quantity is the one that maximizes *net benefit*—total benefit minus total cost—and occurs when 2 acid-rain checks are provided.

The fundamental principles of marginal analysis that you have used to explain how consumers maximize utility and how firms maximize profit can also be used to calculate the efficient scale of provision of a public good. Figure 18.4(b) shows this alternative approach. The marginal benefit curve is *MB* and the marginal cost curve is *MC*. When marginal benefit exceeds marginal cost, net benefit increases if the quantity produced increases. When marginal cost exceeds marginal benefit, net benefit increases if the quantity produced decreases. Marginal benefit equals marginal cost with 2 acid-rain checks. So making marginal cost equal to marginal benefit maximizes net benefit and uses resources efficiently.

Private Provision

We have now worked out the quantity of acid-rain checks that maximizes net benefit. Would a private firm—Arctic Ozone, Inc.—deliver that quantity? It would not. To do so, it would have to collect $1.5 billion to cover its costs—or $60 from each of the 25 million people in the economy. But no one would have an incentive to buy his or her "share" of the acid-rain check system. Everyone would reason as follows: The number of acid-rain checks provided by Arctic Ozone, Inc., is not affected by my $60. But my own private consumption is greater if I free ride and do not pay my share of the cost of the acid-rain check system. If I do not pay, I enjoy the same quality of air and I can buy more private goods. Therefore I will spend my $60 on other goods and free ride on the public good. This is the free-rider problem.

If everyone reasons the same way, Arctic Ozone has zero revenue and so provides no acid-rain checks. Because two acid-rain checks is the efficient level, private provision is inefficient.

Public Provision

Suppose there are two political parties, the Greens and the Smokes, which agree with each other on all issues except for the quantity of acid-rain checks. The Greens would like to provide 4 acid-rain checks at a cost of $5 billion, with benefits of $5 billion and a net benefit of zero, as shown in Fig. 18.4. The Smokes would like to provide 1 acid-rain check at a cost of $0.5 billion, a benefit of $2 billion, and a net benefit of $1.5 billion—see Fig. 18.4.

Before deciding on their policy proposals, the two political parties do a "what-if" analysis. Each party reasons as follows. If each party offers the acid-rain check program it wants—Greens 4 acid-rain checks and Smokes 1 acid-rain check—the voters will see that they will get a net benefit of $1.5 billion from the Smokes and zero net benefit from the Greens, and the Smokes will win the election.

Contemplating this outcome, the Greens realize that their party is too "green" to get elected. They figure that they must scale back their proposal to 2 acid-rain checks. At this level of provision, total cost is $1.5 billion, total benefit is $3.5 billion, and net benefit is $2 billion. If the Smokes stick with 1 acid-rain check, the Greens will win the election.

But contemplating this outcome, the Smokes realize that they must match the Greens. They too propose to provide 2 acid-rain checks on exactly the same terms as the Greens. If the parties offer the same number of acid-rain checks, the voters are indifferent between them. They flip coins to decide their votes, and each party receives around 50 percent of the vote.

The result of the politicians' "what-if" analysis is that each party offers 2 acid-rain checks, so regardless of who wins the election, this is the quantity of acid-rain checks installed. And this quantity is efficient. It maximizes the perceived net benefit of the voters. Thus in this example, competition in the political marketplace results in the efficient provision of a public good. But for this outcome to occur, voters must be well informed and evaluate the alternatives. But as you will see below, they do not always have an incentive to achieve this outcome.

FIGURE 18.4

The Efficient Quantity of a Public Good

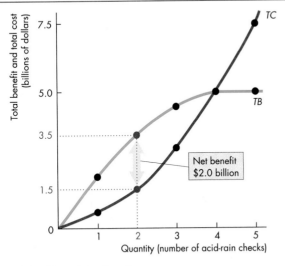

(a) Total benefit and total cost

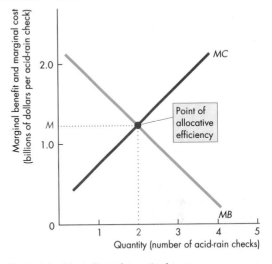

(b) Marginal benefit and marginal cost

Quantity (number of acid-rain checks)	Total benefit (billions of dollars)	Marginal benefit (billions of dollars per acid-rain check)	Total cost (billions of dollars)	Marginal cost (billions of dollars per acid-rain check)	Net benefit (billions of dollars)
0	0		0		0
		2.0		0.5	
1	2.0		0.5		1.5
		1.5		1.0	
2	3.5		1.5		2.0
		1.0		1.5	
3	4.5		3.0		1.5
		0.5		2.0	
4	5.0		5.0		0
		0		2.5	
5	5.0		7.5		−2.5

Net benefit—the vertical distance between total benefit, TB, and total cost, TC—is maximized when 2 acid-rain checks are installed (part a) and where marginal benefit, MB, equals marginal cost, MC (part b). The Smokes would like 1 acid-rain check, and the Greens would like 4. But each party recognizes that its only hope of being elected is to provide 2 acid-rain checks—the quantity that maximizes net benefit and so leaves no room for the other party to improve on.

The Principle of Minimum Differentiation   In the example we've just studied, both parties propose identical policies. This tendency towards identical policies is an example of the **principle of minimum differentiation**, which is the tendency for competitors to make themselves identical to appeal to the maximum number of clients or voters. This principle not only describes the behaviour of political parties but also explains why fast-food restaurants cluster in the same block, and even why new auto models share similar features. If McDonald's opens a restaurant in a new location, it is more likely that Burger King will open next door to McDonald's rather than a kilometre down the road. If Chrysler designs a new van with a sliding door on the driver's side, most likely Ford will too.

The Role of Bureaucrats

We have analysed the behaviour of politicians but not that of the bureaucrats who translate the choices of the politicians into programs and who control the day-to-day activities that deliver public goods. Let's now see how the economic choices of bureaucrats influence the political equilibrium.

To do so, we'll stick with the previous example. We've seen that competition between two political parties delivers the efficient quantity of acid-rain checks. But will the Department of the Environment (DOE) cooperate and accept this outcome?

Suppose the objective of the DOE is to maximize the environment budget. With 2 acid-rain checks being provided at minimum cost, the environment budget is $1.5 billion (see Fig. 18.4). To increase its budget, the DOE might do two things. First, it might try to persuade the politicians that 2 acid-rain checks cost more than $1.5 billion. As Fig. 18.5 shows, if possible, the DOE would like to convince Parliament that 2 acid-rain checks cost $3.5 billion—the entire benefit. Second, and pressing its position even more strongly, the DOE might argue for more acid-rain checks. It might press for 4 acid-rain checks and a budget of $5 billion. In this situation, total benefit and total cost are equal and net benefit is zero.

The DOE wants to maximize its budget, but won't the politicians prevent it from doing so because the DOE's preferred outcome costs votes? They will if voters are well informed and know what is best for them. But voters might be rationally ignorant. In this case, well-informed interest groups might enable the DOE to achieve its objective.

Rational Ignorance

A principle of public choice theory is that it is rational for a voter to be ignorant about an issue unless that issue has a perceptible effect on the voter's income. **Rational ignorance** is the decision *not* to acquire information because the cost of doing so exceeds the expected benefit. For example, each voter knows that he or she can make virtually no difference to the environment policy of the Canadian government. Each voter also knows that it would take an enormous amount of time and effort to become even moderately well informed about alternative technologies. So voters remain relatively uninformed about the technicalities of environment issues. (Though we are using

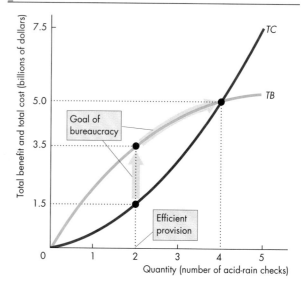

FIGURE 18.5

Bureaucratic Overprovision

The goal of a bureaucracy is to maximize its budget. A bureaucracy that maximizes its budget will seek to increase its budget so that its total cost equals total benefit and then to use its budget to expand output and expenditure. Here, the DOE tries to get $3.5 billion to provide 2 acid-rain checks. It would like to increase the quantity of acid-rain checks to 4 with a budget of $5 billion.

environment policy as an example, the same applies to all aspects of government economic activity.)

All voters are consumers of clean air. But not all voters are producers of the equipment to monitor air quality. Only a small number are in this category. Voters who own or work for firms that produce acid-rain checks have a direct personal interest in the environment because it affects their incomes. These voters have an incentive to become well informed about environment issues and to operate a political lobby aimed at furthering their own interests. In collaboration with the bureaucracy, these voters exert a larger influence than do the relatively uninformed voters who only consume this public good.

When the rationality of the uninformed voter and special interest groups are taken into account, the political equilibrium provides public goods in excess of the efficient quantity. So in the acid-rain check example, 3 or 4 acid-rain checks might be installed rather than the efficient quantity, which is 2 acid-rain checks.

Two Types of Political Equilibrium

We've seen that two types of political equilibrium are possible: efficient and inefficient. These two types of political equilibrium correspond to two theories of government:

■ Public interest theory
■ Public choice theory

Public Interest Theory Public interest theory predicts that governments make choices that achieve efficiency. This outcome occurs in a perfect political system in which voters are fully informed about the effects of policies and refuse to vote for outcomes that can be improved upon.

Public Choice Theory Public choice theory predicts that governments make choices that result in inefficiency. This outcome occurs in political markets in which voters are rationally ignorant and base their votes only on issues that they know affect their own net benefit. Voters pay more attention to their interests as producers than their interests as consumers, and public officials also act in their own best interest. The result is *government failure* that parallels market failure.

Why Government Is Large and Grows

Now that we know how the quantity of public goods is determined, we can explain part of the reason for the growth of government. Government grows, in part, because the demand for some public goods increases at a faster rate than the demand for private goods. There are two possible reasons for this growth:

■ Voter preferences
■ Inefficient overprovision

Voter Preferences The growth of government can be explained by voter preferences in the following way. As voters' incomes increase (as they usually do in most years), the demand for many public goods increases more quickly than income. (Technically, the *income elasticity of demand* for many public goods is greater than 1—see Chapter 5, pp. 98–99.) Many (and the most expensive) public goods are in this category. They include transportation systems such as highways, airports, and air-traffic control systems; public health; education; and national defence. If politicians did not support increases in expenditures on these items, they would not get elected.

Inefficient Overprovision Inefficient overprovision might explain the *size* of government, but not its *growth rate*. It (possibly) explains why government is *larger* than its efficient scale, but it does not explain why governments use an increasing proportion of total resources.

Voters Strike Back

If government grows too large, relative to what voters are willing to accept, there might be a voter backlash against government programs and a large bureaucracy. During the 1990s, the politicians of all parties embraced the idea of a smaller, leaner, and more efficient government.

Another way that voters—and politicians—can try to counter the tendency of bureaucrats to expand their budgets is to privatize the *production* of public goods. Government *provision* of a public good does not automatically imply that a government-operated bureau must *produce* the good. Garbage collection (public good) is often done by a private firm and in some countries experiments are being conducted with private fire departments and even private prisons.

REVIEW QUIZ

■ What is the free-rider problem and why does it make the private provision of a public good inefficient?
■ Under what conditions will competition among politicians for votes result in an efficient quantity of a public good?
■ How do rationally ignorant voters and budget maximizing bureaucrats prevent competition in the political marketplace from producing the efficient quantity of a public good? Do they result in too much or too little public provision of public goods?

We've now seen how voters, politicians, and bureaucrats interact to determine the quantity of a public good. But public goods are paid for with taxes. Taxes also redistribute income. How does the political marketplace determine the scale and variety of taxes that we pay?

Taxes

TAXES GENERATE THE FINANCIAL RESOURCES that provide voters with public goods and other benefits. Five groups of taxes are used:

- Income taxes
- Provincial sales taxes and the GST
- Property taxes
- Employment insurance taxes
- Excise taxes

Figure 18.6 shows the relative amounts raised by these five types of taxes in 1998. Income taxes are the biggest tax source and raised 56 percent of tax revenues in 1998. Provincial sales taxes and the GST are the next biggest revenue source and they raised 22 percent of total taxes in 1998. Property taxes raise about 11 percent of total taxes. Employment insurance taxes raise 7 percent of revenue. And finally, excise taxes raise 4 percent of government revenue. Although they raise a small amount of revenue, excise taxes have a big impact on some markets, as you'll discover later in this chapter. Let's take a closer look at each type of tax.

FIGURE 18.6

Government Tax Revenues

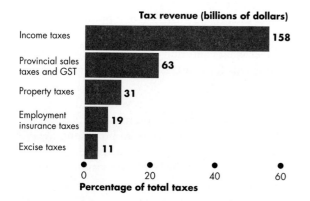

More than half of government revenues come from income taxes. About a third come from provincial sales tax, the GST, and property tax. Excise taxes bring in a small amount of revenue, but these taxes have big effects on a small number of markets.

Source: Statistics Canada, *StatsCan*: Canada; *CANSIM Disc*, March 1999.

Income Taxes

Income taxes are paid on personal incomes and corporate profits. In 1998, the personal income tax raised $73 billion for the federal government and another $46 billion for provincial governments. Corporate profits taxes raised $25 billion for the federal government and $15 billion for the provincial governments. We'll look first at the effects of personal income taxes and then at corporate profits taxes.

Personal Income Tax The amount of income tax that a person pays depends on her or his *taxable income*. Taxable income equals total income minus expenses and other adjustments.

The *tax rate* (percent) depends on the income level and on the province of residence. Provincial income tax rates are defined as a percentage of the federal rate (except for Quebec) and range from 42.75 percent of the federal rate in Ontario to 69 percent of the federal rate in Newfoundland. But surtaxes at both the federal and provincial levels increase these rates. In Ontario, for a single person, and combining federal and provincial basic taxes and surtaxes, the tax rates increase according to the scale:

$0 to $29,590	24.8 percent
$29,591 to $46,747	37.9 percent
$46,748 to $57,184	40.1 percent
$57,185 to $59,180	41.7 percent
over $59,180	47.8 percent

The percentages in this list are marginal tax rates. A **marginal tax rate** is the percentage of an additional dollar of income that is paid in tax. For example if taxable income increases from $20,000 to $20,001, the additional tax paid is 24.8 cents and the marginal tax rate is 24.8 percent. If income increases from $60,000 to $60,001, the additional tax paid is 47.8 cents and the marginal tax rate is 47.8 percent.

The **average tax rate** is the percentage of income that is paid in tax. The average tax rate is less than the marginal tax rate. For example, a single person with a taxable income of $50,000 in 1998 pays $15,138 in income tax. This person's average tax rate is 30.3 percent. A person whose taxable income is $100,000 a year pays $38,366 in income tax, an average tax rate of 38.4 percent.

The average tax rate increases as income increases. When the average tax rate increases as income increases, the tax is called a **progressive tax**. A progressive tax contrasts with a **proportional tax**, which has the same average tax rate at all income levels, and a **regressive tax**, which has a decreasing average tax rate as income increases.

The Effect of Income Taxes   Figure 18.7 shows how the income tax affects labour markets. Part (a) shows the market for low-wage workers and part (b) shows the market for high-wage workers. These labour markets are competitive and with no income taxes, they work just like all the other competitive markets you have studied. The demand curves are *LD* and the supply curves are *LS* (in both parts of the figure). Both groups work 40 hours a week. Low-wage workers earn $9 an hour and high-wage workers earn $170 an hour. What happens when an income tax is introduced?

If low-wage workers are willing to supply 40 hours a week for $9 an hour when there is no tax, then they are willing to supply that same quantity in the face of a 25 percent tax only if the wage rises to $12 an hour. That is, they want to get the $9 an hour they received before plus the $3 (25 percent of $12) that they now must pay to the government. So the supply of labour decreases because the amount received from work is lowered by the amount of income tax paid. The acceptable wage rate at each level of employment rises by the amount of the tax that must be paid. For low-wage workers who face a tax rate of 25 percent, the supply curve shifts to *LS + tax*. The equilibrium wage rate rises to $10 an hour, but the after-tax wage rate falls to $7.50 an hour. Employment falls to 36 hours a week.

For high-wage workers who face a tax rate of 50 percent, the supply curve shifts to *LS + tax*. The equilibrium wage rate rises to $200 an hour, and the after-tax wage rate falls to $100 an hour. Employment decreases to 32 hours a week. The decrease in employment of high-wage workers is larger than that

FIGURE 18.7

The Effects of Income Taxes

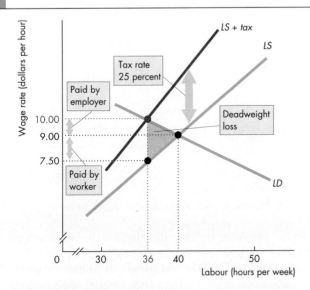

(a) **Lowest income tax rate**

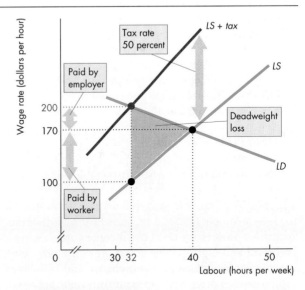

(b) **Highest income tax rate**

The demand for labour is *LD* and with no income taxes, the supply of labour is *LS* (both parts). In part (a), low-wage workers earn $9 an hour and each works 40 hours a week. In part (b), high-wage workers earn $170 an hour and each works 40 hours a week. An income tax decreases the supply of labour and the labour supply curve shifts leftward. For low-wage workers in part (a), whose marginal tax rate is 25 percent, supply decreases to *LS + tax*. Employment decreases to 36 hours a week. For high-wage workers in part (b), whose marginal tax rate is 50 percent, supply decreases to *LS + tax*. Employment decreases to 32 hours a week. The deadweight loss from the high marginal tax rate on high-wage workers is much larger than that from the low marginal tax rate on low-wage workers.

of low-wage workers because of the differences in the marginal tax rates they each face.

Notice that both the employer and the worker pay the income tax. In the case of low-wage workers, the employer pays an extra $1 an hour and the worker pays $1.50 an hour. In the case of high-wage workers, employers pay an extra $30 an hour and workers pay $70 an hour. The split depends on the elasticities of demand and supply.

Notice also the difference in the *deadweight loss* for the two groups. (Check Chapter 6, pp. 118–119, if you need a refresher on the concept of deadweight loss.) The deadweight loss is much larger for the high-wage workers than for the low-wage workers.

Why Do We Have a Progressive Income Tax?

We have a progressive income tax because it is part of the political equilibrium. A majority of voters support it, so politicians who support it get elected.

The economic model that predicts progressive income taxes is called the *median voter* model. The core idea of the median voter model is that political parties pursue policies most likely to attract the support of the median voter. The median voter is the one in the middle—one-half of the population lies on one side and one-half on the other. Let's see how the median voter model predicts a progressive income tax.

Imagine that government programs benefit everyone equally and are paid for by a proportional income tax. Everyone pays the same percentage of his or her income. In this situation, there is redistribution from high-income voters to low-income voters. Everyone benefits equally but because they have higher incomes, the high-income voters pay a larger amount of taxes.

Is this situation the best one possible for the median voter? It is not. Suppose that instead of using a proportional tax, the marginal tax rate is lowered for low-income voters and increased for high-income voters—a progressive tax. Low-income voters are now better off and high-income voters are worse off. Low-income voters will support this change and high-income voters will oppose it. But there are many more low-income voters than high-income voters, so the low-income voters win.

The median voter is a low-income voter. In fact, because the distribution of income is skewed, the median voter has a smaller income than the average income (see Fig. 17.4). This fact raises an interesting question: why doesn't the median voter support taxes that skim off all income above the average and redistribute it to everyone with a below-average income? This tax would be so progressive that it would result in equal incomes after taxes and transfers were paid.

The answer is that high taxes discourage work and saving and the median voter would be worse off with such radical redistribution than under the arrangements that prevail today.

Let's now look at corporate profits taxes.

Corporate Profits Tax   In popular discussions of taxes, corporate profits taxes are seen as a free source of revenue for the government. Taxing people is bad but taxing corporations is just fine.

It turns out that taxing corporations is very inefficient. We use an inefficient tax because it redistributes income in favour of the median voter, just like the income tax. Let's see why taxing corporate profits is inefficient.

First, the tax is misnamed. It is only partly a tax on economic profit. It is mainly a tax on the income from capital. Taxing the income from capital works like taxing the income from labour except for two critical differences: The supply of capital is highly (perhaps perfectly) elastic, and the quantity of capital influences the productivity of labour and wage income. Because the supply of capital is highly elastic, the tax is fully borne by firms and the quantity of capital decreases. With a smaller capital stock than we would otherwise have, the productivity of labour and incomes are lower than they would otherwise be.

Provincial Sales Taxes and the GST

Provincial sales taxes and the GST are levied on a wide range of goods and services. We studied the effects of these taxes on prices, quantities traded, and tax revenue in Chapter 7.

Unlike the income tax, these taxes are *regressive*. The reason they are regressive is that saving increases with income and sales taxes are paid on only the part of income that is spent.

Suppose, for example, that combined provincial sales tax and GST is 15 percent. A family with an income of $20,000 that spends all its income pays $3,000 in sales tax. Its average tax rate is 15 percent. A family with an income of $100,000 that spends $60,000 and saves $40,000 pays sales taxes of $9,000 (15 percent of $60,000). So this family's average tax rate is 9 percent.

We explained the progressive income tax as the outcome of a voting system that places a large weight on the views of the median voter. If the sales tax is regressive, why does the median voter support it? It is the entire tax code that matters, not an individual tax. So a regressive sales tax is voted for only as part of an overall tax regime that is progressive.

Property Taxes

Property taxes are collected by local governments and are used to provide local public goods. A **local public good** is a public good that is consumed by all the people who live in a particular area. Examples of local public goods are parks, museums, and safe neighbourhoods. There is a much closer connection between property taxes paid and benefits received than in the case of federal and provincial taxes. This close connection makes property taxes similar to a price for local services. Because of this connection, property taxes change both the demand for and supply of property in a neighbourhood. A higher tax lowers supply, but improved local public goods increase demand. So some neighbourhoods have high taxes and high-quality local government services and other neighbourhoods have low taxes and low-quality services. Both can exist in the political equilibrium.

Employment Insurance Taxes

Employment insurance taxes are the contributions paid by employers and employees to provide unemployment compensation benefits.

Unions lobby to get employers to pay a bigger share of these taxes and employers' organizations lobby to get workers to pay a bigger share of them. But this lobbying effort is not worth much. For who *really* pays these taxes depends in no way on who writes the cheques. It depends on the elasticities of demand and supply for labour. Figure 18.8 shows you why.

In both parts of the figure, the demand curve LD and the supply curve LS are identical. With no employment insurance tax, the quantity of labour employed is QL^* and the wage rate is W^*.

An employment insurance tax is now introduced. In Fig. 18.8(a) the employment insurance tax is a payroll deduction; in Fig. 18.8(b) the tax is a charge on employers. When the tax is a payroll deduction, supply decreases and the supply of labour curve shifts leftward to $LS + tax$. The vertical distance between the supply curve LS and the new supply curve $LS + tax$ is the amount of the tax. The wage rate rises to WC, after-tax wage rate falls to WT, and employment decreases to QL_0.

When the employment insurance tax is a charge on employers (Fig. 18.8b), demand decreases and the demand for labour curve shifts leftward to $LD - tax$. The vertical distance between the curve LD and the new demand curve $LD - tax$ is the amount of the tax.

FIGURE 18.8

Employment Insurance Tax

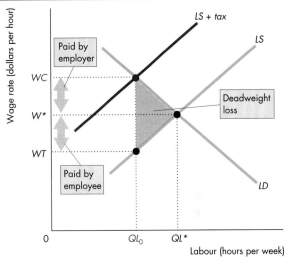

(a) Tax on employees

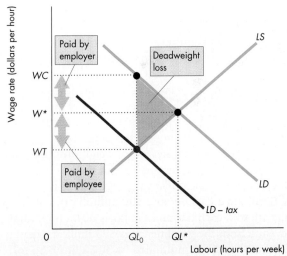

(b) Tax on employers

The labour demand curve is LD and the supply curve is LS. With no employment insurance tax, the quantity of labour employed is QL^* and the wage rate is W^* (in both parts). In part (a), the tax is a payroll deduction. Supply decreases and the supply of labour curve shifts leftward to $LS + tax$. The wage rate rises to WC, after-tax wage rate falls to WT, and employment decreases to QL_0. In part (b), the tax is a charge on employers. Demand decreases and the demand for labour curve shifts leftward to $LD - tax$. The wage rate falls to WT, but the cost of labour rises to WC and employment decreases to QL_0. The outcome is identical in both cases.

The wage rate falls to WT but the cost of labour rises to WC, and employment decreases to QL_0.

So regardless of which side of the market is taxed, the outcome is identical. If the demand for labour is perfectly inelastic or if the supply of labour is perfectly elastic, the employer pays the entire tax. And if the demand for labour is perfectly elastic or if the supply of labour is perfectly inelastic, the employee pays the entire tax. These cases are exactly like those for the sales tax that you studied in Chapter 7 on pp. 137–140.

Excise Taxes

An **excise tax** is a tax on the sale of a particular commodity. The total amount raised by these taxes is small, but they have a big impact on some markets. Let's study the effects of an excise tax by considering the tax on gasoline shown in Fig. 18.9. The demand curve for gasoline is D, and the supply curve is S. If there is no tax on gasoline, its price is 30¢ a litre and 400 million litres of gasoline a day are bought and sold.

Now suppose that a tax is imposed on gasoline at the rate of 30¢ a litre. As a result of the tax, the supply of gasoline decreases and the supply curve shifts leftward. The magnitude of the shift is such that the vertical distance between the original and the new supply curve is the amount of the tax. The new supply curve is the red curve, $S + tax$. The new supply curve intersects the demand curve at 300 million litres a day and 55¢ a litre. This situation is the new equilibrium after the imposition of the tax.

The excise tax creates a deadweight loss made up of the loss of consumer surplus and the loss of producer surplus. The dollar value of that loss is $30 million a day. Because 300 million litres of gasoline are sold each day and the tax is 30¢ a litre, total revenue from the gasoline tax is $90 million a day (300 million litres multiplied by 30¢ a litre). So to raise tax revenue of $90 million dollars a day by using the gasoline tax, a deadweight loss of $15 million a day—one-sixth of the tax revenue—is incurred.

One of the main influences on the deadweight loss arising from a tax is the elasticity of demand for the product. The demand for gasoline is fairly inelastic. As a consequence, when a tax is imposed, the quantity demanded falls by a smaller percentage than the percentage rise in price.

To see the importance of the elasticity of demand, let's consider a different commodity—orange juice. So that we can make a quick and direct comparison, let's assume that the orange juice market

FIGURE 18.9

An Excise Tax

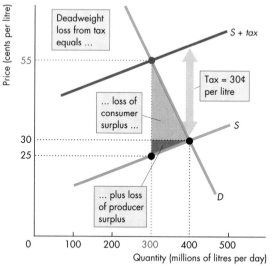

The demand curve for gasoline is D, and the supply curve is S. In the absence of any taxes, gasoline will sell for 30¢ a litre and 400 million litres a day will be bought and sold. When a tax of 30¢ a litre is imposed, the supply curve shifts leftward to become the curve $S + tax$. The new equilibrium price is 55¢ a litre, and 300 million litres a day are bought and sold. The excise tax creates a deadweight loss represented by the grey triangle. The tax revenue collected is 30¢ a litre on 300 million litres, which is $90 million a day. The deadweight loss from the tax is $30 million a day. That is, to raise tax revenue of $90 million a day, a deadweight loss of $15 million a day is incurred.

is exactly as big as the market for gasoline. Figure 18.10 illustrates this market. The demand curve for orange juice is D, and the supply curve is S. Orange juice is not taxed, and so the price of orange juice is 30¢ a litre—where the supply curve and the demand curve intersect—and the quantity of orange juice traded is 400 million litres a day.

Now suppose that the government contemplates abolishing the gasoline tax and taxing orange juice instead. The demand for orange juice is more elastic than the demand for gasoline. It has many good substitutes in the form of other fruit juices. The government wants to raise $90 million a day so that its total revenue is not affected by this tax change. The government's economists, armed with their statistical estimates of the demand and supply curves for orange

FIGURE 18.10

Why We Don't Tax Orange Juice

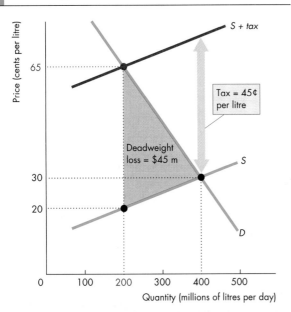

The demand curve for orange juice is D, and the supply curve is S. The equilibrium price is 30¢ a litre, and 400 million litres of juice a day are traded. To raise $90 million of tax revenue, a tax of 45¢ a litre will have to be imposed. The introduction of this tax shifts the supply curve to S + tax. The price rises to 65¢ a litre, and the quantity bought and sold falls to 200 million litres a day. The deadweight loss is represented by the grey triangle and equals $45 million a day. The deadweight loss from taxing orange juice is much larger than that from taxing gasoline (Fig. 18.9) because the demand for orange juice is much more elastic than the demand for gasoline. Items that have a low elasticity of demand are taxed more heavily than items that have a high elasticity of demand.

juice that appear in Fig. 18.10, work out that a tax of 45¢ a litre will do the job. With such a tax, the supply curve shifts leftward to become the curve labelled S + tax. This new supply curve intersects the demand curve at a price of 65¢ a litre and at a quantity of 200 million litres a day. The price at which suppliers are willing to produce 200 million litres a day is 20¢ a litre. The government collects a tax of 45¢ a litre on 200 million litres a day, so it collects a total revenue of $90 million dollars a day—exactly the amount that it requires.

But what is the deadweight loss in this case? The grey triangle in Fig. 18.10 provides the answer. The magnitude of that deadweight loss is $45 million. Notice how much bigger the deadweight loss is from taxing orange juice than from taxing gasoline. In the case of orange juice, the deadweight loss is one-half the revenue raised, while in the case of gasoline, it is only one-sixth. What accounts for this difference? The supply curves are identical in each case, and the examples were also set up to ensure that the initial no-tax prices and quantities were identical. The difference between the two cases is the elasticity of demand: In the case of gasoline, the quantity demanded falls by only 25 percent when the price almost doubles. In the case of orange juice, the quantity demanded falls by 50 percent when the price only slightly more than doubles.

You can see why taxing orange juice is not on the political agenda of any of the major parties. Vote-seeking politicians seek out taxes that benefit the median voter. Other things remaining the same, this means that they try to minimize the deadweight loss of raising a given amount of revenue. Equivalently, they tax items with poor substitutes more heavily than items with close substitutes.

REVIEW QUIZ

- How do income taxes influence employment and efficiency? Why are income taxes progressive?
- Can Parliament make employers pay a larger share of the employment insurance tax?
- Why do some neighbourhoods have high taxes and high-quality services and others have low taxes and low-quality services?
- Why does the government impose excise taxes at high rates on goods that have a low elasticity of demand?

◆ *Reading Between the Lines* on pp. 406–407 looks at the way in which advancing technology changes the balance between public goods and private goods by examining the effect of the arrival of the GPS navigation technology and the public good role of the lighthouses.

In the next two chapters, we are going to look at government economic actions in the face of monopolies and externalities.

Changing Public Goods

NATIONAL POST, MARCH 12, 1999

Lighthouse 'yard sale' coming, group fears

BY GRAEME HAMILTON

Maritime lighthouses that are beacons to mariners and tourists alike will be lost to neglect and foreign ownership if Ottawa doesn't act, a citizens' group warned yesterday.

At a news conference punctuated by the mournful blasts of a nearby fog horn, the group said the federal government is preparing for a "gigantic yard sale" of lighthouses that are no longer needed for navigation.

A debate over the future of the Maritime landmarks has simmered for years as many were rendered obsolete by modern navigational technology. ...

Now as the Coast Guard declares lighthouses surplus, they stand to be sold off at "fair market value," ... Some lighthouses in remote locations will be demolished, the group predicted, and others will be bought up by Americans and Europeans looking for oceanfront real estate.

"What would tourism in the Maritimes be without the lighthouses that are so much a part of our landscape, our culture, and our history," said David Curry, co-chairman of the newly formed Lighthouse Protection Act Committee.

The group wants Ottawa to introduce a Lighthouse Protection Act that would designate all lighthouses built before 1950 as heritage sites and allow community groups to lease them as trustees. Currently, fewer than 20 of the country's 580 lighthouses are protected as heritage structures. ...

Jim Calvesbert, regional director of marine programs for the Coast Guard, said budget cutbacks have made it impossible for the agency to continue looking after lighthouses that aren't needed for navigation. ...

Jim Guptill, who was the last keeper of the Chebucto Head lighthouse before it was automated, said he fears future generations could lose an important piece of Maritime history.

"I want these places to remain open to the public and to be maintained," ...

Essence of the Story

■ A citizens' group is warning that Maritime lighthouses that are no longer needed for navigation will be sold and those in remote locations will be demolished.

■ The group wants the lighthouses to remain as tourist sites.

■ Canada has 580 lighthouses.

■ The Coast Guard does not want to pay the costs of lighthouses that are not needed for navigation.

- When lighthouses were installed along Canada's coastlines, they were public goods used as navigational aids.

- The navigational service could be used simultaneously by everyone and no one could be excluded.

- Figure 1 shows the marginal cost and marginal benefit of lighthouses.

- The marginal cost curve is MC. When lighthouses were used for navigation, the marginal benefit curve was MB_0. The efficient quantity was 580 lighthouses.

- Technological change has resulted in a new global public good for navigation, the Global Positioning System (GPS).

- The GPS, funded and controlled by the U.S. Department of Defense, consists of 24 satellites used by millions of people worldwide.

- The lighthouse as a navigational aid has become obsolete.

- With obsolescence, the marginal benefit of lighthouses has decreased and the marginal benefit curve has shifted leftward to MB_1. The efficient quantity of lighthouses as a navigational aid is zero.

- A lighthouse is no longer a public good.

- By operating a lighthouse as a tourist site and charging admission, it is possible to prevent a person from enjoying all the benefits of the lighthouse. The lighthouse becomes an excludable good—a private good.

- Figure 2 shows the emerging market for lighthouses as tourist sites.

- The marginal cost curve is the same, regardless of the purpose for which the lighthouse is used. So the market supply curve S is the same as the marginal cost curve (MC) in Fig. 1. A private demand emerges, which is shown by the demand curve D_0. The competitive market determines some equilibrium quantity Q_0 (less than or equal to 580 lighthouses) and equilibrium price P_0.

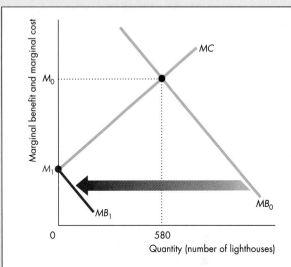

Figure 1 The disappearing lighthouse

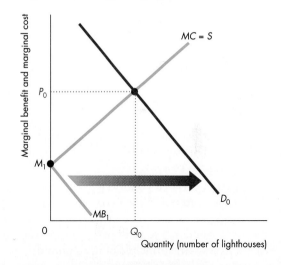

Figure 2 A tourist site market emerges

SUMMARY

Key Points

The Economic Theory of Government
(pp. 392–393)

■ Government exists to provide public goods, regulate monopoly, cope with externalities, and reduce economic inequality.

■ Public choice theory explains how voters, politicians, and bureaucrats interact in a political marketplace.

Public Goods and the Free-Rider Problem
(pp. 394–399)

■ A public good is a good or service that is consumed by everyone and that is *nonrival* and *nonexcludable*.

■ A public good creates a *free-rider* problem—no one has an incentive to pay his or her share of the cost of providing a public good.

■ The efficient level of provision of a public good is that at which net benefit is maximized. Equivalently, it is the level at which marginal benefit equals marginal cost.

■ Competition between political parties, each of which tries to appeal to the maximum number of voters, can lead to the efficient scale of provision of a public good and to both parties proposing the same policies—the principle of minimum differentiation.

■ Bureaucrats try to maximize their budgets and if voters are rationally ignorant, producer interests might result in voting to support taxes that provide public goods in quantities that exceed those that maximize net benefit.

Taxes (pp. 400–405)

■ Government revenue comes from income taxes, provincial sales taxes and the GST, property taxes, employment insurance taxes, and excise taxes.

■ Income taxes decrease the level of employment and create a deadweight loss.

■ Taxes can be progressive (the average tax rate rises with income), proportional (the average tax rate is constant), or regressive (the average tax rate falls with income).

■ Income taxes are progressive because this arrangement is in the interest of the median voter.

■ Property taxes change both demand and supply and can result in high taxes and high-quality service areas and low taxes and low-quality service areas.

■ Employment insurance taxes are paid by the employer and the employee (and sales taxes are paid by the buyer and the seller) in amounts that depend on the elasticities of demand and supply.

■ Excise taxes at high rates on gasoline, alcoholic beverages, and tobacco products create a smaller deadweight loss than would taxes on items with a more elastic demand.

Key Figures ◆

Key Terms

PROBLEMS

*1. You are provided with the following information about a sewage disposal system that a city of 1 million people is considering installing:

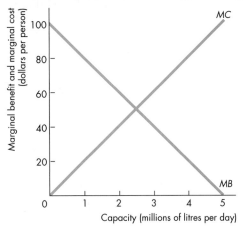

a. What is the capacity that achieves maximum net benefit?
b. How much will each person have to pay in taxes to pay for the efficient capacity level?
c. What is the political equilibrium if voters are well informed?
d. What is the political equilibrium if voters are rationally ignorant and bureaucrats achieve the highest attainable budget?

2. You are provided with the following information about a mosquito control program:

Quantity (square kilometres sprayed per day)	Marginal cost (dollars per day)	Marginal benefit (dollars per day)
0	0	0
1	1,000	5,000
2	2,000	4,000
3	3,000	3,000
4	4,000	2,000
5	5,000	1,000

a. What is the quantity of spraying that achieves maximum net benefit?
b. What is the total tax revenue needed to pay for the efficient quantity of spraying?
c. What is the political equilibrium if voters are well informed?

d. What is the political equilibrium if voters are rationally ignorant and bureaucrats achieve the highest attainable budget?

*3. An economy has two groups of people, A and B. The population consists of 80 percent A-types and 20 percent B-types. A-types have a perfectly elastic supply of labour at a wage rate of $10 an hour. B-types have a perfectly inelastic supply of labour and their equilibrium wage rate is $100 an hour.
a. What kinds of tax arrangements do you predict this economy will adopt?
b. Analyse the labour market in this economy and explain what will happen to the wage rates and employment levels of the two groups when the taxes you predict in your answer to part (a) are introduced.

4. Suppose that in the economy described in problem 3, the proportion of A-types was 20 percent and the proportion of B-types was 80 percent. Everything else remains the same.
a. Now what kinds of tax arrangements do you predict the economy will adopt?
b. Analyse the labour market in this economy and explain what will happen to the wage rates and employment levels of the two groups when the taxes you predict in your answer to part (a) are introduced.
c. Compare the economy in problem 3 with the economy in this problem. Which economy more closely resembles our actual economy?

*5. An economy has a competitive labour market, which is described by the following demand schedule and supply schedule:

Wage rate (dollars per hour)	Quantity demanded (hours per week)	Quantity supplied (hours per week)
20	0	50
16	15	40
12	30	30
8	45	20
4	60	10
0	75	0

a. What are the equilibrium wage rate and hours of work done?

b. If an employment insurance tax of $4 an hour is imposed on employers:
  (i) What is the new wage rate?
  (ii) How many hours are worked?
  (iii) What is the after-tax wage rate?
  (iv) What is the tax revenue?
  (v) What is the deadweight loss?

6. In the economy described in problem 5, the employment insurance tax on employers is eliminated and a new employment insurance tax of $4 an hour is imposed on employees.
  a. What is the new wage rate?
  b. How many hours are worked?
  c. What is the after-tax wage rate?
  d. What is the tax revenue?
  e. What is the deadweight loss?
  f. Compare the situation in problem 5 with that in this problem and explain the similarities and differences in the two situations.

*7. In a competitive market for cookies:

Price (dollars per kilogram)	Quantity demanded (kilograms per month)	Quantity supplied (kilograms per month)
10	0	28
8	4	24
6	8	20
4	12	16
2	16	12

  a. What are the equilibrium price and the equilibrium quantity?
  b. If cookies are taxed $2 a kilogram:
    (i) What is the new price of cookies?
    (ii) What is the new quantity bought?
    (iii) What is the tax revenue?
    (iv) What is the deadweight loss?

8. In the competitive market for cookies in problem 7, the government wants to change the tax on a kilogram of cookies so that it brings in the greatest possible amount of tax revenue.
  a. What is that tax on a kilogram of cookies?
  b. What is the new price of cookies?
  c. What is the new quantity bought?
  d. What is the tax revenue?
  e. What is the deadweight loss?

CRITICAL THINKING

 1. Study *Reading Between the Lines* on pp. 406–407, and then:
  a. Describe the events that have changed the public good status of the lighthouse.
  b. What is the new navigational public good and how is it provided?
  c. Do you think that the provision of GPS satellites is efficient? If not, what must be done to achieve the efficient level of provision?
  d. Use the links on the Parkin-Bade Web site and find out what has been happening to lighthouses. Do you think that the private market for lighthouses as tourist sites is efficient? Why or why not?

2. Use the links on the Parkin-Bade Web site to obtain information about Ontario highways.
  a. Are highways 401 and 407 public goods, private goods, or a mixture of the two?
  b. Which highway, the 401 or the 407, is more public? Why?
  c. Is snow clearing and sanding and salting on highways 401 and 407 a public service or a private service, or a mixture of the two?
  d. Does Ontario have an efficient provision of highway services?

3. Your local city council believes that by installing computers to control the traffic signals, it can improve the speed of traffic flow. The bigger the computer the council buys, the better job it can do. The mayor and the other elected officials who are working on the proposal want to determine the scale of the system that will win them the most votes. The city bureaucrats want to maximize the budget. Suppose that you are an economist who is observing this public choice. Your job is to calculate the quantity of this public good that uses resources efficiently.
  a. What data would you need to reach your own conclusions?
  b. What does the public choice theory predict will be the quantity chosen?
  c. How could you, as an informed voter, attempt to influence the choice?
  d. What does the public interest theory predict will be the quantity chosen?

Chapter 19

Competition Policy

When you consume water, electric power, natural
gas, cable TV, or local telephone service, you
buy from a regulated monopoly. Why do
we regulate the industries that produce
these goods and services? How do we regulate them? Does regulation work in the interests of consumers—the public interest—or does it
serve the interests of producers—special interests? ◆
Regulation extends beyond monopoly to oligopoly. For
example, until 1978 airline prices and routes were regulated. But

Public Interest or Special Interests?

in 1978, domestic air travel was deregulated and the airlines are free to choose their
own routes and fares. Railways, interprovincial trucking, banking, and insurance were
regulated in the past but in recent years they
have been deregulated. Why do we regulate
and then deregulate an industry? ◆ The government used its anti-
combine laws to end Northern Telecom's monopoly on phone equipment
and Bell Canada's monopoly on long-distance phone calls as well as the
installation of phone lines. This action brought competition into all three
markets. Now you can choose where to buy your phone equipment,
which long-distance telephone service to use, and the company to install
your phone line. What are the anti-combine laws? How have they evolved
over the years? How are they used today? Do they serve the public interest
of consumers or the special interests of producers?

◆ This chapter studies government regulation. It draws on your earlier
study of how markets work and on your knowledge of consumer surplus
and producer surplus. It shows how consumers and producers can redistribute the gains from trade in the political marketplace, and it identifies
who stands to win and who stands to lose from government intervention.

After studying this chapter, you will be able to:

- Define regulation, public ownership, and anti-combine law

- Distinguish between the public interest and capture theories of regulation

- Explain how regulation affects prices, outputs, profits, and the distribution of the gains from trade between consumers and producers

- Explain how public ownership affects prices, outputs, and allocative efficiency

- Explain how anti-combine law is used in Canada today

Market Intervention

THE GOVERNMENT INTERVENES IN MONOPO-
listic and oligopolistic markets to influence what,
how, and for whom various goods and services are
produced in three main ways:

■ Regulation
■ Public ownership
■ Anti-combine law

Regulation

Regulation consists of rules administered by a government agency to influence economic activity by
determining prices, product standards and types, and
the conditions under which new firms may enter an
industry. To implement its regulations, the government establishes agencies to oversee the regulations
and ensure their enforcement. The first such economic regulation in Canada was the Railway Act of
1888, which regulated railway rates. Since then and
up to the late 1970s, regulation spread to banking
and financial services, telecommunications, gas and
electric utilities, railways, trucking, airlines and buses,
and dozens of agricultural products. Since the early
1980s, there has been a tendency to deregulate the
Canadian economy.

Deregulation is the process of removing restrictions on prices, product standards and types, and
entry conditions. In recent years, deregulation has
occurred in domestic air transportation, telephone
service, interprovincial trucking, and banking and
financial services.

Public Ownership

In Canada, publicly owned firms are called **Crown
corporations**. The most important Crown corporations are Canada Post, the CBC, CN, VIA Rail, and
Atomic Energy of Canada. There are many provincial
Crown corporations, the most important of which
are the provincial hydro companies. Just as there has
been a tendency to deregulate the Canadian economy
in recent years, there has also been a tendency to privatize it. **Privatization** is the process of selling a publicly owned corporation to private shareholders.
Petro-Canada was privatized in 1991.

Anti-Combine Law

An **anti-combine law** is a law that regulates and prohibits certain kinds of market behaviour, such as
monopoly and monopolistic practices. The main
thrust of the anti-combine law is the prohibition of
monopoly practices and of restricting output in order
to achieve higher prices and profits. In Canada,
unlike the United States, the anti-combine law was,
until 1971, part of the Criminal Code. As a consequence, private lawsuits could not be filed. Also, the
test of guilt is much more stringent under the
Criminal Code than under civil law. As a result,
Canada's anti-combine laws have been used less vigorously than the parallel laws (called "anti-trust
laws") south of the border.

To understand why the government intervenes in
the markets for goods and services and to work out
the effects of its interventions, we need to identify the
gains and losses that government actions can create.
These gains and losses are the consumer surplus and
producer surplus associated with different outputs and
prices. We first study the economics of regulation.

Economic Theory of Regulation

THE ECONOMIC THEORY OF REGULATION IS PART
of the broader theory of public choice that is
explained in Chapter 18. Here, we apply public
choice theory to regulation. We'll examine the
demand for government actions, the supply of those
actions, and the political equilibrium that emerges.

Demand for Regulation

The demand for regulation is expressed through
political activity—voting, lobbying, and making
campaign contributions. But engaging in political
activity is costly and people demand political action
only if the benefit that they individually receive from
such action exceeds their individual costs in obtaining the action. The four main factors that affect the
demand for regulation are:

1. Consumer surplus per buyer

2. Number of buyers

3. Producer surplus per firm

4. Number of firms

The larger the consumer surplus per buyer resulting from regulation, the greater is the demand for regulation by buyers. Also, as the number of buyers increases, so does the demand for regulation. But numbers alone do not necessarily translate into an effective political force. The larger the number of buyers, the greater is the cost of organizing them, so the demand for regulation does not increase proportionately with the number of buyers.

The larger the producer surplus per firm that arises from a particular regulation, the larger is the demand for that regulation by firms. Also, as the number of firms that might benefit from some regulation increases, so does the demand for that regulation. But again, large numbers do not necessarily mean an effective political force. The larger the number of firms, the greater is the cost of organizing them.

For a given surplus, consumer or producer, the smaller the number of households or firms who share that surplus, the larger is the demand for the regulation that creates it.

Supply of Regulation

Politicians and bureaucrats supply regulation. According to public choice theory, politicians choose policies that appeal to a majority of voters, thereby enabling themselves to achieve and maintain office. Bureaucrats support policies that maximize their budgets (see Chapter 18, p. 398). Given these objectives of politicians and bureaucrats, the supply of regulation depends on the following three factors:

1. Consumer surplus per buyer
2. Producer surplus per firm
3. The number of persons affected

The larger the consumer surplus per buyer or producer surplus per firm generated by a regulation and the larger the number of persons affected by a regulation, the greater is the tendency for politicians to supply that regulation. Politicians are likely to supply regulation that benefits a large number of people by a large amount per person. They are also likely to supply regulation that benefits a *small* number of people when the benefit per person is large and the cost is spread widely and not easily identified. But they are unlikely to supply a regulation that brings a small benefit per person.

Political Equilibrium

In a political equilibrium, no interest group plans to use resources to press for changes and no group of politicians plans to offer different regulations. Being in a political equilibrium is not the same thing as everyone being in agreement. Lobby groups will devote resources to trying to change regulations that are already in place. And others will devote resources to maintaining the existing regulations. But no one will feel it is worthwhile to increase the resources they are devoting to such activities. Also, political parties might not agree with each other. Some support the existing regulations, and others propose different regulations. In equilibrium, no one wants to change the proposals that they are making.

What will a political equilibrium look like? The answer depends on whether the regulation serves the public interest or the interest of the producer. Let's look at these two possibilities.

Public Interest Theory   The **public interest theory** is that regulations are supplied to satisfy the demand of consumers and producers to maximize total surplus—that is, to attain allocative efficiency. Public interest theory implies that the political process relentlessly seeks out deadweight loss and introduces regulations that eliminate it. For example, where monopoly practices exist, the political process will introduce price regulations to ensure that outputs increase and prices fall to their competitive levels.

Capture Theory   The **capture theory** is that the regulations are supplied to satisfy the demand of producers to maximize producer surplus—that is, to maximize economic profit. The key idea of capture theory is that the cost of regulation is high and only those regulations that increase the surplus of small, easily identified groups and that have low organization costs are supplied by the political process. Consumers bear the cost of such regulation but the costs are spread thinly and widely so they do not lose votes.

The predictions of the capture theory are less clear-cut than the predictions of the public interest theory. According to the capture theory, regulations benefit cohesive interest groups by large and visible amounts and impose small costs on everyone else. But those costs are so small, in per person terms, that no one feels it is worthwhile to incur the cost of organizing an interest group to avoid them. To make these predictions concrete enough to be useful, the capture theory needs a model of the costs of political organization.

Whichever theory of regulation is correct, according to public choice theory, the political system delivers amounts and types of regulations that best further the electoral success of politicians. Because producer-oriented and consumer-oriented regulation are in conflict with each other, the political process can't satisfy both groups in any particular industry. Only one group can win. This makes the regulatory actions of government a bit like a unique product—for example, a painting by Emily Carr. There is only one original and it will be sold to just one buyer. Normally, a unique commodity is sold through an auction; the highest bidder takes the prize.

Equilibrium in the regulatory process can be thought of in much the same way: The suppliers of regulation will satisfy the demands of the higher bidder. If the producer demand offers a bigger return to the politicians, either directly through votes or indirectly through campaign contributions, then the regulation will serve the producers' interests. If the consumer demand translates into a larger number of votes, then the regulation will serve the consumers' interests.

R E V I E W Q U I Z

- How do consumers and producers express their demand for regulation? What are their objectives? What are the costs of expressing a demand for regulation?
- When politicians and bureaucrats supply regulation, what are they trying to achieve? Do politicians and bureaucrats have the same objectives?
- What is a political equilibrium? When does the political equilibrium achieve economic efficiency? When does the political equilibrium serve the interests of producers? When do the bureaucrats win?

We have now completed our study of the *theory* of regulation in the marketplace. Let's turn our attention to the regulations that exist in our economy today. Which theory of regulation best explains these real-world regulations? Which of these regulations are in the public interest and which are in the interest of producers?

Regulation and Deregulation

THE PAST DECADE OR SO HAS SEEN DRAMATIC changes in the way in which the government has regulated the Canadian economy. We're going to examine some of these changes. To begin we'll look at what the government regulates and also at the scope of regulation. Then we'll turn to the regulatory process itself and examine how regulators control prices and other aspects of market behaviour. Finally, we'll tackle the more difficult and controversial questions: Why does the government regulate some things but not others? Who benefits from the regulation that we have—consumers or producers?

The Scope of Regulation

Regulation touches a wide range of economic activity in Canada. Table 19.1 sets out the major federal regulatory agencies, together with a brief statement of their responsibilities. As you can see by inspecting that table, the predominant sectors subject to regulation are agriculture, energy, transport, and telecommunications.

Provincial and municipal governments also establish regulations covering a wide range of economic activity. Some of these—for example, municipal regulation of the taxicab industry—have important direct effects on the marketplace. Our analysis of the regulatory process and the effects of regulation apply with equal force to price, output, and profit regulation at these other governmental levels.

What exactly do regulatory agencies do? How do they regulate?

The Regulatory Process

Though regulatory agencies vary in size and scope and in the detailed aspects of economic life that they control, there are certain features common to all agencies.

First, the government appoints the senior bureaucrats who are the key decision makers in a regulatory agency. In addition, all agencies have a permanent bureaucracy made up of experts in the industry being regulated and often recruited from the regulated firms. Agencies have financial resources,

TABLE 19.1

Federal Regulatory Agencies

Agency	Responsibility
Atomic Energy Control Board	Administers the Atomic Energy Control Act governing all uses of radioactive material.
Canadian Dairy Commission	Administers national dairy policy, which seeks to give producers an adequate return and keep the price to consumers low.
Canadian Radio-Television and Telecommunications Commission	Regulates all aspects of radio, television, and telecommunications.
Canadian Grain Commission	Regulates grain handling, establishes and maintains quality standards, audits grain stocks, and supervises future trading.
Canadian Wheat Board	Regulates exports of wheat and barley and domestic sales for human consumption.
National Energy Board	Regulates oil, gas, and electrical industries.
National Farm Products Marketing Council	Advises government on the establishment and operation of national agricultural marketing agencies and works with those agencies and provincial governments to promote marketing of farm products. Chicken, egg, and turkey agencies have been established under its aegis.
Canadian Transport Commission	Regulates transports under federal jurisdiction including rail, air, water, and pipeline and some interprovincial commercial motor transport.

Source: Statistics Canada, *Canada Year Book*, 1992.

voted by Parliament, to cover the costs of their operations.

Second, each agency adopts a set of practices or operating rules for controlling prices and other aspects of economic performance. These rules and practices are based on well-defined physical and financial accounting procedures that are relatively easy to administer and to monitor.

In a regulated industry, individual firms are usually free to determine the technology that they will use in production. But they are not free to determine the prices at which they will sell their output, the quantities that they will sell, or the markets that they will serve. The regulatory agency grants certification to a company to serve a particular market and with a particular line of products. The agency also determines the level and structure of prices that the company can charge. In some cases, the agency also determines the scale of output permitted.

To analyse the way in which regulation works, it is convenient to distinguish between the regulation of natural monopoly and the regulation of cartels. Let's begin with the regulation of natural monopoly.

Natural Monopoly

Natural monopoly was defined in Chapter 13 (p. 268) as an industry in which one firm can supply the entire market at a lower price than two or more firms can. As a consequence, natural monopoly experiences economies of scale, no matter how large an output rate it produces. Examples of natural monopolies include local distribution of cable television signals, electricity and gas, and urban rail services. It is much more expensive to have two or more competing sets of wires, pipes, and train lines serving every neighbourhood than it is to have a single set. (What is a natural monopoly changes over time as technology changes. With the introduction of fibre optic cables, both telephone companies and cable television companies will be able to compete with each other in both markets, so what is a natural monopoly will become a more competitive industry.)

Let's consider the example of cable TV, which is shown in Fig. 19.1. The demand curve for cable TV is *D*. The cable TV company's marginal cost curve is *MC*. That marginal cost curve is (assumed to be)

FIGURE 19.1

Natural Monopoly: Marginal Cost Pricing

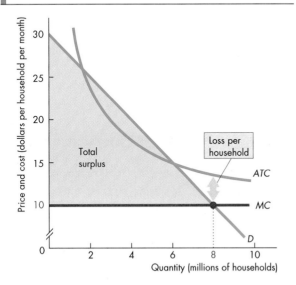

A natural monopoly is an industry in which average total cost is falling even when the entire market demand is satisfied. A cable TV operator faces the demand curve D. The firm's marginal cost is constant at $10 per household per month, as shown by the curve labelled MC. Fixed costs are large, and the average total cost curve, which includes average fixed cost, is shown as ATC. A marginal cost pricing rule that maximizes total surplus sets the price at $10 a month, with 8 million households being served. The resulting consumer surplus is shown as the green area. The firm incurs a loss on each household, indicated by the red arrow. To remain in business, the firm must price discriminate, use a two-part tariff, or receive a subsidy.

horizontal at $10 per household per month—that is, the cost of providing each additional household with a month of cable programming is $10. The cable company has a heavy investment in satellite receiving dishes, cables, and control equipment and so has high fixed costs. These fixed costs are part of the company's average total cost curve, shown as *ATC*. The average total cost curve slopes downward because as the number of households served increases, the fixed cost is spread over a larger number of households. (If you need to refresh your memory on how the average total cost curve is calculated, take a quick look back at Chapter 11, pp. 230–231.)

Regulation in the Public Interest   How will cable TV be regulated according to the public interest theory? It will be regulated to maximize total surplus, which occurs if marginal cost equals price. As you can see in Fig. 19.1, that outcome occurs if the price is regulated at $10 per household per month and if 8 million households are served. Such a regulation is called a **marginal cost pricing rule**. A marginal cost pricing rule sets price equal to marginal cost. It maximizes total surplus in the regulated industry.

A natural monopoly that is regulated to set price equal to marginal cost incurs an economic loss. Because its average total cost curve is downward sloping, marginal cost is below average total cost. Because price equals marginal cost, price is below average total cost. Average total cost minus price is the loss per unit produced. It's pretty obvious that a cable TV company that is required to use a marginal cost pricing rule will not stay in business for long. How can a company cover its costs and, at the same time, obey a marginal cost pricing rule?

One possibility is price discrimination (see Chapter 13, pp. 277–280). Another is to use a two-part price (called a *two-part tariff*). For example, local telephone companies can charge consumers a monthly fee for being connected to the telephone system and then charge a price equal to marginal cost for each local call. A cable TV operator can charge a one-time connection fee that covers its fixed cost and then charge a monthly fee equal to marginal cost.

But a natural monopoly cannot always cover its costs in these ways. If a natural monopoly cannot cover its total cost from its customers, and if the government wants it to follow a marginal cost pricing rule, the government must give the firm a subsidy. In such a case, the government raises the revenue for the subsidy by taxing some other activity. But as we saw in Chapter 18, taxes themselves generate deadweight loss. Thus the deadweight loss resulting from additional taxes must be subtracted from the efficiency gained by forcing the natural monopoly to adopt a marginal cost pricing rule.

Deadweight loss might be minimized by making the natural monopoly cover its cost rather than by taxing another sector of the economy. When a monopoly covers its costs, it uses an average cost pricing rule. An **average cost pricing rule** sets price equal to average total cost. Figure 19.2 shows the average cost pricing solution. The cable TV operator charges $15 a month and serves 6 million households. A deadweight loss arises, which is shown by the grey triangle in the figure.

FIGURE 19.2

Natural Monopoly: Average Cost Pricing

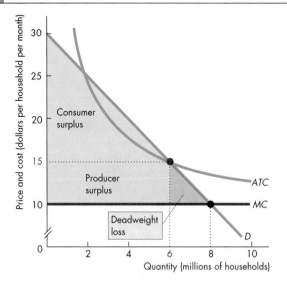

Average cost pricing sets price equal to average total cost. The cable TV operator charges $15 a month and serves 6 million households. In this situation, the firm breaks even—average total cost equals price. Deadweight loss, shown by the grey triangle, is generated. Consumer surplus is reduced to the green area.

FIGURE 19.3

Natural Monopoly: Profit Maximization

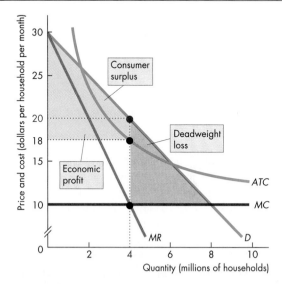

The cable TV operator would like to maximize profit. To do so, marginal revenue (MR) is made equal to marginal cost. At a price of $20 a month, 4 million households buy cable service. Consumer surplus is reduced to the green triangle. The deadweight loss increases to the grey triangle. The monopoly makes the profit shown by the blue rectangle. If the producer can capture the regulator, the outcome will be the situation shown here.

Capturing the Regulator What does the capture theory predict about the regulation of this industry? According to the capture theory, the producer gets the regulator to set rules that work to serve the interest of the producer. But the producer interest is served by being able to operate at the same output and price as an unregulated monopoly. In Fig. 19.3, the monopoly's marginal revenue curve is the curve labelled *MR*. Marginal revenue equals marginal cost when output is 4 million households and the price is $20 a month. At this output and price, the producer makes the maximum profit. So regulation in the interest of the producer maintains the unregulated monopoly outcome.

But how can a producer go about capturing the regulator and obtaining regulation that results in this monopoly profit-maximizing outcome? To answer this question, we need to look at the way in which

agencies determine a regulated price. A key method used is called rate of return regulation.

Rate of Return Regulation **Rate of return regulation** determines a regulated price by setting the price at a level that enables the regulated firm to earn a specified target percent return on its capital. The target rate of return is determined with reference to what is normal in competitive industries. This rate of return is part of the opportunity cost of the natural monopolist and is included in the firm's average total cost. By examining the firm's total cost, including the normal rate of return on capital, the regulator attempts to determine the price at which average total cost is covered. Thus rate of return regulation is equivalent to average cost pricing.

In Fig. 19.2, average cost pricing results in a regulated price of $15 a month with 6 million households being served. Thus rate of return regulation, based on a correct assessment of the producer's average total cost curve, results in a price that favours the consumer and does not enable the producer to maximize monopoly profit. The special interest group will have failed to capture the regulator, and the outcome will be closer to that predicted by the public interest theory of regulation.

But there is a feature of many real-world situations that the above analysis does not take into account: the ability of the monopoly firm to mislead the regulator about its true costs.

Inflating Costs   The managers of a firm might be able to inflate the firm's costs by spending part of the firm's revenue on inputs that are not strictly required for the production of the good. By this device, the firm's apparent costs exceed the true costs. On-the-job luxury in the form of sumptuous office suites, limousines, free baseball tickets (disguised as public relations expenses), company jets, lavish international travel, and entertainment are all ways in which managers can inflate costs.

If the cable TV operator makes the regulator believe that its true cost is *ATC (inflated)* in Fig. 19.4, then the regulator will set the price at $20 a month. In this example, the price and quantity will be the same as those under unregulated monopoly. It might be impossible for firms to inflate their costs by as much as the amount shown in the figure. But to the extent that costs can be inflated, the apparent average total cost curve lies somewhere between the true average total cost curve and *ATC (inflated)*. The greater the ability of the firm to pad its costs in this way, the more closely its profit (measured in economic terms) approaches the maximum possible. The shareholders of this firm don't receive this economic profit because it is used up in baseball tickets, luxury offices, and the other actions taken by the firm's managers to inflate the company's costs.

Public Interest or Capture?

It is not clear whether actual regulation produces prices and quantities that more closely correspond with the predictions of capture theory or with public interest theory. One thing is clear, however. Price regulation does not require natural monopolies to use the marginal cost pricing rule. If it did, most natural

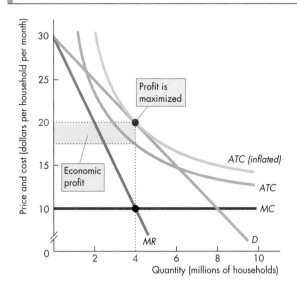

Natural Monopoly: Inflating Costs

If the cable TV operator is able to inflate its costs to *ATC (inflated)* and persuade the regulator that these are genuine minimum costs of production, rate of return regulation results in a price of $20 a month—the profit-maximizing price. To the extent that the producer can inflate costs above average total cost, the price rises, output decreases, and deadweight loss increases. The managers, not the shareholders (owners) of the firm, capture the profit.

monopolies would make losses and receive hefty government subsidies to enable them to remain in business. But there are even exceptions to this conclusion. For example, many local telephone companies do appear to use marginal cost pricing for local telephone calls. They cover their total cost by charging a flat fee each month for being connected to their telephone system but then permitting each call to be made at its marginal cost—zero or something very close to it.

We can test whether natural monopoly regulation is in the public interest or producer interest by comparing the rates of return in regulated natural monopolies with average returns. If regulated natural monopolies have rates of return significantly higher than those in the rest of the economy, then, to some degree, the regulator may have been captured by the producer. There is plenty of empirical evidence that many natural monopolies in Canada do earn higher rates of return than the economy average.

One recent striking example is cable television service; telephone service is another. The rates of return in these two industries exceed 10 percent a year, approaching double the economy average. Perhaps the most dramatic piece of evidence that regulation benefits the regulated firm is the profits of Bell Canada Enterprises (BCE), prior to deregulation of long-distance phone services. BCE is a conglomerate that produced *regulated* long-distance telephone services and *unregulated* phone equipment (Northern Telecom) and financial services (Montreal Trustco). In 1992, BCE made a total profit of $1.4 billion on total assets of $12.3 billion, a profit rate of 11.4 percent. But this total was made up of a profit of $0.9 billion on assets of $7 billion—a return of 12.9 percent—for the regulated Bell Canada and a profit of $0.5 billion on assets of $5.3 billion—9.4 percent—for all BCE's *unregulated* operation.

Until the early 1990s, long-distance telephone service was a natural monopoly, but technological advances in telecommunications have changed the situation. Today, the industry is an oligopoly. But oligopoly is also regulated. Let's examine regulation in oligopolistic industries—the regulation of cartels.

Cartel Regulation

A *cartel* is a collusive agreement among a number of firms that is designed to restrict output and achieve a higher profit for the cartel's members. Cartels are illegal in Canada and in most other countries. But international cartels can sometimes operate legally, such as the international cartel of oil producers known as OPEC (the Organization of Petroleum Exporting Countries).

Illegal cartels can arise in oligopolistic industries. An oligopoly is a market structure in which a small number of firms compete with each other. We studied oligopoly (and duopoly—two firms competing for a market) in Chapter 14. There we saw that if firms manage to collude and behave like a monopoly, they can set the same price and sell the same total quantity as a monopoly firm would. But we also discovered that in such a situation, each firm will be tempted to cheat, increasing its own output and profit at the expense of the other firms. The result of such cheating on the collusive agreement is the

unravelling of the monopoly equilibrium and the emergence of a competitive outcome with zero economic profit for producers. Such an outcome benefits consumers at the expense of producers.

How is oligopoly regulated? Does regulation prevent monopoly practices or does it encourage those practices?

According to the public interest theory, oligopoly is regulated to ensure a competitive outcome. Consider, for example, the market for trucking tomatoes from the fields of southwestern Ontario to a ketchup factory at Leamington, illustrated in Fig. 19.5. The demand curve for trips is *D*. The industry marginal cost curve—and the competitive supply curve—is *MC*. Public interest regulation will set the price of a trip at $20 and there will be 300 trips a week.

FIGURE **19.5**
Collusive Oligopoly

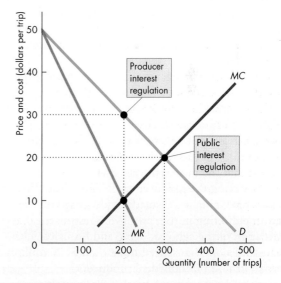

Ten trucking firms transport tomatoes from southwestern Ontario to Leamington. The demand curve is *D*, and the industry marginal cost curve is *MC*. Under competition, the *MC* curve is the industry supply curve. If the industry is competitive, the price of a trip will be $20 and 300 trips will be made each week. Producers will demand regulation that restricts entry and limits output to 200 trips a week, where industry marginal revenue (*MR*) is equal to industry marginal cost (*MC*). This regulation raises the price to $30 a trip and results in each producer making maximum profit—as if it is a monopoly.

How would this industry be regulated according to the capture theory? Regulation that is in the interest of producers will maximize profit. To find the outcome in this case, we need to determine the price and quantity when marginal cost equals marginal revenue. The marginal revenue curve is *MR*. So, marginal revenue equals marginal cost at 200 trips a week. The price of a trip is $30.

One way of achieving this outcome is to place an output limit on each firm in the industry. If there are 10 trucking companies, an output limit of 20 trips per company ensures that the total number of trips in a week is 200. Penalties can be imposed to ensure that no single producer exceeds its output limit.

All the firms in the industry would support this type of regulation because it helps to prevent cheating and to maintain a monopoly outcome. Each firm knows that without effectively enforced production quotas, every firm has an incentive to increase output. (For each firm, price exceeds marginal cost, so a greater output brings a larger profit.) So each firm wants a method of preventing output from rising above the industry's profit-maximizing level, and the quotas enforced by regulation achieve this end. With this type of cartel regulation, the regulator enables a cartel to operate legally and in its own best interest.

What does cartel regulation do in practice? Although there is disagreement about the matter, the consensus view is that regulation tends to favour the producer. Trucking and airlines (when they were regulated by the Canadian Transport Commission) and taxicabs (regulated by cities) are specific examples in which profits of producers increased as a result of regulation. But the most dramatic examples of regulation favouring the producer are in agriculture. An Economic Council of Canada study, based on the situation prevailing in the early 1980s, estimated that regulation of the egg-producing and broiler chicken industries alone transferred more than $100 million a year to just 4,600 individual producers.[1]

Further evidence on cartel and oligopoly regulation can be obtained from the performance of prices and profit following deregulation. If, following deregulation, prices and profit fall, then, to some degree, the regulation must have been serving the interest of the producer. In contrast, if, following deregulation, prices and profits remain constant or increase, then

the regulation may be presumed to have been serving the public interest. Because there has been a substantial amount of deregulation in recent years, we may use this test of oligopoly regulation to see which of the two theories better fits the facts. The evidence is mixed, but in the cases of airlines, trucking, and long-distance phone calls, three oligopolies to be deregulated, prices fell and there was a large increase in the volume of business.

Making Predictions

Most industries have a few producers and many consumers. In these cases, public choice theory predicts that regulation will protect producers because a small number of people stand to gain a large amount and so they will be fairly easy to organize as a cohesive lobby. Under such circumstances, politicians will be rewarded with campaign contributions rather than votes. But there are situations in which the consumer interest is sufficiently strong and well organized and thus able to prevail. There are also cases in which the balance switches from producer to consumer, as seen in the deregulation process that began in the late 1970s.

Deregulation raises some hard questions for economists seeking to understand and make predictions about regulation. Why were the transportation and telecommunication sectors deregulated? If producers gained from regulation and if the producer lobby was strong enough to achieve regulation, what happened in the 1970s to change the equilibrium to one in which the consumer interest prevailed? We do not have a complete answer to this question at the present time. But regulation had become so costly to consumers, and the potential benefits to them from deregulation so great, that the cost of organizing the consumer voice became a price worth paying.

One factor that increased the cost of regulation borne by consumers and brought deregulation in the transportation sector was the large increase in energy prices in the 1970s. These price hikes made route regulation by the Canadian Transport Commission extremely costly and changed the balance in favour of consumers in the political equilibrium. Technological change was the main factor at work in the telecommunication sector. New satellite-based, computer-controlled long-distance technologies enabled smaller producers to offer low-cost services. These producers wanted a share of Bell Canada's business—and profit.

[1]J.D. Forbes, R.D. Hughes, and T.K. Warley, *Economic Intervention and Regulation in Canadian Agriculture* (Ottawa: Department of Supply and Services, 1982).

Furthermore, as communication technology improved, the cost of communication fell and the cost of organizing larger groups of consumers also fell. If this line of reasoning is correct, we can expect to see more consumer-oriented regulation in the future. In practice, more consumer-oriented regulation often means deregulation—removing the regulations that are already in place to serve the interests of producer groups.

R E V I E W   Q U I Z

- What are the main regulatory agencies in Canada?
- Why does natural monopoly need to be regulated?
- What pricing rule enables a natural monopoly to operate in the public interest?
- Why is a marginal cost pricing rule difficult to implement?
- What pricing rule is typically used to regulate a natural monopoly and what problems does it create?
- Why is it necessary to regulate a cartel?
- How might cartels be regulated in the public interest?

Let's now turn to the second method of intervention in markets—public ownership.

Public Ownership

CROWN CORPORATIONS HAVE A SIGNIFICANT AND historical presence in Canadian society. Before Confederation, Crown corporations were used for building canals and operating ports and harbours. The establishment of the Canadian nation involved a commitment to build an international railway to link New Brunswick and Nova Scotia to central Canada. Over the years, vast distances, a sparse population, the presence of a powerful neighbour, strong and distinct national interests, and the existence of two main cultural and linguistic groups nurtured the establishment of Crown corporations.

A Crown corporation is a corporation in which the government has 100 percent ownership. There are federal and provincial Crown corporations, and they are involved in many sectors of the economy,

including transportation; energy and resources; agriculture and fisheries; development and construction; government services; culture; financial intermediaries; telecommunications and broadcasting; provincial lotteries; housing; and alcoholic beverages. Examples of Crown corporations include the Business Development Bank of Canada, the Canadian Museum of Nature, and the Ontario Lottery Corporation.

Public ownership provides another way in which the government can influence the behaviour of natural monopoly. What are the effects of this method of natural monopoly control? How does a publicly owned corporation operate? Let's explore some alternative patterns of behaviour for such corporations.

Efficient Crown Corporations

One possibility is that a Crown corporation is operated in a manner that results in economic efficiency—maximization of total surplus. Let's consider the example of a railway. Figure 19.6(a) illustrates the demand for freight service and the railway's costs. The demand curve is D. The marginal cost curve is MC. Notice that the marginal cost curve is horizontal at $2 a tonne. The railway has a heavy investment in track, trains, and control equipment, so it has large fixed costs. These fixed costs feature in the company's average total cost curve ATC. The average total cost curve slopes downward because as the number of tonnes of freight carried increases, the fixed costs are spread over a larger number of tonnes. To be efficient, a Crown corporation obeys the rule:

Produce an output such that price equals marginal cost.

In this example, that output level is 8 billion tonnes a year at a price—and marginal cost—of $2 a tonne. To be able to operate in this manner, a publicly owned railway has to be subsidized; the subsidy on each unit of output must equal the difference between average total cost and marginal cost. And the subsidy has to be collected other than through the price of the good or service produced—in other words, by taxation. If the government taxes each household a fixed amount, the consumer surplus will shrink to the green triangle shown in Fig. 19.6(a), but consumer surplus will be at its maximum.

The situation depicted in Fig. 19.6(a) achieves an efficient outcome because consumer surplus is maximized. But it is not an outcome that is necessarily

FIGURE 19.6

Crown Corporation

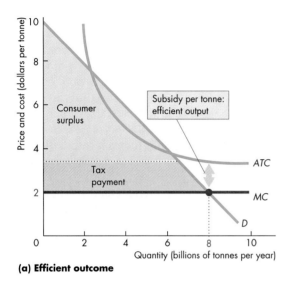

(a) Efficient outcome

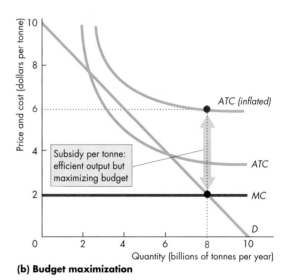

(b) Budget maximization

Part (a) shows a railway operated by a Crown corporation that produces the output at which price equals marginal cost. Its output is 8 billion tonnes a year and the price is $2 a tonne. The Crown corporation receives a subsidy that enables it to cover its total cost and that cost is the minimum possible cost of providing the efficient quantity.

Part (b) shows what happens if the managers of the Crown corporation pursue their own interest and maximize their budget by padding costs. Average total cost now increases to ATC (inflated). If the corporation is required to keep price equal to marginal cost, the quantity produced is efficient, but the managers divert the consumer surplus to themselves.

compatible with the interests of the managers of the Crown corporation. One model of the behaviour of managers is that suggested by the economic theory of bureaucracy. What does that alternative model predict about Crown corporation behaviour?

A Bureaucracy Model of Public Enterprise

The basic assumption of the economic theory of bureaucracy is that bureaucrats aim to maximize the budget of their bureau. The equivalent assumption for the managers of a Crown corporation is that they seek to maximize the budget of the Crown corporation. The effect of budget maximization by the managers of a Crown corporation depends on the pricing constraints under which the managers operate. We will consider two alternative cases:

■ Budget maximization with marginal cost pricing
■ Budget maximization at a zero price.

Budget Maximization with Marginal Cost Pricing If the bureau maximizes its budget but obeys the marginal cost pricing rule, it will produce the efficient outcome. It will produce 8 billion tonnes a year and it will sell its output for $2 a tonne, as Fig. 19.6(b) illustrates. But the corporation will not minimize its production cost. It will pad its costs and become inefficient. It will hire more workers than the number required to produce 8 billion tonnes a year, and its internal control mechanisms, which would ensure internal efficiency, as in a private profit-maximizing firm, will be weak. As a result, the average total cost of the corporation will rise to ATC (inflated).

What determines the limit on the extent to which the corporation can pad its costs? The answer is the maximum amount that the users of the output can be made to pay through taxation. That maximum is the total consumer surplus. That maximum consumer surplus is the area beneath the demand curve and above the marginal cost curve. You can work out how big it is by using the usual formula for the area of the triangle. The height of this triangle is $8 and its base is 8 billion tonnes a year, so the consumer surplus is $32 billion. This will be the upper limit that any government—in a political democracy—can extract from the taxpayer-consumers of the product of this corporation. Spread over 8 billion tonnes, $32 billion gives a subsidy of $4 a tonne, the amount shown in the figure.

Budget Maximization at Zero Price   What happens if a government bureau provides its goods or services free? Of course, it is improbable that a publicly owned railway would be able to persuade politicians and taxpayers that its activities should be expanded to the point of providing its services free. But there are several examples of publicly provided goods that are indeed free. Primary and secondary education and health care are two outstanding examples. For the sake of comparison, we'll continue with our railway, improbable though it is.

If in Fig. 19.6(b) the bureau increases output to the point at which the price that consumers are willing to pay for the last unit produced is zero, output rises to 10 billion tonnes a year. A deadweight loss is created because the marginal cost of production, $2 a tonne, is higher than the marginal benefit or willingness to pay, $0 per tonne. The bureau will be inefficient in its internal operations and inflate its costs. The subsidy will increase to the highest that the public will be willing to pay. The maximum subsidy will equal the consumer surplus. If the subsidy were higher, people would vote to shut down the Crown corporation because the subsidy would exceed the consumer surplus.

Compromise Outcome   There will be a tendency for the corporation to overproduce and to inflate its budget, but not to the extent shown in Fig. 19.6(b). There will be a tendency for consumer interest to have some influence, but not to the degree shown in Fig. 19.6(a). The basic prediction about the behaviour of a Crown corporation, then, is that it will overproduce and be less efficient than a private firm.

Crown Corporations in Reality

How do actual Crown corporations behave? Several studies have been directed to answering this question. One of the most fruitful ways of approaching the question is to compare public and private enterprises in which, as far as possible, other things are equal. There are two well-known and well-studied cases for which other things do seem to be fairly equal. One such comparison is of Canada's public and private railways—Canadian National (CN) and Canadian Pacific (CP). The other is from Australia, which has two domestic airlines, one private and the other public, that fly almost identical routes at almost identical times every day. Economists have studied the costs of these similar enterprises and concluded that each of the publicly owned enterprises operates with a cost structure that is significantly higher than that of the corresponding private firm. In the case of CN and CP, the estimated difference was 14 percent.[2]

Privatization

Largely because of an increasing understanding of how bureaucracies work and of the inefficiency of publicly operated enterprises, there has been a move to sell off publicly owned corporations. Since the mid-1980s, the federal government has sold a dozen companies, including Air Canada. Companies that are too unprofitable to sell, such as CN, are being savagely cut back.

R E V I E W   Q U I Z

- How might a Crown corporation operate efficiently?
- What are the effects of budget maximization by the managers of a Crown corporation?
- What limits the maximum budget of a Crown corporation?

  Let's now turn to anti-combine law.

[2]W.S.W. Caves and Lauritis Christensen, "The Relative Efficiency of Public v. Private Firms in a Competitive Environment: the Case of Canada's Railroads," *Journal of Political Economy* 88, 5 (September–October 1980), 958–76.

Anti-Combine Law

ANTI-COMBINE LAW GIVES POWERS TO THE courts and to government agencies to influence markets. Like regulation, anti-combine law can work in the public interest to maximize total surplus or in private interests to maximize the surpluses of particular special interest groups such as producers. We'll describe Canada's anti-combine law and then examine some recent cases.

Canada's Anti-Combine Law

Canada's anti-combine law dates from 1889. At that time, monopoly was a major political issue and people were concerned about the absence of competition in industries as diverse as sugar and groceries, biscuits and confectionery, coal, binder twine, agricultural implements, stoves, coffins, eggs, and fire insurance.

Canada's anti-combine law today is defined in the Competition Act of 1986, which is described in Table 19.2. The Act established a Competition Bureau and a Competition Tribunal. The Competition Act distinguishes between practices that are:

1. Criminal
2. Non-criminal

Conspiracy to fix prices, bid-rigging, other anti-competitive price-fixing actions, and false advertising are criminal offences. The courts handle alleged offences, and the standard level of proof beyond a reasonable doubt must be established.

Mergers, abuse of a dominant market position, refusal to deal, and other actions designed to limit competition such as exclusive dealing are non-criminal offences. The Director of the Competition Bureau sends alleged violations of a non-criminal nature to the Competition Tribunal for examination.

Some Recent Anti-Combine Cases

Let's see how the Competition Act has been working by looking at some recent cases. The first case we'll examine is important because it confirms the Competition Tribunal's power to enforce its orders.

Chrysler In 1986, Chrysler stopped supplying auto parts to Richard Brunet, a Montreal auto dealer.

Chrysler also discouraged other dealers from supplying Brunet. The Competition Tribunal claimed that Chrysler wanted Brunet's business for itself and ordered Chrysler to resume doing business with Brunet. Chrysler did not resume sending supplies and the Tribunal cited Chrysler for contempt. Appeals against this ruling eventually reached the Supreme Court of Canada, which confirmed the Tribunal's power over contempt for its ruling. But the Tribunal subsequently dropped its contempt charge.

The second case we'll look at concerns aspartame, the sweetener in many soft drinks.

NutraSweet NutraSweet, the maker of aspartame, tried to gain a monopoly in aspartame. It did so by licensing the use of its "swirl" only on products for which it had an exclusive deal. The Competition Tribunal ruled that this action unduly limited competition and told NutraSweet that it may not enforce existing contracts, enter into new contracts in which it is the exclusive supplier, or give inducements to encourage the display of its "swirl." The result of this case was an increase in competition and a fall in the price of aspartame in Canada.

The third case we'll examine concerns a publication you use almost every day: the Yellow Pages.

Bell Canada Enterprises Two subsidiaries of Bell Canada Enterprises have a 90 percent share of the market for the publication of telephone directories in their territories. These companies tie the sale of advertising services to the sale of advertising space in the Yellow Pages. If you want to advertise in the Yellow Pages, you must buy the advertising services of one of these two companies. As a result, other advertising agencies cannot effectively compete for business in Yellow Pages advertising. The Director of the Competition Bureau applied for an order prohibiting the tied-sale practice of these two companies.

Other Recent Anti-Competitive Agreements During 1995 and 1996, the Competition Bureau took action against several anti-competitive agreements. Among such cases were driving schools in Sherbrooke, ready-mix concrete in the Saguenay-Lac St-Jean region, real estate dealing in Calgary, the importing of Australian mandarin oranges, wire for baling pulp, and ambulance services in Alberta.

The Competition Bureau is extremely active in reviewing and, in some cases, blocking mergers. The next cases we examine fall into this category.

TABLE 19.2

Canada's Anti-Combine Law: The Competition Act, 1986

Abuse of Dominant Position

79 (1)   Where on application by the Director, the Tribunal finds that:

   (a)   one or more persons substantially or completely control, throughout Canada or any area thereof, a class or species of business,

   (b)   that person or those persons have engaged in or are engaging in a practice of anti-competitive acts, and

   (c)   the practice has had, is having or is likely to have the effect of preventing or lessening competition substantially in a market, the Tribunal may make an order prohibiting all or any of those persons from engaging in that practice.

Mergers

92 (1)   Where on application by the Director, the Tribunal finds that a merger or proposed merger prevents or lessens, or is likely to prevent or lessen, competition substantially ... the Tribunal may ... [,] in the case of a completed merger, order any party to the merger

   (i)   to dissolve the merger ...

   (ii)   to dispose of assets and shares ...

   [or]

   in the case of a proposed merger, make an order directed against any party to the proposed merger

   (i)   ordering the person ... not to proceed with the merger

   (ii)   ordering the person not to proceed with part of the merger

---

Canada Packers and Labatt   Canada Packers Inc. and John Labatt Ltd. proposed a merger of their flour milling operations that would have made them the biggest miller in Canada and the fifth biggest in North America. The Competition Tribunal stopped this merger saying that the Canadian flour milling business had been run too much like a cartel and that more, not less, competition was needed.

Banks and Airlines   Some attempts to merge are so politically sensitive that they are decided at the highest political level. One example is the decision of the federal government to block an attempted merger by the Royal Bank and the Bank of Montreal. If Canada's two major airlines eventually merge, the sanction of the federal government will be needed.

Public or Special Interest?

The intent of anti-combine law is to protect the public interest and restrain the profit-seeking and anti-competitive actions of producers. On the whole, the overall thrust of the law and its enforcement has been

in line with its intent and has served the public interest. Further, if the recent cases we have examined are setting a trend, we can expect a continuation of pro-consumer decisions from the courts and the Competition Tribunal in future cases.

R E V I E W   Q U I Z

■ What is the Act of Parliament that provides our anti-combine law?

■ What actions violate the anti-combine law?

■ Under what circumstances is a merger unlikely to be approved?

◆ In this chapter, we've seen how the government intervenes in markets to affect prices, quantities, consumer surplus, and producer surplus. *Reading Between the Lines* on pp. 426–427 looks at the recent debate about bank and airline mergers and provides an opportunity to think about that debate using the tools that you've learned and applied in this chapter.

Competition or Monopoly in Banking and Airlines

NATIONAL POST, DECEMBER 15, 1998

Bureau chides banks for not playing ball

BY JILL VARDY

Paul Martin, the finance minister, said the resulting [Competition Bureau] reports are what convinced him to turn down the merger plans of Royal Bank of Canada with Bank of Montreal and Canadian Imperial Bank of Commerce with Toronto-Dominion Bank. ...

Unlike with conventional merger proposals, the competition bureau did not get the final say in this one.

Highlights of the Competition Bureau report include:

• The mergers ... would have lessened competition and caused higher prices, lower service levels, and less choice. ...

• More than half the markets in Canada would see competition between bank branches substantially reduced if the mergers were approved. ...

© 1998 *National Post*. Reprinted with permission. Further reproduction prohibited.

THE CALGARY HERALD, AUGUST 14, 1999

Ottawa opens loophole for airline rivals to talk

BY ANNE CRAWFORD

The federal government has temporarily relaxed the rules of the competition law to allow Canada's two airlines to discuss a dramatic restructuring of the domestic industry, including a possible merger.

Transport Minister David Collenette and Industry Minister John Manley announced the relaxation of competition rules. "Sustaining a more viable air industry while preserving the interest of consumers is a priority for the government," Manley said.

"What we're trying to do is allow an unfettered reorganization of the airline industry," Collenette said. "The development of business proposals for restructuring will be undertaken entirely by the private sector, as ultimately these are business and marketplace decisions." ...

© 1999 *The Calgary Herald*. Reprinted with permission. Further reproduction prohibited.

Essence of the Story

■ Some Canadian banks proposed a merger that was not supported by Finance Minister Paul Martin and the Liberal government.

■ The federal government has relaxed competition laws to allow Air Canada and Canadian Airlines to discuss a possible merger.

■ The Canadian airline industry is facing the possibility of a monopoly.

Economic Analysis

■ A merger of either banks or airlines might:
1. Lower costs but not increase market power
2. Leave costs unchanged and increase market power, or
3. Lower costs *and* increase market power

■ Air transportation is a global business and world-wide competition among airlines is severe. It approaches perfect competition on busy international routes. For example Air Canada, British Airways, and a host of other airlines compete on the routes between Toronto and London.

■ Banking is also a global business and world-wide competition among banks approaches perfect competition in servicing large multinational corporations. The Canadian banking market includes the Canadian banks, foreign banks such as the Hong Kong Bank, and telephone and Internet banking services.

■ Airlines and banks have large fixed costs. They also have high marginal costs that might be lowered by merging and rationalizing two (or more) existing firms.

■ Figure 1 shows the effects of a merger of either airlines or banks, if the industry remains competitive and the merger lowers the marginal cost of delivering the service.

■ Initially, the demand curve D intersects the supply curve S_0 at a quantity Q_0 and a price P_0.

■ Then a marginal cost-cutting merger occurs. With a lower marginal cost, supply increases and the supply curve shifts rightward to S_1. The quantity increases to Q_1, the price falls to P_1, and consumer surplus increases.

■ The outcome in Fig. 1 is the one predicted by the Royal Bank and the Bank of Montreal and the supporters of an Air Canada–Canadian Airlines merger.

■ But airlines serve travellers who live in smaller communities and on many low-density routes, air transportation is a natural monopoly. Canada has many such air routes.

■ Similarly, banks serve customers who live in smaller communities, and in these communities, banking is a natural monopoly. Canada has many such communities.

■ Figure 2 shows the market for air travel from Vancouver to Penticton B.C., or the market for banking services in Penticton, B.C.

■ Again, initially, the demand curve D intersects the supply curve S at a quantity Q_0 and a price P_0.

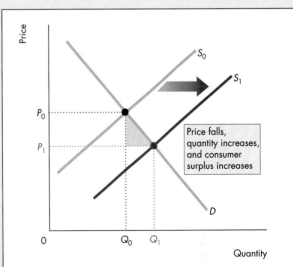

Figure 1 Merger cuts costs

Price falls, quantity increases, and consumer surplus increases

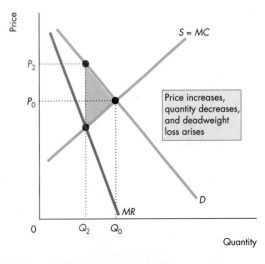

Figure 2 Merger creates monopoly

Price increases, quantity decreases, and deadweight loss arises

■ Then a merger occurs that increases market power but has no effect on costs.

■ With market power, the newly merged firm has a marginal revenue curve MR. And with no change in marginal cost, the firm's marginal cost curve, MC, is the same as the supply curve of the initially competitive market.

■ The firm maximizes profit by decreasing the quantity to Q_2 and increasing the price to P_2. A deadweight loss now arises.

■ Paul Martin and the Liberal government predict the outcome in Fig. 2 in the case of banks but not in the case of airlines.

427

SUMMARY

Key Points

Market Intervention (p. 412)

- The federal government intervenes to regulate monopolistic and oligopolistic markets in three ways: regulation, public ownership, and anti-combine law.

Economic Theory of Regulation (pp. 412–414)

- Consumers and producers express their demand for the regulation by voting, lobbying, and making campaign contributions.
- The larger the surplus per person generated by a regulation, the greater the number of gainers, and the smaller the number of losers, the larger is the demand for the regulation.
- Regulation is supplied by politicians who pursue their own best interest.
- The larger the surplus per person generated and the larger the number of people affected by it, the larger is the supply of regulation.
- Public interest theory predicts that regulation will maximize total surplus; capture theory predicts that producer surplus will be maximized.

Regulation and Deregulation (pp. 414–421)

- Natural monopolies and cartels are regulated by agencies controlled by politically appointed bureaucrats and staffed by a permanent bureaucracy of experts.
- Regulated firms must comply with rules about price, product quality, and output levels.
- Regulation has not lowered the profit rates of regulated firms.

Public Ownership (pp. 421–423)

- More than 100 Crown corporations produce such items as rail transport, hydroelectric power, and telecommunications.
- The economic theory of bureaucracy is that managers maximize their budgets subject to political constraints.

- Crown corporations tend to be inefficient: They overproduce and their costs are too high.

Anti-Combine Law (pp. 424–425)

- Anti-combine law provides an alternative way for government to control monopoly and monopolistic practices.
- The Competition Act of 1986 radically reformed anti-combine law and placed responsibility for enforcement with the Competition Tribunal.

Key Figures and Tables

Key Terms

PROBLEMS

*1. Elixir Springs, Inc., is an unregulated natural monopoly that bottles Elixir, a unique health product with no substitutes. The total fixed cost incurred by Elixir Springs is $150,000, and its marginal cost is 10 cents a bottle. The figure illustrates the demand for Elixir.

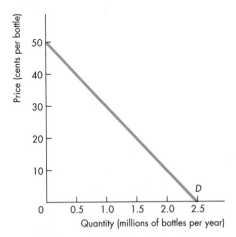

   a. What is the price of a bottle of Elixir?
   b. How many bottles does Elixir Springs sell?
   c. Does Elixir Springs maximize total surplus or producer surplus?

2. Cascade Springs, Inc., is a natural monopoly that bottles water from a spring high in the Rocky Mountains. The total fixed cost that it incurs is $120,000, and its marginal cost is 20 cents a bottle. The figure illustrates the demand for Cascade Springs bottled water.

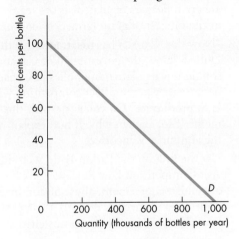

   a. What is the price of Cascade Springs water?
   b. How many bottles does Cascade Springs sell?
   c. Does Cascade Springs maximize total surplus or producer surplus?

*3. The government regulates Elixir Springs in problem 1 by imposing a marginal cost pricing rule.
   a. What is the price of a bottle of Elixir?
   b. How many bottles does Elixir Springs sell?
   c. What is Elixir Springs' economic profit?
   d. What is the consumer surplus?
   e. Is the regulation in the public interest? Explain.

4. The government regulates Cascade Springs in problem 2 by imposing a marginal cost pricing rule.
   a. What is the price of Cascade Springs water?
   b. How many bottles does Cascade Springs sell?
   c. What is the economic profit?
   d. What is the consumer surplus?
   e. Is the regulation in the public interest? Explain.

*5. The government regulates Elixir Springs in problem 1 by imposing an average cost pricing rule.
   a. What is the price of a bottle of Elixir?
   b. How many bottles does Elixir Springs sell?
   c. What is Elixir Springs' economic profit?
   d. What is the consumer surplus?
   e. Is the regulation in the public interest? Explain.

6. The government regulates Cascade Springs in problem 2 by imposing an average cost pricing rule.
   a. What is the price of Cascade Springs water?
   b. How many bottles does Cascade Springs sell?
   c. What is Cascade Springs' economic profit?
   d. What is the consumer surplus?
   e. Is the regulation in the public interest? Explain.

*7. Two airlines share an international route. The figure shows the demand curve for trips on this route and the marginal cost curve that each firm faces. This air route is regulated.

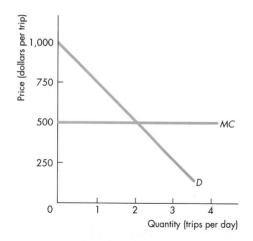

a. What is the price of a trip and what is the number of trips per day if the regulation is in the public interest?
b. What is the price of a trip and what is the number of trips per day if the airlines capture the regulator?
c. What is the deadweight loss in part (b)?

8. Two telephone companies offer local calls in an area. The figure shows the market demand curve for calls and the marginal cost curve of each firm. These firms are regulated.

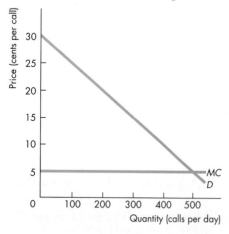

a. What is the price of a call and what is the number of calls per day if the regulation is in the public interest?
b. What is the price of a call and what is the number of calls per day if the telephone companies capture the regulator?
c. What is the deadweight loss in part (b)?
d. What do you need to know to predict whether the regulation will be in the public interest or the producer interest?

CRITICAL THINKING

1. After you have studied *Reading Between the Lines* on pp. 426–427, answer the following questions.
   a. Which parts of the business of an airline might be a natural monopoly and which parts are competitive?
   b. Which parts of the business of a bank might be a natural monopoly and which parts are competitive?
   c. If a merger of two of Canada's largest banks occurred, would there be an increase or a decrease in the efficiency of the banking industry? Who would benefit from and who would pay for the changes?
   d. If a merger of Canada's two major airlines occurred, would there be an increase or a decrease in the efficiency of the air transportation industry? Who would benefit from and who would pay for the changes?
   e. Critically evaluate the decision to block the merger of the Royal Bank and the Bank of Montreal.

2. The government of Canada regulates the production and sale of many goods and services. For example, it regulates the prices of local phone and cable TV services, the acreage that each wheat and cereal farmer can sow, the grain prices paid to these farmers and to whom they can sell the grain. The suppliers of local phone and cable TV services are monopolies, but there are many grain farmers. Why are grain farmers regulated? Is the regulation in the interest of grain farmers or consumers?

3. "Now that Canada has free trade with the United States, the government of Canada should not regulate monopolies in Canada because they are in direct competition with U.S. producers." Do you agree with this argument? If so, explain why. If not, explain why the argument is incorrect.

4. Use the link on the Parkin-Bade Web site to visit Competition Law Review. Look for cases of collusive agreement, abuse of dominant position, and mergers to restrict competition. In each case, describe the means cited as used to lessen competition.

Chapter 20

Externalities, the Environment, and Knowledge

We burn huge quantities of fossil fuels—coal, natural gas, and oil—that cause acid rain and possibly global warming. The persistent and large-scale use of chlorofluorocarbons (CFCs) may have caused irreparable damage to the earth's ozone layer, thereby exposing us to additional ultraviolet rays, which increase the incidence of skin cancer. We dump toxic waste into rivers, lakes, and oceans. These environmental issues are simultaneously everybody's problem and nobody's problem. What, if anything, can government do to protect our environment? How can government action help us to take account of the damage that we cause others every time we turn on our heating or air conditioning systems? ◆ Almost every day, we hear about a new discovery—in medicine, engineering, chemistry, physics, or even economics. The advance of knowledge seems boundless. And more and more people are learning more and more of what is already known. The stock of knowledge—what is known and how many people know it—is increasing, apparently without bounds. We are getting smarter. But is our stock of knowledge advancing fast enough? Are we spending enough on research and development? Do we spend enough on education? Do enough people remain in school for long enough? And do we work hard enough at school? Would we be better off if we spent more on research and education?

◆ In this chapter, we study the problems that arise because many of our actions create externalities. They affect other people, for ill or good, in ways that we do not usually take into account when we make our own economic choices. We study two big areas—the environment and the accumulation of knowledge—in which these problems are especially important. Externalities are a major source of *market failure*. When market failure occurs, we must either live with the inefficiency it creates or try to achieve greater efficiency by making some *public choices*. This chapter studies these choices. It begins by looking at external costs that affect the environment.

Greener and Smarter

After studying this chapter, you will be able to:

- Explain how property rights can sometimes be used to overcome externalities

- Explain how emission charges, marketable permits, and taxes can be used to achieve efficiency in the face of external costs

- Explain how subsidies can be used to achieve efficiency in the face of external benefits

- Explain how scholarships, below-cost tuition, and research grants make the quantity of education and invention more efficient

- Explain how patents increase economic efficiency

Economics of the Environment

ENVIRONMENTAL PROBLEMS ARE NOT NEW, AND they are not restricted to rich industrial countries. Preindustrial towns and cities in Europe had severe sewage disposal problems that created cholera epidemics and plagues that killed tens of millions of people. Nor is the desire to find solutions to environmental problems new. The developments in the fourteenth century of pure water supplies and of garbage and sewage disposal are examples of early contributions to improving the quality of the environment.

Popular discussions of the environment usually pay little attention to economics. They focus on physical aspects of the environment, not costs and benefits. A common assumption is that if people's actions cause *any* environmental degradation, those actions must cease. In contrast, an economic study of the environment emphasizes costs and benefits. An economist talks about the efficient amount of pollution or environmental damage. This emphasis on costs and benefits does not mean that economists, as citizens, do not share the same goals as others and value a healthy environment. Nor does it mean that economists have the right answers and everyone else has the wrong ones (or vice versa). Economics provides a set of tools and principles that clarify the issues. It does not provide an agreed list of solutions. The starting point for an economic analysis of the environment is the demand for a healthy environment.

The Demand for Environmental Quality

The demand for a clean and healthy environment is greater today than it has ever been. We express our demand for a better environment in several ways. We join organizations that lobby for environmental regulations and policies. We vote for politicians who support the environmental policies that we want to see implemented. (All politicians at least pay lip service to the environment today.) We buy "green" products and avoid hazardous products, even if we pay a bit more to do so. And we pay higher housing costs and commuting costs to live in pleasant neighbourhoods.

The demand for a cleaner and healthier environment has grown for two main reasons. First, as our incomes increase, we demand a larger range of goods and services, and one of these "goods" is a high-quality environment. We value clean air, unspoiled natural scenery, and wildlife, and we are willing and able to pay for them.

Second, as our knowledge of the effects of our actions on the environment grows, so we are able to take measures that improve the environment. For example, now that we know how sulfur dioxide causes acid rain and how clearing rain forests destroys natural stores of carbon dioxide, we are able, in principle, to design measures that limit these problems.

Let's look at the range of environmental problems that have been identified and the actions that create those problems.

The Sources of Environmental Problems

Environmental problems arise from pollution of the air, water, and land, and these individual sources of pollution interact through the *ecosystem*.

Air Pollution Figure 20.1(a) shows the five economic activities that create most of our air pollution. It also shows the relative contributions of each activity. More than two-thirds of air pollution comes from road transportation and industrial processes. Only one-sixth arises from electric power generation.

A common belief is that air pollution is getting worse. On many fronts, as we will see later in this chapter, *global* air pollution *is* getting worse. But air pollution in North America is becoming less severe for most substances. Figure 20.1(b) shows the trends in the concentrations of six air pollutants. While lead has been almost eliminated from our air and sulfur dioxide, carbon monoxide, and suspended particulates have been reduced substantially, levels of other pollutants have remained more stable.

While the facts about the sources and trends in air pollution are not in doubt, there is considerable disagreement in the scientific community about the *effects* of air pollution. The least controversial problem is *acid rain*, which is caused by sulfur dioxide and nitrogen oxide emissions from coal- and oil-fired generators of electric utilities. Acid rain begins with air pollution, and it leads to water pollution and damages vegetation.

More controversial are airborne substances (suspended particulates) such as lead from leaded gasoline. Some scientists believe that in sufficiently large

FIGURE 20.1
Air Pollution

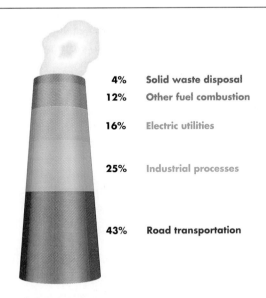

4%	Solid waste disposal
12%	Other fuel combustion
16%	Electric utilities
25%	Industrial processes
43%	Road transportation

(a) Sources of emission

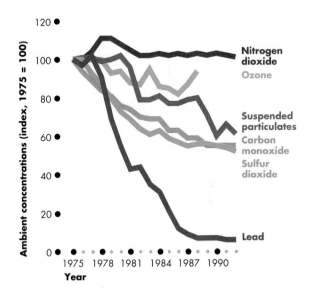

(b) Ambient concentrations

Part (a) shows that road transportation is the largest source of air pollution, followed by industrial processes and electric utilities. Part (b) shows that lead has almost been eliminated from our air and concentrations of carbon monoxide, sulfur dioxide, and suspended particulates have decreased. But nitrogen dioxide and ozone have persisted at close to their 1975 levels.

Source: U.S. Environmental Protection Agency, *National Air Quality and Emissions Trends Report*, 1996.

concentrations, these substances (189 of which have currently been identified) cause cancer and other life-threatening conditions.

Even more controversial is *global warming*, which some scientists say results from the carbon dioxide emissions of road transportation and electric utilities, from methane created by cows and other livestock, from nitrous oxide emissions of electric utilities and from fertilizers. The earth's average temperature has increased over the past 100 years, but most of the increase occurred *before* 1940. Determining what causes changes in the earth's temperature and isolating the effect of carbon dioxide is proving to be difficult.

Equally controversial is the problem of *ozone layer depletion*, which some scientists say results from chlorofluorocarbons (CFCs) used by refrigerators and (in the past) aerosols. There is no doubt that a hole in the ozone layer exists over Antarctica, and that the ozone layer protects us from cancer-causing ultravio-

let rays from the sun. But how industrial activity influences the ozone layer is not understood at this time.

One air pollution problem has almost been eliminated: lead from gasoline. In part, this happened because the cost of living without leaded gasoline, it turns out, is not high. But sulfur dioxide and the so-called greenhouse gases are a much tougher problem to tackle. Their alternatives are costly or have environmental problems of their own. The major sources of these pollutants are road vehicles and electric utilities. Road vehicles can be made "greener" in a variety of ways. One is with new fuels—some alternatives being investigated are alcohol, natural gas, propane and butane, and hydrogen. Another way of making cars and trucks "greener" is to change the chemistry of gasoline. Refiners are working on reformulations of gasoline that cut tailpipe emissions. Similarly, electric power can be generated in cleaner ways by harnessing solar power, tidal power, or geothermal power. Technically possible, these methods are more costly than conventional carbon-fuelled generators. Another alternative is nuclear power. This method is good for air pollution but bad for land and water pollution because there is no known safe method of disposing of spent nuclear fuel.

Water Pollution The largest sources of water pollution are the dumping of industrial waste and treated sewage in lakes and rivers and the runoff from fertilizers. A more dramatic source is the accidental spilling of crude oil into the oceans, such as the *Exxon Valdez* spill in Alaska in 1989 and an even larger spill in the Russian Arctic in 1994. The most frightening is the dumping of nuclear waste into the ocean by the former Soviet Union.

There are two main alternatives to polluting the waterways and oceans. One is the chemical processing of waste to render it inert or biodegradable. The other, in wide use for nuclear waste, is to use land sites for storage in secure containers.

Land Pollution Land pollution arises from dumping toxic waste products. Ordinary household garbage does not pose a pollution problem unless dumped garbage seeps into the water supply. This possibility increases as less suitable landfill sites are used. It is estimated that 80 percent of existing landfills will be full by 2010. Some regions (New York, New Jersey, and other East Coast U.S. states) and some countries (Japan and the Netherlands) are seeking less costly alternatives to landfill, such as recycling and incineration. Recycling is an apparently attractive alternative, but it requires an investment in new technologies to be effective. Incineration is a high-cost alternative to landfill, and it produces air pollution. But these alternatives are not free and they become efficient only when the cost of using landfill is high.

We've seen that the demand for a high-quality environment has grown, and we've described the range of environmental problems. Let's now look at the ways in which these problems can be handled. We'll begin by looking at property rights and how they relate to environmental externalities.

Absence of Property Rights and Environmental Externalities

Externalities arise because of an *absence* of property rights. **Property rights** are social arrangements that

govern the ownership, use, and disposal of productive resources, goods, and services. In modern societies, a property right is a legally established title that is enforceable in the courts.

Property rights are absent when externalities arise. No one owns the air, the rivers, and the oceans. So it is no one's private business to ensure that these resources are used in an efficient way. In fact, there is an incentive to use them more than if there were property rights.

Figure 20.2 shows an environmental externality in the absence of property rights. A chemical factory upstream from a fishing club must decide how to dispose of its waste.

The factory's marginal benefit curve, *MB*, tells us the benefit to the factory of an additional tonne of waste dumped into the river. The *MB* curve is also the firm's demand curve for the use of the river,

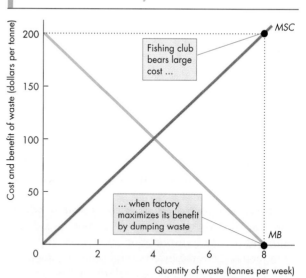

FIGURE 20.2

An Externality

A chemical factory's marginal benefit from dumping its waste into a river is *MB* and a fishing club's marginal cost of having waste dumped is *MSC*. With no property rights, the factory maximizes total benefit by dumping 8 tonnes a week, the quantity at which the marginal benefit of dumping equals the marginal cost (zero). With this quantity of waste, the fishing club bears a marginal cost of $200 per tonne. This outcome is inefficient because the marginal social cost exceeds the marginal benefit.

which is a productive resource. The demand for a resource slopes downward because of the law of diminishing returns (see Chapter 15, pp. 324–325).

Marginal social cost is the marginal cost incurred by the producer of a good—marginal private cost—plus the marginal cost imposed on others—the external cost. The factory bears no cost of dumping. All the costs are borne by the fishing club. The marginal social cost curve, *MSC*, tells us the cost borne by the club when one additional tonne of waste is dumped into the river. Marginal cost rises as the quantity dumped increases.

If no one owns the river, the factory dumps the amount of waste that maximizes *its own* total benefit. Its marginal cost is zero (along the *x*-axis) so it dumps 8 tonnes a week, the quantity that makes marginal benefit zero. The marginal social cost of the waste, which is borne by the fishing club, is $200 a tonne. Marginal cost exceeds marginal benefit, so the outcome is inefficient.

Property Rights and the Coase Theorem

Sometimes it is possible to correct an externality by establishing a property right where one does not currently exist. For example, suppose that the chemical factory owns the river. The fishing club must pay the factory for the right to fish in the river. But the price that the club is willing to pay depends on the number and quality of fish, which in turn depends on how much waste the factory dumps in the river. The greater the amount of pollution, the smaller is the amount the fishing club is willing to pay for the right to fish. The chemical factory is now confronted with the cost of its pollution decision. It might still decide to pollute, but if it does, it faces the opportunity cost of its actions—forgone revenue from the fishing club.

Alternatively, suppose that the fishing club owns the river. Now the factory must pay a fee to the fishing club for the right to dump its waste. The more waste it dumps (equivalently, the more fish it kills), the more it must pay. Again, the factory faces an opportunity cost for the pollution it creates.

Does it matter how property rights are assigned? Does it matter whether the polluter or the victim of the pollution owns the resource that might be polluted? At first thought, ownership seems crucial. And until 1960, that is what everyone thought—including economists who had thought about the problem for longer than a few minutes. But in 1960, Ronald

Coase had a remarkable insight, now called the Coase theorem. The **Coase theorem** is the proposition that if property rights exist and transactions costs are low, private transactions are efficient. Equivalently, with property rights and low transactions costs, there are no externalities. The transacting parties take all the costs and benefits into account. So it doesn't matter how the property rights are assigned.

Figure 20.3 illustrates the Coase theorem. As before, the demand curve for dumping waste is the factory's marginal benefit curve, *MB*. This curve tells us what the factory is willing to pay to dump. With property rights in place, the *MSC* curve is the fishing club's supply curve of river use to the firm. It tells us what the club's members must be paid if they are to put up with inferior fishing and supply the firm with a permit to dump.

The efficient level of waste is 4 tonnes a week. At

FIGURE **20.3**

The Coase Theorem

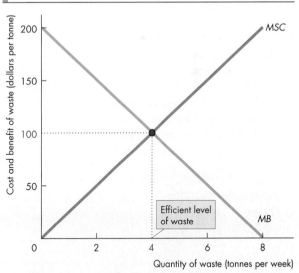

Pollution of a river imposes a marginal social cost, *MSC*, on the victim and provides a marginal benefit, *MB*, to the polluter. The efficient amount of pollution is the quantity that makes marginal benefit equal to marginal social cost—in this example, 4 tonnes per week. If the polluter owns the river, the victim will pay $400 a week ($100 a tonne × 4 tonnes a week) to the polluter for the assurance that pollution will not exceed 4 tonnes a week. If the victim owns the river, the polluter will pay $400 for pollution rights to dump 4 tonnes a week.

this level, the club bears a cost of $100 for the last tonne dumped into the river, and the factory gets a benefit of that amount. If waste disposal is restricted below 4 tonnes a week, an increase in waste disposal benefits the factory more than it costs the club. The factory can pay the club to put up with more waste disposal, and both the club and the factory can gain. If waste disposal exceeds 4 tonnes a week, an increase in waste disposal costs the club more than it benefits the factory. The club can now pay the factory to cut its waste disposal, and again, both the club and the factory can gain. Only when the level of waste disposal is 4 tonnes a week can neither party do any better. This is the efficient level of waste disposal.

The amount of waste disposal is the same regardless of who owns the river. If the factory owns it, the club pays $400 for fishing rights and for an agreement that waste disposal will not exceed 4 tonnes a week. If the club owns the river, the factory pays $400 for the right to dump 4 tonnes of waste a week. In both cases, the amount of waste disposal is the efficient amount.

Property rights work if transactions costs are low. The factory and the fishing club can negotiate the deal that produces the efficient outcome. But in many situations, transactions costs are high and property rights cannot be enforced. Imagine the transactions costs if the 50 million people who live in the northeastern part of Canada and the United States tried to negotiate an agreement with the 20,000 factories that emit sulfur dioxide and cause acid rain! In this type of case, governments use alternative methods of coping with externalities. They use:

1. Emission charges
2. Marketable permits
3. Taxes

In Canada, the federal government has established a government department, Environment Canada, to coordinate and administer the nation's environment policies. Let's look at the tools available to Environment Canada and see how they work.

Emission Charges

Emission charges are a method of using the market to achieve efficiency, even in the face of externalities. The government (or the regulatory agency established by the government) sets the emission charges, which are, in effect, a price per unit of pollution. The more

pollution a firm creates, the more it pays in emission charges. This method of dealing with environmental externalities has been used only modestly in North America, but it is common in Europe. For example, in France, Germany, and the Netherlands, water polluters pay a waste disposal charge.

To work out the emission charge that achieves efficiency, the regulator must determine the marginal social cost and marginal *social* benefit of pollution. **Marginal social benefit** is the marginal benefit received by the buyer—marginal private benefit—plus the marginal benefit to others—the external benefit. To achieve efficiency, the price per unit of pollution must be set to make the marginal social cost of the pollution equal to its marginal social benefit.

Figure 20.4 illustrates an efficient emission charge. The marginal benefit of pollution is *MB* and accrues to the polluters—there is no *external* benefit. The marginal social cost of pollution is *MSC* and is

FIGURE 20.4

Emission Charges

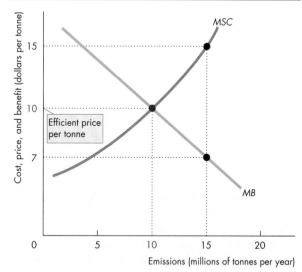

Electric utilities obtain marginal benefits from sulfur dioxide emissions of MB, and everyone else bears a marginal social cost of MSC. The efficient level of pollution—10 million tonnes a year in this example—is achieved by imposing an emission charge on the utilities of $10 a tonne. If the emission charge is set too low, at $7 a tonne, the resulting amount of pollution is greater than the efficient amount—at 15 million tonnes a year in this example. In this case, the marginal social cost is $15 a tonne, and it exceeds the marginal benefit of $7 a tonne.

entirely an external cost. The efficient level of sulfur dioxide emissions is 10 million tonnes a year, which is achieved with an emission charge of $10 per tonne. At this price, polluters do not find it worthwhile to buy the permission to pollute in excess of 10 million tonnes a year.

In practice, it is hard to determine the marginal benefit of pollution. And the people who are best informed about the marginal benefit, the polluters, have an incentive to mislead the regulators about the benefit. As a result, if a pollution charge is used, the most likely outcome is for the price to be set too low. For example, in Fig. 20.4, the price might be set at $7 per tonne. At this price, polluters find it worthwhile to pay for 15 million tonnes a year. At this level of pollution, the marginal social cost is $15 a tonne, and the amount of pollution exceeds the efficient level.

One way of overcoming excess pollution is to impose a quantitative limit. The most sophisticated way of doing this is with quantitative limits that firms can buy and sell—with marketable permits. Let's look at this alternative.

Marketable Permits

Instead of imposing emission charges on polluters, each potential polluter might be given a pollution limit. To achieve efficiency, marginal benefit and marginal cost must be assessed just as in the case of emission charges. Provided that these benefit-cost calculations are correct, the same efficient outcome can be achieved with quantitative limits as with charges. But in the case of quantitative limits, a cap must be set for each polluter. To set these caps at their efficient levels, the marginal benefit of *each* producer must be assessed. If firm *H* has a higher marginal benefit than firm *L*, an efficiency gain can be achieved by decreasing the cap of firm *L* and increasing that of firm *H*. It is virtually impossible to determine the marginal benefits of each firm, so in practice, quantitative restrictions cannot be allocated to each producer in an efficient way.

Marketable permits are a clever way of overcoming the need for the regulator to know every firm's marginal benefit schedule. Each firm can be allocated a permit to emit a certain amount of pollution, and firms may buy and sell such permits. Firms that have a low marginal benefit from sulfur dioxide emissions will be willing to sell their permits to other firms that have a high marginal benefit. If the market in permits is competitive, the price at which firms trade permits makes the marginal benefit of pollution equal for all firms. And if the correct number of permits has been allotted, the outcome can be efficient.

A Real-World Market for Emissions Environment Canada has not used marketable permits but the Environmental Protection Agency (the EPA) has. The EPA first implemented a marketable emission permit program following the passage of the Clean Air Act in 1970. Trading in lead pollution permits became common during the 1980s, and this marketable permit program has been rated a success. It enabled lead to be virtually eliminated from the atmosphere of the United States (see Figure 20.1b). But this success might not easily translate to other situations because lead pollution has some special features. First, most lead pollution came from a single source, leaded gasoline. Second, lead in gasoline is easily monitored. Third, the objective of the program was clear: eliminate lead in gasoline.

The EPA is now considering using marketable permits to promote efficiency in the control of chlorofluorocarbons, the gases that are believed to damage the ozone layer.

Taxes and External Costs

Taxes can be used to provide incentives for producers or consumers to cut back on an activity that creates external costs. To see how taxes work, consider the market for transportation services.

The costs borne by the producers of transportation services are not the only costs. External costs arise from the airborne particulates and greenhouse gases caused by vehicle emissions. Further, one person's decision to use a highway imposes congestion costs on others. These costs also are external costs. When all the external marginal costs are added to the marginal cost faced by the producer, we obtain the marginal social cost of transportation.

Figure 20.5 shows the market for transportation services. The demand curve, *D*, is also the marginal benefit curve, *MB*. This curve tells us how much consumers value each different quantity of transportation services. The curve *MC* measures the marginal *private* cost of producing transportation services—the costs directly incurred by the producers of these services. The curve *MSC* measures the marginal *social* cost, which adds the external costs to the private costs.

FIGURE 20.5

Taxes and Pollution

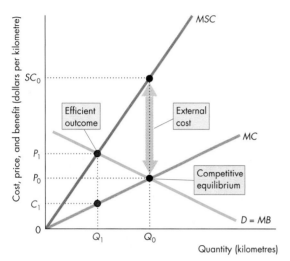

The demand curve for road transportation services is also the marginal benefit curve ($D = MB$). The marginal private cost curve is MC. If the market is competitive, output is Q_0 kilometres and the price is P_0 per kilometre. Marginal social cost is SC_0 per kilometre. Because of congestion and pollution, the marginal social cost exceeds the marginal private cost. Marginal social cost is shown by curve MSC. If the government imposes a tax so that producers of transportation services are confronted with the marginal social cost, the MSC curve becomes the relevant marginal cost curve for suppliers' decisions. The price increases to P_1 per kilometre, and the quantity decreases to Q_1 kilometres. The outcome is efficient.

If the transportation market is competitive and unregulated, road users will balance their own marginal cost, MC, against their own marginal benefit, MB, and travel Q_0 kilometres at a price (and cost) of P_0 per kilometre. At this scale of transportation services, the marginal social cost is SC_0. The marginal social cost minus the marginal private cost, $SC_0 - P_0$, is the marginal cost imposed on others—the marginal external cost.

Suppose the government taxes road transportation and that it sets the tax equal to the external marginal cost. By imposing such a tax, the government makes the suppliers of transportation services incur a marginal cost equal to the marginal social cost. That is, the marginal private cost plus the tax equals the

marginal social cost. The market supply curve is now the same as the MSC curve. The price rises to P_1 a kilometre, and at this price, people travel Q_1 kilometres. The marginal cost of the resources used in producing Q_1 kilometres is C_1, and the marginal external cost is P_1 minus C_1. That marginal external cost is paid by the consumer through the tax.

The situation at the price P_1 and the quantity Q_1 is efficient. At a quantity greater than Q_1, marginal social cost exceeds marginal benefit, so net benefit increases by decreasing the quantity of transportation services. At a quantity less than Q_1, marginal benefit exceeds marginal social cost, so net benefit increases by increasing the quantity of transportation services.

A Carbon Fuel Tax?   A tax can be imposed on any activity that creates external costs. For example, we could tax *all* air-polluting activities. Because the carbon fuels that we use to power our vehicles and generate our electric power are a major source of pollution, why don't we have a broad-based tax on all activities that burn carbon fuel and set the tax rate high enough to give a large reduction in carbon emissions?

The question becomes even more pressing when we consider not only the current levels of greenhouse gases but also their projected future levels. In 1995, annual carbon emissions worldwide were a staggering 6 billion tonnes. By 2050, with current policies, that annual total is predicted to be 24 billion tonnes.

Uncertainty About Global Warming   Part of the reason we do not have a high, broad-based, carbon fuel tax is that the scientific evidence that carbon emissions produce global warming is not accepted by everyone. Climatologists are uncertain about how carbon emissions translate into atmospheric concentrations—about how the *flow* of emissions translates into a *stock* of pollution. The main uncertainty arises because carbon drains from the atmosphere into the oceans and vegetation at a rate that is not well understood. Climatologists are also uncertain about the connection between carbon concentration and temperature. And economists are uncertain about how a temperature increase translates into economic costs and benefits. Some economists believe that the costs and benefits are almost zero, while others believe that a temperature increase of 3 degrees Celsius by 2090 will reduce the total output of goods and services by 20 percent.

Present Cost and Future Benefit   Another factor weighing against a large change in fuel use is that the costs would be borne now, while the benefits, if any, would accrue many years in the future. To compare future benefits with current costs, we must use an interest rate. If the interest rate is 1 percent a year, a dollar today becomes $2.70 in 100 years. If the interest rate is 5 percent a year, a dollar today becomes more than $131.50 in 100 years. So at an interest rate of 1 percent a year, it is worth spending $1 million in 2000 on pollution control to avoid $2.7 million in environmental damage in 2100. At an interest rate of 5 percent a year, it is worth spending $1 million today only if this expenditure avoids $131.5 million in environmental damage in 2100.

Because large uncertain future benefits are needed to justify small current costs, a general tax on carbon fuels is not a high priority on the political agenda.

International Factors A final factor against a large change in fuel use is the international pattern of the use of carbon fuels. Right now, carbon pollution comes in even doses from the industrial countries and the developing countries. But by 2050, three-quarters of the carbon pollution will come from the developing countries (if the trends persist).

One reason for the high pollution rate in some developing countries (notably China, Russia, and other Eastern European countries) is that their governments *subsidize* the use of coal or oil. These subsidies lower producers' marginal costs and encourage the use of fuels. The result is that the quantity of carbon fuels consumed exceeds the efficient quantity—and by a large amount. It is estimated that by 2050, these subsidies will induce annual global carbon emissions of some 10 billion tonnes—about two-fifths of total emissions. If the subsidies were removed, global emissions in 2050 would be 10 billion tonnes a year less.

A Global Warming Dilemma

With the high output rate of greenhouse gases in the developing world, Canada and the other industrial countries are faced with a global warming dilemma (like the prisoners' dilemma in Chapter 14, pp. 299–300). Decreasing pollution is costly and might bring benefits. But the benefits depend on all countries taking action to limit pollution. If one country acts alone, it bears the cost of limiting pollution and gets almost no benefits. So it is worthwhile taking steps to limit global pollution only if all nations act together.

Table 20.1 shows the global warming dilemma faced by industrial countries and developing countries. The numbers are hypothetical. Each country (we'll call each group of countries a country) has two possible policies: to control carbon emissions or to pollute. If each country pollutes, it receives a zero net return (by assumption), shown in the top left square in the table. If both countries control emissions, each bears the cost and gets the benefit. Each has a net return of $25 billion, as shown in the bottom right square of the table. If industrial countries control emissions but developing countries do not, industrial countries alone bear the cost and all countries enjoy a lower level of pollution. In this example, industrial countries pay $50 billion more than they benefit and developing countries benefit by $50 billion more than they pay, as shown in the top right corner of the table. Finally, if developing countries control emissions and industrial countries do not, developing countries bear the cost and industrial countries share

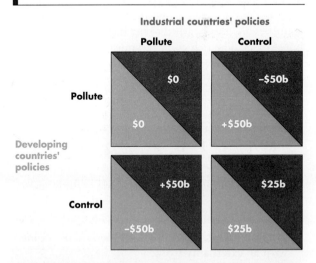

TABLE 20.1

A Global Warming Dilemma

If industrial countries and developing countries both pollute, their payoffs are those shown in the top left square. If both countries control pollution, the bottom right square shows their payoffs. When one group of countries pollutes and the other group does not, the top right and bottom left squares show their payoffs. The outcome of this game is for all countries to pollute. The structure of this game is the same as that of the prisoners' dilemma.

the gains. Developing countries lose $50 billion and industrial countries gain this amount, as shown in the bottom left corner of the table.

Confronted with these possible payoffs, industrial countries and developing countries decide their policies. Each country reasons as follows: If the other country does not control emissions, we break even if we pollute and we lose $50 billion if we control our emissions. Conclusion: Each country is better off individually by polluting. So no one controls emissions, and pollution continues unabated.

Treaties and International Agreements

To break the dilemma, international agreements—treaties—might be negotiated. But such treaties must have incentives for countries to comply with their agreements. Otherwise, even with a treaty, the situation remains as we've just described and illustrated in Table 20.1.

One such international agreement is the *climate convention* that came into effect on March 21, 1994. This convention is an agreement among 60 countries to limit their output of greenhouse gases. But the convention does not have economic teeth. The poorer countries are merely asked to list their sources of greenhouse gases. The rich countries must show how, by 2000, they will return to their 1990 emissions levels.

R E V I E W   Q U I Z

- Why do externalities prevent markets from being efficient?
- How can an externality be eliminated by assigning property rights? How does this method of coping with an externality work?
- How do emission charges and pollution limits work to deal with externalities? Is one preferred over the other?
- How do taxes help us to cope with externalities? At what level must a pollution tax be set if it is to induce firms to produce the efficient quantity of pollution?
- What are the problems that arise when an externality goes beyond the scope of one country?

Economics of Knowledge

KNOWLEDGE, THE THINGS PEOPLE KNOW AND understand, has a profound effect on the economy. The economics of knowledge is an attempt to understand that effect. It is also an attempt to understand the process of knowledge accumulation and the incentives people face to discover, to learn, and to pass on what they know to others. It is an economic analysis of the scientific and engineering processes that lead to the discovery and development of new technologies. And it is a study of the education process of teaching and learning.

You can think of knowledge as being both a consumer good and a productive resource. The demand for knowledge—the willingness to pay to acquire knowledge—depends on the marginal benefit it provides to its possessor. As a consumer good, knowledge provides utility, and this is one source of its marginal benefit. As a productive resource—part of the stock of capital—knowledge increases productivity, and this is another source of its marginal benefit.

Knowledge clearly creates benefits for its possessor. It might also create external benefits. When children learn the basics of reading, writing, and numbers in grade school, they are equipping themselves to be better citizens, better able to communicate and interact with each other. The process continues through high school, college, and university. But when people make decisions about how much schooling to undertake, they undervalue the external benefits that it creates.

External benefits also arise from research and development activities that lead to the creation of new knowledge. Once someone has worked out how to do something, others can copy the basic idea. They do have to work to copy an idea, so they face an opportunity cost. But they do not usually have to pay the person who made the discovery to use it. When Isaac Newton worked out the formulas for calculating the rate of response of one variable to another—calculus—everyone was free to use his method. When a spreadsheet program called VisiCalc was invented, others were free to copy the basic idea. Lotus Corporation developed its 1-2-3 and later Microsoft created Excel, and both became highly successful, but they did not pay for the key idea first used in VisiCalc. When the first shopping mall was built and found to be a successful way of arranging retailing, everyone was free to copy the idea, and malls spread like mushrooms.

When people make decisions about the quantity of education to undertake or the amount of research and development to do, they balance the *private* marginal costs against the private marginal benefits. They undervalue the external benefits. As a result, if we were to leave education and research and development to unregulated market forces, we would get too little of these activities. To deliver them in efficient quantities, we make public choices through governments to modify the market outcome.

Three devices that governments can use to achieve an efficient allocation of resources in the presence of the external benefits from education and research and development are:

■ Subsidies
■ Below-cost provision
■ Patents and copyrights

Subsidies

A **subsidy** is a payment made by the government to producers that depends on the level of output. By subsidizing private activities, government can in principle encourage private decisions to be taken in the public interest. A government subsidy program might alternatively enable private producers to capture resources for themselves. Although subsidies cannot be guaranteed to work successfully, we'll study an example in which they do achieve their desired goal.

Figure 20.6 shows how subsidizing education can increase the amount of education undertaken and achieve an efficient quantity of education. Suppose that all schools are private and that the market for education is competitive. Suppose also that the marginal cost of producing education is a constant $20,000 per student-year. Assume that all these costs are borne by the schools and that there are no external costs. The marginal social cost is the same as the schools' marginal cost and is shown by the curve $MC = MSC$. The maximum price that students (or parents) are willing to pay for an additional year of education determines the marginal private benefit curve and the demand curve for education. That curve is $MB = D$. In this example, a competitive market in private education results in 20,000 students being enrolled with tuition at $20,000 a year.

Suppose that the external benefit—the benefit derived by people other than those who receive the

education—results in marginal social benefits described by the curve MSB. The efficient outcome occurs when marginal social cost equals marginal social benefit. In the example in Fig. 20.6, this equality occurs when 40,000 students are enrolled. One way of getting 40,000 students is to subsidize private schools. In the example, a subsidy of $15,000 per student per year does the job. With a subsidy of $15,000 and a marginal cost of $20,000, schools earn an economic profit if the annual tuition exceeds $5,000. Competition would drive the tuition down

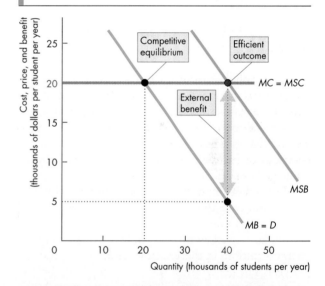

FIGURE 20.6

The Efficient Quantity of Education

The demand curve for education measures the marginal private benefit of education ($MB = D$). The curve MC shows the marginal cost of education—in this example, $20,000 per student-year. If education is provided in a competitive market, tuition is $20,000 a year and 20,000 students enrol. Education produces an external benefit, and adding the external benefit to the marginal private benefit gives marginal social benefit, MSB. Education has no external costs, so MC is also the marginal social cost of education, MSC. An efficient outcome is achieved if the government provides education services to 40,000 students a year, which is achieved by either subsidizing private schools or providing education below cost in public schools. In this example, students pay an annual tuition of $5,000 and the government pays a subsidy of $15,000.

to $5,000, and at this price, 40,000 students will enrol. So a subsidy can achieve an efficient outcome.

The lessons in this example can be applied to stimulating the rate of increase in the stock of knowledge—research and development. By subsidizing these activities, the government can move the allocation of resources towards a more efficient outcome. The mechanism that the government uses for this purpose is a research and development grant. In 1998, through agencies such as the National Science and Engineering Research Council, the Medical Research Council and the Social Sciences and Humanities Research Council, the government spent $620 million. A larger amount was spent in grants to industry.

Another way to achieve an efficient amount of education or research and development is through public provision below cost.

Below-Cost Provision

Instead of subsidizing private schools, the government can establish its own schools (public schools) that provide schooling below cost. And instead of subsidizing research and development in industry and the universities, the government can establish its own research facilities and make discoveries available to others. Let's see how this approach works by returning to the example in Fig. 20.6.

By establishing public schools with places for 40,000 students, the government can supply the efficient quantity of education. To ensure that this number of places is taken up, the public schools would charge a tuition, in this example, of $5,000 a student per year. The government provides this tuition below its marginal cost of $20,000 a student per year. At this price, the number of people who choose to attend school makes the marginal social benefit of education equal to its marginal social cost.

We've now looked at two examples of how government action can help market participants take account of the external benefits deriving from education to achieve an outcome different from that of a private unregulated market. In reality, governments use both methods of encouraging an efficient quantity of education. They subsidize private schools and universities, and they run their own institutions and sell their services at below cost. But in education, the public sector is by far the larger. In research and development, subsidies to the private sector are far larger than the government direct provision.

Patents and Copyrights

Knowledge may well be the only productive resource that does not display *diminishing marginal productivity*. More knowledge (about the right things) makes people more productive. And there seems to be no tendency for the additional productivity from additional knowledge to diminish.

For example, in just 15 years, advances in knowledge about microprocessors have given us a sequence of processor chips that has made our personal computers increasingly powerful. Each advance in knowledge about how to design and manufacture a processor chip has brought apparently ever-larger increments in performance and productivity. Similarly, each advance in knowledge about how to design and build an airplane has brought apparently ever larger increments in performance: Orville and Wilbur Wright's "Flyer 1" was a one-seat plane that could hop a farmer's field. The Lockheed Constellation was an airplane that could fly 120 passengers from New York to London, but with two refuelling stops in Newfoundland and Ireland. The latest version of the Boeing 747 can carry 400 people non-stop from Los Angeles to Sydney or Toronto to Tokyo (flights of 7,500 kilometres that take 13 1/2 hours). These examples can be repeated again and again in fields as diverse as agriculture, biogenetics, communications, engineering, entertainment, medicine, and publishing.

A key reason why the stock of knowledge increases without diminishing returns is the sheer number of different techniques that can in principle be tried. Paul Romer explains this fact with an amazing example. Suppose, says Romer,

> that to make a finished good, 20 different parts have to be attached to a frame, one at a time. A worker could proceed in numerical order, attaching part one first, then part two....Or the worker could proceed in some other order, starting with part 10, then adding part seven....With 20 parts, a standard (but incredible) calculation shows that there are about 10^{18} different sequences one can use for assembling the final good. This number is larger than the total number of seconds that have elapsed since the big bang created the universe, so we can be confident that in all activities, only a very small fraction of the possible sequences have ever been tried.[1]

Think about all the processes, all the products, and all the different bits and pieces that go into each, and you can see that we have only begun to scratch around the edges of what is possible.

Because knowledge is productive and creates external benefits, it is necessary to use public policies to ensure that those who develop new ideas face incentives that encourage an efficient level of effort. The main way of creating the right incentives is to provide the creators of knowledge with property rights in their discoveries—called **intellectual property rights**. The legal device for creating intellectual property rights is the patent or copyright. A **patent** or **copyright** is a government-sanctioned exclusive right granted to the inventor of a good, service, or productive process to produce, use, and sell the invention for a given number of years. A patent enables the developer of a new idea to prevent, for a limited number of years, others from benefiting freely from an invention. But to obtain the protection of the law, an inventor must make knowledge of the invention public.

Although patents encourage invention and innovation, they do so at an economic cost. While a patent is in place, its holder is a monopoly. And monopoly is another type of market failure. To maximize profit, a monopoly (patent holder) produces the quantity at which marginal cost equals marginal revenue. The monopoly sets the price above marginal cost and equal to the highest price at which the profit-maximizing quantity can be sold. In this situation, consumers value the good more highly (are willing to pay more for one more unit of it) than its marginal cost. So the quantity of the good available is less than the efficient quantity.

But without a patent, the effort to develop new goods, services, or processes is diminished and the flow of new inventions is slowed. So the efficient outcome is a compromise that balances the benefits of

more inventions against the cost of temporary monopoly power in newly invented activities.

R E V I E W   Q U I Z

- What is special about knowledge as a consumer good and as a productive resource that creates external benefits?
- What are the external benefits that arise from education and from research and development?
- How might governments use subsidies, below-cost provision, and patents and copyrights to achieve an efficient amount of research and development?
- How might governments use subsidies or below-cost provision to deliver an efficient amount of education?
- Why might knowledge be special in *not* displaying diminishing returns?
- If patents and copyrights can stimulate research, why don't we just award unlimited patents and copyrights to inventors and other creators of new knowledge?

◇ *Reading Between the Lines* on pages 444–445 examines the externalities that arise in collecting and recycling garbage in Vancouver. As you study this topic, try to reflect on all the ideas you've learned in your study of *microeconomics*. You've learned how all economic problems arise from scarcity and involve an opportunity cost. Prices are opportunity costs and are determined by the interactions of buyers and sellers in markets. People choose what to buy and what resources to sell to maximize utility. Firms choose what to sell and what resources to buy to maximize profit. People and firms interact in markets. But the resulting equilibrium might be inefficient and might be viewed as creating too much inequality. By providing public goods, redistributing income, curbing monopoly power, and coping with externalities, public choice modifies the market outcome.

You've now completed your study of *micro*economics. What comes next depends on the type of course that you are taking. You might move from here to study *macro*economics, or you might study *international* economics next. Both will benefit from and draw on the microeconomics you've learned.

---

[1]From Paul Romer, "Ideas and Things," in *The Future Surveyed*, supplement to *The Economist*, 11 September, 1993, pp. 71–72. The "standard calculation" that Romer refers to is the number of ways of selecting and arranging in order 20 objects from 20 objects—also called the number of permutations of 20 objects 20 at a time. This number is *factorial* 20, or 20! = 20 × 19 × 18 × ... × 2 × 1 = $10^{18.4}$. A standard theory (challenged by observations made by the Hubbel space telescope in 1994) is that a big bang started the universe 15 billion years, or $10^{17.7}$ seconds, ago. Although $10^{18.4}$ and $10^{17.7}$ look similar, $10^{18.4}$ is *five* times as large as $10^{17.7}$, so if you started trying alternative sequences at the moment of the big bang and took only one second per trial, you would still have tried only one-fifth of the possibilities. Amazing?

The Market in Recyclables

VANCOUVER SUN, AUGUST 3, 1999

Recycling waste proves more costly than dumping

BY KEN MACQUEEN

Newspapers in blue bag? Check.

Mixed paper and cardboard in yellow bag? Check.

Plastic and metal containers washed and squashed? Check.

Labels removed from cans? Check.

Labels removed from glass. Arrgh! Not even with dynamite. ...

It's garbage day—or if you've got your act together, the night before—time for care and feeding of the blue box. It has become a shared national pastime.

A newly released survey by the Local Government Institute of the University of Victoria found an impressive 74 per cent national participation rate in recycling programs.

But the study also raises hard questions about the economics of the blue box program.

It costs almost three-times as much to recycle garbage as it does to chuck it into the dump, says a survey of the efficiency of recycling in 117 Canadian municipalities.

Garbage bound for dumps costs an average of $48.01 a tonne to collect, while the average net cost of recycling is $124.39 per tonne, ...

The survey raises the hackles of Pamela Nel, recycling coordinator for the Greater Vancouver regional district, who says local recycling programs are not only socially responsible but economically viable.

She said the survey takes a narrow view of the savings of recycling, and no consideration of the costs of stuffing landfills with wasted resources. ...

If grime doesn't pay, why do millions of Canadians stoop in common toil, sifting through their weekly garbage?

Nel of the GVRD said that public's motivation goes far beyond money, although she disputes the narrow way in which the municipal survey calculated costs and ignored benefits of recycling. ...

Residents in the region generated 667,765 tonnes of trash last year, and recycled 34 per cent of it or 228,400 tonnes.

Essence of the Story

■ According to a recent survey, the Canadian participation rate in recycling programs is 74 percent.

■ The survey states that the cost of collecting a tonne of garbage is $48.01 and the average net cost of recycling is $124.39 per tonne.

■ Residents of the greater Vancouver region generated 667,765 tonnes of garbage last year of which 34 percent or 228,400 tonnes was recycled.

■ Pamela Nel of the Greater Vancouver regional district says that recycling programs are socially responsible and economically viable.

■ She says the survey does not take into consideration the costs of filling landfills with wasted resources and ignores the benefits of recycling.

■ Figure 1 shows the private marginal costs and benefits of garbage disposal in the greater Vancouver area.

■ The marginal private benefit curve is *MB*. When we set our garbage out for weekly pickup, the price we pay is zero. So the quantity of garbage disposal services demanded is 668,000 tonnes a week, where the *MB* curve touches the *x*-axis.

■ We'll assume that average cost and marginal cost are constant. With this assumption, marginal cost equals average cost and we can use the numbers in the news article as estimates of marginal cost.

■ The marginal private cost of dumping is $48 a tonne, which is shown by the MC_D curve in Fig. 1.

■ The marginal private cost of recycling is $124 a tonne. But only 34 percent of the greater Vancouver area's garbage is recycled. So the marginal cost of recycling 34 percent and dumping 66 percent is $74 a tonne, which is shown by the MC_R curve in Fig. 1. ($48 × 0.66 + $124 × 0.34 = $74.)

■ If the only benefits and costs of garbage disposal were those shown in Fig. 1, garbage disposal would be inefficient because marginal cost would exceed marginal benefit.

■ But garbage disposal has external benefits and external costs. The external benefit arises because everyone benefits from the hygienic disposal of other people's garbage. The external cost arises because dumping garbage in landfills creates environmental damage and imposes costs on other users of the adjacent areas.

■ Figure 2 shows the private and external costs and benefits of garbage disposal on the assumption that the greater Vancouver area has achieved an efficient use of resources.

■ In Fig. 2, the external benefit of garbage disposal is $74 a tonne. So the marginal social benefit curve, *MSB*, lies above the *MB* curve by that amount.

■ If the external cost of dumping is $26 a tonne and the external cost of recycling is zero, then the marginal social cost is $74 a tonne, shown by the *MSC* curve.

■ Marginal social cost equals marginal social benefit when 668,000 tonnes of garbage are disposed of each week, with 34 percent recycled.

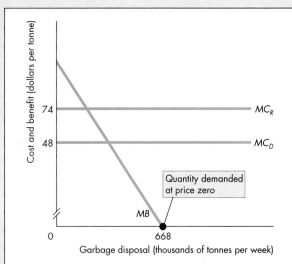

Figure 1 Private costs and benefits

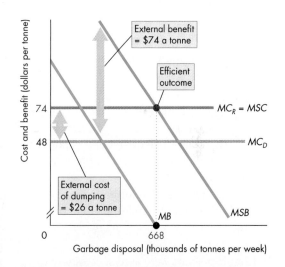

Figure 2 Efficient use of resources

■ If the external cost of landfill exceeds $26 a tonne, Vancouver can become more efficient by increasing the amount of recycling. If the external cost of landfill is less than $26 a tonne, Vancouver can become more efficient by *decreasing* the amount of recycling.

| SUMMARY |

Key Points

Economics of the Environment (pp. 432–440)

- Popular discussion of the environment frames the debate in terms of right and wrong, but economists emphasize costs and benefits and a need to find a way to balance the two.

- The demand for environmental policies has grown because incomes and awareness of the connection between actions and the environment have grown.

- Air pollution arises from road transportation, electric utilities, and industrial processes. In North America, the trends in most types of air pollution are downward.

- Externalities (environmental and others) arise when property rights are absent. Sometimes it is possible to overcome an externality by assigning a property right.

- The Coase theorem states that if property rights exist and transactions costs are low, private transactions are efficient—there are no externalities. In this case, the same efficient amount of pollution is achieved regardless of *who* has the property right: the polluter or the victim.

- When property rights cannot be assigned, governments might overcome environmental externalities by using emission charges, marketable permits, or taxes.

- Marketable permits were used successfully to virtually eliminate lead from our air.

- Global externalities, such as greenhouse gases and substances that deplete the earth's ozone layer, can be overcome only by international action. Each country acting alone has insufficient incentive to act in the interest of the world as a whole. But there is a great deal of scientific uncertainty and disagreement about the effects of greenhouse gases and ozone depletion, and in the face of this uncertainty, international resolve to act is weak.

- The world is locked in a type of prisoners' dilemma game, in which it is in every country's self-interest to let other countries carry the costs of environmental policies.

Economics of Knowledge (pp. 440–443)

- Knowledge is both a consumer good and a productive resource that creates external benefits.

- External benefits from education—passing on existing knowledge to others—arise because the basic reading, writing, and number skills equip people to interact and communicate more effectively.

- External benefits from research and development—creating and applying new knowledge—arise because once someone has worked out how to do something, others can copy the basic idea.

- To enable the efficient amount of education and innovation to take place, we make public choices through governments to modify the market outcome.

- Three devices are available to governments: subsidies, below-cost provision, and patents and copyrights.

- Subsidies to private schools or the provision of public education below cost can achieve an efficient provision of education.

- Patents and copyrights create intellectual property rights and increase the incentive to innovate. But they do so by creating a temporary monopoly, the cost of which must be balanced against the benefit of more inventive activity.

Key Figures ◆

Key Terms

PROBLEMS

*1. A pesticide maker can dump waste into a lake or truck it to a safe storage place. The marginal cost of trucking is constant at $100 a tonne. A trout farm uses the lake and its profit, shown in the following table, depends on how much waste is dumped.

Quantity of waste (tonnes per week)	Trout farm profit (dollars per week)
0	1,000
1	950
2	875
3	775
4	650
5	500
6	325
7	125

a. What is the efficient amount of waste to be dumped into the lake?
b. If the trout farm owns the lake, how much waste is dumped and how much does the pesticide maker pay to the farmer per tonne?
c. If the pesticide maker owns the lake, how much waste is dumped and how much rent does the farmer pay the factory for the use of the lake?

2. A steel smelter is located at the edge of a residential area. The table shows the cost of cutting the pollution of the smelter. It also shows the property taxes that people are willing to pay at different levels of pollution.

Pollution cut (percentage)	Property taxes willingly paid (dollars per day)	Total cost of pollution cut (dollars per day)
0	0	0
10	150	10
20	285	25
30	405	45
40	510	70
50	600	100
60	675	135
70	735	175
80	780	220
90	810	270
100	825	325

Assume that the increase in property taxes that people are willing to pay measures the change in total benefit of cleaner air that results from a change in the percentage decrease in pollution.
a. What is the efficient percentage decrease in pollution?
b. With no regulation of pollution, how much pollution will there be?
c. If the city owns the smelter, how much pollution will there be?
d. If the city is a company town owned by the steel smelter, how much pollution will there be?

*3. Back at the pesticide plant and trout farm described in problem 1, suppose that no one owns the lake and that the government introduces a pollution tax.
a. What is the tax per tonne of waste dumped that will achieve an efficient outcome?
b. Explain the connection between the answer to part (a) and the answer to problem 1.

4. Back at the steel-smelting city in problem 2, suppose that the city government introduces a pollution tax.
a. What is the tax per percentage of waste dumped that will achieve an efficient outcome?
b. Explain the connection between the answer to part (a) and the answer to problem 2.

*5. Using the information provided in problem 1, suppose that no one owns the lake and that the government issues marketable pollution permits to both the farmer and the factory. Each may dump the same amount of waste in the lake, and the total that may be dumped is the efficient amount.
a. What is the quantity that may be dumped into the lake?
b. What is the market price of a permit? Who buys and who sells?
c. What is the connection between the answer to parts (a) and (b) and the answers to problems 1 and 2?

6. Using the information given in problem 2, suppose that the city government issues marketable pollution permits to citizens and the smelter. Each may pollute the air by the same percentage, and the total is the efficient amount.

a. What is the percentage of pollution?

b. What is the market price of a permit? Who buys and who sells?

c. What is the connection between the answer to parts (a) and (b) and the answers to problems 2 and 4?

*7. The marginal cost of educating a student is $4,000 a year and is constant. The figure shows the marginal private benefit curve.

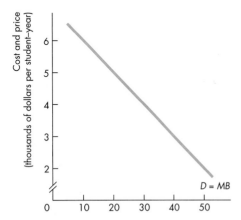

a. With no government involvement and if the schools are competitive, how many students are enrolled and what is the tuition?

b. The external benefit from education is $2,000 per student-year and is constant. If the government provides the efficient amount of education, how many school places does it offer and what is the tuition?

8. A technological advance cuts the marginal cost of educating a student to $2,000 a year and is constant. The marginal private benefit is the same as in problem 7. The external benefit from education increases to $4,000 per student-year and is constant.

a. With no government involvement and if the schools are competitive, how many students are enrolled and what is the tuition?

b. If the government provides the efficient amount of education, how many school places does it offer and what is the tuition?

c. Compare the outcomes in problem 8 with those in problem 7. Explain the differences between the two situations.

CRITICAL THINKING

1. After you have studied *Reading Between the Lines* on pp. 444–445, answer the following questions:

a. What are the main external costs and external benefits that arise from garbage disposal?

b. Could an unregulated market served by private garbage collectors and recyclers provide the efficient quantity of garbage disposal services? Why or why not?

c. If we did leave garbage collection to private enterprise and unregulated markets, what types of property rights would we need to establish to get an efficient outcome?

d. What are the pros and the cons of landfill versus recycling? Where do you stand on this issue and why?

2. Since its foundation 25 years ago, Greenpeace has fought for a cleaner and safer environment. What impact has Greenpeace had on the environment? Has pollution been eliminated? If not, why not?

3. To decrease the amount of over fishing in their territorial waters, the governments of Iceland and New Zealand have introduced private property rights with an allocation of Individual Transferable Quotas (ITQs). To check out the effects of this system, use the link on the Parkin-Bade Web site to visit the Fraser Institute in Vancouver. Then answer the following questions:

a. Would the introduction of ITQs in Canada help to replenish Canadian fish stocks?

b. Explain why ITQs give an incentive to not over fish.

c. Who would oppose ITQs and why?

4. University tuition fees are rising and the federal government is permitting part of the tuition cost as a tax deduction.

a. Why do you think tuition fees are rising?

b. What effect will tax deductions for education costs have on the demand, supply, price, and quantity of education?

c. What are the economic arguments in favour of tax incentives for education? What are the arguments against? Where do you come out on this issue and why?

Understanding Market Failure and Government

Creating a system of responsible democratic government is a huge enterprise and one that can easily go wrong. Creating a constitution that makes despotic and tyrannical rule impossible is relatively easy. And we have achieved such a constitution in Canada by using some sound economic ideas. We have designed a sophisticated system of incentives—of carrots and sticks—to make the government responsive to public opinion and to limit the ability of individual special interests to gain at the expense of the majority. But we have not managed to create a constitution that effectively blocks the ability of special interest groups to capture the consumer and producer surpluses that result from specialization and exchange. ◆ We have created a system of government to deal with four economic problems. The market economy would produce too small a quantity of those public goods and services that we must consume together, such as national defence and air-traffic control. It enables monopoly to restrict production and charge too high a price. It produces too large a quantity of some goods and services, the production of which creates pollution. And it generates a distribution of income and wealth that most people believe is too unequal. So we need a government to help cope with these economic problems. But as the founding fathers knew would happen, when the government gets involved in the economy, people try to steer the government's actions in directions that bring personal gains at the expense of the general interest. ◆ The three chapters in this part explain the problems with which the market has a hard time coping. In Chapter 18, you previewed the entire range of problems and studied one of them, public goods, more deeply. In Chapter 19, you studied competition policy and the regulation of natural monopoly. And in Chapter 20, you studied externalities that arise from pollution (external costs) and from education and research (external benefits). You learned about some of the ways in which externalities can be dealt with. And you discovered that one way of coping with externalities is to strengthen the market and "internalize" the externalities rather than to intervene in the market.

Making the Rules

◆ Many economists have thought long and hard about the issues discussed in this part. But none has had as profound an effect on our ideas in this area as Ronald Coase, whom you can meet on the following page. You can also meet Diane Francis, editor at large of the *National Post* and a provocative contemporary Canadian thinker and commentator on many of the issues that you have just studied.

The Economist

Ronald Coase *(1910–), was born in England and educated at the London School of Economics, where he was deeply influenced by his teacher, Arnold Plant, and by the issues of his youth: communist central planning versus free markets. Professor Coase has lived in the United States since 1951. He first visited America as a 20-year-old on a travelling scholarship during the depths of the Great Depression. It was on this visit, and before he had completed his bachelor's degree, that he conceived the ideas that 60 years later were to earn him the 1991 Nobel Prize for Economic Science. He discovered and clarified the significance of transaction costs and property rights for the functioning of the economy. Ronald Coase has revolutionized the way we think about property rights and externalities and has opened up the growing field of law and economics.*

"The question to be decided is: is the value of fish lost greater or less than the value of the product which contamination of the stream makes possible?"

RONALD H. COASE, *THE PROBLEM OF SOCIAL COST*

The Issues

As knowledge accumulates, we are becoming more sensitive to environmental externalities. We are also developing more sensitive methods of dealing with them. But all the methods involve a public choice.

Urban smog, which is both unpleasant and dangerous to breathe, forms when sunlight reacts with emissions from the tailpipes of automobiles. Because of this external cost of auto exhaust, we set emission standards and tax gasoline. Emission standards increase the cost of a car, and gasoline taxes increase the cost of the marginal kilometre travelled. The higher costs decrease the quantity demanded of road transportation and so decrease the amount of pollution it creates. Is the value of cleaner urban air worth the higher cost of transportation? The public choices of voters, regulators, and lawmakers answer this question.

Acid rain, which imposes a cost on everyone who lives in its path, falls from sulfur-laden clouds produced by electric utility smokestacks. This external cost is being tackled with a market solution. This solution is marketable permits, the price and allocation of which are determined by the forces of supply and demand. Private choices determine the demand for pollution permits, but a public choice determines the supply.

As cars stream onto an urban highway at morning rush hour, the highway clogs and becomes an expensive parking lot. Each rush hour traveller imposes external costs on all the others. Today, road users bear private congestion costs but do not face a share of the external congestion costs they create. But a market solution to this problem is now technologically feasible. It is a solution that charges road users a fee similar to a toll that varies with time of day and degree of congestion. Confronted with the social marginal cost of their actions, each road user makes a choice and the market for highway space is efficient. Here, a public choice to use a market solution leaves the final decision about the degree of congestion to private choices.

Then ...

Chester Jackson, a Lake Erie fisherman, recalls that when he began fishing on the lake, boats didn't carry drinking water. Fishermen drank from the lake. Speaking after World War II, Jackson observed, "Can't do that today. Those chemicals in there would kill you." Farmers used chemicals, such as the insecticide DDT that got carried into the lake by runoff. Industrial waste and trash were also dumped in the lake in large quantities. As a result, Lake Erie became badly polluted during the 1940s and became incapable of sustaining a viable fish stock.

... and Now

Today, Lake Erie supports a fishing industry, just as it did in the 1930s. No longer treated as a garbage dump for chemicals, the lake is regenerating its ecosystem. Fertilizers and insecticides are now recognized as products that have potential externalities, and their external effects are assessed by Environment Canada before new versions are put into widespread use. Dumping industrial waste into rivers and lakes is now subject to much more stringent regulations and penalties. Lake Erie's externalities have been dealt with by one of the methods available: government regulation.

Many people are active participants in the search for better public economic policy and more effective and less intrusive government intervention in the economy. One of these people is Diane Francis, who you can meet on the following pages.

Talking with
Diane Francis

Diane Francis *is editor-at-large of the*
National Post *and a well-known columnist, broad-
caster, and author of best sellers such as* BRE-X:
The Inside Story, Fighting for Canada,
Underground Nation, Controlling Interest: Who
Owns Canada, Contrepreneurs, *and* A Matter of
Survival. *Self-taught and financially independent,
Francis began her journalism career in 1977 after
being a successful entrepreneur. She worked for
many publications and became Editor of* The
Financial Post *in 1991. Throughout the 1990s,
under her direction, the reputation and role of* The
Financial Post *reached new levels. Diane Francis is
a bold and provocative critic of anti-liberal and
anti-competitive forces. And her views on what
Canada must do to survive and prosper cannot be
ignored, either by her supporters or detractors.*

*Robin Bade and Michael Parkin talked with
Diane Francis about a wide range of political-
economic issues that Canada faces today.*

**How did you get interested in business, politics, and
economics?**

I got married as a teenager in the United States to a
very talented graphic designer from Britain. He was
conscripted into the army during the Vietnam War
era, so we came to Canada and started our own art
studio. He was an artist, and I was a natural at business. We worked every hour to build the business.
And when I left it to raise our two kids we had
amassed a good deal of capital so we invested in real
estate and other businesses, sort of venture capital on
a small scale. I just love business.

I started writing about politics and economics as
they affect business. I understand the jargon of economics but not the nuances. I'm interested in business, free enterprise, and democracy. They are my
theology!

**Your writing is full of memorable phrases. An example:
"Canadians are fed up with the red tape and rapacious
taxation policies of successive governments." Can you
elaborate and provide some examples?**

Three examples of over-taxation are capital gains taxes, consumption taxes, and personal income taxes.

We have to compete against Americans whose
capital gains taxes for investors are half our levels.
They changed their capital gains tax some years ago
in recognition of the fact that it was a disincentive.
And ever since, their market has exploded because it
encourages people to stay in markets and earn capital
gains.

We pay bunches more on consumption taxes.
Whether it's gasoline or so-called luxury taxes or sin
taxes, we're paying two to three or four times as
much for liquor, for cigarettes, for gasoline as the
Americans do. And when it comes to regular consumption taxes on goods, we are paying routinely,
except for Alberta, 7 to 9 percent provincial sales tax;
whereas the top sales tax in the United States may be

6 percent and it doesn't apply to all goods. Then we also have the federal consumption tax, which is on services as well as goods, a flat tax of 7 percent everywhere. Americans do not tax services at all. So consumption taxes are onerous.

Then last and most important is personal income taxes, which are excessive at the high end and also at the low end. In most developed countries, income taxes kick in at $12,000 to $15,000. But we start at a much lower level. So at the low end, we tax people earlier and at 17 percent. At the other end, we consider $60,000 plus to be high-high earnings and the income tax rate at the $60,000 plus level is equivalent to what the Americans pay at the $225,000 plus level.

You've described the Canadian health care system and social benefits as being "the most generous but also the most comprehensively mismanaged in the world." Can you tell us what you have in mind?

I think there's an enormous amount of fraud. I did a series of articles on the social services—workmen's compensation, unemployment insurance, welfare, and health care—and discovered that all of these areas were eminently and easily defrauded. Then there's the underground economy that followed the GST—cash for everything.

But the health care stuff: an internal study, which was leaked to me, estimated that $1 out of every $17 was fraud. So $1 billion a year out of every $17 billion Ontario was spending was fraud.

One guy delivered three babies simultaneously in three cities. But the most memorable case was of a woman whose husband took her to an Ontario hospital for a Caesarean section on a Saturday night. Their regular physician was away. When he came back a few days later he said, "This can't be Mrs. So-and-so because I gave her a hysterectomy last year!" It turned out that the "husband" was in the business of smuggling in pregnant women from other countries because once they had a kid here they were entitled to stay. This was a multiple fraud.

Then I did a story about welfare. None of the computers in Ontario's welfare offices were linked. So you could actually get a cheque from every welfare office without one knowing that the other was issuing it to you. Same SIN number!

These programs are just badly engineered, loosely managed, and based on the honour system.

Let's talk about another area that you've written about, Canadian labour law. What's wrong and right with it?

I think the Rand formula, a decision in 1946 by Judge Rand that you don't have to join a union but you do have to pay dues if there's one there, has been a huge disservice to Canada. It has created powerful public sector unions that have been extremely good at getting what they want and has imposed a tax on four million Canadians who are unionized and streamed it into the coffers of a few dozen unions, who have in turn spent this money on political adventures and agenda setting. An elitist and powerful union movement has pulled the agenda towards social democracy European-style without any regard to the interest of the rank and file.

In *Controlling Interest: Who Owns Canada*, you say that 32 families and 5 conglomerates own one-third of Canada's corporate assets. Should we worry about the degree of concentration of ownership, and if we should, what should we do about it?

I think it is always a concern. But we have less reason to worry about it for three reasons. One is free trade with the Americans and another is a tougher Competition Act. We've got both of these in place. The third is just sheer economic growth given the existence of the other two.

...the Rand formula ...that you don't have to join a union but you do have to pay dues if there's one there, has been a huge disservice to Canada.

One of the things I said in the book was, if you don't have a referee on the ice, using the hockey metaphor, then only the goons will play and all the small talented players will be knocked off the ice. Every capitalist I've ever met wants to be a monopolist. Money destroys the system that made him what he was. So you have to have a referee—the cornerstone of a free and open society.

And this spills over into democracy too because

if you have a banana republic owned by three families and they start to own the politicians and the government too, then you lose your freedoms altogether—never mind economic freedom, but all freedom.

So financial feudalism has to be held at bay through the imposition of a very powerful referee who is acting hopefully in the public interest and enshrining competition. If you don't have competition, the cream will not rise to the top, there will not be opportunities, you will lose people or you will bury them, and basically it gets to the heart of the kind of society that you want to live in.

If you don't have a referee on the ice, ... then only the goons will play...

So to me it's part of a theology and you know you're putting a real big spin on it but I don't think it's accidental that the United States, which is unbelievably productive and good for the benefit of the majority of Americans, was the first to bring in very tough antitrust laws in the last century. Every time a company gets huge, whether it's Standard Oil, or AT&T, or Microsoft, they bust it up into little pieces and more opportunities result.

Less fossilization. You know that you just don't want what happened in Britain where the chinless wonders—third generation who were interested in fox hunting—end up with the factories and don't do a good job running them. The whole society suffers.

You've spoken approvingly about the Competition Act. What else has the Canadian federal government got right?

The system. One of the things that I like about the parliamentary system as opposed to an American system, which is the only other system I've lived under and know, is that it is more efficient. It can turn on a dime faster. So that's good.

Canada was faster off the mark in terms of redistributing wealth more fairly to those in need. I think public health care policy is enlightened. I think that it is as important for governments to provide basic health care as to provide basic education. The lower

10 or 15 percent of society has to be supported by the rest proportionately. And the Americans do that. I mean it's not a jungle! But Canada, I think, has done a better job.

To what extent do you think the media (not you, not the *National Post* or *The Financial Post* but the rest of the media!) are responsible for bad economic policy?

The Press is the Press. I think that one of the problems Canada has, vis-à-vis its policy-making process of which the media is a part, is that we're little and a bush league. I mean *60 Minutes'* budget is probably bigger than the CBC's for all of its prime-time programming. I'm just guessing, I'm pulling a figure out of the air. But you know television is an extremely expensive business and so how can you get the best minds, the best producers, the best visuals, the best information for your society unless you pay for it.

Now what's happening is that everything of a world-class or local nature is coming into our living room and people are able to pick and choose the information they need.

But I think that it has impeded decision making here. You know small media, incestuous, group think, drank and slept with the same people, married each other, and you know just hung out with the mandarins and the politicians and all of that—probably about 200 people who literally ran Canada for three generations.

It's changed and I don't want to blow my own horn but I'm an iconoclast and my paper was very iconoclastic. And I think that mixed it up. I think that made all the difference.

How does a student today become a successful economic journalist?

You've got to go journalism school. People are not hired anymore out of general liberal arts or post-graduate areas. The business has become pretty high-tech and capital intensive. If you think you want to become a journalist, get involved in a journalism course right away. You'll soon find out whether you like it or not or if it likes you. And if it doesn't like you, then don't stay in it. It is very important that anybody who gets into journalism is extremely interested in general knowledge of all kinds. Read a wide variety of things from sciences to religions to spirituality to politics to sports as well as current events.

Chapter 35

Trading with the World

Since ancient times, people have expanded their trading as far as technology allowed. Marco Polo opened up the silk route between Europe and China in the thirteenth century. Today, container ships laden with cars and machines and Boeing 747s stuffed with farm-fresh foods ply sea and air routes, carrying billions of dollars' worth of goods. Why do people go to such great lengths to trade with those in other nations? ◆ Low-wage Mexico has entered into a free trade agreement with high-wage Canada and the United States—the North American Free Trade Agreement, or NAFTA. According to Texas billionaire Ross Perot, this agreement has caused a "giant sucking sound" and transferred jobs from Michigan and Ontario to Mexico. Is Perot right? Can we compete with a country that pays its workers a fraction of Canadian wages? Are there any industries, besides perhaps software and movies, in which we have an advantage? ◆ Tariffs—taxes on goods imported from other countries—have been a source of government revenue in Canada since before Confederation and were the centrepiece of Sir John A. Macdonald's national policy of the 1870s. After World War II, a process of trade liberalization brought about a gradual reduction of tariffs. What are the effects of tariffs on international trade? Why don't we have completely unrestricted international trade?

◆ In this chapter, we're going to learn about international trade. We'll discover how *all* nations can gain by specializing in producing the goods and services in which they have a comparative advantage and trading with other countries. We'll discover that *all* countries can compete, no matter how high their wages. We'll also explain why, despite the fact that international trade brings benefits to all, countries restrict trade.

Silk Routes and Sucking Sounds

After studying this chapter, you will be able to:

■ Describe the patterns in international trade

■ Explain comparative advantage and explain why all countries can gain from international trade

■ Explain how economies of scale and diversity of taste lead to gains from trade

■ Explain why trade restrictions reduce our imports, exports, and consumption possibilities

■ Explain the arguments used to justify trade restrictions and show how they are flawed

■ Explain why we have trade restrictions

Patterns and Trends in International Trade

THE GOODS AND SERVICES THAT WE BUY FROM people in other countries are called **imports**. The goods and services that we sell to people in other countries are called **exports**. What are the most important things that we import and export? Most people would probably guess that a rich nation such as Canada imports raw materials and exports manufactured goods. Although that is one feature of Canadian international trade, it is not its most important feature. The vast bulk of our exports *and* imports are manufactured goods. We sell foreigners earth-moving equipment, airplanes, and telecommunication and scientific equipment. We buy televisions, VCRs, blue jeans, and T-shirts from foreigners. Also, we are a major exporter of agricultural products and raw materials. We also import and export a huge volume of services.

Trade in Goods

Manufactured goods account for 50 percent of our exports and 70 percent of our imports. Industrial materials (raw materials and semi-manufactured items) account for 40 percent of our exports and 15 percent of our imports, and agricultural products account for only 5 percent of our exports and 2 percent of our imports. Our largest individual export and import items are capital goods and autos.

But goods account for only 80 percent of our exports and imports. The rest of our international trade is in services.

Trade in Services

You may be wondering how a country can "export" and "import" services. Here are some examples.

If you take a vacation in France and travel there on an Air France flight from Montreal, you import transportation services from France. The money you spend in France on hotel bills and restaurant meals is also classified as a Canadian import. Similarly, the vacation taken by a French student in Quebec counts as a Canadian export to France.

When we import TV sets from South Korea, the owner of the ship that transports them might be Greek and the company that insures them might be British.

The payments that we make for the transportation and insurance are imports of services. Similarly, when a Canadian shipping company transports timber from British Columbia to Tokyo, the transportation cost is an export of a service to Japan. Our international trade in these types of services is large and growing.

Geographical Patterns

Canada has trading links with every part of the world, but the United States is our biggest trading partner for both exports and imports. We buy 77 percent of our imports from the United States and sell Americans 84 percent of our exports. Japan, China, Hong Kong, South Korea, and Taiwan along with Europe and Latin America are our other big trading partners.

Trends in the Volume of Trade

In 1978, we exported 22 percent of total output and imported 20 percent of the goods and services that we bought. In 1998, we exported 36 percent of total output and imported 34 percent of the goods and services that we bought.

On the export side, automobiles, capital goods, and raw materials have remained large items and held a roughly constant share of total exports. But the composition of imports has changed. Food and raw material imports have fallen steadily. Imports of fuel increased during the 1970s but decreased during the 1980s. Imports of equipment and machinery have grown and today are 30 percent of total imports.

Balance of Trade and International Borrowing

The value of exports minus the value of imports is called the **balance of trade**. In 1998, the Canadian balance of trade was a positive $13 billion. Our exports were $13 billion more than our imports. When we export more than we import, as we did in 1998, we lend to foreigners or buy more foreign assets. When we import more than we export, we borrow from foreigners or sell some of our assets to foreigners.

In this chapter, our goal is to understand the factors that influence the *volume* and the *direction* of international trade rather than the *balance* of international trade. And the key to this understanding is the concept of comparative advantage.

Comparative Advantage and International Trade

THE FUNDAMENTAL FORCE THAT GENERATES international trade is *comparative advantage*. And the basis of comparative advantage is divergent *opportunity costs*. You met these ideas in Chapter 3, when we learned about the gains from specialization and exchange between Tom and Nancy.

Tom and Nancy each specialize in producing just one good and then trade with each other. Most nations do not go to the extreme of specializing in a single good and importing everything else. Nonetheless, nations can increase the consumption of all goods if they redirect their scarce resources towards the production of those goods and services in which they have a comparative advantage.

To see how this outcome occurs, we'll apply the same basic ideas we learned in the case of Tom and Nancy to trade among nations. We'll begin by recalling how we can use the production possibility frontier to measure opportunity cost. Then we'll see how divergent opportunity costs bring comparative advantage and gains from trade for countries as well as for individuals, even though no country completely specializes in the production of just one good.

Opportunity Cost in Farmland

Farmland (a fictitious country) can produce grain and cars at any point inside or along its production possibility frontier, *PPF*, shown in Fig. 35.1. (We're holding constant the output of all the other goods that Farmland produces.) The Farmers (the people of Farmland) are consuming all the grain and cars that they produce, and they are operating at point *a* in the figure. That is, Farmland is producing and consuming 15 million tonnes of grain and 8 million cars each year. What is the opportunity cost of a car in Farmland?

We can answer that question by calculating the slope of the production possibility frontier at point *a*. The magnitude of the slope of the frontier measures the opportunity cost of one good in terms of the other. To measure the slope of the frontier at point *a*, place a straight line tangential to the frontier at point *a* and calculate the slope of that straight line. Recall that the formula for the slope of a line is the change in the value of the variable measured on the *y*-axis divided by the change in the value of the variable

measured on the *x*-axis as we move along the line. Here, the variable measured on the *y*-axis is millions of tonnes of grain, and the variable measured on the *x*-axis is millions of cars. So the slope is the change in the number of tonnes of grain divided by the change in the number of cars.

As you can see from the red triangle at point *a* in the figure, if the number of cars produced increases by 2 million, grain production decreases by 18 million tonnes. Therefore the magnitude of the slope is 18 million divided by 2 million, which equals 9. To get one more car, the people of Farmland must give up 9 tonnes of grain. Thus the opportunity cost of 1 car is 9 tonnes of grain. Equivalently, 9 tonnes of grain cost 1 car. For the people of Farmland, these opportunity costs are the prices they face. The price of a car is 9 tonnes of grain, and the price of 9 tonnes of grain is 1 car.

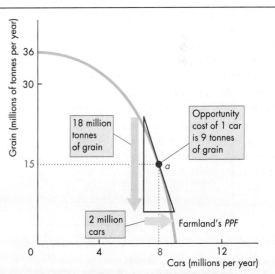

FIGURE 35.1

Opportunity Cost in Farmland

Farmland produces and consumes 15 million tonnes of grain and 8 million cars a year. That is, it produces and consumes at point *a* on its production possibility frontier. Opportunity cost is equal to the magnitude of the slope of the production possibility frontier. The red triangle tells us that at point *a*, 18 million tonnes of grain must be forgone to get 2 million cars. That is, at point *a*, 2 million cars cost 18 million tonnes of grain. Equivalently, 1 car costs 9 tonnes of grain or 9 tonnes cost 1 car.

Opportunity Cost in Mobilia

Figure 35.2 illustrates the production possibility frontier of Mobilia (another fictitious country). Like the Farmers, the Mobilians consume all the grain and cars that they produce. Mobilia consumes 18 million tonnes of grain a year and 4 million cars, at point a'.

Let's calculate the opportunity costs in Mobilia. At point a', the opportunity cost of a car is equal to the magnitude of the slope of the red line tangential to the production possibility frontier, *PPF*. You can see from the red triangle that the magnitude of the slope of Mobilia's production possibility frontier is 6 million tonnes of grain divided by 6 million cars, which equals 1 tonne of grain per car. To get one more car, the Mobilians must give up 1 tonne of grain. Thus the opportunity cost of 1 car is 1 tonne of grain, or, equivalently, the opportunity cost of 1 tonne of grain is 1 car. These are the prices faced in Mobilia.

FIGURE 35.2
Opportunity Cost in Mobilia

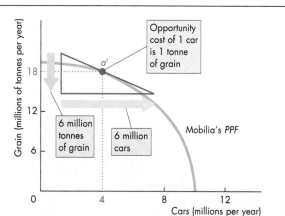

Mobilia produces and consumes 18 million tonnes of grain and 4 million cars a year. That is, it produces and consumes at point a' on its production possibility frontier. Opportunity cost is equal to the magnitude of the slope of the production possibility frontier. The red triangle tells us that at point a', 6 million tonnes of grain must be forgone to get 6 million cars. That is, at point a', 6 million cars cost 6 million tonnes of grain. Equivalently, 1 car costs 1 tonne of grain or 1 tonne of grain costs 1 car.

Comparative Advantage

Cars are cheaper in Mobilia than in Farmland. One car costs 9 tonnes of grain in Farmland but only 1 tonne of grain in Mobilia. But grain is cheaper in Farmland than in Mobilia—9 tonnes of grain costs only 1 car in Farmland, while that same amount of grain costs 9 cars in Mobilia.

Mobilia has a comparative advantage in car production. Farmland has a comparative advantage in grain production. A country has a **comparative advantage** in producing a good if it can produce that good at a lower opportunity cost than any other country.

Let's see how opportunity cost differences and comparative advantage generates gains from international trade.

Gains from Trade

IF MOBILIA BOUGHT GRAIN FOR WHAT IT COSTS Farmland to produce it, then Mobilia could buy 9 tonnes of grain for 1 car. That is much lower than the cost of growing grain in Mobilia, for there it costs 9 cars to produce 9 tonnes of grain. If the Mobilians can buy grain at the low Farmland price, they will reap some gains.

If the Farmers can buy cars for what it costs Mobilia to produce them, they will be able to obtain a car for 1 tonne of grain. Because it costs 9 tonnes of grain to produce a car in Farmland, the Farmers would gain from such an opportunity.

In this situation, it makes sense for Mobilians to buy their grain from Farmers and for Farmers to buy their cars from Mobilians. But at what price will Farmland and Mobilia trade?

The Terms of Trade

The quantity of grain that Farmland must pay Mobilia for a car is Farmland's **terms of trade** with Mobilia. Because Canada exports and imports many different goods and services, we measure the terms of trade in the real world as an index number that averages the terms of trade over all the items we trade.

The forces of international supply and demand determine the terms of trade. Figure 35.3 illustrates these forces in the Farmland–Mobilia international

FIGURE 35.3

International Trade
in Cars

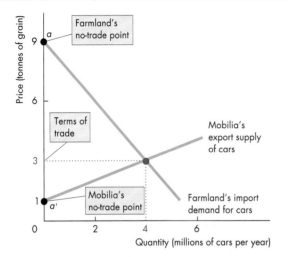

As the price of a car falls, the quantity of imports demanded
by Farmland increases—Farmland's import demand curve for
cars is downward sloping. As the price of a car rises, the quantity of cars supplied by Mobilia for export increases—Mobilia's
export supply curve of cars is upward sloping. Without international trade, the price of a car is 9 tonnes of grain in
Farmland (point *a*) and 1 tonne of grain in Mobilia (point *a'*).

With free international trade, the price (terms of trade)
is determined where the export supply curve intersects the
import demand curve—3 tonnes of grain per car. At that
price, 4 million cars a year are imported by Farmland and
exported by Mobilia. The value of grain exported by Farmland
and imported by Mobilia is 12 million tonnes a year, the quantity required to pay for the cars imported.

car market. The quantity of cars *traded internationally* is measured on the *x*-axis. On the *y*-axis, we
measure the price of a car. This price is expressed as
the *terms of trade*—tonnes of grain per car. If no
international trade takes place, the price of a car in
Farmland is 9 tonnes of grain, its opportunity cost,
indicated by point *a*. Again, if no trade takes place,
the price of a car in Mobilia is 1 tonne of grain, its
opportunity cost, indicated by point *a'*. The no-trade
points *a* and *a'* correspond to the points identified by
those same letters in Figs. 35.1 and 35.2. The lower
the price of a car (terms of trade), the greater is the

quantity of cars that the Farmers are willing to
import from the Mobilians. This fact is illustrated
by the downward-sloping curve, which shows
Farmland's import demand for cars.

The Mobilians respond in the opposite direction.
The higher the price of a car (terms of trade), the
greater is the quantity of cars that Mobilians are willing to export to Farmers. This fact is reflected in
Mobilia's export supply of cars—the upward-sloping
line in Fig. 35.3.

The international market in cars determines the
equilibrium price (terms of trade) and quantity
traded. This equilibrium occurs where the import
demand curve intersects the export supply curve. In
this case, the equilibrium price is 3 tonnes of grain
per car. Mobilia exports and Farmland imports 4 million cars a year. Notice that the price with trade is
lower than the initial price in Farmland but higher
than the initial price in Mobilia.

Balanced Trade

The number of cars exported by Mobilia—4 million
a year—is exactly equal to the number of cars
imported by Farmland. How does Farmland pay for
its cars? It pays by exporting grain. How much grain
does Farmland export? You can find the answer by
noticing that for 1 car, Farmland has to pay 3 tonnes
of grain. Hence, for 4 million cars, Farmland has to
pay 12 million tonnes of grain. Thus Farmland's
exports are 12 million tonnes of grain a year. Mobilia
imports this same quantity of grain.

Mobilia is exchanging 4 million cars for 12 million tonnes of grain each year, and Farmland is doing
the opposite, exchanging 12 million tonnes of grain
for 4 million cars. Trade is balanced between these
two countries. The value received from exports equals
the value paid out for imports.

Changes in Production
and Consumption

We've seen that international trade makes it possible
for Farmers to buy cars at a lower price than that at
which they can produce them for themselves.
Equivalently, Farmers can sell their grain for a higher
price. International trade also enables Mobilians to
sell their cars for a higher price. Equivalently,
Mobilians can buy grain for a lower price. Thus
everybody gains. How is it possible for *everyone* to

gain? What are the changes in production and consumption that accompany these gains?

An economy that does not trade with other economies has identical production and consumption possibilities. Without trade, the economy can consume only what it produces. But with international trade, an economy can consume different quantities of goods from those that it produces. The production possibility frontier describes the limit of what a country can produce, but it does not describe the limits to what it can consume. Figure 35.4 will help you to see the distinction between production possibilities and consumption possibilities when a country trades with other countries.

First of all, notice that the figure has two parts, part (a) for Farmland and part (b) for Mobilia. The production possibility frontiers that you saw in Figs. 35.1 and 35.2 are reproduced here. The slopes of the two black lines in the figure represent the opportunity costs in the two countries when there is no international trade. Farmland produces and consumes at point *a*, and Mobilia produces and consumes at *a'*. A car costs 9 tonnes of grain in Farmland and 1 tonne of grain in Mobilia.

Consumption Possibilities The red line in each part of Fig. 35.4 shows the country's consumption possibilities with international trade. These two red lines have the same slope, and the magnitude of that slope is the opportunity cost of a car in terms of grain on the world market—3 tonnes per car. The *slope* of the consumption possibilities line is common to both countries because its magnitude equals the *terms of trade*. But the position of a country's consumption possibilities line depends on the country's production possibilities. A country cannot produce outside its production possibility curve, so its consumption possibility curve touches its production possibility curve. Thus Farmland could choose to consume at point *b* with no international trade or, with international trade, at any point on its red consumption possibilities line.

Free Trade Equilibrium With international trade, the producers of cars in Mobilia can get a higher price for their output. As a result, they increase the quantity of car production. At the same time, grain producers in Mobilia get a lower price for their grain, and so they reduce production. Producers in Mobilia adjust their output by moving along their production possibility frontier until the opportunity cost in

Mobilia equals the terms of trade (the opportunity cost in the world market). This situation arises when Mobilia is producing at point *b'* in Fig. 35.4(b).

But the Mobilians do not consume at point *b'*. That is, they do not increase their consumption of cars and decrease their consumption of grain. Instead, they sell some of their car production to Farmland in exchange for some of Farmland's grain. They trade internationally. But to see how that works out, we first need to check in with Farmland to see what's happening there.

In Farmland, producers of cars now get a lower price and producers of grain get a higher price. As a consequence, producers in Farmland decrease car production and increase grain production. They adjust their outputs by moving along the production possibility frontier until the opportunity cost of a car in terms of grain equals the terms of trade (the opportunity cost on the world market). They move to point *b* in part (a). But the Farmers don't consume at point *b*. They trade some of their additional grain production for the now cheaper cars from Mobilia.

Figure 35.4 shows the quantities consumed in the two countries. We saw in Fig. 35.3 that Mobilia exports 4 million cars a year to Farmland and Farmland exports 12 million tonnes of grain a year to Mobilia. So Farmland consumes 12 million tonnes a year less grain than it produces, and it consumes 4 million more cars a year more than it produces. Farmland consumes at point *c* in Fig. 35.4(a). And Mobilia consumes 12 million tonnes of grain more than it produces and 4 million cars fewer than it produces. Mobilia consumes at *c'* in Fig. 35.4(b).

Calculating the Gains from Trade

You can now literally see the gains from trade in Fig. 35.4. Without trade, Farmers produce and consume at point *a* in part (a)—a point on Farmland's production possibility frontier. With international trade, Farmers consume at point *c*—a point *outside* the production possibility frontier. At point *c*, Farmers are consuming 3 million tonnes of grain a year and 1 million cars a year more than before. These increases in consumption of both cars and grain, beyond the limits of the production possibility frontier, are the gains from international trade. Mobilians also gain. Without trade, they consume at point *a'* in part (b)—a point on Mobilia's production possibility frontier. With international trade, they consume at point *c'*—a point outside

FIGURE 35.4

Expanding Consumption Possibilities

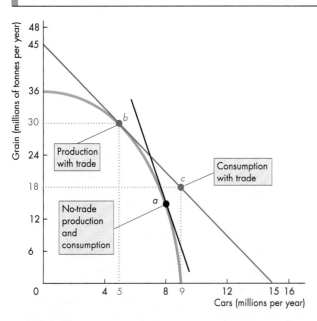

(a) Farmland

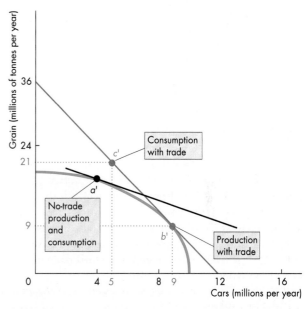

(b) Mobilia

With no international trade, Farmers produce and consume at point *a* and the opportunity cost of a car is **9** tonnes of grain (the slope of the black line in part a). Also, with no international trade, Mobilians produce and consume at point *a'* and the opportunity cost of I tonne of grain is I car (the slope of the black line in part b). Goods can be exchanged internationally at a price of **3** tonnes of grain for I car along the red line in each part of the figure. In part (a), Farmland decreases its production of cars and increases its production of grain, mov-

ing from *a* to *b*. It exports grain and imports cars, and it consumes at point *c*. Farmers have more of both cars and grain than they would if they produced all their own consumption goods—at point *a*. In part (b), Mobilia increases car production and decreases grain production, moving from *a'* to *b'*. Mobilia exports cars and imports grain, and it consumes at point *c'*. Mobilians have more of both cars and grain than they would if they produced all their own consumption goods—at point *a'*.

the production possibility frontier. Mobilia consumes 3 million tonnes of grain a year and 1 million cars a year more than without trade. These are the gains from international trade for Mobilia.

Gains for All

Trade between the Farmers and the Mobilians does not create winners and losers. Everyone wins. Sellers add the net demand of foreigners to their domestic demand and so their market expands. Buyers are faced with domestic supply plus net foreign supply and so have a larger supply available to them.

REVIEW QUIZ

■ In what circumstances can countries gain from international trade?

■ What determines the goods and services that a country will export? What determines the goods and services that a country will import?

■ What is a comparative advantage and what role does it play in determining the amount and type of international trade that occurs?

■ How can it be that all countries gain from international trade and that there are no losers?

Gains from Trade in Reality

THE GAINS FROM TRADE THAT WE HAVE JUST studied between Farmland and Mobilia in grain and cars occur in a model economy—in a world economy that we have imagined. But these same phenomena occur every day in the real global economy.

Comparative Advantage in the Global Economy

We buy TVs and VCRs from Korea, machinery from Europe, and fashion goods from Hong Kong. In exchange, we sell machinery, grain and lumber, airplanes, computers, and financial services. All this international trade is generated by comparative advantage, just like the international trade between Farmland and Mobilia in our model economy. All international trade arises from comparative advantage, even when trade is in similar goods such as tools and machines. At first thought, it seems puzzling that countries exchange manufactured goods. Why doesn't each developed country produce all the manufactured goods its citizens want to buy?

Trade in Similar Goods

Why does Canada produce automobiles for export and at the same time import cars from the United States, Japan, Korea, and Western Europe? Wouldn't it make more sense to produce all the cars that we buy here in Canada? After all, we have access to the best technology available for producing cars. Autoworkers in Canada are surely as productive as their fellow workers in the United States, Western Europe, and Asian countries. So why does Canada have a comparative advantage in some types of cars and Japan and Europe in others?

Diversity of Taste and Economies of Scale

The first part of the answer is that people have a tremendous diversity of taste. Let's stick with the example of cars. Some people prefer a sports car, some prefer a limousine, some prefer a regular, full-size car, and some prefer a minivan. In addition to size and type of car, there are many other dimensions in which cars vary. Some have low fuel consumption, some have high performance, some are spacious and comfortable, some have a large trunk, some have four-wheel drive, some have front-wheel drive, some have a radiator grill that looks like a Greek temple, others look like a wedge. People's preferences across these many dimensions vary. The tremendous diversity in tastes for cars means that people value variety and are willing to pay for it in the marketplace.

The second part of the answer to the puzzle is *economies of scale*—the tendency for the average cost to be lower, the larger the scale of production. In such situations, larger and larger production runs lead to ever lower average costs. Many goods, including cars, experience economies of scale. For example, if a car producer makes only a few hundred (or perhaps a few thousand) cars of a particular type and design, the producer must use production techniques that are much more labour-intensive and much less automated than those employed to make hundreds of thousands of cars in a particular model. With short production runs and labour-intensive production techniques, costs are high. With very large production runs and automated assembly lines, production costs are much lower. But to obtain lower costs, the automated assembly lines have to produce a large number of cars.

It is the combination of diversity of taste and economies of scale that determines opportunity cost, produces comparative advantages, and generates such a large amount of international trade in similar commodities. With international trade, each car manufacturer has the whole world market to serve. Each producer can specialize in a limited range of products and then sell its output to the entire world market. This arrangement enables large production runs on the most popular cars and feasible production runs even on the most customized cars demanded by only a handful of people in each country.

The situation in the market for cars is also present in many other industries, especially those producing specialized equipment and parts. For example, Canada exports illustration software but imports database software, exports telecommunications systems but imports PCs, exports specialized video equipment but imports VCRs. Thus international exchange of similar but slightly differentiated manufactured products is a highly profitable activity.

Let's next see what happens when governments restrict international trade. We'll see that free trade brings the greatest possible benefits. We'll also see why, in spite of the benefits of free trade, governments sometimes restrict trade.

Trade Restrictions

GOVERNMENTS RESTRICT INTERNATIONAL TRADE to protect domestic industries from foreign competition. Governments use two main tools:

1. Tariffs
2. Nontariff barriers

A **tariff** is a tax that is imposed by the importing country when an imported good crosses its international boundary. A **nontariff barrier** is any action other than a tariff that restricts international trade. Examples of nontariff barriers are quantitative restrictions and licensing regulations limiting imports. First, let's look at tariffs.

The History of Tariffs

The Canadian economy has always been protected by a tariff. Figure 35.5 shows the history of that tariff, from Confederation through 1998. The figure shows tariffs as a percentage of total imports—the average tariff. As you can see, the average tariff rate climbed from the early 1870s to exceed 20 percent by the late 1890s. The rate fluctuated but gradually decreased through the early 1920s. It increased again during the Great Depression years of the early 1930s. During these years, most countries increased their tariff rates in what became a "beggar-my-neighbour" policy. The average tariff then decreased through the late 1930s and continued its decrease throughout the years after World War II. Today, the average tariff rate is less than 1 percent.

The reduction in tariffs since World War II followed the signing in 1947 of the **General Agreement on Tariffs and Trade** (GATT). Since its formation, the GATT has organized several rounds of negotiations that have resulted in tariff reductions. One of these, the Kennedy Round that began in the early 1960s, resulted in large tariff cuts starting in 1967. Another, the Tokyo Round, resulted in further tariff cuts in 1979. The most recent, the Uruguay Round, which started in 1986 and was completed in 1994, was the most ambitious and comprehensive of the rounds and led to the creation of a new **World Trade Organization** (WTO). Membership of the WTO brings greater obligations on countries to observe the GATT rules.

FIGURE 35.5

The Canadian Tariff: 1867–1998

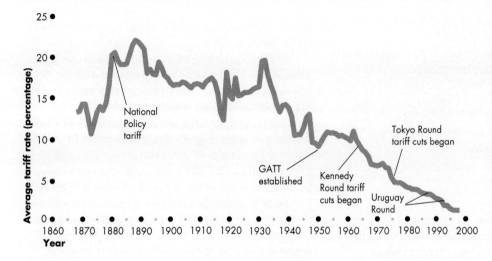

Canadian tariffs were in place before Confederation. Tariffs increased sharply in the 1870s and remained high until the 1930s. Since the establishment of the GATT in 1947, tariffs have steadily decreased in a series of "rounds." The most significant "rounds" are identified in the figure. Tariffs are now lower than they have ever been.

Sources: Statistics Canada, *Historical Statistics of Canada*, Series G485, and *StatCan: CANSIM Disc,* March 1999.

In addition to the agreements under the GATT and the WTO, Canada is a party to the **North American Free Trade Agreement** (NAFTA), which became effective on January 1, 1994, and under which barriers to international trade between Canada, the United States, and Mexico will be virtually eliminated after a 15-year phasing-in period.

In other parts of the world, trade barriers have virtually been eliminated among the member countries of the European Union, which has created the largest unified tariff-free market in the world. In 1994, discussions among the Asia-Pacific Economic group (APEC) led to an agreement in principle to work towards a free-trade area that embraces China, all the economies of East Asia and the South Pacific, Canada, and the United States. These countries include the fastest-growing economies and hold the promise of heralding a global free-trade area. But the Asia crisis of 1997 and other problems with China make it unlikely that free trade will come to APEC in the near term.

The effort to achieve freer trade underlines the fact that trade in some goods is still subject to extremely high tariffs. The highest tariffs faced by Canadian buyers are those on textiles and footwear. A tariff of more than 10 percent (on the average) is imposed on almost all our imports of textiles and footwear. For example, when you buy a pair of blue jeans for $20, you pay about $5 more than you would if there were no tariffs on textiles. Other goods protected by tariffs are agricultural products, energy and chemicals, minerals, and metals. Meat, cheese, and sugar cost more because of protection than they would with free international trade.

The temptation on governments to impose tariffs is a strong one. First, tariffs provide revenue to the government. Second, they enable the government to satisfy special interest groups in import-competing industries. But, as we'll see, free international trade brings enormous benefits that are reduced when tariffs are imposed. Let's see how.

How Tariffs Work

To analyse how tariffs work, let's return to the example of trade between Farmland and Mobilia. Figure 35.6 shows the international market for cars in which these two countries are the only traders. The volume of trade and the price of a car are determined at the point of intersection of Mobilia's export

FIGURE 35.6

The Effects of a Tariff

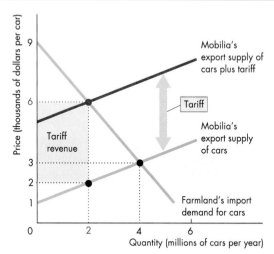

Farmland imposes a tariff on car imports from Mobilia. The tariff increases the price that Farmers have to pay for cars. It shifts the supply curve of cars in Farmland leftward. The vertical distance between the original supply curve and the new one is the amount of the tariff, $4,000 per car. The price of a car in Farmland increases, and the quantity of cars imported decreases. The government of Farmland collects a tariff revenue of $4,000 per car—a total of $8 billion on the 2 million cars imported. Farmland's exports of grain decrease because Mobilia now has a lower income from its exports of cars.

supply curve of cars and Farmland's import demand curve for cars.

In Fig. 35.6, these two countries trade cars and grain in exactly the same way that we saw in Fig. 35.3. Mobilia exports cars, and Farmland exports grain. The volume of car imports into Farmland is 4 million a year, and the world market price of a car is 3 tonnes of grain. Fig. 35.6 expresses prices in dollars rather than in units of grain and is based on a money price of grain of $1,000 a tonne. With grain costing $1,000 a tonne, the money price of a car is $3,000.

Now suppose that the government of Farmland, perhaps under pressure from car producers, decides to impose a tariff on imported cars. In particular, suppose that a tariff of $4,000 per car is imposed. (This is a huge tariff, but the car producers of Farmland are pretty fed up with competition from Mobilia.) What happens?

- The supply of cars in Farmland decreases.
- The price of cars in Farmland rises.
- The quantity of cars imported by Farmland decreases.
- The government of Farmland collects the tariff revenue.
- Resource use is inefficient.
- The *value* of exports changes by the same amount as the *value* of imports and trade remains balanced.

Change in the Supply of Cars   Farmland cannot buy cars at Mobilia's export supply price. It must pay that price plus the $4,000 tariff. So the supply curve in Farmland shifts leftward. The new supply curve is that labelled "Mobilia's export supply of cars plus tariff." The vertical distance between Mobilia's export supply curve and the new supply curve is the tariff of $4,000 a car.

Rise in Price of Cars   A new equilibrium occurs where the new supply curve intersects Farmland's import demand curve for cars. That equilibrium is at a price of $6,000 a car, up from $3,000 with free trade.

Fall in Imports   Car imports decrease from 4 million to 2 million cars a year. At the higher price of $6,000 a car, domestic car producers in Farmland increase their production. Domestic grain production decreases as resources are moved into the expanding car industry.

Tariff Revenue   Total expenditure on imported cars by the Farmers is $6,000 a car multiplied by the 2 million cars imported ($12 billion). But not all of that money goes to the Mobilians. They receive $2,000 a car, or $4 billion for the 2 million cars. The difference—$4,000 a car, or a total of $8 billion for the 2 million cars—is collected by the government of Farmland as tariff revenue.

Inefficiency   The people of Farmland are willing to pay $6,000 for the marginal car imported. But the opportunity cost of that car is $2,000. So there is a gain from trading an extra car. In fact, there are gains—willingness to pay exceeds opportunity cost—all the way up to 4 million cars a year. Only when 4 million cars are being traded is the maximum price that a Farmer is willing to pay equal to the minimum price that is acceptable to a Mobilian. Thus restricting trade reduces the gains from trade.

Trade Remains Balanced   With free trade, Farmland was paying $3,000 a car and buying 4 million cars a year from Mobilia. Thus the total amount paid to Mobilia for imports was $12 billion a year. With a tariff, Farmland's imports have been cut to 2 million cars a year and the price paid to Mobilia has also been cut to only $2,000 a car. Thus the total amount paid to Mobilia for imports has been cut to $4 billion a year. Doesn't this fact mean that Farmland now has a balance of trade surplus?

It does not. The price of a car in Mobilia has fallen. But the price of grain remains at $1,000 a tonne. So the relative price of cars has fallen, and the relative price of grain has increased. With free trade, the Mobilians could buy 3,000 tonnes of grain for one car. Now they can buy only 2,000 tonnes for a car. With a higher relative price of grain, the quantity demanded by the Mobilians decreases and Mobilia imports less grain. But because Mobilia imports less grain, Farmland exports less grain. In fact, Farmland's grain industry suffers from two sources. First, there is a decrease in the quantity of grain sold to Mobilia. Second, there is increased competition for inputs from the now expanded car industry. Thus the tariff leads to a contraction in the scale of the grain industry in Farmland.

It seems paradoxical at first that a country imposing a tariff on imports of cars hurts its own export industry, decreasing its exports of grain. It might help to think of it this way: Mobilians buy grain with the money they make from exporting cars to Farmland. If they export fewer cars, they cannot afford to buy as much grain. In fact, in the absence of any international borrowing and lending, Mobilia must cut its imports of grain by exactly the same amount as the loss in revenue from its export of cars. Grain imports into Mobilia are cut back to a value of $4 billion, the amount that can be paid for by the new lower revenue from Mobilia's car exports. Thus trade is still balanced. The tariff cuts imports and exports by the same amount. The tariff has no effect on the *balance* of trade but it reduces the *volume* of trade.

The result that we have just derived is perhaps one of the most misunderstood aspects of international economics. On countless occasions, politicians and others call for tariffs to remove a balance of trade deficit or argue that lowering tariffs would produce a balance of trade deficit. They reach this conclusion by failing to work out all the implications of a tariff.

Let's now turn our attention to the other tool for restricting trade: nontariff barriers.

Nontariff Barriers

The two main forms of nontariff barrier are:

1. Quotas
2. Voluntary export restraints

A **quota** is a quantitative restriction on the import of a particular good, which specifies the maximum amount of the good that may be imported in a given period of time. A **voluntary export restraint** (VER) is an agreement between two governments in which the government of the exporting country agrees to restrain the volume of its own exports.

Quotas are especially prominent in textiles and agriculture. Voluntary export restraints are used to regulate trade between Japan and Canada.

How Quotas and VERs Work

To see how a quota works, suppose that Farmland imposes a quota that restricts its car imports to 2 million cars a year. Figure 35.7 shows the effects of this action. The quota is shown by the vertical red line at 2 million cars a year. Because it is illegal to exceed the quota, car importers buy only that quantity from Mobilia, for which they pay $2,000 a car. But because the quantity of imported cars is restricted to 2 million cars a year, people are willing to pay $6,000 per car. This is the price of a car in Farmland.

The value of imports falls to $4 million, exactly the same as in the case of the tariff. So with lower incomes from car exports and with a higher relative price of grain, Mobilians cut back on their imports of grain in exactly the same way that they did under a tariff.

The key difference between a quota and a tariff lies in who collects the gap between the import supply price and the domestic price. In the case of a tariff, it is the government of the importing country. In the case of a quota, it goes to the person who has the right to import under the import quota regulations.

A voluntary export restraint is like a quota arrangement in which quotas are allocated to each exporting country. The effects of voluntary export restraints are similar to those of quotas but differ from them in that the gap between the domestic price and the export price is captured not by domestic importers but by the foreign exporter. The government of the exporting country has to establish procedures for allocating the restricted volume of exports among its producers.

FIGURE **35.7**

The Effects of a Quota

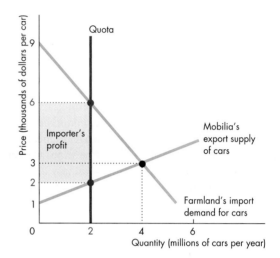

Farmland imposes a quota of 2 million cars a year on car imports from Mobilia. That quantity appears as the vertical line labelled "Quota." Because the quantity of cars supplied by Mobilia is restricted to 2 million, the price at which those cars will be traded increases to $6,000. Importing cars is profitable because Mobilia is willing to supply cars at $2,000 each. There is competition for import quotas.

R E V I E W   Q U I Z

■ What happens to a country's consumption possibilities when it opens itself up to international trade and trades freely at world market prices?

■ What do trade restrictions do to the gains from international trade?

■ What is best for a country: restricted trade, no trade, or free trade?

■ What does a tariff on imports do to the volume of imports and the volume of exports?

■ In the absence of international borrowing and lending, how do tariffs and other trade restrictions influence the total value of imports and exports and the balance of trade—the value of exports minus the value of imports?

Let's now look at some commonly heard arguments for restricting international trade.

The Case Against Protection

FOR AS LONG AS NATIONS AND INTERNATIONAL trade have existed, people have debated whether a country is better off with free international trade or with protection from foreign competition. The debate continues, but for most economists, a verdict has been delivered and is the one you have just seen. Free trade promotes prosperity for all; protection is inefficient. We've seen the most powerful case for free trade in the example of how Farmland and Mobilia both benefit from their comparative advantage. But there is a broader range of issues in the free trade versus protection debate. Let's review these issues.

Three arguments for restricting international trade are:

■ The national security argument
■ The infant industry argument
■ The dumping argument

Let's look at each in turn.

The National Security Argument

The national security argument for protection is that a country must protect industries that produce defence equipment and armaments and those on which the defence industries rely for their raw materials and other intermediate inputs. This argument for protection does not withstand close scrutiny.

First, it is an argument for international isolation, for in a time of war, there is no industry that does not contribute to national defence. Second, if the case is made for boosting the output of a strategic industry, it is more efficient to achieve this outcome with a subsidy to the firms in the industry financed out of taxes. Such a subsidy would keep the industry operating at the scale judged appropriate, and free international trade would keep the prices faced by consumers at their world market levels.

The Infant Industry Argument

The so-called **infant industry argument** for protection is that it is necessary to protect a new industry to enable it to grow into a mature industry that can compete in world markets. The argument is based on the idea of *dynamic comparative advantage*, which can arise from *learning-by-doing* (see Chapter 3).

Learning-by-doing is a powerful engine of productivity growth, and comparative advantage evolves and changes because of on-the-job experience. But these facts do not justify protection.

First, the infant industry argument is valid only if the benefits of learning-by-doing *not only* accrue to the owners and workers of the firms in the infant industry but also *spill over* to other industries and parts of the economy. For example, there are huge productivity gains from learning-by-doing in the manufacture of telecommunication equipment. But almost all of these gains benefit the stockholders and workers of Northern Telecom and other producers. Because the people making the decisions, bearing the risk, and doing the work are the ones who benefit, they take the dynamic gains into account when they decide on the scale of their activities. In this case, almost no benefits spill over to other parts of the economy, so there is no need for government assistance to achieve an efficient outcome.

Second, even if the case is made for protecting an infant industry, it is more efficient to do so by a subsidy to the firms in the industry, with the subsidy financed out of taxes.

The Dumping Argument

Dumping occurs when a foreign firm sells its exports at a lower price than its cost of production. Dumping might be used by a firm that wants to gain a global monopoly. In this case, the foreign firm sells its output at a price below its cost to drive domestic firms out of business. When the domestic firms have gone, the foreign firm takes advantage of its monopoly position and charges a higher price for its product. Dumping is usually regarded as a justification for temporary countervailing tariffs.

But there are powerful reasons to resist the dumping argument for protection. First, it is virtually impossible to detect dumping because it is hard to determine a firm's costs. As a result, the test for dumping is whether a firm's export price is below its domestic price. But this test is a weak one because it can be rational for a firm to charge a low price in markets in which the quantity demanded is highly sensitive to price and a higher price in a market in which demand is less sensitive to price.

Second, it is hard to think of a good that is produced by a natural *global* monopoly. So even if all the domestic firms in some industry were driven out of business, it would always be possible to find several and usually many alternative foreign sources of supply and to buy at prices determined in competitive markets.

Third, if a good or service were a truly global natural monopoly, the best way of dealing with it would be by regulation—just as in the case of domestic monopolies. Such regulation would require international cooperation.

The three arguments for protection that we've just examined have an element of credibility. The counter-arguments are in general stronger, so these arguments do not make the case for protection. But they are not the only arguments that you might encounter. The many other arguments that are commonly heard are quite simply wrong. They are fatally flawed. The most common of them are that protection:

- Saves jobs
- Allows us to compete with cheap foreign labour
- Brings diversity and stability
- Penalizes lax environmental standards
- Protects national culture
- Prevents rich countries from exploiting developing countries

Saves Jobs

The argument is: When we buy shoes from Brazil or shirts from Taiwan, Canadian workers lose their jobs. With no earnings and poor prospects, these workers become a drain on welfare and spend less, causing a ripple effect of further job losses. The proposed solution to this problem is to ban imports of cheap foreign goods and protect Canadian jobs. The proposal is flawed for the following reasons.

First, free trade does cost some jobs, but it also creates other jobs. It brings about a global rationalization of labour and allocates labour resources to their highest-value activities. Because of international trade in textiles, tens of thousands of workers in Canada have lost jobs because textile mills and other factories have closed. But tens of thousands of workers in other countries have gotten jobs because textile mills have opened there. And tens of thousands of Canadian workers have gotten better-paying jobs than textile workers because other export industries have expanded and created more jobs than have been destroyed.

Second, imports create jobs. They create jobs for retailers that sell imported goods and firms that service those goods. They also create jobs by creating incomes in the rest of the world, some of which are spent on imports of Canadian-made goods and services.

Although protection does save particular jobs, it does so at inordinate cost. A striking example of the cost of quotas is that of quotas on the import of textiles. Quotas imposed under an international agreement called the Multifibre Arrangement (that is now being phased out) have protected textile jobs, especially in the United States. It has been estimated that because of the quotas, 72,000 jobs existed in textiles in the United States that would otherwise have disappeared. But each textile job saved cost more than $300,000 a year in added clothing costs!

Allows Us to Compete with Cheap Foreign Labour

With the removal of protective tariffs in Canadian and U.S. trade with Mexico, Texan entrepreneur Ross Perot said he would hear a "giant sucking sound" of jobs rushing to Mexico (one of which is shown in the cartoon). Let's see what's wrong with this view.

The labour cost of a unit of output equals the wage rate divided by labour productivity. For example, if a Canadian auto worker earns $30 an hour

"I don't know what the hell happened—one minute I'm at work in Flint, Michigan, then there's a giant sucking sound and suddenly here I am in Mexico."

and produces 15 units of output an hour, the average labour cost of a unit of output is $2. If a Mexican auto assembly worker earns $3 an hour and produces 1 unit of output an hour, the average labour cost of a unit of output is $3. Other things remaining the same, the higher a worker's productivity, the higher is the worker's wage rate. High-wage workers have high productivity. Low-wage workers have low productivity.

Although high-wage Canadian workers are more productive, on the average, than low-wage Mexican workers, there are differences across industries. Canadian labour is relatively more productive in some activities than in others. For example, the productivity of Canadian workers in producing financial services and telephone systems is relatively higher than in the production of metals and some standardized machine parts. The activities in which Canadian workers are relatively more productive than their Mexican counterparts are those in which Canada has a *comparative advantage*. By engaging in free trade, increasing our production and exports of the goods and services in which we have a comparative advantage and decreasing our production and increasing our imports of the goods and services in which our trading partners have a comparative advantage, we can make ourselves and the citizens of other countries better off.

Brings Diversity and Stability

A diversified investment portfolio is less risky than one that has all the eggs in one basket. The same is true for an economy's production. A diversified economy fluctuates less than an economy that produces only one or two goods.

But a big, rich, diversified economy like that of Canada does not have this type of problem. Even a country like Saudi Arabia that produces almost only one good (oil) can benefit from specializing in the activity at which it has a comparative advantage and then investing in a wide range of other countries to bring greater stability to its income and consumption.

Penalizes Lax Environmental Standards

A new argument for protection is that many poorer countries, such as Mexico, do not have the same environment policies that we have and, because they are willing to pollute and we are not, we cannot compete with them without tariffs. So if they want free trade with the richer and "greener" countries, they must clean up their environments to our standards.

This argument for trade restrictions is weak. First, not all poorer countries have significantly lower environmental standards than Canada has. Many poor countries and the former communist countries of Eastern Europe do have bad environment records. But some countries enforce strict laws. Second, a poor country cannot afford to be as concerned about its environment as a rich country can. The best hope for a better environment in Mexico and in other developing countries is rapid income growth through free trade. As their incomes grow, developing countries will have the *means* to match their desires to improve their environment. Third, poor countries have a comparative advantage at doing "dirty" work, which helps rich countries achieve higher environment standards than they otherwise could.

Protects National Culture

The national culture argument for protection is one of the most often heard in Canada and Europe and just about everywhere else except for the United States.

The expressed fear is that free trade in books, magazines, movies, and television programs means U.S. domination and the end of local culture. So, the reasoning continues, it is necessary to protect domestic "culture" industries from free international trade to ensure the survival of a national cultural identity.

Protection of these industries is common and takes the form of nontariff barriers. For example, local content regulations on radio and television broadcasting and in magazines are often required.

The cultural identity argument for protection has no merit and it is one more example of "rent-seeking" (see Chapter 13, p. 276). Writers, publishers, and broadcasters want to limit foreign competition so that they can earn larger economic profits. There is no actual danger to national culture. In fact, many of the creators of so-called American cultural products are not Americans, but the talented citizens of other countries, ensuring the survival of their national cultural identities in Hollywood! Also, if national culture is in danger, there is no surer way of helping it on its way out than by impoverishing the nation whose culture it is. And protection is an effective way of doing just that.

Prevents Rich Countries from Exploiting Developing Countries

Another new argument for protection is that international trade must be restricted to prevent the people of the rich industrial world from exploiting the poorer people of the developing countries, forcing them to work for slave wages.

Wage rates in some developing countries are indeed very low. But by trading with developing countries, we increase the demand for the goods that these countries produce, and, more significantly, we increase the demand for their labour. When the demand for labour in developing countries increases, the wage rate also increases. So, far from exploiting people in developing countries, trade improves their opportunities and increases their incomes.

We have reviewed the arguments that are commonly heard in favour of protection and the counter-arguments against them. There is one counter-argument to protection that is general and quite overwhelming. Protection invites retaliation and can trigger a trade war. The best example of a trade war occurred during the Great Depression of the 1930s when the United States, Canada, and European countries erected high trade barriers. Country after country retaliated with its yet higher tariff, and in a short period, world trade had almost disappeared. The costs to all countries were large and led to a renewed international resolve to avoid such self-defeating moves in the future. They also led to the creation of GATT and are the impetus behind the WTO, NAFTA, APEC, and the European Union.

R E V I E W   Q U I Z

- Is there any merit to the view that we should restrict international trade to achieve national security goals, to stimulate the growth of new industries, or to restrain foreign monopoly?
- Is there any merit to the view that we should restrict international trade to save jobs, compensate for low foreign wages, make the economy more diversified, compensate for costly environmental policies, protect national culture, or protect developing countries from being exploited?
- Is there any merit to the view that we should restrict international trade for any reason? What is the main argument against trade restrictions?

Why Is International Trade Restricted?

WHY, DESPITE ALL THE ARGUMENTS AGAINST protection, is trade restricted? There are two key reasons:

- Tariff revenue
- Rent seeking

Tariff Revenue

Government revenue is costly to collect. In the developed countries such as Canada, a well-organized tax-collection system is in place that can generate billions of dollars of income tax and sales tax revenues. This tax-collecting system is made possible by the fact that firms that must keep audited financial accounts do most of the economic transactions. Without reliable accounts, the revenue collection agencies (Revenue Canada in Canada) would be severely hampered in their work. Even with audited financial accounts, some proportion of potential tax revenue is lost. Nonetheless, for the industrialized countries, the income tax and sales taxes are the major sources of revenue and the tariff plays a very small role.

But governments in developing countries have a difficult time collecting taxes from their citizens. Much economic activity takes place in an informal economy with few financial records. So only a small amount of revenue is collected from income taxes and sales taxes in these countries. The one area in which economic transactions are well recorded and audited is in international trade. So this activity is an attractive base for tax collection in these countries and is used much more extensively than in the developed countries.

Rent Seeking

The major reason why international trade is restricted is because of rent seeking. Free trade increases consumption possibilities *on the average* but not everyone shares in the gain and some people even lose. Free trade brings benefits to some and imposes costs on others, with total benefits exceeding total costs. It is the uneven distribution of costs and benefits that is the principal source of impediment to achieving more liberal international trade.

Returning to our example of trade in cars and grain between Farmland and Mobilia, the benefits to Farmland from free trade accrue to all the producers of grain and those producers of cars who would not have to bear the costs of adjusting to a smaller car industry. These costs are transition costs, not permanent costs. The costs of moving to free trade are borne by those car producers and their employees who have to become grain producers. The number of people who gain will, in general, be enormous compared with the number who lose. The gain per person will therefore be rather small. The loss per person to those who bear the loss will be large. Because the loss that falls on those who bear it is large, it will pay those people to incur considerable expense to lobby against free trade. On the other hand, it will not pay those who gain to organize to achieve free trade. The gain from trade for any one individual is too small for that individual to spend much time or money on a political organization to achieve free trade. The loss from free trade will be seen as being so great by those bearing that loss that they *will* find it profitable to join a political organization to prevent free trade. Each group is optimizing—weighing benefits against costs and choosing the best action for themselves. The anti-free-trade group will, however, undertake a larger quantity of political lobbying than will the pro-free-trade group.

Compensating Losers

If, in total, the gains from free international trade exceed the losses, why don't those who stand to gain from free trade offer to compensate those who stand to lose so that everyone votes for free trade?

The main answer is that there are serious obstacles to providing direct and correctly calculated compensation. First, the cost of identifying the losers from free trade and of estimating the value of their losses would be enormous.

Second, it would never be clear whether a person who has fallen on hard times is suffering because of free trade or for other reasons, perhaps reasons that are largely under the control of the individual.

Third, some people who look like losers at one point in time may, in fact, end up gaining. The young autoworker that loses her job in Windsor and becomes a computer assembly worker in Ottawa resents the loss of work and the need to move. But a year or two later, looking back on events, she counts herself fortunate. She has made a move that has increased her income and given her greater job security.

Despite the absence of explicit compensation, those who lose from a change in protection do receive some compensation. But compensation is not restricted to the losers from changes in trade policy. In Canada (and in all the other rich industrial countries) elaborate schemes are in place to ensure that people who suffer from economic change receive help during their transition to new activities.

Two major forms of compensation in Canada arise from inter-provincial fiscal transfers and employment insurance. Inter-provincial fiscal transfers result in tax dollars collected in the rich and expanding regions of the country being spent in the poorer regions. Employment insurance provides substantial compensation for workers who lose their jobs regardless of the reason for the job loss. Jobs lost because of changes in international protection are included among those for which benefits are paid.

But because we do not explicitly compensate the losers from free international trade, protectionism remains a popular and permanent feature of our national economic and political life.

Compensating Losers from Protection

There is no general presumption that it is the ones who lose from a tariff cut that should be compensated. Protection brings losses to the consumer and the view might be taken that the winners from protection should compensate the losers from protection. When this perspective is taken, the removal of protection would mean the removal of the compensation of the losers by the winners and there would be no further adjustments needed. What is fair is a tricky matter (as we explain in Chapter 6, pp. 120–123.)

R E V I E W   Q U I Z

- What are the two main reasons for imposing tariffs on imports?
- What type of country benefits most from the revenue from tariffs? Does Canada need to use tariffs to raise revenue for the government?
- If trade restrictions are costly, why do we use them? Why don't the people who gain from trade organize a political force that is strong enough to ensure their interests are protected?

The North American Free Trade Agreement

THE NORTH AMERICAN FREE TRADE AGREEMENT came into effect on January 1, 1994. It was the outgrowth of an earlier Canada–United States Free Trade Agreement, which was signed in October 1987. Both agreements were struck only after several years of intense negotiations and, on the Canadian side of the border, an intense political debate. First, let's look at the terms of the Canada–United States agreement of 1987 and at the progress made in achieving freer trade between two of the world's largest trading partners.

The Terms of the Canada–United States Agreement

The main terms of the Canada–United States Free Trade Agreement are:

- Tariffs to be phased out through 1999
- Nontariff barriers to be reduced
- Free trade in energy products, with energy resource sharing in times of national shortage
- More freedom of trade in services
- Future negotiations to eliminate subsidies
- Creation of dispute-settling mechanisms

Removal of Tariffs   Scheduled tariff cuts began on January 1, 1989 and were completed on January 1, 1998. But tariff protection remains in place and an atmosphere of tension prevails in many areas. Agriculture remains effectively protected with new tariffs that have replaced old quotas. And a series of so-called *countervailing duties* have been introduced to offset the effects of domestic subsidies. Further, several so-called *antidumping duties* have also been introduced in cases in which it is alleged that products are being exported at a price below the cost of production.

Nontariff Barriers   Nontariff barriers such as government procurement policies of buying local products are removed by the agreement. Subsequent to entering into the free trade agreement, Canada and the United States took on additional obligations as members of the WTO, which require the removal of agricultural quotas. So many agricultural quotas have been removed but they have been replaced with tariffs. So despite the free trade agreement, we remain a long way from achieving free trade in agricultural products.

Energy Products   Free trade in energy products existed before the free trade agreement but the agreement ratified the intent to maintain that arrangement. The agreement that scarce energy resources will be shared in times of national shortage became a controversial one. In effect, what the energy sharing clause amounts to is an agreement that governments will not intervene in energy markets to prevent firms from selling their energy to the other country.

Trade in Services   International trade in services has been expanding more quickly than trade in manufactured goods in recent years. The free trade agreement, recognizing this factor and seeking to facilitate further expansion of trade in services between the United States and Canada, incorporates two principles: the *right of establishment* and *national treatment*. The right of establishment means that American firms have the right to set up branches in Canada and Canadian firms have the right to set up operations in the United States. National treatment means that each country will treat the goods and firms and investors of the other country as if they were operating within its own borders.

Future Negotiations on Subsidies   In both the United States and Canada, there are many subsidies, especially on agricultural products. The presence of subsidies causes problems and makes it legitimate under the agreement for the country importing subsidized goods to impose countervailing duties. As we have just noted, several such duties have been imposed.

Dispute-Settling Mechanisms   The Free Trade Agreement included two dispute-settling mechanisms: one to settle disputes relating to all aspects of the agreement and the other to deal with applications of countervailing duties and antidumping laws in either country. For example, the United States has applied for and received permission to impose countervailing duties on Canadian exports of Durum wheat, lumber products, poultry, and live hogs. In each case, the United States accuses Canada of subsidizing these industries unfairly so that Canadian exports are cheaper than U.S. producers can supply them.

The Extension of the Agreement: NAFTA

The North American Free Trade Agreement (NAFTA) is an agreement between Canada, the United States and Mexico that has six objectives. They are to:

■ Eliminate trade barriers
■ Promote conditions of fair competition
■ Increase investment opportunities
■ Protect intellectual property rights
■ Create an effective dispute resolution mechanism
■ Establish a framework for the expansion of the agreement to include other nations in the hemisphere

Effects of the Free Trade Agreement

Working out the effects of an agreement as complex as NAFTA is difficult, and there is no general consensus on what the effects have been. The theory that you have studied in this chapter predicts that the removal of tariffs will produce an increase in the volume of international trade. That is, the theory predicts that Canadians will increasingly specialize in those activities at which they have a comparative advantage and Mexicans and Americans will specialize in a different range of activities and that the three countries will exchange a larger volume of goods and services.

As predicted, trade between the three countries has increased. During the first five years of NAFTA, Canada's trade with the United States increased by 80 percent and Canada's trade with Mexico doubled.

The trade expansion that followed the entry of Mexico in 1995 was especially dramatic. Mexico's exports increased by 31 percent (in U.S. dollar value) in 1995 and by 21 percent in 1996 compared with increases that averaged less than 15 percent a year during the two years before the agreement. But trade expansion with Mexico has not been in one direction. Mexico's imports also increased following the agreement by 23 percent in both 1996 and 1997.

During the 1990s, Canada's exports have expanded from less than 30 percent of total production to 36 percent of production and Canada's imports have increased from 27 percent to 34 percent of total expenditure.

Canada greatly increased its exports of advertising services, office and telecommunication equipment, paper, and transportation services. And its imports of meat and dairy products, communications services, clothing, furniture, and processed foods and beverages also increased by a large percentage.

These huge changes in exports and imports brought gains from increased specialization and exchange. But they also brought a heavy toll of adjustment. Thousands of jobs were lost in the declining sectors and new jobs were created in the expanding sectors. The amount of job destruction in the years following the free trade agreement was historically high and the unemployment rate rose for three successive years. Only during the Great Depression did the rate of job destruction exceed that in the late 1980s and early 1990s. To what extent a high rate of labour market turnover was caused by the free trade agreement is unclear and controversial. But the net outcome of NAFTA appears to be strongly positive. More than a million new Canadian jobs were created between 1994 and 1999.

R E V I E W   Q U I Z

■ By when, under the Canada–United States Free Trade Agreement, were all tariffs on trade between Canada and the United States intended to be phase out? What progress and setbacks have we experienced?
■ What effect has NAFTA had on nontariff barriers?
■ What effect has NAFTA had on trade in services?
■ How has the volume of trade among Canada, the United States, and Mexico changed during the period since NAFTA was established?

◆ You've now seen how free international trade enables all nations to gain from specialization and trade. By producing goods in which we have a comparative advantage and trading some of our production for that of others, we expand our consumption possibilities. Placing impediments on that trade restricts the extent to which we can gain from specialization and trade. By opening our country up to free international trade, the market for the things that we sell expands and the relative price rises. The market for the things that we buy also expands and the relative price falls. *Reading Between the Lines* on pp. 820–821 looks at Canada's international trade experience during 1999 and at the astonishing increases in trade that have occurred under NAFTA.

Net Exports Surplus

NATIONAL POST, AUGUST 20, 1999

Canada's trade surplus continues to rise

Canada's June trade surplus climbed to $2.808-billion, exceeding expectations, as booming U.S. demand for machinery drove exports to their highest level ever, Statistics Canada said yesterday.

Economists had expected a $2.5-billion surplus. May's surplus was revised lower to $2.348-billion from the $2.444-billion reported earlier, StatsCan said. ...

June's surplus reflected an 8% jump in machinery and equipment exports as shipments of aircraft and plane parts increased, the bulk headed to the United States, which takes about 85% of Canada's exports and is completing a decade of economic expansion. ...

June's exports climbed 1.9% to $29.418-billion, topping the May record of $28.880-billion. Exports to the United States exceeded imports by $5.023-billion, up from $4.258-billion in May and surpassing the previous benchmark of $4.594-billion set in March.

Exports to the U.S. surged 2.4% to a record $25.255-billion. ...

Imports, meanwhile, gained 0.3% to $26.610-billion from $26.532-billion, as increased energy and machinery imports were partly offset by lower agricultural and industrial imports.

The trade surplus bolstered expectations that economic growth in Canada is picking up. Yesterday, the Bank of Canada said it expects the economy to expand at a 3.75% pace this year, with little inflation. Earlier this year the central bank forecast growth of closer to 3.25%. ...

Essence of the Story

■ Statistics Canada reported that Canada's trade surplus in June was $2.8 billion. Exports increased 1.9 percent to $29.4 billion and imports grew 0.3 percent to $26.6 billion.

■ June exports are the highest ever.

■ The United States buys 85 percent of Canada's exports.

■ The United States is completing a decade of economic growth.

■ The trade surplus increased expectations that economic growth in Canada is increasing. The Bank of Canada expects the Canadian economy to expand 3.75 percent in 1999.

Economic Analysis

■ Canada's biggest trading partner is the United States. So Canadian exports are strongly influenced by U.S. imports. And U.S. imports are strongly influenced by U.S. real GDP.

■ Figure 1 shows the relationship between U.S. real GDP and Canadian exports to the United States. You can see a strong positive relationship between these two variables.

■ As the United States has experienced real GDP growth throughout the last decade, Canadian exports to the United States have increased.

■ You can also see in Fig. 1 that Canadian exports became more responsive to U.S. real GDP during the 1990s after the Free Trade Agreement came into effect.

■ Canadian imports are determined primarily by Canadian real GDP. Figure 2 shows the relationship between these two variables. You can see a similar pattern to that in Fig. 1. There is a strong positive relationship between Canadian imports and real GDP, and imports became more responsive to real GDP during the 1990s.

■ Figure 3 shows real GDP growth in Canada and the United States. In 1998, U.S. real GDP grew at a faster rate than did Canadian real GDP. The relative growth rates, in part, contribute to the faster growth of Canadian exports than of Canadian imports and lead to the big trade surplus.

■ Because an increase in exports results in an increase in real GDP, other things remaining the same, the article is correct when it states that an increase in the trade surplus raises expectations that Canada's economic growth rate is increasing.

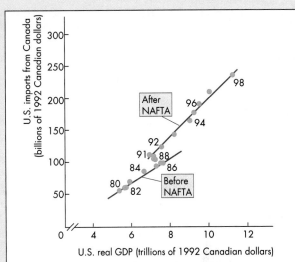

Figure 1 Canadian exports to the United States

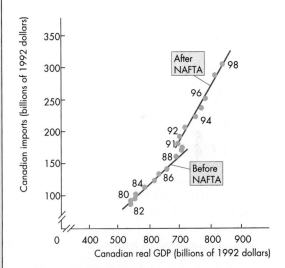

Figure 2 Canadian imports

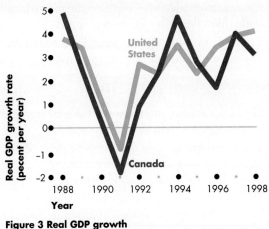

Figure 3 Real GDP growth

821

S U M M A R Y

Key Points

Patterns and Trends in International Trade (p. 802)

■ Large flows of trade take place between countries, most of which is in manufactured goods exchanged among rich industrialized countries.

■ Between 1978 and 1998, the volume of Canadian trade increased from one-fifth to more than one-third of total production.

Comparative Advantage and International Trade (pp. 803–804)

■ When opportunity costs between countries diverge, comparative advantage enables countries to gain from international trade.

Gains from Trade (pp. 804–807)

■ By increasing the production of the goods in which a country has a comparative advantage and then trading some of the increased output, the country can consume at points outside its production possibility frontier.

■ In the absence of international borrowing and lending, trade is balanced as prices adjust to reflect the international supply of and demand for goods.

■ The terms of trade balance the production and consumption plans of the trading parties. At the equilibrium price, trade is balanced.

Gains from Trade in Reality (p. 808)

■ Comparative advantage explains the international trade that takes place in the real world.

■ But trade in similar goods arises from economies of scale in the face of diversified tastes.

Trade Restrictions (pp. 809–812)

■ Countries restrict international trade by imposing tariffs, nontariff barriers, and quotas.

■ Trade restrictions raise the domestic price of imported goods, decrease the volume of imports, and reduce the total value of imports.

■ Trade restrictions reduce the total value of exports by the same amount as the reduction in the value of imports.

The Case Against Protection (pp. 813–816)

■ Arguments that protection is necessary for security, infant industries, and to prevent dumping are weak.

■ Arguments that protection saves jobs, allows us to compete with cheap foreign labour, makes the economy diversified and stable, protects national culture, and is needed to offset the costs of environmental policies are fatally flawed.

Why Is International Trade Restricted? (pp. 816–817)

■ Trade is restricted because tariffs raise government revenue and because protection brings a small loss to a large number of people and a large gain per person to a small number of people.

The North American Free Trade Agreement (pp. 818–819)

■ NAFTA is an agreement between Canada, the United States, and Mexico, which began in 1995 and grew from a previous Canada–U.S. agreement.

■ Under NAFTA, trade has expanded more rapidly than before the agreement.

Key Figures ◆

Key Terms

PROBLEMS

*1. The table provides information about Virtual Reality's production possibilities.

TV sets (per day)		Computers (per day)
0	and	36
10	and	35
20	and	33
30	and	30
40	and	26
50	and	21
60	and	15
70	and	8
80	and	0

a. Calculate Virtual Reality's opportunity cost of a TV set when it produces 10 sets a day.

b. Calculate Virtual Reality's opportunity cost of a TV set when it produces 40 sets a day.

c. Calculate Virtual Reality's opportunity cost of a TV set when it produces 70 sets a day.

d. Using the answers to parts (a), (b), and (c), graph the relationship between the opportunity cost of a TV set and the quantity of TV sets produced in Virtual Reality.

2. The table provides information about Vital Signs' production possibilities.

TV sets (per day)		Computers (per day)
0	and	18.0
10	and	17.5
20	and	16.5
30	and	15.0
40	and	13.0
50	and	10.5
60	and	7.5
70	and	4.0
80	and	0

a. Calculate Vital Signs' opportunity cost of a TV set when it produces 10 sets a day.

b. Calculate Vital Signs' opportunity cost of a TV set when it produces 40 sets a day.

c. Calculate Vital Signs' opportunity cost of a TV set when it produces 70 sets a day.

d. Using the answers to parts (a), (b), and (c), sketch the relationship between the oppor-

tunity cost of a TV set and the quantity of TV sets produced in Vital Signs.

*3. Suppose that with no international trade, Virtual Reality in problem 1 produces and consumes 10 TV sets a day and Vital Signs produces and consumes 60 TV sets a day. Now suppose that the two countries begin to trade with each other.

a. Which country exports TV sets?

b. What adjustments are made to the amount of each good produced by each country?

c. What adjustments are made to the amount of each good consumed by each country?

d. What can you say about the terms of trade (the price of a TV set expressed as computers per TV set) under free trade?

4. Suppose that with no international trade, Virtual Reality in problem 1 produces and consumes 50 TV sets a day and Vital Signs produces and consumes 20 TV sets a day. Now suppose that the two countries begin to trade with each other.

a. Which country exports TV sets?

b. What adjustments are made to the amount of each good produced by each country?

c. What adjustments are made to the amount of each good consumed by each country?

d. What can you say about the terms of trade (the price of a TV set expressed as computers per TV set) under free trade?

*5. Compare the total quantities of each good produced in problems 1 and 2 with the total quantities of each good produced in problems 3 and 4.

a. Does free trade increase or decrease the total quantities of TV sets and computers produced in both cases? Why or why not?

b. What happens to the price of a TV set in Virtual Reality in the two cases? Why does it rise in one case and fall in the other?

c. What happens to the price of a computer in Vital Signs in the two cases? Why does it rise in one case and fall in the other?

6. Compare the international trade in problem 3 with that in problem 4.

a. Why does Virtual Reality export TV sets in one of the cases and import them in the other case?

b. Do the TV producers or the computer producers gain in each case?

c. Do consumers gain in each case?

*7. The figure depicts the international market for soybeans.

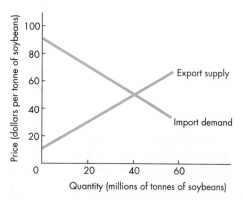

a. If the two countries did not engage in international trade, what would be the prices of soybeans in the two countries?
b. What are the terms of trade if there is free trade between these countries?
c. What quantities of soybeans are exported and imported?
d. What is the balance of trade?

8. If the soybean importing country in problem 7 imposes a tariff of $2 per tonne, what are the terms of trade and what quantity of soybeans gets traded internationally? What is the price of soybeans in the importing country? Calculate the tariff revenue.

*9. If the soybean importing country in problem 7 imposes a quota of 30 million tonnes on imports of soybeans,
a. What is the price of soybeans in the importing country?
b. What is the revenue from the quota?
c. Who gets this revenue?

10. If the soybean exporting country in problem 7 imposes a VER of 30 million tonnes on its exports of soybeans,
a. What are the terms of trade now?
b. What is the revenue of soybean growers in the exporting country?
c. Which country gains from the VER?

CRITICAL THINKING

1. Study *Reading Between the Lines* on pp. 820–821, and then answer the following questions:
a. Why are Canada's exports influenced by the performance of the U.S. economy?
b. Does the U.S. economy exert a powerful influence or a weak influence on Canadian exports? Explain?
c. What effect, if any, does NAFTA appear to have had on Canadian exports and on the U.S. influence on those exports?
d. Why do you think that Canada's exports have expanded more than its imports?
e. Does the performance of the Canadian economy influence U.S. exports?
f. Does the Canadian economy exert a powerful influence or a weak influence on U.S. exports? Explain.

2. Visit the Parkin-Bade Web site and study the *Web Reading Between the Lines* on steel dumping. Then answer the following questions:
a. What is the argument in the news article for limiting steel imports?
b. Evaluate the argument. Is it correct or incorrect in your opinion? Why?
c. Would you vote to limit steel imports? Why or why not?
d. Would you vote differently if you lived in another steel-producing country? Why or why not?

3. Use the links on the Parkin-Bade Web site to visit the Department of Foreign Affairs and International Trade and the Public Citizen Global Trade. Study "Five Years of NAFTA: A Scorecard" and "School of Real-Life Results Report Card." Then answer the following questions.
a. What is the picture painted by the Department of Foreign Affairs?
b. What is the picture painted by the Public Citizen?
c. Whose picture do you think is correct and why?
d. Would you vote to maintain NAFTA? Why or why not?
e. Would you vote to expand NAFTA to include other countries? Why or why not?

Glossary

Glossary

Absolute advantage   A person has an absolute advantage in the production of two goods if that person can produce more of both goods than another person; a country has an absolute advantage if its output per unit of inputs of all goods is larger than that of another country.

Anti-combine law   A law that regulates and prohibits certain kinds of market behaviour, such as monopoly and monopolistic practices.

Average cost pricing rule   A rule that sets price equal to average total cost.

Average fixed cost   Total fixed cost per unit of output.

Average product   The average product of a resource. It equals total product divided by the quantity of the resource employed.

Average tax rate   The percentage of income that is paid in tax.

Average total cost   Total cost per unit of output.

Average variable cost   Total variable cost per unit of output.

Balance of trade   The value of exports minus the value of imports.

Barriers to entry   Legal or natural constraints that protect a firm from potential competitors.

Big tradeoff   The conflict between equity and efficiency.

Bilateral monopoly   A situation in which there is a single seller (a monopoly) and a single buyer (a monopsony).

Black market   An illegal trading arrangement in which the price exceeds the legally imposed price ceiling.

Budget line   The limits to a household's consumption choices.

Capacity output   The output at which average total cost is a minimum—the output at the bottom of the U-shaped *ATC* curve.

Capital   The equipment, buildings, tools, and manufactured goods that we use to produce other goods and services.

Capital accumulation   The growth of capital resources.

Capture theory   A theory of regulation that states that the regulations are supplied to satisfy the demand of producers to maximize producer surplus—to maximize economic profit.

Cartel   A group of firms that has entered into a collusive agreement to restrict output and increase prices and profits.

Ceteris paribus   Other things being equal—all other relevant things remaining the same.

Change in demand   A change in buyers' plans that occurs when some influence on those plans changes other than the price of the good. It is illustrated by a shift of the demand curve.

Change in supply   A change in sellers' plans that occurs when some influence on those plans changes other than the price of the good. It is illustrated by a shift of the supply curve.

Change in the quantity demanded   A change in buyers' plans that occurs when the price of a good changes but all other influences on buyers' plans remain unchanged. It is illustrated by a movement along the demand curve.

Change in the quantity supplied   A change in sellers' plans that occurs when the price of a good changes but all other influences on sellers' plans remain unchanged. It is illustrated by a movement along the supply curve.

Coase theorem   The proposition that if property rights exist and transactions costs are low, private transactions are efficient—equivalently, with property rights and low transaction costs, there are no externalities.

Collective bargaining   A process of negotiation between employers or their representatives and unions.

Collusive agreement   An agreement between two (or more) producers to restrict output so as to raise prices and profits.

Command system   A system in which some people give orders and other people obey them.

Comparative advantage   A person or country has a comparative advantage in an activity if that person or country can perform the activity at a lower opportunity cost than anyone else or any other country.

Complement   A good that is used in conjunction with another good.

Constant returns to scale   Features of a firm's technology that lead to constant long-run average cost as output increases. When constant returns to scale are present, the *LRAC* curve is horizontal.

Consumer equilibrium   A situation in which a consumer has allocated all his or her available income in the way that maximizes his or her total utility.

Consumer surplus   The value that the consumer gets from each unit of a good minus the price paid for it.

Contestable market   A market in which one firm (or a small number of firms) operates but in which entry and exit are free, so the firm (or firms) in the market faces competition from potential entrants.

Cooperative equilibrium   The outcome of a collusive agreement between players when the players make and share the monopoly profit.

Copyright   A government-sanctioned exclusive right granted to the inventor of a good, service, or productive process to produce, use, and sell the invention for a given number of years.

Craft union   A group of workers who have a similar range of skills but work for many different firms in many different industries and regions.

Cross elasticity of demand   The responsiveness of the demand for a good to a change in the price of a substitute or complement, other things remaining the same. It is calculated as the percentage change in the quantity demanded of the good divided by the percentage change in the price of the substitute or complement.

Cross-section graph A graph that shows the values of an economic variable for different groups in a population at a point in time.

Crown corporations Publicly owned firms in Canada.

Deadweight loss A measure of inefficiency. It is equal to the loss in total surplus (consumer surplus plus producer surplus) when output is below or above its efficient level.

Demand The relationship between the quantity of a good that consumers plan to buy and the price of the good, when all other influences on buyers' plans remain the same. It is described by a demand schedule and illustrated by a demand curve.

Demand curve A curve that shows the relationship between the quantity demanded of a good and its price when all other influences on consumers' planned expenditures remain the same.

Derived demand Demand for a productive resource which is derived from the demand for the goods and services produced by the resource.

Diminishing marginal rate of substitution The general tendency for the marginal rate of substitution to diminish as the consumer moves along an indifference curve, increasing consumption of the good measured on the *x*-axis and decreasing consumption of the good measured on the *y*-axis.

Diminishing marginal returns The tendency for the marginal product of an additional resource eventually to be less than the marginal product of the previous unit of the resource.

Diminishing marginal utility The marginal utility that a consumer gets from a good decreases as more of the good is consumed.

Direct relationship A relationship between two variables that move in the same direction.

Discounting The conversion of a future amount of money to its present value.

Diseconomies of scale Features of a firm's technology that leads to rising long-run average cost as output increases.

Dominant strategy equilibrium The outcome of a game in which there is a single best strategy (a dominant strategy) for each player, regardless of the strategy of the other players.

Dumping The sale of a good or service to a foreign country at a price that is less than the cost of producing the good or service.

Duopoly A market structure in which only two producers compete.

Dynamic comparative advantage A comparative advantage that a person or country possesses as a result of having specialized in a particular activity and then, as a result of learning-by-doing, having become the producer with the lowest opportunity cost.

Economic depreciation The change in the market value of capital over a given period.

Economic efficiency A situation that occurs when a firm produces a given output at least cost.

Economic growth The expansion of production possibilities that results from capital accumulation and technological change.

Economic model A description of some aspect of the economic world that includes only those features of the world that are needed for the purpose at hand.

Economic profit A firm's total revenue minus its opportunity cost.

Economic rent The income received by the owner of a resource over and above the amount required to induce that owner to offer the resource for use.

Economic theory A generalization that summarizes what we think we understand about the economic choices that people make and the performance of industries and entire economies.

Economics The science that studies the choices that people make when wants exceed the available resources— when resources are scarce.

Economies of scale Features of a firm's technology that lead to falling long-run average cost as output increases.

Economies of scope A situation in which a firm uses specialized (and often expensive) resources to produce a range of goods and services.

Efficient Resource use is efficient when we produce the goods and services that we value most highly.

Efficient allocation An allocation of resources that occurs when we produce the goods and services that people value most highly.

Elastic demand Demand with a price elasticity greater than 1; other things remaining the same, the percentage change in the quantity demanded exceeds the percentage change in price.

Elasticity of supply The responsiveness of the quantity supplied of a good to a change in its price when all other influences on selling plans remain the same.

Entrepreneurship The resource that organizes labour, land, and capital. Entrepreneurs make business decisions, bear the risks that arise from these decisions, and come up with new ideas about what, how, where, and when to produce.

Equilibrium price The price at which the quantity demanded equals the quantity supplied.

Equilibrium quantity The quantity bought and sold at the equilibrium price.

Excise tax A tax on the sale of a particular commodity.

Exhaustible natural resource A natural resource that can be used only once and that cannot be replaced once it has been used.

Expenditure   The price of a good multiplied by the quantity of the good that is bought is the expenditure on a good.

Exports   The goods and services that we sell to people in other countries.

External benefits   Benefits that accrue to people other than the buyer of the good.

External costs   Costs that are not borne by the producer of the good but borne by someone else.

External diseconomies   Factors outside the control of a firm that raise the firm's costs as industry output increases.

External economies   Factors beyond the control of a firm that lower the firm's costs as the industry output increases.

Externality   A cost or a benefit that arises from an economic transaction and that falls on people who do not participate in that transaction.

Factors of production   The economy's productive resources—land, labour, capital, and entrepreneurial ability.

Farm marketing board   A regulatory agency that intervenes in an agricultural market to stabilize the price of an agricultural product.

Firm   An institution that hires productive resources and that organizes those resources to produce and sell goods and services.

Four-firm concentration ratio   A measure of market power that is calculated as the percentage of the value of sales accounted for by the four largest firms in an industry.

Free rider   A person who consumes a good without paying for it.

Game theory   The main tool that economists use to analyze strategic behaviour—behaviour that takes into account the expected behavior of others

and the mutual recognition of interdependence.

General Agreement on Tariffs and Trade (GATT)   An international agreement designed to reduce tariffs on international trade.

Goods and services   All the things that people are willing to pay for.

Herfindahl-Hirschman Index   A measure of market power that is calculated as the square of the market share of each firm (as a percentage) summed over the largest 50 firms (or over all firms if there are fewer than 50) in a market.

Human capital   The skill and knowledge that people obtain from education and on-the-job training.

Implicit rental rate   The rent that a firm pays to itself for the use of its own assets.

Imports   The goods and services that we buy from people in other countries.

Incentive   An inducement to take a particular action.

Incentive system   A method of organizing production that uses a market-like mechanism inside the firm.

Income   The amount of money that someone earns by working.

Income effect   The change in consumption that results from a change in the consumer's income, other things remaining the same.

Income elasticity of demand   The responsiveness of demand to a change in income, other things remaining the same. It is calculated as the percentage change in the quantity demanded divided by the percentage change in income.

Indifference curve   A line that shows combinations of goods among which a consumer is indifferent.

Industrial union   A group of workers who have a variety of skills and job types but work for the same firm or industry.

Inelastic demand   A demand with a price elasticity between 0 and 1; the percentage change in the quantity demanded is less than the percentage change in price.

Infant-industry argument   The argument that protection is necessary to enable an infant industry to grow into a mature industry that can compete in world markets.

Inferior good   A good for which demand decreases as income increases.

Inflation   A process in which the price level is rising and money is losing value.

Intellectual property rights   Property rights for discoveries owned by the creators of knowledge.

Inverse relationship   A relationship between variables that move in opposite directions.

Labour   The time and effort that people allocate to producing goods and services.

Labour union   An organized group of workers whose purpose is to increase wages and to influence other job conditions for its members.

Land   All the gifts of nature that we use to produce goods and services.

Law of diminishing returns   As a firm uses more of a variable input with a given quantity of other inputs (fixed inputs), the marginal product of the variable input eventually diminishes.

Learning-by-doing   People become more productive in an activity (learn) just by repeatedly producing a particular good or service (doing).

Legal monopoly   A market in which competition and entry are restricted by the granting of a public franchise, government licence, patent, or copyright.

Limit pricing   The practice of charging a price below the monopoly profit-maximizing price and producing a quantity greater than that at which marginal revenue equals marginal cost so as to deter entry.

Linear relationship   A relationship between two variables that is illustrated by a straight line.

Local public good   A public good that is consumed by all the people who live in a particular area.

Long run   A time frame in which the quantities of all resources can be varied.

Long-run average cost curve   The relationship between the lowest attainable average total cost and output when both the plant size and labour are varied.

Long-run industry supply curve   A curve that shows how the quantity supplied by an industry varies as the market price varies after all the possible adjustments have been made, including changes in plant size and the number of firms in the industry.

Lorenz curve   A curve that graphs the cumulative percentage of income or wealth against the cumulative percentage of families or population.

Low-income cutoff   The income level, determined separately for different types of families (for example, single persons, couples, one parent), that is selected such that families with incomes below that limit normally spend 54.7 percent or more of their income on food, shelter, and clothing.

Macroeconomics   The study of the national economy and the global economy, the way in which economic aggregates grow and fluctuate, and the effects of government actions on them.

Margin   When a choice is changed by a small amount or by a little at a time, the choice is made at the margin.

Marginal benefit   The benefit that a person receives from consuming one more unit of a good or service. It is measured as the maximum amount that a person is willing to pay for one more unit of the good or service.

Marginal cost   The opportunity cost of producing one more unit of a good or service. It is the best alternative forgone. It is calculated as the increase in total cost divided by the increase in output.

Marginal cost pricing rule   A rule that sets the price equal to the marginal cost.

Marginal product   The change in total product that results from a one-unit increase in the variable input. It is calculated as the increase in total product divided by the increase in the variable input employed, when the quantities of all other resources are constant.

Marginal rate of substitution   The rate at which a person will give up good y (the good measured on the y-axis) to get one additional unit of good x (the good measured on the x-axis) and at the same time remain indifferent (remain on the same indifference curve).

Marginal revenue   The change in total revenue that results from a one-unit increase in the quantity sold. It is calculated by dividing the change in total revenue by the change in the quantity sold.

Marginal revenue product   The change in total revenue that results from employing one more unit of a resource while the quantity of all other resources remains the same. It is calculated as the increase in total revenue divided by the increase in the quantity of the resource.

Marginal social benefit   The marginal benefit received by the buyer of a good (marginal private benefit) plus the marginal benefit received by others (external benefit).

Marginal social cost   The marginal cost incurred by the producer of a good (marginal private cost) plus the marginal cost imposed on others (external cost).

Marginal tax rate   The percentage of an additional dollar of income that is paid in tax.

Marginal utility   The change in total utility resulting from a one-unit increase in the quantity of a good consumed.

Marginal utility per dollar spent

The marginal utility obtained from the last unit of a good consumed divided by the price of the good.

Market   Any arrangement that enables buyers and sellers to get information and to do business with each other.

Market demand   The relationship between the quantity demanded of a good or service by everyone in the population and its price. It is illustrated by the market demand curve.

Market failure   A state in which the market does not use resources efficiently.

Market power   The ability to influence the market, and in particular the market price, by influencing the total quantity offered for sale.

Microeconomics   The study of the decisions of people and businesses, the interactions of those decisions in markets, and the effects of government regulation and taxes on the prices and quantities of goods and services.

Minimum efficient scale   The smallest quantity of output at which long-run average cost reaches its lowest level.

Minimum wage   The lowest wage rate at which a firm may legally hire labour.

Monopolistic competition   A market structure in which a large number of firms compete by making similar but slightly different products.

Monopoly   An industry that produces a good or service for which no close substitute exists and in which there is one supplier that is protected from competition by a barrier preventing the entry of new firms.

Monopsony   A market in which there is a single buyer.

Nash equilibrium   The outcome of a game that occurs when player A takes the best possible action given the action of player B and player B takes the best possible action given the action of player A.

Natural monopoly   A monopoly that

occurs when one firm can supply the entire market at a lower price than two or more firms can.

Negative income tax A redistribution scheme that gives every family a guaranteed minimum annual income and taxes all income above the guaranteed minimum at a fixed marginal tax rate.

Negative relationship A relationship between variables that move in opposite directions.

Net present value The present value of the future flow of marginal revenue product generated by the capital minus the cost of the capital.

Nonexhaustible natural resource A natural resource that can be used repeatedly.

Nontariff barrier Any action other than a tariff that restricts international trade.

Normal good A good for which demand increases as income increases.

Normal profit The average return for supplying entrepreneurial ability.

North American Free Trade Agreement An agreement which became effective on January 1, 1994 and under which barriers to international trade between Canada, the United States, and Mexico will be virtually eliminated after a 15-year phasing-in period.

Oligopoly A market structure in which a small number of firms compete.

Opportunity cost The opportunity cost of an action is the highest-valued alternative forgone.

Patent A government-sanctioned exclusive right granted to the inventor of a good, service, or productive process to produce, use, and sell the invention for a given number of years.

Pay equity Paying the same wage for different jobs that are judged to be comparable.

Payoff matrix A table that shows the payoffs for every possible action by each player for every possible action by each other player.

Perfect competition A market in which there are many firms each selling an identical product; there are many buyers; there are no restrictions on entry into the industry; firms in the industry have no advantage over potential new entrants; and firms and buyers are well informed about the price of each firm's product.

Perfect price discrimination Price discrimination that extracts the entire consumer surplus.

Perfectly elastic demand Demand with an infinite price elasticity; the quantity demanded changes by a large percentage in response to a tiny price change.

Perfectly inelastic demand Demand with a price elasticity of zero; the quantity demanded remains constant when the price changes.

Political equilibrium The outcome that results from the choices of voters, politicians, and bureaucrats in which all their choices are compatible and in which no group can improve its position by making a different choice.

Positive relationship A relationship between two variables that move in the same direction.

Poverty A state in which a family's income is too low to be able to buy the quantities of food, shelter, and clothing that are deemed necessary.

Present value The amount of money that, if invested today, will grow to be as large as a given future amount when the interest that it will earn is taken into account.

Price ceiling A regulation that makes it illegal to charge a price higher than a specified level.

Price discrimination The practice of selling different units of a good or service for different prices.

Price effect The change in consumption that results from a change in the price of a good or service, other things remaining the same.

Price elasticity of demand A measure of the responsiveness of the quantity demanded of a good to a change in its price, when all other influences on buyers' plans remain the same.

Price floor A regulation that makes it illegal to pay a lower price than a specified level.

Price taker A firm that cannot influence the price of the good or service it produces.

Principal-agent problem The problem of devising compensation rules that induce an agent to act in the best interest of a principal.

Principle of minimum differentiation The tendency for competitors to make themselves identical to appeal to the maximum number of clients or voters.

Privatization The process of selling a publicly owned corporation to private shareholders.

Producer surplus The price a producer gets for a good or service minus the opportunity cost of producing it.

Product differentiation Making a good or service slightly different from that of a competing firm.

Production efficiency A situation in which the economy cannot produce more of one good without producing less of some other good.

Production possibility frontier The boundary between those combinations of goods and services that can be produced and those that cannot.

Productivity Production per unit of resource used in the production of goods and services.

Progressive income tax A tax on income at a marginal rate that increases with the level of income.

Progressive tax A tax on income when the average tax rate increases as income increases.

Property rights Social arrangements that govern the ownership, use, and disposal of resources, goods, and services.

Proportional income tax A tax on income at a constant rate, regardless of the level of income. It is also called a flat-rate income tax.

Proportional tax A tax on income when the average tax rate increases as income increases.

Public good A good or service that can be consumed simultaneously by everyone and from which no one can be excluded, even if they don't pay for it.

Public interest theory A theory of regulation that states that regulations are supplied to satisfy the demand of consumers and producers to maximize total surplus—that is, to attain allocative efficiency.

Quantity demanded The amount of a good or service that consumers plan to buy during a given time period at a particular price.

Quantity supplied The amount of a good or service that producers plan to sell during a given time period at a particular price.

Quota A restriction on the quantity of a good that a farm is permitted to produce or on the quantity of a good that can be imported.

Rand formula A rule (set out by Mr. Justice Ivan Rand in 1945) that makes it compulsory for all workers to contribute funds to the union, whether or not they belong to it.

Rate of return regulation A regulation that determines a regulated price by setting the price at a level that enables the regulated firm to earn a specified target percent return on its capital.

Rational ignorance The decision not to acquire information because the cost of doing so exceeds the expected benefit.

Real income A household's income expressed not as money but as a quantity of goods that the household can afford to buy.

Regressive income tax A tax on income at a marginal rate that decreases with the level of income.

Regressive tax A tax on income when the average tax rate decreases as income increases.

Relative price The ratio of the price of one good or service to the price of another good or service. A relative price is an opportunity cost.

Rent ceiling A regulation that makes it illegal to charge a rent higher than a specified level.

Rent seeking Any activity that attempts to capture a consumer surplus, a producer surplus, or an economic profit.

Scarcity The state in which the resources available are insufficient to satisfy people's wants.

Scatter diagram A diagram that plots the value of one economic variable against the value of another.

Search activity The time spent looking for someone with whom to do business.

Short run The short run in microeconomics has two meanings. For the firm, it is the time frame in which the quantities of some resources are fixed. For most firms, the fixed resources are the firm's technology, buildings, and capital. For the industry, the short run is the period of time in which each firm has a given plant size and the number of firms in the industry is fixed.

Short-run industry supply curve A curve that shows the quantity supplied by the industry at each price when the plant size of each firm and the number of firms remain constant.

Shutdown point The output and price at which the firm just covers its total variable cost. In the short run, the firm is indifferent between producing the profit-maximizing output and shutting down temporarily.

Single-price monopoly A firm that must sell each unit of its output for the same price to all its customers.

Slope The change in the value of the variable measured on the y-axis divided by the change in the value of the variable measured on the x-axis.

Strategies All the possible actions of each player in a game.

Subsidy A payment made by the government to producers that depends on the level of output.

Substitute A good that can be used in place of another good.

Substitution effect The effect of a change in price on the quantity bought when the consumer (hypothetically) remains indifferent between the original and the new situation.

Sunk cost A cost that has been incurred in the past and that cannot be reversed now.

Supply The relationship between the quantity of a good that producers plan to sell and the price of the good when all other influences on sellers' plans remain the same. It is described by a supply schedule and illustrated by a supply curve.

Supply curve A curve that shows the relationship between the quantity supplied and the price of a good when all other influences on producers' planned sales remain the same.

Symmetry principle A principle that states that people in similar situations must be treated similarly.

Tariff A tax that is imposed by the importing country when an imported good crosses its international boundary.

Technological change The development of new goods and better ways of producing goods and services.

Technological efficiency A situation that occurs when the firm produces a given output by using the least inputs.

Technology Any method of producing a good or service.

Terms of trade The quantity of goods and services that a country exports to pay for its imports of goods and services.

Time-series graph   A graph that measures time (for example, months or years) on the *x*-axis and the variable or variables in which we are interested on the *y*-axis.

Total cost   The cost of all the productive resources that a firm uses.

Total fixed cost   The cost of the fixed inputs.

Total product   The total output produced by a firm in a given period of time.

Total revenue   The price of the good multiplied by the quantity sold.

Total revenue test   A method of estimating the price elasticity of demand by observing the change in total revenue that results from a change in the price, with all other influences on the quantity sold remaining unchanged.

Total utility   The total benefit that a person gets from the consumption of goods and services.

Total variable cost   The cost of the firm's variable inputs.

Tradeoff   A constraint that involves giving up one thing to get something else.

Transactions costs   The costs arising from finding someone with whom to do business, in reaching an agreement about the price and other aspects of the exchange, and of ensuring that the terms of the agreement are fulfilled.

Trend   The general direction (rising or falling) in which a variable is moving over the long term.

Unemployment   Resources that are available but are not being used.

Unit elastic demand   Demand with a price elasticity of 1; the percentage change in the quantity demanded equals the percentage change in price.

Utilitarianism   A principle that states that we should strive to achieve "the greatest happiness for the greatest number."

Utility   The benefit or satisfaction that a person gets from the consumption of a good or service.

Value   The maximum amount that a person is willing to pay for a good. The value of one more unit of the good or service is its marginal benefit.

Value of production   The value of the goods and services produced.

Voluntary exchange   A transaction between people, businesses, or countries that is undertaken voluntarily.

Voluntary export restraint   An agreement between two governments in which the government of the exporting country agrees to restrain the volume of its own exports.

World Trade Organization   An international organization that places obligations on its member countries to observe the GATT rules.

Index

Index

Key terms and pages on which they are
defined appear in **boldface type**.

Photo Credits

Chapter 1

Page 2, Realtor and sign, images copyright 1998 PhotoDisc, Inc.; Page 3, Camping, © Parks Canada, Barrett & Mackay, 06.03.07.04 (10); Page 3, Grape harvester, George Rose/Gamma Liaison; Page 3, Baskets of grapes, Owen Franken/Tony Stone Images; Page 4, Doctors, Prentice Hall Inc.; Page 4, Technician, David Joel, Tony Stone Images; Page 4, Cereal boxes, Charles Gupton/First Light; Page 4, Cars, Paul Conklin/PhotoEdit Inc.; Page 5, Construction, MediaFocus International, LLC ; Page 5, GM closure, Chip Henderson/Tony Stone Images; Page 6, Students, images copyright 1998 PhotoDisc, Inc.; Page 6, McDonald's, David Young-Wolff/PhotoEdit Inc.; Page 7, Woman and baby, images copyright 1998 PhotoDisc, Inc.; Page 8, Woman buying, Karl Wu; Page 8, Woman selling, Karl Wu; Page 9, Pentium processor, Photo courtesy of Intel Corporation; Page 9, Fishing boat, Michel Thérien, Department of Fisheries & Oceans; Page 10, Coffee beans, Jack Novak/SuperStock; Page 10, Milkshakes, images copyright 1998 PhotoDisc, Inc.; Page 10, Woman and cell phone, David Young-Wolff/Tony Stone Images; Page 10, Auto plant, Bob Sacha/Aurora/PNI; Page 11, Price change, Dick Hemingway; Page 11, Food display, Steven Weinberg/Tony Stone Images; Page 11, Employment office, Dick Hemingway; Page 12, Close-up on board, Scott Foresman/Addison Wesley Longman, Focus on Sports; Page 12, Sports crowd, Scott Foresman/Addison Wesley Longman, Focus on Sports; Page 13, Scientist, images copyright 1998 PhotoDisc, Inc.; Page 13, Parliament, Government of Canada; Page 14, Weather map, Courtesy of The Weather Network; Page 14, Winter road, images copyright 1998 PhotoDisc, Inc.; Page 14, Running race, David Burnett/Contact Press Images/PNI; Page 15, Highway, Dick Hemingway; Page 15, Christmas shopping, Frank Wood/SuperStock; Page 15, Christmas present, images copyright 1998 PhotoDisc, Inc.; Page 16, Gordon Thiessen, The Toronto Sun.

Part 1 Wrap Up

Page 58, Adam Smith, Corbis-Bettmann; Page 59, Pin factory, Culver Pictures; Page 59, Computer chip, Bruce Ando/Tony Stone Images; Page 60, John Whalley, Alan Noon.

Part 2 Wrap Up

Page 154, Alfred Marshall, Stock Montage; Page 155, Train, Courtesy Stoddart Publishing Co. Limited, from *Canada: The Missing Years*; Page 155, Airplanes, Courtesy Air Canada; Page 156, Lawrence A. Boland.

Part 3 Wrap Up

Page 196, Jeremy Bentham, Corbis-Bettmann; Page 197, Women in factory, UCR/California Museum of Photography, University of California, Riverside. All rights reserved; Page 197, Co-workers, PhotoDisc, Inc.; Page 198, Martin Dooley, Dick Hemingway.

Chapter 10

Page 211, Coke and Pepsi machines, Karl Wu; Page 211, Shoe store, Karl Wu; Page 211, Wheat field, PhotoDisc; Page 211, Windows98 boxes, Dick Morton.

Part 4 Wrap Up

Page 316, John von Neumann, Stock Montage; Page 317, King Monopoly cartoon, Culver Pictures; Page 317, Cable repair, Don Wilson, West Stock; Page 318, Nancy Gallini, Dick Hemingway.

Part 5 Wrap Up

Page 386, Thomas Robert Malthus, Corbis-Bettmann; Page 387, Winnipeg in 1913, National Archives of Canada/PA-030176.

Part 6 Wrap Up

Page 450, Ronald Coase, David Joel/David Joel Photography, Inc.; Page 451, Pollution, © Jim Baron/The Image Finders; Page 451, Lake Erie, Patrick Mullen; Page 452, Diane Francis, Dick Hemingway.